W9-CRA-581

The Russian View of Honolulu 1809-26

Glynn Barratt

Carleton University Press
Ottawa, Canada
1988

THE RUSSIAN VIEW
OF HONOLULU

1809–26

ISBN 0-88629-060-0 (casebound)

Printed and bound in Canada

Canadian Cataloguing in Publication Data
Main entry under title:
The Russian view of Honolulu, 1809-1826

Bibliography: p.
ISBN 0-88629-060-0

1. Honolulu (Hawaii)—History. 2. Honolulu
(Hawaii)—Social life and customs. 3. Russia.
Flot—Officers—Diaries. I. Barratt, Glynn.

DU623.R88   1987   996.9′3102   C87-090287-3

Distributed by:

Oxford University Press
70 Wynford Drive,
Don Mills, Ontario.
Canada M3C 1J9
(416) 441-2941

Available in Hawaii from:

Editions Limited,
1123 Kapahulu Avenue,
Honolulu, Hawaii.
(808) 734-0340

Cover Design: Chris Jackson

Acknowledgements

Carleton University Press acknowledges the support extended to its pub-
lishing programme by the Canada Council and the Ontario Arts Council.
This book has been published with the help of a grant from the Social
Science Federation of Canada, using funds provided by the Social Sciences
and Humanities Research Council of Canada.
Acknowledgement is also made to the National Library of Canada as a
source of illustrations; and to Elmer E. Rasmuson, Library, University of
Alaska, for plate 18.

TABLE OF CONTENTS

APPENDICES

NOTES and BIBLIOGRAPHY

LIST OF ILLUSTRATIONS
(following pages 131, 294)

Plates

1: 'Kamehameha, King of the Sandwich Islands'
2: 'Queen Kaahumanu'
3: 'Teimotu, Brother of Kaahumanu'
4: 'A View of Honolulu Harbour'
5: 'Natives of the Sandwich Islands'
6: 'Arms and Tools of the Sandwich Isles'
7: 'A Men's Dance in the Sandwich Isles'
8: 'Sandwich Islands Craft'
9: 'Helmets and Implements of the Sandwich Islands'
10: 'Natives of the Sandwich Islands' (2)
11: 'Women's Dance in the Sandwich Isles'
12: 'Sandwich Island Woman'
13: 'The Port of Honolulu'
14: 'Interior of a Chief's House in the Sandwich Isles'
15: 'Girl from the Sandwich Islands'
16: 'Kamehameha, King of the Sandwich Islanders'
17: 'Chiefs of Oahu Island Visiting the Sloop *Kamchatka*'
18: 'The Chief Boki'
19: I.F. Kruzenshtern (1770–1846)
20: Iu.F. Lisianskii (1773–1837)
21: The Ship *Neva* in 1805: (Lisianskii)
22: L.A. Gagemeister (1780–1834) and V.M. Golovnin (1776–1831)
23: Armed Sloop of the *Kamchatka* class
24: Armed Transport of the *Blagonamerennyi* class
25: Otto Evstaf'evich von Kotzebue (1787–1846)
26: Adelbert von Chamisso (1781–1838)
27: Hawaiian dwelling and natives
28: Hawaiian natives wearing *kihei*, with animals (rough draft by Choris)
29: Preliminary sketch for portrait of Queen Kaahumanu, by Choris (left);
   Chief Kalanimoku in 1825, near his death (pencil study by Dampier)
30: John Young, Viceroy of Hawaii Island, adviser to Kamehameha I;
   Mission House and Chapel
31: Gleb Semenovich Shishmarev (left) and Ferdinand Petrovich Wrangel (right)
32: Mikhail Nikolaevich Vasil'ev (left) and Fedor Petrovich Lütke (right)
33: The Brig *Riurik* at Tongareva, 1816

Maps

A: The South Part of the Coast of Oahu Island from Waikiki
   Hamlet to the Pearl River, 1817
B: Plan of the Entrance into Honolulu Harbour, on Oahu Island,
   in latitude 21°18′12″N, longitude 157°52′, 1818: (Midshipman Tabulevich)

PREFACE

In June 1804, two Russian Navy vessels, the *Nadezhda* (Captain-Lieutenant Ivan F. Kruzenshtern) and the *Neva* (Captain-Lieutenant Iurii F. Lisianskii), called at Hawaii Island to replenish their provisions.[1] The *Neva* remained a week (June 10–16) at Kealakekua Bay and members of her company were much impressed by the potential of the Islands as a food source for Kamchatka and/or Russian North America (modern Alaska).[2] Reaching Petropavlovsk-in-Kamchatka and Novo-Arkhangel'sk (Sitka) that winter, these far-sighted and imperialist minded individuals reinforced an interest in the Hawaiian Islands that had earlier been shown by Aleksandr A. Baranov (1746–1819), the Chief Manager of Russian-American Company possessions in the North Pacific. Since the mid-1790s, the Chief Manager had been in regular and mutually profitable contact with New England shipmasters whose voyages to Novo-Arkhangel'sk were nearly always interrupted by a sojourn at the Islands.[3] Not a few of these "Bostonians" had brought Hawaiian seamen to the fur-rich Northwest Coast; and most spoke favourably of the resources and potential of Hawaii and Oahu as a mid-Pacific farm.[4]

In June 1806, Kamehameha, king of all the Hawaiian Islands except Kauai and Niihau, sent a New England seaman named George Clark, second mate of the ship *Pearl*, to make a commercial treaty with Baranov. The king proposed that taro, breadfruit, coconuts, pigs, rope, and other local products be exchanged for Russian textiles, timber, and iron.[5] So began Hawaiian-Russian trade in the Pacific, one extraordinary consequence of which — thanks to the parlous state of Russian North America and the arrival on the scene (1815) of Dr. Georg Anton Scheffer (1779–1836), an adventurer and schemer on a grand scale[6] — was an attempt made in the Russian-American Company's name to seize large portions of Oahu and the whole of Kauai. In recent years, these matters have been studied by both Soviet and Western specialists on the basis of the primary materials. One thinks of F.A. Golder, J.R. Gibson, S.B. Okun', R.A. Pierce, I. Kushner, and D.D. Tumarkin (see Bibliography). "Russia's Hawaiian Adventure" of 1815–17 is, in short, a well-tilled field.

But what of Russian naval dealings in the Islands, and on Oahu in particular? Lieutenant Vasilii N. Berkh of the *Neva* and other officers who, on returning to St. Petersburg in August 1806, were enthusiastically supporting the idea of a regular connection between Sitka, Petropavlovsk-in-Kamchatka, and the Islands,[7] were after all in naval service. They and other naval officers gave evidence of a persistent interest in the political and mercantile development of Honolulu, both before and after Scheffer's scheming there.[8] Navy vessels, which had prompted and facilitated Company involvement in the first place, periodically returned to

Honolulu for political and scientific reasons, among others, throughout
the early nineteenth century. Until recently, these matters had been
neglected by historians of Honolulu, the Hawaiian Islands, Russia, and
her Navy. Long preoccupied with Honolulu as a potential source of food
for the ever-hungry settlements of Russian North America,[9] even those
students of the subject who had access to the central naval archives kept
in Leningrad paid no heed, until the early 1980s, to a fact that forms the
basis of this book: the ships and servants of the Russian Fleet frequently
called at Oahu in the early nineteenth century, and have left us valuable
records of their dealings there and of the infancy of Honolulu.

Early in 1983, Soviet scholars started work on a definitive edition of
these records. This edition will present naval materials now inaccessible
to Western students of Hawaii and will cover Russian dealings in the
Islands as a whole, that is, on Kauai, Oahu, and Hawaii. One cannot
suppose that such a valuable book will be neglected in the West, or that
translation will not follow.

By comparison, the scope of this volume is narrow. It presents, not
the entirety of Russian evidence for the political and cultural development of the Hawaiian Islands as a whole, but only those records that
relate to Honolulu in the early 1800s. Honolulu, after all, was the political, cultural, religious and commercial centre of the kingdom by the
last part of Kamehameha's reign. As the hub of North Pacific trade and
commerce, it was visited by Russians fairly often as they came and went
to Sitka or Kamchatka in the North, took on provisions for a passage to
the Baltic, or recuperated pleasantly from scientific work in every part of
the Pacific. This book, in short, focuses on that locale in the mid-Pacific
where Russians called most frequently, between 1809 and 1826; making
a virtue of the fact that Russian narratives describing visits to Honolulu
overlap to some extent. (How was a Russian naval visitor to see new
casts of characters and unexpected scenes, when the most recent Russian
ship had left only a year before?) One can deplore the overlapping of
the narrative and illustrative records of the period, but it is surely more
constructive to collate similar evidence of, for example, the early growth
of Honolulu Harbour, or the widening of missionary power on Oahu, or
the Hawaiian monarchy and, by approaching the material thematically,
to be aware of the swift changes taking place.

"Oahu Passages" appear in different places throughout the dozen Russian narratives now under preparation by the Soviets. That being so,
it is impossible to concentrate on Honolulu as the eight narrators below
describe it and to avoid a piecemeal treatment of the evidence. This lim-
itation argues the need for a selective, complementary, and annotated
treatment of the texts and aquarelles that bear directly on the infant
Honolulu. It is hoped that this account of Russian dealings there from
1809 to 1826, when Russian naval and commercial enterprise in the Pa-

cific was about to enter into a long decline, may complement the Soviet edition of original materials relating to Hawaii.

This book presents the eye-witness accounts of eight highly observant and well-educated men who made a study of the socio-political and economic situation on Oahu between 1809 and 1826. All eight had reached Oahu as officers or scientists on Russian ships. All eight recognized that they were seeing a traditional society at a turning-point in its development. For modern students of the ethnohistory, ethnography, and political and economic growth of Honolulu, it is fortunate indeed that Russian visits should have occurred with greatest frequency during a period that encompassed two major developments in North Pacific history: the rise and fall of Russia's naval venture and imperialist efforts in the North Pacific Basin, and the undermining of traditional Hawaiian culture by New England merchant interests. We see the Honolulu Village of the early 1800s, a potential site of international commerce, change dramatically into the major port and entrepôt of King Kamehameha III's turbulent days. Huts are replaced or overshadowed by prefabricated frame houses from Boston. Schools and taverns draw Hawaiians by the hundreds. *Heiaus* (temples) collapse or are dismantled in the wake of rising missionary zeal.

It is a bonus to scholars that so many Russian officers, who were obliged to keep full records of their stays at Honolulu and surrender them to the imperial authorities at the conclusion of their voyages, should have been predisposed in favour of ethnography.[10] Not every Russian officer was a savant. However, officers in the Russian naval service in the East and in the Pacific in Kamehameha's time formed the élite branch of that service and were better read, more literate, more intellectually curious than any whaling captain of the day.[11] By training as by temperament, they were sober and dispassionate observers of the Islands scene. Almost alone of *haole* visitors to a bilingual (Hawaiian/English-speaking) Honolulu, they had neither *partis pris* where the political and economic tensions between settler and native or New Englander and Briton were concerned, nor axe to grind on missionary triumphs in the Islands of the early 1820s.

Eight narrators have been selected to tell the story of the growth of Honolulu and of the Russian Navy's interest in it over a period of fifteen years. More witnesses could have been called upon and the time-span could have been trebled; there are sufficient primary materials in either manuscript or printed form to take the story to the end of the Hawaiian monarchy. The limitations here are deliberate. Eight is a manageable number — sufficiently small for us to keep the tone of voice and personality of individual narrators and their texts in mind. The eight narrators are, in order of their visits to Oahu: Leontii Adrianovich Gagemeister of the ship *Neva* (1809); Otto Estaf'evich von Kotzebue and Adelbert von

Chamisso of the *Riurik* (1816 and 1817); Vasilii Mikhailovich Golovnin of the *Kamchatka* (1818); Aleksei Petrovich Lazarev and Karl Gillesem of the sloop *Blagonamerennyi* (two visits in 1821); Mikhail Nikolaevich Vasil'ev of the *Otkrytie* (also two visits in 1821); Otto von Kotzebue again, as commander of the *Predpriiatie* (1824–25); and Ferdinand Petrovich Wrangel of the *Krotkii* (1826). In all, the eight narrators made fifteen visits to Honolulu of an average length of twenty-one days. The *Blagonamerennyi* stood at anchor in Honolulu basin twenty-seven days in 1821, the *Predpriiatie* forty-eight days in 1824–25, the *Neva* fifty-six days in 1809. Such stays were long enough to give the visitor an opportunity to write a factually sound report.

Russian narrative and illustrative evidence offers crucial confirmation and correction of New England, British and Hawaiian source materials; for example, the writings of Levi Chamberlain, Maria Loomis, Hunnewell, and Bingham (among local residents), and of Beechey and Paulding (among naval visitors). It shows, for instance, that the growth of Honolulu occurred for at least a quarter of a century between the harbour and the Punchbowl, then northeast along the Nuuanu-Waolani streambeds, and northwest into the rich Kalihi Valley. Around "the Europeans' cemetery" where Chamisso and Kotzebue paid their respects to Isaac Davis, who had died six years earlier in 1810, stretched an empty, swampy plain. The Russian narratives offer pictures of a hundred early buildings (Fort Kaahumanu, the Marin house, the first frame structures, *heiau*, the Reverend Hiram Bingham's misson), and numerous *ali'i*, early settlers, and traders.

There is some overlapping in the Kotzebue, Chamisso, and Golovnin accounts. That overlapping was to grow more obvious to their contemporaries by the early 1820s. From the standpoint of current Hawaiian studies however, it is a fact that must be welcomed, for by concentrating on the same developments, individuals and places, the narratives provide a reassuring depth and sense of texture. In conjunction with the illustrative evidence, that is, the Russian maps and drawings, such a treatment brings us closer to the "truth," or at least to the probable reality. Like pictures overlaid on one another, the narratives offer detail, perspective, and a certain sense of movement. Honolulu, after all, was an organic, not an artificial growth. To read accounts by Russian visitors of sojourns in the period 1816–1825, is to observe that growth through a powerful new lens.

Russian evidence falls into five main areas: the harbour, the monarchy and social order, traditional Hawaiian ways, the development of Honolulu Village, and missionary work at Honolulu. Again, the overlapping is a reflection of reality. As Honolulu Harbour felt the impact of the missionaries' zeal, so did the Reverend Hiram Bingham feel the power of the monarchy which, by the early 1820s, had its seat at Honolulu.

This thematic organization of material might have cost a loss of time sense. Since the elements of growth and continuity are so important in the Russian evidence, allowing us to observe the aging process of the infant Honolulu in some detail, material is arranged chronologically within the five interconnected subject areas. Thus, the development of Honolulu Village is shown in Russian evidence that moves progressively from 1809 to 1826, as is the development of Honolulu Harbour. It is hoped that this arrangement will be useful to those readers with a specific area of concern.

With the same object in view, I annotate the many Russian texts, providing references to materials that bear directly on and complement the points under discussion. In particular, I draw attention to the ethnographic value of the Russian texts and drawings. Finally, I offer data on the sources now available (to those with time and energy enough to track them down in distant cities) on the Russian naval presence at Oahu and more generally on the history of early Honolulu. Soviet archival sources for that history (see Bibliography) are quite extensive and should not be overlooked by anyone with a special interest in the political and economic growth, the international trading rivalry, the ethnohistory, religious life, or the material development of Honolulu Village.

Many of the Russian narratives translated here are presented for the first time in English.[12] The "Oahu Passages" in Kotzebue's narrative of 1821, *Entdeckungsreise in die Süd-See und nach der Berings-Strasse* ... (Weimar, 1821), have been accessible in English since 1821 thanks to Hannibal E. Lloyd's translation: *Voyage of Discovery into the South Sea and Beering's Straits* (London, Longman, Hurst, Rees, Orme, & Brown), I:319–58 and II:195–204. Reprinted by N. Israel of Amsterdam and the Da Capo Press, New York, in their Bibliotheca Australiana series (1967), Lloyd's translation may be found in many libraries throughout the West. It has shortcomings as a translation (see p. 100), but has given generations of American and British readers a correct idea of the *Riurik*'s two visits to Hawaii at a time when Russophobia was very prevalent because of Scheffer.

Volume III of the same work, in Lloyd's translation, offers Adelbert von Chamisso's "Remarks and Opinions" on Hawaii and Oahu (III:229–60). For a relatively recent English version of that poet-scientist's longer account of his experiences on Oahu, we have Victor S.K. Houston's "Chamisso in Hawaii," in the *Forty-Eighth Annual Report of the Hawaiian Historical Society for the Year 1939* (Honolulu, 1940):55–82. This is an adequate translation of the "Kona Coast" and "Honolulu" passages from Chamisso's own *Reise um die Welt mit der Romanzoffischen Entdeckungs-Expedition in den Jahren 1815–1818*. For a discussion of Chamisso's several treatments of his voyage in the *Riurik*, and of material included in his *Tagebuch* but missing from the earlier, official narratives, we have Gisela Menza, 1978:52–53.

Finally, mention must be made of Ella Wiswell's fine recent translation of Vasilii M. Golovnin's account of his voyage in Kamchatka of 1817–19, *Puteshestvie vokrug sveta na shliupe "Kamchatka" v 1817, 1818, i 1819 godakh* (St. Petersburg, 1822). *Around the World on the "Kamchatka," 1817–1819* (University of Hawaii, 1979) follows the chapter layout of the original edition. Annotation complements that provided by V.A. Divin and others for the 1965 Moscow edition of Golovnin's *Puteshestvie* (Moscow, *Izdatel'stvo Mysl'*): 344–56. To summarize, accounts of their experiences on Oahu by Kotzebue, Chamisso, and Golovnin have been available in English for some time, but those of Gagemeister, A.P. Lazarev, Vasil'ev, Gillesem, and Wrangel are to all intents and purposes completely inaccessible to English readers.

Notwithstanding Soviet intentions to publish the Hawaiian narratives of the above, it was decided to include here the "Honolulu Narratives" of Lazarev and Wrangel, and moreover to present both in their entirety. These texts, which are in any case both readable and factually sound, have been less exhaustively exploited than the other narratives in Part Two. Accounts by Golovnin, Lazarev, Gillesem, and Wrangel are presented here on the basis of the first-edition texts (see Bibliography). So too are those of Chamisso and Kotzebue, with the difference that in the case of Chamisso the German texts have been preferred (as being slightly earlier and fuller than the Russian variants); in the case of Kotzebue, the St. Petersburg edition has been chosen. Gagemeister's "Honolulu Passages" are offered in the form in which another early visitor to the Hawaiian Islands, Company Clerk (*prikazchik*) Fedor I. Shemelin, had them printed — as a section in his own description of an earlier Pacific expedition — in St. Petersburg in June 1818. Brief extracts from Vasil'ev's text are given on the basis of the manuscript entitled "Notes on a Stay in the Hawaiian Islands" (1821–22), the holograph of which remains in TsGAVMF in Leningrad (see Bibliography).

ACKNOWLEDGEMENTS

I am grateful to the staffs of many libraries and archives for their assistance, and to many individuals for their constructive criticism of the first draft of this manuscript.

The archives and manuscript repositories include the Central State Archives of Ancient Acts and of the Navy of the USSR (TsGADA and TsGAVMF), each with its dependent library; the Central State Historical Archive in Leningrad (TsGIAL); the Archive of the All-Union Geographical Society of the USSR (AGO); the Archive of the Foreign Policy of Russia (AVPR); the Leningrad Division of the Institute of History of the Academy of Sciences of the USSR (LOII); the Central State Historical Archive of the Estonian SSR (TsGIAE) in Tartu; the Institute of Russian Literature of the Academy of Sciences of the USSR (Pushkinskii Dom, Leningrad); and the Manuscript Divisions of the Saltykov-Shchedrin Public Library in Leningrad and the V.I. Lenin Library in Moscow.

I acknowledge assistance, in the forms of microfilm, photocopies, or expert advice, from the Elmer Rasmuson Research Library of the University of Alaska at Fairbanks; from Harvard University Library; from the Massachussetts Historical Society; and from the Pacific Room and Russian Bibliography Service at the Hamilton Research Library, University of Hawaii at Manoa.

Individuals to whom I am indebted for help of one sort or another include Captain A. Solov'ev, of TsGAVMF; the late S.B. Okun', of Leningrad State University; Irina Grigor'eva, Director of the International Exchange Section of the Saltykov-Shchedrin Public Library in Leningrad; Patricia Polansky of the Hamilton Library, University of Hawaii at Manoa; Mrs. Ella Wiswell of Honolulu; Dr. Marvin W. Falk, Curator of Rare Books at the University of Alaska, Fairbanks; Dr. L.A. Shur of the Hebrew University, Tel Aviv and Meudon, France; Professor D.D. Tumarkin of the Institute of Ethnography, Academy of Sciences of the USSR; Tamara K. Shafranovskaia, of the Peter-the-Great Museum; N.N. Miklukho-Maklai, Institute of Anthropology and Ethnography, Leningrad; and Mrs. Moana Ching of Kailua-Kona, Hawaii.

Ottawa 1988

PRELIMINARY NOTES

A modified form of the Library of Congress system for transliterating the Russian alphabet has been used in this survey, e.g. Andrei, Fedor, Lisianskii. However, recognized anglicized forms are used for proper names, e.g. Alexander, Cossack, Moscow. Rouble values are expressed as silver units. Certain measurements of length and weight are left in the original forms, e.g. *arshin* (= 28 inches), *versta* (= 3,500'), *pood* (= 36 lbs. avoirdupois). Most dates are given in accordance with the New Style (Gregorian) Calendar, which was in use at Honolulu from the earliest days of contact, even though certain of the Russian texts used employ the Julian Calendar that remained in use in Russia and in Russia's possessions in the North Pacific. The difference was twelve days in the nineteenth century. Occasional discrepancies with local Hawaiian sources are to be explained in terms of the ship log and "seaborne time": Russian officers commonly reckoned dates from noon to noon. The following terms may not be familiar to all readers:

ali'i	chief, chiefly class
baidarka	Aleut craft of skins stretched over a frame
haole	European
heiau	temple
ieri (jerry)	chief
kahuna	priest
kanaka	commoner
kapa	stuff made from inner tree bark
kapu	taboo, restraining injunction
Makahiki	Season of festivities and rest in late October-December
morai	temple
prikazchik	Clerk or factor
promyshlennik	Hunter-trader (sea-otter skins etc.) in Russian-American Company lands and beyond

The following (non-English) units of weight, length, and value are also used:

arshin	Russian linear measure, 28 inches
kopek	/100 rouble; approximately 1/2 cent US in 1820
desiatin	.70 acres
piastre	Spanish dollar; approximately $1 in early 1800s
pikul, or *picul*	Chinese measure of weight: 133 1/3 lbs.
pood, or *pud*	Russian weight measure: 36.11 lbs. avoirdupois
quintal	Spanish weight measure: 101 lbs.; loosely used as an equivalent of cwt. (112 lbs.)

rouble	Russian banknote or coin; approximately 50 cents US in 1820.
sazhen'	Russian linear measure: 7 feet or 2.13 m.
thaler	German coin: equalling 3 Marks or $US1
toise	French linear measure: 6.395 feet
versta	.66 miles
vershok	.75 inches

Finally, a few words on the problem of rendering into English Hawaiian proper names which are transcribed in Cyrillic: Russian lacks certain letters, notably "h" and "w". One must accordingly make allowances in Russian texts on encountering *Gavai* or *Gavaii*, for example, or *Ovagu/Ovagi*, even while bearing in mind that Russians in the early 19th century were often rendering into Cyrillic Hawaiian place and personal names on the basis of Cook's and King's terminology. Thus, the English form 'O-Waihi' becomes *O-Vaigi*, and *O-Wahu* becomes *O-Vagu*. However, Russians were inconsistent in the usage of *O-Vagu* and *Ovagu* by the early 1800s, and also confused *Ovagu* (Oahu) with *Ovagi* (a corruption of Hawaii). To further complicate matters, certain Russians and some of their cosmopolitan passengers used the English or even the French forms of place and proper names and did so within a Russian text. Thus, we find Hana-ruru or Hanaruru spelled in latin characters in some Russian manuscripts; and when Cook's and his peoples' attempts at Hawaiian proper names *are* given in the Russian, the results are often inconsistent. Thus: Tameamea, Tammeammea, and Tameiameia as well as Kameamea and Tomi-Omi. By considering the Russians' sources, which were mostly but not exclusively British, we can easily gloss such names as *Atuvai* (Kauai), *Gaul-gana* (Haul-hanna = Olohana, John Young, the former boatswain who frequently shouted "All hands!" in his early days on Hawaii), *Kagamana* or *Kakhumanna* (Kaahumanu), or *Nomakhana* (Nomahana). The origins of such forms as King Tomari (Kaumualii) and Chief Kraimaku or Kareimoku (or even Kalaimoko) are not hard to find in the English-language literature of the 1780s. To explain all such variant forms in a Russian text is perhaps to shed some light on growing Russian knowledge of that literature, but hardly throws light upon Oahu and *its* history. Nevertheless it was resolved to follow international editorial procedures, that is, *not* to standardize all forms of Hawaiian names found in the Russian texts translated.

Other considerations operate where English renderings of Russian and, particularly, Baltic-German surnames are concerned. Widely recognized anglicized forms are accepted, as a principle, especially when bearers of the names that had a "Russian" and "non-Russian" form so signed themselves; hence, Bellingshausen and not Bellingsgauzen, Kotzebue and not Kotsebu. For professional or other reasons, some distinguished Baltic German officers, notably Captain Leontii A. Gagemeister,

so identified with Russia as deliberately to adopt the Slavic version of
their name when signing documents or even letters. Hagemeister is accordingly avoided. In cases like those of the artist Ludovik A. Choris or
Khoris and Admiral Ferdinand P. Vrangel' or Wrangel, when both forms
were employed in different contexts, the "non-Russian," more familiar,
alternative has been preferred.

Part One

PREPARATIONS

CHAPTER ONE

The Russians and Oahu: The Beginnings

COOK AND THE KRUZENSHTERN-LISIANSKII EXPEDITION

The Russian Navy did its best throughout the later eighteenth century to gain such knowledge as it could about Hawaii, among other distant parts, but it remained perforce a second-hand and academic knowledge. Immediate realities were echoed in the fact that, since the mid-1730s, the Imperial Academy of Sciences and not the Navy had held responsibility for the study of such places.[1] More than once, indeed, far-sighted officers in naval service had proposed that Russian ships be sent from Kronstadt in the Baltic to the North Pacific Ocean to train companies of seamen, lend material support to Russia's outposts in Kamchatka, and support the Cossacks' economic ventures in the far northeast of Asia.[2] Once at least, in 1787, a squadron very nearly made the voyage which would probably have brought it to Hawaiian shores.[3] In any event, it was another century that was to witness the beginning (1803) of the connections between Kronstadt and Hawaii, and of Russian circumnavigation proper. By that time, the Russian attitude towards Hawaii and Oahu, as towards seaborne exploration and discovery in general, would have been largely fixed by Captain James Cook and his successor, George Vancouver. For fifty years after his death in 1779, James Cook remained the model of the leader of a voyage of discovery and science for the younger Russian officer of talent.[4]

Paradoxically, Cook reinforced that scholarly, almost disinterested attitude which, of necessity, Russians had earlier adopted towards South Sea Islands and their peoples. Cook's own great achievements were reflected for the Russians, after all, in the most factual and detached descriptions of Hawaii, its topography, resources, and climate.[5] Naval officers especially, numbers of whom had had professional connections with the British in the last third of the century,[6] both recognized Cook's eminence as a commander and were influenced by his approach towards the business of discovery—in short, by Cook the scientist. Second, Cook's abrupt appearance on the Russian empire's easternmost extremity at Unalaska Island in October 1778[7] had disposed the government of Catherine the Great to be receptive to accounts of any voyages into the North Pacific Ocean from the South. Knowledge was potentially economic and strategic power; Russian sovereignty over the Aleutian Islands and her stake in the Pacific-China fur trade were perceived to be at risk.[8] In the last quarter of the eighteenth century, as the activities of Cook and his compatriots made it both possible and necessary, Russian awareness of the Hawaiian Islands grew apace. It grew, moreover, in a North Pacific context of discovery: "soft gold," or otter skins, and northern passages from Europe and the White Sea to the East.[9]

In an age when English was not generally learned by Russian noblemen in childhood,[10] a good number of Russian naval officers could read it. This was the result both of professional connections in the English Channel and the Baltic Sea, and of awareness of the Royal Navy's primacy among the navies of the world. Cook's *Voyages* were also available in French.[11] Nevertheless, the Empress Catherine gave orders for Cook's works to be translated into Russian at the government's expense, under the aegis of the Admiralty College.[12] Her intention was assuredly not to acquaint a Russian readership with the resources and potential of Hawaii, but to recognize political realities and make available new data on the Eastern and Pacific situation. The effect of the accessibility of Cook's three narratives to the whole government and fleet by 1810 was, nonetheless, to send his star into the Russian naval firmament. It also made Hawaii a familiar, if still exotic, word to educated Russian readers. They might well associate it, first and naturally, with the death of Cook; but they at least had a means of filling out the picture in considerable detail and colour. Not until 1820 did the most brilliant of younger Russian officers cease to revere the name of Cook, nor even later would such influential admirals as Ivan F. Kruzenshtern (1770–1846) and Faddei F. Bellingshausen (1778–1852) cease to think of Cook's professional descendants—George Vancouver and Matthew Flinders—with a measure of the same profound respect.[13]

It was to Loggin Golenishchev-Kutuzov (1769–1845) that the task fell of translating Cook's third *Voyage*, that is, the Cook-King text (1784). From a distinguished father Golenishchev-Kutuzov had inherited both maritime and literary interests and attitudes. Regrettably, neither the father nor the son thought literal precision in translating foreign works a worthy altar for the sacrifice of elegance.[14] When dealing with the third *Voyage*, at least, Loggin Ivanovich did not repeat his own decision of a decade earlier when he had based his Russian version of the second *Voyage*, not on Cook's account of 1777 but on Jean Suard's free rendering of it, *Voyage dans l'Hémisphère australe et autour du monde ...* (Paris, 1778).[15] Like Admiral Kutuzov senior, the energetic and prolific Jean-Baptiste-Antoine Suard (1733–1817) had prized fluidity of style. Accuracy was desirable, but secondary in the Paris market of the day.[16]

The relatively gentle pace of Loggin Golenishchev-Kutuzov's (and by 1800 of his helpers') work, which so contrasted with the urgency of Catherine II's orders of another period, was in itself a commentary on the diligence of other French translators: Fréville Jean-Nicolas Demeunier (1741–1814), and André Morellet (1727–1819). All three translators made the details of Cook's discoveries and British dealings in Hawaii quite accessible to French and Russian readerships. Demeunier, especially, was widely known in Russia as the earliest French translator of Cook's final *Voyage*. His translation appeared in July 1785 in Paris. Russian booksellers were stocking it by August.[17] Loggin Golenishchev-Kutuzov's work, together with the offerings of these and other French (and German) paraphrasts, did much to spread at least some knowledge of Hawaii and Oahu Islands among educated Russian readers. Cook's last expedition and the nature of his work thus had particular significance for the development and shaping of Russian interest in the Hawaiian Archipelago. The British visits, first to Unalaska Island, then to Petropavlovsk-in-Kamchatka (April–May and August–October 1779) served as forcible reminders of the relative defencelessness and economic value of Kamchatka and the North Pacific islands.[18] Former members of Cook's final expedition, who were entering the Russian service by the mid-1780s with a view to exploiting their earlier connection,[19] drew the empress's attention to the immense potential of the Coast-to-China fur trade and to the Russians' growing need for a provisioning station in the East or the Pacific, such as the Hawaiian Islands.[20]

News of the enormous sums that Chinese merchants were prepared to pay for even torn sea-otter skins launched many speculative voyages to the localities that Cook had charted and described, including the Hawaiian Islands. Rumours, then reports, of these new speculative voyages not only heightened Russian officialdom's consciousness of the importance of asserting Russia's rights on the Pacific rim, they also offered fresh incentives for discovering what could be learned about Hawaii, and provided the essential means: the published narrative and printed chart.[21] Such men as Petr P. Soimonov, secretary to the empress, and Count Aleksandr R. Vorontsov of the Commercial College were annoyed by the successes of James Hanna and his emulators in the new Pacific fur trade, which they reasonably viewed as detrimental to the Russian interest. They were not slow to see the fur trade and the possible utility to Russia of the fertile Hawaiian Archipelago in a strategic and political, as well as economic, context.[22] As the British minister, James Harris, then in St. Petersburg, wryly put it to the Earl of Sandwich in a long despatch dated 7 January 1780, "The Empress ... expressed a *very* earnest desire of having Copys of such Charts as may tend to ascertain more precisely the extent & position of ... her Empire" and of potentially important provisioning stations further south.[23] The Russians connected Hawaii with Kamchatka, the Aleutians, and the problems of provisioning the Cossack hunter-traders' farflung outposts in North America.

In spring 1786, two British ships commanded by Nathaniel Portlock and George Dixon spent three weeks at the Hawaiian Archipelago, *en route* to the Northwest Coast. They found the natives at Kealakekua on the Kona Coast cool to trading propositions; at Oahu on the other hand they had no trouble getting food and water in exchange for iron nails, cloth, and trifles. Even while Portlock and Dixon were there, the French exploring expedition led by Jean François de la Pérouse put in at Maui.[24] Portlock's and Dixon's *Voyages*, with their reports on the resources and conditions on Oahu, were accessible to Russians by July 1789. La Pérouse's account had to wait several years, but when it did appear in 1800, it was available in Russian as well as in French. Golenishchev-Kutuzov's Russian version, *Puteshestvie la Peruza ...* was received enthusiastically by buyers in St. Petersburg.[25] Appetites for information on Hawaii and the other island groups of the Pacific had been whetted by his recent (1796–1800) free translation of Cook's second *Voyage, Puteshestvie v Iuzhno i polovine zemnago shara ...* and in 1797, by his translation of James Meares' *Voyages from China to the North West Coast*.[26] It was with interest that Russians read how Meares had conveyed one Kaiana, a Hawaiian chief, to China then returned him to his people. Like Kutuzov's and Demeunier's earlier offerings, *Puteshestvie kapitana Mirsa* gave further tantalizing glimpses of Oahu, while continuing to focus on the Kona Coast which, after all, remained the trade and contact centre of the Islands.

What the Russians knew already of Oahu thanks to Cook's associates and Admiral Kutuzov *fils*, however, was dramatically increased in 1800 by Captain George Vancouver and his French translators, Demeunier and Morellet.[27] Suddenly, what little information was available about the *Discovery*'s and the *Resolution*'s two-day stay (27–28 February 1779) in Waimea Bay, was painted over by the story of the storeship *Daedalus*'s visit to that same bay (7–12 May 1792) and of Lieutenant Hergest's murder by "the savagest and most deceitful of the natives" on the archipelago.[28] (Vancouver's narrative reminds us usefully how dangerous Oahu was for *haole* before its conquest by Kamehameha in 1795.[29]) It was Vancouver, through Demeunier and Morellet, who first gave Russians an impression of the south shore of Oahu.

From modern Barber's Point, Vancouver had cruised east across Mamala Bay on 24 March 1793. *Discovery* dropped anchor near Keahi Point, abreast of "the westernmost opening or lagoon" on the island's south shore and called by the natives "O-poo-ro-ah."[30] "Apuroa," in its Russian dress, was Puuloa, the name which survives today as a district of Ewa Beach. The British were not overly impressed by what appeared to be an arid, underpopulated country where the natives had but meagre trade goods. Besides, there was a sandy bar over the opening to what is now Pearl Harbour. A Hawaiian chief aboard observed, however, that at a little distance from the sea the soil was rich. The British saw another opening to the eastward, "called by the natives Honoonoono." This was Honolulu Passage. The chief said it was shallow and a smaller place, so it was not examined carefully. But, reports Vancouver,

I was afterwards informed, by Mr. Brown of the *Butterworth*, that although it is smaller and of less depth of water, yet it admits of a passage
from sea 5 fathom deep between the reefs; and opens beyond them into
a small but commodious bason ... where a few vessels may ride with the
greatest safety.[31]

Honolulu thus came into focus for the Russians.

Both the beginning of the Russian Navy's long-term but eventually
unsuccessful effort to provision Russia's North Pacific colonies and, by
extension, the beginning of the Russian naval presence in Hawaii, are
essentially connected with the name of I.F. Kruzenshtern. Admiral
Kruzenshtern, a Baltic German officer of noble birth, had for a five-
year period (1794–98) served as a Russian Volunteer aboard British
warships.[32] Making use of British contacts and alliances, he had in due
course travelled to Bengal and thence to China. In Canton, he spent nine
months on a systematic study of the workings of the Coast-to-China fur
trade. He himself became the vital human link between St. Petersburg,
Canton, and the Hawaiian Archipelago. In 1800, and again in 1802,
he submitted to the Russian naval ministry a project whereby Russian vessels could supply the Russian outposts from the Baltic, train
whole companies of seamen, and participate directly in the seaborne
fur trade. His designs were viewed with favour by the new court of
Alexander I. The *Nadezhda* and the *Neva* set sail from the Baltic in
August 1803, reaching the Washington (Marquesas) group in April 1804
and the Hawaiian group in May. Kruzenshtern himself commanded the
Nadezhda; Captain-Lieutenant Iurii Fedorovich Lisianskii (1773–1839),
commanded the *Neva*.[33] They were the first of many Russian naval visitors to the Hawaiian Islands in the early nineteenth century who left a
record of the impact of *haole* on the traditional Hawaiian way of life.

Cook's influence and name had permeated Kruzenshtern's and Lisianskii's early service life, during the course of which Cook's *Voyages* had
been repeatedly translated into French, German, and Russian. Kruzenshtern himself encountered members of Cook's final expedition who were
serving in the Russian Baltic Fleet.[34] Thirty, even forty years after
Cook's death at the Hawaiians' hands, the form and very emphases
of his Pacific explorations were not only borne in mind by the ambitious
younger officer at Kronstadt, but were seen as proper to such ventures.
Among these were certain scientific emphases.

Cook had received no orders to concern himself particularly or at
length with "curiosities," as ethnographica continued to be termed, on
setting out on any of his voyages.[35] Nevertheless, both he and those
aboard his ships had shown a lively and persistent interest in the artefacts, languages, beliefs, and social life of the distant peoples they encountered in the North and South Pacific. Officially, the emphasis fell

first upon discovery and the attendant naval sciences (hydrography and
marine astronomy), then on the twin natural sciences (zoology and
botany). In fact, Cook and his people made as full and close a study
of the natives they met as time allowed, gathering artefacts (certain of
which may still be seen in Leningrad),[36] and sketching and recording
as they went. Notice was taken of techniques and customs, diet and
religion, and relations with themselves as Europeans. The example was
not lost on Kruzenshtern in 1802–03, nor had it faded twelve years later
at the outset of another naval venture led by one of his most junior subordinates of 1803–06, Lieutenant Otto von Kotzebue (Kotsebu). Held
intact by Russian officers of academic bent and of another age, Cook's
very spirit was to go with Kotzebue to Hawaii in a way that negated
the intervening thirty years—the age of Bonaparte.[37] Such occupations
as had marked Cook's and Vancouver's visits to Hawaii were resumed,
with few exceptions, by young Russian, and particularly Baltic German,
officers.

Of Kruzenshtern's own venture with the *Nadezhda* and the *Neva* in
1803–06, suffice it to say that as an officer of academic disposition he
was inclined to stress maritime and scientific elements at the expense of
commercial and (hopeless) diplomatic ones.[38] To the extent that the first
Russian seaborne venture in the East was a success, it was successful as
a training voyage and, above all, as a scientific exercise.

For Kruzenshtern, Hawaii proved a disappointment. The Hawaiians
who approached the *Nadezhda* from the south coast of the big island
brought nothing in exchange for iron, cloth, mirrors and other baubles
but a little fruit and one small pig. Not even axes were of interest to
these sophisticated Islanders who had had twenty years of dealings with
commercial travellers from Europe and New England, and who were
loath to part with hogs regardless of a new royal trade monopoly in
them. They wanted money or some "article of luxury" for what they
offered.[39]

Kruzenshtern's and his subordinates' remarks on the Hawaiian Islands' natural resources were precise enough, although not unaffected
by their disappointment. True, the Hawaiians were themselves spoiled
and grasping, but their manners were of slight concern to mariners, and
the Hawaiian group was geographically well placed to meet the provisioning needs of Russian vessels sailing north to either China or the Russian
Northwest Coast of North America. It formed the hub of the Pacific,
being almost equidistant from Japan, the Russian colonies, and Alta
California. For Russians sailing north to Petropavlovsk-in-Kamchatka
or to Sitka from Chile, for example, it might be extremely useful. Barely
ten years later, Russian guns were actually mounted on the shores of
Kauai.[40]

The *Nadezhda* and the *Neva* parted company west of Hawaii Island on 10 June 1804. For Kruzenshtern particularly, time was short. Lisianskii was instructed to proceed to Kodiak without undue delay. He decided first to satisfy his curiosity by looking at the beach where Cook had perished and to barter with the natives for provisions. He did so, observing flattened English bullets in trees near the spot where Cook had fallen. Small-scale, amicable bartering continued for five days aboard the *Neva*, which stood at anchor in Kealakekua Bay: eleven hogs for 90 pounds of iron, fruit for axes, yams for clothing.[41]

Mindful of Vancouver's words about the small, secure harbour on the south coast of Oahu, which had seemingly been visited by half-a-dozen merchantmen besides Brown's *Butterworth*, (the reconfigured thirty-gun French frigate that the *Discovery* had met with ten years earlier[42]), Lisianskii had been thinking of examining the place himself when he anchored at Hawaii Island. In his cabin in the *Neva* were both a copy of the first (London) edition of Vancouver's *Voyage of Discovery* and, more predictably, a set of Hergest's and Vancouver's charts.[43] His inclination to retrace Vancouver's route west to Oahu was, if anything, intensified by King Kamehameha's absence from the Kona Coast in 1804. Lisianskii was disposed to meet the king, survey the troops with which the king proposed to unify and conquer all the islands, and investigate the "Honoonoono" basin, all in one swift visit. As he put it:

> I proposed, on leaving Karakakoa [Kealakekua], to make for Vagu [Oahu] to see the king of Ovaigi [Hawaii], who was there with his army. And such was my curiosity to do so that, fully to satisfy it, I would have sacrificed a few days .... However, I learned that a kind of epidemic disease was rampant on Vagu, so I abandoned the plan ....[44]

Lisianskii passed by Waikiki with some regret, setting a course for Kauai on 16 June 1804. He reached it only three days later, but was met there almost immediately by the local king, Tomari (Kaumualii), who spoke a broken English. Kaumualii sought the Russians' armed assistance in his struggle for continuing autonomy and independence from Kamehameha who, he knew, was planning an attack with a flotilla from Hawaii Island. "In return," Lisianskii noted, "he would gladly have agreed to come, with his island, under Russian domination .... We were not in a position to agree to the king's plan."[45]

In conjunction with such royal willingness to recognize some kind of Russian suzereignty over Kauai, that island's evident fertility and richness of resources made a powerful impression on the people on the *Neva*.[46] At least one of her officers, Lieutenant Vasilii N. Berkh, is known to have considered that a colonizing effort should be made without delay: "These isles do not belong to any European Power, and they *must* belong to Russia ...."[47] He and others on the *Neva*, which passed a cold winter at Kodiak off the Alaskan coast, could see the value of the island and, indeed, the archipelago, as an essential food base for Chief Manager A.A. Baranov's hungry hunters on the Russian Northwest Coast of North America and for the Cossacks of Kamchatka. One small naval craft at least, argued Lieutenant Berkh, should be dispatched to the Hawaiian Islands "every autumn, from Kamchatka. She should winter in the Islands and return to the peninsula in May."[48] It would have been surprising had Lieutenant Berkh's opinion not been sympathetically received in certain Company and even naval circles in St. Petersburg in 1806–07. Not until 1817, however, was he finally in a position to express his views effectively on paper. In a memorandum to the Company Head Office which, internal evidence makes certain, rested squarely on his own journal of 1804, the future annalist of Russia's North Pacific venture as a whole[49] had this to say about Oahu and its people:

> So far-sighted is King Kamehameha's devilish policy that, on possessing himself of Oahu ..., he had the king slaughtered together with all his relatives and retainers .... It was with great pleasure that we heard, on reaching Canton the following year, [1805] that Kamehameha's large army had been scattered by the spread of a disease, so that his design [to seize Kauai] had come to nothing. The king had gone to Oahu the better to prosecute that plan, and had there collected stones suitable for use in slingshots and made other martial preparations. The supply of food on Oahu was inadequate for so great a number of warriors ....
>
> The Sandwich Islanders are graceful, of average build, and—unlike the Kalmucks and other savage tribesmen—quite attractive despite their dark skin. They differ from the North American savages in many respects, being active, capable of any work, docile, obedient, and quite prepared to work aboard European vessels ....
>
> Situated as they are between 18° and 23° N., these islands might be expected to be very hot, like other tropical lands; but because they lie at the very centre of the Pacific, far from the coasts of America, they enjoy a very pleasant climate. Sea breezes blow onshore from dawn to dusk, moderating the sun's heat and cleansing the country of evil vapors .... There is a permanent food supply.[50]

Much though he needed a new, reliable source of foodstuffs for his men along the Northwest Coast and the Aleutian chain, Chief Manager Baranov was in 1805–06 too preoccupied with problems and too short of men and ships to make first contact with Kamehameha (or his royal enemy).[51] In the event, it was Kamehameha who in 1806 took the initiative in giving substance to Hawaiian-Russian contact. Georg Heinrich Langsdorf (1774–1852), the distinguished German naturalist, had sailed in the *Nadezhda* as both secretary and surgeon to the Russian Envoy designate to the Mikado, Nikolai P. Rezanov, and so visited Hawaii, South America, Kamchatka and Japan. He reported that Kamehameha made enthusiastic overtures through the intermediation of unnamed New Englanders who had been trading on the Northwest Coast. The king

> ... made known to von Baranov [sic], at Novo-Arkhangel'sk in Norfolk Sound, that he understood from persons trading to that Coast how much the Russian establishment had sometimes suffered in winter from a scarcity of provisions; that he would therefore gladly send a ship every year with swine, salt, bananas, and other articles of food, if they would in exchange let him have sea-otter skins at a fair price ....[52]

Examination of the lists of trading vessels known to have arrived at Sitka (Novo-Arkhangel'sk) in 1806, direct from the Hawaiian Islands, quickly shows that the O'Cain, a 280-ton Nor'wester owned and operated by the Winships of New York, was the most likely bearer of the royal proposition.[53] First, she had been at Honolulu at the same time as the king. Second, Baranov knew the brothers Jonathan and Nathan Winship as associates of the aggressive Boston shipmaster Joseph O'Cain, whom he had known and personally liked for fifteen years.[54] O'Cain had also visted Baranov in 1806 as commander of the 343-ton Boston ship Eclipse.[55] Third, the brothers Winship stood to profit even more than O'Cain from Hawaiian-Russian trade, so long as Russia had no merchantmen available to carry and expand it.

A small Company vessel, Nikolai, commanded by Pavel or Sysoi Slobodchikov, detoured from San Francisco to Hawaii on her way back to the Russian Northwest Coast in 1806. Her master was received well by Kamehameha, and her holds were filled with foodstuffs in exchange for otter skins.[56] Hawaiian-Russian trade entered a new and crucial phase in which, significantly, fur traders and servants of the Company, who viewed Baranov as their chief, would play a smaller role than servants of the Russian Navy. Even as Slobodchikov was taking the Nikolai back to Sitka with her cargo of Hawaiian products the Neva, now commanded by Lieutenant L.A. Gagemeister (German: Ludwig Karl August von Hagemeister), was on her way from Kronstadt roads to the Pacific. Her return in 1808 marked the beginning of a new stage in the growth of strictly naval Russian influence in the Pacific as a whole and in Hawaii in particular.[57]

RUSSIANS ON OAHU, 1809–1816

When offered the command of the Neva, Lieutenant Gagemeister (1780–1834) was a seasoned officer of barely twenty-six. He had already given ample proof of his abilities in war and peace. His early years of service had in fact followed a pattern reminiscent of Lisianskii's and, particularly, Kruzenshtern's. An ancient Baltic family, the Naval Corps, a spell of Baltic duty, early contact with the British—it was all familiar.[58]

In 1802 he saw action in the Caribbean Sea (St. Lucia, with the *Argo*) and in 1804 with Collingwood and Nelson.[59] He returned to Russia and was promoted in the spring of 1805. On being given the *Neva*, just back from China, his instructions were to sail to the North Pacific settlements with iron, naval stores, and an assortment of supplies. He was a prudent officer: the voyage out to Sitka was conspicuously slow.[60]

Because Lieutenant Gagemeister seemed, at the beginning of his first stay in the Company possessions, to reciprocate Chief Manager Baranov's sympathy, all went more easily than might have been expected. Baranov, who was more than twice his age, and had a jaundiced view of naval officers, appears to have looked on Gagemeister as an erudite and earnest youth. Early in 1808 he issued orders for the *Neva* to take supplies to Kodiak and made allusion to the prospect of a later trading voyage to the Hawaiian Islands. What Baranov said, Gagemeister understood, was on the basis of instructions that the late Nikolai Petrovich Rezanov (1764–1807) had dictated two years earlier, in February 1806.[61] Rezanov, an acquaintance of Tsar Alexander I, nobleman and "Correspondent" (chief administrator) of the Company, had, with his secretary Georg Heinrich Langsdorf, left the *Nadezhda* in Kamchatka in June 1805 and made his way across to Sitka in a leaking, evil-smelling little brig, called the *Mariia*.[62]

By the time Rezanov met Baranov in early August 1805, he had perceived to what extent he and the Company directors in St. Petersburg had been misled for many years, or had perhaps misled themselves, about conditions in the distant colonies. There were no doctors to attend to the disabled and the ailing, who were everywhere in evidence. On the Aleutian outposts, Company employees went in rags. Even at Kodiak, which was supposedly a major Russian colony, there was no bread.[63] At Sitka, meanwhile, Baranov and his men had long been toiling on a new and stronger fort, so placed and armed that Tlingit Indians could never strike again and kill as they had killed in 1802, when an entire Russian outpost had been lost.[64]

Of all the problems that Baranov promptly listed for Rezanov in September 1805, none had impressed him more immediately than the lack of any food-producing territory south of Sitka.[65] More than once, Baranov's people had depended for essential food supplies on the goodwill and business instinct of Americans. (If these had carried only foodstuffs up to Sitka from Hawaii, there would certainly have been no objections; but they traded less in foodstuffs than in guns, powder, and spirits.)[66] Where, then, should hunting-farming settlements be placed? As his detractors emphasized after his death in 1807 on his way across Siberia, Rezanov's plans were no less vague than they were grandiose.[67] On one matter, however, he was clear: the Hawaiian Islands seemed most suitable for the establishment of one or more small farms which might provision both Kamchatka and the Northwest coastal settlements. His plan developed readily in conversation with Baranov; all it lacked was concrete detail. It fell, as seen, to the Chief Manager himself to draft those details twelve months after Rezanov's sudden death.

Lieutenant Gagemeister gathered that Rezanov had proposed that a *de facto* Russian depot-cum-plantation should be placed on one or the other of Kamehameha's (or his rival's) islands, both to guarantee a yearly food supply and to improve the Company's position *vis-à-vis* the North Americans. Ostensibly the Russians would arrive only to purchase salt and other foodstuffs. By coincidence, salt was already badly needed. Gagemeister took his sailing orders from Baranov and, on 10 November 1808, proceeded first west to Kodiak, then to Oahu via Kauai (Waimea Bay) and Maui (Lahaina). He was well received at Honolulu when he arrived on 12 January 1809. His was the only *haole* ship in port, a fact indicative (in the opinion of European residents) of tension between Washington and London. Native chiefs and Boston traders helped the visitors to execute their business, while the latter crammed their journals full with firsthand information, facts, and figures.[68] Gagemeister was, in general, impressed by Honolulu. As he noted five months later (20 June) back in Kamchatka:

> Oahu is the finest of the Hawaiian Islands, and possesses an excellent harbour as well as a most temperate clime .... Honolulu is the port not only for Oahu but also for Maui, Molokai, Lanai, and Kahulawe. It is there that the king has his seat. The harbour, described by Captain Broughton in 1796, has a rather dangerous entrance: it has reefs on either side. However, the basin itself is excellent ....[69]

It was, however, in another letter which he drafted while at sea that Gagemeister dealt or, rather, flirted with the idea of a colonizing effort. As a record of Hawaiian-Russian dealings in the early part of 1809, that letter is a masterpiece of politic omissions, and is certainly misleading. He had this to say eight weeks after departing from Oahu:

> One of those islands can produce food in quantities sufficient to supply a large part of Asiatic Russia .... The Bostonians spread rumours on these islands that the Russians wanted to come and settle there. At first, King Kamehameha was afraid of us, but now he says: "Let the Russians come; we have lived without them, and we can also live with them."
>
> If we were to undertake a settlement, we should start it on the island of Molokai .... The king would be willing to sell us either that or some other island .... If we cannot occupy the whole island now, it is possible to buy part of the land ....
>
> For defence in this locality, it would be sufficient to maintain one or two towers with one or more cannon in each. To occupy this territory would require only about 20 Russians for defence and about the same number

for agriculture. The writer is sure that these islands can be occupied
by friendly methods; but if force is necessary, then two ships would be
sufficient ....[70]

False notes are audible throughout. What king, directors of the Company might well have asked, would sell "us" Molokai? Did Kamehameha
say that he would let the Russians come and build a tower or a fort,
bringing their cannon and their ships? Why does an island now decrease in size to "part of the land," now swell to several islands? But
above all, it is Gagemeister's use of the conditional that interests the
modern reader: had he or had he not arrived with orders to attempt the
purchase of land for a plantation and a fort?

Numerous students of the period have reinterpreted such evidence
as is available for and against Russian designs in 1809.[71] Claims that
Baranov did indeed intend that Gagemeister's visit should result both
in a settlement and in a Russian *point d'appui* were soon put forward
by Archibald Campbell, a passenger aboard the *Neva*.[72] Campbell was
a Scot who had been given working passage on the *Neva* from Kodiak.
In an account of his Pacific wanderings, published in Edinburgh in June
1816, he stated:

> It would appear that the Russians had determined to form a settlement
> upon these islands; at least, preparations were made for the purpose.
> The ship had a house in frame on board, and intimation was given that
> volunteers would be received.[73]

Despite Soviet protestations to the contrary, there is no reason for
dismissing Campbell's evidence as trumpery and brushing it aside.[74]
Though he was not a great admirer of the Russians as a whole, he had
no anti-Russian animus or private axe to grind. All things considered,
it seems probable that Gagemeister's orders were to act where the acquisition of a toehold was concerned only if circumstances favoured an
attempt at semi-permanent colonization.[75] Obviously, the political realities of 1809 obliged him to abandon such ideas and, moreover, to reject
any alliance with "Tomari" (Kaumalii), who again sought Russian aid
and friendship.[76] With the blessing of that local sovereign, the Company
might well have gained its toehold in the Islands, but the cost would have
been far too high — Kamehameha's enmity.

The *Neva* remained almost three months at Honolulu. In exchange for
eighteen hundred otter skins, the Russians took twelve hundred pounds
of salt, some salted pork, and a sufficiency of fruit to meet the crew's own
need. It was agreed, besides, that the Hawaiians would themselves bring
dried taro to Sitka in their own vessel as soon as possible.[77] Kamehameha
once again expressed his friendly sentiments towards Baranov. As in
1806, he had given Sysoi (Pavel) Slobodchikov a fine *ali'i* cloak and

feather helmet to be given to Baranov as a gesture of respect,[78] so now, in 1809, he handed gifts to Gagemeister, sending greetings to the elderly Chief Manager.

It was an error on the part of Baranov not to have gone himself to meet Kamehameha. One must recognize, however, that his reasons for dispatching Gagemeister were entirely adequate. He was himself no longer young or even fit. He had logistical and other problems to exhaust him in the northern settlements. Gagemeister spoke good English, which Kamehameha and his rival understood, and was an officer of wide experience. But Gagemeister was at best a lukewarm advocate of Company control in the Pacific and America. Indeed, he was concerned about it only insofar as Russian influence in the Pacific Basin was dependant on the welfare of the Company. Lastly, his private attitude towards that Company as an agent of the State had somewhat changed since his arrival in the colonies as the result of everything that he had seen. It was the pattern of the future.[79]

The actual results of Gagemeister's sojourn at Oahu, disregarding acquisition of a little salt and pork and the surveying of half-a-dozen bays, are summarized by the American historian, Harold W. Bradley:

> In February 1810, thirteen months after the arrival of *Neva*, an English whaler touched at Honolulu. When it departed in March, it carried Archibald Campbell, to whom Kamehameha entrusted a letter to George III. In this letter, the British monarch was reminded of the promises made on his behalf by Vancouver, and he was requested to send a man-of-war to the Hawaiian Islands. In August, Kamehameha addressed a second communication to King George, ...again requesting some tangible evidence of British protection.[80]

Possibly incidents occurred after the *Neva* sailed from Honolulu and before the whaler came that gave Kamehameha reason to believe that he was threatened by an outside force. The likely truth, however, is that royal interest in British suzerainty, (which of course Kamehameha may have understood quite differently from the British on Hawaii or in London), was a consequence of pleasant memories of other times coupled with happenings during the *Neva*'s stay at Oahu. Doubtless, there were European residents of Honolulu ever ready to persuade Kamehameha that whatever misgivings he might have about the presence of a well-armed Russian warship at Oahu, were well grounded.[81] That the king never again regarded Russians with naive and open friendliness and as essentially distinct from, say, New Englanders, has been shown by recent students of the rise and fall of Georg Anton Scheffer as the petty-king of Kauai.[82] Even by 1810, friendly relations between King Kamehameha and Baranov had collapsed. Baranov sent no word of explanation for Lieutenant Gagemeister's attitudes or actions, and Kamehameha was unable to dismiss from mind the rumour, fanned consistently by English and New England settlers and traders on Oahu, that the Russians had indeed future designs upon Hawaiian independence. Very possibly, the *Neva* came to Oahu (and to independent Kauai) on a mission of reconnaissance. The supposition is supported by remarks made ten years later (6 April 1818) in a letter to the Company Head Office in St. Petersburg by Gagemeister: "After my first voyage was the right time [to exploit Kauai], but no one then paid any heed ...."[83] But is not evidence of a reconnaissance by foreigners itself enough to put the independent ruler on his guard?

It was at this uncertain juncture in Hawaiian-Russian contact that hostilities broke out between Great Britain and the anglophobe United States (the War of 1812). From those hostilities, predictably and logically in view of Honolulu's function as the new Pacific *entrepôt*, commercial hub, and focus for Pacific rivalries, arose developments in the relationship between the Russians of the Northwest Coast and King Kamehameha. Symbolically, these new developments revolved around a ship, the *Atahualpa*, as familiar in Honolulu Harbour as at Sitka.[84] She was wrecked, flying the Company's own flag, at Kauai.

One result of the new war, coming so hard upon the heels of the Napoleonic Wars, was that Baranov found himself once more in personal control of all the Company affairs on and about the Northwest Coast. Matters went far more easily for him on the political and economic planes than the directors of the Company could reasonably have expected.[85] The war disrupted trade and posed new problems of supply, but these he handled with a practised pragmatism. He did not regard American free traders as his foes simply because their government was fighting Britain, Russia's ally in the European struggle of the day. For years certain Bostonians had dealt fairly with him. European news took many months to reach the Northwest Coast; in the interim another war could have erupted between the Russians and some other power.

Numerous New England merchantmen were idling at Honolulu and Canton, fearful of capture by a British man-of-war if they put out to sea. Baranov passed the word that if Americans could reach the Russian settlements, they and their crews would all be hired and might sail under the Company's own flag. Within five months, five Yankee masters had arrived in Sitka Sound. Baranov bought two vessels outright, *Lydia* (*Il'men*), a brig and the *Atahualpa* (*Bering*), a Boston-registered three-master that had traded on the coast in Honolulu and Canton since 1801.[86] Thanks to the War of 1812, he had by March 1814 some seven ocean-going craft at his disposal—an unusual state of affairs. He dispatched the *Bering* (ex-*Atahualpa*) to the Hawaiian Islands, still commanded by her former owner, James T. Bennett, but with Aleut hunters and a Cossack crew aboard. In January 1815 the *Bering* underwent repairs in Honolulu Harbour. Four days after her departure, on the 25th, she stopped at Kauai (Waimea Bay). There, on the 31st, a gale beached and damaged her. As he considered proper and correct, King Kaumualii took possession of her and appropriated all her cargo.[87] Bennett and his men passed ten unpleasant weeks on Kauai but were rescued by another Boston ship, the 165-ton *Albatross* (Captain William Smith). Smith, a Virginian who had just left Honolulu, took them speedily to Sitka.[88]

Captain Bennett's reappearance with the news of the disaster at Waimea Bay was soon followed by other troubles. Wilson Price Hunt (1784–1842), the leader of an expedition sent to Fort Astoria in 1810 by the New York-based merchant John Jacob Astor in support of his "Columbian adventure," had been protected by Baranov since the outbreak of the war between Great Britain and the United States. However, Hunt had taken his ship the *Pedlar* and traded firearms and powder for the Tlingits' otter skins in Sitka Sound, and in July 1815 Baranov had impounded her.[89]

These mini-crises were observed by the commander of a Russian sloop, the *Suvorov*, with a mixture of amusement and disgust. Lieutenant Mikhail Petrovich Lazarev (1788–1851), who had arrived at Novo-Arkhangel'sk from Kronstadt roads the previous November, was a thoroughgoing advocate of naval jurisdiction over Russian colonies in the Pacific. From the outset, he refused even to recognize civilian authority, that is to say, Baranov's, over the *Suvorov*. Passions mounted when the "Navy" and the "Company" adherents demonstrated their respective loyalties. Lieutenant Lazarev's own supercargo, the *Suvorov*'s surgeon, Dr. Georg Anton Scheffer, disappointed him by siding with the Company. Exasperated by his treatment at Baranov's hands and by an inability to overrule a Company directive, the lieutenant openly supported Hunt. The fortress guns of Novo-Arkhangel'sk were then trained on the *Suvorov*,[90] whose commander was now threatened with removal from his post if he would not obey instructions. Lazarev slipped anchor in the night and stole away leaving behind his supercargo, Dr. Scheffer, as a pledge of future troubles for Baranov. When the latter had recovered from his rage, he welcomed Scheffer who he knew had not been Lazarev's well-wisher and who was certainly an educated, widely-travelled man.[91]

It was not long before Baranov, shorthanded as ever, had dismissed a passing doubt about the stranger and entrusted him with the important mission of recovering the cargo of the *Bering* from Kauai.[92] So, with help from the American and British governments, James Bennett, Wilson Hunt, and—more immediately—Mikhail Petrovich Lazarev and the enraged Baranov, the scenario was set for Dr. Scheffer's and the Company's adventure in Hawaii. In October 1815 Scheffer sailed for the Islands as a passenger aboard the *Isabella* (Captain Tylor).[93] All the players were in place.

"Russia's Hawaiian adventure" has been dealt with recently in English, on the basis of the primary materials. Accordingly, no effort will be made to tell the story once again. It must be borne in mind, however, that the doctor's bright imperialist vision formed the backdrop to the many naval visits of the ten-year period (1816–25) with which this study is concerned. From it stemmed the problems with which a dozen naval officers, who owed allegiance to the Crown and not to the Company, were forced to cope. In particular, it fell to Otto von Kotzebue (Kotsebu) of the *Riurik*, who stopped in Honolulu both in 1816 and in 1817, to disassociate the Russian State from Dr. Scheffer and his schemes and to allay a streak of russophobic fear on Oahu which the doctor had inspired. One must recognize, in short, that Scheffer's schemes coloured Hawaiian attitudes towards the Russians, at the same time modifying Russian conduct in, and hopes of, Honolulu.

Dr. Scheffer, then, was sent to Kauai both to repossess a salvaged cargo and, as Peter Corney put it, to secure "a footing" for the Company and Russia in the Islands.[94] Footloose, clever, and ambitious, he arrived only to face stiff opposition in the person of the aging English seaman, John Young or Olohana (1742–1835) who was Kamehameha's chief *haole* advisor. Suspecting that the Russo-German visitor was not the simple botanist he claimed to be, Young immediately warned the king against him. So too did several New England shipmasters, including William Hunt, who feared an encroachment on their privileges.[95] But, by drawing on his medical ability and natural persuasiveness, the doctor soothed the king, who even ordered that a house be built for him and land allotted for a Company-owned factory and depot on Oahu.

Queen Kaahumanu in particular, whom many Russian captains were to visit in the next ten years and whom other doctors were to treat for liver problems and obesity, was much taken by Scheffer. As the king's chief consort, she was powerful enough to make the land grants on Oahu more significant than they might otherwise have been. Scheffer was duly given an extensive parcel in the Koolaupoku district on the southeast of the island, and another in the Hoaeae district on the (modern) Pearl River to the west of Honolulu. The latter was presented, at the queen's behest, by her brother Kuakini, known to foreigners as John Adams. In addition, Scheffer gained all fishing rights along a four-mile stretch of seashore on the south side of Oahu, and a flock of sheep and goats. He moved immediately to his house where, surrounded by a breadfruit grove, he played the role of busy botanist and waited for the ships earlier promised by Baranov: the 300-ton settlements-built *Otkrytie* and *Kad'iak* (ex-*Myrtle*).[96] Without them, he could make no further moves.

Scheffer's situation grew more difficult as weeks went by. Provisions were supplied irregularly, and his movements were increasingly restricted. He was right to blame these changes for the worse on English-speaking residents and traders. But at last, on 5 May 1816, the *Otkry-tie* arrived at Honolulu, where Kamehameha had assigned one of his own storehouses for the Company's immediate and future use. Six days later, another Russian brig, the *Il'mena* (ex-*Lydia*) came in, direct from California.[97] The doctor's spirits soared. Commanding the *Otkrytie* was Lieutenant Iakov A. Podushkin, an impoverished but able naval officer who, like his predecessor Gagemeister of the *Neva*, had been seconded to the Company. Not an hour went to waste, if we believe Podushkin's journal for the period, once the *Otkrytie* had anchored in the waveless "inner port" of Honolulu: "I lowered the topmast, repaired the rigging, caulked the deck, repaired the hull of the ship as far as possible, and replenished the water supply ....")[98] Scheffer sailed for Kauai, by way of Hawaii, in the *Otkrytie*; the climax of his meteoric ride in the Pacific was at hand.

On Kauai, he soon secured the goodwill of Kaumualii and a promise that the *Bering*'s cargo would in due course be surrendered. Within ten days he had gone further by persuading the king to place his islands under Russian suzerainty and to grant the Russian Company a full monopoly of trade in sandalwood on Kauai, Niihau, and whatever other islands he might conquer with the Russians' armed assistance. Russian warships would assist him in this venture.[99] Scheffer then had blockhouses erected at Waimea and at Hanalei.[100] For almost a year, he was *de facto* lawmaker on Kauai.

Trouble, however, was already brewing on Oahu. It boiled over when, on 4 September 1816, after acquiring another ship (to be presented to his chief associate, King Kaumualii), Scheffer asked a large party of foreigners to dinner at the Russian factory at Honolulu. All were struck, and some were angered, by the sight of well-armed sentries at its entrance and a Russian flag flying above.[101] There was a bitter argument. Scheffer returned to Kauai not long after and, in mid-September, ordered the construction of a lava blockhouse, Fort Elizaveta. He remained in perfect harmony with Kaumualii who, delighted by the purchase of another merchantman, the *Avon* (Captain Isaac Whittemore), gave him further lands and gifts. At Honolulu, on the other hand, he had already overplayed his cards. The Russian factory had been destroyed by arson. Kamehameha was urged by the influential "minister" John Young and other European residents, to take some steps to counter Scheffer's modest military force at Honolulu. Young and Chief Kalanimoku, also known as Billy Pitt, started construction of another, more substantial fortress.[102] Thus Scheffer and his scheme contributed to the assertion of Hawaiian independence and defensive capability.

But Kauai, not Oahu, was the Scheffer stronghold. By October, he had raised the Russian flag in Hanalei, started work on earthen forts there, renamed a dozen places, given Russian statesmen's surnames to *ali'i* and, for good measure, secured further land grants on the banks of the Waimea, Makaweli, and Hanapepe Rivers.[103] An American attempt to haul the hated Russian flag down at Waimea was forestalled by native sentries, placed by Kaumualii. Such, in broad terms, was the situation when, late in November, word arrived in Kauai that the Russian armed brig *Riurik*, commanded by Lieutenant Otto von Kotzebue, was at anchor in the port of Honolulu.

CHAPTER TWO

Honolulu in the Russian Navy's
North Pacific Plans, 1816–26

Otto Evstaf'evich von Kotzebue (1787–1846), who had sailed with Kruzenshtern while still an adolescent, was the living measure of the change in Russian naval thinking at the close of the Napoleonic Wars. His voyage in the *Riurik*, a fir-built brig of only 210 tons fully laden,[1] was designed to bring new glory to the State, as well as useful mercantile and strategic information. It gave new expression to the international rivalry that had, for decades, been pursued by other means, and it brought Kamehameha's rising Honolulu once and for all into the framework of the international maritime and economic strategy of post-Napoleonic Europe. New emphasis on commerce and the sciences connected with discovery did not break up the underlying continuity of outlook among forward-looking servants of the Russian (or the French or British) Navy. Kotzebue's sailing orders merely showed that, yet again, the pattern of overall intention had been rearranged by war and its conclusion. He himself was representative of both change and continuity in the Pacific naval context. Like his mentor, Kruzenshtern, he was a native of Estonia and a pupil at the Baltic German *Domschule* in Reval (modern Tallin); like Lisianskii, Gagemeister, and the bulk of their lieutenants, he did well at the Cadet Corps, read voraciously, and felt foreign influences.[2] Though he never served abroad as a volunteer, he was based at Arkhangel'sk, the Russian port with the most ancient Western European links. When offered the command of the *Riurik* by Count Nikolai Petrovich Rumiantsev (1754–1826), Russia's Chancellor, he was a well-known, well-connected, rising officer of twenty-seven.[3]

Kotzebue's reputation, as became a Baltic German protégé of Kruzenshtern, the founding father of the Russian Navy's venture in the East and Oceania, was that of an extremely able scientific seaman. The *Riurik*'s mission was in fact to set new precedents in the field of Russian scientific expeditions.[4] Yet at the same time it revived past naval practices and old preoccupations. In the first place, it was organized to solve the ancient problem of a navigable Arctic passage to the Orient. Second, it had been largely planned by Kruzenshtern, Rumiantsev, and Johann Casper Hörner, the astronomer—all men linked with the *Nadezhda*. Third, it was an offshoot of the western expeditionary experience since Admiral Lord Anson's day. As for the wealthy Russian Chancellor's own interests in maritime and scientific questions, they were far from new and had been nurtured and sustained by naval officers, including Kruzenshtern himself, since 1806. With the return of peace to Europe, they

had suddenly put out new shoots.[5] As chief advisor to the Chancellor on
naval matters, Kruzenshtern was privileged to decide, within wide margins, to which questions Kotzebue should address himself in Oceania.
He kept his personal experience of the Marquesas and Hawaiian Islands,
Cook's example, and his own love of cartography, firmly in mind. As he
expressed it in 1818:

> Even supposing that the wished for discovery of a connection between the
> two seas [Atlantic and Pacific] should not be made, ... many important
> advantages would accrue from it .... The crossing of the South Sea twice,
> in quite different directions, would certainly not a little contribute to
> enlarging our knowledge of this great Ocean, as well as of the inhabitants
> of the numerous islands scattered over it.[6]

More than ever, in this postwar period, Pacific service was to be
distinct from other branches of the Russian naval service. On the one
hand, it was linked even more firmly with prestigious social circles and
societies including the academies of Sciences and Arts and with the
Russian Court itself. On the other hand, it was linked to an expenditure
unthinkable to the majority of Admiralty bureaucrats—for what the
indolent and courtly naval minister, Jean François de Sausac, Marquis
de Traversay, would not disburse on the *Riurik*, Rumiantsev would. The
brig was built in Abo, Finland, at the Count's private expense; her shell
alone cost 30,000 roubles.[7]

Count Rumiantsev also paid the salaries of all appointed to the *Riurik*. These included Lieutenant Gleb S. Shishmarev of the Navy; the
precocious Russo-German artist Ludovik or Louis Choris (1795–1828);
the Franco-German soldier-savant Louis (Adelbert) von Chamisso (1781–
1838); and, as surgeon, the young Dorpat entomologist and doctor,
Johann-Friedrich Eschscholtz (1793–1831).[8] Kotzebue's was a cosmopolitan and youthful company. In short, old chords were struck during the
course of preparations for the voyage that was finally to bring the Russian Navy's flag, and not the Company's, to Honolulu Harbour. Use of
English instruments and maps, the Baltic German contribution, ethnographic interests, the invitations sent abroad but the appointment of a
wholly Russian crew—all were familiar from 1804. It fell to Kruzenshtern to underline the *un*traditional and novel aspect of the first of
Kotzebue's two Pacific expeditions:

> Now, in a period when Russia will enjoy all the blessings of a lasting peace
> thanks to the high sentiments of the Emperor Alexander, how could our
> sailors be better employed? Though they have all the requisite qualifica-
> tions, my companions aboard the *Nadezhda* are unemployed today, save
> only *Riurik*'s company and two other men ....[9]

One thinks of the contemporary outlets for the British naval officer seeking adventure of the patriotic sort and fearful of unemployment in a shrinking navy—Arctic or African work. Captain Parry far northwest of Davis Strait, Otto von Kotzebue and Mikhail N. Vasil'ev (1820) north and east of Bering Strait—all three answered the unaccustomed challenge of a period of international peace by sailing north.

The *Riurik* sailed from Kronstadt on 30 July 1815,[10] rounded Cape Horn in January, paused at Chile, then proceeded to Kamchatka and Alaska. By August 1816, Kotzebue was discovering the great Alaskan bay still known as Kotzebue Sound. It was a disappointment that there proved to be no passage east. September found the *Riurik* at Unalaska Island where her company was entertained and fed by the civilian authority.[11] She sailed on 14 September, the same week that Scheffer's fort at Honolulu was destroyed. Kotzebue did not lay his course direct for the Hawaiian Islands, as he had earlier intended, but by way of San Francisco.[12] Thus, unwittingly, he allowed the swell of anti-Russian feeling on Oahu and Hawaii to increase for three more weeks while he unhurriedly approached from the east.

On coasting down towards Kailua, where he wished to meet Kamehameha, Kotzebue realized that there were problems. Four hundred native warriors, he learned, were armed and waiting for him in anticipation of a raid or an attempted occupation. Scheffer's actions, and the local British and American reactions, predisposed Kamehameha to be chilly when Kotzebue eventually met him face to face. However, Kotzebue speedily assured him that Russia had "no colonizing objects" or ambitions in Hawaii and, moreover, that his sovereign had certainly not sanctioned Scheffer's warlike and imperialist acts.[13] Kamehameha was convinced and much relieved. A toast was drunk to Alexander, tsar and high chief of the Russians (*ali'i nui Rukkini*). Food was sent aboard the *Riurik* in which, accompanied by an intelligent and anglophone Hawaiian chief named Manuia, whom the king had sent to aid him in Oahu, Kotzebue made his way to Honolulu. He arrived on 27 November 1816.[14]

Kamehameha's representative, Kalanimoku, and his minister, John Young, received the Russians with civility by Honolulu's waterfront (Pakaka Landing). But there was tension in the air. Many natives, in canoes and on the shore, watched with spears in their hands, and many yelled at Kotzebue in a less than friendly way. Kalanimoku had already met Manuia and so immediately had the visitors surrounded by a native guard for their protection. None too soon the heavy atmosphere grew lighter. Kotzebue's friendly motives were announced to the Hawaiians. The *Riurik* moved closer in, coming to anchor by the *Albatross*.[15] On 29 November the Russians were supplied with taro, yams and coconuts, bananas, watermelons, and enormous hogs in accordance with Kamehameha's order of the week before. It was too soon, nevertheless,

for the Hawaiians' deep misgivings and suspicions to have vanished altogether, and the Russians had a shock when Vasilii S. Khramchenko,
first mate of the *Riurik*, went with a party to survey the harbour's edge.
No sooner did he set up poles with pennants fluttering and start surveying than a crowd of angry natives gathered round. Scheffer's poles and
flagposts and his recent desecration of an old *heiau* on a property that
had been ceded to him by the king were well remembered. The poles
were speedily replaced by sweeping brooms, and laughter followed.[16]

Over the next few days, the Russians—and the French or Franco-
Germans in their midst—made a deliberate and careful study of the
Honolulu scene. They paid attention to traditional Hawaiian ways, the
impact of *haole* ways, the workings of the sandalwood and other trades,
the natural resources and topography, the climate, and, above all, the
potential of Oahu. Choris was a skilful artist and recorded many scenes
and individuals in pen and ink, or aquarelle. Journals were filled with
firsthand data. Local artefacts were bought and stowed aboard. Hawaiian chiefs, escorted by their wives, were well received on the *Riurik*'s
quarterdeck. The naturalist Chamisso was especially busy. He attended
a traditional religious ceremony as a guest of Chief Kalanimoku, spoke
with educated residents, collected specimens, took measurements, observed, and wrote unceasingly.

Accompanied by Khramchenko and Eschscholtz, Kotzebue made a
two-day trip on foot through Mauna Loa village and across the hills
northwest of Honolulu to Waiau by the Pearl River and back.[17] Significantly, he was given a Hawaiian escort and was kept under surveillance
by Captain George Beckley, the British commandant of the new Honolulu fort.

Kotzebue and his people liked Oahu and its natives, whom they described thoroughly, more for the interest than for the practical advantage of their countrymen, just as irreparable cracks were visibly growing
across the structure of the old Hawaiian culture.

Local skills proved very useful to the Russians. For example, native
divers with experience of raising pearls examined and repaired the *Riurik*'s hull, remaining underwater for considerable periods. Likewise,
a number of the Europeans then in Honolulu, notably the Spanish
botanist-entrepreneur Francisco de Paula Marin, the New Englander
Oliver Holmes, and Captain Alexander Adams of the *Albatross*, proved
civil once the Scheffer situation had been clarified.

Lieutenant Kotzebue's attitude towards the Islanders *en masse* and
the *ali'i* in particular was no less sensible than Scheffer's was provocative;[18] nor did he stint his admiration of their skills as, for example, when
he came across a coastal reservoir for sea fish (*lokoi'a*), made of coral
stone, and artificial taro fields (*lo'i*). Relations with the native governor,
Kalanimoku, grew more cordial as days went by. The Russians were in

general approving of the native monarchy and social order that they saw, and they were grateful for a plentiful supply of foodstuffs. As a group, they were intelligent observers of the Honolulu scene; Choris and Chamisso especially proved worthy of their predecessors, Langsdorf and Tilesius von Tilenau.[19]

The *Riurik* left Honolulu on 14 December, and made straight for the Otdia Islands of the Ratak Chain in Micronesia (Eastern Carolines), where Kotzebue had already made discoveries six months before.[20] As she was towed out of the harbour, there was formal gunfire: the Russians gave a seven-gun salute thereby, as Kotzebue put it, consecrating Honolulu's royal fort. The royal brig *Kaahumanu*, rocking gently at her mooring only yards away, likewise responded with a seven-gun salute.[21]

Unannounced and rather brief though it had been, the first of Kotzebue's five Oahu visits had allayed Kamehameha's and his governors' increasing fears about Scheffer. Indeed, it emboldened them to take new measures to control events on Kauai which the *Riurik* had pointedly avoided on her passage out. Then came the information that Baranov had disavowed Scheffer's new treaties, signed by Kaumualii and his followers, and would not pay for any of the three merchantmen which Scheffer thought he had acquired for the Company.[22] Scheffer himself went on his grandiose, conspiratory way, seemingly oblivious to the clouds gathering thick on the horizon.

The beginning of the end came late in April 1817. Kaumualii did not raise the Russian flag, was taking large amounts of goods out of the Company-owned warehouse, and often met with Scheffer's old and new Yankee antagonists, such shipmasters as Isaac Whittemore, Dick Ebbets (1789?-1824), Dixey Wildes, and William Heath Davis. On 8 May, the king gathered his ministers, called out a thousand warriors, and ordered Scheffer and his men to leave Kauai.[23] An angry Scheffer hoped to make a stand at Hanalei, where in fact he claimed the whole island for Russia; but, aware of strong and mounting opposition, he was forced to flee the island in the practically unseaworthy old *Kad'iak* (ex-*Myrtle*). He arrived at Honolulu five days later. Here too his days were numbered, and on 7 July he took the avenue of escape offered, unexpectedly, by Captain Isaiah Lewis of the large Rhode Island trader, *Panther*.[24] Lewis, still obliged to Scheffer for some medical attention in the past, offered a passage to Canton. At Kauai, where the brig stopped briefly, Scheffer knew the final ignominy of avoiding being seen by any native.[25]

Kotzebue, in the meantime, had been active in the Carolines and, since July, in Arctic survey work. His orders were, on coming south again, to look for islands that the Dutch explorer Jacob Roggeveen claimed to have sighted in the eighteenth century. This he did and, in the process, found new islands and examined others in the Kwa-

jalein, Aur, Erikub, and Ailuk groups in the Ratak chain.[26] His Arctic
work came to an end off the St. Lawrence Islands, where a storm struck
suddenly and he was injured. Chamisso was not convinced that Kotzebue was in truth so ill, or delicate in health, that he could justifiably
abandon all attempts to find a navigable passage in the Arctic ice. In
Chamisso's opinion, Kotzebue had already lost his stomach for the freez-
ing latitudes.[27] However that may be, it is apparent that Kotzebue had
not long been pondering his next movement from Unalaska when he recognized the absolute necessity of a return to Honolulu. It was on the way,
he argued, to Manila(!) and, besides, could furnish plants that might
be usefully transplanted on the Ratak chain.[28] His pleasant recollections
of Oahu, and the contrast that it made with Bering Strait, may be discerned in every justifying line of his account. Again by way of Kona, on
the west coast of Hawaii Island ("Teiatatua," or Kailua), where again
he was hospitably received and questioned by Kamehameha, Kotzebue
entered Honolulu Harbour for the second time at 4 p.m. on Wednesday,
13 October 1817. Barely three months had passed since Scheffer had
been ignominiously carried off to Canton.[29]

The *Riurik*'s second stay at Honolulu, lasting fourteen days, was a
reflection of the first in most respects. Again, Kalanimoku, Young, and
the *ali'i* present were obliging and again the Russians took a close look
at the Boston-Northwest-China trade, which made Oahu so important
to New Englanders. Much to his pleasure, Chamisso was allowed into
a *heiau* "fifty fathoms square" in area. He left a colourful description
of "colossal idol heads," decaying pork, and laughing priests. Again
Choris made sketches, while Hawaiians gazed with open curiosity at
Kadu, Kotzebue's friend and principal informant from the Eastern Carolines, whom he had brought to Honolulu at his own request. He shared
Kalanimoku's pleasure that the Scheffer episode was at an end, and
the spectacle of the *Kad'iak* beached on a shoal neither embarrassed
nor disturbed him. He was civil to the Aleuts and Cossacks, ably led
by the intelligent *promyshlennik* Timofei Tarakanov, whom misfortune
had marooned at Honolulu. They were tense, angry, and hungry; understandably, the natives would not feed them *gratis*, and they had no
funds.[30] Having delayed two days at Chief Kalanimoku's own request,
the Russians sailed on 27 October. As a friendly gesture, four American
(New England) shipmasters, John Ebbets of New York, Thomas Meek,
Thomas A. Brown, and W.H. Davis, sent their boats to pull the *Riurik*
out of harbour.

Kotzebue left Manila three months later and proceeded through the
Sunda Strait towards South Africa, entering Table Bay on 29 March
1818. After an amicable meeting with the French Captain Louis Claude
Desaulses de Freycinet of the *Uranie*, he pressed on home by way of
Portsmouth, Copenhagen, and his native Reval. On 3 August, the *Riurik*

stood at anchor facing Count Rumiantsev's mansion on the bank of the Neva.[31] More plainly even than Lieutenant Mikhail Petrovich Lazarev's successful voyage in the *Suvorov*, Kotzebue demonstrated that the final restoration of political stability to Europe heralded another era for the Russian, as for other Western European, navies in the North Pacific area. It showed, moreover, that the principal non-diplomatic objectives of the Kruzenshtern-Lisianskii expedition of twelve years before— supplying and supporting the American, Aleutian, and Kamchatkan outposts physically and morally, and furthering discovery, hydrography, and trade—were to be energetically, but also more selectively, pursued in the new age.[32]

Kotzebue's homecoming was gratifying, both to him and to his patron. Traversay and the Academy of Sciences commended him, and he was soon promoted to captain. Yet, the air of his reception was not altogether gay. There were no patriotic scenes as there had been aboard the *Nadezhda* and the *Neva* in 1806. There was no reaction at the Naval Ministry or in the Company Head Office to Shishmarev's report on the Scheffer-Kaumualii crisis, and responses to Kotzebue's statements that Kamehameha had been told that Tsar Alexander had not ordered Scheffer's actions and was altogether ignorant of them, were yet more muted and equivocal.[33] Though he could not have known it, Kotzebue had in fact returned at a time when the Company directors were in confusion and a regular political campaign against their board, led by a naval group, was in its crucial phase. Even while the *Riurik* had been docking, Traversay, the naval minister, had been arranging new political alignments with the virtual directors of the Company directors, Captain-Lieutenant Vasilii Nikolaevich Golovnin (1776–1831) and Admiral Gavriil A. Sarychev. The year 1817–18 was a turning point in the Pacific for both Navy and Company alike. Even while the *Riurik* had been at Honolulu in October 1817, Kotzebue learned, the sloop *Kamchatka* (Captain Golovnin) had crossed the line and made for Rio de Janeiro *en route* for Chile, Petropavlovsk, and the Russian settlements.[34]

Golovnin had long contended that no merchant company should represent the Russian Crown in the Pacific and America.[35] Officially, his orders were to take supplies and stores to Petropavlovsk and the colonies, survey uncharted stretches of the coasts of what is now southeast Alaska, and inspect the Company's establishments and operations. In reality, this last instruction was the overriding one. It was his aim to gather evidence of inefficiency, incompetence, and even cruelty against the Aleuts to be used against the Company directors in conjunction with the evidence he had amassed in 1810 during his first Pacific voyage in the *Diana*.[36] Golovnin was to devote two years, if he judged it necessary, to the survey of islands, bays, and inlets that had yet to be examined. At the same time, it was tacitly acknowledged in his group that he was to undermine every Company position and contention to be properly or honourably representing Russia. Thus, the groundwork would be laid for a naval takeover at Novo-Arkhangel'sk.

Profoundly prejudiced against the Company though Golovnin might be, he was among the very ablest naval officers in Russia, a distinguished navigator, and a man of comprehensive curiosity. His journals are models of their kind, exhaustive, sober, and controlled. From the perspective of Hawaiian studies, his appointment to the *Kamchatka* must be viewed as fortunate. Like Kruzenshtern and Gagemeister, he spoke fluent English, having served on British warships (1802–05)[37] and had longterm British contacts dating from his adolescence. Captain James Trevenen's influence had been particularly strong, and it had been while serving with Trevenen, formerly of Cook's *Discovery* and now captain of the ship *Ne Tron' Menia*, that Golovnin had read Cook's *Voyages*. Twice in the mid-1790s, his facility in English and his competence in signaling resulted in his serving as liaison officer between the Russians and British in the English Channel where their fleets were on blockade.[38] No Russian officer who visited Oahu in the early nineteenth century was better able to converse with anglophones or was more conscious of the English-language literature on that island.

Like Lisianskii, the youthful Golovnin had made a study of colonial administration on the British Caribbean Islands and was aware of the significance of long-range seaborne commerce.[39] Honolulu was of interest to him as an important trading entrepôt and as a likely point of friction between trading companies and nations. This awareness of the significance of trade was complemented by an interest in native cultures. Just as Kruzenshtern and Iurii Lisianskii had had firsthand dealings with Marquesan Islanders at Taio-hae Bay on Nuku Hiva (April 1804) before approaching the Hawaiian chain,[40] so Golovnin had had *his* earlier encounters with Pacific Islanders. Significantly, those encounters had themselves had their associations with the *Discovery* and Cook.

Coming up to the New Hebrides (Vanuatu) in mid-July 1809, Golovnin had called at Resolution Bay in Tanna. Heavy jungle lay all around and, intermittently, volcanic rumblings were heard. The native craft that finally approached were, however, just as Cook and the Forsters described them thirty years earlier.[41] Barter ensued: fruits, vegetables and firewood for Russian mirrors, beads, and knives. Few artefacts were taken by the *Diana*. Golovnin was under pressure. Even so, he left an excellent account of what he heard and saw on Tanna. For example, we are told what weaponry was laid aside by groups of natives when, mistrustfully, the Russians took their fifty casks of water from a pond described by Cook; what body ornaments and native clothing were in evidence; what structures and canoes were to be seen. A practised linguist, Golovnin drew up a local word-list that remains of ethnological significance today.[42] He was himself, perhaps, no savant of the Chamisso or Langsdorf sort, but he was well-disposed to natural and other sciences by instinct as by policy, and chose the brightest of subordinates. Among *Kamchatka*'s midshipmen when she arrived at Honolulu on 27 October 1818, were Friedrich Lütke (Litke, 1792–1882), later admiral and president of the Academy of Sciences; and future governors of Russian North America, Arvid Etolin (Etholen, 1799–1876) and Ferdinand von Wrangel (1796–1870), later captain of the round-the-world ship *Krotkii* and, like Lütke, a full admiral and eminent geographer.[43] It might be said of Golovnin even more justly than of Kruzenshtern in 1803, that he was carrying the future of the Russian naval venture in the North Pacific Ocean. And for this modern students of Hawaii may be grateful.

Golovnin had spent eight months surveying and inspecting in the North before proceeding to the port of Monterey in California. There, he met with Gagemeister,[44] the new Governor of Russian North America. From Monterey, the *Kamchatka* doubled back to Port Rumiantsev and Fort Ross, the Russian outposts in "New Albion," then on 27 September headed for Hawaii.[45] Like his predecessors, Golovnin called first at Kealakekua Bay to pay a visit to Kamehameha I (21–23 October). Since the king was at Kailua, the Russians went there too. Kalanimoku, who had earlier reported to the king on the *Riurik*'s second stop at Honolulu and remembered Kotzebue well, was in attendance. Guns were fired in salute, and Golovnin was promised that in Honolulu he would certainly be given what he needed. Having carefully examined Golovnin's and his subordinates' cocked hats and highly polished shoes, the king excused himself. He wished to play a game. The Russians gazed at his obese and idle heir, "Lio-Lio," at his wives, and at his admiralty yard, expressed their gratitude for ten enormous hogs, and filled their sails for Oahu.[46]

Golovnin's 1818 account of life in Honolulu is among the fullest and most circumstantial written by a European naval captain of his age.[47] It deals at length with the trade and commerce that revolved around the harbour front, with social and political developments, with European-native dealings and the evident decline of the traditional Hawaiian ways, and with local customs and techniques. It is, in short, of major ethnographic value. But the reader must be left to judge these matters for himself (see Part II). Suffice it to emphasize the *pattern* in the Kotzebue, Chamisso, and Golovnin accounts. All three reported on the subjects listed above, and were anxious to present a sober, factual description of the Honolulu scene. All three made trips on foot out of the settlement, collected Hawaiian artefacts, and held lengthy conversations both with native chiefs (*ali'i*) and with well-travelled Americans in port. Nor does the pattern end with textual accounts; as Chamisso's and Kotzebue's narratives had been enriched by Louis Choris, so was Golovnin's to be enriched by watercolours from the brush of Mikhail Tikhanov, artist on the *Kamchatka*.[48]

Like his predecessors, Golovnin examined local husbandry and agriculture, carefully described the square stone fort beside the harbour,
entertained friendly *ali'i* (in his case, Ka-Hekili Ke'eaumoku and Boki),
and was begged by young Hawaiians to accept them as additional and
unpaid seamen. Golovnin, unlike the cautious Kotzebue, saw no reason
for not taking one Hawaiian youth back to St. Petersburg. He gave a
passage to an Islander named Lauri, renamed Terentii, as a potential
intermediary between Russia and Hawaii and, perhaps, as an apologist
for Russia. (Lauri was not to disappoint him. Having spent a winter in
St. Petersburg, he was returned to Honolulu where he praised various
aspects of Russian life.)[49]

Lieutenant Kotzebue's voyage out in the *Riurik* had come as no surprise in England, nor had any effort been made to keep the expedition
secret. Even so it was disturbing, as had been the news of Scheffer's
scheming, brought to England on 8 June 1817 by the *O'Cain* (Captain
Robert McNeil). It lent substance to the rumours of the previous six
months, that Russian influence was spreading in Hawaii, and to Lieutenant A. M'Konochie's *Considerations on the Propriety of Establishing
a Colony on One Side of the Sandwich Islands*.[50]

In Britain, no one knew what an impression had been made on Kotzebue and Shishmarev when they learned, while in Oahu in November
1816, that "a fine ship" was being built in New South Wales for Kamehameha's use in peace or war.[51] Had it been known that Kotzebue viewed
the building of that vessel, the *Prince Regent*, as a pledge of British
readiness to intervene should other Powers grow too bold in their pretensions in the Islands,[52] and moreover, that his view would be accepted
by the Russian Foreign Ministry, McNeil's news of Scheffer would have
been softened. As it was, rumour and apprehensions flourished. There
were Russians, it appeared, on the Kuril and Aleutian Island chains,
by San Francisco, on Oahu, Kauai, Molokai, and along the Northwest
Coast to an uncertain point of latitude.[53]

Profoundly though he scorned the Russian government as inefficient
and tyrannical, Sir John Barrow (1764–1848), Secretary to the Admiralty Board in London, was provoked to action by the news of Kotzebue's
Arctic enterprise. He had himself long been involved in the attempt to
find a navigable Northern Passage, and considered that he had a public
duty to perform where exploration was concerned. It was vexatious that
the Russians had such a hold on the Hawaiian Islands, or on some of
them at least; but the Americans were also present in increasing numbers. There were certainly no plans in 1817–18, to establish British
rule at Honolulu.[54] Possible Russian domination of a navigable passage
to the North Pacific Ocean, on the other hand, called for effective action. The mere *finding* of a passage by the Russians would be bad. "It

would," wrote Barrow testily, "be mortifying if a naval power of but yesterday should complete a discovery in the nineteenth century which was so happily commenced by Englishmen in the sixteenth."[55] The House of Commons sympathized and, mindful of the harm that Russian triumphs in the North might do to Britain's China trade, offered a very handsome prize for the discovery of any navigable northern passage to the Orient. The golden age of Arctic exploration had begun—an exploration that would once more bring Russian Navy ships to Honolulu.

In May 1818 when news arrived of the Buchanan-Franklin naval expedition to the North and of the Ross and Parry venture north and west through Baffin's Bay, the Russian Admiralty recognized that it was time for Russia to win laurels and political advantage, if not economic profit, from another major scientific venture. What was needed was another, even grander undertaking on the lines of Kotzebue's but supported generously by the State. Unlike the British or Americans, the Russians could not compensate for failure by activity in South America or in the South or mid-Pacific. It was recognition of this hard reality that led to the adoption by December 1818 of the concept of a double expedition.[56] While one Russian squadron sought a navigable passage in the North linking Pacific and Atlantic tidal waters, a second would head south where not one Western European expedition had done any work whatever since James Cook's return in 1775. In Antarctica, a Russian naval officer might hope to emulate that hero of discovery and even complement his work.

The Naval Ministry offered command of the Antarctic expedition first to Kruzenshtern, who pleaded illness, then to Makar Ivanovich Ratmanov, first lieutenant of the *Nadezhda*. He too pleaded ill health and recommended Faddei (German: Fabian) von Bellingshausen, 1778–1852), former fifth lieutenant on the *Nadezhda*, who accepted the position. It was a happy choice for Bellingshausen was to lead his ships—the *Vostok* (sloop) and the *Mirnyi* (reconfigured transport) to conspicuous success if not glory in Antarctica and Polynesia.[57] For the simultaneous Pacific-Arctic venture, Captain-Lieutenant Mikhail N. Vasil'ev was appointed to the sloop *Otkrytie*, Lieutenant Gleb Shishmarev, late of the *Riurik*, to the reconfigured transport ship *Blagonamerennyi*. Their orders were to pass through Bering Strait and to do their best to find a passage to the northeast.[58]

What Vasil'ev and Shishmarev hoped to do was an impossibility, but circumstantial factors made their Arctic failure the more certain. Neither was of Kruzenshtern's or Kotzebue's calibre as an aggressive scientific officer or equal to a Lazarev or Golovnin in terms of seamanship. Though recently and strongly built (the *Otkrytie* was, like the *Vostok*, 130 feet in length and 33 feet in the beam, her consort only ten feet shorter), their ships were far less suited to their task than the *Riurik* had been. No doubt, their officers and crews were competent. Besides two scions of successful Anglo-Russian naval families, Lieutenant Roman Petrovich Boil (Boyle) and Midshipman Roman Gall (or Hall), Vasil'ev had an eminent astronomer, Pavel Tarkhanov, and a first-rate artist, Emel'ian Korneev on the *Otkrytie*.[59] The subordinates of Shishmarev included Mikhail Petrovich Lazarev's brother Aleksei, his own distinguished nephew Nikolai,[60] and an excellent young second-in-command, Ivan Ignat'ev. Neither solid ships nor competent subordinates, however, made a difference when in July 1820 at latitude 71°6'N, Vasil'ev met drifting ice-sheets. Since the *Otkrytie* lacked any longboat or *baidarka* (kayak) in which the shallow coastal waters to the east might be explored, he and Shishmarev headed south to the St. Paul Islands and Unalaska.[61] It was obviously necessary to obtain a shallow-draughted boat. Shishmarev had the parts and/or the needed spares aboard. Vasil'ev therefore went to Sitka, where he left Ivan Ignat'ev to construct that boat. He and Shishmarev, meanwhile, made for San Francisco harbour where they wintered very comfortably (November 1820 to 17 February 1821). It was *en route* from San Francisco to the Sitka boatyard that in late spring 1821 (25 March–7 April) Vasil'ev, Shishmarev, and their companies called in at Honolulu on the first of two surveillance and provisioning visits.

Certainly, there was good reason for a passing Russian sloop to show the flag at Honolulu. Captain Matvei Murav'ev, the latest Governor of Russian North America, had reached the colonies in 1820 with instructions to enforce an isolationist and even xenophobic policy. This was calculated to enflame whatever complications might already be developing in the Pacific as a consequence of Spain's decline as a world power. Murav'ev's was the unhappy task of implementing a decision, reached on Golovnin's and Gagemeister's earlier advice, aimed at closing Russia's North Pacific islands, shores, and harbours to intrusive foreign traders. In particular, New England poachers were at last to be excluded from the Russian territories.[62] In the Governor's instructions lay the seeds of disaster for the Russian Navy's hopes and aspirations in the North Pacific Ocean.

The British and U.S. governments were both annoyed by, and refused to recognize imperial *ukazes* of September 1821 claiming exclusive rights and sovereignty over territory in America down to the 51st degree of latitude, extending to 115 miles offshore on both the North American and Asian sides of the Pacific.[63] Tensions arose in the North Pacific Basin and negotiations were held in St. Petersburg, from which in 1824–25 derived conventions between Russia, on the one hand, and Washington and London on the other, that would fix the size of Russian North America and modern Alaska. These developments were in the future when the *Otkrytie* first sailed into Honolulu Harbour. To Vasil'ev, however, it was obvious that Russian interests at Novo-Arkhangel'sk could not be furthered by a full eclipse of Russian trading interests in the Hawaiian Islands. Foodstuffs would be needed for the settlements that could not feed themselves. Since the future of Fort Ross, the Company's outpost in California, looked more uncertain every month in view of anti-monarchist and even revolutionary sentiment in Upper California,[64] what North Pacific source of foodstuffs was more promising to Novo-Arkhangel'sk than Honolulu? At the very least, the Russian Navy should attempt to counteract whatever anti-Russian sentiments and policies entrenched American or British residents of the Hawaiian Islands might be fostering.[65]

When he had called at San Francisco five years previously (1816), Kotzebue had been drawn into a dialogue with the provincial Spanish governor, Pablo da Sola, on the matter of Fort Ross and illicit Russo-Spanish trade.[66] The fact was, as officials of the Russian Foreign Ministry well knew, that Fort Ross was an illegal settlement "wedged into Spain's possessions on the coast of California." Monterey, the local Spanish capital, was "barely 1° away from it."[67] For ten years the question had been festering, a sore on Russo-Spanish amity. No Russian officer who called there could argue ignorance of its potential as the core of a considerably larger Russian colony and mid-Pacific base for Russian shipping (though perhaps not as the major source of grain that Nikolai Petrovich Rezanov and Chief Manager Baranov had envisaged in the fall of 1806).[68] On the other hand, no naval officer since Kotzebue's time would have been unaware of the possible results of Russia's seizure of what some powers regarded as Spanish territory. In 1817–1818 Golovnin and Gagemeister had been forced to listen patiently to complaints from the colonial authorities at Monterey and San Francisco. Spanish patience was exhausted.

However in the spring of 1821, the need to deal with Madrid—over the question of Fort Ross, at least—was diminishing. Revolution in Madrid seemed possible, though not yet likely, to Tatishchev, Russia's minister to Spain.[69] Even these considerations showed the prudence of developing goodwill at Honolulu where a new, unstable king, Kamehameha II (also known as Liholiho) had no history of friendship with Baranov. What concessions could Russia gain from a provocatively forward policy in New Albion, Fort Ross, and California in 1821? Russia still supported Spain in South America, and Spain had few supporters in her struggles with colonial insurgents.[70] Fort Ross might reasonably be abandoned if Spain gave Russia trading rights in perpetuity in Upper California.[71] In any case, whether or not a just accomodation was arrived at over Fort Ross and the trading problems, and regardless of the ultimate success or failure of the local revolutionaries, the Russians on the Northwest Coast could almost certainly draw benefit from a continuing, and correct relationship with the Hawaiian monarchy.[72]

Vasil'ev's and Shishmarev's officers had almost daily dealings with Kamehameha II and his stepmother, Kaahumanu. They were also brought into immediate, and vexing, contact with the king's French secretary, the adventurer Jean Rives (Ioane Lunahine); with Kalanimoku and the rather older Boki; with Reverend Hiram Bingham and his missionary colleagues from New England; and with certain of the new king's wives. Ubiquitous though evidence of European contacts and acculturation were, in Honolulu the Russians were impressed by the resilience of ancient ways, especially at court. The king acknowledged the usefulness, in certain spheres, of the missionaries, whose compound lay "three *versts* off" to the east of Honolulu quayside.[73] Kamehameha II was quite at home in the New England merchants' two-storey plank houses, one of which quartered Kaahumanu and her courtiers in 1821.[74] He was also perfectly conversant with the international trade in sandalwood from which he drew a yearly revenue of thirty-five or forty thousand *piastres* according to Karl Gillesem, a midshipman on the *Blagonamerennyi*. Nevertheless, Hawaiian ways and attitudes were strong. Kamehameha II and *ali'i* close to him ate, dressed, and were housed in traditional fashion when they were not in the company of foreigners. Polygamy was general, *kapu* were still observed, dancing and singing had not noticeably been affected—yet—by the Americans in black whom Gillesem mistakenly referred to as Moravians.

Both curiosity and duty led the Russians to investigate the state of readiness and composition of the royal fleet and army. The fleet now consisted of nine brigs, five schooners, and a great flotilla of canoes. The infantry had forty thousand rifles in an arsenal above the town which was defended by a harbour fortress mounting thirty-two serviceable pieces, one of forty-eight-pound calibre.[75] The Hawaiians recognized that the fort was badly placed and had such deficient ramparts that a single warship could have silenced its guns.[76] The day was over, on the other hand, when Russian policy might even contemplate such an attack. Significantly, by spring 1821, it was not Vasil'ev's emperor but the Americans who Kamehameha II feared might seize Oahu. Only six weeks before the Russian squadron's coming, we read in the instructive journal of Maria Loomis, the wife of a New England mission helper, that Kamehameha II had asked a young Hawaiian who had recently returned from the United States to estimate the likelihood of a U.S. invasion by frigate.[77] For the distant Tsar Alexander, Kamehameha II felt a measure of affection, idly wondering if he might even visit him.[78]

The trade in sandalwood was, by comparison with these political and military questions, of minor interest to the Russian visitors in 1821. Nevertheless, the Russian records are of major interest today because, albeit incidentally, they describe that trade at its zenith. By the spring of 1822, it was already in decline.[79] In passing comments the Russian narratives give evidence that the New England traders were engaged in bitter, ceaseless competition with each other to get sandalwood either from Kamehameha II or, more often, from the "favoured chiefs" whom he permitted to participate in the monopoly.[80] They saw the vessel, *Cleopatra's Barge*, which the now hard-pressed partnership, Bryant & Sturgis, had induced the king to purchase in November 1820 for a good pile of that dense and valuable timber.[81] Despite its gilt mirrors and shining brasswork, it was obviously not worth eighty thousand Spanish *piastres*, the reported selling price.[82] The profits in Canton for such small quantities of sandalwood as the New Englanders could still obtain on the Hawaiian Islands, so the Russians learned, were lately much reduced: wood bought for six or seven *piastres* a *picul* might be sold for only nine or ten.[83] As for the ploy of giving ships for sandalwood, there was a limit to the number of attractive brigs that Kamehameha II and his chiefs could use.[84] The Honolulu market was already overstocked with merchandise. The golden days of easy profits had passed.

At least a few New England merchants and Hawaiian chiefs emulated John Jacob Astor's efforts to extract a profit from the hungry Russians on the Northwest Coast.[85] As the *Otkrytie*'s own officers admitted, Russia's North Pacific settlements continued to be basically dependent on the outside world for foodstuffs and manufactured goods. Their needs could not be met from Fort Ross and round-the-world provisioning was inefficient and extremely costly.[86] As the Russians studied Honolulu, so, in 1821 and on the basis of their comments, did the Honolulu traders closely study the potential of the Sitka and Kamchatka markets. From the *Otkrytie*'s and the *Blagonamerennyi*'s first visit to Oahu, early symptoms of declining sandalwood profitability and a depressed Hawaiian market, sprang new schemes for Honolulu-Russian trade in which the Boston firm Marshall & Wildes took the lead.[87] Within three months of the Vasil'ev-Shishmarev stay, a group of enterprising chiefs had sent their vessel *Thaddeus* to Petropavlovsk-in-Kamchatka with a large amount of salt.[88] She traded profitably in the North, and returned to Oahu with a mixed cargo of canvas, cordage, iron tools, and salted fish.[89] So promising a start was prematurely ended, to the chiefs' regret, by the *ukazes* of September 1821. These closed all coastlines under Russian jurisdiction north of 51°N and banned foreign vessels from approaching within a hundred miles of Russian ports.

The *Otkrytie* and *Blagonamerenny* returned to Unalaska Island in June 1821. Vasil'ev passed Cape Lisburne on 1 August but was stopped by solid ice and high winds four days later at 70°40'N, 161°27'W). He instead sailed south to Petropavlovsk. Shishmarev called at Cape Mulgrave, Alaska, then went west towards Cape Serdtse Kamen' which was sighted on 4 August. He too was repelled by ice and storms, and so withdrew to Petropavlovsk. Shishmarev did survey both the St. Lawrence and St. Matthew Islands on his way. Frustrated for a second time, the squadron left for Kronstadt in October. However its difficulties in the North were not yet over. Barely three days out from Petropavlovsk, both vessels were shrouded in a thick mist. They soon lost contact with each other, and proceeded individually to Oahu, the designated rendezvous *en route* for South America. Shishmarev brought the *Blagonamerennyi* back into Honolulu Harbour on 24 November 1821. The *Otkrytie* arrived three days later.[90]

News of the imperial *ukazes* had not yet reached the Hawaiian Islands. Although they were aware of the approaching quarantine of Russian outposts in Kamchatka and along the Northwest Coast, which was to last three years (1821–24) and cause great hardship,[91] neither Vasil'ev nor Shishmarev spoke of it publicly at Honolulu. As before, they and their people were hospitably received by the *ali'i*, by established foreign residents, and by the Reverend Hiram Bingham now the *de facto* head of the New England mission lately founded on Oahu.

The Russians supported Bingham's work in public fashion and attended both his chapel and his school for the Hawaiians. Thus they strengthened the missionaries' hand at a particularly awkward time, a fact which Bingham himself openly recognized in later years.[92]. Well rested and handsomely provisioned, the Russians sailed on 20 December 1821 for Cape Horn, Brazil, and home.[93] They entered Kronstadt roadstead on 1 August 1822.[94]

Having issued the imperial *ukazes* of September 1821, threatening seizure of offending foreign merchantmen, confiscation of their cargoes, and imprisonment of unrepentent officers, the Russian Crown was forced to recognize their naval implications. If "poachers" were in fact to be arrested in so vast an area, at least one naval squadron was immediately required for that duty. This was plain to Count Karl V. Nesselrode (1780–1862), the Russian foreign minister, by April 1822.

Two formal British protests were followed by an angry diplomatic note from the United States referring to the freedom of the high seas and illegal annexations.[95] It was not in Russia's interest to clash with Britain over such an issue. At this time the objective of Tsar Alexander I was to bring "order" to the Balkans as a whole, and British neutrality was needed. On the other hand, the Company for whose specific benefit the *ukazes* had been promulgated was in deep financial difficulties.[96]

Ukazes could not be ignored if the imperial authority was to remain unquestioned. Steps were thus taken that the government itself would have regarded as impolitic a year before. The sloop *Apollon* (Captain Irinarkh Stepanovich Tulub'ev) had not long before left Kronstadt for the colonies, and was expected to arrive by August 1822.[97] Like both the *Kamchatka* and the *Otkrytie*, she was a well-equipped and manned vessel of about 900 tons. She mounted thirty-two new guns and was the nucleus for a Pacific squadron.[98]

Further steps were also taken. The frigate *Kreiser* (Captain Mikhail P. Lazarev) and the *Ladoga* (ex-*Mirnyi* of the Bellingshausen-Lazarev Antarctic expedition) were ordered to the Russian Northwest Coast laden with eighteen months' provisions. Their instructions were to join the *Apollon*, patrol the Russian waters in dispute, and stop American free traders' depredations.[99] The fifteen days between the *Otkrytie*'s return to Kronstadt and the *Kreiser*'s departure were sufficient for Vasil'ev, an old associate of Lazarev, to brief him fully on the Coastal and, no doubt, the Californian and Hawaiian situations.

The *Apollon* reached Sitka in October 1822. By then the government had authorized the building of a new 750-ton armed sloop, the *Predpriiatie* (*Enterprise*), expressly for the purpose of cruising in the North Pacific waters claimed by Russia, and delivering supplies and stores to Sitka and Kamchatka. But it was late to lay the keel of any ship with that in view: earlier bans on trade with foreigners within the Company's domains in the Pacific were reducing Sitka and the other coastal outposts to despair. It was no longer possible to purchase what was needed, year by year. Governor Matvei I. Murav'ev was forced to take what came from Kronstadt—it could hardly be rejected and returned as rotten, broken, or not wanted. It was becoming obvious that the system of supplying from the Baltic was an economic failure. Goods from Kronstadt cost far more than Americans had charged for better and fresher goods from California or Hawaii. They came too late, and could be sent only if international tensions posed no threat to their delivery, as had occurred in 1809–12. It cost the Company some 700,000 roubles to dispatch a cargo worth 200,00 roubles in its ship *Kutuzov* (1820–21).[100] There was hunger in the settlements from Novo-Arkhangel'sk to the Pribylov Islands even by the early weeks of 1822. By 1823 Governor Murav'ev saw no alternative to stating that "necessity altered the rules" and sending the *Golovnin*, a small company schooner, to Oahu for provisions.[101]

Crisis reigned in the Pacific settlements until the reappearance of American free traders in the wake of the conventions signed by representatives of the United States, Russia, and Great Britain (1824–25). Those conventions, which delimited the Russian border on the Northwest Coast (Alaska's "panhandle") and gave U.S. and British subjects liberty to take their ships up Russian rivers to the source of furs,[102] made the *Predpriiatie*'s proposed policing work superfluous. It was however inconceivable that she should not be put to use without delay. As an investment she had yet to earn her keep, and there were always cargoes to be taken to the colonies and coastlines to be charted. Captain Kotzebue took command of her in January 1823 and sailed from Kronstadt six months later on 27 July.[103]

It was Kotzebue's luck to be released from all surveillance and pa-

trolling duties. He was finally allowed to give free rein to his academic
and investigative instincts. As a consequence, Hawaiian studies are the
richer for the records of his final double visit to Oahu, of 14 December 1824 to 31 January 1825 and 14 to 19 September 1825. As he had
in the *Riurik*, in the *Predpriiatie* he made a scientific passage through
the Ratak group and a visit to Oahu. On the *Riurik* he had been a
junior lieutenant; now his rank and reputation gave him influence and
he was able to select eight of the brightest midshipmen in Russian service and six "scientific gentlemen." Among the latter were his old Reval
(modern Tallin) acquaintance, Dr. Johann Friedrich Eschscholtz (1793–
1831) of the *Riurik*, Heinrich Seewald (Russian: Zival'd, 1797–1830) the
zoologist, two Russo-German naturalists, Emil (Russian: Emilii Khristianovich) Lenz (1804–65) and Ernst Karlovich Hoffmann (Russian: Gofman, 1801–71), and the Dorpat-based astronomer and mathematician
Wilhelm Preis (1793–1839). Half of his lieutenants later attained flag-
rank.[104]

The *Predpriiatie* was the largest vessel ever to have entered Honolulu's inner harbour. Her arrival caused a stir. Kaahumanu was away
from Honolulu. Kotzebue found himself much in the company of Queen
(Lydia) Namahana, a widow of Kamehameha I whom he had met on 28
October 1817 at Kailua on the Kona Coast.[105]

Kinau was now the Island's governor, and there were other major
changes which discouraged the Russians. Hiram Bingham and his fellow
missionaries had acquired an ascendancy over Queen Kaahumanu and
were enforcing a compulsory and rigid program of education on Oahu.
Gin shops and public drunkenness were far more evident than they had
been in 1817, despite the missionaries' oppressive presence. Shopkeepers, now semi-permanently based in Honolulu, were exploiting would-be
purchasers of ribbons, laces, necklaces, and porcelain.

Still, the Russians were received with every kindness and were happy,
on 17 January 1825, to see the influential chief Kalanimoku entering the
harbour with a regular Hawaiian fleet. He and Kotzebue spoke at length
of the idolatry still practised in the highlands of Oahu, of the missionary
impact, and of the present king's great father, Kamehameha I.[106] With
Queen Namahana, Kotzebue spoke of the Hawaiian Lauri's experience
in Russia, of Russian painting, and of Mr. Bingham.

Soon before the *Predpriiatie*'s departure for Sitka Sound, Kaahumanu
and her suite returned to Honolulu from Kauai. She too remembered
Kotzebue, whom she visited aboard his ship several times and showered
with parting gifts. As Surgeon Ivan Kovalëv of the *Otkrytie* had tended
her and other members of the royal family successfully in April 1821,[107]
so now Kalanimoku took the advice of Dr. Eschscholtz. Of the early
Russian visitors to Honolulu with a surgeon in their company, few failed
to secure the honest gratitude of members of that family.

Kotzebue's eight-month absence from Oahu coincided with a series of political upheavals which resulted directly or indirectly from the deaths of Kamehameha II and his consort, Kamamalu.[108] HMS *Blonde* (Captain Lord Byron) had arrived at Honolulu with surviving members of the ill-starred royal group in May and had departed on 8 June.[109] A third Kamehameha had been recognized and Kalanimoku retained influence as co-regent with Queen Kaahumanu; but in fact Kalanimoku's power had diminished as his strength had ebbed away, and Hiram Bingham had kept the king "under the strictest surveillance" while he "meddled in affairs of state."[110] The Kotzebue narrative speaks eloquently for itself (see Part II). The Russians were disgusted by the missionaries' confiscation of a set of puppet-booths and magic lanterns brought by Captain Byron as an entertainment for the Hawaiians.[111]

Kotzebue's final stay at Honolulu was by far the least agreeable. Kalanimoku was apparently approaching death, and Queen Namahana was unfriendly thanks to Bingham's influence. Thus it was with mixed relief and sadness that the Russians left for home. As though in public recognition of the fact that a most happy royal era in Hawaiian-Russian intercourse had ended and another started, Kotzebue spent his last free time on shore in conversation, not with any representative of the Hawaiian dynasty, but with the captain of an English whaler.[112] Henceforth, Honolulu was, in the minds of Russian officers in the Pacific, only an entrepôt and supply station—nothing more.[113]

With the reopening of Russian coastlines north of 51°N to foreign traders, there ensued a brief flurry of interest in Sitka and Kamchatka on the part of leading Honolulu merchants, as potential markets for their goods. Marshall & Wildes and especially Bryant & Sturgis did their best in 1826–28 to re-establish profitable trade with Russian settlements which would "always be in want of certain articles" that Honolulu could provide.[114] Their efforts brought limited rewards; the Honolulu-Sitka trade was in decline even by 1827 and continued to decline throughout the 1830s. In any year between 1825 and 1838, never more than four American controlled and registered free traders had been active on the Russian Northwest Coast.[115] By 1826 the new form of Hawaiian-Russian dealings had been settled by the visit of the naval transport *Krotkii* (Captain Ferdinand Petrovich Vrangel' or Wrangel) to Oahu.

Wrangel had left Kronstadt in August 1825 with a cargo of supplies for Petropavlovsk-in-Kamchatka and the Company possessions in America. He had arrived on 11 June 1826 by way of Rio de Janeiro, Valparaiso, and the Marquesas Islands (where Nukuhivan warriors had killed four of his men).[116] The *Krotkii* was partially unloaded in Kamchatka and arrived at Novo-Arkhangel'sk in September 1826. Because in the opinion of the governor, her presence there was superfluous, Wrangel was readying for home within two weeks. He sailed to Honolulu on 13 October.

Having vainly sought "Maria Laxara Island" which was still marked on his chart (27°6N, 139°20E) though its existence had been suspect even twenty years before, and hindered by opposing winds for days, he did not enter Honolulu until the third week of November. At the centre of at least two dozen merchantmen, each one flying the Stars and Stripes, he saw a smart "naval corvette, mounting twenty-four 32-pounders."[117] She was the USS *Peacock* (Captain Thomas ap Catesby Jones). Thus the Russians were made aware of American commercial and political involvement in the Islands.

The *Peacock* had been sent to the Hawaiian Islands in response to claims that U.S. lives and property were being threatened there. More specifically, the growth of a considerable whaling fleet since 1821 had led to mass desertions; murderous ex-seamen, it was claimed, had joined with natives and were now as great a problem as the collection of the debts incurred by chiefs in years past.[118] Since 1817 *ali'i* had been buying goods on credit, giving notes for stands of sandalwood that were as yet uncut. Often their debts remained after the wood at their disposal had been carried off to China.[119]

Wrangel reported on these concerns in his account of *Krotkii*'s one-week stay at Honolulu. He throws a welcome beam of light on the uncomfortable position of the first British consul on Oahu, Richard Charlton, during the *Peacock*'s visit. Consul Charlton was surrounded by proof of the United States' fast-growing influence at Honolulu. Yet, because Thomas ap Catesby Jones came in the interests of civic peace and economic order, to examine "claims for property"[120] and not American imperialist claims to the Hawaiian Archipelago, Charlton was obliged to put a pleasant face on his dilemma and associate with John C. Jones, Marshall & Wildes' local agent, a man he much disliked.[121] In Wrangel's presence, Charlton felt obliged to be polite towards Americans against whom, in reality, he was "most bitter."[122] Wrangel, Charlton, Jones, and ap Catesby Jones shared at least one friendly dinner in the course of which the commodore gave Wrangel news of the "rebellion" then raging in Tahiti. There were other pleasantries and courtesies, but Wrangel understood that, fundamentally, ap Catesby Jones and Charlton were both determined that a measure of Hawaiian independence should continue to exist if the alternative was British or American possession.[123] He himself was scrupulously neutral on such questions, dealing equitably with the British and Americans. If Wrangel and his lieutenants were obliged for hospitality and lodging to a Yankee shipmaster, John Meek of the *Tamaahmah*, it was excusable; they had encountered him at Sitka three months earlier,[124] and Meek had long had amicable trade links with the Russians.

In other ways too, the *Krotkii*'s visit followed the *Riurik*'s pattern. As had Kotzebue and the naturalist Chamisso, Wrangel and his officers went up into the hills behind the town of Honolulu, made a study of traditional Hawaiian husbandry and diet, and disliked their escort's "taro dough." Like Kotzebue, Chamisso, and Golovnin before them, they had lengthy audiences with King Kauikeaouli (Kamehameha III), "a boy of twelve or so," the younger brother of Kamehameha II, who had died two years earlier,[125] and made their estimates of royal strength. They cast a cool, appraising eye over the missionaries whom, they knew, both ap Catesby Jones and Boki, now Oahu's governor, were criticizing privately and publicly.[126] Boki had formed a sentimental tie with Wrangel on the *Kamchatka*'s first visit to Honolulu eight years earlier.) Like Surgeons Eschscholtz, Kovalëv, and Zaozerskii of the *Riurik*, *Otkrytie* and *Blagonamerennyi*, the *Krotkii*'s Dr. Kiber tended Billy Pitt and other native courtiers.[127]

Hawaiians and Americans alike rendered assistance to the *Krotkii*'s crew, as they would help that of the *Amerika* (Captain Ivan Ivanovich fon-Shants) in 1835[128] in full knowledge of Russia's unaggressive and innocuous position *vis-à-vis* the Hawaiian monarchy and semi-independence. Thus Russians benefited by the imperial withdrawal from an intercontinental power struggle in the North Pacific Basin, the political and mercantile elements of which had almost fused in 1820.[129] Necessarily, Hawaiian attitudes towards the Russian Crown and Navy underwent another change when, at the outbreak of the Crimean War (part of which was fought in the Pacific) the strategic implications—for Hawaii as for Britain—of a full Russo-American *entente* were understood.

The very fact that there was tacit understanding between Russia and the anglophobic United States in 1853–54 was enough to strip the passing Russian of his mantle of neutrality.[130] However, this was far ahead in Kotzebue's, Golovnin's, and Wrangel's Honolulu days. As they themselves drew daily benefit from Russia's even-handed policy towards the British and Americans in the Hawaiian Archipelago and recognition of Hawaiian independence, so, today, we draw advantage from their balanced and objective narratives. Having no personal or nationalistic axe to grind, they painted Honolulu as it was, not as they thought it should be seen.

CHAPTER THREE

The Sharper Focus:
Russian Contacts and Activities at Honolulu

Thus far, the place of Honolulu in the pattern of the Russian Navy's North Pacific enterprise has been considered from the general but Eurocentric standpoint of that navy's economic and strategic needs and objectives. This chapter will survey Russian dealings in and near Honolulu from 1809 to 1826. The Russian ships and officers who visited there will be more specifically examined, and Russian contacts, movements, and activities ashore will be brought into sharper focus.

RUSSIAN SHIPS AT HONOLULU, 1809–26

Seven Russian vessels paid eleven visits to Honolulu during this period. The ships were the *Neva* (1809), the *Riurik* (1816 and 1817), the *Kamchatka* (1818), the *Otkrytie* (twice in 1821), the *Blagonamerennyi* (1821 twice), the *Predpriiatie* (1824 and 1825), and the *Krotkii* (1826). The small Russian-American Company vessel *Nikolai* called at Hawaii Island (1806), then made a short visit at Honolulu.[1] The *Neva*, too, had visited that island in 1804, but as seen in Chapter One, avoided Waikiki because of the pestilence (*oku'u*) then decimating the assembled fleet and army of Kamehameha.[2] Other Company-owned vessels also called at Honolulu in the 1830s, sailing straight from Sitka (Novo-Arkhangel'sk) on the Russian Northwest Coast of North America or by way of Upper California.[3] Among the round-the-world vessels to pause at Honolulu in the 1830s were the *Amerika* (1835) and the *Nikolai* (1838).[4]

The *Neva* alone flew the Russian-American Company flag when she called at Oahu. The *Riurik*'s status was complex, as she belonged to Count Rumiantsev, Chancellor of Russia, and was carrying a company who were effectively in his employ, yet—with the tsar's permission—flew the naval ensign. Her commander, Kotzebue, expected to be treated as the captain of a warship and at Honolulu as in other places was in fact so treated.[5] The other Russian ships which stopped at Honolulu up to 1826 were naval vessels, fully armed although perhaps on discovery or expeditionary work, and well equipped at Admiralty dockyards in the Baltic.

The *Neva*, which Gagemeister brought to Honolulu Harbour on 12 January 1809,[6] had been built by the English on the River Thames in 1801 and bought for the Kruzenshtern-Lisianskii expedition around the world (see Chapter One) in 1802. Originally named the *Thames*, she was a sloop of 370-odd tons.[7] Modified in London for lengthy voyaging, she crossed the North Sea on her maiden voyage under Russian ownership at the creditable rate of eleven knots in variable winds.[8] To good sailing qualities she added the advantage of a large hold. When coasting off Oahu in June 1804, she had a company of fifty-three. Sailing more economically in Company employ, Gagemeister brought her back five years later with a company of only forty-three, with no recorded loss of manoeuverability or safety.[9] The *Neva* was also a versatile ship, equally capable of serving as a fighting ship or transport. In the spring of 1809 she carried furs to Honolulu, and returned to the North with salt and food supplies.[10]

Kruzenshtern wrote of the construction of the brig *Riurik*, which Kotzebue brought to Honolulu even as Georg-Anton Scheffer was pursuing his imperialist dream on Kauai (see Chapter One):

> It had been resolved to have a vessel of 70 or 80 tons ... built of oak in the imperial dockyard by the able shipwright Razumov. This plan could not be executed, however, as there was no private dockyard in St. Petersburg and oak timber is the exclusive possession of the Admiralty. The only alternative was to purchase abroad a ship built of oak, which would be too expensive, or to have one built of fir .... Lt. Kotzebue accompanied me to Abo, in Finland, and at the end of May, 1814, I contracted with the shipbuilder Erik Malm to build us, for the sum of 30,000 roubles, a vessel of 180 tons burthen, which should be launched at the beginning of May in the following year. I bespoke the astronomical and physical instruments in England, of the justly celebrated Troughton.[11]

The admiral also ordered in London two large telescopes by William Tully, a contemporary "log-sounding machine by Mr. Massey," and maps by James Horsburgh (1762–1836), John Purdy (1773–1843), and Aaron Arrowsmith (1750–1823). These were to be used in North and mid-Pacific waters. The brig was launched in 1815.

At 180 tons, Kotzebue's *Riurik* was less than half the size of the *Neva*. It would be wrong to think however that she was diminutive beside the other foreign ships then or recently at Honolulu. In the three-year period preceding her arrival most foreign vessels (*en route* to or returning from the Northwest Coast or China) had been brigs or schooners in the same range as herself. The *Bordeaux Packet*, *Albatross*, *Abaellino*, *Traveller*, and *Colonel Allan*, among other merchantmen, were lighter than the *Riurik*, while the *Pedler*, *Isabella*, and *Atahualpa* (to name but three New England vessels met by Russians in the period 1813–16) were of less than 230 tons.[12] It was a rare ship, like the American brig *Panther* (430 tons), that approached even half the tonnage of the next two Russian sloops at Honolulu, the *Kamchatka* and the *Otkrytie*, or even matched the *Neva* in spread of canvas and dimensions.[13]

The *Riurik* had been designed and built for scientific and investigative purposes. The *Kamchatka* had been modified for survey work. The *Suvorov* had been modified for trade. None had impressive armament, yet all had unmistakable political significance in the Pacific. In the post-Napoleonic age, as in the time of *Resolution* and the *Discovery*, "the aims of science and of empire were essentially one and the same."[14] Knowledge was power.

The *Riurik*'s mission was essentially exploratory and scientific. It was Count Rumiantsev's hope that a navigable northern passage would be found connecting North Pacific and Atlantic waters. Kruzenshtern hoped that Russians would complete the mapping of the North Pacific Basin by discovering whatever other island-chains remained unknown to Europeans.[15] Even so, the brig mounted eight guns, and so was able to salute Fort Kaahumanu, to the joy of the *ali'i*, on 14 December 1816 (see Narrative 12).

The *Kamchatka* and the *Otkrytie* were sloops of the same class and had very similar specifications. Both were of 900 tons and were a shade over 130 feet from stem to stern and 33 feet across the beam. Both were built in St. Petersburg yards by the shipwright Stoke with Pacific and expeditionary work in mind. Both could comfortably carry lower decks of a hundred hands and more. (The *Kamchatka* actually reached Honolulu with 119 lower ranks, the *Otkrytie* with only 63 because some men had been transferred to the escorting sloop, the *Blagonamerennyi*.)[16]

Such dimensions and companies merit attention. Foreign warships like the *Kamchatka* and the *Otkrytie* not only dwarfed the other ships in Honolulu Harbour when they came, but also overshadowed them in terms of personnel. Thus the significance of their arrivals and their local influence was doubled. Few vessels had come to Honolulu with more trained men than the *Kamchatka* (136) or the *Predpriiatie* (121). Such visitors could hardly fail to exert a major social, economic, and strategic influence in the Hawaiian Islands for as long as they remained—or longer.

Other Russian naval visitors sustained Russia's presence at Oahu, though of course they could not give it continuity. The Russians came and went but the New Englanders were in continuous and ever growing residence in the Islands. The *Blagonamerennyi*, sister-ship to Mikhail P. Lazarev's *Mirnyi* as the *Otkrytie* was sister-ship to Faddei F. Bellingshausen's South Pacific and Antarctic prober, the *Vostok*,[17] was a capacious, well-armed transport of 530 tons. Built by the shipwright Kupreianov at Lodeinoe Pole yard outside the capital, she was 115 feet long and 29 feet broad. Originally named the *Svir'*, she mounted twenty guns and was little slower than the *Otkrytie* in normal winds. Like her, she had a solid copper sheath.[18] Ninety feet in length and fractionally broader in the beam than the *Blagonamerennyi*, the naval sloop *Krotkii* was a larger vessel than the *Neva*. She was armed and rigged as a bark. The *Predpriiatie* at 750 tons was 130 feet in length and 34 feet in the beam.

Like the *Kamchatka* and the *Otkrytie*, the *Predpriiatie* had been newly and specifically built for a Pacific expedition in 1823. Originally she was to have taken stores to the *Kamchatka* and then undertaken surveillance cruises off the Russian Northwest Coast, where "Yankee poachers" were at work.[19] Scientific and exploratory objectives had been almost afterthoughts. Anglo-Russian and Russo-American conventions had settled the Northwest Coast dispute, and determined the modern outline of Alaska and its panhandle. Thus the *Predpriiatie* had been released for geographical and other scientific work.[20]

The broad pattern of Russian naval visits to Oahu was an accurate reflection of Russia's growing naval, economic, and political ambitions in the North Pacific Basin. The arrivals of the *Riurik*, the *Otkrytie*, and the *Blagonamerennyi* were linked to Russian hopes of yet discovering a navigable northern passage over Asia or America. While not devoid of strictly naval and strategic aims (as seen, the *Predpriiatie* had been diverted from patrol duties off Sitka at the last minute), the Honolulu visits of the *Kamchatka*, the *Predpriiatie*, and the *Krotkii* were immediately linked with the well-being and security of settlements on Russia's Northwest Coast.[21] Russian-American Company interest in a direct Kamchatka/Sitka-Honolulu trade link, represented by the visit of the *Neva* in 1809, developed in the maritime and scientific context of the post-Napoleonic period. That process in itself reflected the Navy's growing pressure on the Company to gain control of Russia's North Pacific venture (1812–21). Russians traded at Honolulu (buying foodstuffs and supplies for the Kamchatka and American possessions) less because of Company directives than because of passing naval officers' need for provisions.[22] Perhaps inevitably, the collapse of Russia's naval and imperial ambitions in the North Pacific Ocean and America in 1824–25 signalled the rapid winding down of the series of Oahu visits documented here. Few Russian naval visitors arrived at Honolulu to revictual *or* to satisfy their scientific curiosity for years after the *Moller* left in 1826.

Below are details of the Russian ships and Honolulu visits under discussion. Arrival date is taken as the date of entry into Honolulu Harbour, *not* the first day of arrival at Oahu. Many, if not most, *haole* vessels were obliged to anchor or to beat to windward in Mamala Bay outside the harbour entrance until the calm at dawn let them in under tow (as described by Kotzebue, Narrative 2). Dates are given in accordance with the modern calendar. Russian ships' logs and many journals of this period indicate dates by the Old Style (Julian) calendar then thirteen days behind the Gregorian Style that had been in use at Honolulu since the 1790s. Some of the printed Russian texts reckon dates by the new calendar, and Russians and others reaching Honolulu from the settlements of Russian North America, where Old Style reckoning was still employed,

Details of Russian Ships at Honolulu

Vessel	Officers	Dates of Arrival–Departure	Length of Stay (days)
Russian-America Company Ship *Neva*, 370 tons	Lt. L.A. Gagemeister Lt. M.A. Berkh Lt. A.P. Kozlianinov Mate Ivan Vasil'ev Second Mate Efim Klochkov Lower deck: 36	12 Jan.–8 Mar. 1809	56
Brig *Riurik*, 180 tons	Lt. O.E. von Kotzebue Lt. G.S. Shishmarev Lt. I.I. Zakharin Mate Vasilii Khromchenko	27 Nov.–14 Dec. 1816 1–14 Oct. 1817 (second visit)	17 14
Sloop-of-war *Kamchatka*, 900 tons	Capt. V.M. Golovnin Lt. M.I. Murav'ev Lt. N.G. Filatov Lt. F.F. Kutygin Mate G. Nikiforov Lower deck: 119	26–30 Oct. 1818	5
Naval sloop *Otkrytie*, 900 tons	Capt.-Lt. N.M. Vasil'ev Lt. A.P. Avinov Lt. P. Zelenoi Lt. R.P. Boil' Mate M. Rydalev Lower deck: 63	21 Mar.–7 Apr. 1821 27 Nov.–20 Dec. 1821 (second visit)	17 24
Naval sloop *Blagonamerennyi*, 530 tons	Capt.-Lt. G.S. Shishmarev Lt. I.N. Ignat'ev Lt. A.P. Lazarev Mate V. Petrov Lower deck: 71	20 Mar.–7 Apr. 1821 24 Nov.–20 Dec. 1821 (second visit)	18 27
Naval sloop *Predpriiatie*, 750 tons	Capt.-Lt. O.E. von Kotzebue Lt. T.I. Kordiukov Lt. N. Rimskii-Korsakov , Lt. P. Bartashevich Lt. N. Pfeifer Mate Grigor'ev Lower deck: 99	14 Dec.–31 Jan. 1824–25 13–19 Sept. 1825	48 6
Naval sloop *Krotkii*	Capt.-Lt. F.P. Wrangel Lt. M. Lavrov Mate M. Pashinnikov Lower deck: 42	?23 Nov.–?2 Dec. 1826	?9
Naval sloop *Moller*	Capt.-Lt. M.N. Staniukovich Lt. A. Leskov Lt. A.S. Leontovich Mate A. Rydalev Lower deck: 75	6 Dec.–9 Feb. 1827–8	64
Naval transport *Amerika*	Capt.-Lt. I.I. von Schants Lt. E.A. Berens Lt. V. Zavoiko Lt. M. Duhamel Mate A. Gavrilov Lower deck: 52	11–13 Nov. 1835	3

Notes:
Further details may be found in Ivashintsev, 1980:137–48.

Vessels listed here were on round-the-world voyages, not sailing direct from Sitka (Novo-Arkhangel'sk).

were highly conscious of discrepancies. Chamisso, who reached Oahu via Unalaska Island off Alaska in October 1817, had this to say:

> The Europeans on the Sandwich Islands were getting their time chronology, so to speak, from west to east, via Canton; but we were bringing our time reckoning from east to west and so were a day ahead of them, as we had been in Kamchatka and the settlements. This same time difference exists between neighbouring San Francisco and Port Bodega. But it is rather difficult to come to terms with real time, if one looks at east-west time chronology, Greenwich time and shipboard time, intermediate and "real" time, time by the sun and by the stars, the astronomical day, and so forth ....[23]

By "shipboard time," Chamisso meant time reckoned from dawn but dated from noon to the following noon, which itself requires adjustments on the part of Russian visitor and modern editor alike.

Ships' Companies

At the outset of the Russian Navy's North Pacific enterprise in 1802–03, an effort had been made by Navy, Company, Academy officialdom and the Court to give the new Pacific branch of naval service an exclusive stamp. In Kruzenshtern's opinion it was vital to establish an *esprit de corps*.[24] Pay was high, equipment sound, and only seamen with the brightest records and skills additional to those usually expected were accepted.[25] Both the Navy and the Company intended that the new Pacific service should be élite with an enviable promise of swift advancement for the few. The tone thus set by Kruzenshtern was faithfully maintained, first by his *protégé*, Lieutenant Kotzebue, and then by V.M. Golovnin. This resulted in Russian officers and ordinary seamen on Oahu in the early 1800s being among the ablest, best educated, and potentially most influential in the Russian Fleet.

As Kruzenshtern had chosen Lisianskii as his second-in-command because he knew him to be loyal and accomplished,[26] so did Gagemeister choose Lieutenant Moritz Berkh for the *Neva* in 1806, and Kotzebue, Lieutenant Gleb Shishmarev for the *Riurik*. All three commanders looked for steadiness of temper and a first-class service record. Such lieutenants were inevitably specialists devoted to the service. It was right that the Hawaiians should regard them as *ali'i*, very different from Nor'westers' mates (see Narrative 17). So too were surgeons, pilots, carpenters, and ordinary seamen chosen; Kruzenshtern and his successors all attempted to exclude the malcontent and to compose, to the extent that they were able, a harmonious society. Perhaps it was with thoughts of Captain Bligh in mind, as well as of the need to run a calm and ordered ship that could for months or even years serve as laboratory and office for an expedition's scientists and training school for midshipmen of promise, that the Admiralty emphasized the virtues of "attachment and obedience."[27] And in the same humane, pragmatic spirit, officers also saw to it that their subordinates received the very best available supplies. Like Kruzenshtern they tended to select junior officers well known to them and of the same background and outlook as themselves. To the extent that they could choose their lower decks, they valued youthfulness and practical experience. The Admiralty College itself ordered the Commandant of Kronstadt Port to crew the *Otkrytie* and the *Blagonamerennyi* with "the healthiest men, not more than 35 years of age, such being better able to withstand hardship at sea, but men also possessing some skills above and beyond their duties."[28]

To survey the names of officers who called at Honolulu in the early nineteenth century is to appreciate the value of the Baltic German element in Russia's naval and Pacific enterprise. Among the Baltic Germans on Oahu in 1809–1826 were Gagemeister (von Hagemeister), Moritz Berkh (Berg), Surgeon Karl Mordhorst of the *Neva*, Kotzebue, Dr. Johann Friedrich Eschscholtz (1793–1831) of the *Riurik* and the *Predpriiatie*; Midshipmen F.P. Lütke and F.P. Wrangel of the *Kamchatka*; Lieutenant N.A. Pfeifer, Heinrich Seewald (1797–1830), Ernst Hoffman (1801–71), and Emil Lenz (1804–65), the last three of Dorpat University (modern Tartu) serving on the *Predpriiatie*. To these names must be added Chamisso and the memoirist Karl Gillesem (Hulsen) of the *Blagonamerennyi*, the *Predpriiatie*'s distinguished and bilingual (though humbly-born) Wilhelm Preis (1793–1839), and Dr. August Kiber of the *Krotkii*. Kiber and Hulsen were of Prussian origin. Seewald was as much a product of Berlin and Heidelberg as of the Dorpat University where, like his colleagues Eschscholtz, Lenz, and Hoffman, he won prizes and distinction.

The representatives of a nobility based in Estonia loomed disproportionately large among the Russians on Oahu, as they did by 1825 on Russia's Naval Staff and at the Admiralty College in St. Petersburg. As scions of a caste long and well favoured in that city, such young officers as Gagemeister, Moritz Berkh, and Kotzebue lent a usefully prestigious aura to those voyages that brought the Russians to Oahu. For contemporaries, their names had social and political as well as academic significance.[29] Lenz, Hoffman, Preis, and Eschscholtz of the *Riurik* and the *Predpriiatie* preceded Chamisso in publishing results of scientific work (zoology, geology, astronomy and botany) that had been done, at least in part, at Honolulu.[30] As for socio-political importance and professional success among the Honolulu visitors, Gleb Shishmarev of the *Riurik* and the *Blagonamerennyi*, Lieutenant Matvei Murav'ev and Midshipmen Lütke and Wrangel of the *Kamchatka*, Vasil'ev of the *Otkrytie*, and Lieutenants Timofei Kordiukov and Nikolai Rimskii-Korsakov of the

Predpriiatie attained flag-rank. A dozen of their comrades reached the rank of full captain.

One other aspect of this manning of Pacific expeditions merits notice—that of the returner. A relatively high proportion of the men in Russian ships at Honolulu in the early 1800s returned to the Pacific Basin. Efim Klochkov, Gagemeister's second mate in the *Neva* in 1809, returned as the commander of the *Riurik* in 1822.[31] Both Gleb Semenovich Shishmarev, Kotzebue's first lieutenant aboard the *Riurik*, and Vasilii S. Khramchenko, his mate, returned as captains of their ships, the *Blagonamerennyi* (1821) and the *Amerika* (1832).[32] Others who returned were Lutkovskii, Lütke, Wrangel, Nikiforov, Kozmin and Tikhanov of the *Kamchatka*, Petrov of the *Riurik*, and Midshipman Karl Nol'ken of the *Krotkii*.

Thanks largely to the work of Rear-Admiral Nikolai A. Ivashintsev, the hydrographer and student of the Russian Navy, it is possible to name all officers, midshipmen, naval cadets, mates, scientists, and other individuals aboard the Russian ships that called at Honolulu in the early nineteenth century (see Table 1). The careers of those naval visitors to Honolulu who remained some time in Russian naval service may be checked in the official "Navy List" of the Imperial Russian Navy, *Obshchii morskoi spisok*.[33] The officers and ordinary seamen who arrived with Russian ships at Honolulu represented the élite of Russia's navy. Even ordinary seamen like Egor' Kiselëv of the *Vostok* (Captain Bellingshausen) were with few exceptions literate and capable of recording their impressions of the Pacific Islanders.[34] Their officers were cultivated men, able and willing to do scientific work and make shore contacts on Oahu of a kind not mentioned in their orders.

Shore Contacts

Russian naval visitors to Honolulu sought out individuals of six broad types or categories:

• the representatives of the traditional Hawaiian ruling class, including kings, queens, and their children, chiefs of highest rank, and wives and favourites of chiefs;
• *haole* who were or had been in the royal service and in favour;
• *haole* merchants semi-permanently settled in the Islands and possessing houses or property at Honolulu;
• passing shipmasters, notably masters of ships bound for or coming from the Northwest Coast or China or the whaling grounds found off Japan in 1820;
• representatives of the American mission at Honolulu; and
• *kanakas* or Hawaiian commoners.

Two classes are conspicuously absent from the list: *konohiki* or lesser chiefs managing the estates of kings, and native priests (*kahuna*). On the Kona Coast of Hawaii Island in 1804, Lisianskii and his people had had many dealings with both classes.[35] There were no extensive royal lands in the immediate vicinity of Honolulu, however, like those at Kaawaloa which Lisianskii had seen. As for the lack of contact with *kahuna*, it is in large measure explained by the timing of the Russian visits, which in broad terms coincided with the *Makahiki* season when services in the principal *heiau* ceased.[36]

Russians were well received at Honolulu by Kamehameha II (Liholiho), Kamehameha III (Kauikeaouli), Queen Kaahumanu and Queen Namahana Piia, and the chiefs Boki, Kinau, Kuakini, Ka-Hekiri Ke'eaumoku (Hekiri), and Kalanimoku. The most frequent and intimate contact was with Kalanimoku, Governor of Oahu when Kotzebue first arrived and, with Kaahumanu, Co-regent of the Hawaiian Islands from 1823 until his death in 1827. Russian sources are unanimous in praise of him and underline to what extent by 1821 he was responsible for all business involving foreign visitors and residents in Honolulu.[37] The frequent references by Russians to Kalanimoku, as well as to Namahana and Kaahumanu, comprise valuable and hitherto unused biographical material. Russians had encounters with Boki in 1818, 1821, and 1824–26 (see Narratives 25, 85, and 129), with Kinau in 1824 (see Narratives 54 and 55), and with Kalanimoku on almost every visit to Oahu from 1816 to 1826. Kamehameha II (Liholiho) received Russian guests in 1821 (see Narrative 127) and made a better impression on them than he had on Chamisso's informants of 1816 (see Narrative 40). Kamehameha III (Kauikeaouli), "a boy of perhaps twelve," made a positive impression upon Wrangel in 1826, though his gifts seemed rather meagre and his household troops too ostentatious (see Narrative 129). The representatives and agents of the Hawaiian monarchy and Russian officers were well-disposed towards each other and were pleased with what they saw. The Russian officers were deeply monarchist in outlook, and the Hawaiian kings were appreciative of the political advantages of friendship with the tsar.[38]

Among the English settlers whose fortunes had been made by royal patronage, John Young, George Beckley, and Alexander Adams had the most contact with the Russians on Oahu. As Kamehameha I's most trusted *haole* adviser, Young exercised vast influence at Honolulu (see Narratives 1, and 6–8). Beckley was Commandant of Fort Kaahumanu guarding Honolulu Harbour (see Narrative 8); Adams was the captain of the royal brig *Kaahumanu* (ex-*Forester*) (see Narratives 3 and 11).

Other English settlers of lesser rank met by the Russians included Harbottle and Warren, the pilots at Honolulu Harbour (Narratives 1–2, 25), and unnamed tavernkeepers of 1824–26 (see Narratives 111 and

113). Many Russians also had dealings with the entrepreneurial horticul-
turist and breeder, Francisco de Paula Marin or Marini (see Narratives
98–99, 102, 108 and 121). The prosperous Spaniard was interpreting
for Namahana and Kalanimoku in 1824–25 (see Narratives 54 and 58),
and had been in royal service during his early years in the Islands. Unlike Beckley and Adams, however, Marin was by 1816 living as if, as
Chamisso puts it, he were then "independent of the king and not enjoying his particular favour" (see Narrative 98). Numerous Russian visitors
admired his vineyard, garden plots, botanical experiments, and herds of
cattle, sheep, and horses. Inevitably Russians also came across the native wives and the half-caste children born to Marini, Beckley, Harbottle,
and other *haole* residents (see Narrative 99). In 1818, Golovnin found
half-castes numerous but easily distinguishable from the pure Hawaiians
by their mastery of English and by certain crafts or trades (see Narrative
105).

By the early 1820s, the Russians were in close contact with another
sort of settler: the successful shipmaster or shipowner who had decided
to remain in the Islands, having prospered in the trade and commerce
of the North Pacific Basin. Not surprisingly the Russians had especially
close dealings with New England masters who had previously traded
at Kamchatka or on the Russian Northwest Coast. Such men as John
and Thomas Meek, John Ebbets, and William Heath Davis, all of whom
had bases and/or families at Honolulu, had for ten or fifteen years traded
periodically at Sitka. Their vessels, the *Isabella, Mercury, Pedler, Alert,
Brutus* and *Enterprise*, were as familiar to Russians in the North as to
their agents in Canton or their suppliers on Oahu.[39] By extension, they,
and men like Golovnin, had many mutual acquaintances. Mindful of
these profitable dealings with the Russians, Thomas Meek went to much
trouble to assist and entertain visiting Russians on Oahu, even moving
temporarily out of his house in Honolulu (see Narrative 129). As Meek
was useful to Wrangel, so Davis went out of his way to help Golovnin
(see Narrative 18).

The fourth group with whom Russians had dealings—shipmasters
and seamen who chanced to be in port at the same time—was considerably larger. Most of these men were U.S. citizens engaged in the
Coast-to-China or sandalwood trades or, after 1820, in North Pacific
whaling. All were resting and reprovisioning at Honolulu. They and the
visiting Russians exchanged news and, sometimes, goods as well (see
Narratives 29 and 127). Relations were cordial, though the conduct of
Russian common seamen ashore was more correct than that of the New
England crews or than the Hawaiian Islanders were used to. Among
other captains met by Russians in 1816–21 were James Smith Wilcox
of the *Traveller*, John Brown of the *Cossack*, Andrew Blanchard of the
Bordeaux Packet, David Nye of the *Brutus*, John Suter of the *Mentor*

(see Narratives 3, 15 and 18), and, in 1821, the pioneer Yankee whaler off Japan, Joseph Allen of the ship *Malo* (Narrative 24). As Russian narratives reflect the crisis and incipient decline of the Hawaiian sandalwood trade in 1821–24 (see Narrative 27), so too do they reflect the early stages of commercial readjustment caused by Captain Allen's huge whaling success in 1820.[40]

Appended to this group of foreign mariners in port were Captain Thomas ap Catesby Jones, USN, and the officers and men of his corvette, the USS *Peacock*. Wrangel arrived at Honolulu in November 1826 to find the *Peacock* already there (see Narratives 36–37 and 148). It was the first time that the Russians had found another *haole* warship in the harbour, and the first time that American and Russian naval officers had met at Honolulu. Baron Wrangel, Captain Jones, and their lieutenants met on several occasions and were guests together at the homes of the U.S. Commercial Agent on Oahu, John C. Jones, and of the British Consul, Richard Charlton. Wrangel was unquestionably conscious of the tension between Charlton and the two New England Joneses,[41] but was scrupulous in his avoidance of all partisan remarks. The Russian government had, after all, yet to retreat from full support of the Hawaiian Kingdom's independence or, indeed, to give political expression to a broadly pro-American position in the North Pacific area.[42] Thus, Wrangel merely noted cautiously that Captain Jones and Charlton were apparently both seeking "to determine the islands' degree of independence from England and from the United States ..." (see Narrative 129).

Already, Wrangel knew, the American Board of Commissioners for Foreign Missions had unwittingly done much to reinforce the political position of the United States in the Islands. The Reverend Hiram Bingham had been virtually ruling, through the agency of Kaahumanu, even by 1824 (see Narratives 124–125). The mission's power had expanded in 1825–26. Like Kotzebue, Wrangel had personal misgivings about Bingham and disliked the joylessness imposed on the Hawaiian populace (see Narrative 129). Though strict Lutherans themselves, both deplored the severity with which Bingham was pursuing his programme of conversion and reform. The Russians also met the Reverend Charles S. Stewart, whom they liked (Narrative 125), the mission printer, Elisha Loomis, and two Hawaiian assistants whom Bingham had returned to the Islands from the mission school in Cornwall, Connecticut (see Narrative 127). Kotzebue was impressed by the missionaries' determination both to learn and to speak Hawaiian, but he doubted if Oahu boasted many Christian converts. In general, Russians regarded Christianity as desirable in itself but almost unavailable to Hawaiians through the agency of Bingham, "so untalented a madcap" (see Narrative 125).

Russians had few and brief encounters with Hawaiian native priests in 1816–17. In 1821 and later, they apparently had none whatever, such already were the pressures brought to bear against revivals of the old religious practices. The *Riurik*'s two visits to Honolulu were both in the *Makahiki* months of October and November.[43] "Services at all the *heiaus* of the chiefs were omitted for two months and twenty-six days; after which all the chiefs returned and worshipped."[44] The timing of the Russian visits goes some way towards explaining many aspects of the 1816–17 narratives, and throws light on those by subsequent "October-and-November" visitors including Golovnin, Lieutenant A.P. Lazarev, and Gillesem. The Hawaiians' refusal to eat pork aboard the *Riurik*, for instance, may be understood in terms of *kapu Kane*, (30 November) and the *makahiki* constraints associated with that whole month (*Welehu-Kaelo*). These are discussed by David Malo in his study of Hawaiian "antiquities."[45] November was, besides, the month for chiefs to practise games and public sports, and more specifically, the time for sham battles (*Lono-maka-ihe*) with blunted spears.[46] Kotzebue and Golovnin were both entertained by such fights which would assuredly have taken place even in their absence.

Fellow spectators of these spectacles were the Hawaiian common people. Russian texts do not elaborate on contacts between Russians and Hawaiian commoners unless the latter had specific skills. Thus we see references to pearl-divers (repairing the damaged copper bottom of a ship (Narrative 32), to skilled seamen (Narrative 31); and to successful cultivators of Oahu's gardens (see Narrative 129). Like the men whom Russian officers saw horse-racing bareback in Honolulu, these were commoners or *makaainana* and possessed real talents.[47] Other commoners were taken on as guides or paddlers by Chamisso, for instance, on his trip up the Pearl River of 1817, and by Wrangel on his hike towards Puu Konahuanui in 1826.[48]

Trained to be thorough and observant, Russian officers thought it their duty to describe the houses (see Narrative 92), tattooing and ornaments (see Narrative 79), clothing (see Narrative 93), and diet (see Narratives 94 and 97) of these people. Always moving in the background, Honolulu *kanakas* provide perspective for the Russians' canvas. If the foreground of that canvas was invariably filled by kings and chiefs, and not by the lowly-born majority, that was in keeping with the Russian and Hawaiian sense of protocol and order.

Russian contacts with Hawaiians were of course linked with their maritime requirements (repairing, provisioning, and watering of vessels, for example), or with scientific interests (botany, zoology, geology, astronomy, linguistics, and surveying). Meetings of political or socio-political significance were secondary to naval needs. It was in the hope of faster and more satisfactory provisioning (and with an element of curiosity), that Russian officers passed hours in the company of native kings and chiefs at Honolulu. As their maritime or naval needs and contacts were with few exceptions met within the harbour, so were their social needs met within the settlement, but scientific work took them beyond to the hills north and west.

RUSSIAN MOVEMENTS AND ACTIVITIES IN HONOLULU AND SURROUNDING AREAS (1816–26)

By examining the narratives and maps presented here, it is possible to trace the movements and activities of Russian visitors to early Honolulu. It is pleasant in itself to have the possibility of such precision at so great a distance from the time and place, but there are also practical advantages and applications for Hawaiian studies. First, we are able to confirm the Russians' records of their movements and activities against each other and against local sources. Any likelihood of error or omission, for example in a claim that a Hawaiian chief or Yankee trader met a given Russian seaman on a given day or that a certain Russian officer was in a temple on a given day, is thus removed. Second, the Russians can be trusted to illuminate the physical development of Honolulu proper. For example, certain of the Russian narratives (see Narratives 110, 111, 129) throw light on the precise chronology of the construction of the first prefabricated buildings, and their uses. Other texts combine to offer a precise visual record of the growth of Honolulu's first stone fort (see Narratives 8, 12, 13, 18, 26 and 127). Third, the precise and concrete quality of Russian evidence for Russian scientific, maritime, and economic enterprises in Honolulu lends it value as new source material.

What, then, did Russian visitors see of Oahu? For convenience, their movements are surveyed by area: Honolulu Village; north and northeast of Honolulu; and west of Honolulu.

Honolulu Village

Numerous Russians strolled from one end of the village to the other, making notes on what they saw. It was easy to do so, even in the later 1820s and despite the fact that it "seemed large, because even the poorest Sandwich Islanders" might have "two huts."[49] When, on 15 December 1824, Kotzebue went from Namahana's residence beside the harbour to the mission church west of the Punchbowl in a carriage pulled by cheerful youths and with the queen beside and pressing hard against him ("grasped me firmly ... with a powerful thick arm"), the journey took a quarter of an hour and the carriage went up all the village streets.

Together Russian maps and narratives indicate the settlement's swift growth. Even in 1826 when Wrangel made the second of his visits, Honolulu was an entity distinct from both Waikiki to the east and Mauna-Loa (or Moanalua) to the west. (In modern terms, Moanalua settlement stood north of the Keehi Lagoon Beach Park, 200 metres southeast of the Salt Lake.) Russian evidence confirms New England and Hawaiian source materials that show Honolulu's growth to be, at least for a quarter of a century, between the harbour and the Punchbowl, then northeast along the Nuuanu-Waolani stream beds and northwest into the rich Kalihi valley. Not until later in the century were structures built in any number in the (modern) Moiliili area, that is, between the Punchbowl's southern slopes and Waikiki. The "European cemetery," where Chamisso and Kotzebue paid respects to Isaac Davis who had died six years earlier (see Narrative 103), was still surrounded by an empty, swampy plain.[50]

Between 1816 and 1826 Russian vessels stayed an average of eighteen days at Honolulu. It was long enough for Russian officers and seamen to thoroughly explore the village, even allowing for the necessity of large repairs on some vessels and the need to reprovision, water, stow supplies, and socialize with representatives of the Hawaiian monarchy. They concentrated on the areas around Kamehameha's houses on Pakaka Point, Fort Kaahumanu, and "America," as Marin called his solid whitewashed homestead-depot-farmhouse, which had thick stone walls and a picturesque red roof. In little groups, or individually, Russians pressed north and east in the direction of Reverend Bingham's mission (see Narratives 110–127). The Punchbowl itself, now the National Memorial Cemetery of the Pacific, also drew attention. It was barely fifteen minutes' walk from the Honolulu landing-stage (put up by Marin for the use of Stephen Reynolds, David Nye, and other shipmasters and traders from New England who, by 1810, were boarding in "America") and offered panoramic views over the settlement and ocean. Better yet, it offered shade and novel plants. "On undertaking my first botanical excursion," comments Chamisso, "I climbed the burnt-out volcano right behind the town, so entering the woods [on Puu-o-waina]."[51] Like other Russian officers who followed him to Bingham's mission compound in the 1820s, Gillesem took particular note of the large hill behind it (Narrative 110). It was a hill on which there had been human sacrifices in the recent past; the memory remained fresh in local minds.

The Russian narratives translated here are, like Choris's Oahu illustrations, full of concrete information about structures. The native huts, (see Narrative 92), the native school buildings of 1824 (Narrative 116), the earliest storehouses (Narrative 111), an example of the very early haole-managed Honolulu inn (Narrative 129), and the layout of the mission are described in detail. Many Russian narratives offer a glimpse of Marin's house and thereby complement other contemporary European visitors' accounts and local sources. By comparing Russian texts moreover it is possible to see the changing functions of the celebrated house built by Antonio Ferreira, the Portugese stonemason called by the

Hawaiians *Aikona*. In 1816, when the *Riurik*'s people walked across the waterfront area then known as Kapu'ukolo, "America" was already surrounded by the "guesthouses" of ship captains staying with Marin while their vessels were in port; but it was still publicly recognized as royal property. (Marin, who was the stonemason Ferreira's father-in-law, had served as supervisor of construction in 1809–10; construction started shortly after the *Neva* left Honolulu.) Russian visitors of 1821–24 saw the building in regular use both as a store for trade goods that belonged to Kamehameha II and to Marin and as a business office. But by then the wealthy Marin had erected the additional large storehouse on Pakaka Point described by Midshipman V. Tabulevich of the *Kamchatka* as "the American shipmasters' house" (see Map B).

To Chamisso and Kotzebue we owe pictures of the physical condition and essential furnishings (*hale pahu* or drum-house, *makaiwa* images, etc.) of that hundred-metre-square *heiau* in Honolulu which, they learned, had been laid out within the past few months (see Narratives 72 and 104). It was Kamehameha I who informed them that an older temple on the site having been desecrated by the acts of Dr. Georg Anton Scheffer and his people in 1816, had been destroyed and replaced.

Russian descriptions of activities and buildings in Honolulu Village complement contemporaneous American and British narratives, for instance, those of Levi Chamberlain, Maria Loomis, James T. Hunnewell and Bingham (among the local residents), and Captains A. Duhaut-Cilly, F.W. Beechey and Hiram Paulding (among the naval visitors). The Russian texts augment the value of these French- or English-language sources.

Archaeology tells us where the Russians passed some time. We know the sites of Fort Kaahumanu (near the Aloha Tower), of Marin's house (500 metres north by Marin Street), the "European cemetery" (on Pensacola Avenue) and Bingham's house and church. Of other places often seen by Russian officers, nothing remains. The texts themselves nevertheless provide a record of the two-storey plank houses brought to Honolulu Village by the merchant company, Marshall & Wildes, for example, and acquired in August 1821 by Kamehameha II. Kotzebue found the huge Queen Namahana and her retinue in one of them in 1824 (see Narrative 54 and 110). Russian narratives speak eloquently of Thomas Meek's and William Heath Davis's permanent Hawaiian residences. Like Meek's own brother John and the New Yorker John T. Ebbets, among other Yankee shipmasters of substance[52] who had prospered in the North Pacific (Coast-to-China) trade since 1810 and were hospitable to Russian passersby,[53] both men were comfortably settled at the heart of Honolulu (see Narratives 17–18 and 129).

North of Honolulu

Chamisso had not been in Honolulu long before he was exploring the wooded hills that lay beyond. These walks drew him northeast onto the slopes of (modern) Pacific and Makiki Heights. His first longer excursion took him straight into the thick woods of Makiki Heights from which he returned some hours later, his kerchief crammed with botanical specimens, "through the valley below, which had most skilfully been irrigated with a view to taro cultivation."[54] This was the valley through which the Waolini and the Nuuanu Streams still flow today. By 29 November 1816, Chamisso was every day striding alone over these hills. "I walked every single day through this area and over these mountains, so I will not describe my lonely rambles further ...."[55]

"While hiking through the fertile valley behind Honolulu" on another day, Chamisso chanced upon Marin's new experimental rice-paddy and exchanged words with its zealous local guardian who saw him picking shoots and was annoyed. This entire country, just northeast of modern Palama district, was in 1817 covered by "empty fields, left and right." The fields would attract golfers in another age. Dr. Eschscholtz, the *Riurik*'s surgeon, also wandered along "narrow passes between taro fields, over ditches, down irrigation lines and the embankments." This and comparable passages by Chamisso and Kotzebue (see Narratives 70 and 74) illustrate the classical descriptions of traditional Hawaiian taro fields by John Ii and David Malo.[56]

As the days passed, Chamisso was attracted to the higher land with "tree-like lianas, whose nets were spread above the low-growing scrub." He ventured off "the regular [pre-European] path," shown on the map of 1817 (Map A), swinging west over the rocky spur (due north of modern Iwilei) that separated the Kalihi and the Honolulu valleys. From here, there were views of the Makiki Heights and mountains far beyond to the north and east. Chamisso had stamina and was an energetic climber. "I found myself suspended now over the slope of a rock, standing, as it were, in a hammock high over an abyss ...."[57]

Professional duties and curiosity alike kept Chamisso in Honolulu settlement in early December during the *kapu Ku*.[58] He witnessed a religious ceremony, not in the old Pakaka *heiau* near the fort where such activities had been suspended during *Makahiki*, but in Honolulu's newest *heiau*, completed only months before.[59] He also observed *Hulahula* spectacles on 4 and 6 December; but on 7 December he learned that Kotzebue was intending to embark upon a sightseeing and hunting expedition overland to the Pearl River. He quickly sought out escorts from Kalanimoku for a venture of his own to Oahu's northern coast. Chamisso set out from Honolulu early on 8 December.

The three men "climbed to the ridge of the mountain situated behind Honolulu." This is enigmatic, but by far the largest mountain that might reasonably be described in such a way was, and remains, Mount Tantalus; and the quickest northward route was through the modern Honolulu Watershed Forest Reserve (Highway 13, Nuuanu Pali Road). From these heights, the party then descended "by the slope on the north coast, climbing down on bare feet just as it is done in Switzerland."[60] The night was passed in a Hawaiian settlement on Kaneohe or perhaps Kailua Bay. Chamisso returned to Honolulu "via a more westerly and much higher mountain pass and so through a valley." Any practical experience of hiking on Oahu will suggest that Chamisso returned by the nearest travelled pass then to his west, that is, through what is now Kaneohe Forest Reserve and so into Kalihi Valley. He arrived back in the evening, barely missing *kaua kio* demonstrations (mock battle with traditionally blunted spears made of sugar-cane) in which, Malo informs us, the Hawaiian aristocracy often "indulged" throughout this season of festivity.[61] Kotzebue had returned from his own trip and had been entertained with *kaua kio* demonstrations by Chief Kalanimoku.

The next major Russian push northeast of Honolulu came ten years later, when Baron F.P. Wrangel trekked—initially along the very route that Chamisso had taken—to a point near Puu Konahuanui. From that exposed and windy elevation, he admired the Pacific Ocean to the northeast, off Kailua Bay.[62] Wrangel made his trip inland escorted by the surgeon of the *Krotkii*, Avgust Kiber, two or three young Russian seamen, and four members of Kamehameha III's native guard. They forded the Honolulu River west of modern Highway 61, then pressed northeast across the taro fields, following winding paths. These were tracks along the banks of hard-packed earth that held the water in the irrigated patches. The Russians perforce crossed many irrigation streams (*au wai*) while gaining height. "To the sides, at a little distance, the bare slopes of low mountain ridges could be seen."[63] The level valley below was quite covered with "yellowed grasses." This was late November, the *Hoo-ilo* season when, as Malo expresses it, "the herbage died away."[64]

The party rested in a hut after two hours, devouring watermelon and admiring strings of *kukui* nuts to be used at dusk as candles. Cabbage for the Honolulu market grew nearby. They then pressed on another ninety minutes, still heading northeast, "by an extremely difficult track, descending finally into a shady ravine."[65] It was about 10 a.m. and the Hawaiians set down the "huge calabash" (*'umeke pohue*) they had carried up these hills. In the calabash bowl was a doughlike mass of "earlier prepared taro" (*pa'i'ai*).[66] There was fresh water as well as shade in the ravine, and the native guides added some water to their dough, making a *poi* mix as Wrangel watched. The visitors themselves having in due course breakfasted on chicken, duck, yams, taro, and potato, washed down with wine *and* gin, the group proceeded on their way.

Soon they were faced by even steeper rocky rises. The Hawaiians removed their hats and prepared to meet winds which struck with force, "roaring dreadfully and ceaselessly." Ahead, to the northeast, "surged the ocean, while under our feet and behind to the southwest stretched out the whole valley we had crossed, Honolulu Harbour with its ships looking like little boats, and the distant sea."[67] Around stood high and jagged cliffs. "We could not hear our own voices, such were the noise of ocean rollers smashing against the coral reefs that encircle this eastern shore of the island and the howling, whistling, and roaring of the winds as they struck the steep walls of these pyramidal cliffs ...." It was in this unlikely locality that Wrangel had his first unexpected encounter with up-country natives "going to the settlement on the east coast, below the mountain on which we now stood." "The sun was already passing through the meridian, and we were still seven miles distant from Honolulu [settlement]."[68] The Russians returned to their ship by the same route, arriving tired and muddy, at approximately 5 p.m. Kiber, like Chamisso, had ferns and flowers to examine, classify, and stow. Wrangel made notes on the condition, diet, clothing, body ornaments, and missing teeth of the Hawaiians he had seen.

Even from the upper slopes of Mount Tantalus (2,013 feet), Wrangel could have seen the ocean in the far northeast, looking north of Mount Olympus. From there, however, he could hardly have been deafened by the surf on Kailua or Lanikai reefs. He must therefore have gone towards the peak called Puu Konahuanui (3,105 feet). From Honolulu Harbour to that peak is seven miles, by way of Wrangel's approach (modern Nuuanu St. and Alewa Heights spring). Wrangel could not have known that there were actually several Hawaiian settlements along the east coast of the island.

West of Honolulu

While Chamisso was visiting the north coast of Oahu, on 8–9 December 1816, Kotzebue, Surgeon Eschscholtz, and the first mate of the *Riurik*, Vasilii S. Khramchenko, made an excursion west towards the Pearl River. They were escorted by George Beckley, the English commandant of Fort Kaahumanu, and by two of his Hawaiian soldiers.[69] The six men took a route marked on the 1817 map of "the southern part of the coast of Vagi [Oahu] Island" (see Map A). Crossing the Honolulu River in the area of modern Kalikimaka Kila Mall, they went west "through a beautifully cultivated valley ... bounded to the north by wooded hills" and to the south by the ocean (see Narrative 74). This was the "Taurea Valley" (modern Kahili Valley), the stream of which flowed into the eastern end of Chief Kalanimoku's massive fishpond.

Keeping west behind extensive taro fields, the party came to the

Moanalua Stream and crossed it south of modern Lunalili Freeway. Passing through a village then almost as large as Waikiki, they climbed a hill yet further west and broke the journey. A view of Honolulu Harbour opened up over the coconut and breadfruit groves below, and Kotzebue took some careful sextant readings.[70] Here, the party left the shoreline, skirted a large salt lake and moved north. The route was approximately that now followed by Moanalua Road, south of Halawa Heights.

There were other settlements of no great size and other coconut plantations, as well as properties presented by Kamehameha I to his "minister," John Young and to a well-respected Massachusetts man, Oliver Holmes (see Narratives 1, 5, 7–8, 99 and 101). The estates were beautifully tended by Hawaiian labourers. Even though the sun was high, the air was suddenly made noisy by Hawaiian bats ('ope'ape'a), and Kotzebue shot one so that he could examine it. The travellers entered their lodgings for the night in "Wauiau" (Waiau) village at 5 p.m., having walked perhaps ten miles (but only six along a straight line from the Riurik).[71]

The shoreline west of Honolulu Harbour and certain topographic features have changed considerably since 1817. Land has been reclaimed, and the coastal fishponds, the original part of Anuenue (Sand) Island, and two low islands in Mamala Bay south of the "Wauiau" [Waiau] village, have disappeared entirely. In particular, the laying out of Honolulu International Airport and the Fort Kamehameha Military Reservation to the south of Hickam Air Force Base has changed the countryside that Kotzebue saw. Nevertheless, we can retrace his steps with adequate precision. Moving west along the modern Moanalua Road, Kotzebue turned south into what is now Camp Catlin Naval Reserve. Aliamanu Crater was approximately due east of him. Crossing a tributary of Waiau River by the modern Navy and Marine Golf Course, he followed the (now vanished) little river south-southwest into what is now the Hickam Air Force Base. By 5 p.m. on 8 December 1816, he was near the Pearl Harbor Entrance and in modern Ewa District. The rapid stream that emptied then into Mamala Bay due west of Kumumau Point (the "Wauiau River") was diverted in comparatively modern times into two large drainage channels which empty into the ocean between Hickam Harbor and Ahua Point. (Landfilling turned the western part of century-old fishponds into Keehi Lagoon Park.)

Kotzebue, Eschscholtz, and Khramchenko were entertained with baked piglet, fresh fish, and taro in the village which belonged to Kalanimoku. They could not, however, hire a canoe in which to enter the Pearl River. Frustrated, they returned to Honolulu the next day by way of Moanalua village (see Narratives 43 and 76). Putrifying pigs hung down from trees where, today, stand the giant terminal and cargo storage buildings of Honolulu International Airport.

Chamisso had better luck in his attempt to see the Pearl River in mid-October 1817 during the *Riurik*'s second visit to Oahu. His goal was not the river itself but the Waianae Range, "the western massif of the island," quite invisible from Honolulu.[72] Having first sought the advice of Marin and the practical assistance of Kalanimoku, Chamisso set out from Honolulu Harbour on 7 October, skirting Kapalama and passing south of the fishponds. "Accompanied by a guide and one boy, I went by canoe along the coral reef that encircles the beach. Sometimes we were inside the breakers, sometimes outside them. Reaching the Pearl River, we ascended it, moving in towards the foot of the mountain I had wished to visit."[73] We may conclude that Chamisso was heading for the (modern) Honolulu Forest Reserve from the fact that there are three full days and a botanical collection to account for, and no other destination fits the phrase "western massif."

Having collected specimens inland, Chamisso and his Hawaiian guides returned to water, placed his plants in a canoe, and paddled to the reef lying southeast of the Pearl Harbor Entrance. "At one time," they went "quite far out to sea over the coral reef, because the craft had to be taken out beyond it." Here, outside the breakers, they paused to watch Hawaiians who were fishing from several canoes in ten to fifteen feet of water. These were local men, probably hoping to catch mullet. Bright-coloured butterfly fish (*Chaetodontidae*) and other fish were being taken. Chamisso's guide and his boy "supplied themselves with fish here, having obtained Kalanimoku's permission to do so. They were still eating them, raw and unclean, even three days later—by when they were spoiled and full of insect larvae."[74] Though no longer young, Chamisso was tough enough to deal easily with all the rigours of this trip. He noted the darkening of water by the Pearl River's mouth, and even capsized. When drenched by thunderstorms northwest of Pearl Harbor, he simply stripped until he dried. Chamisso painstakingly collected fern and flower specimens, employing a technique he had perfected ten months earlier:

> During my trip, I made no use of botanical cases made of tin but only of handkerchiefs. One spreads out the cloth, puts the collected plants on it, presses them down with one hand, and ties with the other hand and the mouth. Two opposite ends of the handkerchief are thus knotted, the third or lower corner is then knotted to them, and one carries the whole by the fourth. On a larger expedition, with guides and porters, one brings along a book of blotting-paper, to secure the fragile plants immediately. My store of plants had been wetted by these rains now and I feared decay. So, when we reached our night's quarters, I reserved one room or hut (that is, placed a *kapu* on it) in order to spread the plants out overnight. Such a *kapu* is considered sacred and will be observed; but on board our ship there was no protection from any *kapu* — and my entire four-days' harvest had to be "secured", that is, had to vanish, whether wet or dry.[75]

In the course of this excursion, Chamisso made careful notes, some later used in his *Bemerkungen und Ansichten*,[76] some never published. Incidentally, he gained new insights into daily life among Hawaiians—how, for example, they traditionally coped with sopping wet *malo* and cloak:

> A heavy rain, indeed, a kind of violent downpour, welcomed us on top of one mountain. The Hawaiians' clothing, being made of bark, met the rain like unsized paper. To shelter their clothing, my people turned to the top of the tree called *Dracaena terminalis* [*Cordyline fruticosa*]. *Malo* or loincloth and *kapa* cloak were tightly wrapped around the tree trunk; the wide leaves were then bent backward, spread out, and secured with a piece of string. So fastened round this trunk, their garments looked like a turban. I myself removed all my drenched clothes and we went down from this hill in the "national dress of the savages."[77]

The south coast of Oahu west of Honolulu was surveyed, albeit fleetingly, by several of the young scientists who came with Russian expeditions to the Islands in the 1820s. Ernst Karlovich Gofman (1801–71) geologist and mineralogist of Dorpat University and a naturalist serving on the *Predpriiatie* in 1823–26, in January 1825 passed Oahu *en route* for Mauna-Loa on Hawaii Island. Eschscholtz, too, looked west of Honolulu, as did Lieutenant Pavel I. Zelenoi, of the *Otkrytie* in 1821. It would have been surprising only had such men *not* done so. They were living in the area for weeks on end and had professional as well as temperamental curiosity to satisfy. Staff-Surgeon Grigorii Zaozerskii of the sloop *Blago-namerennyi* was an amateur palaeontologist, and dug when opportunity arose—for example, at Sydney, Australia and on Oahu. The *Predpri-iatie*'s astronomer, Vil'gel'm Preis (1793–1839), had a lifelong interest in the technology of weaving, a result of time spent in a weaving-shop during his straitened youth. Like Gillesem, four years earlier in 1821 (see Narratives 54 and 108), Preis studied local *kapa*-making when his duties (in a hut-observatory) allowed.

CHAPTER FOUR

Hawaiian-*Haole* Relations in the Early 1800s: The Russian Evidence

GENERAL OBSERVATIONS

Even as late as 1810, the British maritime explorers (and exploiters) of the later eighteenth-century Pacific (Cook and King, Portlock and Dixon, George Vancouver, and their many published officers) continued to exert a major influence on Russian attitudes toward Hawaii. British influence was evident, for instance, in the Russian consciousness of the supreme importance—to the *haole* as visitor and would-be trader—of Kamehameha's "civilizing mission." No Russian narrative of 1810–26 fails to praise at least some aspects of that mission. Second, British influence was patent in Russian confidence that notwithstanding the Hawaiian "savagery" that had resulted in attacks on foreign shipping at Oahu in the mid-1790s, those who visited in friendship and who treated King Kamehameha with correctness could obtain peacefully all that a Russian crew and vessel needed. Third, it was apparent in Russian readiness to make the passage to Oahu in a philanthropic spirit. Of course, the Russians also came for food and water and were hoping to obtain them for the lowest price; but, like their British predecessors, Kotzebue, Golovnin, Vasil'ev, and Wrangel thought it proper to distribute on the Islands what they felt would bring Hawaiians intellectual and material advantages. In short, they brought a breath of eighteenth-century "Enlightenment" to Honolulu in another age.

For thirty years after his death at the Hawaiians' hands, James Cook had been the Russian Navy's model of the leader of a voyage of discovery and science. Still, in 1810, the form and very emphases of *his* Pacific explorations were not only borne in mind by the ambitious Russian officer like Kotzebue, but were treated as the norm for such large ventures. And among those emphases were scientific ones. Cook, and Vancouver after him, had shown an active interest in Hawaiian "curiosities," as in their social structure, language, and beliefs. Preserved intact by Russian officers like Gagemeister, Golovnin, and Kotzebue—too young to have known even Cook's junior subordinates (Trevenen, Billings, Ledyard) who had entered Russian service to exploit their own connections with the *Discovery*—Cook's very spirit went with the *Riurik* to Honolulu in a way that set at nought the intervening forty years—the Age of Bonaparte. Such occupations as had marked Vancouver's visits to Hawaii were resumed by Russian seamen in the last years of Kamehameha's life.

In general, the Russians thought Kamehameha an exemplary and even admirable king. His "childish" acts, thought Golovnin, were balanced by "mature judgement and action, which would not disgrace even a European monarch" (Narrative 45). Russian officers were deeply sympathetic to the principle of monarchy itself, as well-embodied (in their European judgement) by the king; but they were also much in sympathy with the *de facto* abolition of particular traditional Hawaiian customs (local raids and inter-island warfare). Though the Russians met Kamehameha only on the Kona Coast and not at Honolulu, they were always deeply conscious of his power on Oahu. Thanks to him alone, they knew, the Russian visitor ashore was safe, trade was secure, and the economic propects of the Islands were superb. Royal pilots watched over the harbours (Narratives 1–2). Royal orders were transmitted by a regular and twofold method that the Russians thought efficient (Narrative 46). Royal Governors and troops maintained tranquility and order, day by day. Kalanimoku and Manuia considered it their duty and their pleasure to put any royal edict into instantaneous effect.[1] These were aspects of Hawaiian monarchy that Russian officers could understand and thoroughly approve.

As for the king's many monopolies and wealth, in weaponry and other goods, they seemed to Russian naval officers both natural and proper, if the Islands' independence and political stability were to be maintained. Even officers like Golovnin and Wrangel who deplored the heavy burden on the commoners whose labour brought Kamehameha wealth (e.g., by felling and transporting sandalwood and bringing salt to Honolulu for American or Russian use), treated that burden as a fair price for order. As the Russians had recourse to Russian terms (*monarkh* or monarch for Kamehameha, *starshina* or elder for *ali'i* like Hekiri and Boki), so they thought of the Hawaiian commonality as Pacific peasantry. It is of note in this connection that when Chamisso asked Don Francisco de Paula Marin to describe Hawaiian social rank or order, the Spaniard referred to four classes or "castes": *de sangue Real, de hidalquia, de genta media,* and *de baxa plebe* (Narrative 42). Again, the Russians could and did think of Kamehameha's people, as did Englishmen and Frenchmen, in their own national terms. *Ali'i ai moku* were relations of the sovereign or *gosudar'*; Marin's *hidalquia, ali'i nui,* were equated readily with the *dvorianstvo* or Russian landowning nobility; the "middle people" were, perhaps, the Russian merchants, guild members, and priests' descendants; while the islanders *de baxa plebe* were the *kauwa*, the lowliest of Russian serfs.

It is essentially because the Russians were unable to dissociate Hawaiian social systems from their own experience of other systems, that their evidence of social customs and relationships is far less useful to ethnography today, than what they saw of the Hawaiians' material (and so describable and solid) culture. This is true of Russian records for the earlier post-contact period in many parts of Polynesia.

With occasional exceptions, Russian visitors to Honolulu in the early 1800s took the kindest view of chiefs who, like Kalanimoku and John Adams Kuakini, were themselves the truest agents of Kamehameha's policy of full cooperation with the *haole*—and by extension the most Europeanized *ali'i*. They did not respect the chief who clung tenaciously to ancient attitudes. In that regard, their sympathies were more with Reverend Hiram Bingham and the missionaries who came in 1820, than with chiefs who represented the traditional Hawaiian way (*Ka moolelo Hawaii*). Of course, the very fact that Bingham, John Young, and Isaac Davis, were *haole* with chiefly powers and prerogatives at Honolulu, complicated Russian feelings—more particularly when, as in the case of "Mr. Young," the Russians' sense of social order was affronted by the man's own humble status, as a common sailor. No such problems were experienced when a Hawaiian chief behaved in a chiefly style, while adopting European technology and morality.

Judging the natives of Oahu by the standards of their own morality or, more precisely, by the moral code they publicly endorsed, the Russian visitors of 1809–1826 found much to damn. But they reserved their indignation for the *haole* (beachcombers, trading captains, whaling crews, New England merchants) who encouraged immorality as Europeans understood the term (Narratives 83 and 127). It was a fact that some Hawaiians sold their wives' and daughters' favours to the *haole* (Narratives 4, 9, and 107), and used the proceeds to obtain New England rum. It was a fact that human sacrifice was practised in the temples, although perhaps on a reduced scale and altered basis (Narrative 120) by 1817. The problem was, could immorality that had religious sanction be destroyed by Christian forces? In itself, the use of force would very likely lead to bloodshed or internal violence, and not salvation as the Reverend Bingham knew it (Narrative 119). All in all, the Russians were uncomfortable condemning the Hawaiians' immorality and were more disposed to dwell on Bingham's bigotry than on his flock's licentiousness (Narratives 124–25).

It is, indeed, a more positive quality, Hawaiian honesty, that Russian records emphasize. Because the Russians came to barter, they were often judging the natives' honesty as traders at Oahu. There were thefts on rare occasions (Narrative 119), but in general the Russians found Hawaiians upright dealers (Narrative 76). It appeared, however, that thefts from *haole* were less condemned by the Hawaiians than were thefts among themselves and that, as years passed, such crimes had grown more common (Narratives 113 and 127). Still, in Kotzebue's view, the Europeans at Oahu had themselves shown the example of commercial trickery (Narratives 115 and 124); Hawaiian theft was on a smaller scale. And despite the black examples and extortions that the *haole* had brought to the Hawaiians' lives, the latter were in general submissive (Narratives 54 and 127) and hospitable to strangers (Narratives 76 and 96). The Russians who had time and opportunity to study the Hawaiians in the broadest social spectrum and at close quarters, as Kruzenshtern had not in 1804, thought very well of them.[2]

The Hawaiian Monarchy and Other States

Russian officers observed and heard a good deal about the Hawaiian kings' relations with, and attitudes toward, the governments and public of Great Britain, the United States, Russia, China, France and Spain from Kamehameha, Liholiho, Davis, Young, and Marin, certain English-speaking chiefs, and from New England settlers. They sought the information, in connection with the possible expansion of Hawaiian-Russian links, once Dr. Scheffer's own imperialist game was at an end.

Visiting Honolulu in January 1809, Captain-Lieutenant Gagemeister promptly recognized New England traders' readiness to worry both Kamehameha and Kaumualii (then the independent ruler of Kauai-Niihau) by reporting Russian plans to colonize and settle in Hawaii. When reporting this to Company Main Office, Gagemeister chose to maximize New Englanders' malevolence and minimize Kamehameha's actual concern about the Russians (Pierce, 1965:38). Nevertheless, he gave an accurate reflection of the two Hawaiian kings' growing awareness of Russia as potential friend or enemy. Thanks to the *Neva*'s visit to Kauai (June 1804), Kaumualii was more conscious of the Russian North Pacific settlements and of the Russian Navy in the early 1800s than was his rival on Hawaii. For Kamehameha, Russia was embodied rather later—and in less impressive shape—by the little *Nikolai* commanded by Slobodchikov (1806).

Arriving in Hawaii ten years later, Kotzebue and his people felt the pressure of an anti-Russian sentiment born of Scheffer's actions on Oahu and particularly on Kauai, which Britons and Americans had fostered. Young was helpful in this crisis (Narrative 5). Kotzebue very speedily dissociated the *Riurik* from all Scheffer had done since his arrival in the Islands, and apparently convinced Kamehameha that the tsar had no designs on his possessions. Kamehameha's later dealings with official representatives of Russia, that is, with officers (whom he distinguished from traders in a way that Russian officers liked very much: see Narrative 40), were not as warm as with the British but were pleasant and correct (Narrative 46). Liholiho showed more *bonhomie* toward the Russians as a whole than did his father, and an equal generosity to Russian individuals who took his fancy (Narratives 49 and 127). More significantly, Liholiho also took more interest in putting flesh around the bones of such commercial and political connections as existed between Russia and Hawaii by the early part of 1821. And in response to an approach by Captain Rikord, then commander in Kamchatka, he authorized regular trade links with the Russians. Liholiho had had dealings with the *haole* since infancy, was literate, intelligent, and had considerable knowledge of geography. It was accordingly predictable that he was willing to approach Tsar Alexander, once the latter had repeated his displeasure with Scheffer; and he did in fact write to the tsar (Narrative 127).

Russians found that time had not tarnished Kamehameha's deep attachment to Great Britain. The Hawaiian flag reflected that attachment (Narrative 127), which was patently emotional as well as naval or strategic in its nature; and the likes of Young and Isaac Davis were embodiments of British influence at Honolulu. Kotzebue (and the Russian government taking its cue from him) regarded Britain as the actual controller of Hawaii, notwithstanding protestations by the British that they recognized Hawaiian independence (Narrative 8); but the Russians fully recognized that British citizens, whose old allegiance to their motherland survived new oaths of loyalty to a Hawaiian king, had not seized power and did not hold positions of authority by force. Rather, the king had welcomed them and made them powerful. The question thus arose: to what extent, and in what sense, were Young and other chiefs of foreign origin Hawaiian subjects? Golovnin answered the question one way (Narrative 105), Baron Wrangel in another.[3] Fundamentally, Russians believed that English residents at Honolulu, like New Englanders, were agents of their native land and that their loyalty to King Kamehameha was a transient and purchased one. But that Kamehameha recognized Great Britain's special claims as the "discovering" and patronizing European Power, was apparent; and the Russians were correct to see political significance in Consul Richard Charlton's growing struggle (1826–27) with American national/commercial interests at Honolulu (Narrative 129).

Many Russians saw the sense in Kamehameha's policy of equal opportunity and steady hospitality for Britons and Americans alike (Narrative 20). They sympathized with his and his successor's sensible objective of exploiting both national groups. They understood that, although Hawaiians generally left on Yankee vessels for the Northwest Coast and China, and although Britons were outnumbered on Oahu by Americans by 1810–12, Kamehameha nonetheless held the United States in less esteem than Britain. Young sustained the king's pro-British attitude, even interpreting State documents from London (Narrative 8). Other Englishmen substantiated his belief in the particular utility of links with Britain by assisting the Hawaiian king's personal trade with merchants in Canton (Narratives 3 and 21). Vasil'ev was right to conclude (Narrative 48) that Kamehameha's aim had been to foster friendly links with

every Power, and with Britain in particular, but to retain the reins of
State in his own hands. He had, in keeping with that policy, refused
to make hereditary land grants (Narrative 105) even to his chief *haole*
advisors: Oliver Holmes, Davis, and Young.

Aleksei P. Lazarev's account of his 1821 visits to Oahu contains remarks to the effect that Liholiho was not well-disposed towards "the
Spaniards" (presumably of California and South America, whence came
Captain Hypolito Bouchard and the "Spanish patriot ships" of 1818: see
Narrative 127). It also contains a suggestion that Marin was, for reasons
of his own, willing to flatter Russian visitors by overstating Liholiho's
awareness of Russia (as a source of useful missionaries). That suggestion
in itself serves to remind us that politicking was practised in the Islands,
first and foremost, by the European residents themselves, who more or
less appreciated the complexities of formal diplomatic ties. The Russian texts draw our attention to Kamehameha's diplomatic skill, based
upon shrewdness that was not the least diminished by his ignorance,
initially at least, of European diplomatic protocol. Coincidentally, they
also emphasize the durability of the impression that James Cook and
other early British visitors had made on the *ali'i nui*. A New Englander
like Ebenezer Townsend could remark with disapproval, in 1798, that
Kamehameha entertained an overblown opinion of the English ("from
the circumstance that English ships ... have been the king's, and in lieu
of bartering ... do all by presents, on a very liberal scale").[4] Golovnin
came twenty years later, but was bound to recognize that Britain's star
was still ascendant in Hawaii, since Kamehameha's memory of personally gratifying contacts with the officers of British men-of-war in other
times was as fresh as it had been in Townsend's day—so powerful had
been the influence of the the *Discovery*.

Attitudes of the *Ali'i nui* to the *Haole*

Russian records offer information on the attitudes of Kalanimoku,
Boki, Kinau, Kaahumanu, Namahana Piia, and Hekiri toward naval
callers, toward New England merchants, and especially toward the Honolulu mission.

For eleven years (1816–1826), all Russian visitors to Honolulu found
Kalanimoku acting as Kamehameha's representative and, in effect, the
chief responsible for dealings with themselves and other *haole*. As Governor, as commanding officer at the fort in Beckley's absence, as a royal
protégé of other times, he was "second in command after the king himself" when Kotzebue came (Narrative 2), and so remained even when
Liholiho reigned (Narrative 58). His friendly attitude toward the *haole*
echoed Kamehameha's own, and he went further than his master judged
expedient in lending comfort to the Christian missionaries in Polyne-

sia. Though already middle-aged, he learned to read and write, was baptized in 1824, and took pride in those achievements.[5] However, he did not abandon the traditional Hawaiian dress in favour of an English uniform (Narrative 7). Again, he followed royal precedent (Narrative 49) and his own sense of self-respect. He obliged his Russian visitors in many ways: providing them with foodstuffs *gratis*, with the services of skilled men (Narrative 32), with security and nights lodgings inland (Narrative 76). He had even treated Scheffer's people kindly, not desiring "to return evil for evil" (Narrative 43) where *haole* were concerned. To judge by Kotzebue's narratives, he was particularly cordial toward the officers of the *Riurik* (Narrative 44).

The Russian texts of 1824–26 do not portray Kalanimoku as a zealous convert to the missionaries' faith. It is by no means plain from Russian texts, indeed, that he appreciated fully the significance of having been baptized a Roman Catholic aboard the French ship *L'Uranie* (1819). Like many chiefs, Kalanimoku looked on Christianity and literacy as essential ties with *haole* beliefs and strengths; that is, pragmatically (Narrative 122). He was at no time Bingham's pawn as Namahana had gleefully become, by 1824 (Narrative 124). He is reported to have recognized the need for Christianity for the Hawaiians, while regretting that the old and "sacred things" had been so suddenly destroyed (Narrative 58). The Russian evidence suggests that after 1824 he found it prudent—under pressure from his Co-regent Kaahumanu—to accept communion at Honolulu; but that certainly his life had not been changed dramatically by fresh conversion. He continued to be friendly to opponents of the Honolulu mission while supporting its activities in 1825.

Kalanimoku won the Russians' confidence and was well liked by them. The Russian evidence corroborates the view of John C. Jones, Marshall & Wildes' agent on Oahu, and of Gilbert Mathison the traveller, that little business could be done at Honolulu by a foreign ship unless Kalanimoku knew about it and approved. Because he helped the Russians in their watering, provisionment, and other needs, he was himself helped in his illness by at least three Russian surgeons (Narrative 129) and received assorted valuable gifts.

Boki Kamameule and Hekiri, too, are represented in the Russian texts as loyal agents of the king (Narratives 18–19), but neither seems to have impressed the naval visitors as did Kalanimoku. Gillesem shows Boki as a dandy (Narrative 50) and a questionable influence on Liholiho (1821). Five years later, Wrangel shows him hovering about the twelve-year-old Kauikeaouli (Kamehameha III) and in an obvious position of authority (Narrative 129). By contrast, Kinau appears in a warmer light: hospitable, clad only in his waistcoat, heavy boots, and *malo* (Narrative 54), he obeyed the king (or queen) without demur. Intensely loyal to Kamehameha, whom he grieved most painfully (Narrative 56), he welcomed foreign naval officers. But other times brought other patriotic duties and, directed by Kaahumanu, he attended Bingham's sermons (Narrative 124).

As for Queen Kaahumanu, Russian narratives offer a record of her ultimate subjection to the Gospel as presented by Reverend Hiram Bingham that is hardly less affecting than the missionaries' record. From the outset it is evident that Kaahumanu shared Kamehameha's deep respect for *haole* skills and knowledge. *Palapala* was an aspect of superiority that she could recognize (Narrative 123). Acculturating steadily, she wore *haole* clothes (Narratives 51 and 62), wholly abandoning Hawaiian dress by 1824, studied the rudiments of writing, and at last received communion from Bingham to their mutual contentment.

Much has been said of Kotzebue's sharp and public criticisms of the Honolulu mission as embodied by the energetic Bingham (Narratives 124–26). The missionary William Ellis, though himself an Englishman and not a countryman of Bingham, joined with Tyerman and Bennet in indignant refutation of the charge of tyranny that Kotzebue laid. That Kotzebue felt an animus against Bingham is obvious and, in itself, does not invalidate the message of his narrative of 1830: that Kaahumanu's regency was in reality the (modified) continuation of Kamehameha's absolutist rule. She had accepted Bingham's doctrine and advice, so it was logical that she should recklessly enforce moral reform of which some foreigners—for instance Kotzebue, John C. Jones, and other merchants on Oahu—disapproved. Like Kotzebue, Wrangel was a witness to a logical result of her emergence, in the early 1820s, as "the new and good Kaahumanu."[6] What the Russians might deplore or view askance, New England visitors could see in other ways; and even Wrangel understood that Queen Kaahumanu's absolute support of Bingham's programme (Narrative 129) had positive effects, as well as obvious political potential.

Namahana Piia, by contrast, is presented by the Russians as an unimpressive figure, unsuccessfully adopting *haole* dress, a blind adherent to the missionary code (Narratives 54 and 123). Indeed, her total acceptance of the code had less political significance, for the Hawaiians as a whole, than had Kaahumanu's. Kotzebue's narrative is nonetheless of interest to the extent that it presents us with a portrait of a chieftess in a time of psychological and social crisis. Namahana, like Kaahumanu, saw continuance of the "Kamehameha policies" toward the *haole* as crucial (Narrative 61). Even so, she had a slight and superficial understanding of the world beyond her Islands, of the Gospel, and of *haole* ambitions. She was typical of powerful *ali'i* in the time of Liholiho, recognizing the political and cultural significance of literacy and of Christianity as talismans connecting her with the world of Hiram Bingham, Captain Byron of the *Blonde*, and Beritane.

Russians were impressed by the submissiveness of the *ali'i nui*, and Hawaiians as a whole, to the new mission. But as Chamisso had sensed the possibility of socio-political disorder on the first Kamehameha's death (Narrative 41), so Kotzebue sensed that deep resentment against Bingham's Christian Order which was afterwards to burst into flames with the approval of the third Kamehameha (Narrative 65). One regrets that he did not attempt to verify the stories he heard (with satisfaction, it would seem) about the groundswell of resentment against Bingham.

Hawaiian-*Haole* Trade and Barter

By the standards of the late eighteenth century, the Russians traded on a quite extensive scale in the mid- and South Pacific in the early 1800s. Articles for barter had been stowed in quantity aboard the *Riurik*, *Otkrytie*, *Blagonamerennyi*, and *Predpriiatie* in Kronstadt roads, before they left for Oceania. Because the Russians were so late upon the Polynesian scene, they had examples to assess where the provisionment of vessels and the gathering of "native products" were concerned. Cook, for his part, had taken "Toys, Beeds, and glass Buttons" *inter alia*, specifically in order to exchange them for provisions and, if any "Beeds" remained after his ships had all they needed, for "the native curiosities" (see Beaglehole, 1955:520–21). At Nukuhiva in the Washington-Marquesas group, and off the Kona Coast, in 1804, Captain-Lieutenant Kruzenshtern had let his whole ship's company barter for Polynesian products, once the matters of provisionment and watering had been attended to. Among the youths aboard the *Nadezhda* who observed the whole procedure—from initial contact, naming of offical barter officers or supervisors, and controlled exchange of goods to free and unrestricted trade—had been both Bellingshausen and the brothers Kotzebue. But the *Nadezhda*'s store of trinkets, like the *Neva*'s of 1804, had been exiguous compared with the store aboard the *Blagonamerennyi*, *Otkrytie*, or *Predpriiatie* in 1821–24. As Commander of the Northern Division of the Russians' double polar expedition of 1819–22, M.N. Vasil'ev received these orders with regard to the collection of Pacific artefacts and provisionment in Oceania:

> In order to induce the native peoples to deal with us in friendly fashion, and to permit us to obtain from them through barter fresh provisions and hand-made articles of various sorts, objects have been supplied from St. Petersburg. These items are such as have been calculated to please peoples still in an almost primitive state of nature, viz.:

Knives, miscellaneous	400
Knives, garden sized	20
Saws, one-man	10
Saws, cross	10
Chisels	30
Gimlets	125
Rasps and Files	100
Axes	100
Scissors	50
Steel flints	300
Small bells, whistles	185
Fringes, various hues	60 *arshin*
Striped ticking	100 *arshin*
Tumblers	120
Copper wire	100 lbs
Iron wire	80 lbs
Horn combs	250
Needles, various	5000
Rings	250
Garnets	5 strings
Beads, various	20 strings
Wax candles	1000
Mirrors, various	1000
Red flannelette	218 *arshin*
etc.	

(Bellinsgauzen, 1960:66)

Like the *Vostok*, bound for the farthest South in 1820–21, the *Otkrytie* carried thirty-eight other varieties of trade goods around the globe, to very different effect in different localities where barter was attempted. Like the ships in Bellingshausen's South-bound squadron, the *Otkrytie* and the *Blagonamerennyi* had ample room for "trinkets" in their holds. The *Riurik* was cramped indeed, at 180 tons; but the *Predpriiatie*, the first ship built in Russia under cover and ashore, was the largest to have entered Honolulu's inner harbour since the *haole* had known of its existence. There was certainly no need for Russian visitors in Liholiho's day to choose which articles to stow (although in fact few bulky artefacts were taken from Oahu to St. Petersburg), or to surrender other Polynesian objects to make room for new Hawaiian ones as, in his day, Cook had been virtually forced to pass up *tapa* from Tahiti in return for Maori arms and ornaments.[7] There was space enough for natural history collections, rocks, and artefacts, as well as edible supplies, aboard such ships. The question was, did the Hawaiians—who were hardly "primitive" in their demands of *haole* travelling salesmen by now, and hardly likely to want heavy Russian candles when Oahu was overstocked with the New

England whalers' spermaceti candles—have a taste for what the Russian ships had brought? The Russian texts are full of data on the matter, and reflect the mixed experience that many Russians had at Honolulu. Unprepared for the sophisticated wants of the Hawaiians, and *ali'i* in particular, they nonetheless scored a hit by bringing beads like those the *Discovery* had brought, but which no merchantman had carried for a quarter of a century. Unversed in local trading practices, they were assisted by New England trading captains with experience of Honolulu markets—and the Sitka market too. And more than once, they were presented with the foodstuffs they needed and supposed they would be buying, as a gift. We turn, first, to the question of what goods were in demand at Honolulu; that is, readily exchangeable for food, Hawaiian artefacts, or services.

"Toys and Beads"

Regarding Kotzebue as a Russian Vancouver and commander of a man-of-war, Kamehameha undertook to supply him with foodstuffs *gratis*.[8] Nonetheless, the Russians did distribute many ornaments and other "trifles" on Hawaii and Oahu, and observed the greater joy that they occasioned at a distance from the port of Honolulu.[9] Strings of Russian beads were well-received not just by children but by adults too. The artist Louis Choris had arrived with many strings of multi- coloured and, particularly, dark red beads.[10] Such beads had not been seen at Honolulu since Vancouver's visits and, because Kaahumanu took a liking to them, they acquired sudden value. Several swine were offered for a single string of them. New England captains made belated trading offers to the queen and others even tried to buy up Choris's entire stock. These deep red beads were very soon associated with a silken neckerchief, of the fashionable sort worn by John Young's native wife (Narrative 7). Such small silk neckerchiefs had been imported by Americans from China,[11] and were now used in conjunction with another *haole* ornament or two: if not a string of Russian beads, perhaps a mirror or a tiny pipe (Narrative 79).

Fashion was capricious and dependent upon royal whim. Hawaiian necklaces especially were subject to such whims. In 1824, glass beads were in demand once more (Narrative 115): a single string could fetch two dollars. Honolulu merchants sold such ornaments on easy credit and, in Kotzebue's view, engaged in trickery to sell them off (Narrative 124). Russian ships came well-supplied with rings and mirrors, and apparently left many on Oahu, thus depressing local prices; but inflation had been obvious in the Hawaiian trinkets market since the *Discovery* and the *Daedalus* had visited in 1793.[12] With regard to necklaces and fashion, it is noteworthy that Gagemeister was impressed by the Hawaiians' readiness to purchase walrus tusks (for *lei pala'oa*) from the *haole* (Narrative 97). For all the social connotations of those whale-tooth ("ivory") pendants,[13] it is apparent that by 1809 Hawaiians also viewed them in the "Toys and Beads" (prestigious and aesthetic) context. Russians duly carried walrus tusks to Honolulu.

Iron and Ironware

Even in 1804, the Russians found scant interest in Hawaii in iron nails. Peaceful times had caused the chiefs to lose their interest in the materials of war: only on Kauai, where Kaumualii was awaiting the Kamehameha onslaught, was the *Neva*'s iron required. Russian cloth was the prerequisite for purchase of provisions.[14] Matters did not change in 1804–1820. Chamisso was told, indeed, that certain chiefs were buying weapons on their own account (Narrative 41), despite Kamehameha's long-term defensible monopoly of the Hawaiian "*haole* weapons" market. It is probable, however, that Kalanimoku had been slandered by the visitor's unnamed informant. It is plain, in any event, that European weaponry was sold month after month in considerable volume to Kamehameha, who had arsenals well-stocked with guns and ammunition by the early 1800s (Narratives 22 and 26). On the rare occasions when a Russian visitor was asked for iron, it was for royal use alone.[15] The broken iron hoops which Russian ships carried to Taio-hae Bay on Nukuhiva—until at least the 1820s—were as worthless on Oahu as in Europe.

Certain finished iron goods, by contrast, had a market on Oahu. Both American and other merchantmen brought plenty in the early 1820s. Even Frenchmen were exporting to Hawaii what the Mexicans and Chileans had not yet bought (Narrative 29). Iron utensils were beginning to be used, and iron plates and porcelain were ousting coconut- or gourd-based articles (holders and bowls). In 1821, Russians exchanged small adzes for foodstuffs; but their knives, saws, chisels, bells, and other iron-based supplies were simply spurned by the Hawaiians (Narrative 127). Five years later, Baron Wrangel pleased Governor Boki by accepting local foodstuffs in exchange for Baltic clamp-supported booms (*poderzhannye utlegar i bom-utlegar'*), of which Hawaiians had no store.[16] As finished ironware had ousted iron scraps and nails as commodities by 1810, however, so within five years Hawaiian kings and princes were rejecting iron articles in favour of more complex foreign products: ships and houses. (On Kamehameha's purchase of the *Cleopatra's Barge* in 1820, see Narratives 28 and 127; on the royal brig *Kaahumanu* (ex-*Forester*), see Narratives 2 and 3; on the frame-houses sent to Oahu by the firm Marshall & Wildes, and admired by Kamehameha's widows and relations, see Narratives 54 and 110.)

"The evolution of the wants of the Hawaiian people as revealed by demands in barter," comments Harold Whitman Bradley,[17] "is an interesting commentary upon the spread of civilization." Nowadays, we would perhaps prefer to qualify the word "civilization," used so easily by Bradley half a century ago; but the validity of his remark is undeniable as it applies to *haole* iron. Ships and houses sent from Boston to Oahu for immediate disposal were of course riddled with nails, which the native purchaser failed to see: the whole was more than all its (iron, glass, and wooden) parts.

Cloth and Clothing

Calling in 1809, Gagemeister found "broadcloths of lesser quality" in demand (Narrative 97). New Englanders had successfully been bartering woollen cloth, blue and red thread, and canvas, obtaining foodstuffs from Kamehameha in exchange.[18] Gagemeister saw that Hawaiians would use Russian cloth to make *malo* and *pa'u* and that, furthermore, the colour was not of significance. At Kealakekua in June 1804, Lisianskii had noted a local preference for red material. Gagemeister noted that the Hawaiians looked for a close-woven material. In itself, the thickness was not important (Narrative 97). Brightly-dyed *haole* cloth, and colourful threads corresponded with traditional stuffs dyed in "extremely bright tones" (Narrative 93). The Russians managed to barter cloths and canvas periodically until 1825. In March 1821, the *Blagonamerennyi* acquired livestock and vegetables in large amounts (Narrative 127), in exchange for homespun woollen cloth called *kolomianka* and small adzes. The cloth was that officially described as flannelette.

It was not cloth as much as finished Russian clothing, however, that the Hawaiians valued. The *ali'i* prized dress uniforms (Narrative 127). Other Islanders took any sort of clothing (Narrative 115). As time passed, Hawaiians built up larger wardrobes and no longer thought themselves well dressed if they were clad in one or two *haole* garments (Narrative 54). Golovnin observed the former situation (Narrative 87), emphasizing the Americans' ability to profit from their own worn and discarded pants and jerseys. Wrangel, who returned to Honolulu in 1826, observed the change (Narrative 129). The higher a Hawaiian's rank, the more likely it was that he or she would wear imported *haole* clothes on ceremonial occasions (Narrative 7). Namahana, Kamamalu, and Kaahumanu, among other high-born women, had a number of voluminous velvet and satin dresses by the early 1820s (Narratives 50 and 112). *Haole* dress retained its value as a trade good as the value of material itself declined.

Alcoholic Spirits

The Russians were in general reluctant to sell spirits in the Islands, but occasionally did so. Alcohol was legal tender on Oahu, and Americans would give a bottle for a kid (Narrative 88). Rum was allegedly required for the *makahiki* season, and the Russians saw a great deal of drunkenness at Honolulu (Narratives 50 and 113). *Haole* spirits and the Islands' own distilleries produced more lasting and deplorable effects than, in the Russian view, the use of *'awa* had (Narratives 83 and 88). Gillesem and Kotzebue thought that nobles had in general rejected *'awa* in favour of imported rum. Although the Russians were reluctant to supply their hosts with rum or vodka, they themselves acquired spirits from New Englanders in port (Narrative 127).

Tobacco

Kotzebue and Chamisso found children smoking tobacco and adults smoking to excess and falling senseless to the ground.[19] Pipe-heads, hung by the Hawaiians' sides on cords, were items of prestige. Choris depicts one (Plate 9, Figure 3). *Ali'i nui* could afford the prices charged by the New Englanders for briar pipes mounted with brass. Kaahumanu and other high-born women smoked with zeal. The Russians associated smoking with disease and even population shrinkage. Chamisso was offered tobacco as he hiked to the interior by commoners, not chiefs. There is no evidence in Russian texts, however, that tobacco was exported by Hawaiians, although it was quite abundant by 1816 (Narrative 99). Marin certainly had hopes of major profit from his own tobacco field, the cigars being, in Golovnin's opinion, "not inferior to those from Panama" (Narrative 108). But the tobacco industry was in its infancy, and shaky manufacturing technique delayed its growth until the early 1830s.[20]

Hawaiian Articles and Services Available to Foreigners at Honolulu

The Russian narratives provide much information on the articles and services Hawaiians offered in the early 1800s, in exchange for *haole* goods like the above. Specifically, they offer data on the vegetables and fruit, livestock, Hawaiian artefacts, natural salt, and sandalwood provided by Oahu, and on such local services as diving, labouring, and prostitution. This material is usefully collated with the many English-language records for the period concerned. Russian narratives not only underline the growing number of *haole* settlers (Narrative 20) and seaborne traders (Narrative 124) in the Islands, Oahu in particular, but also illustrate the capital available by Liholiho's reign to purchase services and goods. One whaler found at Honolulu by the *Predpriiatie* in mid-September 1825 had whale-oil aboard her worth some $25,000 (Narrative 34). Even four years earlier, writes Lazarev, the celebrated whaling captain Allen of the *Maro* was anticipating profit of at least $12,000 for himself (Narrative 24), and was intending to return to Honolulu. For the past several years, writes Gillesem, Hawaii's kings have earned approximately $40,000 annually from the sale of sandalwood (Narrative 27). New England shipmasters imported quantities of North American and Chinese manufactures to Oahu. It was true that, intermittently, their profits from Canton were more potential (in the form of Chinese goods to be disposed of in New England) than in monetary form, so that a scarcity of cash in Honolulu boosted barter;[21] but in the main there was a good deal of money circulating on Oahu by the early 1820s (Narrative 115). Since the Russians were in any case obliged to buy provisions for themselves at Honolulu, it was natural they should be keenly interested in the market for provisions and, in general, alive to local bartering and trade.

Food Gifts and Gift Exchange

Certain Russian captains were given free supplies while in Hawaii. Kamehameha undertook to feed the *Riurik*'s company as long as they remained in his possessions.[22] More commonly, a captain's food requirements were met in part by royal gifts. Thus, Golovnin was given twenty hogs, a boatload of fresh greens, and other goods.[23] Royal precedent was followed by *ali'i*. In October 1817, for instance, Kalanimoku made a gift of fish and fruit to Kotzebue (Narrative 44), and in 1821 Kaahumanu made a gift of twenty hogs, greenstuffs, and fruit to Captain Shishmarev (Narrative 51). These gifts were made without clear provisos or conditions. Even so, the Russians felt obliged to make reciprocal and no-less-formal gifts. So gift exchange was a variety of barter, in the Russians' view at least. Because the Russians had appropriate (and not too valuable) articles aboard with which to recompense Hawaiian hospitality, they saw no major problem in such barter. Even so, they realized that the initiative lay always with their hosts, and that responses might be needed any time.

Occasionally, individual officers engaged in gift exchange with *ali'i nui*, or the king himself. Having received an unsolicited but welcome article, they were constrained to give an object in return—*noblesse oblige*. Lieutenant Lazarev gave Liholiho motley and exotic clothing in exchange for a Hawaiian model craft and other things (Narrative 127). In Wrangel's name, Lieutenant Mikhail Lavrov presented Kauikeaouli with a silver watch, two wine glasses and glass decanters, three Morocco hides, and an impressive looking-glass (Narrative 129), in return for royal kindness since the *Krotkii* had arrived at Honolulu, and in hopes of further "presents" to be eaten in the future. Baron Wrangel was, in this respect, much disappointed by the livestock that arrived a little later.

Hawaiian gift exchange was unpredictable and largely uncontrollable as well. The feather cloaks Kamehameha had been giving to selected *haole* commanders in the late 1790s were no longer on the shelf when Golovnin admired them; nor could such presents be solicited—or even purchased for a modest sum (Narrative 90). Though not essentially a problem, gift exchange with its inevitable burden of political and social obligation was a frequent complication in the Russians' bartering at Honolulu. All in all, regular barter in which both parties expressed plain expectations of return for items offered was much simpler. Then the problem was to find the needed *thalers* which, by 1820, Honolulu natives were requiring in exchange for anything (Narrative 127).

Livestock

The Hawaiian trade in live hogs was a royal monopoly in theory, and frequently in practice too. Lisianskii had, in 1804, managed to overcome it by appealing to the greed of the *ali'i* and the common sense of Young, then on the Kona Coast; but he had had to cope with it. In 1809, Gagemeister met the same monopoly and found that hogs were paid to Kamehameha by the chiefs as part of their annual "land tax," while many commoners had never tasted pork—although they raised hogs in their huts (Narrative 35). Thus, the ownership of swine tended to gravitate toward the highest-ranking chiefs and the kings. The latter, certainly, had very large numbers of animals at their disposal in the care of commoners (Narratives 43 and 76). A hog could always be found, and stifled, in honour of a passing Russian officer (Narrative 85).

Kamehameha's control of the sale of hogs affected many Russian visitors, who were obliged at times to pay for them in cash (Narrative 97), sometimes at a higher rate than certain natives would have charged (Narrative 106). New Englanders inflated prices by accepting hogs at local rates, say, seven or eight dollars, while pretending that a trifle to be given in exchange was worth the same. In 1818, Golovnin was forced to offer fifteen dollars for two average pigs (Narrative 106), and recommended that in future Russian ships in the mid-Pacific look to other likely ports for such supplies. They did not do so; and in fact the growing herds being developed by Oahu chiefs, Oliver Holmes, Marin, and other *haole*, along with the relaxation of the royal monopoly on livestock markets in the reign of Liholiho, exercised a downward pressure on the price of hogs and pork.

In 1821, the *Blagonamerennyi* took on live hogs at five dollars apiece (Narrative 127). Smaller animals were two dollars, and piglets were one dollar. As they had since the *Riurik*'s visits, the Russians stowed their hogs live—despite the noise and inconvenience of shipboard pens or sties.[24] They did, however, purchase salt-pork from the enterprising

Marin. Understandably, they were reluctant to reduce their store of fresh meat for an imminent long voyage. As purchaser for the *Blagonamerennyi* in 1821, Lazarev bought sows at Honolulu, and a litter was produced at sea. Several hogs were still alive when Lazarev returned to Kronstadt in the Baltic Sea in August 1822.[25] Russian visitors observed the gusto with which Hawaiian women during the '20s ate pork, which had previously been *kapu* (Narratives 78, 84 and 123).

Dogs remained numerous at Honolulu in the early 1800s but were not, it seems, an article of trade with foreigners. Baked dogs were served at feasts attended by Russian officers, and the latter were offered dog on other occasions also (Narratives 84 and 86). Queen Kamamalu enjoyed roast pup, in 1821, as Kamehameha I had enjoyed it (Narrative 127). The dog-tooth leg ornaments drawn and purchased by the Russians (see Plates 7 and 11, commentary in Chapter 13) offer confirmation of Reverend William Ellis's assertion (1839:347) that in 1823–24 large numbers of the animals were being bred for food and for canine teeth.

Hens, on the other hand, were raised specifically for trade with foreigners. In 1821, Hawaiians would sell five birds or twenty-five hens' eggs for a dollar (Narrative 127). And by 1824, "European domestic poultry" was being raised "everywhere" (Narrative 111). Two years later, Wrangel saw Hawaiians bringing hens over the mountains from the east coast of Oahu, to be sold at Honolulu (Narrative 129). It was evidently a routine trek for the individuals observed, whose industry had been directed to another source of profit.[26]

Other imported animals were also sold by native owners, by the time of Liholiho. Even so, the Russian evidence suggests that Marin's sheep and cattle herds were both the largest and the best until that time (Narrative 99). Marin's cattle were indeed a local spectacle in Honolulu: Choris drew part of his herd with a native drover on his horse (Plate 13). Such stock needed a watchful eye; descendants of Vancouver's gift cattle, and of more recently escaped beasts, were roaming mountains on Hawaii and Oahu. Russian visitors of 1804 had been informed of the problem (Korobitsyn, 1944:171–72). Marin's sheep and cattle herds caught Russian eyes even in 1824–25 (Narrative 111); but hogs or goats were more amenable to shipboard life and cheaper than cattle, so the Russians generally took the smaller stock. In 1821, a nanny-goat went for a dollar and a half (Narrative 127). The Russians necessarily took on hay to feed their goats and other animals at sea (Narrative 129).

Vegetables and Greenstuffs

"Greens" were provided in quantity for all Russian ships at Honolulu (Narratives 51 and 106). Cabbage and other greenstuffs were grown by Marin for such trade (Narrative 106), and his example was adopted by Hawaiians, so that "European vegetables" were fairly widespread on Oahu by the early 1820s (Narrative 111). In 1818, Golovnin was favourably struck by the cabbage, cucumber, garlic, and mustard grown there (Narrative 108). Other vegetable varieties were being introduced in 1817–21, and with the *haole* in mind. For two dollars the *Kamchatka* acquired fifty head of cabbage, most of which were pickled on the spot. In 1821, the *Blagonamerennyi* took on cabbage enough to fill three naval casks (Narrative 127) at Honolulu. Cucumber was then being produced in "the residents' plantations" (by Hawaiians as well as *haole*) north of the town (Narrative 110). The mission on the eastern plain grew vegetables in 1821–25, but there was little surplus once the missionaries' own needs had been met.

The Russians, like other *haole* visitors, also bought sweet potatoes (*Ipomoea batatas*) and yams (*Dioscorea alata*). In 1809, the burden of taxation/confiscation had induced the commoners to cultivate them on a number of remote and scattered plots (Narrative 38). Sweet potato production increased in 1810–20, but yams were not grown on a large scale on Oahu. The wild species, *hoi*, was eaten only in times of famine. Hawaiians were evidently influenced by the fact that yam is too mealy to be mashed into poi (Narrative 94). Gagemeister saw sweet potatoes being cultivated "by transplant" (Narrative 66); that is, propagated from cuttings of an old vine and planted in holes. He seems not to have purchased tubers for *Neva* as Golovnin had for the *Kamchatka* nine years later. Gillesem saw sweet potatoes "the size of a human head" at Honolulu (Narrative 110), but found their taste too sickly. Enforced school attendance by entire families in 1825 reduced supplies of sweet potatoes, at the same time boosting prices (Narratives 65 and 116). This in turn drove many whalers from Oahu to Lahaina on Maui, which enjoyed a major boom. The effects of greenstuff shortages were still being felt a year later, when the *Krotkii* was unable to purchase all the greens required for a passage to Manila (Narrative 129).

Russians also purchased taro on Oahu. On the whole, they found it difficult to share their hosts' enthusiasm for that food (Narratives 35 and 50). However, Gagemeister's observation that taro could be treated in a way that made it "similar to flour," and that it was of some importance,[27] did result in modest purchases for use in Company possessions. Gagemeister did not doubt that on Oahu alone there was enough taro for all possible foreign and Hawaiian needs (Narrative 66). Neither Chamisso (Narrative 70) nor Kotzebue (Narrative 74) suggests that Hawaiians grew taro for export. It was, essentially, the national staple (Narratives 94 and 96). Except perhaps in 1824–26, it was available in quantity; but Russians did not care to purchase much, despite a certain similarity with Northern European swedes (Narrative 110).

Among other foodstuffs also offered to the Russians, and accepted periodically in modest volume, were breadfruit, sugar-cane, and gourds. Few Russian vessels were at Honolulu in the main fruiting season of the breadfruit (June to September), so few Russians could see mature fruits being picked when they were most inviting. Even Waiau's breadfruit groves were unimpressive in December (Narrative 100). As for sugar-cane, the Russian visitors of 1804–09 had entertained expansive visions of supplying Transbaikalia in its entirety with Island Crops, or at least Russian North America and Kamchatka.[28] When the *Riurik* arrived, sugar-cane was certainly grown with trade in view, as well as for pigfeed and domestic use (Narratives 74 and 101). Golovnin mentions it, together with exotic fruits, as a crop produced in bulk (Narrative 108), and it was grown for foreign use by the *ali'i* (Narrative 110) and commoners alike (Narrative 129). Gagemeister saw Hawaiian sugar-cane as a potential source of rum as well as sugar,[29] echoing the view of Peter Puget of HMS *Chatham*.[30] And he actually bought some local rum, while objecting to Kamehameha's price (Narrative 66). Hawaiian rum was also purchased by the Company in 1824.[31] In 1826, Wrangel was interested to learn of Boki's attempt to produce sugar in marketable quantity, for which reason Boki brought John H. Wilkinson from England in the *Blonde*. The Russians were told of Wilkinson's factory and sugar plantation in upper Manoa Valley only weeks after the Englishman had died (Narrative 129). In 1821, sugar had sold for two dollars a cane (Narrative 127) and Lazarev had purchased many canes.

Fruit

Bananas, breadfruit, and coconuts were sold routinely to foreign ships at Honolulu. Cultivated varieties of banana were sold to the Russians (Narratives 111 and 129), who merely noted the wild varieties (Narrative 66) that flourished in the hills. Bananas were cultivated on a growing scale for export, but retained their religious uses until 1820 (Narratives 74 and 83), and their use as ornament, platter, and raw material for woven artefacts far longer (Narratives 72 and 93).

Gagemeister believed that coconut palms were all Kamehameha's, and that commoners were given few coconuts (Narrative 66). He purchased few or none. In later years, coconuts were sold in quantity at Honolulu, as a food easily stored and a cheap commodity. *Haole* captains also prized coconut-fibre cords (Narrative 23). The *Blagonamerennyi* took on bananas, coconuts, breadfruit, and *pisang* (Narrative 94).

But increasingly, the Russians bought imported fruits at Honolulu: grapes, oranges, lemons, watermelon, melons (Narrative 108). Much of Marin's wealth came from his exploitation of imported fruits (Narrative 98), and he was evidently the Russian captains' main supplier of such fruits. However, others also sold them melons, watermelons, and pineapple by 1821 (Narrative 110). A dozen melons, watermelons, or gourds could by then be purchased for one dollar, an indication of a relative abundance of supply even in early spring or winter (Narrative 127). In the hills due north of Honolulu, and in Manoa, the very landscape suggested the purchase of fruit (Narrative 74).

To judge by Russian records, both the Navy's and the Company's own ships tended to purchase a variety of fruits and vegetables at Honolulu, notwithstanding price levels at any given time. Russian captains were concerned about their companies' diet and health. Typically, Gagemeister took not only sugar-cane but also taro on his passage north to Kodiak in 1809.[32] Dried taro was given to *promyshlenniki* long after the *Neva*'s people had eaten all the fresh fruit from Oahu.[33] Coconuts were taken in their natural, mature form; but in the year 1824, at least, coconut oil, too, was transported to Sitka.[34] Thirty-nine barrels of oil, *inter alia*, were paid for in fur-seal pelts and specie. There is evidence that Russians took small quantities of candlenut (*kukui*) oil, of the sort seen by Vasil'ev in 1821 (Narrative 72), from Honolulu. It was certainly available, though not exported in the '20s as it was a decade later.[35] It was merely that the Russians had no use for it at sea or on the Northwest Coast, where animal-based oils were abundant. Even so, Baranov thought it worthwhile to draw *kukui* nuts to the attention of Lieutenant Iakov A. Podushkin of the *Otkrytie*, when drawing up his sailing order of 15 February 1816.[36] Kaumualii had proposed them as an article of trade two years earlier,[37] and, if we credit Dr. Scheffer, they were in demand in Europe in 1817 for their medicinal properties: eleven roubles had been charged for 18 ounces in St. Petersburg.[38]

Sandalwood

The Russians had no use for sandalwood, but left good records of the Honolulu-China trade as it was then being developed by New Englanders and by Kamehameha and the leading chiefs. Taken together, Russian narratives of 1817-26 provide a wealth of information on the place of Honolulu in the trans-Pacific trade of that whole period, and in the sandalwood-for-China enterprise especially. It was a trade, as Chamisso records, which the Americans controlled without much threat from other Powers (Narrative 14). Russians recognized the daring and commercial ingenuity demanded by the trade, and were themselves ready and willing to report such geographical discoveries as the New Englanders might make in the Pacific (Narrative 11), but were frequently censorious, nevertheless, of the considerable profits being turned. In this respect, Lieutenant Lazarev's remarks were very mild (Narrative 127).

Kamehameha's own venture in China, with the brig *Kaahumanu* in

1817, was of special interest to European visitors. Golovnin discovered all he could from the *Kaahumanu*'s English-born commander Alexander Adams (Narrative 21). Even in December 1816, the *Riurik*'s people had been told that sales of sandalwood to the Americans had brought the king enormous riches (Narrative 41); they themselves saw all too well what drudgery the king's monopoly of sandalwood was causing for the natives, who had left their fields and villages to fell timber in the hills (Narrative 83). In 1821, Gillesem learned that sandalwood exports produced a revenue of $30,000 annually for the Crown (Narrative 27), and that the timber bought for $5 to $7 for a *picul* could be sold to Chinese merchants for $11 or a little less. By then, however, the Pacific whaling fleet was more in evidence, and commercially a more potent force at Honolulu than timber-carrying Bostonians. The Russian narratives reflect this fact, describing the local consequences of the West Pacific whale hunt, begun in 1820 by Captain Allen (Narratives 24 and 34), and—understandably given the writers' naval calling—emphasizing the New Englanders' desperate efforts (1819–22) to persuade the leading chiefs to part with sandalwood for ships, or even manufactured goods of which they plainly had no need. A disproportionate amount of space is given, in the texts, to the Hawaiians' acquisitions of the *Forester*, *Bordeaux Packet*, *Albatross*, and *Cleopatra's Barge* (see Narratives 2–3, 21, and 28).

In October 1817, Kotzebue looked over the *Bordeaux Packet*, which Andrew Blanchard had managed to sell to Kamehameha the month before.[39] He was impressed by such evidence of the value placed on sandalwood by the Chinese. While he watched, Hawaiian commoners brought loads of sandalwood to Honolulu's landing-place, Pakaka. There it was sorted, weighed, and put in boats for shipment. It was sold in pieces only three inches across (Narrative 27). Perhaps Hawaiian sandalwood was of a poorer quality than that available in Timor, as was claimed by Captain Beechey[40] and confirmed by Gilbert Mathison.[41] Still the Chinese were prepared to purchase it, as Golovnin reports, to make cases, little boxes and the like, for coffin-making, and for temple oil (Narrative 105). It was sold in three or four grades, and the worst was shown to purchasers first. In 1818, reports Golvnin, there were still very considerable stands of sandalwood on the Hawaiian Islands as a whole, but the very fact that it grew well on higher land meant that natives had to bring it "forty *versts* or more" to Honolulu or another port.[42] Kamehameha's anxiety to purchase *haole* vessels that could readily be reconfigured as Hawaiian warships, had induced him to require Kaumualii of Kauai to send him, as an annual tribute and *de facto* sign of fealty, a shipload of that wood.[43] As a result, Kauai Islanders were forced to cut the timber for Kamehameha, Kaumualii, and foreigners alike. A European supervised the operations in the north of Kauai.[44]

Chief Manager Baranov's instructions to Scheffer of 1 October 1815, written on the eve of Scheffer's sailing for Hawaii, had specifically alluded to the need to have Kamehameha grant the Russian American Company the right to trade in sandalwood, on the conditions by which William Heath Davis and the Winships had been trading, or on other terms.[45] Baranov returned to that theme several times over the coming eighteen months, and plainly hoped that Russians too could sell Hawaiian sandalwood at nine dollars a *picul* in Canton.[46] By January 1817, Scheffer himself was dreaming of the day when Russian subjects would control the Canton trade in sandalwood, setting a higher price.[47] But it was not to be; a lack of ships and personnel, political uncertainties,and mounting pressure from the British and Americans already resident or trading in the Islands, shattered the dream. As Golovnin was on his way to Honolulu, via Petropavlovsk-in-Kamchatka and the Northwest Coast, Governor Gagemeister bitterly reported to the Company Main Office in St. Petersburg that, Scheffer's faults apart, the "North Americans" had stripped the hills of Kauai of better sandalwood.[48]

As for Oahu, there had never been a likelihood that Russians would effectively combat the trade advantages secured by the New Englanders in 1810–12.[49] But although non-participants themselves in any China-centred trade, the Russian visitors of 1809–26 were keen observers of New England enterprise of every kind; and as it chanced, the greatest frequency of Russian naval visits to Oahu (1818–21) coincided with the heyday and first panic in the Honolulu–China trade in sandalwood.[50] The Russian records should accordingly be used to supplement New England data on that subject as, unfortunately, they have not. All the texts translated here complement Samuel Eliot Morison's Maritime History of Massachusetts (Boston, 1921), Bradley's The American Frontier in Hawaii (Stanford, 1942), or—among older works—Charles Gutzlaff's Sketch of Chinese History (London, 1834) and Peter Corney's Voyages (Honolulu, 1896), where that branch of trade and commerce is concerned.

Artefacts

Cook had received no orders to concern himself at length with "curiosities" in the Pacific, as he sailed on his first mission in the *Endeavour*. His orders were first, to gaze on Venus in Tahiti; second, to discover if a southern continent existed as geographers supposed; and third, to execute botanical objectives. Even so, both he and Joseph Banks had shown a lively and objective interest in native peoples they met; and the pattern was repeated on the second and final voyages, even though Cook's orders with regard to ethnographica had been reiterated word for word each time. Cook's attitude toward Pacific "curiosities" was, by the standard of the later eighteenth century, enlightened and professional.

His countryman, Samuel Wallis, R.N., of HMS *Dolphin*, had not wanted to obtain Tahitian artefacts in 1767, and had tried to return a barkcloth gift from Queen Oberea as "of very little use to us and certainly a great loss to them."[51] Other contemporaries looked on "curiosities" as of the slightest worth, if any, to be sent into "the rag-and-bone Department" of museums and forgotten.[52]

Cook and his people, on the other hand, had made as close and full a study of the natives as time allowed, collecting representative Hawaiian artefacts, recording, sketching, and in other ways surmounting obstacles in order to advance the infant science. "*Endeavour* was a relatively small vessel, whose cargo-space ... considerably limited the amount of bulky ethnographica that could be taken back. Again, the primary task of Banks and Solander was natural-historical study. If they were short of space, it would have to be utilized primarily for herbaria, shells, and other 'naturalia'."[53] Nonetheless, a very large collection of Pacific artefacts had come to England (where, alas, they were dispersed or relegated by museums to obscurity and, frequently, mistreated). While the expeditions had continued, at least, proper attention had been paid to the description and depiction of the artefacts in question; and Sydney Parkinson, George Forster, William Hodges, and John Webber drew other objects brought from Polynesia to England at that time.[54]

These examples proved influential in St. Petersburg as, at the dawn of a new century, the Russian Admiralty readied the *Nadezhda* and the *Neva* to take their place on the Pacific stage. They weighed especially on I.F. Kruzenshtern, the moving spirit and commander of the coming Russian round-the-world voyage of 1803–06. Lieutenant Kruzenshtern had served in his adolescence with James Trevenen, a distinguished youthful veteran of Cook's third voyage. He had long perceived Cook's greatness as a seaman and was marked indelibly by Cook's approach to the business of discovery; in short, by Cook the scientist. Of Kruzenshtern's and Iurii Lisianskii's expeditions in the *Nadezhda* and the *Neva*, which brought the Russians to Hawaii for the first time (June 1804), it suffices here to observe that Kruzenshtern insisted on its maritime and scientific elements at the expense of its commercial and its (hopeless) diplomatic ones, and that his bartering procedures and collection of Pacific artefacts at Nukuhiva set a precedent to be followed in Hawaii by his countrymen throughout the early nineteenth century.

It is because the Russian visit to the Washington-Marquesas group in 1804 so influenced later procedure and particularly attitudes towards Pacific artefact collecting by a younger generation (Kotzebue, Golovnin, and Wrangel being major representatives at Honolulu), that it is important to the study of those officers' subsequent visits to Hawaii. However, these realities have all been touched upon in recent books.[55] Suffice it to quote briefly from the instructions issued to the *Nadezhda*'s company as they were nearing Nukuhiva (Taio-hae Bay) in 1804:

> It would only be natural if, on our arrival, new objects inspired in many
> the desire to possess them. And you, for your part, would willingly barter
> European goods, consisting mostly of trinkets, for the various curios of
> these people. But lack of caution might have the most unhappy results ....
> It is therefore prohibited for any man to barter with these natives on the
> ship. Only when we have furnished ourselves with all provisions necessary
> for the continuation of our voyage ... shall I give sufficient notice for every
> man to begin bartering his own things for others, according to his means
> and inclinations .... It is emphatically reaffirmed that no member of the
> lower deck will use a firearm, aboard or ashore, without specific orders to
> that effect from th officers ....[56]

It is not easy to exaggerate the scientific and political importance of
this order, every line of which reflects Cook's influence on Kruzenshtern
and so on younger officers. Orderly bartering for foodstuffs at the outset,
the appointment of official purchasers to supervise it, a complete ban on
the use of firearms except in crisis; later, freedom to amass local collections with the captain's public blessing and encouragement: all might be
seen in full effect at Honolulu in the early 1800s. Day by day, through
peaceful barter, officers and men of both the *Nadezhda* and the *Neva*
obtained Marquesan and, a month later, Hawaiian artefacts. So, too, in
later years did the officers and men of other ships; and as the visitors
of 1804 had avoided the misfortunes then foreseen with trepidation—
theft, familiarity, and bloody retribution by the gun—so too did those
of 1809–26.

As Kruzenshtern, Lisianskii, and their people had in 1804 deliberately and persistently acquired artefacts by barter at Hawaii,[57] so too
did Kotzebue, Vasil'ev, Golovnin, and their companies, as well as later
callers. Kotzebue's orders for the *Riurik* referred specifically, as Kruzenshtern expressed it, to the certainty that trans-Pacific crossings would
contribute "not a little to enlarge our knowledge of ... inhabitants of
... islands scattered over" the Pacific.[58] In Vasil'ev's instructions for the
Otkrytie, several articles are broad and imprecise. Whenever possible,
however, he and all his officers were to engage in scientific work, nor
was the work to be invariably nautical or naval. Thus, Vasil'ev had
the discretion both to interpret and emphasize the scientific provisions
in his instructions. And as had Cook and Kruzenshtern, he chose to
read them in a way that favoured study of the Polynesian Islands and
their peoples, while encouraging his officers to do the same. Perhaps
his "Notes on a Stay in the Hawaiian Islands" (*Zapikski o prebyvanii
na Gavaiskikh ostrovakh*: TsGAVMF, *fond*, 213, op. 1, *delo* 104), and
the essay by Roman P. Boyle, Third Lieutenant of the *Otkrytie*, "A
Note on the Nature, History, Mores and Customs of the Natives of the

Sandwich Islands" (*Zapiska o prirode, istorii, nravakh, i obychaiakh* ...,
ibid. delo 113), lack the penetrating quality and ethnological correctness
of Hawaiian observations made by Chamisso and published that same
year (1821). The point, however, is that Boyle and Vasil'ev were alive
to opportunities to study the Hawaiians in their dealings with the *haole*
and in their own culture. Once again, Hawaiian artefacts were taken
back to Kronstadt for delivery to the Academy of Sciences' museum and
the Admiralty museum. And once again, Hawaiian artefacts were drawn
by a particularly able Russian artist, Emel'ian Kornéev. (See Appendix
C).

We may regret that the most versatile and energetic scientist in any
ship participating in the Russian Navy's polar expedition of 1819–22,
Ivan Mikhailovich Simonov (1794–1855), sailed aboard the southward-
bound *Vostok* with Bellingshausen, and so did not visit Oahu. It is
probable that, had he sailed in the sister sloop *Otkrytie*, Simonov would
have collected objects there that today would grace the cabinets of the
Kazan' State University together with his other Oceanic artefacts.[59]
Again, Hawaii would have figured in the articles and letters that he published on his personal experiences in Pacific waters,[60] and the interest
properly shown in his Pacific ethnographic work by Soviet historians and
others,[61] would have thrown a welcome light on the material and social
culture of Oahu in the time of Liholiho. Honolulu's loss, in this respect,
is Fiji's and New Zealand's gain. But, like the early loss of Emel'ian
Kornéev's whole portfolio of Polynesian, Arctic, North American, and
other aquarelles, it is amply compensated for by the abundance of extant
Russian materials on Honolulu. That abundance stemmed directly from
the orders under which Russian captains sailed from the Baltic around
the world.

Here are extracts from the third and fourth sets of instructions issued,
simultaneously and in duplicate, to Captains Bellingshausen and Vasil'ev
in May and June 1819. Set Three, from the Admiralty Department,
Article 15 reads:

> An astronomer, naturalist, and draughtsman are setting out with you,
> and they have their own particular orders from the Academy of Sciences
> .... The draughtsman is to make views of all remarkable places he happens
> to visit, also portraits of native peoples, their dress and their amusements.
> All collections of articles, of whatsoever sort, ... shall be handed to the
> Division Commander at the close of the expedition, and he shall present
> every object without exception to the Emperor as represented by the
> naval minister.[62]

Set Four, Secondary Instructions from the naval minister, Paragraph 23
reads:

Navigators shall at no time lose any opportunity to research and make observations on anything whatever that may contribute to the advancement
of science in general or to particular areas thereof ....[63]

The Russian visitors to Honolulu in the years 1809–26 were well placed
to collect Hawaiian artefacts. They were acquainted with large portions
of the British naval literature on Hawaii, came with quantities of European articles for large-scale barter, and were predisposed to barter for
Hawaiian "curiosities." Their hand was weakened, as Lisianskii's narrative forewarned them, by New Englanders' commercial enterprise: by
1809, the trickle of New England goods being imported at Oahu had
become a steady stream. By 1817, it was a flood. Still, the *ali'i* and the
commoners alike remained quite willing to dispose of certain artefacts
to Russian seamen, for a price. The Russians often met that price if it
did not, as was increasingly the case, have to be paid in specie: *piastres*
or *reals* (see Narrative 127).

> It is [writes Adrienne L. Kaeppler] one of the unfortunate accidents in
> the history of museums that although the British Museum probably has
> the most extensive collection from the voyages of Captain Cook existing
> anywhere, much of it cannot be identified .... The problem is not missing
> objects, but missing documentation.[67]

The Leningrad "pre-1828" Hawaiian *fond* cannot remotely be compared with London's (or with Göttingen's or Bern's) eighteenth-century
Hawaiian collections. But, *mutatis mutandis*, Kaeppler's words, are just
as relevant to the Museum of Anthropology and Ethnography (MAE)
in Leningrad as to the British Museum. For in Leningrad/St. Petersburg, as in the early nineteenth-century British Museum, complete and
accurate documentation was not provided for Hawaiian objects. Of the
great majority, no more can confidently be asserted than that by 1828
they had been moved to the Academy of Sciences' *Kunstkammer* from
the Admiralty's own crowded museum.[65] Which specific Russian ship or
expedition brought a given artefact back to St. Petersburg from 1806
(when the *Nadezhda* and the *Neva* returned to base) to 1827 (when
the *Moller* too returned with her Hawaiian contribution), can in general be ascertained only by reference to the contemporary narratives of
those participating in the voyages and/or to aquarelles or sketches by
the artists on the ships in question. Thus, the MAE collection gives
an overall impression of the sorts of "curiosities" that the Hawaiians
would surrender to such *haole* visitors in 1809–26; but for details of the
provenance and value that an owner had attributed to any single artefact, we must turn to the contemporary texts. The following remarks
merely scratch the surface of a topic that requires special treatment,
of the kind well demonstrated by Miss Kaeppler. Further observations

are made (Chapter 13) in connection with the ethnographic value of the "Honolulu drawings and watercolours" done by Mikhail Tikhanov and Louis Choris.

In 1818, Golovnin wished to acquire a feather cloak and so offered both Boki and Hekiri a gun of English make, complete with case and "all the fittings," and a large telescope, if they would give him one (Narrative 47). The chiefs refused, because that trade was a royal monopoly. The Russians made enquiries of John Elliot de Castro, whom Kotzebue had transported to Hawaii from a Spanish-Californian jail, and who had won Kamehameha's trust. They were assured that the king did sell such garments, but that Americans had driven the price up to $800 (Narrative 90). Thwarted, Golovnin focused on utilitarian and smaller artefacts, notably *'ahu* cords and fish-hooks (see Narrative 23). New England skippers bought a good deal of native cordage, as a substitute for hempen ropes, and used it on their voyages—in which Hawaiian seamen commonly took part (Narratives 11, 22, and 31)—along the Northwest Coast of North America. Such voyages increased the limits and the danger of the slave-trade.

In March 1821, the *Blagonamerennyi* was surrounded by Hawaiians with "various trifles for sale" as soon as she arrived (Narrative 127). The vendors wanted cash. So, too, did men of higher social standing who arrived a little later. These brought out "mats, spears, and other objects," and would accept in return "almost nothing but *thalers*" (Narrative 127). American shipmasters, the Russians thought, had made Hawaiians over-particular and inflated local prices, both for foodstuffs and for artefacts. Frequent intercourse with *haole* had made Kamehameha especially, but also the *ali'i* in general, shrewd traders (Narrative 105).

Salt

It was to get salt, among other things, that Chief Manager Baranov sent the *Neva* to the Hawaiian Islands at the close of 1808.[66] Slobodchikov, lately returned to Sitka in the *Nikolai*, had brought that commodity so that Baranov could approve its quality. And it was King Kamehameha who, in 1806—according to Georg Heinrich Langsdorf[67]—had offered salt (and a variety of foodstuffs) to the Russians in exchange for otter skins. The Russian-American Company required large amounts of salt, not for human consumption, but in order to cure peltry on the northwest Coast, on the Aleutian Islands, on the Kurils, in Kamchatka, and elsewhere. There were salt-mines in Kamchatka, but the difficulty of conveying the salt to Sitka led Baranov to consider other sources. Fedor Ivanovich Shemelin and Nikolai Ivanovich Korobitsyn, the two Company clerks (*prikazchiki*) who had accompanied the *Nadezhda* and the *Neva* respectively, on their Pacific voyages of 1804–05, had both reported that Hawaii could provide salt in abundance in addition to vegetables and meat.[68] Gagemeister bartered 1,805 fur-seal skins and some walrus tusks for Hawaiian goods, including approximately twenty-two tons of local salt.[69] Over the following ten years, Baranov also acquired salt from Upper California, but in modest volumes. The Company recognized the high quality of crystallized salt from Oahu. Those New Englanders like William Heath Davis of the *Isabella* who sold salt to the Company (represented by Baranov) in the years 1809–17, most likely brought it from Oahu.[70] In that period, 2,500 *poods* or slightly over 40 tons of salt were obtained for Company use in the Pacific,[71] most from Oahu, some from California.

As salt had first interested Baranov in Oahu, so eight years later it induced him to respond to an offer made by Kaumualii from which evolved the abortive Scheffer adventure. Writing to Baranov through Captain James Bennett of the *Atahualpa* on 27 December 1814,[72] Kaumualii offered salt and numerous other commodities from Kauai in exchange for a ninety-ton brig, naval supplies, and firearms. By 1816, we find Baranov cautioning Lieutenant Iakov A. Podushkin of the ship *Otkrytie*—not to be confused with the ship of the same name commanded by Vasil'ev in 1819–22, which was three times her size—not to get too much Hawaiian salt[73] unless it could be had for less than fifty kopeks a *pood*. Podushkin took some aboard all the same.

The Aliapaakai and Moanalua lakes near Honolulu, in particular, attracted the attention of Podushkin, Gagemeister and, inevitably, Scheffer. ("What a boon for the Russian holdings on the Northwest Coast" it would be, if the Company controlled the Islands: "If we take only half of the most moderate price for which this substance ... is sold in these places, it could easily yield an annual profit of 100,000 Spanish *piastres* ...."[74] So Scheffer continued to calculate throughout 1817.) Hiking westward toward Waiau and the Pearl River, Kotzebue passed a salt lake, probably Aliapaakai, and found its shores "covered with the most excellent salt" (Narrative 101). He was informed that the *ali'i* who owned the lake received a large income from that commodity. It was the labour of commoners to carry the salt thence to Honolulu, for shipment abroad.

Still, in 1821, the Russians prized Oahu salt. Responding to an advance by Captain Petr Ivanovich Rikord, then Governor of Kamchatka, who had stressed the logic of Hawaiian-Kamchatkan trade (Narrative 127), Liholiho and a group of wealthy chiefs commissioned the *Thaddeus* (Captain William Sumner) to carry a cargo of salt to Petropavlovsk. The salt was well-received by Rikord, and cordage, canvas, axes, and salt-fish made a good impression on the trading chiefs when the *Thaddeus* returned.[75] The salt-fish especially pleased the Hawaiians, who, says Gillesem, had not learned the Cossack/Aleut preparation technique (Narrative 52).

The ever-growing number of American ships in port, however, had by 1822 driven the prices of essential food provisions on Oahu higher than they were in New England. An inflationary trend noted by Golovnin in 1818 had reached a higher plane. Company Head Office accordingly reminded Captain Matvei Murav'ev, then Governor of Russian North America, that salt was really the only Island product that could usefully be carried to the settlements. And salt could well be had in California, together with badly needed grains.[76] Still, the Company did obtain more than a hundred tons of Honolulu salt in 1824–25,[77] some of it being carried in the *Riurik* and the *Lapwing*.[78] Hawaiians benefitted from the selling price of 1.75 *piastres* a *pood*.

Russian records indicate that the Pacific salt trade was a smaller burden on the commoners than was the trade in sandalwood. Nevertheless, it fell exclusively upon their shoulders, and in 1823–25 from 400 to 600 barrels were laboriously brought out annually from Moanalua Lake. The Reverend William Ellis was assured that "quantities of it" had been sent off to Kamchatka for the curing of skins.[79] He found the chiefs regarded salt as an important export item after sandalwood and food (Narrative 27).

Personal Services by Hawaiians

Russian visitors were offered services, as well as goods, in exchange for Russian goods. These services were offered, not by the *ali'i*, but by commoners who often were not allowed to retain the Russian goods but had to turn them over to the chiefs. Often, commoners laboured for the *haole* on the instructions of their chief; salt might be carried to the harbour-side, or divers might investigate the damaged copper sheathing of a ship or a submerged part of a hull attacked by worms (Narrative 32). The former were ordinary labourers, the latter—men with special skills or training. But by far the largest service offered to the *haole*, Russians included, was the company of women.

The Soviet historian, Daniel D. Tumarkin, has this to say on the subject:

> The sailors who had first visited the Hawaiian Islands had reported that, to the evident pleasure of the seamen, many women came out in craft or swam out to them. These visits were explained not only in terms of curiosity but were also, evidently, a manifestation sui generis of hospitable hetaerism, such as may be met among many peoples at an analogous level of development .... Naturally, the colonizers took advantage of that custom, as also of the relative freedom of extramarital relations on the Islands; and with gifts, they encouraged women to come out to their ships and gradually changed these visitations into the most loathsome trade .... Russian navigators attempted to fight against this debauchery. Thus

Iu. F. Lisianskii, who participated in the Russians' first voyage round
the world, recalls that when the *Neva* had arrived in 1804 at Kealakekua
Bay (Hawaii Island), she had been surrounded "by the numerous forces
of Venus," but that not a single woman had been allowed onto the ship
....[80]

Making use of unfavourable remarks by Archibald Campbell, William
Broughton, and George Vancouver, Tumarkin rightly stresses that this
"trade in women" had considerably worsened between 1778 and 1793;
that British and American seamen had actively fostered prostitution,
with or without the active collaboration of Hawaiian men; and that
they had continued to look for, and to pay for, prostitution in the Islands in the early 1800s. One may note the highly selective use of such
comments—out of context—by early Russian visitors (Iu.F. Lisianskii,
Nikolai I. Korobitsyn) who, in Tumarkin's presentation of the case at
least, were typically "correct" in all their dealings with the young "forces
of Venus" and were scandalized by what the British and Americans had
done. But one concurs with both Tumarkin and Vancouver that, indeed,
haole visits had encouraged trade in sex.

There are, however, certain aspects of Tumarkin's treatment of this
topic that demand to be refuted. First, the matter of Hawaiian *geterizm*
(hetaerism): if this term is taken to mean a state of society in which
women are held in common, or a state of promiscuous concubinage, or
that such conditions characterized certain societies, it is decidedly inap-
plicable to Hawaii. Like Tumarkin's passing reference to "many peoples"
who, in other times, shared their wives or daughters with important visitors, and like his hints elsewhere in *Vtorzhenie kolonizatorov* that the
Hawaiians, too, had *Areoi* societies, his use of such a term in such a
context, is most unfortunate.

Second, the matter of the Russians' perfect record in attempted (or
required) abstinence from sexual relations in Hawaii, indeed in Oceania at large, requires comment. Soviet prudery is justified, at least in
part, by the unquestionable fact that Russian companies in Polynesia
did comport themselves with more reserve and discipline than any other
European seamen of that age. It is a fact that Russians were too late
to have brought venereal disease to the Hawaiians. In general, Russians
may boast that their compatriots did not encourage prostitution on the
Islands as the British and Americans unquestionably did. It does not
follow from this, however, that Russian seamen did not sometimes look
for intimate relations with Hawaiian (and other Polynesian) women.

Since Tumarkin holds the *Neva* up as an example of Russian correctness in the first years of the century, the private journal of that vessel's
sharp-eyed priest, the Archpriest Gedeon, may be employed to show
that Russians were highly susceptible to the Hawaiian maidens' charms

in 1804 (see Tumarkin, 1979 on Gedeon's MS). Again, Tumarkin quotes the captain of the *Nadezhda* as rejecting the advances of a father who had hoped to sell his daughter's favours to the Russians (Kona Coast), and then proceeds to emphasize the Russians' horror at the practice.[81] It does not follow from this that the *Nadezhda*'s company did not enjoy personal contact with the girls of Polynesia when they could. At Taio-hae Bay on Nukuhiva, according to Fourth Lieutenant Emel'ian E. Levenshtern (whose private diary is unusually frank), such opportunities had soon been found by certain men. "Our sailors don't miss a thing. They even try it in the water ...."[82] The *Nadezhda*'s deck, it seems, looked like a hospital at dawn, save that the bodies were attractive. One should not exaggerate such incidents. But one should also recognize that Polynesians looked for joy in sexual relations, and that Russians, too, could sometimes "fall from grace." Not even Kotzebue thought it necessary to deny that, after sixteen days at Honolulu on the *Riurik*'s first visit, local women had had connections with his crew. "All day long," on 13 December 1816, "the ship was surrounded by swimming women, who tenderly took their leave of their own friends."[83]

According to Chamisso (Houston, 1939:63), the *Riurik* was quickly approached on her arrival at Honolulu by "insistent" women, who were soon shouting their offers. Kotzebue adds that they were visibily annoyed when not allowed aboard (Narrative 4), but that they all returned, day after day. Contacts thus made were followed up ashore; and Russians were on occasion left alone with Hawaiian "wives" (Narrative 9).

Two years later, Golovnin found that his ship, like all the European ships at Honolulu, was surrounded by craft "bringing out young women ... as the principle trade article" (Narrative 107). At least when Captain Broughton had come to Hawaii in 1796, local craft had brought out women and fresh fruit.[84] Cash was requested for these women's favours: ironware did not suffice, as once it had, nor was cloth acceptable in an increasingly sophisticated market.[85] Golovnin believed, however, that "only the commoners" engaged in this trade in 1818, and states that chiefs would "not trade their daughters or wives for any sum" (Narrative 107). The Russians saw many Europeans residing at Honolulu, more or less permanently, with native women, as well as naked half-caste children (Narrative 105). Few such women had been married in a public ceremony that a Russian might have recognized as binding. Chamisso believed that on the north shore of Oahu, away from Honolulu, he saw evidence of "more patriarchal and unspoiled customs" (Narrative 118). He also held that chastity (*die Reinheit*), as a virtue, was and always had been foreign to Hawaiians.[86]

By 1821, the trade in sexual favours had become raucous and strictly cash-based (Narrative 127). The Russians declined to buy, thus causing offense. In Lazarev's view, the New England missionaries had managed

to do nothing yet (1821) to control the renting out of daughters (Narrative 127). Vasil'ev charged Marin with doing so, conceding that it was
a universal Hawaiian practice.[87] But Bingham's progress is recorded by
both Kotzebue and Wrangel. By 1826, "only the lower class of women,"
thought Wrangel, could be "reproached with licentiousness" (Narrative
129). Kaahumanu kept watch on young women's movements and dress;
even the neck had to be covered. Kotzebue deplored the prostitution he
had seen at Honolulu, but like other visitors believed Bingham had gone
too far in outlawing traditional Hawaiian songs and dancing while enforcing inactivity on Sunday.[88] Wrangel described repressions that would
lead to rebellion against the mission's rigid mores within two months of
his departure from Oahu.[89] Then, Hawaiian girls would again dance the
hula.

Kotzebue's criticisms of Bingham were intense. However, they accurately anticipated a crisis that the mission's recent ban on prostitution
was about to cause.[90] The *Predpriiatie* left Honolulu on 19 September
1825. Within three weeks, New England whaling crews were threatening
to seize women by force, if they could not be had by any other means.
The trade in sex was too entrenched at Honolulu to be ended, once and
for all, even by edicts promulgated by Kaahumanu—Baron Wrangel's
"severe Vestal" (Narrative 129).

Hawaiians Under *Haole* Control

Russian records of the early nineteenth century provide a tolerably
comprehensive picture of the ways in which the European settlers and
shipmasters at Honolulu were controlling, and exploiting, the Hawaiian
common people. In particular, the Russians show Hawaiians being used
as common labourers; as skilled labour on the land or sea, and as invol-
untary students in the *haole* school of life. Of the Hawaiians' servitude,
which meant felling and carrying sandalwood, collecting and carrying
salt and foodstuffs to the harbour, and in general providing manual
labour for their chiefs and rulers, there is little more to be said. "The
condition of the common people," as Malo observes (1903:87), "was that
of subjection, ... burdened and oppressed, some even to death." The
Russian narratives corroborate this testimony (see Narratives 27 and
86).

The Hawaiians served their European masters—Young and Marin,
Holmes and Davis, Rives and Beckley—in more skilful ways than by
labour alone. Some served as herdsmen (Narrative 43), and as tenant-
watchmen on plantations.[91] Others served as guides in the interior. Still
others were hired fishermen. George Beckley had Hawaiian common
troops to train and drill. The many cameos of such employment contained in the Russian texts are a valuable record of evolving race re-

lations. More significant however, and of greater interest to Russian officers themselves, are those vignettes that show Hawaiians as crewmen on New England trading ships, on the Northwest Coast itself, or—in the case of Terentii (Lauri) and Kanehoa, aboard Russian ships. It was predictable that naval officers would take a sympathetic interest in the Hawaiians' universally acknowledged love of voyaging to other lands. That they should do so in the very years when Hawaiians were most regularly active in Bostonians, and able to report to their compatriots on all the wonders of St. Petersburg, the Northwest Coast, and China, is a bonus for historical and wider Polynesian studies.

From the outset, Russian visitors had (favourably) noted the Hawaiian willingness to serve at sea. In 1804, Lisianskii had opined that scores of Islanders would "give all they had" to work on *haole* ships as crewmen.[92] Not a few had proved their usefulness to the Americans in the Pacific trade, which had encompassed the Hawaiian Islands since Captain Colnett's day.[93] Lisianskii's observations were amplified by Langsdorf.[94] While on the northwest coast of North America in 1806, adds Langsdorf, "I saw and talked with several natives of Owhyhee serving as sailors on board vessels from Boston, who received as pay ten or twelve *piastres* per month."

The New England vessels encountered by Langsdorf at Novo-Arkhangel'sk on Sitka Island were the *Juno* (Captain John D'Wolf) and the *O'Cain* (Captain Jonathan Winship, Jr.). The *O'Cain*, at least, which had left Boston in October 1805 and arrived on the Coast while Dr. Langsdorf and Rezanov were at San Francisco,[95] had had the opportunity to take on a few Hawaiians.[96] They presumably returned when the *O'Cain* called at the Islands on her passage to Canton in 1807.

But in any case, the Russians and their passengers were well aware of the Hawaiians' readiness to leave their homes and, with Kamehameha's blessing, gain experience and skills across the water. Like John Turnbull in 1802,[97] the Russians with the *Riurik* in 1816 met individuals who had not only seen the Russian Northwest Coast and Tlingit Indians, but had also saved enough Spanish *piastres* from their pay to purchase property and live in comfort in Hawaii.[98] Choris reports that such adventurers related their extraordinary doings in the north to their compatriots' admiration and astonishment. Kotzebue similarly comments on Hawaiian gullibility, but in connection with the tall tales that the Hawaiian native Lauri told Namahana Piia about the mansions in St. Petersburg "so large that he had walked three days in one of them," but not run out of rooms![99]

In October 1818, Golovnin was informed that the reliability of Islanders and their attachment to their captain (or *ali'i haole*) induced New England masters who proposed to capture Tlingit Indians to have Hawaiians by their side (Narrative 22). In case of mutiny, Hawaiians regularly took the captain's part. Golovnin's major informant with experience of slaving was Captain David Nye, of the brig *Brutus* (see Narrative 18). Nye had a reputation as a brutal captain,[100] and provided Golovnin "with certain curious information" about Hawaii and its people. Alexander Adams, an Englishman, made much of the American expansion of the slave-trade on the Northwest Coast, in conversation with Kotzebue (Narrative 11). It is evident, however, that Vasil'ev had solid grounds to speak of some New England skippers, in 1821, as men "inhuman enough" to trade in life (Narrative 109). Hawaiians certainly engaged in the New England Coastal raids, and some no doubt were killed as a result.

By 1821, several hundred Hawaiians were employed aboard the royal squadron. All the vessels in that squadron except one, the *Ha'aheo o Hawaii*, still had European captains[101] in the last years of Kamehameha's reign. But the Europeans "could not say enough in praise of the agility and sharpness of their men" (Narrative 52). The Russian records emphasize that the Hawaiians had retained their glowing early reputation as efficient sailors. One is not therefore surprised to find Captain Charles Wilkes, USN., of the United States Exploring Expedition, enlisting fifty-odd Hawaiians (1841) to replace seamen whose terms had then expired—and commending the Hawaiians in the very terms reported by Russians from Lisianskii to Vasil'ev.[102]

Russian texts reveal relations between Hawaiians and a number of influential early settlers, notably John Young (Olohana), Francisco de Paula Marin, George Beckley, Oliver Holmes, William Heath Davis, Isaac Davis, Alexander Adams, Jean Rives, and Thomas Meek. They also illuminate relations between Reverend Hiram Bingham and his native hosts.

In 1816, Young was a senior chief directing the arrival of shipping at Honolulu (Narrative 1), his relations with Kalanimoku being very sound (Narrative 5). It was Kotzebue's opinion, as it had been that of Captain William Shaler ten years earlier,[103] that Young was universally respected on Oahu as an upright man. Once a common seaman, he was reading letters from, or at least in the name of, King George III (Narrative 39) and enjoyed extraordinary influence and prestige. Marin, too, controlled many Hawaiians and acted as a chief (Narrative 19) and interpreter (Narratives 50 and 54). Although living far from Kamehameha I in the post-Napoleonic years, and jealous of such independence from the king as he could keep, Marin was in frequent contact with the royal family during the 1820s. The Russians found him often associated with Boki and Kalanimoku (Narrative 58). Hawaiians worked his plantations, as labourers and watchmen, and herded his livestock; others were his tenants, Kamehameha having granted him *koele* (estates on kula land) for medical and other services.[104] He was considered a demanding master.

While not effusive or over-enthusiastic in offering help to foreign visitors, notes Chamisso (Narrative 98), Marin was helpful enough. The Hawaiians respected him as a butcher, mason, carpenter, cigar-maker, and vintner. Kamehameha and Liholiho esteemed him rather as a physician.

As Commandant of Fort Kaahumanu, Captain George Beckley was in immediate control of (more or less untrained) Hawaiian "troops" (Narrative 127), and retained full authority over minor chiefs in Liholiho's reign (*ibid*). It was he who appointed military escorts to Russian wanderers, thus maintaining loose but adequate surveillance over them on Oahu.

The Russians seem not to have met Oliver Holmes of Plymouth, Massachusetts (and sometime Governor of Oahu), after 1816. They were aware of his large land holdings however, and Baranov was just as conscious as other would-be traders in the Islands during that period[105] of Holmes's influence as an advisor to Kamehameha. In February 1816, Lieutenant Iakov A. Podushkin of the Company vessel *Otkrytie* was specifically advised to "show kindness" to him, and to Marin, lest either prejudice the king against him.[106] As a powerful chief on Oahu, Holmes was able—and apparently willing—to assist Scheffer during that year. Scheffer's testimony must be treated gingerly, but it would appear that there was some strain and even coolness between Holmes the American and John Young the Englishman.[107]

Gagemeister alone could have met Isaac Davis, the sailor left on Hawaii in 1790 whom Kamehameha so trusted[108] and who served there as Governor. Davis died in 1810 (Narratives 8 and 103), and Chamisso visited his grave. Russian records indicate that Davis's memory was honoured long afterwards. His namesake, William Heath Davis, the shipmaster and merchant-settler at Honolulu, is shown in a favourable light by Golovnin (Narrative 18). The two were friends (Narratives 85 and 106). The visitors of 1821, however, do not substantiate Golovnin's high opinion of this Davis as a regional philanthropist. On the contrary, he was considered a harsh exploiter of Pacific Islanders. As early as October 1815, Baranov had been aware of William Heath Davis's successful exploitation of Hawaiian natives and resources (sandalwood), and was hoping that his Company could gain some like privileges.[109] Other Russians, too, became aware of that trader's hard-nosed use of the Hawaiians, whom he carried to Canton and to the Northwest Coast as crewmen in the *Isabella*, the *Eagle*, and the *Brutus*. He is implicitly included in the list of New Englanders drawn up in 1822 by Mikhail N. Vasil'ev of "Bostonians" who not only took Hawaiians to the country of the Tlingit Indians, but also sold some into slavery.[110]

The Company administrator and annalist Kiril T. Khlebnikov has likewise damning comments to make on the New Englanders' propensity to carry off Hawaiians (and particularly women) for abuse and exploitation in the North.[111] Kotzebue and Vasil'ev were equally prepared to believe that American slavers or, rather, traders indulging incidentally in the Pacific Coast slave-trade, were carrying off Hawaiians (Narratives 11 and 109). William Heath Davis, in any event, maintained his contacts with the Russians,[112] had two sons by Oliver Holmes's daughter, and died at Honolulu in 1823. From 1818 onward, he was associated by his Russian visitors with Captain Thomas Meek of the *Eagle* (Narratives 127 and 129). Meek, like Davis, had longstanding connections with Baranov[113] and prospered in the early 1820s with assistance from the Russians. He was conscious of a degree of indebtedness to the Chief Manager, who died in 1819, and was in any case a gentler and more civilized "Bostonian" than Davis. By 1825 he was contributing annual sums of money to support the mission work at Honolulu.[114] The following year, he had both the resources and the inclination to provide a grateful Wrangel with a temporary house in Honolulu (Narrative 129).

Russian encounters with the French-born settler, Jean Rives, date from 1821 (Narratives 49–50). Secretary and companion of Liholiho, the Frenchman made a poor impression on Lazarev, but was evidently liked by the royal party and perfectly bilingual in French and Hawaiian. Like other *haole* chiefs, he exerted his influence by carefully maintaining his connection with the king.

CHAPTER FIVE

Russian and Russo-German Science on Oahu
(1816–26)

INTRODUCTORY REMARKS

Surveys are offered here of the botany, zoology, cartography, hydrography, and mineralogy that Russians and/or Germans in their midst, undertook on Oahu or en route to it. Marine astronomy has been subsumed by its resultant sciences (or arts); and since the physics and especially the oceanography of Emil Lenz have been discussed in many histories of science and Pacific exploration, and have only incidental bearing on Oahu, they are touched on very briefly. Interested readers are directed to the works of Otto Krümmel, *Handbuch der Ozeanographie* (Stuttgart, 1907, vol. I), S.O. Makarov, *"Vitiaz" i Tikhii okean* (St. Petersburg, 1894), and Sir Joseph Prestwich, "Tables of Temperatures," *Proceedings of the Royal Society*, XXII (London, 1874): 462–68. Surveys of Lenz's oceanography of 1824–25 with *Predpriiatie* (Captain Otto von Kotzebue) may be found also in Friis, 1967:193, and in Fersman, 1926:95–96. Little important or original astronomy was undertaken by the Russians on Oahu. What was done there by the two well-trained astronomers who did have shore observatories in Honolulu in the early 1800s—Pavel Tarkhanov of the sloop *Otkrytie* (1821) and Vil'gel'm Preis of the *Predpriiatie* (1824–25)—was wholly practical, relating to their naval duties. (Both were on secondment to the Navy, Preis from Dorpat University, Tarkhanov from his post at the Academy of Sciences: see Lazarev, 1950:27 and 87; and Kotzebue, 1981:317.)

In the view of his contemporaries, Lenz and the geodesist Academician V.K. Vishnevskii, Preis's actual astronomy in the Pacific was completely overshadowed by his observations of theodolite and pendulum (see Kotzebue, *New Voyage*, I:3 and Kotzebue, 1981:318). The interested reader is in any case directed to Preis's monograph, *Astronomische Beobachtungen auf des ... zweiter Reise um die Welt in den Landungsplatzen angestellt* (Dorpat, 1830).

The largest scientific contribution made by Russians or their German fellow-travellers at Honolulu (and omitted here), is indisputably the contribution to linguistics. Chamisso's Hawaiian language studies in particular have long been recognized as valuable. For that reason, Samuel H. Elbert treated them in detail when introducing a contemporary reprint of Chamisso's *Über die Hawaiische Sprache* (Amsterdam, Halcyon Antiquariaat, 1969). Linguists of a younger generation have been scanning Russian *Voyages* for other such materials, collating work

by the New England missionaries at Honolulu with the (different) Hawaiian word-lists in Lisianskii's *Puteshestvie* of 1812, and in his own English translation of that work (see "A Vocabulary of the Language of
the Sandwich Islands," *Voyage Round the World*, London, 1814:326–
28). In the USSR, also, such materials have recently been studied or are
shortly to be published. The Hawaiian word-list and appended notes
compiled in 1821 by Lieutenant Aleksei P. Lazarev of the *Blagonamerennyi*, for instance, which remain at TsGAVMF (*fond* 213, op. 1, *delo* 43),
are scheduled to be published by the Soviet authorities—in a collection
of Hawaii-based materials and documents—by 1990. In these circumstances, it appears best to leave linguistics, like astronomy, out of this
sketch. We turn, then, to the role of Kotzebue, captain of the ships
that carried Chamisso and Johann Friedrich Eschscholtz to Oahu, as
the incidental patron of the twin natural sciences, zoology and botany.

THE ROLE OF KOTZEBUE AS A SCIENTIFIC INTERMEDIARY

Otto Evstaf'evich von Kotzebue was a cultivated naval officer, an accurate recorder of Pacific Island life, and an effective diplomat; but he
was not an eminent scholar.[1] It is not to his discredit as a naval officer that his essential contribution to Hawaiian studies was to bring to
Honolulu and the Big Island far greater scientists and scholars than himself. Four of his academic passengers aboard the *Riurik* (1816–17) and
the *Predpriiatie* (1824–25) who had extended stays at Honolulu, were
famous in their lifetimes and remain well-known today. These were
Johann Friedrich Eschscholtz (1793–1831), the Dorpat doctor and zoologist who served as naturalist on the *Riurik*;[2] his colleague Adelbert
von Chamisso (1781–1838), the multitalented and cosmopolitan chief
representative of natural (and other) sciences aboard that ship; Ernst
Karlovich Gofman (1801–71), mineralogist and naturalist with the *Predpriiatie*; and the distinguished geophysicist and oceanographer, Emilii
Khristianovich (German: Heinrich Friedrich) Lenz (1804–65).[3] All in
their different ways made the resources and the natural conditions of
Hawaii better known to Europeans, particularly to educated readers of
that time.

Among half-a-dozen lesser scientists or surgeons whom those vessels
also brought to Honolulu in the company of Dr. Eschscholtz, (who, like
Kotzebue, visited there four times in 1816–17 and 1824–25), were the
Predpriiatie's able astronomer, Vil'gel'm Preis (1793–1839); the naturalist Heinrich Seewald (Russian: Zival'd), also voyaging in *Predpriiatie*; and the most brilliant assistant navigator to arrive in Polynesia
on a Russian ship during this period, Vasilii S. Khromchenko, marine
surveyor.[4] All these men were under orders to pursue the naval, natural, and even human sciences, collaborating fully with the *Riurik*'s

and *Predpriiatie*'s official artists and scholars, and simultaneously to maintain detailed journals of their doings on the far side of the globe. As Kruzenshtern observed three months after the *Riurik*'s return from Polynesia to St. Petersburg (November 1818):

> It was supposed that crossings of the whole of the Great South Sea, twice and in entirely different directions, would assuredly do much to increase our knowledge of that ocean and of peoples inhabiting the many islands strewn across it. Furthermore, a rich harvest of objects of natural history was anticipated, since Count Rumiantsev had appointed not only a ship's surgeon but also a competent naturalist to accompany the expedition. The coming venture was accordingly of very great significance to science ....
>
> (Kotzebue, *Puteshestvie*, I:x)

At the instigation of Kruzenshtern, who was Rumiantsev's unofficial naval-maritime adviser, Johann Casper Hörner wrote "Instructions for the Physical and Astronomic Operations" that the men with the *Riurik* were to perform in the Pacific and in the Arctic. Hörner, who had sailed to Hawaii with the *Nadezhda* (Captain Kruzenshtern) in 1804, sent detailed notes from Switzerland: "regarding estimates of latitude and longitude," "surveying coasts," "determining refraction on horizons," and "dipping needles."[5] Chamisso and Dr. Eschscholtz had the liberty to organize their own (natural) sciences. It was an independence jealously, but sometimes vainly, guarded: Kotzebue was uncomfortable with Chamisso's prerogative to take instructions only when they related to the working of the ship, or the successful prosecution of the voyage as a whole.[6] Still, there was scarcely any risk that Chamisso, or Eschscholtz, would be idle where their scientific duties were concerned. So, too, in 1823–24 the very presence of so large a group of scientists (details in Ivashintsev, 1980:144), under a captain resolved to gain more laurels for discoveries in the Pacific, augured well for certain sciences at least. (To glance at Kotzebue's preface to the 1830 Weimar edition of his *Neue Reise um die Welt* ... is to appreciate which sciences he favoured: "We were amply supplied with astronomical and other scientific instruments, and had two pendulum apparatuses besides a theodolite made expressly for our expedition by the celebrated Reichenbach ...").[7] The Baltic German element was stronger in the *Predpriiatie* than aboard the *Riurik*. The University of Dorpat (modern Tartu) was about to make another contribution to Pacific studies: Eschscholtz, Gofman, and Lenz were all alumni of that venerable Swedish-Russian institution, and would all return to it in one capacity or other at the expedition's end.[8]

The following does not purport to be a comprehensive study of the sciences undertaken by the Russians on Oahu in the early 1800s. It is rather an attempt to draw attention to the Russian contributions to zoology and botany, which Western scholarship continues to ignore in the context of Oahu; and to emphasize the work still to be done on Chamisso's Hawaiian botany and on hydrography. For Gofman's mineralogy and practical geology in the Hawaiian Islands (1824–25), see Kotzebue, *New Voyage* (1830), II:246–47. The lava samples taken from the region of Mauna Loa and Oahu were taken to the Geological Museum of St. Petersburg's Academy of Sciences, and there added to samples of "scoriaceous lava" that the energetic Eschscholtz had collected in a lava stream from Mount Hualalai (modern Kaupulehu Forest Reserve), miles northeast of Kailua Bay. Eschscholtz's two samples had both been picked up on 28 September 1817, on his second visit to the Kona Coast (see Kotzebue, *Voyage of Discovery*, II:191 and III:352). His interest in Hualalai, like Kotzebue's own, lay in the fact that it had erupted with terrible effect in 1801, destroying villages and taking lives. As a botanist and doctor, Eschscholtz also recognized the local work and exploration of Vancouver's surgeon, Archibald Menzies (1754–1842), who had climbed Hualalai, at the same time introducing many food plants.[9] For development of geological collections in St. Petersburg, see *Geologicheskii muzei, osnovan v 1716 godu* (Leningrad, 1925).

Zoology

The ablest Russian zoologist to visit the Hawaiian Islands in the early nineteenth century was Johann Friedrich Eschscholtz. One regrets that circumstances did not favour zoology at Honolulu. At 180 tons, the *Riurik* was cramped below her deck, so that no large beasts could be stowed aboard her for investigation later.[10] Chamisso and Eschscholtz had, in any case, a large number of animals, notably fish, medusae, velellae, sea birds, and butterflies, that had not yet been dealt with properly when the *Riurik* first called at Honolulu.[11] In particular, Eschscholtz was busy with Brazilian and Californian butterflies, Pacific *Holothuria*, and Arctic flora from St. Lawrence Island, when he visited Oahu (see Kotzebue,. *Voyage*, III:295–300, 325, 378–84, etc.). He had little opportunity, therefore, to investigate Hawaiian fauna. What time he did manage to spend ashore, it appears was devoted to assisting Chamisso on his botanical-cum-ethnographic rambles to the north of Honolulu (see Houston, 1939:79).

Nor were matters any better ten months later (October 1817), when the *Riurik* returned to Honolulu from the Arctic. Lacking assistants trained in the tasks of sorting, rapidly describing, and preserving specimens, both Chamisso and Eschscholtz were preoccupied with shipboard work and were all too conscious of the scientific opportunities slipping by them on Oahu. Eschscholtz's Hawaiian call of 1824, in the *Predpriiatie*, followed hard on exhilarating weeks of zoologizing in Micronesia's

Ratak Chain, and on a stay at San Francisco that had likewise brought a sizeable collection to his cabin.

Finally, we must bear in mind that *Acalephen*, not *Mammalia* or any other land-based creatures, formed the core of Eschscholtz's Pacific work. His book, *System der Acalephen* (Berlin, 1829) has no connection with Oahu; nor, predictably perhaps, do Hawaiian fauna occupy positions of importance in his magnum opus, *Atlas Zoologischer, enthaltend Abbildungen und Beschreibungen neuer Thierarten ...* (Berlin, 1829–31). Such zoology as Eschscholtz did pursue at Honolulu forced itself on his attention, like the butterfly *Vanessa Tameamea* that fluttered round the harbour. ("The lower wings ... are on the under side a dirty green, with darker scalloped bands ...": full description and illustration appear in Kotzebue, *Entdeckungsreise* (1821), III:207 and Plate V). As Eschscholtz himself remarked, that butterfly much resembled *Vanessa atalanta Linn.*, and was a mid-Pacific representative of huge and globally distributed *Vanessa genus* (tortoise-shells of Europe and America) (*ibid.*, III:207). The closest relation to *Vanessa Tameamea*, however, is *Vanessa Californica* or *Carye* (Hübner),[12] found as far north as Vancouver Island and as far south as Peru. Merely noted by lepidopterists of W.J. Holland's generation in the West, between the two World Wars, Eschscholtz's "Honolulu butterfly" has been the object of more analytic interest in recent years for the reason stated (1948) by Elwood Zimmerman:

> The cosmopolitan butterfly genus *Vanessa* is represented in Hawaii by a single endemic species. Its larva is so distinct from other *Vanessa* larvae as to make it appear almost to belong to a different genus .... It appears most probable that it has been derived from a comparatively recent (geologically speaking) natural immigrant.[13]

Eschscholtz's data on *Vanessa Tameamea* have been used by modern lepidopterists to demonstrate a theorem advanced by R.C. Perkins in 1913; that "many endemic genera that contain a single or few species are offshoots from other, ... larger endemic genera, ... which have diverged more widely in structure than the average" (Perkins, 1913:cxlv). Without much effort, Eschscholtz happened on the solitary Hawaiian species of *Vanessa* in the family *Nymphalidae*, thus making a significant albeit minor contribution to the study of Hawaiian lepidoptera. In recognition of the hospitality that had been shown him by Kamehameha and other Hawaiian chiefs, Eschscholtz gave the names of Kalanimoku (Kraimoku) and Manuia (Manuja)—two chiefs whom he had personally met numerous times at Honolulu—to other butterflies. *Apatura Kraimoku* and *Idea Manuja*, to give their antiquated name forms, were respectively from Guam and from Brazil (Kotzebue, *Entdeckungsreise*, III:208–10).

Chamisso, for his part, paid less attention to zoology than to botany while on Oahu. Even so, he noted fauna while ashore, as he had noted "spouting whales" (*Physeter*) in the Kaiwi Channel, west of Molokai, on his approach (Houston, 1939:62). It was second nature for him to observe and to describe. Here are passing comments from "Bemerkungen und Ansichten" ("Remarks and Observations") in the third volume of Kotzebue's narrative of 1821, Section: "Die Inseln Sandwich—die Johnstone-Inseln":

> The only original wild quadrupeds of the Sandwich Islands are a small bat and a rat. To these we must add our common mouse now, besides the flea, certain kinds of *blatta*, and other noxious parasites .... But the ocean teems with fish, many species of which are embellished with hues of a marvellous splendour .... Among the crabs, one distinguishes the beautiful *Cancer squilla* and the *Palinurus* species .... Sea-worms and zoophytes, though, probably compose the richest and most interesting part of the fauna. In general, the local species appear to be quite different from those at Radak. (pp. 145–46)

Chamisso had opportunity to study the Hawaiian bat (*'ope'ape'a*), as Kotzebue shot a few near Waiau, six miles west of Honolulu, on 8 December 1816. ("I shot one on the wing, and as the mouse fell dead, all the natives there marvelled greatly at my skill": Kotzebue, *Puteshestvie*, II: 64. Russian renders "bat" as "flying mouse"). As for the native rat, it swarmed on Oahu in the early 1800s, disturbing the Russians when they tried to sleep ashore on mats (see Narrative 87), and giving sport to the Hawaiian chiefs who had for centuries been hunting them with bow and arrow (Buck, 1957:376). The gun of Kotzebue brought Hawaiian birds to the *Riurik*, some for the pot and some for science. That same afternoon, we know, native Hawaiians pleased the Russians by contributing to the expanding zoological collection. ("They managed to shoot a pair ... of divers of a species which, though flightless, is hard to take since the bird will dive the instant that the powder flashes in the pan": *ibid.*, II:62). From Kotzebue's references to habitat and very swift diving, it is clear that the bird was *Fulica americana sandwichensis*—that is, that native *'alae*. A coot of the family *Rallidae*, this bird was called a mudhen by the *haole* and was eaten by the Hawaiians (see Malo, 1951:37–38) long before George Beckley stalked it on Aliamanu Pond.

Like the mudhens, *Vestiaria coccinea* (*'i'iwi*) were obtained and stowed aboard for later study in St. Petersburg.[14] Chamisso refers to the *'i'iwi* as "the *Nectarina coccinea*, whose highly-valued feathers form part of the tribute" paid to kings (Kotzebue, *Voyage*, III:238). Golovnin was likewise interested in this bird (see Narrative 101), describing its capture by glue. Whether or not *'i'iwi* specimens now held in Leningrad (Institute of Zoology, Academy of Sciences of the USSR: Division of Ornithology Museum, 1 University Quay) were brought by Kotzebue and his people, or aboard another Russian ship, cannot be stated.[15] From the labels (*etiketki*) on the older specimens, however, as from labels on *Sericulus chrysocephalus* from New South Wales (cabinet XX, 4–7/3, 93369) it is certain that *'i'iwi* were transferred to the Academy servants of the Admiralty in the early 1800s.

The fate of the botanical and zoological collections that arrived with the *Riurik* (1818), was an uncertain one because, although she flew the Russian Navy flag, and was regarded as a warship both in Russia and abroad, the *Riurik* was actually Count Rumiantsev's property. Had the *Riurik* been sailing on a standard naval mission, as was the *Predpriiatie*, all such collections would—together with related logs and journals—have been handed to the naval ministry.[16] But Kotzebue, his lieutenants, and his crew were on secondment from the Navy and in Count Rumiantsev's personal employ.[17] So indeed was Chamisso, though he had left Russia for Germany within a few months of the expedition's end, taking botanical and other objects with him. In the circumstances, it was unavoidable that zoological, botanical, and ethnographic specimens should be presented to the Count, not the Academy, and that in due course some should pass into the Count's private museum—and from there, in 1826, be moved to Moscow.[18] Many specimens no doubt stayed in St. Petersburg; but there is reason to believe that zoological as well as ethnographic objects from the South and mid-Pacific were eventually lost as a result of their transferal to Rumiantsev's (and the subsequent Moscow Public) Museum.[19] Other specimens travelled with Eschscholtz to the University of Dorpat, in Estonia, to form a basis for a major zoological collection which, deplorably, was lost to fire.[20]

Based in Honolulu Harbour, Russians naturally took an interest in fish. They netted fish themselves, were given fish by the *ali'i*, and consumed fish. Russian texts are sprinkled with allusions to specific species. Here is Golovnin: "Among the fish here is a certain poisonous species. It is called *pikhi* by the natives and is so noticeable that it may readily be recognized without any drawing or description, for the form of its head bears an extraordinary likeness to that of an owl ..." (Golovnin, 1949:397). The fish in question is the *Tetraodon* (swell or puffer) fish called, not the *pihi*, but the *keke*. (Russian cursive *k* and *p* are not dissimilar, and Golovnin's MS offered the typesetters of 1822 numerous textual-palaeographic posers.) What is striking is that Golovnin should have regarded the *'o'opu hue* (*keke*) as *the* most dangerous Hawaiian fish. He had presumably been warned of it while visiting Honolulu. The warning was sound (see Malo, 1903:73 and Beckley, 1883:2). The fish's "owl-like look" is echoed in the standard ichthyological descriptions of the species; for example, in D.S. Jordan and B.W. Evermann's *Aquatic Resources of Hawaiian Islands*: "Head and snout broad, ... jaw ... forming a sort of beak" (1903:424).

While on his way to the Pearl River's mouth by canoe on 7 October 1817, Chamisso saw several Hawaiian craft fishing outside the reef in "ten or fifteen feet of water" (*Werke*, 1836, I:344). Numerous *Chaetodontidae* (Hawaiian: *kihikihi*) had been caught in trawling nets. Chamisso took note of them as best he could, given his awkward situation at the time. Such fish, we learn from Kepelino (*Ka moolelo o na i'a Hawaii*; MS in Bernice P. Bishop Museum Library), were "considered delicious to Panaha'eke," i.e., delicious to Panaha-the-humble; or when nothing better might be had (p. 52). Angular *kihikihi* (*Zanclus canescens linn.*) and *Lau wiliwili*, the two most common *Chaetodon* forms at Oahu in the early nineteenth century, as now, were to be found along the non-acroporitic coastal reefs of the Hawaiian Islands. Specimens of both kinds are in Leningrad today. So, it is worth noting in passing, are small samples of Hawaiian reef of coral genuses *porites* and *pocillopora*, all of early nineteenth-century and naval provenance. It was in just such coral reef, in shallow depths, that Chamisso would have observed his *Squilla raphidea*, a foot-long giant relative of mantis shrimps, and *Palinurus argus* (family: *Alpheidae*; suborder: *reptantia*), the Pacific spiny lobster. Both attracted his attention in the early part of winter, to the west of Honolulu town and harbour (Kotzebue, *Voyage*, III:238).

There can be little doubt that other zoological material from the Hawaiian Islands reached St. Petersburg, with Russian Navy ships, during the early nineteenth century. We know, for instance, that the Staff-Surgeon of the *Blagonamerennyi*, Grigorii A. Zaozérskii, was a natural historian and palaeographer of talent. While at Sydney (April 1820), he "uncovered two skeletons of animals no longer living in New Holland," which were duly stowed aboard and found their way to the St. Petersburg Academy of Sciences.[21] Lieutenant Aleksei P. Lazarev of the same vessel shared his interests and was apparently a zealous ornithologist. "For friendship's sake," Lieutenant Phillip Parker King, R.N., presented him with a collection "of the birds and insects of that country [New South Wales], which he had himself collected carefully ...."[22] Such officers would have pursued their interests, duty permitting, on Oahu as at Sydney twelve months earlier. The very volume of the "natural historical and ethnographic articles" that crammed the Navy's own museum by the late 1820s, makes it obvious that most men followed orders and surrendered their collections to the Crown at the conclusion of their voyages.[23] Such articles filled forty-five large cabinets.[24] Much work has to be done in tracking down Hawaiian zoological (and other) specimens in Soviet museums.

Botany

The wardrooms of the Russian ships that visited Oahu in the early 1800s contained many amateur but knowledgeable botanists. One such was Gagemeister, who in 1809 made short descriptions of Hawaiian husbandry and horticulture for the benefit of bureaucrats in European Russia.[25] Another was the artist, Louis Choris of the *Riurik*, whose Honolulu aquarelles belie his eye for vegetation. However, it is not in *Voyage pittoresque autour du monde* but in his later *Vues et paysages des Régions équinoxiales* that Choris the observer of the plant kingdom is seen. A third was Dr. Geinrikh Zival'd of the *Predpriiatie*, a fourth—the surgeon of the *Krotkii*, Avgust Kiber. "Surgeon Kiber," writes Wrangel of a hike up to the Koolau Range (northeast of Honolulu) in December 1826, "even here found objects from the plant kingdom that merited his attention" (Wrangel, 1828:100). But all these amateurs together did not make even a fraction of that major contribution to Hawaiian botany, indeed Hawaiian studies, that was made by Chamisso. His name looms over others in the field.

Chamisso spent a total of thirty-two days on Oahu, and a mere forty-one in the Hawaiian Islands. Well might he have urged the unobliging Kotzebue to allow him to remain there until the *Riurik* should return from Arctic exploration work a year later (Kotzebue, *Voyage*, III:243). There was work to last a lifetime. Forced to do it all within one month, he botanized with unrelenting vigour, almost always unaccompanied by anyone but native guides and making journeys to the north, northwest, and west of Honolulu. His approximate routes have been surveyed in brief (Chapter 3).

Suffice it to note that most of Chamisso's productive botanizing was conducted in a time of sudden showers, in the Nuuanu and Manoa valleys or in Waianae in the general direction of Kaala. He was thus collecting not in arid scrubland but in dry forest and rain forest; and when in dry forest, he mostly worked in streams and gulches (in the Nuuanu region, for example). On his hikes, he paid particular attention to the ferns and forest lichens and to swamp flora, ignoring dry strand vegetation and exotic blooms. He focused first on one locality, then on another. In November 1816, we can say, he worked deliberately in the region of today's Pacific and Makiki Heights ("I walked every single day through this area and over these hills ...": Chamisso, *Werke*, 1836, I:222). A few days later, he was botanizing north of modern Iwilei, searching stream-beds and ascending rocky spurs. For a man of thirty-six, he was an energetic climber in the bush, ("I found myself suspended over the slope of a rock, standing, as it were in a hammock high over an abyss"). On 8 December, he pushed into the rain forest and higher valleys further north, penetrating to the north coast of Oahu (Kaneohe or Kailua Bay) and returning by the Kaneohe Forest Reserve of today.

Like Wrangel ten years later, Chamisso was traveling "in *Hoo-ilo* season ... when the herbage died away" (Malo, 1903:53), so that Oahu's "yellowed grasses," ferns, and lichens caught his eye as they might not have done in the Hawaiian spring (Wrangel, 1828:100). As for Chamisso's most enterprising and protracted expedition—to the Waianae range and Mount Kaala in October 1817 (see Narrative 82)—suffice it to note that it brought to him forest vegetation. He worked almost naked as he collected over the Pohakea pass (see Ii, 1963:23 and 96, on that Waianae trail), using handkerchiefs instead of boxes to preserve his specimens.

> On a larger expedition, with guides and porters, one brings along a book of blotting-paper to secure the fragile plants immediately. My store of plants had been wetted by the rains and I feared decay. So when we reached our night quarters, I reserved one side of the house and made it *tabu* (*kapu*)—and there I spread my specimens out overnight. Such a *tabu* (*kapu*) is considered sacred and will be observed; but on board our ship there was no protection from any *tabu* (*kapu*), and yet my entire four-days' harvest had to be 'secured', that was, had to vanish whether wet or dry in the quickest possible time. Such was the iron rule ....
>
> (Chamisso, *Werke*, 1836, I:347)

Such comments merely hint at shipboard strains, but throw light on the tension that existed between Chamisso and Kotzebue by this time.

In sum, it may be said that Chamisso worked principally in zones of rain forest and swamp, at least 1,000 feet above sea-level. The closed canopy forest of the Waianae foothills and the northeast of the island had, in those days, a luxuriant understory of ferns—including large treeferns (*hapuu*)—and a covering of lichens, moss, and fungi. He himself speaks thus of the lianas to be found above the Nuuanu Valley, not far from Honolulu:

> With regard to giant arboreal creeping vines, it should be noted that the plant kingdom is there represented chiefly by herbaceous, air- and bean-bearing species, which create a mesh just above the low bush. On one occasion, I was in the mountains and slightly off the path and became entangled in such a net. I was trying to push on when I realized, at the last moment, that I was suspended in that net over the brink of a rocky precipice.
>
> (Chamisso, *ibid.*, I:222)

Chamisso's enjoyment of these rain forest excursions was evident; he had been cooped up at sea too long. But he had scientific reasons also for concentrating on Hawaiian alpine flora. First and foremost was the fact that neither Archibald Menzies, who had visited the Islands with Vancouver, nor any other botanist, had made that alpine flora known to Europeans—notwithstanding Joseph Banks's acknowledged hospitality towards *savants* who wished to view his plant collections. "What the learned companion of Vancouver, Archibald Menzies, succeeded in collecting on various trips to the heights of Hawaii and Maui Islands, still lies buried with so many other treasures in the Banks herbarium ...," wrote Chamisso in 1820 (Kotzebue, *Puteshestvie*, III:144). As was logical under those circumstances, he himself had first collected on another island, with a view to complementing Menzies's work, and now proposed to publish. To his great regret, Chamisso failed to publish any volume on Hawaiian alpine flora. Time and energy were lacking during a period of terrible activity and labour in his life, as has been shown by E. du Bois Reymond (see *Adelbert von Chamisso als Naturforscher*, 1889: Chaps. 3–4). We turn perforce to the botanical remarks in the "Bemerkungen und Ansichten" printed in 1821, albeit printed to the author's justified dissatisfaction (see Kotzebue, *Voyage*, III: 436). The St. Petersburg edition of his work as the *Riurik*'s naturalist was, in fact, replete with typographical and other errors. Here, to suggest the breadth of Chamisso's botanical horizons, are a few lines from that work:

> The flora of Hawaii has nothing in common with that of the nearest continent, on the Californian coast. Leafless forms of *Acacia*, the species *Metrosideros, Pandanus, Santalum, Aleurites, Dracaena, Amomum, Curcuma* and *Tacca*, all bear the stamp of their origin and natural relationships. The predominant families here are the *Rubiaceae, Contortae*, and *Urticae*: several species of this last grow wild and are used in the manufacture of various sorts of bast material. (*Broussonetia papyrifera*, the paper-mulberry tree, is indeed cultivated in the Sandwich Islands as in most of the South Sea Islands, for that purpose. But it is an error to suppose that bark cloth is made only from the bark of that tree.) A number of milky, arborescent *Lobeliaceae* are also to be distinguished. The exterior limits of Hawaii Island produces rather few kinds of grass and shrub, but the flora of the interior is luxuriant—though not comparable with the rich abundance of Brazilian soil. Only low trees descend into the valleys, among them the *Aleurites triloba* with its whitish foliage ....
> Oahu is the most fertile of all the Sandwich Islands ... and the cultivation of the valleys that lie behind Honolulu is remarkable .... Many foreign trees and plants are being reared in Marin's plantations; and several of those he has introduced may already be found growing wild in many places: for example, *Portulacca oleracea*, (only two other species of which kind belong to the native flora).
>
> (Kotzebue, *Entdeckungsreise*, III:144)

Chamisso spent some time in Francisco de Paula Marin's company. He saw the value of imported Asian purslane (*Portulaca*), cooked as greens, as of the "rice sprouted from Chinese seeds," some shoots of which he had himself plucked by mistake—to the annoyance of the

Spaniard's native watchman. "Manini," records Chamisso, "did not meet me with effusion, but I found him always helpful and instructive when I looked him up; quickly grasping the point that I was driving at, he taught me most of what I know [about Hawaii]" (Houston, 1939:64). Fluent in Spanish, Chamisso was able to discuss with Marin the techniques and problems of transplanting in the Tropics. What he learned was promptly passed on to Kadu, for use in Eastern Micronesia (Ratak Chain). It was self-evident to Chamisso that Marin's vineyards, like his goat- and cattle-herds, were an important contribution to the life of all Hawaiians of the future. Even so, he took less interest in Marin's horticultural and business innovations than in local native flora, and, essentially relying on his own forays, he built up his botanical collection in the hills.

Because his efforts to assist the Marshall Islander Kadu to introduce Hawaiian plants to Micronesian low atolls in 1817 were fundamentally botanical, they may be summarized here. The *Riurik* had first called at the Ratak chain (Taka and Utirik atolls, in lat. 11°11'N, long. 190°2'W) in May 1816 (Kotzebue, *Voyage*, I:172–78). Returning to that part of Micronesia eight months later, Kotzebue made a series of discoveries and visited not only Wotje, Ailuk, and Aur atolls in the Ratak Chain, but also "Erikub" (Maloelap? See Ivashintsev, 1980:28). Chamisso and Kotzebue spent a week at Wotje atoll, whence the Russians sent their launch on explorations to the south, and whose inhabitants were welcoming (Kotzebue, *Voyage*, II:59–87). To Kotzebue, Wotje was "beloved Otdia," a place of peace and plenty; to the botanist, it was a challenge in its flora and its shortcomings alike. There and elsewhere in the Ratak chain, Chamisso "distributed" Hawaiian seeds from Honolulu to the natives, demonstrating "processes" of basic care (*ibid.*, II:106 and 118). That same month, the Russians met Kadu the Carolinean, whom they in due course brought to Queen Kaahumanu in Hawaii. In November 1817, they brought him back to Wotje in the Ratak chain (*ibid.*, II:192 and 206–08).

Chamisso's and Kotzebue's efforts to alleviate the Ratak people's shortages of food by introducing new and useful plants, were in the spirit of eighteenth-century Enlightenment. Though only partially successful, they were philanthropic efforts that rebound Russia's credit even now. Chamisso records these details of the transplanting or other propagation of Oahu plants to Micronesia:

> The real object of our return visit was to be useful to our friends. We brought them goats, hogs, dogs, cats, domestic hens, and sweet potatoes (*Ipomoea tuberosa Lour. Coch.*) from the Sandwich Islands, as well as melons, water-melons, gourds of different sorts, ... sugarcane, grapes, and pineapples. We also brought them the apple-tree of the Sandwich Islands

(not an *Eugenia*), the *ti*-root (*Dracaena termin.*), the lemon tree, and the seeds of quite a few other useful plants of the Sandwich Islands, including the *Aleurites triloba*, (nuts from which are used as tapers and yield both oil and stuff for dying), and a couple of shrubs whose bast goes to manufacture cloth ....

(Kotzebue, *Entdeckungsreise*, III:120)

Many of these plants and seeds had only recently been introduced to the Hawaiian chain by Marin or by other *haoles*; but some had reached Hawaii with the Polynesians centuries before. For instance, *ko* (*saccharum officinarum*) and *'uala* (*Ipomoea batatas*), among others, were indigenous to the Hawaiian Islands, not to Eastern Micronesia (see Buck, 1957:5–7). And in this respect, Chamisso's decision to import *kukui* or candlenut trees (*Aleurites moluccana* or *triloba*), and Oahu mountain apples (*Eugenia malaccensis*, despite Chamisso), is of significance. *'Ohia'ai* (mountain apples) were a famine food at Honolulu, though their bark was still occasionally used for dying purposes (*ibid.*, 187). Chamisso doubtless supposed they would survive and be of use on Ratak's "poor and dangerous" low atolls (Kotzebue, *Voyage*, III:176).

Kotzebue was distressed, on his return to Wotje atoll (31 Oct. 1817), to be told that four-legged "and human rats" had totally destroyed the "Russian garden" planted there. He was therefore supervising when, next morning, Chamisso gave a compulsory and public lesson to the Islanders. Besides the plants mentioned above, the Wotje Islanders were left with orange trees, taro, and sprouting yams from Honolulu (*ibid.*, II:211). Finally, the Russians gave a feast at which Hawaiian roots were served, boiled and ready to be eaten, to their Micronesian hosts. Large numbers of *'uala* were consumed with healthy appetite. As for the watermelons brought from Honolulu, seeds were given to a trusted native named Lagediak. The man promised to make a garden "upon pillars," to protect the watermelons from the ravages of rats that the Hawaiian cats had failed to arrest. Kadu then promised to attend to the plantations with affection, and to call the foreign plants by Russian names. Future visitors to Wotje and adjacent atolls, noted Kotzebue at the time (*ibid.*, II:216), would "therefore find, instead of yams, taro, and potatoes, timaros, tamissos, and totabus." "Totabu" was Kotzebue, —"Tamisso"—Chamisso.

Plant Specimens Collected on Oahu: The Chamisso Collection (now in Leningrad)

Chamisso left Russia for Berlin in early winter, 1818. Part of his botanical collection stayed behind, part went to Germany. Like Choris, he maintained a correspondence with I.F. Kruzenshtern but felt no urge to return to Russia. In Berlin, he was received with royal hon-

ours and appointed Curator of that city's well-financed Botanic Garden.
His herbarium was large; but its Pacific Islands section did not capture his attention. His discovery (1819) of metagenesis in organisms of
the subclass *Salpae* steered him in different directions. His Hawaiian
specimens were ultimately lost in World War II. Such specimens as the
St. Petersburg Academy of Sciences obtained from Count Rumiantsev
or from Chamisso himself in 1818, on the other hand, survived. They
are today held at the L. Komarov Institute of Botany of the Academy
of Sciences, in Leningrad. The present writer found them there (May
1985), with the assistance of the systematicist and leading Soviet authority on J.R. Forster's and his son's herbaria, Andrei E. Bobrov, research
associate of that same institute.

The following twenty-five specimens are held in storage cupboards.
All are mounted on stiff folio sheets with other specimens of the same
plant, of other provenance, and individually labelled. Labels are, however, not in Chamisso's own hand, so annotations that were made in
recent times have been omitted.

1 *Bidens sandwichensis Less.* Family: *Compositae* Group: *Campylotheca*
(Beggar-tick; from a 4-foot high shrub with herbaceous upper branches:
see *Linnaea*, VI: 508. From Nuuanu Valley very probably. DTH 9237.
A214.)

2 *Bidens Chinensis Less.* Family: *Compositae* Group: *Bidens*
(Probabaly *Bidens pilosa*. DTH 9237a. Collected by Eschscholtz and
not in 1816–17, but in 1824. Hawaiian: *ko'oko'olau*, used medicinally
or as a tea: see N 844.)

3 *Sonchus oleraceus Less.* Family: *Compositae* Group: *Sonchus Ci-
chorium*
(Sow thistle or *pualele*; weedy herb, hollow stems, milky sap; a European native. DTH 9595. N 860. Leaves and roots used medicinally
by Hawaiians. Collected by Choris.)

4 *Bidens micranth Gaud.* Family: *Compositae* Group: *Campylotheca*
(Beggar-tick; shrub, 2–3-foot high, reddish stem. Described by Gaudichaud in *Voyage*, V:464. DTH 9237 N 216. From Eschscholtz in
1824 and used medicinally, like No. 2.)

5 *Adenolepis pulchella Less.* Family: *Compositae* Group: *Campylotheca*
(Description in *Linnaea*, VI:510. DTH 9237. A212. From Oahu,
1817.)

6 *Polypodium hymenophylloides Kaul.* Family: *Filices* Group: *Polypodium* (Referred to by Chamisso as *Amphoradenium hymenophyl.*:
see DTH 114. Kaulfuss, *Enumeratio Filicum*:118. A556. A creeping
rhyzome found on trees above 3,000 feet above sea-level. Hawaiian:
pai.)

7 *Polypodium tamariscinum Kaul.* Family: *Filices* Group: *Polypodium*

(Chamisso's *Amphoradenium tamarr.*: see DTH 114. Kaulfuss, *Enumeratio*:117. Gaudichaud in *Voyage*, V:365. A rhyzome known as *wahine noho mauna*. A556.)

8 *Aspidium unitum.* Family: *Filices* Group: *Aspidium*
(Kaulfuss's *Aspidium resiniferum*. DTH 20 A573. Hawaiian: *neke*. A swamp-loving rhyzome.)

9 *Aspidium cyatheoides Kaul.* Family: *Filices* Group: *Aspidium*
(Native Hawaiian fern, *kikawaio*, used for food and medicine; A571. N 21. Further evidence of Chamisso's awareness of ethnobotany. Grated roots resemble okra.)

10 *Dicksonia prolifera.* Family: *Filices* Group: *Asplenium*
(This is Chamisso's *Athyrium proliferum Moore*. DTH 53. Kaulfuss, *Enumeratio*:225. A615. An edible tree-fern, most probably from the Nuuanu Valley. N 10 and 25.)

11 *Cibotium Chamissoi Kaul.* Family: *Filices* Group: *Cibtioum*
(The Hawaiian tree-fern, *hapu'u i'i*, named for Chamisso by Kaulfuss: *Enumeratio*:230. DTH 7. A547. N 10. Frond stems are mealy and the trunk core is farinaceous.)

12 *Selaginella arbuscula Spring.* Family: *Lycopodiaceae* Group: *Selagin*
(Referred to by Chamisso as *Lycopodium arbuscul.*: see DTH 155. A648. Described by Spring, 1850, II:183. Still growing in Nuuanu. A small club-moss from damp forestland; Hawaiian: *lepelepe a moa*. N 5.)

13 *Lycopodium polytrichoides Kaul.* Family: *Lycopodiaceae* Group: *Lycopod*
(Kaulfuss, *Enumeratio*:6. DTH 154. A643. Hawaiian: *wawaeiole*. A rare epiphyte, from Waianae and Halawa on Oahu. Complete data in Otto Degener, *Flora Hawaiiensis*, Honolulu, 1935, I: family 19. Given in N 2 as *Lycopodium cernuum L.*)

14 *Polypodium spectrum Kaul.* Family: *Filices* Group: *Polypod*
(Chamisso's *Microsorium spectrum*. DTH 106. A559. The large, three-lobed fan-fern, *pe'ahi*; from damp forests or gulches. N 26.)

15 *Polypodium pellucidum Kaul.* Family: *Filices* Group: *Polypod*
(Hawaiian *'ae*, a common endemic polypod; fern fronds up to 15 inches long. Kaulfuss, *Enumeratio*:101. A557. N 25–26.)

16 *Pteris irregularis Kaul.* Family: *Filices* Group: *Pteris*
(A native Hawaiian sword-brake fern, *mana*. In deep gulches, 1,000–3,000 feet above sea-level. Kaulfuss, *Enumeratio*:189. A628. DTH 96. N 16–17.)

17 *Vittaria elongata rigida.* Family: *Filices* Group: *Vittaria*
(The grass-like fern described in A551 and Kaulfuss, *Enumeratio*:193. Not *Tetraplasandra kauaiensis Sherff*, also known to Hawaiians as *'ohe'ohe*.)

18 *Carex Oahuensis Kunth.* Family: *Cyperaceae* Group: *Carex*
(Referred to by Chamisso as *Carex flaviceps*. DTH 525. A487. A native sedge in the range 3,000–5,000 feet above sea-level on the Waianae Range. C.S. Kunth, *Enumeratio Plantarum*, II:515.)

19 *Tetramolopium Chamissonis.* Family: *Compositae* Group: *Tetramol*
   (A Hawaiian native aster, with purplish ray florets, growing mostly above 3,000 feet; bush-like. Identical with Lessing's *Tetramol. lepidotus*: see *Linnaea*, VI:502. DTH 8920. A199)

20 *Tetramolopium tenerrimum Nees.* Family: *Compositae* Group: *Tetramol*
   (Low shrub, from Waianae—Mount Kaala area; aster-like, pink or purplish florets. Nees von Esenbeck, *Genera et species Asterearum*:203 and Lessing in *Linnaea*, VI:120. A198. N 834.)

21 *Phyllostegia mollis Benth.* Family: *Labiatae* Group: *Phyllosteg*
   (A native Hawaiian mint; collected by Chamisso in Waianae. DTH 7228. A352. Hawaiian: *kapana*.)

22 *Phyllostegia glabra Benth.* Family: *Labiatae* Group: *Phyllosteg*
   (A white-flowered mint, from Oahu, above 2,000 feet. Data in *Linnaea*, VI:79. *The Botanical Register* (London), Vol. XV: no. 1292. Bentham's *Phyl. glabra var. Macaei*?)

23 *Phyllostegia Chammisoi Benth.* Family: *Labiatae* Group: *Phyllosteg*
   (This appears to be the mint species described by Gaudichaud in *Voyage*, V:452 and table 64. Related to *kapana*. A352.)

24 *Plantago princeps Cham. & Sch.* Family: *Plantaginaceae* Group: *Plantago*
   (A native species of plantain, medium to high altitude, near bogs; Chamisso and Schlechtendahl in *Linnaea*, I:167. Hawaiian *ale*. DTH 8116. A363.)

25 *Naias major All. angustifolia.* Family: *Naiadaceae* Group: *Naias*
   (A floating aquatic herb. See A. Braun in B. Seeman, ed., *Journal of Botany, British and Foreign*, II:275. DTH 64. A458.)

Key to References

A   W. Hillebrand *Flora of the Hawaiian Islands: A Description of their Phanerogams and Vascular Cryptogams* (Heidelberg, 1888)

DTH   *Register zu De Dalla Torre et Harms: Genera Siphonogamarum ad Systema Englerianum conscripta ...* (Weinheim, 1958)

Kaulfuss, Georg Friedrich   *Enumeratio Filicum quas in itinere circa terram legit Adalbertus de Chamisso ...* (Lipsiae, 1824)

N. Neal, Marie C.   *In Gardens of Hawaii* (Honolulu, Bernice P. Bishop Museum Special Publ. 50, 1965)

Voyage   Gaudichaud, Beaupré, in "Botanique du Voyage autour du monde sur l'Uranie et la Physicienne ..." *Voyage autour du Monde ... par ... de Freycinet* (Paris, 1827–39): vol. V.

Linnaea   Ein Journal für die Botanik in ihrem ganzen Umfange (Halle, 1826–62)

The Leningrad "Chamisso Collection" from Oahu mostly dates from the *Riurik*'s two visits to that island (1816–17). Annotations on the labels under Nos. 2 and 4 (only) indicate that Eschscholtz took those specimens in 1824, and that No. 3 (alone) was plucked by Choris. Chamisso is thus accredited, at BIAN, with 22 Oahu specimens. Two plant families, *Compositae* and *Filices*, predominate in the collection (7 and 10 representatives respectively). Of the remaining eight, three are mints or *Labiatae*, and two are club-mosses or *Lycopodiaceae*. The aquatic *Naiadaceae*, the sedges, and the plantains have a single representative apiece (Nos. 25, 24, 18). Botanically, the emphasis is heavily on ferns, high forest shrubs, and mosses, and by no means on exotic blooming plants. Only the beggar-ticks or Spanish needles and the asters (Nos. 1, 2, 4, 19 and 20) might be said to have dramatic bright-hued flowers in their season.

Like BIAN's important "1820 Sydney-Parramatta" plant collection, brought to Russia from Australia in 1822 and largely made by I.M. Simonov and F.F. Bellingshausen of the ship *Vostok* (see Bellingshausen, *Voyage*, 1945, II:348–49), Chamisso's (and Eschscholtz's) collection from Oahu is a record of the collectors' tastes, true scientific interests, and movements. As observed, the Russians were familiar with Dr. Menzies's botany on Maui and Hawaii (1793), and accordingly intent on botanizing elsewhere in the archipelago if opportunity arose (see Kotzebue, *Voyage of Discovery*, III:234).

It is impossible indeed to "match" the specimens now held in Leningrad with such fragmentary (but precious) data as we have of Chamisso's main hikes over Oahu: to the North Shore, to the Mount Kaala region, in the Nuuanu Valley, the Manoa Hills, and so forth (see Chapter 3 for surveys of his itineraries). Nevertheless, the likely provenance of certain specimens is quite apparent. For example, No. 21 (the *Phyllostegia mollis*) grew in Waianae; No. 1 was almost rampant in the Nuuanu Valley in the early 1800s, but retreating by the later nineteenth century. It will be obvious that certain of the plants in the collection have survived in those particular localities where Chamisso or Eschscholtz found them, but that many have retreated in the face of spreading suburbs and pollution. So the Leningrad material has value in the context of historical ecology. But it has even more importance as an echo of Hawaiian ethnobotany when used together with the Chamisso collection from Oahu that was once part of the Willdenow Herbarium in Prussia. For although, as noted, that collection was itself destroyed in World War II, we have an excellent idea of its holdings as they were in 1820.

The Former Chamisso Botanical Collection from Oahu in Berlin

From the scientific standpoint, the timing of Chamisso's arrival in

Berlin was happy. After ten tormented years, in the course of which
the Prussian State's stability was shaken—like the poet-botanist's own
life—by the Napoleonic Wars, Berlin was free again (1815). The occupying forces had departed, and the recently established Friedrich Wilhelm
University was complemented by a major new museum. The Botanic
Garden, too, had undergone a renaissance thanks to Karl Ludwig Willdenow (1765–1812), the botanist whose ceaseless energy had brought his
plant collections European fame, and had expanded his herbarium to
20,000 specimens before he died. Chamisso brought his Pacific plants to
a herbarium enlarged by recent contributions from the greatest French
and German botanists and travellers: Bonpland, La Billardière, Humboldt, and Klein. Nor did his fortune end at that; he very soon established contact with a range of fine collaborators, men like Georg Friedrich
Kaulfuss (1773–1830) and George Bentham (1800–84), who were among
the ablest *sistematiki* of their respective generations.

It was Kaulfuss who undertook the listing and minute description
of the *Filices* in Chamisso's collection, (the *Enumeratio ...* Lipsiae,
1824). As for the brilliant young Bentham, whose father Samuel had
worked in Russia as a naval architect and whose more famous uncle
Jeremy, the eminent philosopher, employed him as a private secretary,
he was available and willing to describe Chamisso's family of mints (see
his "De Plantis in expeditione speculatoria Romanzoffiana ... Labiatae
..." in *Linnaea*, VI:76–82). Thanks to Bentham, European science was
acquainted (1831) with all six mints collected by the Russians on Oahu
(five *Phyllostegia* and *Plectranthus parviflorus W.*). Thanks to Kaulfuss,
Oahu's club-mosses and ferns were better known than the related species
found on any other South Sea Island.

But the work of Kaulfuss and Bentham both depended upon that
of Chamisso's distinguished publisher, the German botanist Diedrich
Franz von Schlechtendal (1794–1866). It was Chamisso's good luck that
Schlechtendal was (scientifically and fiscally) in a position to be launching *Linnaea: ein Journal für die Botanik*, in 1825–26, as it was Schlechtendal's to have the voyager's material to offer in his first several issues.
From the botanists' collaboration sprang a comprehensive, ten-part listing and description of the plants brought from the *Riurik* expedition
to Berlin. That work, which treated plants by family and genus and
was introduced by Chamisso himself, had the general title: "De Plantis expeditione speculatoria Romanzoffiana observatis: rationem dicunt
Adalbertus de Chamisso et Diedericus de Schlechtendal." Each family
is in turn provided with a geographically ordered preface. To find those
specimens taken from Oahu, one therefore refers first to "*Insulae ae-
quinoctiales Oceani magni: O-Wahu*" or "*Insulae Sandwichenses*," and
then to a generic index with page references.

The following twenty-seven specimens were, in the present writer's view, indisputably collected on Oahu Island and not on the Big Island. Two further plants are omitted as duplicates of Nos. 24 and 25 in the Leningrad list above. No doubt Chamisso gathered other speciments in duplicate, leaving one in St. Petersburg and taking another to Berlin in 1818. In general, however, the Berlin collection from Oahu differs strikingly from the extant Leningrad collection, having no *Lycopodiaceae* or *Filices* but no less than eight members of the coffee family (*Rubiaceae*). Of those eight, moreover, half belong to the genus *Kadua* or *Hedyotis*, named by Chamisso in order to preserve the name and memory of the intelligent and helpful Ratak Islands refugee who was his friend.

Such heavy and distinctive emphases within the two collections from Oahu seem to show that they do not result from chance divisions and haphazard allocation of the specimens that went to Kronstadt in the *Riurik* (1818). On the contrary, it seems that Chamisso divided his material according to a plan. As a result, it is essential to consider both collections to achieve an overview of Chamisso's Hawaiian botany. In this connection, one should note that passing comments in the Latin texts attached to specimens in *Linnaea* sometimes illuminate the provenance of plants now held in Leningrad (and elsewhere in the world). No. 7 below, for instance, is said to have been gathered *in rupestribus montium insulae O-Wahu* (that is, among rocks on the hills of Oahu Island). That is the usual but not inevitable habitat of *Vaccimium cereum F.* and other relatives of the *'ohelo* shrub sacred to the goddess Pele.[26] Again, Nos. 8 and 10 were found together *in clivis aridioribus ad radices montium circa Hana-ruru insulae O-Wahu* (on arid slopes by the foothills around Honolulu on Oahu Island. See *Linnaea*, I:527–28, 539–40; II:36). No. 10 is *'ulei* (*Osteomeles anthyll.*), the native rose much used by Hawaiians to make their musical instrument, the *'ukeke*, as well as fishnet hoops, and fish-spears. An evergreen shrub, it is found nowadays in dry parts of the Big Island at altitudes up to 4,000 feet. Yet Chamisso saw it *ad radices montium*, far nearer sea-level, and close to Honolulu. It was in association with *maiele* or *pukiawe* (*Styphelia tameiameia Ch.*). That heath-like shrub, the burning of which could free *ali'i* from *kapu* so they could mingle with the common people, is today prolific near Kilauea Volcano. But, again, the Russians saw it right by Honolulu.

   1 *Arabis owaihiensis Nob.*   Family: *Cruciferae*
     (Native Hawaiian mustard, used as food. *Linnaea*, I:17–18.)
   2 *Lepidium owaihiense.*   Family: *Cruciferae*
     (Pepper-grass or *'anaunau*; mustard-like weed. *Linnaea*, I:32.)
   3 *Schiedea lingustrina N.*   Family: *Caryophyllaceae*   Group: *Alsineae*
     (Native Hawaiian member of the pink family, shrub. *Linnaea*, I:46–47. A33.)
   4 *Viola Chamissoiana.*   Family: *Violaceae*

(Native viola. *Linnaea*, I:408. A17. Collected in 1817.)
5 *Viola tracheliifolia Ging.* Family: *Violaceae*
(Hawaiian: *pa makani*. 6-foot high shrub with woody stem. Closely related to No. 4. *Linnaea*, I:409.)
6 *Vaccinium cereum F.* Family: *Ericaceae*.
(Member of the heath family; leathery leaves; edible cooked; related to *'ohelo. Linnaea*, I:527–28. A271–72.)
7 *Cyathodes Tameiameia Nob.* Family: *Epacridaceae* Group: *Styphel*
(Native shrub, *maiele. Linnaea*, I:539–40. A272.)
8 *Argemone mexicana L.* Family: *Papaveraceae*
(Mexican poppy, orange flowers. Not *pua kala* or Hawaiian prickly poppy, *Argemone glauca P. Linnaea*, I:552. A9.)
9 *Osteomeles anthyllidifolia Lindl.* Family: *Rosaceae* Group: *Pomace*
(Hawaiian *'ulei*, evergreen shrub; white flowers. *Linnaea*, II:36. N 387.)
10 *Potamogetones pauciflorus.* Family: *Potamogetonaceae*
(Hawaiian native pondweed, seen by Chamisso in *lo'i* or taro ponds above Honolulu—*in agriis aqua irroratis*; opaque, floating leaves. *Linnaea*, II:177.)
11 *Ruppia maritima L.* Family: *Ruppiaceae*
(Hawaiian tassel pondweed, found submerged in brackish ponds or taro pools. Extremely narrow leaves. *Linnaea*, II:233.)
12 *Lythrum maritimum Kunth.* Family: *Lythraceae*
(Hawaiian crape myrtle called *pukamole*; prostrate smooth perennial. *Linnaea*, II:357. A131.)
13 *Herpestis monnieria Kunth.* Family: *Scropulariaceae*
(A water hyssop found by the Russians in the marshes of Waikiki in trailing mats; identical with *Bacopa monnieri L.P. Linnaea*, II:572. A323.)
14 *Polygonum glabrum Willd.* Family: *Polygonaceae*
(Native Hawaiian buckwheat. Eaten by Hawaiians and called *kamole. Linnaea*, III:46. A378.)
15 *Rumex giganteus Aiton.* Family: *Polygonaceae*
(Hawaiian sorrel, *pawale*; weedy, dock-like herb. *Linnaea*, III:61. A377.)
16 *Viscum articulatum.* Family: *Loranthaceae*
(Chamisso refers to this Hawaiian mistletoe as *Viscum moniliforme Blum*. Growing on host trees near Honolulu. *Linnaea*, III:202. A392.)
17 *Heliotropium curassavicum L.* Family: *Boraginaceae*
(A seaside heliotrope called *nena* or *kipukai*; prostrate and smooth perennial herb, seen on Oahu salt marshes. Once it provided a tea used as a tonic. *Linnaea*, IV:456. N 718.)
18 *Cordia subcordata Lam.* Family: *Boraginaceae*
(The evergreen *kou* tree, on Oahu seashores; fruit in hard, enlarged calyx. *Linnaea*, IV:474. N 714.)

19 *Tribulus cistoides L.* Family: *Rutaceae* Group: *Tribulus Zyg*
(Hawaiian: *nohu.* Low-spreading coastal perennial weed; spiny fruits.
Linnaea, V:44. N 477.)

20 *Straussia Kaduana N.* Family: *Rubiaceae* Group: *Psychotrac*
(Chamisso's *Coffea Kaduana,* an endemic Hawaiian coffee with in-
conspicuous flowers; seen in forest shade—*in nemorosis montium O-
Wahu: Linnaea,* IV:33–34. A179.)

21 *Straussia Mariniana N.* Family: *Rubiaceae*
(Chamisso's *Coffea Mariniana;* Hawaiian *kopiko. Linnaea,* IV:35–
36.)

22 *Hedyotis Menziesiana N.* Family: *Rubiaceae* Group: *Hedyotis*
(Called *Kadua Menz* by Chamisso. *Linnaea,* IV:161. A164.)

23 *Hedyotis kaduae affinis.* Family: *Rubiaceae*
(Another coffee species on Oahu, shade-loving, non-endemic; *Linnaea,* IV:164.)

24 *Hedyotis cordata.* Family: *Rubiaceae*
(Coffee species. *Linnaea,* IV:160. A161.)

25 *Hedyotis acuminata Nob.* Family: *Rubiaceae*
(Coffee species: Chamisso's *Kadua Acuminata;* opposite leaves, stip-
ules between leaf bases; shrub. *Linnaea,* IV:163. A159.)

26 *Morinda citrifolia L.* Family: *Rubiaceae*
(Indian mulberry or *noni;* small evergreen shrub with ovoid fruits
resembling tiny breadfruits; on forest-edge; bark gave a red dye, roots
gave a yellow dye. *Linnaea,* IV:149. A177.)

27 *Burneya Gaudichaudii N.* Family: *Rubiaceae*
(Hawaiian coffee species. *Linnaea,* IV:190.)

Just as the Leningrad collection from Oahu may be practically characterized as one of ferns, mosses, and mints, so may the collection (now
lost) which Chamisso took to Berlin be described as one of bright flowers,
coffees, and water weeds. Plants conspicuously absent from the Soviet
collection—that could be found in taro fields, on the brackish coastal
land of Waikiki, even in Honolulu harbour by the *Riurik*—were in Berlin
(e.g., Nos. 10–13, 17–19). But in Berlin there were apparently no "Honolulu ferns." As for the *Rubiaceae* brought from Oahu and removed
from Russian custody, they formed a major subcollection of botanical
importance far exceeding that of Chamisso's two violets. (Nevertheless,
those violets were treated with a half-a-dozen others from Kamchatka,
Unalaska, and from Chile, in a rigorous description of the family *Violaceae* as represented in the Berlin collection, by the botanist Gingins:
see "Description de quelques espèces nouvelles de violacées, reçues de
M. Adelbert de Chamisso", *Linnaea,* VI:406–13.) Again, one is impressed by the collector's consciousness of native uses of his specimens,
as ordinary or famine food, material for artifacts, a source of dyes, or
medicine. It is unfortunate that recent works on that subject, for example, B.H. Krause's *Ethnobotany of the Hawaiians* (Honolulu, 1974),
take no comparable note of Chamisso's large contribution to the field.

Hawaiian botany awaits proper development, in a local context, of the data used a century ago by E. du Bois Reymond and published in his *Adelbert von Chamisso als Naturforscher* (1889).

In conclusion, one may ask *why* the Berlin herbarium was bare of Polynesian *Filices* gathered by Chamisso—for they are absent in the *Linnaea* descriptions of the later 1820s. Almost certainly, Oahu *Filices* (and many others) were entrusted to the author of *Enumeratio* ... Georg Friedrich Kaulfuss, whose seminal account of them appeared, not in Prussia but in Halle, in 1824. That being so, it is improbable that no Oahu *Filices* survived to modern times.

Cartography and Hydrography

The *Nadezhda* and the *Neva* had not put in at Honolulu in June 1804, but did establish precedents for later visitors where naval science was concerned. By their attitudes and actions Lisianskii and particularly Kruzenshtern went far toward determining the nature of the mapping undertaken by their Russian followers in the Hawaiian Archipelago from 1809 to 1826.

To turn, first, to the matter of particularly able personnel with scientific interests and skills: Kruzenshtern's officers, Makar' I. Ratmanov, Fedor Romberg, Petr Golovachev, and Emel'ian E. Levenshtern (von Loewenstern), were all specialists. It was solely on the basis of their service records that such officers, or others, gained a berth aboard the *Nadezhda* and the *Neva* in 1803. As for the expeditionary scientists, Wilhelm Gottfried Tilesius von Tilenau (1769–1857), naturalist, Johann Caspar Hörner, astronomer, and Dr. Karl Espenberg, the surgeon, they comprised a glowing circle of distinction at the expedition's core. Kruzenshtern wanted, and finally obtained, the very best equipment and supplies; it was his object to establish an esprit de corps by handsome pay, good food, and high expectations. With this in view, he turned to the St. Petersburg Academy of Sciences, of which he was himself a corresponding member, for assistance in the area of science. It was Kruzenshtern's achievement at the outset of the Russian Navy's South and mid-Pacific enterprise, to overcome his lack of rank and turn his multipurpose voyage, which had earlier been mercantile in its scope, into a scientific venture of importance to the academic world—and to hydrography especially. Using the data he himself collected, and reports by many others in the coming twenty years, he prepared one of the finest nineteenth-century Pacific atlases: *Atlas Iuzhnogo Moria* (*Atlas of the South Sea*: St. Petersburg, 1823–26).[27]

With regard to cartography and hydrography in Oceania, Kruzenshtern's instructions from the Main Administration of the Russian-American Company (dated 29 May 1803) contained these lines:

> All that you discover and acquire during your voyage by observation, bearing on geography, navigation, and other sciences, as well as all maps and descriptions whatsoever, you will of course submit to the American Company; but knowing of your zeal in these areas, we think it superfluous to go into greater detail ...[28]

The Company's trust was well placed; Kruzenshtern appointed his scientists on the best advice (Tilesius was recommended by Count Manteufel of Berlin, Hörner by Baron Franz von Zach of the Seeberg Observatory of Gotha), and looked for the most modern instruments.[29] The latter were in due course purchased, not in Russia, but in London. In 1815, the instruments were taken to Honolulu in the *Riurik* and used by Kotzebue, Chamisso, and Khramchenko to good effect.

Kruzenshtern's (and Lisianskii's) choice of instruments for measurement by sea and land was deeply influenced by their experience as Russian Volunteers with the British Navy (1793–98).[30] While serving in HMS *Thetis* and HMS *L'Oiseau* on the North America station, both had become familiar with certain timepieces, reflecting-circles, sextants, telescopes, and naval quadrants.[31] That familiarity in turn led to the use of instruments by British makers on Oahu until at least the 1820s, by the people of the *Riurik*, *Kamchatka*, *Otkrytie*, and *Krotkii*. Specifically, Kruzenshtern ordered chronometers by John Arnold (1736–99), an 18-inch quadrant by George Adams the younger (1750–95), and a whole set of instruments (reflecting circle, two 10-inch sextants, two artificial horizons, two azimuth compasses, artificial magnet, and other scientific equipment) by the greatest astronomical instrument-maker then active in England, Edward Troughton (1753–1835).[32] Inasmuch as these measuring instruments set precedents for Russian naval practice in Hawaii and in other distant parts throughout the early nineteenth century, and were employed aboard the *Neva* in 1804 as she was coasting off Hawaii and Oahu (see Lisianskii, *Voyage*:98–100, 112, 362), they merit further consideration here.

As a youthful Volunteer with the British Fleet in 1793–96, that was, as lieutenant under Rear-Admiral George Murray, Kruzenshtern had read the essays and textbooks of George Adams, then mathematical instrument-maker to George III. Among these, *Geometrical and Graphical Essays, containing a Description of the mathematical Instruments used in Geometry, civil and military Surveying, Levelling and Perspective* (London, 1790) drew his attention to the writer's own mechanical abilities.[33] His respect for Adams's astronomical quadrants was shared by Johann Caspar Hörner, astronomer aboard the *Nadezhda* in 1803–06, and thus a ten-year-old quadrant capable of either vertical or horizontal use was duly taken around the world.[34]

As for the four chronometers made by the late John Arnold, also carried by the *Nadezhda* and the *Neva*, they had been specially designed for use in East India Company ships for the determining of longitude at sea. All had such refinements as the new expansion balance and detached escapement. Kruzenshtern and Lisianskii had observed their use aboard the Indiamen *Bombay Castle* and *Royalist* in 1799–1801.[35] The timepieces were checked upon arrival in St. Petersburg by Kruzenshtern's older associate in the Academy of Sciences, the German-born geodesist-astronomer Friedrich (Russian: Fedor Ivanovich) Shubert (1758–1825). Since his own recent election as a corresponding member (13 April 1803), Kruzenshtern had had much contact with the man soon to be head of the St. Petersburg Observatory. As the author of *A Guide to Astronomical Observations used in Determining Latitude and Longitude* (St. Petersburg, 1803), and sponsor of classes at the eminent Academy for younger naval officers (whose duties called for maritime astronomy), Fedor I. Shubert seemed to Kruzenshtern the very model of the practical *savant*.[36] Shubert found nothing to criticize in the chronometers of Pennington or Arnold, but had sensible suggestions for their use by Navy men.

Kruzenshtern also had several personal meetings with Edward Troughton, whom he much admired as an artist and a man.[37] As he knew, Troughton had invented the reflecting circle (1796) and perfected the marine barometer, theodolite, and transit-circle. Aware of the Russian Government's full satisfaction with the large theodolite with which the *Nadezhda* and in 1815 the *Riurik* had been supplied, the British government itself selected it for use in the American Coast Survey (1815–16) and in other distant geodesic work in South America and India. As for Kruzenshtern himself, he did not hesitate in 1814–15 to speak for "the justly celebrated Troughton" (Kotzebue, *Voyage*, I:16), and to order sextants, compasses, and other instruments for use in the Pacific and the Arctic.

The Soviet naval historian V.V. Nevskii summarizes the astronomy required of the *Nadezhda*, the *Neva*, and other vessels bound on oceanic missions in the early nineteenth century:

> Longitude at sea was already established with the aid of chronometers. Each ship usually carried two, three, or even more chronometers, as the constantly fluctuating physical and meteorological conditions produced significant errors in the readings. The error margin would normally increase when a ship passed into the Tropics, where it would be necessary to alter the chronometers' movement often. The mean of the readings from two or three chronometers was usually considered true. Chronometers' readings constantly had to be emended on the basis of precise astronomical observations. But the very best way of reckoning longitude of a place in those times was by establishing the angle between the moon and various stars by a sextant. In addition, it could be measured by the octant, which gave a different reading from the sextant's by a minute or two.

Such measurings were performed in great number. The calculations were usually made on the basis of lunar tables, for which plenty of time was needed .... Golovnin's companion on expeditions in 1807–13, P.I. Rikord, writes that the precision with which Kruzenshtern fixed points could be compared with the measurements of Greenwich Observatory ....

(Nevskii, 1951:39)

Like Kruzenshtern in 1803–06, Gagemeister in 1809, and Kotzebue in 1816–17 made use of the lunar tables by Bürg, "which had gained the First Consul's prize at the National Institute" in Paris (Kruzenshtern, *Voyage*, I:9). All three captains reckoned their latitude, while out of sight of land, by estimating the meridianal height of the sun or certain stars, and took multiple compass bearings around the Hawaiian Islands when feasible. Kruzenshtern briefly discusses the degrees of error produced by use of his British timepieces on his passage to Hawaii, taking Cook's and Vancouver's fixes for the longitudes of the easternmost and southernmost points of the Big Island to be correct (*ibid.*, I:190–91, 195–96, 199–200). Further details of this initial Russian astronomy and hydrography in Hawaii are contained in the *Nadezhda*'s log and in Kruzenshtern's own journal for May–June 1804, now held in TsGIAL (*fond* 15, op. 1, *delo* 2), in Leningrad. Microfilm of portions of the log, replete with astronomical and meteorological data on a daily basis, may be found in the Shur Collection (Reel 79), Elmer E. Rasmusen Research Library, at the University of Alaska in Fairbanks.

Besides "several sextants, compasses, two marine barometers, a dipping-needle, an aerometer" and other meteorological equipment, Kruzenshtern in 1815 ordered for Kotzebue a "log and sounding-machine invented by Massey, a Six-thermometer, and a camera lucida," the latter made by Thomas Jones (Kotzebue, *Voyage*, I:16). To these were added telescopes by the London maker Tully, a box-chronometer by Hardy with compensatorium mechanism, and a little pocket chronometer by Barraud. The *Riurik* was better equipped to make correct determinations of position, and hence to undertake sound hydrography, than the *Nadezhda* herself had been. And, like the *Nadezhda*, she carried to Hawaii "an excellent collection of charts and a well chosen library" (Kruzenshtern, *Voyage*, I:9). Among the charts supplied to her, we know, were those in *Directions for Sailing to and from the East Indies, China, New Holland ...* (London, 1809–11) compiled by the hydrographer James Horsburgh (1762–1836); others published to supplement the *Map of the World* on globular projection, first published by Aaron Arrowsmith (1750–1823) in 1794; and yet others by the eminent British hydrographer John Purdy (1773–1843), including the recent *Chart of the Atlantic Ocean* (1812). The *Riurik* had sailed before the Russian Admiralty could obtain, fresh off the press, his *Tables of Positions, or of the Latitudes and Longitudes of Places* (London, 1816); but Golovnin's *Kamchatka* took them East in August 1817.

As he approached Oahu for the first time, however, Kotzebue made less use of Arrowsmith's and Purdy's work than of Vancouver's. In the *Riurik*'s wardroom was a much-consulted copy of the first London edition (1798) of Vancouver's *Voyage*, with its supplement of charts. As navigators (*shturmany*), it was Vasilii S. Khromchenko's and Mikhail Kornéev's duty to assist their First Lieutenant, Gleb Shishmarev, in his reading of the two plates that bore directly on Honolulu Harbour and the Russians' safe approach to "Whyteete." The plates were Nos. 15, "A Chart of the Sandwich Islands, as Surveyed during the Visits of His Majesty's Sloop *Discovery* and the Armed Tender *Chatham* ... in the Years 1792, 1793, & 1794, and prepared ... by Lieutenant Joseph Baker," and No. 16, "Views of the Sandwich and Other Islands: Whyteete Bay, Woahoo, in Lat. 21°17'N and Long. 202°10'E." The former, like charts accompanying Cook's and King's published accounts of their manoeuverings about the Islands, showed the track of the *Discovery* in March 1793, since like the *Riurik* she crossed Mamala Bay. The latter, drawn by Sykes, had the particular advantage of depicting Honolulu from a spot two miles south-southwest, that was precisely where the Russians found themselves by 1 p.m. on 27 November 1816 (Kotzebue, *Voyage*, I:320). Cartography began at once.

By "meridional solar reckonings" that day and every day the *Riurik* remained at Honolulu, the harbour there was fixed at 21°17'57"N, or almost a minute further north than had been reckoned by Vancouver twenty-three years earlier (*ibid.*, I:357). The accepted modern reading is 21°18'N. Taking the mean of repeated lunar observations and calculating by Bürg's lunar tables, the Russians then fixed its longitude at 157°452'W, magnetic needle variation being 10°57'E, compared with *Discovery*'s variation of 8°E. By conversion, Vancouver's determination of the same spot may be seen to have been 157°90'W. The accepted modern reading is 157°51'W, one minute east of the *Riurik*'s reckoning.

It may be said without exaggeration that the *Riurik*'s determination of the geographical position of the harbour, from where she stood, was as precise as any made during the early 1800s. In October 1818, however, yet more accurate readings by the officers of the *Kamchatka* (Captain V.M. Golovnin) allowed Naval Cadet Vikentii Tabulevich of that ship to draw a "plan" of the harbour entrance and describe it (see Map B and notes below) as lying in latitude 1°18'12"N, longitude 157°52'W of Greenwich. This was hydrography and map-making of the highest quality, performed with the best available equipment. Kotzebue and Golovnin alike allowed a great deal of time for astronomic observations, for the use of lunar tables, and for practical surveying in the field.

The survey posts set up around Honolulu's inner harbour at the start of the *Riurik*'s first visit (29 November 1816), reminded the Hawaiians of attempts by Scheffer to acquire land—and very nearly resulted in a clash (see Narrative 5). The compass work essential for surveying of the kind that Tabulevich was instructed to perform is described by Kotzebue. From a point northwest of Honolulu harbour and overlooking it, he writes, "the compass was set up, and I took some angles with my sextants, at which the inhabitants ... expected to see some work of conjuration" (Kotzebue, *Voyage*, I:341). The sextants, like those used in the *Kamchatka*, were made by Edward Troughton (*ibid.*, I:16).

Troughton's instruments produced no sorcery (see Narrative 113) but did produce useful maps of Honolulu Harbour, published in Golovnin's *Puteshestvie vokrug sveta sovershennoe na voennom shliupe Kamchatka v 1817, 1818 i 1819 godakh* (St. Petersburg, 1822), and of the two-and-a-half mile stretch of Oahu's south coast examined by Kotzebue and Khramchenko—first published in the atlas accompanying Kotzebue's *Puteshestvie v Iuzhnyi okean i v Beringov proliv* (St. Petersburg, 1821–23)—but sadly omitted from Nikolai Grech's edition of that work in compact single volume, also of 1821–23. As the Soviet historian V.A. Divin justly remarks, "the charts and descriptions compiled by Russian seamen during the sloop *Kamchatka*'s voyage are distinguished by their great accuracy and detail in presentation .... For Golovnin recommended that seamen take a critical attitude towards their predecessors' charts, at the same time pointing out that ignorance of old charts is inadmissable .... Golovnin paid special attention to checking the coordinates of geographical points indicated on earlier maps" (Golovnin, 1965:15).

Nor was surveying in the hands of only one or two men while *Kamchatka* stood at anchor in "the Port of Gonoruru." On the contrary; inspection of the hands represented—in materials now held at TsGAVMF (*fond* 7, op. 1)—indicates that several were charged with meteorology, astronomy, and keeping up the logs. As Navigator Grigorii Nikifórov was the principal, but not exclusive, keeper of the *Kamchatka*'s log at Honolulu, making four entries per day, so Tabulevich was the principal, but not the sole surveyor then ashore. The *Kamchatka* was also, as Golovnin intended, a seaborne school for young cadets and midshipmen of scientific inclination (see Ivashintsev, 1980:139). A dozen youths contributed to the hydrography of 1817–19, as all available and able personnel in the *Riurik* had been expected to follow Hörner's detailed "Instructions" dated 20 June 1815. Essentially, wrote Hörner, Kotzebue and his people were "attentively to observe, and circumstantially to describe, every unusual appearance, and especially *to measure every thing mensurable*" (see Kotzebue, *op. cit.*, I:41). There followed detailed descriptions of procedures for correctly fixing latitude and longitude and for surveying coasts (*ibid.*, I:42–56).

Vasil'ev and Shishmarev too, in their turn, reached Oceania with clear orders from the Russian Admiralty to perform as "zealous, Russian-born" hydrographers. The relevant instructions have been twice reprinted in the 1949 and 1960 Soviet editions of the 1831 account by Belling-shausen of the voyage to Antarctica and Polynesia of the sloops *Vostok* and *Mirnyi* (see Bellingshausen, 1960:75–78). Those instructions were the same for Bellingshausen's South-bound and Vasil'ev's Northern "di-visions" of 1819–21, where naval science was concerned. The following is an excerpt from Section 1:

> Astronomical, mathematical, and physical instruments are wanted for this voyage. Some have been issued from the store of those prepared here, but those here unavailable will be received upon your arrival in England. The naval minister has written to the Russian Ambassador there, to the effect that they be readied ....

> *(Ibid.*, 75)

At Honolulu, the *Otkrytie's* log was kept by Mikhail Rydalev, the *Blagonamerennyi's* by Vladimir Petrov, formerly of the *Riurik*. Survey-ing was done by Lieutenant Roman P. Boyle, Cadet Grigorii Pagava, and others. Chronometers and astronomical instruments were taken ashore and remained in the care of the *Otkrytie's* astronomer, Pavel Tarkhanov. Data obtained by all these expeditions were incorporated by Kruzenshtern in his *Atlas of the South Sea* (St. Petersburg, 1823–26: 2 Pts. and supplements). Not even then did Russian captains cease to verify and modify coordinates for points in the Hawaiian Islands. Leav-ing Honolulu on 9 February 1828 after a ten-week stay, for instance, Captain-Lieutenant Mikhail N. Staniukovich of the sloop *Moller*, made systematic visits to all points of the Hawaiian Archipelago from Kauai to Pearl, Hermes, and Maro Reefs, precisely fixing latitude and longitude as he proceeded west (Ivashintsev, 1980: 89). His orders were to question all coordinates, and to persist with astronomic observations over periods of months, not days or weeks (instructions in *Zapiski Admiralteiskago Departamenta*, St. Petersburg, pt. I).

But what of measurement on Oahu? Though he lacked the time to do it, Golovnin understood the urgency of mapmaking in the Hawaiian Islands. As he drily noted, Captain King had used the presence of un-melting snow on Mauna Loa and a questionable volume by a Frenchman as the basis for imagining that great volcano to be 18,400 feet in height (Golovnin, 1965:226). How could that be? In 1804, the *Nadezhda's* officers had reckoned it to be 2,254 French *toises*, or 13,524 feet high (Krusenstern, *Voyage*, I:193); and though the people of the *Kamchatka* could not know it, Kotzebue had in 1817 re-measured it, and reckoned it was 2,284.4 *toises*, or 13,694 feet above sea-level (Kotzebue, *Voyage*, I:318). That it should rise 5,000 feet above the Russians' estimation was ridiculous; and yet no European resident or visitor had yet seen fit to take a mercury barometer and so confirm the principles of trigonometry! As for the distances within the Islands and across them, they were still being guessed at in 1820.

Kotzebue, Golovnin, and Kruzenshtern made minor but important contributions to contemporary knowledge of Oahu's geographical realities. Chamisso reckoned the height of Mount Kaala in the Waianae Range by barometric method, arriving at the figure 3,786 feet. Today, the peak is reckoned to rise 300 feet above that level, indicating that the German was not measuring the summit proper but a point southeast of it. Kotzebue found the tide at Honolulu Harbour to be just less than a fathom (ebb to full). Tabulevich of the *Kamchatka* marked the spots of Marin's "white stone house," Fort Kaahumanu, and assorted other *haole* and native structures (see Map B), providing data on the early growth of Honolulu town. The value of his "plan" and of the Khramchenko survey and map, in this respect, is treated separately (see below, Chapter 13).

Russian illustrative records sometimes complement cartography. The Russian State Museum in Leningrad holds, in its "Drawings Section," the portfolio compiled by the artist Pavel Nikolaevich Mikhailov (1780–1840) during his voyages around the world in the *Vostok* (1819–21) and the *Moller* (1826–29).[38] Among the 300-odd pen sketches, aquarelles, and other illustrations are a number showing scenes in or near Honolulu in the early weeks of 1828. (Moller sailed on 9 February). One is a semi-finished watercolour, 21 cm. high and 35 cm. across, entitled "A Waterfall on Ganarura [Honolulu] Rivulet, on the Island of Avagu [Oahu]." It is dated 8 February 1828, and shows some thirty Hawaiians swimming or jumping in the Honolulu River. The painting relates well to the stream shown on Map A (1817) flowing southwest towards the Honolulu Harbour. That attractive waterfall cannot be seen today, alas.

Meteorology

While at Hawaii in 1804, the *shturmany* (navigators) of the *Nadezhda* and the *Neva* kept systematic records of air temperature, wind strength and direction, humidity, and currents in the ocean. Logs contain two or more daily entries. Kruzenshtern's and Hörner's example was followed rigorously by the people of the *Riurik*, *Kamchatka*, and *Otkrytie* when they, in turn, came to the Islands.

Lisianskii had ordered meteorological instruments from Edward Troughton while in England in 1803, including a maritime barometer and a large hygrometer. It was Hörner however who, besides getting a portable barometer from Troughton, and other instruments by Continental makers (an electrometer by Saussure and an elegant hygrometer by Jean de Luc, both available in Hamburg at the time), supplied the *Nadezhda* with thermometers patented by Mr. Six. These were designed to show the minimum and maximum temperatures in the absence of observers at a given spot; and another type the measurement of water temperatures.[39] Thus the Russians were able to investigate the ocean temperature at many depths in the Pacific, and compare Six's thermometer's results with a pre-checked regular mercury thermometer. This work devolved on Hörner himself, whose subsequent paper, "The Degrees of Temperature of Sea Water at Various Depths," was incorporated in Volume Three of Kruzenshtern's *Puteshestvie* of 1809–12 (pp. 263–64).

Assisted by Kruzenshtern, Hörner found that "at first the warmth diminishes imperceptibly, then more rapidly; then, at great depth, it drops more slowly again; and finally it remains constant" (*ibid.*, 3:277). The problems raised by these data, (which bore directly upon climatic and/or physical conditions in Hawaii), were correctly viewed by Hörner, and attracted the attention of the pioneering oceanographers, notably Iurii M. Shokal'skii, in the later 1800s.[40] As Shokal'skii observes in his classic work, *Okeanografiia* (Petrograd, 1917), Hörner doubled the value of his data by making observations at four spots in the Pacific on a vertical series of temperature readings.[41]

Hörner also determined the specific weight of water samples at thirty-three points in the Pacific, and concluded that salinity is not the same in the Hawaiian latitude and further north. He also rightly estimated the specific weight of water in the mid-Pacific area as higher than in the several "adjacent seas" (the Seas of Okhotsk, Japan, and South China).[42] During 1804–05, no less than 340 observations were made from the *Nadezhda* on the speed and direction of Pacific Ocean currents (Kruzenshtern, 1809–12, 3:149–83). Kruzenshtern and the English Captain Hunter independently, and almost simultaneously, came across the east end of the current now known as the "equatorial countercurrent" (*ibid.*, I:229 and 3:165). Meteorological data was set out by Kruzenshtern on 127 pages of tables in his *Puteshestvie*, certain of which bear directly on Hawaii. Anglophile though he was, it may be mentioned here, Kruzenshtern's own Six-thermometer which did such sterling work in Oceania, was not of British manufacture. It was made by I. Sheshúrin in St. Petersburg and was transferred to Kruzenshtern by Admiral V. Ia. Chichagov (1726–1809), his old commander in the Baltic (Barratt, 1981a:108).

The meteorology performed by the *Nadezhda* and the *Neva*, in sum, was highly competent by the contemporary standard. It was wanting in a few respects, however; and these are listed by the Soviet historian V. Nevskii (e.g., barometric mercury shifting because of sea-movements, breaks in continuous observation of the ship's way: see Nevskii, 1951:41). But such shortcomings merely strengthened the position of the scientists with the *Riurik* a decade later. Gone, by then, was any prospect of the simultaneous employment of barometers marked by the Fahrenheit and Reaumur scales, which had marred the Russians' first mid-ocean science. Kotzebue's scientific orders were, as seen, drafted by Hörner (Kotzebue, *Voyage*, I:41–83). They referred specifically to many areas of meteorology: to the control of barometric oscillation (pp. 67–68), to the proper use of wind-gauges at sea (p. 69), to the measurement of ocean tides and currents (pp. 70–73), and to depth-sounding at sea (pp. 73–75).

In addition, Kotzebue was required to investigate the sea's salinity, to use the Six-thermometer for underwater temperature levels, and to check marine phenomena then little understood—for instance, surface fluorescence, "falling stars," and "fire-balls" (p. 82). He did so systematically, the final volume of his *Puteshestvie* (1821) being embellished with significant "Areometric Observations," giving air and ocean temperatures, specific gravity of water samples, latitude and longitude, and aerometric weight, between 18 July 1816 and 13 April 1818. For Hannibal Evart Lloyd's English translation, see Kotzebue's *Voyage of Discovery* (London, 1821, 3:403–24). Figures for the periods of *Riurik*'s two stays at Honolulu, 27 November–13 December 1816 and 1–13 October 1817, are annoyingly omitted from the text. We see, however, that the sea (surface) temperature fell 0.4 degrees while the *Riurik* remained in Honolulu harbour on her first visit (*ibid.*, 3:406), and fell 1.1 degrees over the second (3:411). On the other hand, the atmospheric temperature was steady, fluctuating in the range of rather less than one degree on both occasions. Nights were mild; the mean height of the *Riurik*'s thermometer while she remained at Honolulu (1816) was 75 Fahrenheit, and the mean barometric pressure was 29 inches and eighty lines (Kotzebue, *Voyage*, 1:357). *Riurik* was perhaps the first ship to use the Woltmann wind-gauge on Oahu. Implications for the growth of oceanic climatology were stressed by Hörner and perceived by Chamisso, to whom the wind-gauge's results gave compensation for the failure of the Troughton dipping-needle.[43]

Kotzebue's study of the physical conditions in Hawaii and elsewhere in Oceania was taken up by Golovnin, though his was not a scientific expedition like the *Riurik*'s or the *Otkrytie*'s, in 1818. His narrative of 1822 contains, in H.R. Friis's words, "abundant material about ... the inclination of the magnetic needle, hydrography of coastal waters, winds, and currents."[44] It is unfortunate that Soviet editions of that volume have omitted basic scientific data of significance to Polynesian studies. There has always been a tendency, however (in the West too), to omit 'dry' lists of figures from editions or translations that are not aimed at the specialist. Thus, Kruzenshtern's imposing scientific-cum-professional appendices were simply cut when Richard Hoppner and the publisher John Murray brought his *Voyage Round the World* into the English library (1813). And Georg Heinrich Langsdorf's text was modified and marginally shortened into *Voyages and Travels* in that same year.

Instructions for the *Predpriiatie* of 1823 required a minimum of three barometric observations daily at 6 a.m. or 8 a.m., at midday, and at 10 p.m. Barometric pressure and air temperature were moreover to be fixed at the same moment—an important innovation. The *Predpriiatie* was issued with a maritime barometer by Peter Dollond (1730–1820). Dissatisfaction with it led the Russians to prefer another one, made by the Russian craftsman Samoilov.[45] That small instrument was used at Honolulu in 1824. Meteorological and other data may be found, not in Kotzebue's *New Voyage ...* (St. Petersburg and Weimar, 1830), but rather in the briefer and persistently neglected Russian narrative of 1828.[46]

The *Predpriiatie* was better equipped and manned for oceanographic and meteorological work than any previous ship in Oceania. As Kotzebue drily put it, at the expedition's end (*New Voyage*, I:2–3), 'We were accompanied by Professors Eschscholtz and Lenz as Naturalists; Messrs. Preus and Hoffman as Astronomer and Mineralogist; and ... we were richly stored with astronomical and other scientific instruments.' H.R. Friis discusses the successful use by Lenz of the bathometer designed by himself and I.E. Parrot of Dorpat for the sampling of sea-water at depth and estimation of specific water weight:

> These two inventions can well be regarded [i.e., depth-gauge plus bathometer –GB] as the beginning of an exact oceanographic technique .... A theory of oceanic water circulation formulated by him as an explanation of the appearance of lower temperatures at great depth was based on factual data observed on the *Riurik* and on his own tests on the *Predpriiatie* ....[47]

Certain of Lenz's other conclusions, which have since been found to be correct, help to explain Hawaii's physical conditions. Lenz posited, for instance, the existence of 'salinity maxima' both north and south of the Equator and of 'minimal salinity localities' between; rightly explaining the phenomenon in terms of more intense evaporation in the areas of trade-wind, and of calm within the lowest latitudes. Again, he posited continuous but ever shrinking drops in water temperature in the Hawaiian latitudes, at least to nineteen hundred metres.[48] Such conditions predetermined the mobility (in depth) of ocean fauna and, by obvious extension, of the natural resources man might find.

Meteorological records kept by Russian ships in Hawaii in the early nineteenth century remain largely unpublished. What value they may have for climatology has been well demonstrated by the Soviet geographer, Vasilii Mikhailovich Pasetskii. While preparing a work on the geography performed by the Decembrists, Pasetskii in 1975–76 consulted nineteenth-century official publications giving data on the science undertaken by those Russian Navy vessels (*Ladoga, Vostok, Kreiser* and *Apollon*) in which future Decembrists (M.K. Kiukhel'beker, D.I. Zavalishin, K.P. Torson, and F.G. Vishnevskii) had arrived in Oceania in 1822–24.[49] Among these publications were *Meteorological Observations Made During the Voyage Round the World of the Frigate 'Kreiser' in 1822–1824* (St. Petersburg, 1882) and *Meteorlogical Observations Made During the Voyage Round the World of the Sloop 'Apollon'* (St. Petersburg, 1882). *Apollon* wintered in 1823–24 at San Francisco. *Kreiser* also called there (21 November–21 December 1824), so that the bulletins of 1882 have patent value for a study of the Californian climate over time. *Kreiser* was also in Tahiti (Matavai Bay: 9–20 July 1823). It remains for climatologists with mid-Pacific and Hawaiian interests to use materials in *Meteorological Observations made During the Voyage Round the World of the Sloop "Kamchatka", Commanded by Captain 2nd Grade Golovnin in 1817–1819* (St. Petersburg, 1873) and the sister publications on the meteorology performed by *Otkrytie* (St. Petersburg, 1873) and *Krotkii* (St. Petersburg, 1882). Associated bulletins, giving surveys of meteorological data collected on board many Russian Navy ships in Polynesia in the nineteenth century, are referred to by W. Wiese in A. Fersman, ed., *The Pacific: Russian Scientific Investigations* (Leningrad, ANSSSR, 1926:119). Unpublished meteorological data in the logs of such ships are still held in the Archive of the Main Hydrographic Department, Leningrad.[50]

By comparison, earlier naval records of Pacific Ocean water density and temperature have been used extensively; and certain Russian studies of the later nineteenth century have relevance to the Hawaiian Islands, (though in general the emphasis is on the North Pacific Ocean and connected seas).[51] Chief of these are *"Vitiaz" and the Pacific Ocean* (*"Vitiaz" i Tikhii okean*: St. Petersburg, 1894) and the preceding hydrological and hydrographic essays by Stepan O. Makarov. Having himself collected quantities of data on a voyage round the world in 1886–89, Makarov turned to those in logs and journals of the early 1800s. For *"Vitiaz" and the Pacific Ocean*, he used records of surface water temperature from 78 ships, including those at Honolulu or the Kona Coast in 1804, 1816, 1818, and 1821. "The vastness of the number of figures may be judged by the fact that, in arranging the data referring to the temperature of the surface water, the Pacific Ocean was divided into 8,000 one-degree squares, some of which had been traversed by as many as 20 ships per month."[52]

'Kamehameha, King of the Sandwich Islands'

'Queen Kaahumanu'

'Teimotu, Brother of Kaahumanu'

'A View of Honolulu Harbour'

'Natives of the Sandwich Islands'

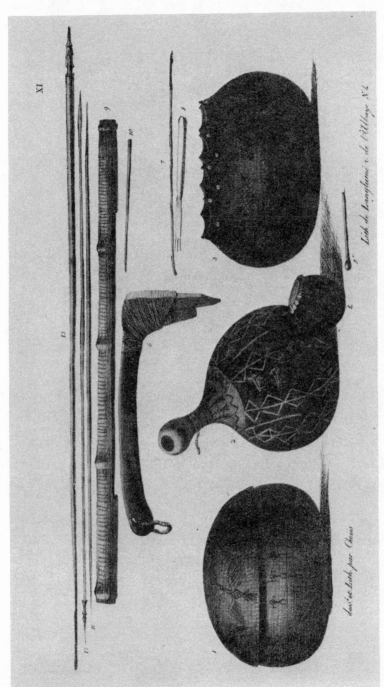

'Arms and Tools of the Sandwich Isles'

'A Men's Dance in the Sandwich Isles'

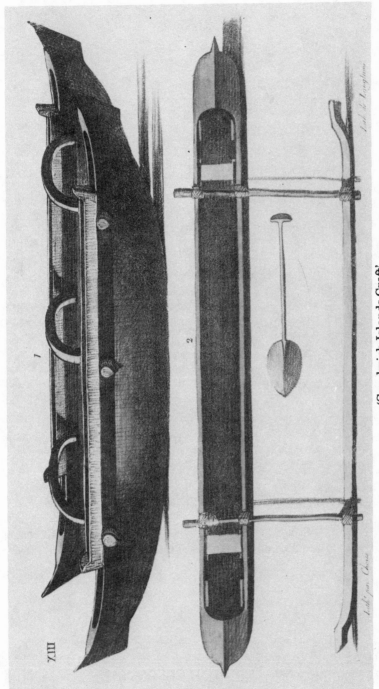

'Sandwich Islands Craft'

'Helmets and Implements of the Sandwich Islands'

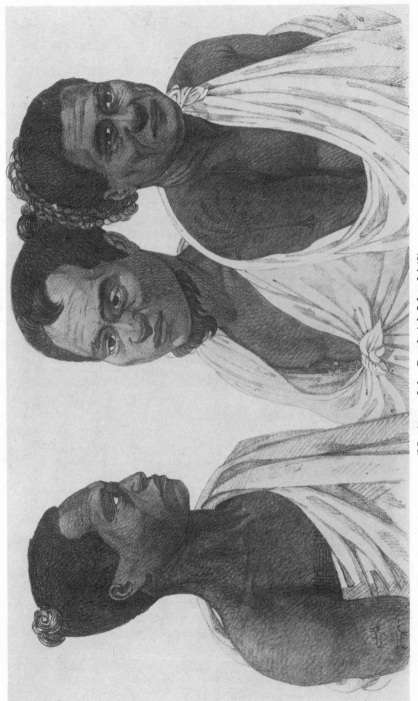

'Natives of the Sandwich Islands' (2)

'Women's Dance in the Sandwich Isles'

'Sandwich Island Woman'

'The Port of Honolulu'

'Interior of a Chief's House in the Sandwich Isles'

'Girl from the Sandwich Islands'

'Kamehameha, King of the Sandwich Islanders'

'Chiefs of Oahu Island Visiting the Sloop *Kamchatka*'

'The Chief Boki'

Part Two

THE RUSSIAN NARRATIVES

CHAPTER SIX

Honolulu Harbour

INTRODUCTION TO THE NARRATIVES OF
OTTO EVSTAF'EVICH KOTZEBUE

The translation below is from the first Russian edition of Kotzebue's *Puteshestvie v Iuzhnyi Okean i v Beringov proliv* (St. Petersburg, 1821), Part II:42–74. The passage in question is contained in pages 318 to 358 of the first volume of Hannibal E. Lloyd's contemporaneous English version of that work, *A Voyage of Discovery into the Sea and Beering's Straits, for the Purpose of Exploring a North-East Passage* (London, Longman, Hurst, Rees, Orme & Brown, 1821: Chapter X: "From the Coast of California to the Sandwich Islands"). In general, Lloyd's translation is sound. In his own words (*A Voyage*, I:vi,) he "endeavoured to put [Kotzebue's original German text] into such natural and manly language as it would become an English naval officer to write ...." The following remarks by Lloyd, however, indicate that even had the German text been taken as the basis for the present work, the "Honolulu Passage" of *A Voyage* would have been inadequate to modern needs:

> In the orthography of proper names of persons and places, the *Edinburgh Gazeteer* has been followed for the geographical part; and for the names of Lieutenant Kotzebue's new discoveries, and of persons whom he has occasion to mention, his own orthography has been preserved, as an attempt to accomodate them to English pronunciation would probably have produced combinations of letters very different from those which an Englishman would form, from hearing them pronounced by the natives themselves. (*A Voyage*, I:vi)

Thus, German "*ei*" becomes English "long i," German "*ie*" usually appears as English "ee," and so forth. Such problems may be avoided by a reference to Kotzebue's own Russian text which is more complete than the German text, *Entdeckungsreise in die Süd-See* (1821).

The first part of the tenth chapter of Kotzebue's work, translated below, deals with the *Riurik*'s voyage to Hawaii Island from San Francisco Bay and with transactions on Hawaii. It offers useful descriptions of Kamehameha himself, Kaahumanu, and Kamehameha II. It also touches on Hawaiian responses to Scheffer's designs, Hawaiian-*haole* relations on the Kona Coast, New England enterprise there, Hawaiian social and political organization, *kapu*, and material culture.

Having sailed from San Francisco on 1 November 1816, the *Riurik* laid a course directly for the Islands. Mauna Loa came in sight on 21

November. On the advice of John or João Elliot de Castro, a peripatetic Portuguese taking a passage back to the Hawaiian Islands with the Russians, Kotzebue made for Kawaihae Bay, where the influential English adviser of Kamehameha I, John Young, was said to live. Elliot de Castro had served as physician to Kamehameha I in 1812–14, won royal favour, and had been granted property. In January 1814, however, he had restlessly moved on to Sitka and from there, as supercargo in the brig *Il'mena* (ex-*Lydia*), sailed to Spanish California where the Spaniards had imprisoned him for thirteen months.

Kotzebue supposed that Elliot de Castro's acquaintance with Kamehameha I would be useful. In the event, it defused a potentially explosive situation. Because of Georg Anton Scheffer's words and actions, Kamehameha I was ready to take the *Riurik* as a hostile man-of-war; 400 armed warriors stood ready for a fight on 23–24 November. With Elliot de Castro's help, Kotzebue speedily disassociated both himself and the imperial authorities from Scheffer's threatening behaviour on Oahu. A friendly two-day visit to Kailua ensued. When Choris, artist aboard the *Riurik*, had done the king's portrait and a large meal had been consumed, the Russians took their leave. On Kamehameha's orders, a young Hawaiian chief named Manuia boarded the *Riurik* as royal messenger and to avert unpleasantness at Honolulu, where again Scheffer had brought the Russian name into disrepute.

The *Riurik* stood becalmed northwest of Kona all day on 25 November. Kotzebue and his crew took the opportunity to reckon the heights of Mauna Loa, Mauna Kea, and Haleakala on Maui, among other cloud-free peaks, and brought their journals up to date. The southern shores of Kahoolawe were passed by 3 a.m. next day; fires were seen along the coast. By 6 a.m. on 26 November, Lanai was plainly visible. But because the winds had died down, Oahu was not seen until the afternoon, and was still five miles off at 6 p.m. Aware that he could not enter Vagititi (Wahititi, modern Waikiki) Bay or harbour that same day, and reassured by the presence of Manuia and Elliot de Castro, Kotzebue ordered that the brig stand out to sea till dawn next day.

1.   *26–27 November 1816*

Because I could not expect to reach harbour this day, I now decided to pass the night in the locality of Vagititi [Waikiki] Bay, with which Vancouver had sufficiently familiarized us.[1] It was there that a new harbour was said to lie. We had been told on Ovaigi [Hawaii] that the sea-current at Vagu [Oahu] flows so powerfully to westward that one must be careful not to get in the lee of that island. I experienced the very opposite, however, discovering at dawn that we had been borne eight miles southeast by the current, and that despite the fact that a pretty stiff wind blew from that quarter and that a high sea was rocking the ship.

My travelling companion, Manuia by name, had been seasick during the night. His own servant, a fourteen-year-old Islander, could not even move. I had earlier invited Manuia to sit at our own table since he always conducted himself very properly and seemed to know the use of knives, forks, and spoons. He consumed whatever was served him with a hearty appetite and was not loath to drinking quite a few glasses of wine. All in all, indeed, his behaviour gave the impression that he had frequently been on European vessels.[2]

Early on 27 November, I laid a course to the western point of Vagititi Bay, which is unmistakable because of the conical mountain standing there. The English call this mountain Diamond Hill because of certain crystals found there which were at first supposed to be diamonds. It is still believed that the place does contain diamonds, and for that reason the populace are not permitted to visit it. Mr. Young[3] gave me one of these crystals and opined that, even if it were not a true diamond, it might yet be another variety of precious stone. So faint was the breeze by this time, however, that we could not double the point until almost noon.[4]

Vagu is recognized by both Europeans and natives to be the most fertile island in the entire group. It is known as the garden of the Sandvichevy [Sandwich] Islands and it certainly has a right to that appellation in view of its considerably cultivated state and extreme natural beauty. Rugged and sharp-topped cliffs rise 529 *toises*[5] from the sea to form the southeast portion of the island, and these do, indeed, seem to argue against the island's high fertility; but you can hardly round the yellow Diamond Hill before your gaze is struck by the most beautiful landscape. Right at the shoreline, you see verdant valleys full of banana trees and palms, among which are scattered the natives' dwellings. Beyond these the land rises little by little and all the hills are covered by a thick mantle of green. Signs of careful industry are apparent everywhere.[6] And here you have opened up before you the southern part of this island which stretches twenty miles in a straight line, east to west; over this expanse, the soil is practically uniform. In the northwest part of Vagu, the island's most magnificent mountain is visible, whose peak, by my measurements, reaches a height of 631.2 *toises*.[7] We had now sailed past Vagititi village, near the place where Vancouver, not even suspecting that he was near a very convenient harbour, had dropped anchor in a very risky way.[8] Through our telescopes, we could see the village of Gana-rura [Honolulu] beyond, near the harbour of the same name. A canoe with three men in it came out to us. Having first called out a few words to these men, Manuia leapt into the water and, being a first-rate swimmer, soon reached the canoe with which he went ashore to announce our arrival to the chiefs and to get us a pilot.[9] We had need of a pilot in view of the harbour's difficult entrance.

By now we were near Gana-rura and could see a number of houses built in the European manner. They made a striking contrast with the native huts. The environs of Gana-rura are, assuredly, very attractive. In the harbour itself was a fort, flying Tameamea's [Kamehameha] flag.[10] Several vessels lay at anchor near it, and the whole would have had quite a European air, had the palm trees and bananas not suggested another portion of the globe [Plate 13]. The Governor duly sent us a pilot at 2 p.m. He proved to be an Englishman, Gebottel [Harbottle] by name, who was in the royal service. It was the man's business to bring all vessels that arrived there safely into harbour.[11] We ourselves had by now reached its entrance and so, as he asked, dropped anchor in eight fathoms of water, coral and sandy bottom. Such is the lie of the land here that a wind prevails from the harbour all day long. Ships are accordingly forced to wait till morning; a calm falls just before sunrise, and advantage is taken of it to tow ships in. I found it most unpleasant to lie thus at anchor. Ships are on occasion lost in very high southerlies, and those winds are frequent at Vagu. Barely 100 fathoms from us was a reef, and the sea-swell was breaking on it with violence.[12] This, however, is the only position where ships can lie at anchor. A little further out, the water is unfathomable.

Our cables suffered considerably in the course of the twelve hours that we waited here, so bad was the sea-bottom. The entire coast, in fact, is encircled by coral reefs which, in a number of places, stretch a mile or more out to sea. It is behind these that nature has formed the beautiful harbour of Gana-rura. Were its entrance not too shallow for large ships, it might be called the finest in the world, entirely sheltered as it is on the ocean side from the fury of the waves. A glance at the map appended here[13] will give the reader a clear idea of this harbour.

Kotzebue

COMMENTARY

1. Kotzebue had aboard the *Riurik* a copy of Vancouver's *Voyage of Discovery* (London, 1798), and was following Vol. II:214–18. Vancouver had not acquainted his readers with Waikiki, but both Kotzebue and Chamisso knew about the districts of O-poo-ro-ah and Honoonoono, and recalled that Captain Brown of the *Butterworth* had found the latter very serviceable as a harbour (*ibid.*, II:216; and Dibble, 1909:54–55).

2. Manuia, son of Kamauawahine and Alapai and a youthful companion of Kamehameha I's son, Liholiho (later Kamehameha II) (see Ii, 1963:53, and 86) was the young chief put aboard the *Riurik* on the Kona Coast by the king to ensure the Russians a polite reception at Honolulu (see Kotzebue, 1821, II:40–42). Manuia had indeed had frequent dealings with Europeans, learning the English that now proved useful to Kotzebue from Jean Rives (Ioane Luwahine) in 1811–12. It was under his influence that Hawaiian youths had, on 24 November 1816, in the smooth sand of Kamakahonu Bay, Kailua, made a stick drawing of the *Riurik* under full sail. Manuia maintained his connections with both Kamehameha II and foreign ships, voyaging to London in 1824 as steward of the royal Hawaiian party (Sinclair, 1976:73) and later visiting Canton.

3. John Young, boatswain of the *Eleanora* (Captain Simon Metcalfe) in 1789, was marooned at Kealakekua on the Kona Coast in March 1790 (Bradley, 1942:16–17). Young was the most trusted of Kamehameha I's *haole* advisers, serving at times as Governor of Hawaii and Oahu. Unlike the other ex-seaman who had acquired vast influence as Kamehameha's counsellor, Isaac Davis (Aikake), Young was generally well disposed towards the Russians. (Davis had in 1809 discouraged the king from entering into formal trade relations with Captain Gagemeister of the *Neva*. See Ii, 1963:79). Most Russian naval visitors to Hawaii or Oahu in 1809–21 had dealings with Young and found him honourable. "Diamond Hill"

was modern Diamond Head (Leahi).

4. The *Riurik* had been driven slightly east of Kaalawai-Kahala by the combination of easterly current and breeze failure.

5. For foreign units of weight and length, see Preliminary Notes above.

6. From his position at 1 p.m. Kotzebue saw and admired Palolo Valley, Puuo Manoa, Ualakaa, and the Punchbowl. The *Riurik* was moving westward along the Kalia shoreline.

7. Taking one (old French) *toise* as 6.395 feet, Kotzebue reckoned Mount Ka'ala in the Waianae range to rise 4,036 feet above sea level. The measurement was extraordinarily precise by the standards of 1816. Today the mountain is reckoned to be 4,030 feet high.

8. Vancouver, 1798, II:218.

9. Manuia was well aware of the urgent need to dispel, or at least to counteract the anti-Russian feeling aroused at Honolulu three months earlier when Dr. Georg Anton Scheffer, acting in the name of the Russian-American Company, had posted Russian guards and raised an unfamiliar flag. Details are in Corney, 1896:46–48, 70–72; Mehnert, 1939:27–30; and Pierce, 1965:12–13.

10 This was Fort Kaahumanu, built in 1816 by Chief Kalanimoku (or "Billy Pitt" to the *haole* residents) and John Young, specifically with a view to forestalling any further Russian incursions (Emerson, 1900: 11–14). Its first commandant was the Englishman George Beckley whom Russian visitors to Honolulu met almost invariably in this period. See Ballou, 1905:5–11 on the "Jack and Bars," the Hawaiian flag of red, white and blue horizontal stripes with the Union Jack in the upper quarter by the masthead. The artist in the *Riurik*, Ludovik Choris, depicted it from afar (Choris, 1822: "Port d'Hanarourou").

11. John M. Harbottle's career in the Islands had long been linked with the ship *Lelia Byrd*, which had in 1803 brought the first horses to Hawaii (Cleveland, 1850:204–10) and which was purchased by Kamehameha I, renamed *Keoua Lelepahi*, and much used by the royal family in 1812–14. Harbottle was retained as her captain (Ii, 1963:105; Bradley, 1942:30–31). Corney met Harbottle, much as Kotzebue had, in 1818 (Alexander, 1907:14). Like William Warren, his assistant at Honolulu Harbour in 1817–22, Harbottle—whom the Russians name Gebottel or even Botl'—was supposed by Americans to be American (*Columbian Centinel*, 6 Nov. 1816).

12. This was the surf along the reef encircling Kuloloia Beach produced by the swell of Mamala Bay (Ii, 1963:65 and 90, maps by Paul Rockwood).

13. See Map A. The map was actually drawn up in 1817, but the *Riurik*'s assistant navigator (later Captain) Vasilii Stepanovich Khromchenko began surveying the harbour itself on 29 November 1816. See Narrative 5.

2. *27 November 1816*

We reached the harbour of Gana-rura [Honolulu] at noon on 27 November. Manija [Manuia] left for the mainland with the first returning canoe and shortly afterwards the royal pilot, an Englishman by the name of Gerbottel [Harbottle] came out and gave us permission to anchor outside the reef. Because of the way the wind regularly dies away before sundown, every ship needs to be towed in here.

The captain went ashore as soon as the *Riurik* rode at anchor. An American schooner, the *Traveller* of Philadelphia, Captain Vilcoks [Wilcox],[1] was just then setting sail. Beyond the surf, we could see an attractive town, the thatched roofs overshadowed by palm trees [Plate 4]. There were Hawaiian-style huts and European-style houses, with white walls and red roofs.[2] The town interrupts an expanse of sunny plain which surrounds the foot of the hills. Woods envelop those hills and descend low on their slopes.

There were two ships in harbour belonging to the chiefs of the Islands. One set out for O-Waihi [Hawaii] on the morning of the 29th, laden with taro. The other, named *Kahu-manu* [*Kaahumanu*] after Tameiameia's [Kamehameha] noble wife, was a small, elegant, and graceful sailing brig. She had been built in France as a pirate ship. Originally known as *La Grande Guimbarde*, she had been taken by the British and renamed *Forester*. Acting as guard-ship, *Kahu-manu* fired the customary retreating shot at sundown.[3]

The captain returned to the ship none too pleased with the reception he had received. The populace were still angry with the Russians, and the Governor had expressed the same prejudice against them. Mr. Iung [Young] had been helpful though.[4] Kareimoku [Kalanimoku], the Governor, also called Mr. Pitt by the British,[5] was second-in-command after the king himself on these Islands, and he had promised the captain to carry out Tameiameia's order punctually.

On the morning of the 28th, we called for the canoes to pull us into harbour. We knew, by means of a cannon-shot, that they were available to us [Plate 8]. The pilot came out with eight canoes, each carrying the owner and sixteen to twenty paddlers.[6] Mr. Iung escorted them in another small native craft. The anchor was weighed and the *Riurik* was taken in tow by the noisily playful and laughing Islanders, with such strength and ease that our sailors could not conceal their surprise. We went at three knots, by the ship's log, and dropped anchor right below the fort.[7] Mr. Iung then came aboard to request payment for services rendered to us, persons not in the king's employ.[8]

Chamisso

COMMENTARY

1. James Smith Wilcox, or Wilcocks, a Philadelphia merchant in the China trade, was in Canton by 1790. His brother Benjamin Chew Wilcocks (1776–1845), mentioned by Kotzebue (see Narrative 3), was in 1812–22 U.S. Consul in Canton. On his schooner *Traveller*, lately arrived from Macao, see Bancroft, 1884; 1:335–36; and Howay, 1973:122.

2. For a map of the area east of Nuuanu Stream showing the sites of *haole* and native houses, see Ii, 1963:65. See also Map B, prepared by crew on the *Kamchatka* (Captain V.M. Golovnin) in October 1818. It shows the site of the whitewashed and red-roofed (second) house of the pioneer and influential *haole* resident, Francisco de Paula Marini. The house observed so quickly by Chamisso was solid evidence of the Spaniard's frugality and prosperity, which later made him unpopular (Mathison, 1825:427; Paulding, 1831:227).

3. The *Forester* was a French privateer purchased from the British by the wealthy New York merchant John Jacob Astor. She was commanded by William J. Piggott in 1813–14 and by Alexander Adams in 1816. She was sold to Kamehameha I on 6 April 1816 (Porter, 1931, II:641–42; Pierce, 1965:233–34).

4. Manuia had assured the Governor that the *Riurik*'s commander had dissociated himself from Scheffer's actions of 24–26 August in Honolulu, which had angered Young (Pierce, 1965:13).

5. Kalanimoku was not of noble Hawaii Island lineage but from Maui. Having served Kamehameha I well as a warrior and counsellor since 1795, he was as influential as any living *ali'i* in 1815–27. Russian visitors concurred with other foreigners in regarding Kareimoku [Krymakoo]—who was Co-regent of the Hawaiian Islands in 1823–27—as a reliable and upright chief (*MHSP*, LIV:33–36, John C. Jones to Marshall & Wildes, 6 July 1821; Mathison, 1825:424). Chamisso himself discusses Kalanimoku's ancestry and powers in Kotzebue, *Voyage*, III:240–241.

6. These were *wa'a kaulua* (double canoes with two equal hulls) of the kind drawn by Choris (Choris, 1822: "Bateaux des îles Sandwich" and "Vue du port Hanarourou"). The dugout underbodies made from single tree trunks and heavy cross-booms required sizeable crews, but vessels of 500 tons were being towed into the harbour at Honolulu. See Plates 4, 8 and 13 here.

7. Fort Kaahumanu. See Narratives 8, 12, 13, and 18.

8. These charges fluctuated over the years, as did the royal port duties (Ellis, 1828:427; Stewart, *Private Journal* 1828:124; and Narrative 4.

3. *27 November 1816*

Three vessels were lying in harbour, and two belonged to Tameamea [Kamehameha] who had acquired them in exchange for sandalwood. One was a handsome brig, the other a sizeable three-master, the *Al'batros* [*Albatross*], which was used at that time for transporting supplies from Vagu [Oahu] to Ovaigi [Hawaii].[1] It was planned to send her in the future, flying the king's flag, with sandalwood for Canton where Chinese wares might be taken in exchange. The English Government has undertaken to respect Tameamea's flag everywhere and, moreover, to support his commerce with Canton.[2] Should this trade prosper, the Hawaiian Islanders will unquestionably make rapid progress toward civilization. As for the brig, she was the *Kagumana* [*Kaahumanu*]. She was built to carry eighteen guns and modelled on the lines of a warship, with speed in view. Tameamea uses her as a warship, in fact, and she is said to be very fast .... Captain Pikkord [Piggot], who had made a number of voyages in her as *Forrester* [*Forester*] of London, notably from the West Coast of America to Canton, had come with her to the South Seas, where a bargain was struck with Kamehameha.[3] Captain Pikkord's second-in-command, Alexander Adams, entered the king's service once the ship was his, becoming her new captain.[4] As such, he today receives a salary of fifty *piastres* a month plus all sorts of fresh provisions, which are sent out to him *gratis* each day. There are six Europeans in his crew, besides several natives.

The third vessel in harbour, *Travellor* [*Traveller*] of Philadelphia, a schooner under the American flag, was just making sail when I arrived with the *Riurik*.

Her owner, who paid me a visit, proved to be a brother of the American Consul in Canton, Mr. Vil'koks [Wilcox].[5] He himself had left Canton some years previously, filling his ship with Chinese wares with a view to conducting a contraband trade with the Spanish colonies on the western littorals of America. However, he had had poor luck. He had very nearly lost his ship, at Valparaiso, only escaping jail by fortunate chance.[6]

Kotzebue

COMMENTARY

1. Notably, taro (see Narrative 108). On the *Albatross*, formerly commanded by Captain Nathan Winship, and now known as *Makanimoku*, see Bradley, 1968:29–31; Howay, 1973;10, 1963:106.
2. Kotzebue knew of the letter of 30 April 1812 from the Earl of Liverpool to Kamehameha. It was in reply to a letter of August 1810 from Kamehameha I to King George III. (*HRA*, Ser. 1, 7:475–76; and 8:625).
3. Porter, 1931, 2:641; Bradley, 1968:85n; and Pierce, 1965:159 and 242.
4. *Kaahumanu*'s log for the Canton venture of 1817, kept by Alexander Adams, appeared in print in 1905 (*Hawaiian Almanac and Annual*: 51). Both William Piggott (or Pigot) and his former navigator in the brig *Forester-Kaahaumanu*, Adams, had had frequent dealings with the Russians in the three years prior to their encounter with the *Riurik*. Both had been at Sitka in April 1814 and in Kamchatka five months later. In 1815 Piggott had made an exhausting overland journey to St. Petersburg hoping to sell a cargo (Porter, 1932:278ff). It was not surprising that he and Kotzebue found matters to discuss.
5. See Narrative 2.
6. Bancroft, 1884, 2:283–85.

4. *27–29 November 1816*

We were in the harbour within half an hour, the *Riurik* having made three knots by the log; and we cast anchor in eight *sazhen* [fathoms] of water just a musket-shot from shore and facing the local fortress. At this juncture, Iung [Young] came on board and told me that, as the canoes that had pulled us did not belong to the king, we were obliged to pay each canoe proprietor the sum of three *piastres*. As commander of a ship-of-war, however, I was exempted from anchorage dues. (Present law requires all merchantmen to pay one *piastre* per foot drawn, by way of anchorage fee). We had no choice but to submit and pay forty *piastres* in all, though I thought it peculiar that I had not been told of these dues beforehand [Plate 25].[1]

The *Riurik* had scarcely dropped anchor before a crowd of Sandvichan [Sandwich Islanders] was surrounding her. Some were in canoes, others swam out. All wished to come aboard and all were annoyed when they were forbidden to do so. In order to get the necessary work finished, I had already declared the ship *tabu* [*kapu*] for several days, in fact. The fair nymphs sang us a few additional love-songs, then turned back, amazed by our hardness of heart.[2]

On the 29th, they began to supply us with foodstuffs in accordance with Tameamea's order. Every day, now, we received an abundance of taro, yams, coconuts, bananas, and watermelon. As for the hogs, they were so large that our entire crew could not eat one in two days. More than half of what we had been promised remained over, so I ordered part of the livestock to be salted down, part stowed aboard alive. A certain Spaniard by the name of Marini [Manini], (who has already lived here many years and who was formerly greatly in the royal favour), salts pork quite excellently. I even carried some of his salt pork back to St. Petersburg, and it was not in the least spoiled. Meat is not salted in the Spanish American colonies, because the opinion there prevails that it begins to spoil even as it is being salted down. In Khili [Chile] ships usually provision with meat dried in the sun, which does not actually contain much nutritional value and has no taste.[3] Certainly, great care must be taken when salting meat in hot climates so that all the bones are removed and the blood squeezed out by means of some sort of heavy press.

Kotzebue

COMMENTARY

1. On the development of these port dues, first recorded here, see Ellis, 1826:398; Stewart, 1828:97–98; and Graham, 1826:157–59.
2. Soviet commentators make much of Russian rectitude in the face of this Polynesian hetaerism (Tumarkin, 1964:77–78). The scene might have been painted by Cook, 1785, 2:543; or Vancouver, 1798, 2:40.
3. Kotzebue had called at Talcaguano in Chile, 13 February to 9 March 1816 (*A Voyage*, I:124–32), and had been unimpressed by it.

5. *29 November 1816*

We were given food, in accordance with Tameiameia's [Kamehameha] order, for the first time on 29 November. They brought us vegetables and fruits in great abundance, and pigs so huge that we could not consume the half of them. The leftovers were pickled. Some hogs were taken aboard still alive.

It was on this day that the captain undertook the mapping of Hana-ruru [Honolulu] Harbour.[1] He had Chramtschenko [Khromchenko][2] place signal poles with flags on in various positions. But these flags reminded the natives of another flag which had been hoisted at the time of [Scheffer's] occupation.[3] Everyone thereupon took up their weapons, hoping for a battle of the sort that those happy people, who enjoy bearing arms, seemed to have missed as a diversion. Luckily, Haul-hana[4] was told what was going on in time to intercede and managed to calm Kareimoku [Kalanimoku] down too. He himself came aboard the *Riurik* to warn our captain of the development, and so became our guardian angel. All flags were removed and war was abandoned.

Chamisso

COMMENTARY

1. See Map A.
2. The *Riurik*'s mate. On ships' companies at Oahu, see Ivashintsev, 1980:137ff and Table 1.
3. See Chapter 1.
4. John Young. "Haul-hanna" is evidently a version of Olo-hana or Olohana, itself an approximate local rendering of "All hands!" Young was a former navy boatswain. Young's son John, Minister of the Interior of the Kingdom of Hawaii in the 1850s, was known as Keoni Ana or Keonihana. The "surname" was thus preserved (Carter, 1923:51–53).

6. *29 November 1816*

A misunderstanding occurred to raise the people against us. The natives would indeed have taken up their weapons and the whole business might well have had serious consequences, had Iung [Young] not become an intermediary in time.[1] The cause was this: as a survey of Gana-rura [Honolulu] Harbour had never been made by anyone, so far as I knew, and as it was then known only to a small number of mariners, I decided that I would draw up a plan of it. To that end, I sent our mate, Khramchenko,[2] to erect long poles at various points. The poles had flags attached. The appearance of these flags brought the natives to despair, for only a short while before this, Sheffer [Scheffer] had raised the Russian flag, saying: "I take possession of the island." In view of all this, the natives had no doubt that I was taking the first step towards conquest. Iung [Young] came out to me and asked insistently that the flags be taken down. I explained my innocent intent and ordered the poles to be replaced by brooms;[3] and by that means I restored tranquility. The more surely to gain the confidence of the populace, I sent to ask Kareimoku [Kalanimoku] to consider doing us the honour of dining on board the *Riurik* on the morrow.

Kotzebue

COMMENTARY

1. This is a reflection of the potency of Kamehameha's annoyance at Scheffer's imperialistic actions in 1816. Neither S.B. Okun' nor D.D. Tumarkin, the principal Soviet authorities on these events (see Bibliography), places proper stress on the close escape from "serious consequences" experienced by the *Riurik*'s company in November 1816, while Scheffer was still on Kauai.
2. Vasilii S. Khromchenko, or Khramchenko (1792–1842), pursued a highly successful naval career in the North and South Pacific. In 1821 he surveyed Bristol Bay, Alaska; in 1828–30 he commanded the *Elena*, calling at Port Jackson and the Marshalls *en route* to Sitka (Ivashintsev, 1980:101–02). In 1832 he returned to Oceania as captain of the transport *Amerika* (*ibid.*, 110), again calling at Sydney and again crossing the Marshalls.
3. Russian: *veniki*, besoms or bath-brooms, used on deck.

7. *30 November 1816*

Having accepted my invitation, Kareimoku [Kalanimoku] came to see me at about noon with his wife, Mr. Iung [Young], and the most important noble *geri* [*ali'i*], among them the brother of Queen Kagumana [Kaahumanu].[1] Iung also brought along his wife, a near relation of Tameamea [Kamehameha]. The severity of Kareimoku, whose earlier mistrust of us had vanished, had turned into kindness. He pressed my hand in a friendly manner and said several times, *Aroha* [Aloha], "God bless you." My guests had decked themselves out in their best clothes; Kareimoku I scarcely recognized in the uniform of an English navigator complete with polished boots and a cocked hat on his head. All this clothing, however, was so tight on him that he could hardly make a movement and, particularly in this time of midday heat, he was in danger of stifling. With no less pride, but with the same difficulty, the other *geri* [*ali'i*] moved about in their European dress.[2] They presented a strange mixture, some being clad as sailors, others as fashionable dandies, and others again as *Gerngut* [*Herrenhut* or Moravian brethren]. Such attire placed all these persons in a most painful situation and brought to mind a picture of dressed up monkeys. The dress of Tameamea's ministers, consisting simply of a frockcoat, was far preferable.

Fashion now reigns to such a degree here that even people of the lower class consider it necessary to have at least *some* European clothing. It is for this very reason that on these islands one can meet with the most comical figures. One man goes in only a shirt, another in trousers only, while a third plays the fop in his waistcoat. There is no question but that Americans buy up all the out-of-date clothing they can in their cities and sell them here at great profit. One of my guests was wearing an exceedingly long frockcoat with buttons the size of a teacup, which he was constantly admiring. The ladies, on the contrary, still wrap themselves entirely in a material *tappa* [*kapa*] of their own manufacture, only sporting a silken kerchief at the neck. Mrs. Iung alone, as the wife of a European, is in this regard distinguished from the other women, being dressed with rich Chinese silks but in the European fashion.[3] Mrs. Iung's pleasant face and, for a semi-savage, very modest behaviour, especially pleased us. Kareimoku's spouse, on the other hand, who was a woman of considerable height and breadth, and of extremely powerful build, was positively masculine in face as in conduct.

Kotzebue

COMMENTARY

1. This was "Teimotu, of the war race of Owhyee," as Chamisso refers to John Adams Kuakini (Kotzebue, *A Voyage*, III:241). Kuakini, an able and intelligent governor of Hawaii at this time (Bradley, 1942:95 and 198), was visiting Oahu together with his sister. Both were children of the warrior chief Keeaumoku (see Ii, 1963:53; Dibble, 1909:44). The chief was drawn by Choris [Plate 3]. This noble party disembarked for the *Riurik* from Pakaka Beach, Kalanimoku's houses then standing well in view of her, along Kuloloia Beach (Ii, 1963:65). The Russian *geri* [*ali'i*] reflects the usage of Cook and his officers.

2. See Narratives 51, 79, and 87 on the spread of European clothing at Honolulu in 1816–21.

3. Chinese silks had been imported direct from Canton since the early 1790s by New Englanders, but most remained in the hands of the king and chiefs.

8. *30 November 1816*

I had intended to go into the fort, but a sentry shouted out to me, *Tabu* [*Kapu*], and so I was obliged to return. In the course of time, I discovered that access to that fort is prohibited to all strangers, especially to Europeans. Kareimoku [Kalanimoku] is always resident in it, and work is still going on there.[1] As the natives of Vagu [Oahu] are not skilled in the operation of cannon, an Englishman, George Bekli [Beckley],[2] has been appointed fortress commandant. He formerly served in a merchantman. The fort itself is nothing more than a rectangle with cannon all round it. The walls are two fathoms high and built of coral stone. I called on Iung [Young], who allowed me to read over a letter from the King of England to Tameamea [Kamehameha] which Mr. Vil'koks [Wilcox] had brought from Port Dzhakson [Jackson].[3] The letter was in English and Tameamea was honoured in it by the title, Your Majesty. The main content was the following: George, King of England, expresses to his Majesty the King of the Sandvichevy [Sandwich] Islands his sincere gratitude for a feather cloak sent to him by the frigate *Kornvallis [Cornwallis]*. He assures him of his friendship and protection and informs him that all English naval forces have been instructed to show every respect to vessels sailing under the flag of His Majesty King Tameamea.[4] Finally, mention is made of a vessel being built for him at Port Dzhakson and of the gifts sent to His Majesty.[5] It is clear from this letter that Tameamea is recognized as a real king by the English Government. All papers received by the king are put in the keeping of Mr. Iung, who enjoys his particular confidence and the respect of the people. Old age and infirmity, however, make it probable that he will soon follow into the grave his comrade Davis,[6] known to us from Vancouver's *Voyage*.

Kotzebue

COMMENTARY

1. Kalanimoku continued to live in the fort intermittently until 1824, when his stone house was erected at Pohukaina nearby (Ii, 1963:143). On progress in the fort itself in 1816–17, see Emerson, 1900:12ff.

2. Cox, 1832:36–39; see also Narrative 1, n. 10 above.

3. This was the Earl of Liverpool's letter to Kamehameha dated London, 30 April 1812 (original in PRO: State Papers; copy in Archives of Hawaii, Foreign Office and Executive Papers: 2). Discussion in Bradley, 1942:48–49. James Smith Wilcocks had called at Port Jackson, modern Sydney, Australia, in the *Traveller* earlier in 1816 (Pierce, 1965:190), *en route* from Canton.

4. This cloak had been taken to England in the frigate HMS *Cornwallis* (Captain Charles Johnstone) which had in fact called at Kealakekua on 2–6 December 1807, and not, as Gagemeister claimed, in May 1809, a full year later (Pierce, 1965:38).

The Liverpool letter had not, as Young wanted Kotzebue to suppose, contained any definite offer of British protection. The vital phrase had been, "the effect of securing your Dominions from any attack or molestation by other Powers." Not unreasonably, given the British claim to the Islands through prior discovery or on the basis of cession, and in view of Britain's post-Napoleonic pre-eminence in the world and in view of such letters as John Young could produce, Kotzebue understood Liverpool to have meant *pokrovitel'stvo* or "protection" (Kotzebue, 1821, II:54) and so reported to the Russian government.

5. The vessel in question was the 70-ton schooner *Prince Regent*, which Governor Lachlan Macquarie of New South Wales was indeed attempting to have built. She finally reached Kamehameha II on 1 May 1822, and was promptly run aground by Kalanimoku (Mathison, 1825:424 and 462; and T.G. Thrum, "Hawaiian Maritime History," *Hawaiian Almanac*, 1890:66–79). Wilcocks evidently made it plain to Kotzebue that the vessel was to be well-armed for her size. King George's other gifts to Kamehameha I included a British cocked hat and full-dress uniform and a "great quantity" of assorted spikes and nails (*HRA: Series 1*, VII:475–76). Kotzebue's own cultural and service background predisposed him to regard the Islands, in these circumstances, as a *de facto* dependency of Great Britain. John Young skilfully presented the "evidence" in such a way as to convince Kotzebue (and others) that this was so.

6. Isaac Davis, lone survivor of the Hawaiian massacre of the crew of *Fair American* (Captain Metcalfe) in 1790, was protected and promoted to positions of great power by Kamehameha I, Co-regent of Hawaii in 1795 (Vancouver, 1798, II:140; III:65–66; Shaler, 1808:162; and Ii, 1963:83–84). The Russians inspected the grave of "Aikake," whose funeral procession Ii describes.

9. *6–7 December 1816*

Our work on the ship had been executed quite successfully by 7 December, but we discovered that the copper sheath had again been damaged in several spots and particularly in a part where the water was so deep that the most skilful diver had to be used in repair work. When all the efforts of my most expert swimmer to attach a copper plate had proved vain, Kareimoku [Kalanimoku] sent us one of his own people who brought the work to a happy conclusion. To our amazement, the man remained three or even four whole minutes underwater, surfacing only for a moment to draw breath before diving down again.[1] A companion handed him nails, but used the time while they were being hammered in to inhale air on the surface of the water. Our own aforementioned expert diver found, on inspection of the entire ship's keel, that there were many damaged places which could be repaired only by means of careening her.

Our relations with the natives of Gana-ruru [Honolulu] were excellent; every day, many nobles or *geri* [*ali'i*] would visit us, they alone having permission to come out to the *Riurik* at any time. Often they would bring out gifts, taking nothing from us in return. And from morning to evening, the ship would be surrounded by the fair sex.[2] Our seamen, who remained ashore for days on end, never had the least cause to complain of the natives, who always received them with great hospitality, even, sometimes, leaving them alone with their wives without the least indication of distrust [Plate 5].[3]

Kotzebue

COMMENTARY

1. Oahu fishermen were accustomed to deep diving, not for pearls but for turtles, lobster, and some fish. See Malo, 1903:277; Buck, 1957:302–03; and Ii, 1963:63 ("the game of staying under water as long as possible").
2. Compare Narratives 107, 118, 127 and 129.
3. Such passing remarks combine with more specific observations by Lieutenant Emel'ian E. Levenshtern, of the *Nadezhda*, to cast doubt on Soviet assertions (see Narrative 4) that Russian crews had no sexual relations whatever with Hawaiian women (Levenshtern, *Putevoi Zhurnal*, TsGIAE, *fond* 1414, op. 3: *delo* 4:8–9 June 1804).

10. *13–14 December 1816*

By 13 December, we were ready to leave. The Europeans on the Sandwich Islands, incidentally, were setting their time from the west, via Canton, while we had brought our time from east to west. Therefore, we were one day ahead of them, as if we had been in Kamtschatka [Kamchatka] or the Russian settlements.[1] The same time difference exists between neighbours at San Francisco and Port Bodega. It is rather hard to come to terms with real time ....

On the morning of 14 December, we communicated with the pilot by cannon shots. He came out with several double canoes, and we were taken out of the harbour.[2] Kareimoku [Kalanimoku] came aboard us.

Chamisso

COMMENTARY

1. Chamisso ignores the additional complication that the Old Style (Julian) calendar, not the Gregorian calendar, remained in use in the Russian outposts. In the Pacific, he and others aboard Russian ships normally used Gregorian-style dates in journals, but it may be necessary to add thirteen days to synchronize Russian and Hawaiian source material.
2. These Honolulu *wa'a kaulua* had features of the craft used on long sea voyages (three stout cross-booms, median bow covers, etc.). However, they lacked significant bow and stern pieces, and their relative size was merely to accomodate the sixteen, twenty, or more paddlers who towed large vessels in and out of the harbour (see Narratives 1 and 4). Choris drew them several times in 1816–17 (see Plates 4, 8, 13).

11. *13 December 1816*

Today there dined with us Captain Alexander Adams, an intelligent man who has travelled pretty widely. His conversation was accordingly very pleasing to us. Adams told us, *inter alia*, that Americans from the United States discovered some years ago a certain island near the coast of California which, because of the huge number of sea-otters found on it, they have called Otter Island. Its southern extremity lies in 33°17'N latitude, and reckoned by lunar distances its longitude is 240°50'E from Grenvich [Greenwich]. The circumference is fifty or sixty miles, and a dangerous reef is said to lie north-northwest of this island.[1] Adams also told us that, whereas in Europe efforts are being made to abolish the slave-trade, citizens of the United States of America are exerting all their energy to strengthen it. To buy slaves, American vessels proceed to latitude 45°N on the Northwest Coast of America, where the population is large. Having learned by experience they will be paid far more for men than for peltry, the natives of those parts have turned to that dreadful hunt. As American merchants have provided them all with firearms, they easily overpower the unfortunate races living in the interior of that country, then give their captives to shipmasters in exchange for various items of clothing. Moving instances of filial love are not rarely encountered among those persecuted tribes, but their inhuman persecutors draw advantage even from this, out of avarice. When, for instance, a son hears of the captivity of his own father, he runs to the slavers to offer himself in exchange. And the barbarians willingly accept this magnanimous proposal, as a young man is of more use to them than an old one.[2] When a ship is thus sufficiently laden with slaves, she sets off north to latitude 55° where the Coast Indians take the unfortunates for their own service in exchange for sea-otter skins. The Europeans sell these for a good profit in China and rejoice at their gains, so shamefully made. The same shipmasters also take much pleasure in abusing the trust of Tameamea [Kamehameha]. One American master, for instance, to whom the king had entrusted a vessel laden with sandalwood to be delivered to China, did not return at all.[3] And every year, a number of seamen are put off at these Islands because of their bad conduct. Since these men can only serve as bad examples, and generally cause harm, it must be supposed that the Sandwich Islanders' good disposition will soon be completely corrupted by them.[4]

Adams enjoys the king's particular confidence and had been sent by him in a brig that had previously stood at Ovaigi [Hawaii][5] to Vagu [Oahu] Island to forestall any insurrection there. The king does not fear anything on Ovaigi as he was born there and, in the natives' belief, was confirmed by the gods in his royal status. By contrast, the natives of Vagu Island seem to him dangerous, inasmuch as he himself conquered them.[6]

Kotzebue

COMMENTARY

1. San Nicolas, in the Santa Barbara Group due west of Los Angeles. The "reef" was Begg's Rock.
2. See also Narrative 109, and Morison, 1961:135ff on slavers.
3. The allusion is to Captain Nathan Winship and the *Keoua Lelepali* [ex-*Lelia Byrd*). In reality, Winship's contract with Kamehameha I had been more complex that Kotzebue knew. The king had indeed had to wait three years for his $10,000,

but it was finally brought to him (Ii, 1963:113, 128; Snyder, 1937:B65; C. Davis, "Sandwich Islands," in *North American Review*, III, May 1816:52–53). John Young was almost certainly Kotzebue's informant and it was he who, in the summer of 1813, had persuaded Kamehameha I to repudiate the sandalwood contract he had made with the Winships in 1812, i.e., the monopoly of that trade (Howay, ed. *The Voyage of the New Hazard ...* by Stephen Reynolds, Salem, 1938:108–14; *Niles Weekly Register*, 18:418). This is another example of Young's ability—and readiness—to present his own versions of recent events to the Russian visitors.

4. See Narratives 107, 113, 115, 119 and 124.

5. This was the *Kaahumanu* (ex-*Forester*) in which—before his own arrival in the Islands in February 1816—Adams had sailed to Kamchatka, Sitka, and along the California coast. Russian sources confirm John Papa Ii's statement (Ii, 1963:128) that, since entering Kamehameha's service in April 1816, Adams had been in close and frequent contact with Kalanimoku.

6. At the Battle of Nuuanu in 1795 (Ii, 1963:14–15; and Dibble, 1909:56–57).

12.   *13–14 December 1816*

It was made known in Gana-rura [Honolulu] that we meant to leave Vagu [Oahu] Island on the morrow; and for that reason we were visited by many distinguished persons today [13 December] who wanted to bring us gifts and wish us a prosperous voyage. All day long, the ship was surrounded by swimming women taking tender farewells of their friends. Kareimoku [Kalanimoku] had ordered that I be requested, by Bekli [Beckley], to salute the fort when I set sail, thereby in some way consecrating it, as he wished. I readily agreed to fulfil that request.

At 6 a.m. on the 14th, we fired to request a pilot, who shortly afterwards appeared with a number of large craft.[1] We weighed anchors and the *Riurik* was towed out of the harbour. Just as soon as Kareimoku came on board, I gave orders for the fort to be saluted with a seven-gun volley. This gave him such intense pleasure that he embraced me several times. In the fort itself, they did not delay to reply to my courtesy; and when they had fired off their rounds, the brig *Kagumana* [*Kaahumanu*] began firing a salute—which we returned with an equal number of guns. And in this way, a European custom had been introduced to the Sandwich Islands. It was very pleasing for me to be the first European to exchange salutes with that fort.[2] Should Gana-rura become, in time, a flourishing city, then people may say that it was Russians who first consecrated their fort, and that its first shot was fired in honour of the Emperor Alexander I.

At 8 o'clock we were already out of the harbour. Kareimoku promised to entreat the gods that the sun might escort us by day and the moon by night, and then left us with our guides. As the latter put off, they three times shouted: hurrah! We moved away from the shore with a faint easterly wind. I ordered a southwest course to be set, and by noon we had already lost sight of the highest point of the Island of Vagu.[3]

Observations Made During Our Stay at the Island of Vagu [Oahu]

The mean of many noon observations gave, as the latitude of our anchorage:	21°17'57"N
The mean of lunar observations, taken on several consecutive nights, indicated the longitude of our anchorage as:	157°52'W
Compass inclination:	10°57'E
Magnetic needle variation:	43°39'00"
The time of high water, at new and full moon, was found to be 2 hours 55 minutes; and the greatest rise in sea water level was 6 feet.	
Mean barometer reading:	29 inches, 80 lines
Mean thermometer height:	75° Fahrenheit

... ...

I must further mention here that throughout our stay at the island of Vagu, Manuia followed precisely the instructions of the king. He never left the ship without my permission, guarded her against theft of any sort, and invariably assisted us in the purchase of local rarities. When I had need of anything, he did not hesitate to leap into the water and would not rest ashore until he had carried out my instructions. In order to supply me with firewood, he quickly brought together a hundred Islanders, who felled timber, brought it to the ship, and cut it up. All this would have been exhausting work for my sailors in so hot a climate. We rewarded him generously, on parting; but he regarded it as a special honour to have been entrusted by me, with things intended for Tameamea [Kamehameha I].[4]

Kotzebue

COMMENTARY

1. Double canoes; see Narratives 1–2.
2. Details in Emerson, 1900:11–25. Fort Kekuanohu, dismantled in 1857, later stood on this site.
3. Mount Kaala, in the Waianae Range (4,030 feet). The *Riurik* now made, by a circuitous route and with discoveries in view, for the Radak and Ralik chains of the Caroline Islands in Micronesia. (Kotzebue, *A Voyage*, I:355–56; Ivashintsev, 1980:28).
4. Manuia was rewarded for loyal service. Remaining in Kamehameha II's entourage, he accompanied him to London in 1823–24 as steward of the royal party. Surviving measles there, he returned to Oahu and served in various capacities during the governorship of Boki, e.g., commandant of Fort Kaahumanu: see A. Frankenstein, *The Royal Visitors* (Portland, Oregon Historical Society, 1963); Sinclair, 1976:73;

Ii, 1963:104, 145. He was among the most widely travelled Hawaiian chiefs of his generation.

TRANSLATOR'S NOTE ON THE MOVEMENTS OF THE *Riurik* IN 1816–17

In the nine and a half months since she had gone from Honolulu (14 December 1816 until 13 October 1817), the *Riurik* and her company had covered at least 8,000 miles. In the Carolines, significant discoveries and contacts had been made, and in the person of Kadu, a Radak native of intelligence and charm whom Kotzebue had encountered on 23 February 1817 (see *A Voyage*, 2:121–31) these new connections became reality for the Hawaiian Islanders. Brought to Hawaii like an unexpected Micronesian envoy, Kadu made an impression on his Polynesian hosts and, in particular, on Queen Kaahumanu (*ibid.*, 2:192–94) and her suite.

Among the clusters in the Carolines examined in the first nine weeks of 1817 had been Otdia ("the Rumiañtsevs"), Kwajalein ("the Arakcheevs"), and Erikup ("the Chichagovs"). More recently in April, Kotzebue had arrived at Unalaska; and from there, once repairs had been completed to the brig and the seamen were rested, an exhausting Arctic survey was begun (see Ivashintsev, *Russian Round-the-World Voyages*; 28–30). It was off the St. Lawrence Islands in the middle of July that Kotzebue saw the need to hasten south. Chamisso later publicly cricitized this decision. Whether or not this was a justified decision has been weighed, with mixed results, by many Soviet and Western specialists since 1932, when A.C. Mahr published his views (see *The Visit of the "Riurik"*:12–13). Possibly Kotzebue's chest weakness and the bruise sustained in an accident during the voyage, had grown far worse in Arctic latitudes. It is accepted that his final illness and death were connected with that weakness.

What has relevance to the *Riurik*'s return to the Hawaiian chain, in any event, is that her captain and her leading scientist were not getting on well together. This emerges from the Kotzebue narrative and Chamisso's own *Tagebuch*. These strains themselves perhaps stemmed from the *Riurik*'s Arctic voyage, in particular, its unsuccessful end. To read the "Honolulu section" of the second part of Kotzebue's *Puteshestvie*, Chapter XIII: "From the St. Lawrence Islands to Guakhan," (Guam,) is to be conscious of its author's brittle mood. Much though he relished the provisions, warmth, and friendliness of Honolulu, Kotzebue was already mentally *en route* to Europe by October 1817. A two-week stay more than sufficed. That he remained in port as long as that was largely due to local victualling patterns and to Chief Kalanimoku's great civility.

As in 1816, so now the Honolulu visit was preceded by a visit to the Kona Coast, Hawaii. Reaching Kawaihae Bay on 27 September, the *Riurik* coasted to Kealakekua and a meeting with Kamehameha I (Kotzebue, *A Voyage*, 2:189–94) which, again, passed off quite easily. The Russians left the king a little iron and departed, with a three-man escort, for Oahu. The passage was difficult and the *Riurik* was utterly becalmed off Lanai for twenty hours. Chamisso, impatient to continue with the botanizing and with other scientific work—cut short when Kotzebue had declined simply to leave him on Oahu nine months earlier—was forced to wait a little longer. Had his own wishes been granted, by a captain whom he privately accused of lacking scientific vision, he would have spent the best part of a year on the island stretched before him. He was determined not to waste a single hour when he got ashore once more.

13. Early October 1817

The fort situated at the rear of Hana-rura [Honolulu] Harbour, put up by Mr. Iung [Young] without great expertise, is simply a square.[1] It is built of dry stone, lacks ditches, and has neither towers nor bastions on its walls [Plate 13]. Certainly, it will not answer to the two-fold objective of the island Governor—to offer defence against either an outside or an internal enemy. The fort should be regularly built on its present site, in my view, and there should also be a battery on the outer limit of the reef to cover the harbour entrance. The natives have a good supply of arms and ammunition indeed; but even so, they are still unfamiliar with the management of field-pieces or, in fact, with European military practice.[2] One might think that a serious attempt at occupation would prove decisive here. In reality, though, a conqueror would only have won the earth in which he might rest, for the Hawaiians will not submit to foreigners. They are moreover far too strong, warlike, and numerous to be speedily wiped out, as were the natives of the Mariana Islands [Plate 6].[3]

Chamisso

COMMENTARY

1. See Plate 4 and Alexander, 1907:13–15.
2. With regard to the "good supply of arms and ammunition," the Russians had reported as early as 1804 that Kamehameha I had such quantities of both in his armories that even Russian striped ticking material was much preferred to either (Lisianskii, *Voyage*:99, 102, 115–16; Kruzenshtern, *Voyage*, I:196–97). Under Beckley's and other settlers' supervison, the problem of cannon practice was being tackled in 1816; a gun drilling field had been laid out beside an older spear-throwing field, 300 yards back from Kalanimoku's houses on Kuloloia Beach (Ii, 1963:65).
3. The Chamorros, who were on Chamisso's mind because the *Riurik* had in 1817 called at Guam (24–28 November) as well as at numerous islands of the Ratak chain, and had witnessed the effects of Spanish colonialism. See my *Russian Exploration in the Mariana Islands, 1816–1828* (Saipan, Micronesian Archaeological Studies, 1984) and Kotzebue, *Voyage*, III:76–80.

14. Early October 1817

It is asserted that two hundred vessels from the United States of America are occupied with trade in this latitude of the Pacific Ocean. It seems to us, though, that the number is exaggerated. The main branches of trade are the carrying of contraband along the Spanish coasts of North and South America, which is conducted by monks on the Spaniards' side;[1] the fur-trade on the Northwest Coast; the exporting of the same variety of goods, collected in the Russian-American Company's colonies; and the sandalwood trade from the Sandwich, Fidji [Fiji], and other Islands.[2] Here, the field is open for the most daring undertakings ....

Canton is the intermediate point or depot for all this trade; Hana-ruru [Honolulu] is its free port and storage point. For the most part, a shipmaster manages his own business, so there is no need to fear those disputes which often occur between captain and supercargo when those offices are separated from each other. The trade along the Northwest Coast is fraught with dangers, honesty being observed by neither side.[3] All precautionary measures must be taken always, lest one suffer from the firearms that have been sold to natives there.

                                                                    Chamisso

COMMENTARY

1. Barratt, 1981b:149–52; Gibson, 1976:174–97.
2. Bradley, 1968:26–32.
3. Full treatment in Morison, 1961 and Gibson, 1976:158–62. Chamisso was familiar with Lisianskii's and Langsdorf's recent accounts of their Pacific voyages of 1804–1805, and well knew that many Hawaiians had sailed to the Northwest Coast in New England vessels (Lisianskii, Voyage:128; Langsdorf, 1813, I:187; Franchère, 1854:85; Bradley, 1942:20, 33).

15. 1 October 1817

At daybreak on 1 October, we caught sight of Vagu [Oahu], and by 5 p.m. we had reached Gana-ruru [Honolulu] anchorage. Shortly after we dropped anchor, a brig flying the American flag, which we had seen earlier passing from the north through the channel between Vagu and Mororai [Molokai], came up close to us. I afterwards learned that this vessel was indeed an American one.[1] Mr. Baranov had hired her in Sitka to carry a cargo of furs from Okhotsk; having executed his duty in that regard, her captain was now on his way back. As soon as I had anchored, I went ashore. I had been preceded there by the young Kareimoku [Kalanimoku] who had gone ahead in a canoe belonging to the local natives. We found everything in motion in the harbour. Eight ships stood at anchor. Six of them flew the North American flag, one flew the flag of Tameamea [Kamehameha I], and the eighth, belonging to the Russian-American Company, was sitting on a sandbank.[2] When I was near this little fleet, they greeted me with gunfire from the American ships. This courtesy was shown me as the commander of a Russian warship.

At the landing-place,[3] I was met with great civility by the captains of the aforementioned vessels, and led to Kareimoku's residence. He was delighted to see me once more. Even while I was some way off, he cried out to me

Aroha! [*Aloha*] "Welcome!" Three guns then fired in the fortress, and with each one he pressed my hand, repeating the word, *Aroha!* Through Iung [Young], he told me that he had already received Tameamea's instruction by messenger, but that in any case, simply out of love for the *Riurik*, he would have taken care of everything. I asked him for boats to tow our ship into the harbour's interior; but the captains of the American ships asked me to use their boats, promising to send them the next morning [2 October]. In accordance with the general practice here, we fired a gun at dawn and craft immediately came out to tow us in. We were brought to anchor in the same spot that we had occupied the previous year. And we had scarcely arrived there before Kareimoku accompanied by Iung came aboard, followed by a large canoe laden with vegetables, fruit, and a pig. Kareimoku was much pleased to be received on deck with a three-gun salute. The fort then fired a seven-gun salute, to which we responded with the same number.

Kotzebue

COMMENTARY

1. Probably the *Brutus* of Boston (Captain Thomas Meek); see Corney, 1896:73; Roquefeuil, 1843, 2:93–94.
2. .The *Kad'iak*, ex-*Myrtle*; see Howay, 1973:78–79. Among the other vessels found at Honolulu by the Russians were the *Cossack* (Capt. J. Brown), the *Bordeaux Packet* (Capt. Andrew Blanchard), and the *Alert* (Capt. Lemuel Porter); see Judd, 1929.
3. Just north of the foot of Nuuanu St.; see Ii, 1963:65. In 1825 a sunken hulk formed the first solid wharf there. It was replaced in 1837 by a regular wharf or jetty built under the supervision of Captain John Meek. On the Meeks, see Narratives 17 and 120 here.

16.   *6 October 1817*

Today, 6 October, there arrived the American brig *Boston*.[1] Having rounded Cape Horn and looked in at Sitka, her captain was intending to continue on his voyage from Oahu to Canton. For a good price he let us have a certain amount of biscuit, of which we were entirely out.

Kadu[2] meanwhile had made numerous friends here, where a number of things greatly astonished him. Once, for example, he was greatly scared by the sight of a man on horseback, whom he took for some frightful monster.[3] The islanders took pleasure in teaching Kadu, though; and since he took particular interest in the cultivation of the land, it was my hope that he could become the intermediary whereby the Radak Islanders could learn about certain plants which I proposed to take there with me from here.[4]

On the 8th, the master of an American schooner concluded an agreement with Kareimoku [Kalanimoku], offering him a copper-bottomed vessel in exchange for a shipload of sandalwood.[5] From this, one well sees what a good price the Americans get for their sandalwood in China. Several ships lying at anchor here, in fact, were getting cargoes of this timber in exchange for goods or coin, the wood being delivered right to them in the presence of Kareimoku, up to the specified weight.[6]

Kotzebue

COMMENTARY

1. This vessel had been captured by a band of Tlingit Indians at Nootka Sound on 12 March 1803, and all but two of her crew had been murdered. Kotzebue learned of this from her new master and from men of the schooner *Lydia*, which had rescued the two survivors in 1805. The *Boston* was one of many New England vessels that were plying between the Hawaiian Islands and Russian North America in these post-Napoleonic years (see Appendix B here). According to statistics provided by K.T. Khlebnikov in 1833 (Gibson, 1972:11–13), twelve of the eighteen foreign vessels that called at Sitka in 1818–23 had the Islands as their final destination; and of these eighteen, no less than five had actually started trading voyages at Honolulu, loading up with goods thought likely to appeal to the Company authorities at Novo-Arckangel'sk precisely as John Jacob Astor's *Forester* had done in 1813–14 (Porter, 1931, II:641; Bradley, 1942:76–77). There was frequent and friendly contact between the Russian Northwest Coast and Honolulu in this period. Chief Manager Baranov and his heirs were, comparatively speaking, well informed of recent happenings on the Hawaiian Archipelago and ignorant of those in Europe.
2. An adaptable and intelligent Radak Islander brought from Micronesia in the *Riurik* (see Kotzebue, *Voyage*, II:122–31).
3. Honolulu's first horses had been brought in 1803 by the *Lelia Byrd*, (now Kamehameha's *Keoua Lelepali*; see Cleveland, 1850:204–10,) and had at that time alarmed Hawaiians who subsequently took pleasure in a Caroline Islander's apprehensions.
4. Chamisso is the principal source regarding Kadu's Honolulu sojourn and subsequent exploitation of his Hawaiian experience; see Kotzebue, *Voyage*, III:107 (his ability to converse with Hawaiians), 109 (his regret that he did not learn even more at Honolulu), and 175 (his care of melon, watermelon, gourd, *kukui*, and other seeds entrusted to him at Honolulu and sown on Otdia Island in the Radak chain in 1817).
5. The *Bordeaux Packet*, sold by Captain Andrew Blanchard (Hunnewell, 1895:8).
6. *Maka'ainana* were effectively being forced to carry the timber right from the interior of Oahu to the quayside.

17. *12 October 1817*

By asking me to stay a few days longer, Kareimoku [Kalanimoku] took from me the possibility of leaving Vagu [Oahu] the next day, (the 12th) as I had earlier planned. There was to be a *tabu* [kapu] the following day,[1] and it would end only the day after that; so he would be unable to accompany me. Besides this, he represented to me that my voyage would be unfortunate if I started on it before the *tabu* had ended. Since he had invariably dealt with me in a friendly way, I could not refuse this request of his. Meanwhile the ship was brought to a state of readiness to put to sea, and all foodstuffs were taken aboard. When, finally, a good number of animals such as goats, pigs, dogs, pigeons and cats, were added to these other supplies, the *Riurik* looked exactly like Noah's Ark.

We were ready to leave harbour at dawn on 14 October. The captains of American vessels, whose names I here mention with gratitude: William Davis, John Gebet [Ebbets], Thomas Brown, and Thomas Mik [Meek],[2] sent me their boats to tow us out. Soon after this, Kareimoku also made his appearance; he had just returned from the *morai*.[3] Greeting me with an *Aroha!* [*Aloha*], he assured me that in response to his insistent requests the gods had promised to protect us during our voyage, so that we might reach our own land with whole heads and healthy limbs .... He brought us watermelons as well as fish from his own artificial pond,[4] and generally behaved with far more courtesy towards us than towards the captains of merchantmen, in his relations with whom he maintained a certain pride.

Kotzebue

COMMENTARY

1. This was *kapu Hua*, by Hawaiian reckoning. The Russians frequently came up against *kapu* restrictions in 1809–18, and showed the necessary patience. *Kapu Hua* was about to commence on 12 October 1817 because by Hawaiian reckoning the next day was *mohalu*. (There was a discrepancy of the sort that led Chamisso to reflect on the difficulty of knowing "correct" time in the Pacific, on the far side of the globe from Greenwich. Aboard the *Riurik*, it was already 12 October, but Kalanimoku and the *kahuna* ashore estimated that the twelfth night of the month would fall at the close of the next day). Kotzebue's and Chamisso's dating of this *kapu* thus fails to tally exactly with that given by W.D. Alexander in Malo, 1903:55, 58; but it supports the statement that the *kapu* lasted two days. Chamisso had witnessed the observance of *kapu Ku* at Honolulu the previous November (see Narrative 72). Then, following W.D. Alexander's data (Malo, 1903:58), he had witnessed its potency throughout the first (*hilo*) and second (*hoaka*) days of December. Another day, the sight of a woman's corpse floating in Honolulu Harbour brought home to him still more forcefully the fact that the traditional *kapu* remained "in undiminished power" (Kotzebue, *Voyage*, III:249). Aware that Lisianskii and his British predecessors had touched on the subject of the Hawaiian calendar and time divisions, Chamisso decided not to write a special paper on *kapu* and on their sequence; but he did deal with those matters tangentially in his study, *Über die Hawaiische Sprache*, printed in 1837 and reprinted in 1969 (Amsterdam, Halcyon Antiquariaat) with an introduction by Samuel H. Elbert.

2. William Heath Davis, Sr. was now owner and master of the *Eagle*, admired by the *Riurik*'s company, in which Thomas Meek was in 1818 to carry a mixed cargo to Sitka (for 1,211 fur-seal pelts; Khlebnikov, 1976: 57). Meek himself was in the *Brutus*, a 190-ton brig finally sold outright to the Russian-American Company (Pierce, 1965:231). John Ebbets, a New York shipmaster employed by Astor at intervals since 1809, had sold his *Albatross* (now known locally as *Makanimoku*) to Kamehameha I on 16 October 1816 (*ibid.*, 232) and was now on

the *Enterprise*. Details of movements are in Khlebnikov, 1976:57–58; and Howay, 1973:119–21. Thus, only David Nye was missing from the tightly-knit group of Americans who dominated trade between the Islands and Sitka in 1817–19. Not surprisingly, these men who were so friendly towards Kotzebue were precisely those most willing to oblige Captain Vasilii M. Golovnin of the *Kamchatka* in October 1818. See Narrative 18.

In general, Russian material tells us more about New England shipmasters at Honolulu than the latter tell us about Russians. Names are frequently mangled: John Ebbets becomes Gebet (Kotzebue, *A Voyage*, II:198), John Harbottle becomes Botl (Gillesem, 1849:217), and so forth. The journal of James Hunnewell of 1817–18, as edited in 1895 by his son James ("Voyage in the *Bordeaux Packet*," *HRS, Papers*, no. 8, 1909:3–19), typifies such New England manuscript material in that it is faulty and incomplete. Hunnewell asserts that a Russian vessel called the "Cretie" reached Honolulu from Hawaii on 10 April 1818, sailing again on 5 May (*ibid.*, 17). The name faintly echoes *Otkrytie*, which had indeed been at Oahu two years earlier. No mention whatsoever is made of the *Riurik*, which *was* at Honolulu—together with James Hunnewell—in mid-October 1817.
3. On problems of identifying this *heiau*, see Narratives 68 amd 104.
4. These were by the River Mauna Loa's mouth, north-northwest of Honolulu Harbour. See Map A.

18. *27 October 1818*

In the harbour at the time were four merchantmen from the United States of America and two brigs which belonged to the Hawaiian king. There were also, lying on their sides, the Russian-American Company ship *Kad'iak*, which had earlier foundered, and an American vessel which had been sold to the king.[1] These craft were standing in the harbour by the entrance to which there was a square stone fort mounting fifty-two guns. This whole spectacle far surpassed anything we had seen in the Russian or Spanish settlements in these parts of the globe; and when we bore in mind that the stone fort, vessels, and cannon that we were seeing belonged to a people who still went naked, and that these even had their national flag, we could only wonder at their advances in civilization.

On our arrival in the bay, two captains of American vessels had immediately come out to visit me. One of them, Nay [Nye] by name, I already knew.[2] They provided me with certain curious information bearing on the country we were in. After dinner, there came out to us yet another American captain, Devis [Davis], an old acquaintance of mine[3] and one of the most obliging and straightforward men I know, and the Spaniard Manini [Marini] who had lived on these islands for more than twenty years. They undertook to show me everything of interest here and to give us necessary information.

I went ashore with some of my officers on 27 October at 8 a.m. As I passed by the American vessels, they each fired a seven-gun salute in my honour; and another salute, of five guns, was fired from the fort as we stepped ashore. We later replied to these salutes from our sloop .... We were not permitted into the fort itself, but we walked right round it. It stands right by the shore and has been built of coral stone or blocks. The wall is some seven feet high, and it has a parapet on the seaward side of almost the same height. There are also gun embrasures in the wall facing the sea. The purpose of this fort is to defend the harbour's entrance and it is well-situated for that.

I dined with Captain Devis, where all his other comrades had gathered, as well as the island's governor and the local naval commander. The former is called Bokki [Boki], the latter—Gekiri [Hekiri].[4] The English, however, have given Gekiri the name Mr. Coxe, and he likes that very well. Bokki executed the royal orders punctiliously this same day, sending us hogs and greenstuffs.

Golovnin

COMMENTARY

1. The *Kad'iak*, beached at Honolulu since June 1817, had originally been the *Myrtle* (Captain Henry Barber): see Howay, 1973 for her movements on the Northwest Coast (1807–16) and her several visits to Sitka. She had been leaking alarmingly as early as July 1816, when Scheffer had her. The American vessel on her side was the *Bordeaux Packet*, sold in September 1817 by Andrew Blanchard.

2. Captain David Nye had assumed command of the *Brutus* in 1818 and taken her to the Northwest Coast, where in August his path had crossed the *Kamchatka*'s. He returned in 1819 and traded at Sitka for 2,700 seal skins (Khlebnikov, 1976:58; and Pierce, 1965:231). But he and Golovnin had apparently met in 1811 while the brig *New Hazard* and the *Diana* had been visiting the Northwest Coast.

3. William Heath Davis, Sr. had been at Sitka with the *Isabella* (now Kamehameha I's *Enepalai*) in July 1810. Thus his meeting with Golovnin had been recent, in 1818, with the *Eagle*; see Ivashintsev, 1980:19, 38; also *Materialy dlia istorii* 1861, pt. III:passim, on Golovnin's brushes with New Englanders and their influence while on the Northwest Coast.

4. Boki Kamauleule was Kalanimoku's brother but not always his ally in Hawaiian politics. They were descendants of the same Hawaiian chief, as was Kamehameha I (see Ii, 1963:53). Admiral Kahekili Ke'eaumoku (or Keeaumokuopio or "Hekiri") and his own brother, John Adams Kuakini, came of another but connected lineage.

19. *29 October 1818*

Saying farewell to the Americans towards evening, I returned to the sloop, and shortly afterwards Manini[1] [Marini] also came out, to settle up with me for articles that had been supplied to us [Plate 22]. He brought with him two Sandwich Islanders, whom Bokki [Boki] judged it necessary to send with me to Atuai [Kauai] Island, to calm its people with regard to our arrival. They might otherwise have thought we had come to carry out threats of vengeance made by Dr. Shefer [Scheffer], who had established a Company settlement in their midst but who had later been expelled by them.[2] A third Sandwich Islander, an agile young man, volunteered his services to us, insistently asking us to take him along also. Since these natives are not forbidden to leave their fatherland, and as we knew from the Americans that they were very keen to work on European vessels, I took him on. I calculated that when he had learned Russian he might be highly useful to the [Russian-] American Company in its commerce with the Sandwich Islands. The name of this Sandwich Islander was Lauri.[3] We turned it into a surname, and named him Terentii, in honour of the saint whose day it then was.

Golovnin

COMMENTARY

1. Francisco de Paula Marini complemented his horticultural enterprise and experimentation with commercial enterprise, acting as a virtual wholesaler and supplying both the *Riurik* and the *Kamchatka* with vegetables and salt-pork in 1816–18. Encouraged by successes with the Russians and with other *haole* visitors, Marini expanded his business, acquiring large herds of cattle, goats, and swine, and flocks of sheep: see Mathison, 1825:427; and Paulding, 1831:227. Golovnin himself admired Marini's vineyard, and the live tobacco plants, wheat, and other cereals in store (Golovnin, 1949:393–94).
2. Golovnin in fact called in at Waimea on the south shore of Kauai (30 October 1818), hoping to find the *Enterprise*. He had a letter from William Heath Davis for the interpreter—said to be aboard that vessel—who was requested to assist the Russians in an audience with Kaumualii (Golovnin, 1949:375–76). Neither the interpreter nor the king were nearby and Golovnin was unwilling to wait for their return from the north of the island where sandalwood was being felled.
3. On Lauri, see Appendix A.

20. *Late October 1818*

Such frequent and protracted visits [by Americans] soon familiarized the Sandwich Islanders with the use of many European things and even with the customs of enlightened nations. This was the more true because of the natives' present ruler, whose strong desire it is to educate his people [Plate 16]. By his honest and correct dealings with Europeans and kindness to them, that ruler has attracted many seamen from merchantmen and even a number of skilled tradesmen, who have settled among the Sandwich Islanders, taking wives from among the island girls. When Vancouver was here [from 1791 to 1794], the king already had eleven Europeans in his service. But now there are about 150 of them on the Sandwich Islands,[1] and they include shipwrights, locksmiths, boilermakers and joiners, as well as many carpenters and blacksmiths.

Golovnin

COMMENTARY

1. This tallies with figures given by Bradley, 1968:34; and Tumarkin, 1964:94. See also Narrative 105.

21. *Late October 1818*

On the advice of Europeans in his service, he [Kamehameha I] dispatched a brig to Canton with a cargo of sandalwood. (This brig is called the *Kugamanu* [*Kaahumanu*], after the king's favourite wife [Plate 2]; he had four formerly and has lately taken another, a young girl). It was a two-masted vessel, commanded by an American but flying his own flag.[1] As is well known, the Chinese charge visiting foreign ships extremely high port dues, even running into thousands of roubles, just for the right to drop anchor in their ports. Whether or not any goods are actually sold is of no concern to the Chinese. When, on this brig's return, Tameamea [Kamehameha I] found out that such a sum had been paid simply for anchorage in a Chinese harbour, he observed that it was very steep. But he decided then and there that if other nations were extracting such sums from his vessels, he must do the same—to a certain point only.[2] All European ships coming into Gonolulu's [Honolulu] outer harbour, he determined, should henceforth pay him sixty *piastres*, and those coming into the inner harbour, where they could anchor more tranquilly, should pay eighty *piastres*.[3]

Golovnin

COMMENTARY

1. *HAA*, 1905:51; *Columbian Centinel*, 6 Dec. 1817; Narrative 11.
2. Ellis, 1826:398.
3. In addition, there was a twelve dollar pilot's fee (Alexander, 1907:14–15; Stewart, *Private Journal*, 1828:124; and Kotzebue, *New Voyage*, II:193).

22.   *26–28 October 1818*

The king's other brother, Gekiri [Hekiri] by name, has command of the naval forces, which consist of two or three brigs purchased from Americans, and a number of schooners and sizeable longboats fitted with decks. All are armed with cannon or falconets. The seamen on these craft are all from among the Sandwich Islanders, and natives also command many of them, the trips being between islands.

These people have great abilities .... They in fact like to work on European vessels, and the Americans always have a few of them aboard and praise them highly as keen, obedient, and steady hands who, moreover, show great attachment to their commanders.[1] In incidents of general mutiny on merchantmen, they have always taken the captain's side. It is for that reason that American shipmasters who suspect their crews of some dangerous plot against themselves take on a few of these Islanders on their way to the Northwest Coast of America. Tameamea [Kamehameha I] willingly releases them, hoping that on their return they may be useful to him, having picked up knowledge on the voyage ....[2]

It is Tameamea's wish to earn the amity and trust of Europeans by all means. With a view to the safety of vessels that call on him, he has appointed a pilot to every roadstead. These pilots have certificates, written out in English over his sign (as he cannot write), attesting to their skill.

Golovnin

COMMENTARY

1. Kahekili Ke'eaumoku was Kamehameha I's distant cousin, but treated as a close relation (Ii, 1963:53). These comments echo those of Lisianskii (1814:128) and Langsdorf (1813, 1:187). See also Narrative 14, n. 3.
2. Turnbull, 1805, 2:70–71. Golovnin had himself seen Hawaiian crewmen and labourers on the Northwest Coast where they had had occasional contact with the Russians since at least 1806 (Bradley, 1942:20, n. 74). In the 1820s and 1830s far fewer Hawaiians remained in Russian North America than in the Oregon Territory (*ibid.*, 227–28).

23.   *28 October 1818*

In addition to its fruit, which provides the natives with pleasant food and drink, the coconut palm furnishes them with ropes for rigging on their craft and for other needs. These ropes are woven from the fibres on the exterior of the coconut shell in such quantity and in such lengths that the natives can sell them to visiting ships. They brought very large numbers of them out to us,[1] and American captains often buy such cordage for use as light tackle. They buy it, not out of necessity, but because they find that it is hardly inferior to hempen rope in strength and may be had far more cheaply.[2]

Golovnin

COMMENTARY

1. No early specimens are on view, however, in the Peter-the-Great Museum, N.N. Miklukho-Maklai Institute of Anthropology & Ethnography, Leningrad. See Likhtenberg, 1960.
2. See Shaler, 1808: 166; and Langsdorf, 1813, 1:187. MAE does hold, in its "pre-1828" collections (Nos. 505, 736, 750, etc.) examples of Hawaiian cordage associated with clothing and fish-hooks, such as edge-cords and fishing-lines (Nos. 736–220, 736–221), which may or may not have been brought to Russia by the *Kamchatka* (Likhtenberg, 1960:168–69, 193–94). Lisianskii, while on the *Neva*, had brought one line, in 1806 (No. 750–6—an item illustrated in *Sobranie kart i risunkov* (St. Petersburg, 1812) that complemented his *Voyage*). Golovnin was mistaken in thinking the *'ahu* cordage admired by New England shipmasters had been made exclusively from coconut-husk fibres or coir. *Olona*, *hau* bark, and other materials were in everyday use (Buck, 1957:290, 296, 310).

24.   *24 November 1821*

Almost right up to the time of our arrival in the Sandwich Islands, the Americans had not engaged in whaling at all in the Pacific Ocean but had usually gone for whales along the coasts of Tierra del Fuego, or off Patagonia and Khili [Chile]. As the whales producing spermaceti had become very scarce in those parts, however, Captain Allen of the *Malo* [*Maria*] and his companions had decided to try their luck in the Pacific off the shores of Japan, where, he had heard, such whales might be found in quantity. This had been in 1820. Allen's first attempt proved a success and he had grown quite wealthy. In the next year, 1821, nine vessels had set off there after his example and had hunted most successfully, especially Allen himself, who had taken as much as 200 tons of pure spermaceti in a total of seventeen months .... Captain Allen believed that the share of the cargo collected by him and his comrades in 1821 would be about 12,000 *piastres*. And besides this profit, the construction of ships and the upkeep of his people had cost him nothing. The hunt of which I here speak is pursued between 30° and 35°N and longitudes 160° and 170°W from Grinvich [Greenwich]; and the whalers have selected the Sandwich Islands as their resting place.[1]

Lazarev

COMMENTARY

1. These data confirm accounts in Starbuck, 1876:95ff; and Bingham, 1847:134. See also Bradley, 1968:80.

25. *21 March 1821*

By 21 March we were so near the shore that we could use the land-breeze which had sprung up to enter the harbour. That harbour is actually formed by a coral reef which is quite submerged at high-tide and stretches in an arc from north to south. (We know that there is only one entrance on the south side.) In view of all this, the captain[1] ordered a flag hoisted on the foretop-gallant-mast for safety's sake, and we fired a gun to request a pilot. Soon we spotted a number of canoes paddling towards us from inside the harbour. In one of them were two Englishmen, sailors called Botl' [Bottle] and Uorn [Warren].[2] Coming on board, the former introduced himself as His Hawaiian Majesty's pilot for Ganaruru [Honolulu] Harbour, and he presented Uorn as his apprentice .... The wind began to fall off, so Botl' decided to bring us in without waiting for a reply from Poki [Boki], especially as a refusal could hardly be expected. We safely passed through the entrance, which is no more than 100 fathoms wide, with the aid of a tow-rope, dropping anchor in nine fathoms of water immediately opposite Kagumanna [Kaahumanu] fort.[3] That fort immediately gave us an eight-gun salute, receiving the same number from us in reply. The *Otkrytie* entered the harbour shortly afterwards. She received the same mark of respect.

Gillesem

COMMENTARY

1. Captain-Lt. Gleb Semenovich Shishmarev (Rear-Admiral, 1829, died 1835), Kotzebue's second-in-command on the *Riurik*, 1815–1818, now commanding the transport *Blagonamerennyi*; described by Chamisso as "a man who spoke Russian only; with a face serenely beaming, like a full moon, agreeable to behold; a man who had not forgotten how to laugh" (Chamisso, ed. Bartels, *Werke*, 1836, III:18; also Mahr, 1932:12). Further on his career and on his voyage of 1819–22, see

Lazarev, 1950:29–30; and Kuznetsova, 1968:237–40. Crossing Mamala Bay from the southeast, Lazarev could see the shore reef stretching north-northwest from Diamond Head towards Honolulu. The "arc, from north to south" refers to the reef comprising the actual entrance into the harbour.

2. Captain John M. Harbottle and William Warren; see Narrative 1, n. 11. According to W.D. Alexander (1904:24), Harbottle had arrived as early as 1794.

3. Approximately opposite modern Nuuanu St. The anchorage was actually in five fathoms of water, as Lazarev says (Lazarev, 1950:253) and as Kotzebue's chart of 1817 indicates (Map A).

26. *21 March 1821*

Kagumanna [Kaahumanu] Fort, so named for the present king's stepmother, is not built right by the harbour entrance but on the low shoreline facing the very centre of that harbour. It now[1] consists of a square redoubt with a low earthen rampart, on which are mounted thirty-two iron field-pieces of various calibres, from 12-pounders right up to a 48-pound monster. All these pieces are on naval gun-carriages. The engineer in charge of the fort was evidently a native, for a worse position could not have been selected for it. The shore on which it stands, and the rampart itself, are so low that cannonballs from the very smallest of warships could easily knock the guns from their carriages, so silencing them.[2]

Ganaruru [Honolulu] Harbour itself, which shares its name with a settlement behind this fort, is not very large; it will accomodate no more than fifty ships. However, it is very safe, for the reef protecting it from the sea swell has left so narrow an opening that the swell simply cannot penetrate, more particuarly as the passage in is situated on the more westerly side of the island and the waves generally roll from the east in the tropics, where the trade winds prevail ....[3] Since coral reefs spread at a gradual rate, the harbour entrance must in time close up completely. Several old men among the natives could tell us that it had once been three times wider than at present.[4]

Gillesem

COMMENTARY

1. Gillesem wrote in the mid 1820s, but on the basis of his 1819–22 journal. Russian accounts reflect the development of the fort, from year to year (Emerson, 1900:11ff).

2. Compare Narratives 8, 13 and 18.

3. Another instance of the unreliability of Gillesem's account compared with, for example, Chamisso's or Golovnin's. Honolulu actually lies east of the centre of Oahu's south coast, and Leahi Point by no means eliminates the ocean swell (or waves) moving westward into Mamala Bay.

4. This seems exceedingly unlikely!

27. Late March 1821

Since the island on which the king resides must provide him and a sizeable court with foodstuffs, that ruler frequently moves from one island to another. For the most part, though, he lives on Gavaie [Hawaii] or Vagu [Oahu].[1] Other islands are, for this same reason, occasionally required to send provisions to the royal place of residence.[2] Another source of royal income, nowadays, is the sale of sandalwood which may either be exchanged for specie or bartered for goods of many sorts.[3] The sandalwood tree grows plentifully on all these Islands, and it belongs to the king. American traders pay him from five to seven *piastres* a *picul*, and sell the timber in Canton for nine to eleven *piastres*. The wood is so dense that a piece one fathom long and only three inches thick weighs a *picul*. The king earns 30,000 or 40,000 *piastres* annually from sandalwood exports. A third source of royal income used to be salt, collected by the seashore in great quantity. The sandalwood is not felled with axes but is sawn down, lest material be lost in the form of chips and splinters. Both that labour and the gathering of salt is still done by the commoners, who work on duty details.[4]

Gillesem

COMMENTARY

1. One half-truth followed by another: Kamehamea II had indeed spent most of his time on either Hawaii or Oahu in 1819–21, but this was for political or religious reasons.
2. But see Ii, 1959:75–76 and Handy, 1953:11–14 on the collection of food taxes during *Makahiki*.
3. See Narrative 127.
4. See Bradley, 1968:70–71 (forced labour), 78 (salt for the Russians).

28. 24 March 1821

On 24 March, we saw a whole squadron of little craft coming into Ganaruru [Honolulu] Harbour, all flying the Sandwich Islands flag. This squadron consisted of two brigs and four schooners, one of which, moving ahead of the rest, was serving as the king's personal yacht.[1] He was aboard her. The king had bought this yacht from some American merchants for 80,000 *piastres*. Though the vessel was indeed finished internally with gilt mirrors and did mount sixteen brass twelve-pounders, she was certainly not worth that huge sum. The king was escorted by his mentor, Karimoku [Kalanimoku], who had been appointed to him by his father, the late king. As soon as he reached shore, the monarch went to pay a visit to his stepmother,[2] who was ill.

Gillesem

COMMENTARY

1. *Cleopatra's Barge.*
2. Kaahumanu. The king is Kamehameha II. Gillesem and others followed him to the queen's two-storeyed house (see Narrative 49). She had lately acquired

it from American merchants and now used it in preference to her older house, Kapapoko (Ii, 1963:66), when in Honolulu. In 1824 Kaahumanu occupied yet another house—also visited by Russians—that stood next to Reverend William Ellis's residence at the corner of King and Punchbowl Sts. (Ii, 1963:143).

TRANSLATOR'S NOTE ON KOTZEBUE'S THIRD VISIT TO HONOLULU

Kotzebue's third visit to Honolulu, with the armed sloop *Predpriiatie* in December 1824, took place more than three years after the *Otkrytie*'s and *Blagonamerennyi*'s departure. Contact between Oahu and the Russian Northwest Coast had been maintained during that period by John and Thomas Meek in the brigs *Pedler* and *Arab* (Khlebnikov, 1976:59–60). Kotzebue was himself older and drier now, and Honolulu settlement had changed dramatically. His record of this 1824 visit, *A New Voyage Around the World ...* (London, 1830) illuminates the nature of that change. Kotzebue was no sentimentalist, but he was glad to recognize old faces here and there in the new, and mission-dominated, town. Two such acquaintances were Alexander Adams and the chief Kalanimoku.

As he had in November 1816 (but not in 1817), Kotzebue had arrived at the Hawaiian group by way of San Francisco Bay, giving his scientists and crew an opportunity to work ashore and to relax in California. For details of his movements west and schedule, the reader is referred to Ivashintsev, 1980:76 and *A New Voyage*, 2:153–55. On the background of the voyage itself, see Chapter 2.

29. *14 December 1824*

As soon as the pilot arrived on board, I recognized him as Alexander Adams, the Englishman who had had command of King Tameamea's [Kamehameha] ship *Kakkumanna* [*Kaahumanu*] at the time of my previous visit in the *Riurik*. He was now the chief pilot here. The wind did not allow us to run into the harbour at once, but it changed in our favour after a few hours and our skilful pilot brought us safely through the intricacies of its narrow entrance. Our ship was the largest ever to have passed through this channel, which would be impassable for first-rate vessels.

Some of the ships that we found in harbour were English or American whalers, which had called in for provisions. Others were on their way to trade on the Northwest Coast of America for peltry or were now returning from that coast with their cargoes. Others again had arrived from Canton and were laden with Chinese goods for which the Sandwich Islands offer a good market.[1] One ship, finally, was French from the port of Bordeaux. She had taken a cargo of ironware to Chile, Peru, and Mexico, and had brought the unsold portion here to Ganaruru [Honolulu]. All the captains visited me, hoping to hear European news, but many of them had left Europe after we had, so they could oblige us by giving us sight of their London newspapers ....

Ganaruru Harbour is almost completely European in its character now, one is surprised to find. Only the somewhat scanty dress of the natives reminds one of the little time that has passed since they first became acquainted with our ways.

Kotzebue

COMMENTARY

1. Details of these vessels in U.S. Dept. of State, Consular Letters, Honolulu vol. 1, J.C. Jones to Clay, 1826, passim; see also *MHSP*, 44:41–42. Judd, 1929 is incomplete where 1824 visits to Honolulu are concerned.

30. *Mid-December 1824*

Our arrival had created quite a sensation on the island. A foreign warship is not a common sight here, and a Russian one even less common. And naturally enough, the attempt of the unbalanced Dr. Shefer [Scheffer] to raise the island of Otuai [Kauai] against Tameamea [Kamehameha I] in 1816, in hopes of annexing it to the Russian empire, had left an apprehension of other such schemes—even though the ridiculous plan had been completely dismissed by the Emperor Alexander.[1] The English too, however, have contributed even in print to the dissemination of the strange idea that Russia was eyeing the independence of the Sandwich Islands, and that Liolio [Liholiho or Kamehameha II] had undertaken his voyage only with a view to imploring England to lend him support against the Russian government.[2] Judging by the protective attitude that England has taken towards these islands for quite some time, it seems likely that she herself is secretly entertaining just such designs against their independence, and is only awaiting a suitable opportunity to put them into effect. The English, though, always profess to recognize the full sovereignty of the native ruler, and the King of England himself, when writing to Tameamea, addresses him as "Your Majesty. ..." [3] But the natives' nervousness about us had been even further increased by a paragraph in a paper from Mexico which had lately arrived and which offered a fresh variant of the English fiction ....

Not once throughout my whole stay at this island, however, did I have the least reason to be displeased with the conduct of my seamen, despite all the temptations to which they were exposed through the evil example of other sailors.[4] Everyone who could be spared from the ship was allowed ashore every Sunday. This routine being common knowledge in Ganaruru [Honolulu], a crowd of Vakhu [Oahu] natives was always waiting to welcome the arrival of our ship's boat.

Kotzebue

COMMENTARY

1. Pierce, 1965:26–29.
2. Apparently a reference to Graham, 1826:72. In fact, the British government was more concerned about American interest in Oahu (Bradley, 1968:94–102). Kotzebue was writing—on the basis of his own and other officers' journals and

the *Predpriiatie*'s own log—after 1827, not in 1824. He was accordingly and rightly more disposed to emphasize the British government's apparent willingness to represent Kamehameha II's visit to Great Britain as connected with a hope for some "support against the Russian government." George Canning was widely known to have observed to George IV immediately after Kamehameha II's death in London that Russia was "known to have Eyes upon those Islands" (text in Hawaiian Historical Commission, *Publications*, I, no. 2, 1925:33); and the matter of "protecting" the Hawaiians against Russian (or American) advances had been publicly discussed by William Ellis (1826:426–27).

3. All this is disingenuous since Kotzebue knew quite well that Great Britian had a claim to the Hawaiian Islands through prior discovery and cession and moreover, in terms of *Realpolitik*, the British recognition of Kamehameha II's and his successor's sovereignty was by no means incompatible with a "protective attitude." The passage had a significance, however, as a modified restatement of Kotzebue's own position on the "independence question" of 1818 (Kotzebue, *Voyage*, I:325–26). It appears to have strengthened the offical Russian view that the Hawaiian Islands *were* indeed a British suzerainty. From this evolved a Russian willingness to take a vaguely pro-American position, where Hawaiian and other Pacific Island issues were concerned (Golder, 1926; R.W. van Alstyne, "Great Britain, the United States, and Hawaiian Independence, 1850–1855," *PHR*, 4 (1935):15–24; and Barratt, 1983: 55–74). Kotzebue thus played his part in the imperial authorities' later perception of a Russo-American entente, especially in the Pacific basin, as a particularly useful lever to be used against Great Britain, there and elsewhere in the world. But, of course, British officials, naval officers, traders, and missionaries were equally ready to cry wolf and to accuse Russia of imperialist designs in Hawaii and even Tahiti (Tyerman & Bennet, 1832, II:216), as well as in New Zealand and Australia (Barratt 1981c, passim).

4. Paulding, 1831:226; C.O. Paullin, *Diplomatic Negotiations of American Naval Officers*, 1912:336 (on drunken and licentious sailors, shore riots, etc.).

31. *17 January 1825*

Given the Sandwich Islanders' partiality for the sea life[1] and the geographical situation of their islands, it seems likely that, in time, they will become a force at sea. Tameamea [Kamahameha I] has left more than a dozen ships to his successor, and all are manned by native crews. These people obtain first-rate nautical training on United States merchantmen plying between America and Canton; and the Americans, who equal the English as seamen, will bear witness to the Islanders' abilities.

Kareimaku [Kalanimoku] arrived at Ganaruru [Honolulu] Harbour's entrance, on 17 January with a regular squadron of two- and three-masted ships and many troops. He had brought a campaign on Kauai to a satisfactory conclusion.[2] The fleet, being unable to enter the harbour because the wind was contrary, was obliged to cast anchor outside. I immediately sent an officer over in my launch to congratulate the king's deputy on his safe arrival. Kareimaku and his new, young wife returned in my launch.

Kotzebue

COMMENTARY

1. Compare Narrative 22. Also Bradley, 1942:33, 227.

2. By seeing Kaikioewa, formerly guardian of Kauikeaouli (Kamehameha III) installed as its temporary Governor, the late King Kaumualii having died in exile on Oahu the previous May. (Bingham, 1847:146–48; Stewart, 1828:97–98; Lydgate, 1916:35–36. On the "campaign" itself, Dibble, 1909:169–73.)

32. 19 January 1825

Kareimaku's [Kalanimoku] arrival proved very useful indeed to us, for we had just made the unpleasant discovery that a large part of the copper with which the ship was bottomed had worked loose.[1] To have repaired this in the ordinary way, it would have been necessary to unload laboriously and keelhaul the vessel; but our noble friend, on hearing of our problems, enabled us to manage the business in an easier way. He sent me three very expert divers who attached new copper plates to the submerged hull. Two of them brought down the hammers to drive in the nails, while the third held the materials. These men, we discovered, could keep working forty-eight seconds at a time, though their eyes were always red and protruding when they did come up, as a result of the effects of enormous strain on the optic nerve of keeping the eyes thus open underwater.[2] We had some skilful divers of our own among the crew members who, although they could not have attempted this piece of work, were at least able to examine what had been done by the natives of Vakku [Oahu]. They reported that it had been done properly.

Kotzebue

COMMENTARY

1. This was a tiresome repetition of the problem with the *Riurik*'s copper-sheathing in December 1816 (Kotzebue, *Voyage*, I:337–38), itself a reflection of the Russian Admiralty yards' infamous graft and the penny-pinching of the post-Napoleonic years (Barratt, 1981a:178; Veselago, 1939:290–91). Kotzebue's new ship had been launched in 1823 and spent less than five months in tropical waters (Ivashintsev, 1980:75–76), but was ravaged by *teredo navalis*, the shipworm that had plagued the *Endeavour* half a century before.

2. This was considered a game (Ii, 1963:63).

33. 31 January 1825

On 31 January 1825 we left Ganaruru [Honolulu] Harbour accompanied, to our pleasure, by our friend Karimaru [Kalanimoku]. With the help of our surgeons,[1] he felt well enough now to venture out that far. He took out with him several large double canoes;[2] and these, as there was no wind, towed us clear of the harbour and, indeed, quite far enough out to sea to obviate any danger from the reefs. Only then did Kareimaku take his leave of us with the warmest expressions of friendship.

Kotzebue

COMMENTARY

1. Heinrich Seewald (Russian: Zival'd, 1797–1830), surgeon of Dorpat, and Johann Eschscholtz (1793–1831), anatomist and professor of the same city (Tumarkin, 1981:317). Also, for data on ships companies, see Ivashintsev, 1980:136ff. Kalanimoku was suffering from *opu'ohao* (dropsy): see Ii, 1963:48.
2. *Wa'a kaulua*; see Narratives 1, 10 and 89.

34. *13–19 September 1825*

Our second visit to Honolulu proved as unpleasant as the first one had been agreeable. Even our best friend, Nomakhanna [Namahana],[1] seemed entirely different and received us with coolness and great reserve. So we took on our provisions and supply of fresh water with all possible speed, and we were glad to be free to leave a country where happiness and gaiety had been driven quite out by one wrong-headed man.[2]

A number of whalers were lying at anchor in the harbour, and one of them was commanded by the Englishman whom we had encountered at San Francisco.[3] Then he had had no luck, but fortune had since been more kind to him and he was now on his way back from the coasts of Japan with a valuable cargo of spermaceti—$25,000 worth of it. He had just called in here to take on provisions for his homeward passage ....

We made sail on 19 September as the first rays of the sun were gilding the romantic hills of Vakku [Oahu], and took our final leave of the Sandwich Islands, heartily wishing them what they so sorely need: another Tameamea [Kamehameha I], not in name merely, but in spirit and action.

Kotzebue

COMMENTARY

1. Lydia Namahana Piia, mother of Kaahumanu *ma*; sketch in Ii, 1963:100.
2. Reverend Hiram Bingham, the New England missionary.
3. See Kotzebue, 1981:231, and Narrative 24.

Further observations for late November 1826 are contained in the narrative of Ferdinand Wrangel, Chapter 11, Narrative 129.

CHAPTER SEVEN

The Monarchy and Social Order

35. *January–March 1809*

 The land and the surrounding sea (for purposes of fishing) are all divided up among native courtiers and grandees and other deserving persons.[1] The king personally has large tracts of cultivated land, and he frequently takes land even from those to whom he has presented it—or else he does so through his minister. Sometimes he will take only part of the land, sometimes all of it.[2] He thus rules through a nobility that obeys him not so much out of true attachment as through fear. The grandees themselves have every right to farm out their lands, and a tax-farmer or tenant then works them. The farmer may himself give up some of his profits to another man, and so live at ease. Land taxes, which are paid to the king as well as to the grandees, take the form of swine, dogs, fish, *maro* [*malo*], *pau* [*pa'u*], and *kappa* [*kapa*], that is, capes or cloaks made from bark material and used by men and women alike in times of cold or rain. In truth, the position of the common farmer on the Island is a wretched one and very hard, for the king will sometimes, regardless of all the circumstances, take as much as two-thirds of all the taro and sweet potatoes he has grown. Natives now deliberately cultivate both these crops on various little plots, with a view to the king's taking produce from one or two of them but not all. There are many who have never had the chance to eat their own meat, or even sample it, despite their possessing a sufficient number of pigs and dogs.[3] And in addition to these oppressive and heavy taxes, by which his subjects are already too burdened, the present king has now placed another load on their shoulders: he often assembles cultivators even from remote corners of the Island, some to work his own lands, others to help in building seagoing craft, barns, and other structures. Not only does the king pay them nothing for their labour; he even declines to feed them. Much evil springs from such unskilled government and such extreme burdens. One result has been insufficiencies in the food supply, and hunger has killed many people even in recent times. Formerly, there were as many as 150,000 people on Ovaigii [Hawaii] Island alone, but today there are barely 100,000 on all the Sandwich Islands together.[4] Settlements of the poor are situated right by the seashore, where the common people can at least nourish themselves on fish as well as taro.[5]

Gagemeister

COMMENTARY

1. Several scholars have concerned themselves over the past half-century with the political significance of Gagemeister's visit to Oahu of 1809 (Golder, 1930:40–41; Mehnert, 1939:20; Pierce, 1965:3–4; Tumarkin, 1964:137–38). Specifically, attention has been focused on the question of whether Gagemeister had indeed been ordered—as his Scottish passenger Archibald Campbell later claimed (Campbell, 1816:117)—to make a settlement or Russian outpost on the Islands. Certainly,

Gagemeister did discuss the ways and means by which a settlement or colony could be established there. Part of one relevant letter, to the Russian-American Company directors dated 1 May 1809, appears as Document No. 1 in Pierce, 1965:37–39. What has commonly been overlooked in Soviet and Western scholarship is the fact that, as an officer seconded to that Company, Gagemeister was especially concerned with trade potential and the natural resources of the Islands. In his reports of 1809–10 to the directors in St. Petersburg, more space and emphasis is given to resources and/or economic matters than to strategic or political concerns (reports now in Perm District State Archive, *fond* 445 K.T. Khlebnikova, op. 1, *delo* 58). Gagemeister's three-month sojourn in the Islands gave him time to study the feudal land ownership system, here summarized. (For bibliography, see Bradley, 1942:4–5.) Perhaps because *haole* residents at Honolulu regarded the temporary absence of American vessels there as "a sign of conflict between the Republic and the English" (Pierce, 1965:39 citing Gagemeister), the Russian visitors did not receive the full assistance of all settlers (Ii, 1963:79). That probability makes the correctness of Gagemeister's data on Oahu more commendable.
2. The reference is to *keole* (land divisions set aside for the king): see Malo, 1903:258. The Russians would have seen the "large tract of cultivated land" owned personally by Kamehameha I which lay near Nuuanu, close to Honolulu Village: see Ii, 1963:69 (the royal farms called *keoneula*).
3. All essentially correct: see Malo, 1903:191, 199, and 272; Dibble, 1909:72–76.
4. Discussion in Kuykendall, 1938: 336.
5. The Russians saw *maka'ainana* along the coast (Malo, 1903:88).

36.   *27 November 1816*

As soon as we had cast anchor, I went ashore to pay my respects to Governor Kareimoku [Kalanimoku]. Even though Manuja [Manuia] had landed before us, announcing both our amicable intentions and the king's instructions, the appearance of a Russian warship produced general and great unease among the natives and induced them to take up arms. The Englishman Iung [Young] met me right where my boat stopped, even as the armed Islanders were yelling in a most dreadful way. (One of the most trusted of the king's confidential servants, Iung has already spent more than twenty years on these Islands and had now been sent to Vagu [Oahu] to build a fort. The circumstances of his life are known from Vancouver's *Voyage*.)[1] When I hesitated to step out of my launch, Iung told me I had nothing to fear and he himself helped me ashore. Escorted by a large troop of soldiers, who shielded us from the importunity of the populace, we went into Iung's neat and attractive house, where Kareimoku and the principal nobility shortly afterwards also appeared.

Kareimoku and his suite were dressed in the local fashion, in a variety of broad white cloaks made of stuff woven from tree bark and thrown over the right shoulder, after the Roman manner [Plate 10].[2] Besides this, they had a cartridge-box and a brace of pistols tied round their naked bodies. They had come straight from the fort where, in case of an attack, all defensive preparations had already been made. The Roman attire was becoming on Kareimoku with his Herculean figure and stately appearance. His face bespoke intelligence; and as he is indeed a sensible man, the English living here had given him the name Pitt. He greeted me in the European manner, shaking my hand. Once he had invited me to be seated, and when he and his suite were also sitting down, my very first business was to persuade him that the mistrustful attitude taken toward us should be abandoned. Iung explained to him the aim of our voyage. His dark expression only then lightened a little, and he instructed Iung to say the following to me: "The gods are our witnesses that we never caused Russians any harm."[3] I assured the chief that all Sheffer's [Scheffer] actions here (and he particularly complained about that person) had been done in opposition to the will of our emperor; and, at the same time, I tried to reassure him about the future, for he still remained apprehensive on that score. Our conversation ended with his promising me that he would fulfil Tameamea's [Kamehameha I] orders, which were sacred to him, and said that the following morning at 4 a.m. I might fire a gun as a signal to the boats instructed to tow me into harbour. Upon this, we parted amicably.

Kotzebue

COMMENTARY

1. See Vancouver, 1798, 2:136ff.
2. Actually, they were worn over the left shoulder as drawn by Choris (Plate 10, "Habitans des îles Sandwich") and described by Buck (1957:210), or else simply wrapped around both shoulders (see Plate 5). Choris illustrates both the plain white *kihei*, referred to by Kotzebue and made of several basic *kapa* strips (*punana*), and the *kihei* embellished by stamped designs. The left-hand figure of Plate 5 sports an impressed chevron and triangular bands of classical form (Buck, 1957:195ff).
3. The 1821 German edition continues: "And yet they have rendered us evil for good." Such minor, yet significant, omissions and additions account, to a large degree, for the difference between the 1821 Weimar and St. Petersburg editions.

37. *27 November 1816*

After many vain yet dangerous attempts to dispose of his goods in South America, Mr. Vil'koks [Wilcox][1] had sailed to Botanibei [Botany Bay] in order to recuperate from extreme exhaustion after so long a voyage, and to take on provisions. There, at Port Dzhakson [Jackson], the Governor had handed him a letter from the King of England to Tameamea [Kamehameha I] and various gifts also intended for the latter, including some rich, full-dress uniforms embroidered in gold.[2] Mr. Vil'koks further informed me that there was being built at Port Dzhakson, on instructions from the English government, a fine ship for Tameamea.[3] From all this, it may be concluded that, having taken the Sandvichevye [Sandwich] Islands under her special protection, England perhaps already considers them secretly her own—and will certainly lose no suitable opportunity to possess herself completely of them. It was now Mr. Vil'koks' intention to sail to the shores of California and try his fortune there. Before we parted company, he informed me of a chain of islands discovered by the ship *Amerika* [*America*] of the United States, commanded by Captain Andrei Valter [Andrew Walter] in the course of a voyage from the Markizskie [Marquesas] Islands to Canton. According to him, this chain consists of low coral islands, overgrown with thick woods, and about thirty miles in circumference. The captain had found a convenient anchorage on the west side and had landed in order to leave a few goats ashore. The latitude of this island was fixed by observations as 3°48′N; longitude as reckoned by chronometers is 159°15′W of Grenvich [Greenwich].[4]

At daybreak on 28 November a gun was fired, and shortly afterwards the royal pilot, Mr. Gebottel [Harbottle] appeared, accompanied by eight double canoes, each manned by sixteen to twenty paddlers. In each craft came the owner, here called *geri* [jerry] by the English, to see that order was maintained during the towing. Old Iung [Young] sat in a little skiff and supervised the whole operation. The high spirits aboard these craft was most entertaining; people joked and laughed, and even the work itself seemed done as if in play, the adult Sandvichane [Sandwich Islanders] appearing to us like sportive children.

Kotzebue

COMMENTARY

1. James Smith Wilcox, Philadelphia merchant in the China trade since 1789, brother of Benjamin C. Wilcox, U.S. Consul in Canton (1812–22): see Narrative 3.
2. See Pierce, 1965:190–91. The Governor of New South Wales was Lachlan Macquarie.
3. The *Prince Regent*, finally delivered to Liholiho in 1822.
4. This was Fanning Island, a large and thickly wooded broken atoll in 3°51′N, 159°12′W, which had been discovered by Edmund Fanning when taking the *Betsey* northwest from the Marquesas Islands in 1798 (Sharp, 1960:182). The island was "discovered" again by Captains Mezick of the *Sidney* (R.G. Ward, ed., *American Activities in the Central Pacific, 1790–1870*, Ridgewood, NJ., 1967, II:324–25) and Andrew Walter of the *America*. Like Golovnin and Vasil'ev, Kotzebue was at pains to pick up geographical data from American shipmasters at Honolulu (see Narrative 11). Data thus acquired were assessed and sometimes used. See Kruzenshtern's classic *Atlas Iuzhnogo moria* (*Atlas of the South Sea*), St. Petersburg, 1823–26.

38. Late November 1816

The drawing that Choris had earlier made of Tameiameia [Kamehameha I], which bore a great likeness to him indeed, produced quite extraordinary pleasure [Plate 1].[1] Everyone recognized him, and was happy. But the artist had put a woman of the middle class next to the king on the page in his drawing-book [Plate 12]; and Mr. Jung [Young], who saw the sketch first, had doubts about this juxtaposition. He advised our friend to separate the two portraits, or not to show them at all. The drawing was duly cut down the centre before the drawing of the king was shown to the natives. Choris distributed several copies of his successful portrait, and when we arrived at Manila a year later, we noticed that American merchants had got hold of one and had it copied by Chinese painters for trade purposes. Choris purchased one sample of this Chinese export.[2]

Chamisso

COMMENTARY

1. Plate 1 is a portrait based on the 1816 sketch. On Louis Choris, artist in the *Riurik*, see Chapter 13 and Charlot, 1958. On the sitting, see Kotzebue, *Voyage*, I:314–315.

2. Choris played an important role in the Europeans' fast developing familiarity with the Hawaiian people in the 1820s (see Chapter 13). Choris discusses the lithography and publication of Hawaiian watercolours, *inter alia*, in a series of letters to I.F. Kruzenshtern in 1821–1822 (TsGIAE: *fond* 1414, op. 3, *delo* 42: reel 118 in the Shur collection microfilm at Elmer E. Rasmusen Library, University of Alaska at Fairbanks). Choris purchased his American-Chinese copy of his portrait of Kamehameha I at the close of 1817, probably from an American merchantman then anchored at Cavite (see Kotzebue, *Voyage*, II:260).

39. *8 December 1816*

The islanders have a very high opinion of writing skills, and a letter seems to them an exceedingly important thing.[1] Bekli [Beckley] gave me the following illustration of this. While still on the island of Ovaigi [Hawaii], he had written a letter to a friend on Vagu [Oahu] and handed it to a *kanaka* (peasant) who was going there. The latter joyfully promised to undertake the mission but in fact, kept the letter, and preserved it as a precious article. A few months later a European ship arrived, and the *kanaka* hurried out to her with his treasure, offering it for sale to the captain—for a pretty high price. Fortunately, the captain was an old friend of Bekli, and recognizing the handwriting, he bought the letter, which by that means came again into the hands of the original writer.

They[2] had prepared sleeping places for us on extremely clean matting, but the friskiness of the rats, which jumped across our faces, robbed us of sleep. And after a night so unpleasantly passed in vigil, we had the further dissatisfaction of learning that it would be impossible to find a craft for us, so we would be obliged to return without seeing the Pearl River. The mouth of this river, where there are several islands, is so deep that the very largest ships of the line could lie at anchor only a few *sazhen* [fathoms] from the shore; and so broad that 100 ships could easily stand in it simultaneously. The entrance into Pearl River is the same as that into Gana-rura [Honolulu] Harbour,[3] but the windings between the reefs render the passage even more difficult. If it were a European possession, then of course means would be found to make this harbour one of the finest in the world. In the so-called Pearl River itself, there are extremely large sharks, and there have been several instances of their swallowing bathers. The natives have built on its banks an artificial pond of

coral stones in which they keep one large shark to which, so I was told, they
sometimes throw adults or more commonly children, as victims.

On my way back, I was amazed to see almost decayed swine hanging from
various trees. I learned that herdsmen did this in order to prove to their
masters that the livestock had died naturally, not been killed and eaten by
themselves.[4] Towards evening, we returned safely to the *Riurik*.

Kotzebue

COMMENTARY

1. *Palapala* was already associated with *haole* power; and this was reinforced by the
   New England missionaries in 1820–25, so that Liholiho and most *ali'i* studied
   writing (Bradley, 1942:135; Narratives 123 and 126).
2. The commoners at Waiau near Pearl River, among whom Kotzebue spent the
   evening and night of 8 December 1816 (see Narrative 76).
3. A surprising error.
4. The Russians were favourably impressed by the obedience that Hawaiian commoners habitually showed to their chiefs. See Malo, 1903:84 and 258 (hogs with
   mutilated ears on *koele*); and Dibble, 1909:72–76.

40. *9 December 1816*

9th December. Today Kareimoku [Kalanimoku] invited me, through Manuia,
to come and watch a spear-throwing exercise.[1] Iung [Young] was greatly surprised that the Governor should have agreed to yield to my request in this
respect, regarded it as a mark of particular goodwill on his part, and thought
that I owed it entirely to my rank as commander of the first warship to have entered Gana-rura [Honolulu] harbour. I had occasion, subsequently, to observe
quite often that Sandwich Islanders make a great distinction between naval
and merchant vessels.[2] With the latter, they are fairly bold in their behaviour,
having seen through the European traders' strenuous efforts to deceive them
in every way and, in consequence, having lost all respect for them.

Kareimoku had excellent grounds for declining to grant me the spectacle
of the spear-throwing exercise which I had requested; for since the time when
Tameamea [Kamehameha I] had taken possession of Vagu [Oahu] Island, the
spirit of rebellion prevailed amongst its natives. They seize any good opportunity, indeed, to attempt a revolt. Only noble individuals may participate in
this exercise, which usually ends with unpleasant consequences—inevitably,
there are killed and wounded. When Tameamea himself had visited Vagu two
years previously, and organized just such a warlike exercise, he had had soldiers at hand with loaded muskets; and these had pretty soon been obliged
to put an end to the rising fury of the warriors. From all this, it will be evident that Kareimoku was right when he agreed to grant me the spectacle only
having secured my promise to support him with my ship's company.

After lunch, we set off for the shore and found, at the assembly point, more
than sixty nobles ready for the spectacle of combat. Their spears, however,
which were made from sugar-cane ends, were fairly harmless [Plate 6].[3] They

divided into two parties, the combat began, and even though Kareimoku—who took part in the amusement himself—did not permit it to get to the point of a real and decisive struggle, it was found at the end that there were several seriously wounded men.[4]

Kotzebue

COMMENTARY

1. *Lono-maka-ihe*, much practised during the *makahiki* months of November and December: see Narratives 77 and 85; and Ii, 1963:66 (the usual site for practice).

2. Kotzebue was struck by this more than once (Narrative 44).

3. These were *kaua kio* spears, light, with blunted ends, specially made for the occasion (Buck, 1957:417).

4. As was usual each year (Malo, 1903:93).

41. *Early December 1816*

Tameiameia [Kamehameha I] has amassed very great riches by making full use of the position of his kingdom and the sandalwood tree that grows in it.[1] He buys weapons and ships for ready money and is building small vessels for himself which, when he does not choose to find copper enough for sheathing, are dragged on shore ... But after the death of this old hero, the state which he created and has maintained by force will fall to pieces; for already its partition has been settled on and even prepared for.

Kareimoku [Kalanimoku], also called Naia (Bill Pitt by the English), a scion of the royal line of the island of Mouwi [Maui], was still a child when that island was conquered by Tameiameia. The latter spared him, treated him kindly, and educated him. He granted him the power of life and death over others; and always, he found Kareimoku loyal to him. This Kareimoku, Governor of O-Wahu [Oahu] Island and commandant of Hana-ruru [Honolulu] fort on that island, which is the most important of the islands because of its harbour, has nonetheless armed himself with the intention of seizing it [Plate 3]. He is purchasing weapons and ships on his own account. Teimotu,[2] descended from the warriors of O-Waihi [Hawaii] and brother of Queen Kahumanu [Kaahumanu], is bound to him by close friendship and harmony of ideas, and is to have the island of Maui as his portion. The king of Kauai Island is to retain his hereditary kingdom. As for Tameiameia's natural heir, the weak and soulless Liholiho (the Prince of Wales of the English), grandson of the last king of O-Waihi and a son of Tameiameia and the majestic Queen Kahumanu, before whom his father alone may appear bareheaded, he will be given only the hereditary island of Hawaii as his domain. Although indeed some of the most powerful chiefs and most noble vassals are among the Europeans, yet not one of those Europeans can have the least pretension to sovereignty over the native inhabitants.

Chamisso

COMMENTARY

1. See Narratives 14, 27, and 127.
2. See Narrative 71 and Plate 3. This passage appears to be a libel against Kalanimoku, who was certainly loyal to Kamehameha in 1816.

42. *October 1817*

The relations of social order, which are founded not on any written laws or rights but rather on faith and customs, and which are stronger than any authority, may be understood and interpreted in various ways. Mr. Marini [Marin] supposes there to be four castes within the Hawaiian people: those *de sangue Real*, or princes; those *de hidalguia*, or nobility; those *de genta media*, or of middling condition (constituting the greater part of the population); and those *de baxa plebe*, that is, the rabble, a small and despised group. In former days, every white man was considered the equal of the nobles; now, his position depends upon his personal qualities.

The word *hieri, ieri, erih, ariki,* or *hariki,* meaning chief, head, or commander, may best of all, perhaps, be translated as master. The king is *ieri ei moku,* or master of the island or islands. Each powerful prince is *ieri nui,* or great master; and Tameiameia [Kamehameha I], Kareimoku [Kalanimoku], Haulhana (Mr. Jung [Young]), and others are called so, without distinction.

All the land belongs to the master of an island, and nobles possess the ground only in the form of fiefs. These fiefs, though hereditary indeed, are inalienable from the crown and, should a line become extinct, they revert to the king ...

Peasants and workers move from place to place as they wish. Every man is free; he may be killed, but he may not be sold or forcibly detained. Nobles who do not have lands are in the service of the more powerful lords. The master of an island has many such retainers, and the men who paddle for him are drawn exclusively from that caste. The castes are so separated one from another that, as is natural, it is impossible to pass from one to another. Nobility that can be given and removed is, after all, no nobility. The wife does not share the husband's rank. The condition of children is determined by certain very precise laws, principally on the basis of the mother's own rank but also on that of the father.[1]

Chamisso

COMMENTARY

1. Golovnin made enquiries into these same questions, in 1818 (Narrative 105). In general, he and Chamisso give correct information. See Malo, 1903:79–83; Ellis, 1826:394–98.

This passage exemplifies Chamisso's ability to maximize the usefulness of local informants by putting questions to them on the basis of his own previous knowledge. As he interviewed John Young and Marin in Honolulu, so he spent productive hours with Kadu and Don Luis de Torres at Guam and in the Micronesian Islands: see Kotzebue, *Voyage*, III:76–139. Unfortunately, Heinz Kelm's 1951 dissertation on Chamisso's large contribution to the general ethnography of Polynesia ("Adelbert von Chamisso als Ethnograph der Südsee": Bonn, 1951), has not been published. We therefore await fuller studies of the subject than those offered in René Riegel's *Adelbert von Chamisso, sa vie et son œuvre* (Paris, 1934) or Julius Schapler's venerable *Chamissostudien* (Arnsberg, 1909).

43. *1 October 1817*

Kareimoku [Kalanimoku] next informed me, with great pleasure, that the king and natives of Atui [Kauai] had expelled Dr. Sheffer [Scheffer] from that island and that, not long before, he had arrived on Vagu [Oahu] with his whole company—consisting of a hundred Aleuts and a few Russians—aboard the *Kadiak*, now sitting on a shoal. The ship had been in such a sorry condition that her crew had been obliged, on the passage from Atui to Vagu, to pump out water ceaselessly to stop her from foundering, and had been forced to run her aground on entering the harbour.[1] Kareimoku told me that he had received the unhappy Aleuts and Russians kindly, since he did not wish to return evil for evil. Even Sheffer himself had not been prevented from taking passage in a vessel of the United States which was bound for Canton, only a few days before our own arrival.[2]

Kareimoku had hardly finished his account before Tarakanov, a Russian-American Company agent,[3] came aboard together with a number of that Company's officers. In accordance with Baranov's orders, Tarakanov had been placed completely at Sheffer's disposal. He now expressed his personal disapproval of developments on Atui Island—through which they had all had their lives placed in jeopardy—and said he considered it a miracle that in their retreat from Atui only three Aleuts had been shot. Tamari [Kaumualii] had considered them his true enemies and could easily have killed many more.[4] He also mentioned his dangerous voyage hither and the fact that, since they were naturally unable to obtain provisions unless they paid for them, they now found themselves in a truly wretched situation. Luckily, I had stowed aboard such a quantity of fish while at Unalashka [Unalaska] Island that I could supply these unhappy men with enough to last a month. Tarakanov, who struck me as a sensible fellow, had already concluded an arrangement with Mr. Gebet [Ebbets], the owner of two vessels lying at Gana-ruru [Honolulu]. By the terms of that contract, Gebet bound himself to clothe and feed the Aleuts for one whole year on condition that he take them across to Kaliforniia [California] where they should busy themselves in hunting sea-otters on the nearby islands. Gebet was then to convey the Aleuts to Sitka and hand over to the Company one half of the skins obtained.[5]

Kotzebue

COMMENTARY

1. These events had occurred four months earlier, in June 1817: see Narrative 30 and Pierce, 1965:22. Scheffer had arrived on Oahu with more than forty Aleuts.

2. The *Panther* (Captain Isaiah Lewis) had left Oahu on 7 July (Pierce: 23 and Howay, 1973:115–16).

3. Timofei Tarakanov, an able and literate *promyshlennik* in the Russian-American Company's employ, who had arrived in the Hawaiian Islands on the *Il'mena* (ex-*Lydia*) on 12 May 1816 and then taken orders from Scheffer, mostly on Kauai, for fourteen very difficult months (Pierce, 1965: passim).

4. Pierce, 1965:94.

5. John Ebbets had had close dealings with Baranov at Sitka since 1802, when he had ransomed prisoners from Tlingit Indians and brought them up to Kodiak. In 1810 he had carried Company-owned furs to Canton on commission (Khlebnikov, 1976:4 and 11). On Russo-American exploitation of the sea-otters along the Upper California coasts, and Hawaii's role in it, see Bradley, 1939; Ogden, 1941; and Wheeler, 1971. The "nearby islands" were not the Farallons off the Golden Gate of San Francisco Bay, chiefly exploited by the Russians for their fur seals (Khlebnikov, 1976:122–23), but the Santa Barbara (or Channel) Islands. New England shipmasters like Ebbets were familiar with them by 1817–20, as Russian-American Company servants were not. Ebbets duly took the Aleuts seen by Kotzebue to those islands (December 1817), and from there to northern Chile, then delivered them (and the precious peltry) to Baranov back at Sitka.

44. *14 October 1817*

Kareimoku [Kalanimoku] brought us watermelons and fish from his artificial pond,[1] and was generally far more attentive to us than he was to the captains of merchantmen. In his relations with the latter, he maintained a certain pride. On parting, I presented him with a portrait of Tameamea [Kamehameha] which, it seemed, gave him great delight.[2] He left us, having cordially pressed my hand, once more commending us to the protection of his gods. To the young Kareimoku, who had been constantly with us, we entrusted gifts for the king. I made him a gift of one of my embroidered uniforms. When he had put it on, he could not express his joy loudly enough.

Kotzebue

COMMENTARY

1. A kilometer northwest of Honolulu Harbour: see Map B. and Narrative 74; Alexander, 1907:13–15.

2. Choris had drawn Kamehameha on 24 November 1816: see Plate 1. Details of the sitting in Kotzebue, *Voyage*, I:314–15. Kotzebue was like other Russian officers of the same period in basically approving of the Hawaiian monarchical and feudal social systems. Not only was he conscious of the "certain pride" with which Kalanimoku treated Yankee shipmasters who had no pretensions to warrior status (see Narrative 40); he himself differentiated between Hawaiians. John Young presented him with a problem in that regard, because although now an *ali'i nui*, he was once a low-born sailor. (Young is sometimes referred to in the Russian texts as "G. Iung," that is, "Mr. Young," at other times merely by surname, the polite *gospodin* being omitted.)

45. *26–28 October 1818*

Tameamea [Kamehameha I] is already very old: he claims to be seventy-nine years old [Plate 16]. It is probable that his precise age is unknown even to him; but his appearance indicates that there cannot be a great disparity between his estimate and the reality. However, he is alert, strong, and active. Temperate and sober, he never takes strong spirits and he eats very moderately.[1] In him one sees a marvelous mixture of childish conduct and the most mature judgement and action, which would not disgrace even a European monarch ....

The readying of the defences of his kingdom also greatly preoccupies Tameamea.[2] I have already referred to the number of firearms delivered to him by Europeans. It is necessary to add that these include mortars and howitzers. The former, though, can hardly be put to use for want of men who know how to handle them. Cannon, on the other hand, they load very quickly and well ...

Although these troops are trained by Europeans, Tameamea does not give the latter command of them. His army is commanded by his chiefs, the first of them, that is, the commander-in-chief, being a brother of the king's first wife. His name is Karua [Kalua].[3] This Karua, who is still young, though extremely tall and stout, is a man of great gifts. He came out to visit me on the sloop and I was very surprised by the freedom with which he could express himself in English. I even thought at first that he had been in America.

Golovnin

COMMENTARY

1. Campbell, 1816:215 confirms this; but see Turnbull, 1805, 2:65–66 on earlier royal orgies fuelled by rum.
2. See Narravites 52 and 127.
3. Plate 17 depicts a strikingly tall chief (centre, rear view), who may be identified tentatively as "Karua" (Kekuanaoa?).

46. *27–28 October 1818*

The civil administration of the Sandwich Islands is, as yet, hardly organized at all; for almost nothing has been introduced to the native laws from Europe save taxes which, in certain respects, resemble ours. They were instituted by Tameamea [Kamehameha I] on the advice of his Europeans[1] without, however, destroying the earlier financial system which operates as follows. As soon as the king has need of foodstuffs or anything else, it is proclaimed that some or all districts must deliver what is required, just as the master of a house might order his servants to bring him this or deliver it to someone else. Such decrees are still carried out with great exactness and without any complaining.[2] But, as I say, a permanent tax has also been introduced, on the European model. Landowners, for instance, are now obliged to pay an annual tax depending on the number of workers they may hire ... And each canoe must pay one *piastre*

for the right to fish by the shore during the fishing periods which occur in
various seasons of the year.

Whenever Tameamea issues an order to one of his "governors," he does so
through a chief of lower rank, who invariably delivers the order orally. But
at the same time, Eliot [Elliot][3] issues a written order to the same effect, and
the king affixes his sign, which never changes, to it. The recipient of an order
examines the sign and compares what the envoy has already said with what
the royal secretary is telling him, and if they agree, puts the order into effect.
Should they differ, he sends for a repetition of the order. The royal order that
ten hogs and a boatload of greenstuffs should be delivered to me on Voagu
[Oahu] was issued in this manner, and personally brought both the messenger
and the order aboard my sloop [Plate 23].[4]

Golovnin

COMMENTARY

1. Campbell, 1816:212; Patterson, 1817:70; Roquefeuil, 1823, 2:341–42, on Kamehameha's growing wealth after 1804.
2. See Narrative 27.
3. John Elliot de Castro, English-speaking Portuguese physician to Kamehameha in
   1812, royal adviser after 1817. On his Russian and Californian connections, see
   Pierce, 1965:233. On the estates of "governors" and "landowners" (*kuakua*) on
   kula land—see Malo, 1903:258 and 271.
4. Golovnin, 1964:373.

47. *27–28 October 1818*

From the feathers of a small red bird, described in such detail in various
Voyages, the chiefs make their ceremonial capes or mantles which, even now
and after the introduction of European clothing, have not been abandoned and
are still used on all ceremonial occasions. Boki, the Governor of Voagu [Oahu]
Island, who is one of the highest chiefs of noble rank in the royal service,
being the brother of Tameamea's [Kamehameha I] prime minister, and Gekiri
[Hekiri], the commander of the naval forces and brother to the first queen,
visited me dressed in such cloaks [Plate 17]! I wanted to purchase one of them
and offered for it a good English hunting gun in a case with all the fittings and
a large telescope, but they told me that all such garments belong to the king
and that without his permission they cannot be disposed of. And when on
Ovaigi [Hawaii] Island I tried to acquire a similar garment through Eliot, he
also told me that no one but the king may sell them—and that Tameamea will
not accept less than 800 *piastres* for one now, since the captains of American
vessels will buy them from him at that price. *They* are not losing on the deal,
however, since they pay in kind and so most likely give the king 50 *piastres* in
cash, not 800; and these articles are purchased for sale to collectors of rarities.
I had no wish, I concede, to pay 4,000 roubles for an object fit only for display
before the curious.

Golovnin

COMMENTARY

1. The *Kamchatka*'s artist, Mikhail Tikhanov, drew Boki in traditional *ahuula* and *mahiole*: see Plate 18. The little bird is the *i'iwi* (*Vestiaria coccinea*): see Narrative 90. Hekiri was Ka-Hekili Ke'eaumoku, known to the English as "Mr. Cox."

2. Golovnin develops this theme: see Narrative 90 and Golovnin, 1964: 396. His comments underline the fact that American shipmasters were exporting many Hawaiian feather cloaks for profit by 1816–18. Many such cloaks, e.g. the "Starbuck," remain in the Peabody Museum, the British Museum, and other institutions of world renown. MAE in Leningrad has five feather cloaks of major interest from the standpoint of ethnohistory and of technique: see Likhtenberg, 1960:198–99, Plates VIII and IX. Besides four garments associated with, and almost certainly acquired on Cook's third expedition (Nos. 505–18, 505–19, 505–12, 505–17), MAE boasts the "Baranov cloak" presented to the Russian-American Company's Chief Manager by Kamehameha I in 1807 and forwarded to the Academy of Sciences' *Kunstkammer* in 1810 by the Chairman of the Board, Mikhail M. Buldakov. The "Baranov cloak" and a wide-crested helmet (*mahiole*) associated with it form a tiny collection of their own (No. 517) at MAE, and are on permanent public display on a mannequin in the Peter-the-Great Museum in Leningrad. The Leningrad cloaks have been studied thoroughly by Adrienne Kaeppler, 1978.

48. *March 1821*

Seeing the advantages enjoyed by the Europeans the king showed them much kindness, with a view to increasing the level of education of his own people; but he gave them no real power ...[1]

As for Marini [Marin], he has many daughters and gives them out to skippers for cash, while himself living in a stingy manner, always on the sharp look-out for a profit ... By all his actions, he shows himself to be a man of low qualities.[2]

Vasil'ev

COMMENTARY

1. This was true to the extent that all lands reverted to the Crown, on the death or departure of a *haole* "landowner;" and Vasil'ev had rightly been as impressed by this Hawaiian policy as Chamisso had been five years earlier (see Narrative 41). Even so, Young, Davis, and Holmes, among other Europeans and New Englanders, obviously did enjoy "real power" in Hawaii under the royal aegis.

2. Mathison (1825:427), Paulding (1831:227), and other *haole* visitors to Honolulu criticized Marin's extreme frugality; but Vasil'ev's is perhaps the most extreme criticism of all. See Narratives 54, 58, 102, and 108 on Marin's kindness and willingness to share his expertise, at least to a point; also Narrative 121, on Vasil'ev's own biases.

49. *24 March 1821*

We were taken to the upper floor [of the residence of Queen Kaahumanu]. Great was our surprise when we cast our eyes over bare walls and a large empty room.[1] The floor was spread with mats, however, and the sick queen was lying on them in the middle of this chamber. Old women were tending her in local fashion, that is, were pressing their knees down onto her stomach with all their might. Not only they but also a dozen other old women, meanwhile, wailed and cried in soul-rending voices; and these cries were answered, in the same way, by a huge crowd of natives gathered below.

As the king entered this room, his stepmother raised her head and began to weep. This was a fresh signal for general lamentation, in which the king and his retinue joined. This went on for perhaps half an hour. The king then drove everyone from the chamber and knelt down by his stepmother who, having spoken to him for awhile, asked us for a surgeon. Dr. Kovalëv, surgeon of the *Otkrytie*, was with us and immediately set to work. He cured the queen of her ailment in a few days.[2] The queen, a woman of fifty or so, was a real giantess ... The king then went off to his own hut, inviting us along.

Reaching it, his first business was to remove all his clothing—a white flannel jacket, shirt, shoes, and a round straw hat—and to put on instead his *maro* [*malo*].[3] He then lay down on mats and invited us to do the same. The king began to question us, through his interpreter, the Frenchman Rives,[4] about Russia. He expressed the desire, incidentally, to call on the Emperor Alexander. He asked us about our American colonies,[5] which were known to him through the expedition of the adventurer Sheffer [Scheffer] ... and, lastly, about own our objectives, which he could not understand at all. What could it signify to our Emperor, he asked, if there were land or water in the farthest North?

Gillesem

COMMENTARY

1. See Narrative 28, on Kaahumanu's several houses and fondness for moving.
2. The Russians encountered traditional Hawaiian medical treatment on more than one occasion (Kotzebue, *Voyage*, I:342). The "soul-rending" wails were probably of religious significance (Malo, 1903:145), as a form of invocation of the god of medicine. Kaahumanu's illness, passed over so briskly by Gillesem, had political significance. In the first place, it improved relations between the Russians and the American missionaries who saw that the queen's illness and potential cure would incline her to view the new mission's work more kindly. In the second, it sealed Kaahumanu's good opinion of Russian naval officers at large. Bingham himself, as his account of the Russian surgeons' visits makes plain (1847:148), was afraid that the "paroxysms" shaking Kaahumanu might kill her and was impressed by Kovalëv's skill in December 1821, when he dealt with another royal attack. Gillesem comments on another April session:

We were quite ready to sail, on 3 April, when the king suddenly sent and asked that our surgeons be sent. His favourite wife had been taken very ill ... so we sent our two surgeons ashore. They ascertained that the symptoms were indeed dangerous, and so our departure was postponed. She remained in danger till the 7th, then improved; and we made haste to quit that beautiful island ... (Gillesem, 1849:224–25).

The royal sufferer this time was Kamamalu. Her recovery gave relief and pleasure to Liholiho. The Russians' cure of Kaahumanu however, had more meaning for the missionaries, towards whom the queen had formerly been rather cool. Bingham reverts to Kovalëv's and Zaozerskii's role in influencing Queen Kaahumanu (and so enhancing the mission's spiritual and temporal power), in his narrative (1847:150).

3. For treatment of royal adoption and adaptation of European dress, see Tumarkin, 1964:91–92.

4. Jean Rives (Ioane Luwahine), secretary and companion to Liholiho and, on the king's death in England in 1824, sponsor of a group of French missionaries and artisans on Oahu (Blue, 1933:85–89; Annales, 8:5–6; Yzendoorn, 1927:28–31; Ii, 1963:86–87, 143).

5. Along the Northwest Coast (modern Alaska).

50. 25 March 1821

The next day, His Hawaiian Majesty honoured us with a visit, appearing in an English admiral's uniform, a straw hat, and shoes on bare feet. He was accompanied by Kareimoku [Kalanimoku], Governor Poki [Boki], who also wore English naval dress, and his favourite wife, called Kamegamega.[1] The latter wore a white satin dress, though her head was adorned in the Hawaiian style and her feet were unshod. The Spaniard Marini [Marin] was acting as interpreter on this day. The whole party went into our cabin and sat at table with us, eating our dishes with a keen appetite, without however neglecting their own beloved taro which they had brought out with them. They drank little wine, much preferring rum, with the result that, on leaving table, they were nearly all drunk ....[2]

We called on the king the next day. A table set in the European manner in one of his large huts was gleaming with silver and crystal. The dinner was of the English sort. Besides us, there were present some missionaries, resident Europeans, and three American shipmasters. The Frenchman Rives was master of ceremonies,[3] and the meal itself was prepared by the cook from one of the American vessels.

Gillesem

COMMENTARY

1. Queen Kamamalu. See Narratives 25, 85, and 129 on Boki.

2. See Narratives 67 and 69 also, on the heavy drinking of queens and female chiefs; and 83, 88, and 113 on the results.

3. See Narrative 49, n. 4. Both Gillesem (1849:224) and Vasil'ev (1821:44) regarded Rives as little better than a thieving adventurer whose hand was in the royal coffer. Their view was fully shared by Freycinet and his wife, who referred to

Rives as an impudent *fripon*: see Blue, 1930:59–60; and Tumarkin, 1964:35. The Russian narratives underline the favoured position enjoyed by Rives, or Ioane Luwahine, in Liholiho's court in this period. Ii (1963:86) explains how the French beachcomber in 1810 had become a companion of the young chief Liholiho and, together with the Manuia whom Kotzebue had met and liked, spent time in a little school at Honolulu.

51. *29 March 1821*

On 29 March, the completely recovered Queen Kagumanna [Kaahumanu] came out to visit us again,[1] bringing twenty hogs and a good quantity of greens and fruit to each sloop, as gifts. She wore a black velvet dress, but her entire retinue of eight ladies wore no other clothing than the *pau* [*pa'u*], a sort of skirt wrapped around the body several times and made of native stuff dyed bright yellow, green or crimson.[2] At the back, their hair was plaited in two tresses, but at the front it was cut short and smeared with lime, over the brow [Plate 12].[3]

Gillesem

COMMENTARY

1. Eight months later, she was in good enough health to marry the deposed king of Kauai, Kaumualii; but, like Queen Namahana, she was again to be tended by visiting Russian doctors. See also Narrative 49.
2. Compare Narrative 93. See Buck, 1957:186–89 on natural dyes.
3. This was observed by Cook's people (Cook, 1784, 3:134), and depicted by Choris: see Plate 12. Webber recorded long hair "plaited in tresses" which was actually false hair (Buck, 1957:562).

   Kaahumanu appears repeatedly in Russian texts of 1816–21, which reflect the development of her tastes in clothing and housing, and her attitude towards the *haole* in general. Choris depicts her wearing a voluminous *pa'u* of the sort she still favoured in 1823 (Sinclair, 1976:18), when not experimenting with velvet [Plate 2].

52. *26 March 1821*

The armed forces of the king consisted at this time [1821] of several thousand troops stationed on all the Islands. These troops were in red English uniforms minus the lower part or the headgear. Muskets were kept in a fort built on a hill behind Ganaruro [Honolulu] village,[1] and numbered 40,000.[2] Also stored in this fort were a number of fieldpieces with proper caissons and all appurtenances. The royal fleet now consisted of nine brigs and four schooners, besides the yacht.[3] These craft were commanded by Englishmen,[4] but the crews were all native and the captains could not say enough in praise of the agility and sharpness of their men. The voyages of these Hawaiian craft now extend beyond the Islands: they have been at Canton[5] and next year the king means to dispatch a brig loaded with salt to Kamchatka, in order to get there some dried salt-fish.[6] Hawaiians are very fond of this but do not know how to prepare it.

Gillesem

COMMENTARY

1. Not Fort Kaahumanu, but the Puu-o-waina arsenal.
2. Compare Arago, 1822, 2:135–36.
3. The *Cleopatra's Barge*; see Narratives 31, 127, and 129.
4. Incorrect: the *Ha'aheo o Hawaii*, brig, had a Hawaiian captain: see Golovnin, 1822, 1:340–41; and Ellis, 1826:465.
5. The *Columbian Centinel*, 6 December 1817; (Ellis, 1826:398).
6. Salt from Aliapaakai or the Moanalua saline lake was by far the most important article in Hawaiian exports to the Russian settlements until the 1830s. Very large amounts were easily obtained from Moanalua Lake: Ellis (1827:28) speaks of 400–600 "barrels of fine, clear, hard, crystallized salt" annually. Of the Russians' use for it, Ellis says: "Quantities of it have been sent for sale to Kamtschatka, and used in curing seal skins at the different islands to which the natives have sent their vessels for that purpose, or sold in the islands to Russian vessels ..." Natural salt from Oahu was indeed distributed on the Aleutian Islands, for use there when Aleut hunters delivered sea-otter or seal skins; but the Aleuts were hardly sending "their vessels" to such centralized curing points. As always, they had only their skin-on-frame *baidarki* (kayaks).

53. *26 March 1821*

As for the royal income, it is not yet fixed but depends upon circumstances, there being no regular collections of taxes.[1] When the king needs funds, he orders a new hut to be built for him and has the former residence destroyed. On moving into this new hut, he has large earthenware pots placed by the entrance, with sentries by them. Couriers are then dispatched to all places on the island to spread the news. Every male subject more than ten years of age must cast one Spanish *piastre* into the pot.[2]

Gillesem

COMMENTARY

1. See Narratives 27 and 46.
2. See Bradley, 1968:58–59 on royal wealth in specie. Earthenware pots were certainly *not* traditionally used in Hawaii, for this or any other purpose, since suitable clay was missing and the Hawaiians had no knowledge of pottery. Gillesem was probably told of a recent modification of old tax-gathering procedure.

54. *15 December 1824*

On the morning after our arrival, I went ashore with some of my officers

to pay my respects to Queen Nomakhanna [Namahana]. On the quay, we
were met by the Spaniard Marini [Marin], who, in his capacity as interpreter,
conducted us to Her Majesty. On the way, I came across many of those whose
acquaintance I had made on my earlier visit here. They greated me with a
friendly *Aroa* [*Aloha*].

The residence of Nomakhanna was situated by the shore, not far from
the fort. It was a delightful little two-storeyed house with a balcony, built
of planks in the European manner.[1] It had been embellished with paint and
had large and attractive windows. By the steps of this house, I was met by
Khinau [Kinau], Governor of Vakhu [Oahu].[2] He appeared before us in the
most complete *déshabille*, wearing only an unbuttoned waistcoat of red cloth,
which was by no means suited to so huge a figure, and heavy boots such as are
generally worn by our fishermen. These cramped his movements considerably.
The Governor extended his hand to me in a most kindly manner, with
repeated *Aroa*, then led me up to the second floor, where everything had a
very tidy and elegant appearance.

All the way up the staircase and right to the door leading into the queen's
room, there were children, adults, and even old people, of both sexes. Under the direction of Nomakhanna herself, they were diligently practising their
reading from a spelling-book and trying out their writing on slates. Phi-
lanthropy of such a kind does the queen honour. The Governor also held a
spelling-book in one hand,[3] and on it lay an elegant bone pointer. Some of
the old men evidently came not so much for learning's sake as in order to give
a good example.[4] They held their books upside down, but even so they gave
the impression of being engrossed in their reading.

Kotzebue

COMMENTARY

1. This was one of two frame houses sent to Honolulu by the merchant company,
   Marshall & Wildes, in July 1821 and purchased by Liholiho: see Harvard University Library, Marshall MSS: Jones to Marshall & Wildes, Oahu, 5 October 1821.
   See also Narratives 110 and 129. The house stood near the corner of King and
   Punchbowl Streets.
2. Kahoanoku Kinau, son of Kamehameha I and father of Kekauonohi, *not* Kin-
   auwahine: see Ii, 1963:37, 49–50, and 89.
3. This was "the easy reading lessons of Webster's spelling book," selected by Mrs. Bingham the previous year: see Holman, 1931:30; and Bingham, 1847:104.
4. See Westervelt, 1912:18ff.; Mathison, 1825:428–29; Thurston, 1921:66; also Narratives 127 and 144 on Queen Namahana and Narrative 63 on Kinau.

55.   *15 December 1824*

The room was furnished in the European manner, with chairs, tables, and
mirrors. In a corner stood a huge bed embellished with silk curtains;[1] and the
floor was covered with beautiful fine mats.[2] On one such mat, in the middle
of the room, lay Nomakhanna [Namahana]. She lay on her stomach, stretched

out fully. Turning her head toward the door, she raised herself with her arms on a silk cushion.[3] Two young girls in light clothing sat cross-legged on either side of the queen and drove off the flies with large bunches of feathers attached to long, stick-like handles.[4]

Nomakhanna was not more than forty years old. She stood six feet two inches tall and was more than two *arshin* in girth.[5] She wore a blue silk dress of slightly old-fashioned European cut. Her hair, black as tar, was plaited and laid round the top of her head, which was as round as a ball ... When the queen recognized me, she laid to one side a book of psalms that she had been reading before my arrival. Changing her position from a horizontal to a sitting one with the aid of several servants, she extended her hand to me ... Her memory was better than mine, for she immediately recognized me as a Russian officer who had visited the late king Tameamea [Kamehameha I] on Ovai [Hawaii] Island. I had, in fact, been presented to the queens then.[6] Nomakhanna had grown so round since that time, however, that I had failed to recognize her. The queen remembered how highly I esteemed her late husband; and for that reason my appearance provoked in her memories of the departed ruler. As she spoke of Tameamea's death, tears sprang from her eyes. "The people lost a father and protector in him," she said. "What will become of these islands now, only the Christian God knows."

Kotzebue

COMMENTARY

1. A major Chinese import to Honolulu by 1820.
2. Choris depicts one such large, chief's mat, apparently *moena makaloa*, in Plate 14 ("Interior of a Chief's House"). See Buck, 1957:130–35, for details of technique.
3. Likewise an import, replacing the plaited pandanus pillow (*uluna*) also drawn by Choris.
4. These were *kahili*, emblems of royalty; but the girls wielding them, whom Malo calls *haa-kue* (1903:86), were not Namahana's *kahili*-bearers (*ibid*.:107).
5. More than 56 inches (142 cm.).
6. On 28 September 1817: see Kotzebue, 1821, 2:191–92. See Bradley, 1942:135–41 on the printing of Hawaiian books and their use in 1822–24.

56. *15 December 1824*

"What would Tameamea [Kamehameha I] say, if he saw the changes that have taken place here!" exclaimed Nomakhanna [Namahana] with a profound sigh. "We no longer have gods or temples—all has been destroyed. In Tameamea's time, everything was far better. No, we shall never again have such a king." And again tears welled up in her eyes.

Baring her right arm, she showed me, tattooed on it in Latin letters but in the Hawaiian language, the inscription: "Our good King Tameamea died on 8 May 1819." This sign of mourning, which we saw on numerous natives, cannot be taken off as we remove a piece of crape.[1] The Sandwich Islanders, mourning their beloved monarch, will carry it to their death, which of itself bears witness to the depth of their esteem for his memory. The more convincingly to demonstrate the depth of that grief, they also knocked out a front tooth on the day of Tameamea's death.[2] It is for that reason that all the Sandwich Islanders speak with a whistle. There are even those whose words of mourning were tattooed on the tongue. Khinau [Kinau] obliged me to recognize this; sticking his tongue out, he showed me the aforementioned inscription.[3] It is marvelous that that painful operation, which would normally result in a very serious swelling, had no harmful consequences.

Kotzebue

COMMENTARY

1. As in European mourning.
2. See Narrative 97; also Narratives 75 and 78 on death rites.
3. Compare Narrative 54 (queenly mourning). Ellis (1839:181) saw Liholiho's widow, Queen Kamamalu, having a black mourning line tattooed on her tongue.

Merely watching caused him pain. The Namahana with whom Kotzebue had several encounters was Lydia Namahana, also known as Piia, daughter of Keeaumoku and sister of Kaahumanu (see Ii, 1963:53 and 141). She should not be confused with her mother, also Namahana, daughter of Haalou (*ibid.*:141). Namahana Piia was baptized in Honolulu on 4 December 1825 and remained under Bingham's powerful influence when Wrangel and the *Krotkii* arrived there in 1826.

57. *15-20 December 1824*

Having mastered the art of writing, the queen has grown passionately fond of it.[1] She greatly valued the fact that she had acquired the possibility of conversing not only with persons close by, but also with those at a distance.[2] Nomakhanna [Namahana] promised to write me a letter in order, as she said, that I might show everyone in Russia that she was familiar with that mystery ....

I shortly afterwards had occasion to grow quite convinced that Nomakhanna was the possessor of a gigantic appetite. I frequently visited the queen, usually in the morning, and always found her occupied with the same task. Fully extended on the floor, she was writing me her letter. It was evidently causing her much trouble. Once however I chanced to call on her at her dinner time. When I entered her dining-room, the queen was lying on her stomach on a fine mat opposite a large looking-glass. Ranged in a semicircle right by the royal mouth, there were many dishes of various sorts, all in closed porcelain tureens. Solicitous servants pushed now one, now another dish up to her, and Her Majesty, making energetic use of her hands, swallowed everything with a truly wolfish appetite ... Later, with the aid of her servants, she was turned over onto her back. By hand signals, she summoned a tall and powerful servitor. The latter, well knowing his duty, instantly leapt onto the queen's belly and began unceremoniously to pummel it with knees and fists, precisely as if he were kneading dough.[3] During this very severe working over, the aim of which was to facilitate digestion, Her Majesty groaned a little ... Nomakhanna generally finds people too lean and advises them to move about less, the better to gain in size. Varied indeed are our ideas about beauty. Here, a female figure a fathom tall and of immense girth is considered fascinating.

Kotzebue

COMMENTARY

1. *Missionary Herald*, 19 (April 1823):100–01; Mathison, 1825:422–23; Thurston, 1921:66–67.
2. As Kuakini had conversed with Bingham on 8 February 1822, the day written communication in Hawaiian had begun: *Missionary Herald*, 19 (June 1823):183.
3. The Russians had seen Queen Kaahumanu similarly treated in 1821: see Narrative 49. Further on Namahana, see Narratives 54, 56, 112, and 123; popular sketch in Richard Tregaskis, *The Warrior King: Hawaii's Kamehameha the Great* (NY, 1973):289. Namahana was known as Piia ("child mountain") because of her size.

58. *17 January 1825*

Kareimaku [Kalanimoku] appeared to be very glad to see me again. After embracing me sincerely, he introduced me to his young and pretty wife.[1] Next, having asked me to show him my ship,[2] he examined it with the greatest attention, always expressing pleasure on seeing some object that was new to him. Finally, he exclaimed: "How great is the difference between this ship and ours. And how I would like to see ours in such fine condition: O Tameamea [Kamehameha I], why did you die so early?"

Sitting in my cabin, Kareimaku spoke much more about the death of his friend, the late king. Marini [Marin] declined to translate his words, declaring that it was impossible to convey in another tongue such deep meaning and such strength of feelings ... Kareimaku touched also on the change of religion that had taken place here. "Our present faith," he said, "is better than the old one; but the common people living in the hills will take some time to understand that. It will be necessary to take strong measures in order to restrain them from a revolt. The king should not have destroyed all the old sacred things so suddenly; as a result, he was obliged to set off to foreign parts,[3] for he no longer felt safe in his own country. God alone knows how it will all end. I personally fear a bad outcome. The people love me and do much for my sake, but I am very ill. The state, which I have with difficulty held back from ruin, may fall apart after my death. Then blood will flow again and every man will strive to seize as much as possible for himself. Even now, while I still live, a revolt has erupted on Otuai [Kauai] Island."

These fears of Kareimaku would appear to be well grounded, for they are shared by Islanders and foreigners alike. Many *ieri* consider that the partition of the country after Kareimaku's death is, indeed, inevitable; and certain chiefs have already indicated the districts that they intend to seize, not even concealing their objectives. Even so, the aging and sick Kareimoku is still maintaining order in the country,[4] for everybody knows that not one rebel would go unpunished.

Kotzebue

COMMENTARY

1. See Narrative 31.

2. The *Predpriiatie* (*Enterprise*).

3. This reported speech is of interest in several respects, but must regrettably be considered through the prism of Marin's translation; and even Kotzebue suspected that Marin was not as competent an interpreter as he pretended. Kalanimoku was certainly correct to fear civil disturbances, if not civil war, in the near future, and at the time of the *Predpriiatie*'s visit suspected Boki Kamauleule of sedition (Ii, 1963:145; Bradley, 1942:183–84). He was aware of the depth of his illness (*'opu'ohao*, or dropsy, with complications), and disturbed by the aftermath of Keeaumoku's appointment as Governor of Kauai. Kotzebue himself knew about the latter (see Narrative 31). But did Kalanimoku truly believe that Liholiho had gone to England because "he no longer felt safe in his own country?" If so, he was mistaken (Sinclair, 1976:51–53; Dibble, 1909:165–67): the king was motivated less by fear than by natural restlessness. Kalanimoku, who had himself advised strongly against the royal visit to England that had ended fatally, was indulging in a little revisionism.

59. *17 January 1825*

During my previous visit here the artist Choris, who was then accompanying me and was subsequently murdered in Mexico,[1] had drawn a successful portrait of Tameamea [Kamehameha I]. I now presented the venerable Kareimaku [Kalanimoku] with an engraving made from that portrait. The old man's joy was truly affecting. He examined the engraving with indescribable delight, covering it with kisses. Large tears rolled down his cheeks. Taking leave of me, Kareimaku asked me to send him a surgeon and complained that he did not feel well.[2] Pressing my hand, he said: "I too am a Christian, and I can read and write." It is highly significant that the hero and statesman should have alluded precisely to those accomplishments of his, remaining silent about others. The Sandwich Islanders regard Christianity and literacy as ties connecting them with the civilized nations.[3]

Kotzebue

COMMENTARY

1. On Choris, see Chapter 13.

2. His health deteriorated after 1825 and he died early in February 1827.

3. Here and elsewhere, the Russian texts emphasize the great importance of Kalanimoku, Co-regent of the Hawaiian Islands, as "the uniform friend of the missionaries" (Bradley, 1942:145) and supporter of both literacy and Christianity. It is equally plain, however, that Kotzebue (and Vasil'ev) liked Kalanimoku's restrained and dignified *style* of government—a style reflected in his lack of enthusiasm for public demonstrations of loyalty to Hiram Bingham and "the Christian God."

60. *17–18 January 1825*

For a whole day, great excitement reigned in Ganaruro [Honolulu]; and all conversation revolved around the fact of Kalanimoku's return. The natives discussed his heroic deeds and spoke of the rebel, Tomari's [Kaumualii] son, who had been taken captive and brought to Ganaruro. The latter was called Prince Dzhordzh [George].[1] I managed to see him and talk to him several times. He was a young man of about twenty-five, of none too pleasant appearance. He dressed entirely in the European manner. Although this "prince" had been educated in the United States of America,[2] he seemed no more knowledgeable than a common seaman. On the other hand, he was said to have mastered many vices. Kareimoku [Kalanimoku] maintained a constant watch over Dzhordzh, and had appointed two *ieri* to follow his every step. In addition, the prisoner had been warned that he would be strangled at the first attempt to flee.[3]

Kotzebue

COMMENTARY

1. George Kaumualii. On the bloodless revolution of 1824 on Kauai, see Stewart, 1828:97ff.; Bingham, 1847:146–48; and Lydgate, 1916:34–36.
2. Returning to the Islands with the American missionaries in 1820: *Missionary Herald*, 17 (June 1821):169–70; Bingham, 1847:97–98; Christison, 1924:652–55.
3. Such a death disgraced the *ali'i*.

61. *21? January 1825*

Everything that Nomakhanna [Namahana][1] saw on board our ship gained her approval, but my cabin pleased her most of all. Seating herself on a sofa there, she immediately broke it. A portrait of the Emperor Alexander drew her particular attention. Placing herself before it on the floor, in order to cause no further damage, the queen scrutinized the portrait with much interest, then said: "Maitai ieri nui Rukkini!" ("The great sovereign of the Russians is very handsome!") Nomakhanna assured me that she was excellently informed about life in Russia: she had been told much about Petersburg, and especially about the tsar himself, by the Sandwich Islander Lauri, who had made a voyage there in 1819 with Captain Golovnin on the Russian ship *Kamchatka*,[2] and had later returned to his native land. The queen further assured me that she herself would gladly have visited Russia, had she not feared the frosts there, which, according to Lauri, were truly frightful.

From Lauri she had learned that the people in that country wrapped themselves up in furs from head to foot but were still subject to the risk of losing an ear or nose. He had also related that the frost there transforms water into glass, on which people travel in large chests drawn by horses, since the glass does not shatter. In Lauri's words, houses in Russia are as high as hills and amazingly spacious; he had wandered about in one for three days without coming to the end of it. From this, it is evident that Lauri exaggerated a little, but Nomakhanna had believed his tales implicitly.

Kotzebue

COMMENTARY

1. On Namahana Piia, see also Narratives 112 and 123.
2. See Appendix A., and Narrative 19.

62. 27–28 January 1825

Having finished her business on Otuai [Kauai], Kakhumanna [Kaahumanu] returned to Ganaruro [Honolulu] with a handsome thirteen-year-old boy, a brother of the late king.[1] I paid her a visit and was most kindly received. Kakhumanna is quite tall and stout, but she is not as enormously wide as Nomakhanna [Namahana], and is considerably older than her. Her face shows traces of her former beauty. Kakhumanna is always dressed entirely in the European style and has adopted our customs with far more success than has the other queen.[2] Her half-stone, half-wooden house is a more spacious one than Nomakhanna's, but no more luxuriously appointed. It also has two storeys and a balcony. Near her residence stands the house of the missionary, Binkhem [Bingham]. On Kakhumanna's arm, as on Nomakhanna's, is tattooed the date of Kamehameha I's death.[3] The queens have no other tattoos and, in general, one sees signs of the existence of that custom very rarely now—only on elderly people.[4] Kakhumanna honoured me with visits to our ship a number of times.

Kotzebue

COMMENTARY

1. Kauikeaouli (Kamehameha III).
2. She was actually baptized and admitted to communion that same year, 1825: see Bradley, 1968:144–45: also Narrative 51, n. 3, on clothing.
3. See Narrative 56, (Namahana's tattoos); also Narratives 49 and 75 (traditional mourning); and Narrative 79 and Plate 14 (tattooing).
4. Details of the decline of this practice in Emory, 1946:235ff.

63. Mid-September 1825

In the short time of our absence, some extremely important changes had taken place here. My readers will know, perhaps, that the king and queen of the Sandwich Islands, having paused at Rio de Janeiro on their way, had safely reached London and there been received with the greatest of attention by the English government; but that both had shortly afterwards died there, expressing the wish to be buried in their native land ...[1] A few days after the arrival of Lord Byron, on 11 May 1825,[2] both coffins had been brought ashore with great ceremony, while an artillery salute roared out from the English frigate *Blonde* and from the fort ... Immediately behind the coffins walked the heir to the throne, the thirteen-year-old brother of the late king, dressed in a European uniform ...[3] Later, the whole procession went to a small stone chapel, and there the two coffins were interred. Soon afterwards, Kareimoku [Kalanimoku] proclaimed the heir Tameamea [Kamehameha] III as king of the Sandwich Islands.[4] Until he reached his majority, the country was to be governed, as previously, by Kareimoku and Queen Kakhumanna [Kaahumanu].[5]

Thus, the regents remained the same as before.[6] In reality, however, Kareimoku has almost lost the very possibility of engaging in State affairs, such is the poor condition of his health; and the ambitious Kakhumanna has fallen entirely under the influence of the missionary, Bingkhem [Bingham]. By acting through her, that cleric has gained such vast power over the people that, within seven months, the Vakhu [Oahu] Islanders have become unrecognizable.[7]

Kotzebue

COMMENTARY

1. Full details in Graham, 1826:103–61; Bloxam, 1925:23–49.
2. An error: HMS *Blonde* reached Honolulu on 6 May.
3. Kauikeaouli, who was actually eleven, not thirteen.
4. It was his prerogative to do so, as co-regent since Liholiho's departure for England in November 1823.
5. Bingham, 1847:203; Dibble, 1909:168.
6. Bradley, 1968:143, n. 99.
7. See Narratives 125, 126, and 129.

64. *14 September 1825*

Wishing to give pleasure to the Islanders, Lord Bairon [Byron] had brought from England all kinds of games: dolls, a shadow theatre, etc. When he gave orders for the appropriate preparations to be made ashore, however, Bingkhem [Bingham] came to hear of the intended spectacle and forbad the public performance. According to him, it ill became God-fearing Christians to find pleasure in such worldly things ...[1]

That a people so naturally gay and cheerful should bear without even a murmur, the bigotry laid upon them, shows how generally accustomed these good-natured people have become to executing any desire of their rulers with obedience. For this very reason, a wise government might so easily have introduced true civilization here. One feels like crying, with Kareimaku [Kalanimoku], "Tameamea [Kamehameha I], you died too soon!"[2]

Kotzebue

COMMENTARY

1. See also Narrative 127 for the results of this attitude. Kotzebue's comments here prefigure those published in 1828 by Reverend Charles S. Stewart, whom the Russians met and liked (Kotzebue, *A New Voyage*, II:256), and whose deep antipathy towards Bingham's pleasure-banning brand of Calvinism was (publicly) shared by *haole* merchants also met by Kotzebue. Stewart may have discussed with the Russians Byron's stay at Honolulu (see Stewart, 1828:277–83), about which he had quite similar views.

2. Kotzebue's public criticisms of New England missionary enterprise in Hawaii and British missionary work on Tahiti provoked equally public and heated rebuttals in 1830–32. (For Reverend Daniel Tyerman's and George Bennet's responses to his uncomplimentary remarks about their proselytizing at Matavai Bay in April 1824, see Tyerman & Bennet, 1832, II:216–17: "either misunderstood or misrepresented what he saw ...," etc.) Most European naval visitors to Oahu shared Kotzebue's distaste for Bingham's thoroughness where prohibition of ancient Hawaiian practices was concerned (Beechey, 1831, II:101–03; Duhaut-Cilly, 1834–35, II:290ff). The criticisms levelled against Bingham and his colleagues by officers of Byron's HMS *Blonde*, however, (which Kotzebue merely amplified), had already produced a published defence of the New Englanders by 1827: see *An Examination of Charges against the American Missionaries at the Sandwich Islands, as Alleged in the Voyage of the Ship "Blonde"* ... (Cambridge, Mass., 1827). The continuation of that defence, in *North American Review*, XXVI (January 1828):59–111, adumbrated the very charges that Kotzebue was to level two years later.

65. *Mid-September 1825*

The queen has been urged to such tyranny by Bingkhem [Bingham] who most likely already considers himself absolute ruler of all these islands. He has, however, miscalculated his own strength. If the bow-string is drawn too tightly, the bow will surely snap. I predict to Bingkhem that one fine day his star will fall and he will instantly lose his authority. Even now, there are many malcontents.

The summoning of natives from the countryside[1] to Ganaruro [Honolulu] has led to a sharp increase in food prices; and those prices will continue to rise, both because of the increase in the number of consumers and because the studying and incessant praying are hindering agricultural work. So material deprivations are being added to the spiritual yoke. This will drive the natives to free themselves yet more quickly from their heavy chains. I myself heard numerous *ieri* [*ali'i*] express their dissatisfaction.[2] As for the farmers, who regard Bingkhem's religion as the source of all their trials,[3] they once burned a church by night. The fire was soon extinguished and so caused no damage; but the guilty parties were not found.

Kotzebue

COMMENTARY

1. In the late summer of 1825; see Bradley, 1968:144, 146.
2. See Bloxom, letter of 6 September 1825, in *HAA*: 1924:73 (Kaahumanu's word as law).
3. See Narratives 64 and 127 (religious oppression).

Kotzebue was right in predicting that the virtual abandonment of agriculture on Oahu would lead to food shortages and exorbitant price levels. Duhaut-Cilly saw the predictions realized (1835, II:283–84). And there were indeed many who studied and prayed reluctantly and superficially (see Bradley, 1942:148–50), "expressing their dissatisfaction" to sympathetic foreigners when it seemed safe to do so. It is obvious, however, that Kotzebue had developed a *parti pris* against Bingham by January 1825, that it was now being strengthened, and that he heeded the missionary's opponents on Oahu. From this bias sprang an evident predisposition to idealize pre-contact Polynesian and, especially, Hawaiian life and culture.

For additional observations on the monarchy and social order in 1821, see the narrative of Aleksei Lazarev, Chapter 11, Narrative 127. For later 1826, see the narrative of Ferdinand Wrangel, Chapter 11, Narrative 129.

CHAPTER EIGHT

The Traditional Ways

No Russian officer, scientist, or passenger aboard a Russian ship at Honolulu in the period in question had been *trained* as an ethnologist. The discipline did not exist as such in European universities. No officer or scientist at Honolulu, on the other hand, failed to do as Cook had been enjoined to do, that is, "observe the Genius and Temper, Disposition and Number of the Natives" he encountered (Beaglehole, 1955, I:cclxxxiii). As professional observers and recorders of phenomena that were at times unrecognized by them, the naval officers regarded it, moreover, as an obvious and usual part of their duty to record at least the visible components of the material and social cultures of Hawaii. Not for them, by 1810–20, the Rousseauesque romantic fascination with the islands of *La Nouvelle Cythère*, South Sea havens of the Noble Savage. Gagemeister, Golovnin, Vasil'ev and Kotzebue might be strikingly dissimilar in temperament and style, but in *this* they agreed: it was their duty to leave factually accurate and comprehensive records of their stays at Honolulu and, if time permitted, also of traditional (and new) Hawaiian ways.

But what of Chamisso, a poet, an admirer of Johann Gottfried Herder, and a man who *was* disposed to view Hawaiians as more "natural" (in every sense) than Europeans? Did his deeply sympathetic interest in *ka Moolelo Hawaii*, to borrow the title of David Malo's classic book (Honolulu, 1903), so cloud his picture of traditional Hawaiian ways as to invalidate them? On the contrary, it was his sympathy with those much threatened ways that reinforced his resolution, as a genuine *savant*, to paint them soberly and fully while he could. As Chamisso poignantly expressed it,

> Should we not call out to these missionaries who are so pious, that thirst for knowledge ... is divine, and it is not a sin for men to wish to glance back at their history, in which God has revealed himself in progress ... (*Werke*, 1856, 2:364)

66. *January–March 1809*

The Islanders' main foods are taro root and sweet potato or *uvara* ['*uala*]. Taro is cultivated in pools dug six feet deep. The earth excavated from the centre is placed round the edges to form slopes up to the sides of these pools. Fresh water is introduced by way of narrow ditches, when they are quite ready; and when the bottom is flooded, the natives stamp on it with their feet to soften it further and so render it the more suitable for planting. Well-established grassy stems cut from a taro root are then planted out in the pool at a distance of one foot from each other. The taro ripens in six months unless prevented from doing so by a prolonged drought. For the complete ripening of the root, the plant above should stand in two feet or more of water.[1] Sweet potatoes are similarly cultivated by means of the transplant. They are placed in the earth itself, at a shallow depth. Around the ponds in which taro is growing, the natives also grow bananas, burying the young cut stems up to half their height in the ground. There are quantities of wild bananas growing in the hills, as indeed of indigenous taro also; and the latter is very good, though taro is certainly better and firmer when cultivated in the aforementioned pools. In other parts of the island, there are many coconut palms and breadfruit trees. Rope is made from the former, albeit in small quantities. The king, who has possessed himself of all coconut palms here, gives the Islanders one kernel apiece (sic) with which to make this rope.[2]

Breadfruit, or apples, are kept in pits for two months when not quite ripe. After that time, they are ready for use. Quite an amount of sugarcane is also cultivated, although it serves mainly as pig-feed. Moreover plenty of sugarcane grows wild in the hills ... where one also finds a wild root called *ti* [*ki*]. The natives distill a good deal of rum from it.[3] *Ti* leaves are used here instead of plates and to wrap up fish or meat when being cooked. The dry *ti* root may weigh up to ten pounds. When cooked, it has a treacly odour but becomes quite pleasant if it is left awhile. The king has several casks of it which have stood for years and are hardly inferior to good Brazilian rum—if they do not excel it. However, the price is high ....

A fair amount of tobacco grows wild, too, and some is planted. Our sailors bought some at ten pounds a *piastre*. It was not fumed but the leaf was quite large and thick. *Curcuma* or Indian saffron, with its yellow root, well-known to medicine and commerce, does grow, but these natives cultivate little, having no great need of it.[4] They use it only to dye their *maro-pau* [*malo* and *pa'u*] a bright yellow. The *maro* is a belt or sash worn by men, the *pau* is worn by women and reaches to the knee.

Gagemeister

COMMENTARY

1. An excellent description of traditional taro cultivation: see Malo, 1903:270; and Buck, 1957:10.
2. *Aha niu*. See Malo, 1903:108.
3. This was not traditional but had been demonstrated by William Stevenson, an ex-convict from Botany Bay; see Campbell, 1816:146–47; and Alexander, 1891:157.
4. On *'olena* dyeing, see Buck, 1957:186–87 and Narratives 51 and 93.

67. *30 November 1816*

Because my cabin was small for so numerous a group, I ordered a table to be prepared on the quarterdeck;[1] but it was in vain that our cooks made their most assiduous efforts to give the Sandvichan [Sandwich Islanders] a good impression of a Russian feast: they ate nothing. I did not know, unhappily, that pork must be consecrated in a temple before it may be eaten; and for the same reason not only the pork but also all the other dishes were *tabu* [*kapu*], inasmuch as they had all been prepared over the same fire.[2] And so my guests, sitting in their droll attires, remained unfed observers of a European dinner until, finally, at my insistent request, they were willing to sample cheese, biscuits, and fruit. Wine and vodka, it seemed were not *tabu*, for they frequently emptied their glasses. It must be regretted that these Islanders are passionately fond of strong spirits; Europeans have not neglected to spread the poison even here, at the same time setting them a sorry example.[3] The natives drink a whole bottle of rum at one go, quite easily, and it is incredible how much of it they can carry.[4] The ladies, who could eat nothing because their husbands were present, stuck to the wine the more diligently for that very reason.[5]

Kareimoku [Kalanimoku] did not neglect to drink to the health of our sovereign, the Emperor, and to Tameamea [Kamehameha I] also. The ship and her internal arrangements pleased everyone and Kareimoku in particular. He examined everything with great attention. An excellent portrait of my father[6] hanging in the cabin produced a state of confusion in all my guests, for they mistook it for a living being and could only convinced themselves that it was not by touching it. Mr. Choris showed them the portrait of Tameamea, which they immediately recognized and which gave them great delight. When it became known on the island that we had Tameamea on paper, we were daily visited by a crowd of people who wanted to see him.[7] At four o'clock my guests left the ship, very pleased with their reception—the more so because I had attempted to make amends for the failure of the dinner by giving them various presents.

With sunset today, a *tabu* lasting one night and two days begins for Kareimoku and the most noble chiefs.[8] The higher a person's rank is here, the more sacred are the duties imposed on him; and such a *tabu* takes place at every new and full moon.[9] As soon as the sun approaches the horizon, they go into a *murai* [Tahaitian: *morai*, or temple], nor do they leave it till the appointed time has elapsed.

Mr. Chamisso, at his request, received permission from Kareimoku to remain in the *murai* the whole duration of the *tabu*. There is no doubt that he is the first European to have succeeded in obtaining such consent.[10] From the appendix to his *Voyage*, readers may learn what occurred in that holy place.

Kareimoku's visit aboard finally convinced the natives of my peaceable intent, so that I was able to examine the whole island freely and without the least danger.

Kotzebue

COMMENTARY

1. Choris's illustration of the *Riurik*'s stern (Plate 33) shows how crowded her quarterdeck was for this international meeting.

2. Pork did not necessarily have to be "consecrated in a temple" before consumption. As Kotzebue and Chamisso both supposed (Kotzebue, *Voyage*, III:249), the problem was that the *haole* had prepared the pork in, as it were, a single *imu* (the ship's galley). But pork was in any case *kapu* for women of even the highest rank, and the Russians had arrived in the *makahiki* period. In that period (October to January), *ali'i* abstained from fresh pork (see Malo, 1903:188). All in all, the visitors could not have offered a less appropriate repast.

3. See Turnbull, 1805, II:62 (local rum production from sugar cane); Campbell, 1816:146–47, and 185; and Alexander 1899:157 (its widespread abuse); also Narrative 66, n. 3. See Narrative 45 on Kamehameha's personal sobriety by 1816. Kotzebue's cheese came from California.

4. Vasil'ev and Shishmarev in 1821 offered Hawaiian notabilities less alcohol, unless Liholiho was present in person.

5. See Narratives 78, 84, and 117 on *kapu* that affected women's diets; also Malo, 1903:83–84; also Narratives 47, 73 and 74 on *mua* and penalties for infringements of associated *kapu* procedures.

6. The German dramatist and publicist, August von Kotzebue, shot by a revolutionary-minded student in 1819; a high-ranking Russian spy, in his enemies' view: studies by Doring (1830) and Rabany (1893).

7. Painting, like writing (*palapala*), was regarded by most Hawaiians as having magical qualities associated with *haole* (see Narratives 46 and 59 on the potency of written messages). On the portrait of Kamehameha I and its distribution in 1816, see Narrative 38 and Charlot, 1958.

8. *Kapu ku.*

9. A half-truth; see Malo, 1903:83–84; Ii, 1963:59, and 95.

10. A patent error: by 1816 there were dozens of *haole* living more or less settled lives on the Islands, many of whom had been there 20 years or more (Bradley, 1942:33–35). Some had thrown their lot in with particular chiefs and had acquired both the status and the privileges of *ali'i* for themselves (Campbell, 1816:165–66). It is exceedingly implausible that not one of these had ever attended religious observances in a *heiau* from start to finish. Chamisso was certainly among the first to *report* such observances to the learned (Eurocentric) world.

68. *30 November 1816*

The sun was almost setting when I went past the temple which Kareimoku [Kalanimoku] had just entered, accompanied by Mr. Chamisso and several *geri* [*ieri*]. This temple, situated not far from Ganarura [Honolulu], had been built very speedily since the natives had been obliged to destroy an older one which Sheffer's [Scheffer] people had desecrated by bursting in.[1] The fury of the natives had then been unlimited; and there is no question that if Iung [Young] had not entered into the crisis as intermediary, Sheffer's servants would have paid for their bold action with their lives.

While entering the temple, all the persons named observed the very strictest silence. Soon afterwards, several people came out from all four sides, raised their arms heavenward and, it seemed, invoked someone from thence with a loud shout.[2] When they had repeated this a few times, they went back into the temple. After this, two men rushed out like madmen and ran round the temple, with all their strength, in opposite directions. I went off, in order to have no contact with them; for in that event, they would have imparted their sanctity to me and I would have been obliged, with them, to observe the mysteries of *tabu* [*kapu*] in the *morai*. I willingly declined this, as my curiosity could be satisfied for me by Mr. Chamisso.[3]

Kotzebue

COMMENTARY

1. See Pierce, 1965:17; and Thrum, 1923:33–34 (Honolulu *heiau*).
2. Rites associated with *kapu puli* or *pule*, then just starting (30 November 1816).
3. See Narrative 72. The Pakaka *heiau* was closest, a bare 50 metres from the fort; it was owned by Kinau. It is tempting to try to determine exactly which *heiau* in Honolulu was visited by Chamisso, but, on the basis of Hawaiian sources (Malo, Kamakau, and Ii), one can only venture cautious statements. As Kotzebue plainly says, it had certainly been erected within the past five months, in the king's absence, and had been finished swiftly. Mau'oki *heiau* in Waikiki was a large stone structure (Ii, 1963:144). "Several people," observes Kotzebue further, "came out from all four sides" ("vyshlo ... iz vsekh chetyrykh storon") and shouted in invocation, perhaps in the spirit described by Ii (1963:39, 43). A *heiau luakini* had a single entrance, and the Russians do not mention any walls around this "temple." Kaheiki *heiau* had substantial palisading. This one evidently had a smaller and lower enclosing fence. On the other hand, Chamisso's narrative (see Narrative 82) makes evident that the *heiau* in question had several structures in it, including an eating house (an earth-oven house, *hale umu*), and a *mana* house in which was kept a feather god (*'aumakua hulu manu*) of classical type (Buck, 1957:503–12), with pearl-shell eyes and dogs' teeth. Finally, the Russians' *heiau* lacked any oracle tower and huge wooden images of the variety observed and drawn by Choris at the Ahuena *heiau* in Kailua, Kona, six days earlier (Ii, 1963:117–22; Buck, 1957:488–95). Kotzebue and Chamisso were careful observers and both would hardly have omitted to mention such striking features of "their" *heiau*, had they been present. In sum, the Russians saw a simple palisaded *heiau*, almost certainly not a *heiau luakini* and almost certainly nearer to Honolulu Harbour than to Waikiki.

   Kotzebue sheds light on the matter in a passage describing his own subsequent visit, of 11 October 1817, to "the temple:" see Narrative 104. Moved by curiosity, the *Riurik*'s captain decided to look over a *heiau* from which came "the sound of a dull drum." (The *heiau* thus had the usual *hale pahu*, as well as *mana*, *hale umu*, and other buildings.) What he saw indicated the rites of Lono, rather than Ku, and certainly gave no indication of recent human sacrifice. But this applied equally to Chamisso's experience; there was no great stress or fear, rather ritual associated with the *makahiki* season, which itself had deep Lono associations. ("The Lono ritual was milder, the service more comfortable;" Malo, 1903:208.)

This in turn gives rise to questions regarding the possible asynchronism between Russians' and Hawaiians' calendars; Kalanimoku and his people were about to observe a two-night *kapu* or, as Malo terms it, *pule*. Malo further remarks (1903:188) that "when the *Ku-tabu* of the month of *Welehu* had come, it went without religious service." This might indicate that the *Kane kapu* was about to be observed, it being the 28th day of the month by local reckoning.

Returning to the subject of his visit to a *heiau* "as Kareimoku's guest," and summarizing Hawaiian *heiau* (Kotzebue, *Voyage*, III:248), Chamisso observed that "every great chief has his peculiar gods (*akua*), the idols of which are represented in his morai." This might certainly be taken as an indication that the *heiau* visited had been Kalanimoku's; for Kalanimoku had himself supervised the construction of that *heiau* in 1816. This in turn argues against Pakaka, a *heiau po'okanaka* (dedicated by human sacrifice: see Kamakau, 1976:145–46) and in any case associated not with Chief Kalanimoku but Kinau. And so we turn again to the attractive possibility that the *heiau* defiled by Scheffer and his people had in fact been a *Hale o Lono*. Ku was associated with Kamehameha I, indeed, and Kalanimoku was a loyal warrior and keeper of Fort Kaahumanu, all of which suggested Ku observance; but his *personal* religious obligations also called for proper deference to Lono in the *makahiki* period. (It is in any case merely implied, not stated, that Kalanimoku went with Chamisso into the *heiau* and stayed there.)

Other factors lend support to a selection of the principal *Hale o Lono* as "the temple" that the Russians saw. First, Chamisso "presented himself"at Kalanimoku's house just before sunset, on 30 November 1816, and was very quickly taken to the "temple," the ceremonies beginning "at sunset." Time was lacking to walk over to Kupalaha or Leahi *heiau* at Waikiki, by way of trails through Kalia (See Ii, 1963:93). Second, the *Hale o Lono* slightly east of the Nihoa shipyard and Pakaka landing-point (*ibid.*, 65) stood very close to the site of Fort Kaahumanu and therefore close to the scandalous events of late August 1816. Third, that "temple area" was about one hundred metres square, just as described by Kotzebue (Narrative 104).

69. *4 December 1816*

Since I had long before expressed a wish to see the dancing of the natives of Vagu [Oahu] Island, Kareimoku [Kalanimoku] invited us today, on the 4th,[1] to such an entertainment. They conducted us to his house, before which a large area had been prepared for the ceremony. It was already surrounded by many spectators. Mats had been spread for us in the middle of the circle. It struck me as most odd that I did not find my host there, but Iung [Young] soon came up to me and said, "The Governor excuses himself for not being here, but his wife got so drunk that he cannot leave her." Strange though this excuse was, it was quite true, and I had to be content with it. The women here are generally more inclined to drunkenness than the men.[2] We seated ourselves, and the dancing began thereafter.

The music was made by four men who struck hollow gourds with small sticks, so producing a dull sound that could serve to beat time for the song. Three public dancers, who travel from one island to another and demonstrate their skills for money, now stepped out completely naked but for arm bracelets of hogs' tusks and half-armour for the feet made of dogs' teeth [Plate 7]. These dancers stood facing us, beside each other, and gave an expresion of the song's meaning by means of various skilful body movements.[3] Their principal art was to make instant facial changes, suiting the facial expression to the movements of the whole body. The spectators were enraptured and, at every pause for rest, would enter the circle itself to give gifts to the dancers. Such was their ecstasy that eventually they even presented these mountebanks with their silk kerchiefs.

After the men had sufficiently distinguished themselves, there was a change of scene and many young girls arranged themselves in three rows. The head and shoulders of each was beautifully ornamented with wreathes of flowers, and the neck with beads and various fantastic objects. Only the lower body was covered with motley *tappa* [*kapa*] material. This group had a very pleasing effect, especially when making the most delightful movements to the monotonous music. The back rows imitated the front row, repeating their gestures. The entire spectacle bore the imprint of unsullied nature,[4] and entertained me more, indeed, than would the most skilfully executed European ballet. The place had been enclosed by a fence of bamboo canes, a small house lying concealed behind it. Before this house, a large pig was strolling, guarded by two *kanakas*; and every person of rank who passed by this house would stroke the pig tenderly. Such caresses surprised me. I found out from Iung [Young] that in the house there was a nine-month-old son of Tameamea [Kamehameha I], whose education had been entrusted to Kareimoku [Kalanimoku]. The pig in question I learned was *tabu* [*kapu*] and would be sacrificed to the gods when the young prince fulfilled his first sacred duties in the *murai* [*morai*]. The festivity and the dances had been given, on this day, in honour of the young son of the king;[5] for, though he has no right to participate in these entertainments or even to show himself before a certain age, still the nobility of his birth requires that such feasts often be given in his honour.

Kotzebue

COMMENTARY

1. December 1816.
2. See Narratives 67, 69, and 129.
3. This scene is depicted by Choris (Plate 7 here) and has frequently been reproduced as a classic representation of the Hawaiian *hula pahu*. The professional dancers demonstrate their art "before the rich in order to obtain gifts from them:" Malo, 1903:303. (The rich include the Russians.) Choris's work and the dance itself are discussed in Chapter 13. Drumming (*ka'eke*) was much in favour at Honolulu because it was a skill in which Liholiho excelled (see Ii, 1963:137). The Russians were treated to performances on both "knee drums" and composite *ipu hula*, or gourd drums, as well as *'uli'uli* gourd rattles fitted with handles and shield-like frontal ornament (see Buck, 1957:411–14). These gourds contained a few pebbles which made "a not unpleasant sound" in Choris's judgement. See also Narrative 73.
4. See Plate 11 and Narrative 80. The Russians recognized that the female dancers

wore "a special costume," as Choris puts it: see Chapter 13 for discussion of his illustrations. Abundant but very soft *pa'u* were specially dyed and stamped. It is some indication of Choris's interest in these dances that he should have made two or even three watercolours of such performances. In addition to "Danse des femmes dans les îles Sandwich" (Narrative 11 and Plate XVI in *Voyage pittoresque autour du monde* (1822), we have another and related scene in *Vues et paysages* (1826). It too has been reproduced in numerous works of late (e.g., in Tregaskis, 1973: Plate 5, without acknowledgement). There, striped *kapa* is worn for obvious aesthetic effect. See Malo, 1903:74–75, on ways of staining and printing *pa'u* and various names accordingly applied to them. Another description of *hula* dancing, complete with commentary on the accompanying songs heard in 1821 (despite Reverend Hiram Bingham's known disapproval), was left in 1822 by Mikhail N. Vasil'ev of the *Otkrytie* ("Zapiski o prebyvanii na Gavaiskikh ostrovakh," Ts-GAVMF, *fond* 213, op. 1, *delo* 104:54–55). Later Russian visitors to Honolulu deplored the virtual extinction of traditional *hula* in romantic fashion, welcoming whatever glances of it they could get: see, for instance, the emotive remarks of Surgeon A. Vysheslavtsov in *Ocherki perom i karandashom iz krugosvetnogo plavaniia v 1857, 1858, 1859 i 1860 godakh* (St. Petersburg, 1867:411).

5. This was Kauikeaouli, aged almost four: Kamakau, 1961:260ff. on the *kapu* and circumstances surrounding his early childhood.

70. *28–29 November 1816*

The peace-greeting, *Arocha!* [*Aloha*] is offered by everyone and returned by everyone. Every call being answered by a similar one, a person continues on his way without ever turning around. One day, when I went botanizing in the taro plantations outside Hana-ruru [Honolulu],[1] I noticed that these greetings of *Arocha!* would not stop—even though I had passed all the houses and could see nothing but empty fields to left and right. These *Arochas* continued in various versions, and I continued to reply naively. When I looked around, unobserved, I saw a crowd of children following: they were making fun of me, by having me reiterate *Arocha* all the time. Just you wait, I thought. And I kept the greetings up, making the children follow me up into the narrow passes of the taro fields, over ditches, over irrigation channels and earthbanks.[2] Then, suddenly, I turned and rushed toward them with a terrible howling, by arms raised. Startled, they fled, tumbled over each other, and fell right into the water channels.[3] I laughed at them, and we parted friends. *Arocha!*

                                                                                    Chamisso

COMMENTARY

1. Actually, one km. due north of the inner harbour and on either bank of the Honolulu River: see Map A.

2. Described in some detail by Kotzebue in Narrative 74.

3. See also Narratives 74, 94, 97, and 108 on taro cultivation. Details of the "water channels" (*au wai*) in Malo, 1903:39 and 271; Buck, 1957:10.

71. *30 November 1816*

On 30 November, the captain invited Kareimoku [Kalanimoku] and the
highest-ranking chiefs, Teimotu,[1] brother of Queen Kahumanu [Kaahumanu],
and Haulhana, for luncheon aboard the *Riurik*. Kareimoku was most cordial
and arrived with peace greetings. The men were all dressed in European style,
not the latest perhaps,[2] but very respectably; and their behaviour at table was
very proper and mannerly. We, on the other hand, acted as bungling idiots. It
is a social duty to make inquiries about the habits and customs of those whom
we invite as guests, and to prepare things accordingly. The pig that we had
ready for our guests had not been blessed in a temple and was therefore, to put
it in European terms, not kosher.[3] A bit of dry bread and a glass of wine was
all they were permitted to enjoy. And they had to watch us eat without even
being able to walk about; such was our hospitality. They behaved far better
than *we* should have done, recognizing our goodwill. Kareimoku toasted the
Emperor of Russia with an *Arocha!* [*Aloha*]; and we returned the toast in
honour of Tameiameia [Kamehameha I], so becoming fast friends.

Chamisso

COMMENTARY

1. Keeaumoku (?); see Narrative 40.
2. See Narratives 106 and 115 (sale of outmoded clothes).
3. Chamisso *was* correct in this, though he evidently knew little of the complex
   injunctions or the four regular *kapu* (*Hua* on the 13th and 14 days of the month,
   Kaloa on the 23rd and 24th, *Kane* on the 27th and 28th, and *Ku* on the 4th–
   6th. Because it was not the *makahiki* season, temple use was modified: see Malo,
   1903:56, 188, and 251.

72. *30 November 1816*

At sundown on 30 November, the festivities of *Tabu-pori* [*kapu pule*] began,
ending at sunrise three days later.[1] I was eager to be present and so addressed
myself to Kareimoku [Kalanimoku], who made no difficulties and invited me
to go as his guest, for as long as the feast lasted, in the sacred shrine of their
temple. He left the ship at about 4 p.m., and I rejoined him at sunset ...

I would like to point out the gaiety with which the native liturgy was performed; it made our masquerades look like a funeral. The religious offices
proper only lasted a few hours. Just as in the Catholic liturgy, the people
partly join in the singing with the priest. Intermissions were occasions for
cheerful conversation, and meals were served. I was served according to our
European customs, receiving baked taro instead of the customary mash. During dinner and the accompanying conversation, one lies down on mats in the
eating-house.[2] One lies in two rows on the stone floor, head toward the central
corridor. The food, brought in on banana leaves, is eaten by hand. The sticky
taro mash, which represents our bread, is simply licked from the fingers; but
water for washing is brought before and after each meal. Torches made from
kukui nuts [*Aleurites triloba*] stand on poles and throw a bright light during

the night.[3] In the *morai*, everything is just as at home. If one wants to leave the sacred area, one is escorted by a small boy carrying a little white flag as a warning; a woman now touched by a man would have to be killed at once ...

Choris has a picture of a Hawaiian temple idol in his *Voyage pittoresque*. The type represented repeatedly in Plates VI, 4; VII, 3; and VIII, 1 and 3 seems to me to have a hieroglyphic function as well as being an archaic and national structure. The figure made of basket-work and dressed in red feathers is kept in the holy of holies of the temple and appears during the *tabu-pori* [*kapu pule*].[4] I believe the wide mouth contains real dog-teeth. A few youths actually brought this figure out to me, so that I could look at it closely. Eager to find out everything possible, I put my hand in the figure's mouth. A sudden turn by the person holding the idol caused my hand to be swallowed up. Naturally, I withdrew my hand very fast! Everyone broke into laughter.

Chamisso

COMMENTARY

1. This was possibly *kapu Ku*, first of the regular *kapu* observed monthly. Details in Malo, 1903:56. See Narrative 68 n. 3.
2. Buck, 1957:520–21 on these temple houses.
3. These were flambeaux, *ma-ko'u*, of *kukui* nuts; also seen in use by Vasil'ev, 1821:24, and 31.
4. Choris's plates are discussed in Chapter 13. The "basket-work" figure was an *'aumakua hulu manu*, the foundation material being split *'ie'ie* rootlets, rather than wicker: see Buck, 1957:503–09.

73. *4 December 1816*

Kareimoku [Kalanimoku] arranged a *hurra-hurra* [*hulahula*] or dance for us on 4 December, and another on the 6th ... We barbarians! We apply the term savage to talented people with a greater sense of beauty than ourselves, and we permit our ballet to drive the shamefaced poet and mourning mimic actor from our halls supposedly dedicated to all the arts ....

On the 4th three men danced, on the 6th a group of girls, among them many beauties. It was not the girls who left a lasting impression on me, however, but the men, who were much more artistic ....[1] Never have I seen anywhere, at any other festival, an audience so overwhelmed and intoxicated with joy as the Hawaiians were at this performance. They showered the dancers with gifts, clothing, jewels ....[2]

We were promised yet another spectacle—one in which the princes and nobility would demonstrate the national weapon practice.[3] This is not without danger, the mock battle often resulting in a genuine fight as a result of these people's lively temperament. The weapon, of course, is the spear. It is not catapulted with arm raised as was done in ancient Greece, however, but is thrown with lowered arm, near the ground. The back of the hand is turned upwards, the thumb backward. From this position, the spear is cast upwards.[4]

Chamisso

COMMENTARY

1. Ellis, 1826:48–49; Damon, 1925:208; Dibble, 1909:100–02; also Narratives 69 and 80; and Ii, 1963:137.
2. The Russians were seeing a *hula pahu* (Malo, 1903:303), which was much enjoyed in the *makahiki* season.
3. *Lono-maka-ihe*. These sham fights also took place for pleasure, in November-December: see Malo, 1903:93 and 281.
4. Chamisso saw the blunted spear of sugar-cane stem, cut for these mock fights and so thrown, as well as *hau* wood spears. There were established and recognized practice fields for these sham spear-fights, in the Honolulu of the time: see Ii, 1963:66. Choris drew three varieties of short spear that he saw in 1816–17: see Plate 6. It is unfortunate that he declined to comment on them, in his *Voyage pittoresque ...*, p. 24; but two are obviously *ihe laumake* or barbed spears of the sort seen by Cook and well described by King (Cook, 1784, III:151–52) before Choris or Kotzebue had been born. The third appears to be an *ihe pahe'e*, used in the game of *pahe'e* that Choris and Chamisso saw being played at Honolulu. Both ends are trimmed to blades and the cross-section is symmetrical and balanced. No doubt because the "mock battle" was put on (see Ii, 1963:65–66 for the location) on or immediately beside the prepared level ground set aside for that game, on the *kahua pahe'e* (see Ellis, 1838:197–98 for a good description), and on the same day, Chamisso confused the "battle" and the game. As Chamisso says, the spear or dart was thrown underhand, so that it would slide as far as possible across the field. See also Buck, 1957:374–75 on the darts.

MAE in Leningrad would appear to have no *ihe pahe'e* misplaced amongst other spears or game sticks (though 4302-5, an old Hawaiian artefact transferred from the Naval Museum only in 1931, does resemble a giant *ihe pahe'e*: see Likhtenberg, 1960:203 and SMAE, XXXIX, 1984:20). It does however boast five "game stones" (see Likhtenberg, 1960: Plates XV and 204), as the MAE records describe quoits including *'ulumaika* stone discs. And two of these, 736–222 and –223, were collected in Hawaii before 1828; their slightly concave upper and lower faces are exactly as seen by early European visitors to the Islands and described by Reverend William Ellis (Ellis, 1839:198). The officers of the *Blagonamerennyi* also saw *'ulumaika* (and *noa*) being played in the centre of Honolulu: see Narrative 127.

The MAE collections amplify and complement Chamisso's verbal description and Choris's painting of a dance by three expert dancers in other ways. There are, for instance, a boar's tusk bracelet (505–16) and a dog-tooth ornament (750–5) that were in St. Petersburg even before Kotzebue reached Hawaii in the *Riurik*, to judge by MAE and LOAAN records, as well as assorted necklaces. It would be useful to examine other articles associated by Choris with the public dances of 4 December 1816 and painted by him; for instance, the musical instrument that figures as "9" on his Plate XI in *Voyage pittoresque autour du monde* (Plate 6 here). Choris's own annotation (p. 24 and Chapter 13) makes plain that he believed it to be a hula stick (*ka la'au*) of an unusual variety, with notches for percussive effects. Essentially however, it is an unfinished *'ohe ka'eke* or bamboo pipe of the classical kind, described by Nathanial B. Emerson in 1909 (see his *Unwritten Literature of Hawaii*: Bureau of American Ethnology, Bulletin 38: Washington, D.C.:144).

None of the articles on Choris's plate entitled "Armes et ustensils des îles Sandwich," however, are to be found in MAE today; and all were almost certainly
among those presented to Count N.P. Rumiantsev in 1818 and transferred after
his death, together with hundreds of other ethnographic items, to Moscow and
the Rumiantsev Museum: see *Sbornik materialov dlia istorii Rumiantsovskago
Muzeia*, (St. Petersburg, 1882), bk. 1:108ff. and *Piatidesiatiletie Rumiantsovskago Muzeia v Moskve, 1862–1912: istoricheskii ocherk* (Moscow, 1912):164–66,
etc. According to the Soviet historian of ethnography, Tat'iana V. Staniukovich
(meeting with the writer on 21 May 1985), those Hawaiian artefacts were stored
in various Moscow buildings during the Great Patriotic War (World War II) and
lost as a result of the turmoil of that time.

74. *8 December 1816*

From the [Honolulu] River, the way led west through a beautifully cultivated valley which, being bounded to the north by wooded hills, offers a
spectacle of delightful, wild emptiness to the traveller's gaze.[1] To the south, it
is bounded by the ocean. Artificial fields planted with taro root, which might
very well be called lakes, attracted my attention. Every one of them forms a
square of about 160 feet and, like our basins, is bounded with stones. This
field (or pond, for so it might be termed), is covered by two feet of water,
and in that boggy ground the natives plant taro roots, which will only grow
in such wet conditions. Each pond is fitted with two sluices, to let water in
on one side and out on the other and into the adjacent pond, and so on. The
fields are slightly lower than one another, so that the same water, flowing
out of a single elevated reservoir (which is fed by springs), may irrigate very
sizeable plantations. When the taro is planted, water is usually run off until
no more than 6 inches remains. Into this bog they plant a slip of a plant from
which the roots have been cut; and this new slip soon takes root itself, so that
another harvest is possible after only three months. Taro needs a good deal of
room, since it puts out great roots. It has long stalks and large leaves, which
seem to swim on the water surface and for that reason have a rather strange
appearance. The spaces between the fields, which are from 3 to 6 feet wide,
are planted on both sides with sugar-cane or bananas, which form pleasant
shady alleys.[2] And these taro fields offer the natives yet another advantage:
fish caught in distant streams and introduced to the water in them, thrive
wonderfully.[3] In precisely the same manner that the Islanders keep river fish
here, they keep sea fish in the sea itself, where they sometimes take advantage
of the surrounding reefs. By building a coral-stone wall from the latter to
the shore, they form convenient stews in the ocean.[4] To make such a reservoir
certainly requires much labour, but it does not call for the skill needed for taro
fields. To make the latter, both effort and skill are wanted. I myself saw whole
hills covered with such fields, through which water was gradually flowing; each
sluice formed a tiny waterfall as the water descended to the next pond between
alleys of sugar-cane or banana trees, affording the most delightful spectacle.

Kotzebue

COMMENTARY

1. This was the "Taurea Valley," through which the small river of that name flowed due south into the eastern limit of Kalanimoku's fish-ponds. See Map A.

2. Kotzebue was crossing terraces (*lo'i*) to the west of the Kalihi Stream (see Buck, 1957:10); the sluices controlled artificial streams called *au wai*. The path Kotzebue was following took him along a firm embankment, known as *kuakua*, between the ponds (see Malo, 1903:39).

   The passage is almost perfectly echoed in Campbell, 1819:145. Archibald Campbell examined the same taro fields in 1809, when Gagemeister brought him to Honolulu in the *Neva*. It was then March, and he found the water, introduced "by drains or aqueducts," only "twelve or eighteen inches" deep; but the embankments planted with sugar-cane, the paths along the shady alleys thus made, and the germination rate were as found by Kotzebue seven years later. Kamakau (1976:33–37) indicates that the Russians were seeing "pond field" taro cultivation, the embankments (*kuauna*) having been raised in the ancient Hawaiian manner.

3. *Awa, pua, 'ama'ama, 'o'opu,* and *aholehole* fish, says Kamakau: *ibid.,* 34.

4. These were shore ponds (*loko kuapa*) of the kind seen and drawn in pencil by William Dampier while walking near the Pearl River mouth: see Ii, 1963:25. Oahu boasted many such ponds, most of which were ancient and had been built with much labour. The largest seen by the Russians near Honolulu were *loko kuapa* or *loko kai pu'uone* owned by Kalanimoku (see Kamakau, 1976:48–50).

75. 8 December 1816

We heard a loud sobbing reverberating in several houses, and discovered that it was sick men being bewailed by their wives. It is the custom here that as soon as a husband falls sick, his wives and female relations gather round his resting place, loudly bemoan his situation, tear out their hair and scratch their faces, in hopes of thereby affording him some relief, indeed, a complete cure.[1] Nor has the custom been discontinued here of burying a dead *geri's* [*ieri*] principal favourite with him, still alive. Beckley informed me that the priests had already determined who would accompany Tameamea [Kamehameha I] into his grave, and did not conceal their fate from them since the victims, proud of their destiny, gladly purchase the honour by that most dreadful death.[2]

I myself had occasion to meet on Vagu [Oahu] Island one of these condemned men. Despite his situation, he was always calm and gay. On the death of the king, such men were brought, bound, into the royal *murai* [*morai*], where, with many solemn rites, they died at the hands of a priest.

The river Mauna-Roa [Mauna Loa], which is probably one of the broadest rivers in all these islands, derived its name from the mountain Mauna-Roa [Mauna Loa] on the island of Ovaigi [Hawaii]. The literal translation of the name is: high mountain. It is asserted that opposite the village there lies a convenient harbour, the entrance to which however is between reefs and, so, very dangerous. I saw this harbour very clearly, as it lay before me, and so I have indicated it on the chart.[3] Some seaman may well appear who wishes to investigate it. Having rested sufficiently, we now set off on the return journey, leaving the shore and cutting across a spur of land extending far into the sea where the road led us over a high hill. On this elevation, the exhausting heat was modified somewhat by the northeast trade wind; but this wind sometimes gusted so strongly that it threatened to cast us from the height where we walked.[4] We observed here several plantations of the tree from whose bark material is made locally.[5] The preparation of this stuff is very tedious, for the bark must be beaten in water until it becomes fine enough.[6] Only old women occupy themselves with this work; the young ones have the right to live in idleness and spend all their time receiving court from men. Thus, this onerous toil is added even to the burden of old age, and the poor old women have nothing left to them but the memory of a gaily spent youth.

Kotzebue

COMMENTARY

1. See Narrative 49, n. 2; also Malo, 1903:130–31, and 146–49 (religious and supernatural associations of care for the sick); and Ii, 1963:47 (ancient cures).
2. See Narratives 78 and 120. The matter of selecting those privileged to die with the king had in fact been dealt with by the chief *kahuna* of the powerful Kanalu class, Hewahewa (see Ii, 1963:39, and 91; and Dibble, 1909:67–69). The proximity of his houses to Fort Kaahumanu and Kuloloia Beach (Ii, 1963:90) would have made it difficult for Beckley to ignore his existence and considerable influence. Reverend Sheldon Dibble took a quasi-professional interest in accounts of Kamehameha I's death and in the attendant ceremonies; he learned that one man, Keamahulihia, had died in the king's honour (*op. cit.*, 68). See Malo, 1903: Chap. 29 on the *kuni* ceremonies, in which Kotzebue and many other foreigners took a somewhat ghoulish interest.
3. See Map A.
4. Baron Wrangel felt the force of this northeast wind, in November 1826: see Wrangel, 1828:102.
5. *Broussonetia papyrifera*, or *wauke*, was cultivated northwest of Honolulu until the 1850s or later. See Ellis, 1839:109–10 (on women's work).
6. Kotzebue evidently did not see the first-stage beating (*ho'omo'omo'o*) of *kapa*, as he would have known that the bast is not beaten in sea water, but is soaked in it: Buck, 1957:180–81. See Likhtenberg, 1960:200 for a description of MAE's "pre-1828" *I'e kuku* or second-stage beater (No. 750–2).

76. *8 December 1816*

Having covered about ten miles, though we were no more than six from Gana-ruru [Honolulu] on a straight line, we reached our night's quarters. We found ourselves in a pretty village belonging to Kareimoku [Kalanimoku] and known as Vauiau [Waiau], a name taken from the rapid stream that flowed from there down into the sea.[1] I wanted to pass the night here in order to move on by water, next morning, to the nearby Pearl River; and with that in view, I ordered my guides to hire a boat at once. Their efforts to find a boat were vain, however, since the natives had left the shore for several days to fish.[2] There was only one craft there, the property of a *geri* [*ieri*] in Gana-ruru; and since his people did not dare to let me borrow it, I was forced to be patient till the following day.

The inhabitants of this village had had orders from Kareimoku to entertain us well. Their first care, therefore, was to prepare dinner for us. A piglet was baked in the ground, with taro and ground apples; fish was brought from the taro fields; and we ourselves could supply wine. Since we were very hungry, the meal seemed to us princely. Curiosity brought many onlookers to us, and to some of them we gave wine which they loved, though it was the very first time they had ever drunk it. All our guests were in excellent spirits, and an evening was passed in singing and dancing.

Afterwards, it transpired that despite all our precautions a knife had been stolen from us. The guides whom Kareimoku had provided for us, who were now responsible for the natives' behaviour, vainly tried to find the thief. Sandwich Islanders rarely rob each other, and such an action is punished by general scorn or, on occasion, by death; but the theft of some object from a European brings great honour to the thief, who does not even scruple to boast about it.[3]

Kotzebue

COMMENTARY

1. One mile east of the Pearl River's mouth: see Map A. The hamlet was on a much-frequented trail from Waimalu and Aliapaakai pond to settlements listed by Ii (1963:97, para. 1). Young, Holmes, and Marin all had property in the area (*ibid.*, 95 and Kotzebue, *Voyage*, I:345).

2. On their fishing, see Narratives 81 and 91. The mere duration of this fishing expedition makes it plain that local fishermen had gone out beyond the reefs. Ten months later, Chamisso saw men using long drag nets in the same locality (*Werke*, 1836, I:344: expedition of 7–10 October 1817), in ten to fifteen feet of water. Numerous craft stood outside the breakers but not far from the reef formation, and a wide range of fish was caught including *kihikihi*. See Buck, 1957:289–312 and Kamakau, 1976:59–65 on nets and bags. Chamisso was impressed by the quantity of fish caught in what he terms *langen schleppenden Nessen*, and struck by the fact that *Chaetodon-Arten* (flying fish) were especially (*besonders*) in evidence in the nets and canoes. *Langen* might be interpreted here as "wide," rather than "deep," and we see wide flying-fish bag nets (*hano malolo*) or simply *kolo* bag nets (see Buck, 1957:311). Long seine nets were also used in waters near but beyond the reefs, though normally in depths of more than ten feet. In any case, these men from the locality were *lawai'a*, experts who had often and regularly fished that coast and had good gear; and Kotzebue, like Chamisso, called on them in the *Ho'oilo* season when there was much sea fishing (Kamakau, 1976:14; Buck, 1957:286).

Because the Hawaiians were generally using their own (in any case expensive) nets when Russians observed them, they were far less willing to part with them in exchange for Russian wares than to part with spare hooks. As a result, MAE in Leningrad has not a single "pre-1828" Hawaiian fishing net or bag, but several composite hooks with or without a line (Likhtenberg, 1960:193–94). Both Kotze-

bue and Golovnin were impressed by fishing lines and other cordage that they
saw in the Hawaiian Islands in 1816–18 (see Narrative 23). It is thus significant
that MAE has three such lines, all transferred from the Naval Museum in 1931
(Nos. 4302–3, 3, 1) and all described, in MAE *opisi*, as "very old."
3. See Narratives 76, 113, and 119 on Hawaiians' thieving, etc.

77. 9 December 1816

The day appointed for this lance-exercise[1] is announced well in advance, so
that nobles may gather from all parts for this demonstration of their bravery
and agility. Often, more than a hundred men assemble. Dividing into equal
parties, they choose a large open space for the field of combat. Both parties
then take up their positions, the leader of each advancing to the middle of
the area. The latter commence battle by attempting to strike each other with
lances, of which they hold several in their hands. Twisting in the most skilful
manner, each does his best to avoid the other's blows; and both men are in
constant motion, now leaping to one side, now the other, stooping, bending
the body in every possible way, and flinging spears at the same time. Both
groups of warriors, in the meantime, stand quietly and motionless, awaiting
the outcome. A high spirit animates the party whose leader is victorious, for
this is considered a good omen.

After this prelude, the troops grow more lively: one party advances against
the other and, in an instant, all is action and the air is filled with innumer-
able blunted spears—for only such spears may be used in these exercises.[2]
Their true martial art consists of breaking through enemy lines, falling on the
scattered units with maximum force, and taking warriors prisoner. For this
reason, the skilful leader never fails to take advantage of his enemy's errors,
and, by cunning, tries to persuade the enemy to draw his main force to one
side. In that case, the enemy's weakest part will become his prey. When
such a stratagem is successful, the issue is settled; the deceived party is vanquished. These natives act in exactly the same way in real battles, only with
the difference that the spears are then pretty sharp and can pierce an enemy
at ten paces. In addition, they also throw stones and wield hardwood clubs[3]
during real struggles. Since firearms have now been introduced here, however,
it is likely that spears will soon pass out of use.[4] Tameamea [Kamehameha
I] is generally considered to be the most skilful spear-thrower. In order to
improve *his* skill, he would often order fourteen spears to be aimed at his
chest simultaneously, and though each blow might have proved a fatal one, he
would always most dexterously deflect them or avoid them all. The renown
of his invincible courage assisted him in the conquest of the Islands. When
he appeared with his fleet before Vagu [Oahu], the king of that island fled
into the mountains, being sure that the custom of putting the vanquished to
death would be practised on him. "I must die," he said to those with him,
"but I shall not die by the hand of my conqueror, whom I wish to deprive
of that triumph. I will render myself a victim to the gods." His body was
subsequently found in a cave on the summit of a mountain.[5]

Kotzebue

COMMENTARY

1. See Narratives 40 and 85 on sham fights (*kaua kio*). The spectacle put on for the Russians was rather tamer than the one Vancouver had seen on 4 March 1793 (*Voyage*, 1798, II:150–54); but the skills exhibited had hardly decreased since those times (see Portlock, 1789:188–89 on the spear avoidance demonstration staged on his quarterdeck by Namaateerae).
2. David Malo describes the sham fights in complementary fashion: see Malo, 1903:93–94. On the spears used, see Buck, 1957:417–23.
3. *La'au palau'*: Buck, 1957:438–40.
4. Golovnin could confirm this, two years later in 1818: see Narrative 85.
5. On the Battle of Nuuanu and the subsequent death of Kalanikupule, see Ii, 1963:15; and Dibble, 1909:56–57. John Young was Kotzebue's probable informant, and had himself participated in the battle: survey in Tregaskis, 1973:261–62.

78. *Early December 1816*

Human victims, who were killed here according to the ancient custom at the death of a king, prince, or distinguished noble, and buried with him, were of the very lowest class. In certain families of this caste, there still exists the hereditary destiny, as it were, of dying together with one or other member of a noble house, in accordance with precise and fixed laws. It is established which of them will become a victim and at whose death. These victims know their fate, and their lot appears to terrify them not in the least. Given the progressive spirit of the times, however, this custom is already falling into decay and may now be followed only on the occasion of the death of the most sacred chiefs. When three victims offered themselves to fulfil their destiny at the death of Queen Kahu-manu's [Kaahumanu] mother, Karemoku [Kalanimoku] would not allow it and no human blood was spilled. Certainly, people are still making sacrifices but it would be unjust to reproach the Hawaiians for that. They sacrifice criminals to their gods, and do we in Europe not sacrifice them to Justice?[1]

Every great chief has his own gods or *akua*, whose idols are placed in all his temples. Other chiefs have other gods. But the worship of these idols seems to be more an external parade than a genuine rite of worship. As for the common people, they may have no such gods but they choose various objects to worship; for example, birds or fowl. Superstition reigns in many different guises in the Sandwich Islands ... We were expecting the populace to observe a certain moderation and humility in times of prayer and sacrifice, and were much amazed by the prevailing spirit of impropriety and the indecorous sport made of the idols and the low tricks with which they chose to amuse us throughout the sacred rites. It may positively be said that children play with their dolls with greater sedateness.[2]

All the restrictive laws of the *tabu* [*kapu*], however, are preserved in their full, inviolable strength ...[3] The two sexes may not share meat from the same animal. The consumption of pork (but not dog meat, which is no less valued), turtle meat, and certain fruits—for instance, coconuts and bananas—is forbidden or *tabu* to women.[4] Male and female attendants of women are in many regards under the same restrictions as the women themselves. We ourselves saw floating round our ship the corpse of a woman who had been put to death because, when in a drunken state, she had entered a house that served as her husband's dining place ....[5] Intercourse with Europeans has thus far had very little influence on the outward social order, way of life, or customs of these people.

Chamisso

COMMENTARY

1. See Narratives 75 and 120; and Buck, 1957:527.
2. See Narratives 72 and 104; and Buck, 1957:466ff. (gods).
3. See Narratives 75 and 117.
4. Compare Lisianskii, 1812:194–96; and Ellis, 1825:391–93.
5. Malo, 1903:51.

79. Early December 1816

The Hawaiians are tattooed little and irregularly. It is remarkable that they should have borrowed foreign designs for that national ornamentation. Goats and muskets, sometimes even letters, a name or birthplace may be seen tattooed along the arm. The men shave the beard and cut the hair in the form of a helmet, the crest of which is dyed a light brown or whitish colour.[1] The women cut their hair short, leaving only an edging of long hairs around the forehead. These are bleached white with lime and stand up like bristles.[2] Often, too, they leave a fine, long bunch in the centre of the forehead, which is dyed violet and combed back. Some, wanting to please Europeans, grow their hair longer and tie it up behind in a plait like that ordered by the Prussian army regulations of 1800. Sensibly, the Hawaiians have retained their national dress and way of life. It was purely in our honour that the princes would attire themselves, very well, in fine English tunics, imitating our ways with much propriety.[3] At other times, at home, they dressed in their own manner; and only visiting foreigners were entertained with porcelain and silver.[4] However, fashion reigns even in the Hawaiian Islands and with all its caprices and whims—particularly over the women. Ornaments worn by the queens or noble ladies promptly increase in value to marvellous extents.[5] At present, all the women are wearing around their necks a little mirror and pipe wrapped up in a European kerchief.

Chamisso

COMMENTARY

1. This was an ancient style: see Cook, 1784, 3:134.
   Russian evidence of Hawaiian ornament in 1816–26 is far sparser and less satisfactory than that collected by Kruzenshtern's and Lisianskii's people in 1804: see Barratt, 1987: pt. 3. This is particularly true of tattooing, which even Chamisso treats in a cursory fashion, so that Choris's sketches and watercolours contain the bulk of information (see Plates 7, 10, and 14) on the subject. Suffice it to note

that the banded, regular tattooing running (diagonally) across the face, neck, and left-hand upper torso of the central dancer in Plate 7 ("Danse des hommes dans les îles Sandwich") bears similarities to the more complex design tattooed across Liholiho's right-side upper torso (Plate 14: "Intérieur d'une maison d'un chef …") As for the toga-ed figures of Plate 10, described by the artist himself (Choris, 1822:15) as having imbibed too freely of *kava* (and showing the air of semi-drunken men), their exposed upper arms are tattooed with a palm frond and two goats. Such as it is, this and related narrative evidence from 1816–18 provided by the Russians does substantiate material in Emory, 1946. The very paucity of the Russian evidence for the later period, however, reflects the decline of tattooing, at least near Honolulu. Kotzebue recognized this fact (see Narrative 62). Choris did think to illustrate tattooing (marking) instruments (Plate 6, figs. 7–8); but his description does not suggest that he saw the operation being performed in Honolulu, or viewed the matter as deserving the attention that both Georg Heinrich Langsdorf and Tilesius von Tilenau had given it, when the *Nadezhda* and the *Neva* crossed Polynesia in May–June 1804: see Langsdorf, 1813–14, I:116–23, 183; Tilesius von Tilenau, "Izvestie o … sostoianii zhitelei ostrova Nukugivy," *Tekhnologicheskii zhurnal*, 3 (St. Petersburg, 1806), pt. 4.

2. Natural lime was mixed with the mucilaginous juice of the *ti* root and *kukui* gum.

3. Golovnin confirms this: Golovnin, 1822, 1:310.

4. See Narrative 50.

5. See Narrative 115.

80. *4 December 1816*

The spectacle of the *hurra* [*hula*] and dancing of the Hawaiians, performed at feasts, filled us with wonder.[1] The words of these songs, for the most part, celebrate the fame of some prince or other just like Pindaric odes. Our knowledge of their language was too poor to allow us to judge the poetry. The singing itself was monotonous. By that singing, as by the accompanying drumbeat, the turns of the dance were measured. Fusing into a whole, the music does attain a peculiar higher harmony.

In a quiet dance, the human body adapts itself, by this rhythm, to the most wonderful forms, taking on all humanly possible and most delightful positions. Movements are constant and quite unconstrained. One seems to see the antique brought to life. The dancer's feet barely touch the ground …. Drummers sit in the background, the dancers before them in one or more rows.[2] The voices of all combine in a single chorus. This singing starts slowly and softly, only gradually and little by little speeding up and gaining in force as the dancers advance and their actions grow animated. All the dancers make one and the same movements, so that it seems as if but one dancer, repeated several times, were standing before us …. At these festivals, the Hawaiians are beside themselves with joy.[3]

Chamisso

COMMENTARY

1. Compare Narratives 69 and 73; also Ii, 1963:137; and Malo, 1903:303.
2. Shown in Plate 6. Compare Ellis, 1839:100. Reverend William Ellis saw an almost identical performance at Kailua, Hawaii, in 1822. Details of the double gourd drum, *ipu hula*, in Buck, 1957:405–07.
3. This was precisely what disturbed the missionaries under whose influence the *hula* practically vanished from Honolulu, if not outlying districts of Oahu, in the 1820s: see Dibble, 1909:101 ("... exhibitions of licentiousness and abomination ...", etc.)

81. *7–10 October 1817*

I had been planning to visit the western range of Oahu Island. Mr. Marini [Marin] gave me some advice and Kareimoku [Kalanimoku] his support, so that I was able to undertake the trip, on 7–10 October 1817.

A canoe carried me, my guide, and a boy along the coral reef surrounding the beach at Hana-Ruru [Honolulu]. Sometimes we were outside the breakers, sometimes inside.[1] We went up the Pearl River toward the foot of the mountain I had wanted to see ....

At one point, we went quite far beyond the reef and out to sea. Several craft were outside the breakers and busy fishing in a depth of ten or fifteen feet of water. Various kinds of fish were being caught in long trawling nets, including a variety of *Chaetodon* of the most wonderful hues.[2] My crew supplied themselves with fish here, having Kareimoku's permission to do so.[3] And they were still eating them, raw and unclean, even three days later when they were spoiling and already full of insect larva.

When we returned and crossed the breakers again, incompetent handling filled the canoe with water. Fish we had just caught were swimming around my feet and my crew were swimming in the sea around the canoe. But all was very soon under control.

                                                                          Chamisso

COMMENTARY

1. Chamisso's trip to the Waianae Range is reflected in Chapter Five.
2. Strictly, *Chaetodontidae*: butterfly fish, small but used as food by the commoners. See Narrative 76, n. 2 on fishing.
3. Fishing rights were strictly guarded: see Narrative 46.

82. *7 October 1817*

A heavy and violent downpour of rain awaited us on top of the mountain [west of Honolulu]. My Hawaiians' clothing, being made of bark, resisted the rain as though made of unsized paper. To protect it, they used a *Dracaena terminalis* treetop.[1] *Maro* [Malo] and *tappa* [kapa] wrap were pulled tightly around the little trunk, the wide leaves being bent backwards, spread out, and tied with string ... I myself removed all my clothes, which were soaked, and we went down the mountainside naked, that is, in "the national dress of a savage!"

It has been mentioned so many times that the Hawaiians are more sensitive than we are to the cold that the fact is scarcely noteworthy now and I should not touch on it. I merely add that for me, as a collector, it was *not* a helpful thing. Rain fell again, when we made a second crossing of the mountain range over a higher pass,[2] so that we had no view of the surrounding country all that time. Descending again to an inhabited area, I made myself decent by covering parts of my body with two handkerchiefs. My escort was satisfied with an even smaller covering, his whole attire consisting of a piece of string about three inches long ....

I have actually always used handkerchiefs, and never carried botanists' tin boxes on my excursions. One spreads out the kerchief, places the collected plant specimens across it, presses them with one hand, and with the other hand and mouth then ties the opposite ends of the kerchief into a knot. The lower end can then be tied to the others and the fourth end can be used for carrying. On longer expeditions, of course, when one has both a guide and a bearer along, one can take a bound book of blotting-paper in which to secure the delicate specimens at once. On this particular occasion, the heavy rain had completely soaked my plant collection and I feared it would rot. So when we reached a house, one side of it was made *kapu*—and there I spread my specimens out overnight .... I returned from this expedition on 10 October, and on the 12th undertook one final trip into the hills.

Chamisso

COMMENTARY

1. *Cordyline terminalis* or *ti* tree. Chamisso's escorts associated the leaves of *ti* with protection from rain, the *ti*-leaf rain cape being much used, especially by the common people, in rainy months.
2. This would have been Kolekole Pass, a little southwest of Mount Kaala, the more southerly and lower pass across to Waianae being Pohakea Pass, used by Liholiho and the Hawaiian annalist John Papa-Ii in his childhood (Ii, 1963:23, 27, and 96). Chamisso had followed the usual trail from the Pearl River's upper reach toward Kunia. His botanical collection, part of which remains at the Institute of Botany of the Academy of Sciences of the USSR, in Leningrad, reflects his route up to the rain forest.

83. *11–12(?) October 1817*

In the evening, when the air grew fresher, I would take a daily walk, which may here be done without any danger whatever.[1] For although one often encounters drunk persons, they are mainly cheerful and affectionate when in that state. They get drunk on *kava* ['*awa*] root, which is prepared here exactly as on other South Sea Islands, the only difference being that here only old women chew the actual root; young women soak it in saliva, to dilute the pap.[2] The harmfulness of frequent use of this root is shown by the ulcers with which the natives here are constantly afflicted. The nobles prefer to intoxicate themselves with rum, which they get by barter from the Americans.[3]

There are now many fields left uncultivated, since the natives are obliged to be cutting sandalwood.[4] On my way to the plantations, I was met by two boys carrying large bunches of bananas. These boys halted every hundred paces and, with a loud cry, drew the attention of the people all around to themselves. Men immediately threw themselves to the ground, covering their faces with both hands, and did not get up until the boys had moved further on; but far more was expected of the women. On catching sight of these boys, they were obliged immediately to undress. I was told that an important *tabu* [*kapu*] was to begin that evening,[5] and that the bananas were being taken to a temple as an offering to the gods.

                                                                        Kotzebue

COMMENTARY

1. Matters were different by 1825: see Narrative 113.
2. See Narrative 88 and Ii, 1963:107, and 128 on *'okolehao*.
3. Gillesem confirms this: Narrative 94.
4. See Narrative 27, n. 1; Malo, 1839:126–27; Ellis, 1826:375–76; and Mathison, 1825:451 (commoners' sufferings).
5. *Kapu pule*, or more precisely *kapu Hua*. Observance of *kapu Hua* in *makahiki* was indeed associated with propitiation of the deity and his progress, in idol form, around the island: see Malo, 1903:188ff. Kotzebue witnessed the effects of *kapu moe*, the prostration *kapu*: see Ii, 1963:51, 95. Either the god itself was about to pass, its arrival being loudly proclaimed at short intervals by the boys (lest the unwitting not prostrate themselves and/or disrobe, so endangering their lives), or some *kapu* chief was walking in daytime.

84.   *11 October 1817*

In front of one house, I found a large gathering of ladies who had placed themselves around a fire on which they had roasted a dog. Most politely, they invited me to take part in the feast; but on this occasion, I did not have time. The female sex, to whom pork is forbidden, eat dog's flesh instead,[1] and with this in view, the dogs are fed only on fruit. These dogs, which would appear to belong to the same breed as our hound, have the peculiarity of never attaching themselves to people. For that reason, they are always kept together with swine.[2]

                                                                        Kotzebue

COMMENTARY

1. See Narrative 123 (Namahana enjoying pork).
2. Russian evidence confirms that dogs were being raised as "an article of food," in Reverend William Ellis's phrase (Ellis, 1839: 347), on a considerable scale.

85. *28 October 1817*

The following day, 28 October, I again passed the morning ashore. We were shown how the Islanders prepare food for themselves in a pit, using hot stones.[1] To this end, they roasted a small pig, some fish, and vegetables, undertaking the entire operation in our presence, beginning with the stifling of the piglet. One should explain that the natives do not kill animals with knives, but instead tie up the mouth and so stifle them ...

On the 19th I was again ashore and dined with Devis [Davis].[2] Before the meal, Bokki [Boki] ordered his Islanders to entertain us with a sham battle. For this, they used spears and bows made of sugar-cane sticks. The battle was more like a game than military manoeuvres ...[3] Later, fist-fights started; but only two pairs fought, and rather poorly at that.[4] Many came forward but could not agree to fight, each man considering himself weaker than his opponent. The Americans told me that the Sandwich Islanders had altogether lost their courage and their skill with hand weapons. Finding firearms far preferable, they took to our guns and pistols, without however learning to handle them properly, while abandoning their own weaponry.

Golovnin

COMMENTARY

1. See also Narrative 94.
2. Captain William Heath Davis, Sr., master and owner of the merchantman *Eagle*, formerly *Isabella*: Howay, 1973:121; and Pierce, 1965:232.
3. See Narratives 39 and 77.
4. *Mokomoko*, Hawaiian boxing in which an opponent's blow was received on the fist if possible, often caused broken arms. It was traditionally practised in the *makahiki* season, unlike the more savage *kui-alua*, in which every effort was made to maim.

86. *Late October 1818*

If Tameamea [Kamehameha I] would pay as much attention to the rights of his subjects as he does to those of Europeans living with him, or indeed even half as much, he might greatly alleviate the present burdensome situation of the common people, whose life and property are now at the absolute disposal of the chiefs. The rights and the properties of the latter are, on the other hand, hereditary.

These chiefs keep very careful track of their own pedigrees, and trace back the origins of each family. Their system of kinship has yet to be fully understood by us Europeans. While we were in the king's residence, for instance, the king's own son[1] came and sat on the threshold of the door. I gestured to him to enter and be seated beside us; but I was informed that he could not enter his father's house, since his natural mother was a member of the noblest family on the island of Hawaii, and he was hence of nobler antecedents than his father ....[2]

The chiefs own all the land, and they alone have the right to eat meat and certain kinds of the better fish forbidden to commoners ... Tameamea himself prefers dog meat to pork; almost every day, he is served a fat roasted pup for dinner ... As far as women and commoners are concerned, all injunctions pertaining to food are strictly observed. But many of the chiefs do not observe the prohibitions that relate to themselves. At certain times, for instance, they may not eat pork, fowl, etc.; but they disregard everything and eat whatever they feel like ....[3] Eliot [Elliot] told me that the more important the chief is, the less he will follow such injunctions, and that these free-thinking chiefs, so to speak, are more attached to Europeans and get along with them better. A woman, however, no matter how noble she is, may not break a single one of the prohibitions imposed on her sex.

Golovnin

COMMENTARY

1. Liholiho.
2. Compare Narrative 41. On Keopuolani, Kamehameha's sacred wife, see Sinclair, 1976.
3. Confirmed by Kotzebue, 1821, 2:247; and Vasil'ev, 1821:36; see also Simpson, 1847, 2:31; and Tumarkin, 1964:96–98.

87. *Late October 1818*

When they see a European dressed in an outfit consisting of several separate garments—for instance, a dress-coat, waistcoat, etc.—they do not realize that by our standards it is improper to appear without a coat, no matter how rich and attractive the rest of the outfit may be; that is, that all is required. They ascribe it to vanity and say that we want to show off as much clothing as possible at one time. Therefore on formal occasions they do the same thing.[1] At other times, they may wear only underclothing, without stockings or anything else; and a second man may sport only a vest and a loincloth around his middle;[2] and a third may have merely a tunic thrown over his naked body. This is accepted among them as ordinary everyday clothing is among us. But this people's favourite clothing is an ordinary white shirt with cuffs, or a long coat. The chiefs mostly walk about in one garment: shirt or coat.[3] Otherwise, they wear nothing from head to foot. The common people often dress themselves up in old sailors' jerseys or pants, which they get by barter from Americans.

Golovnin

COMMENTARY

1. Attitudes had changed by 1826: see Narrative 129; also Narratives 7, 50 and 112 (selective use of clothing).
2. Kinau, Governor of Oahu, met Kotzebue so dressed in 1824: see Narrative 54.
3. Franchère, 1854:64; Campbell, 1816:136–37.

88. Late October 1818

Chiefs are beginning to adopt European customs in their mode of life. For instance, they now drink tea twice daily, usually in the morning and towards evening.[1] And some dishes are prepared for their table in our way, boiled or roasted .... But unfortunately strong spirits are in too general use among them now; and numerous chiefs have become inveterate drunkards.[2] Even the king's son and heir, a young man, and the king's first counselor or minister, a relative of his favourite wife, drink immoderately and so cause grief to old Tameamea [Kamehameha I] who, though a very sober man himself, cannot restrain them.

The common people are likewise addicted to this pernicious vice and now, on Voagu [Oahu] Island, where more ships call than at any other island, certain foodstuffs are purchased with strong spirits as if on a fixed rate of exchange. For one large goat, for instance, Americans now give two bottles of rum, for a kid one bottle.[3] We ourselves were at Voagu just a few days before the biggest of their festivals, which starts in the first half of November and continues for twenty-one days.[4] During this time the natives do not occupy themselves with any kind of work, and are forbidden even to go out in their craft. They pass the time eating, drinking, and playing games. For this reason the chiefs, whom I offered articles I had stowed in exchange for fruits and vegetables, turned me down, asking instead for rum. They said that a protracted festival was approaching, during the course of which they had absolutely to be drunk every day ....

It should be noted, however, that in bringing strong spirits and cards, the Europeans merely spread drinking and cardplaying, but did not actually introduce them to the Sandwich Islanders.[5] The latter had, after all, been quite at home with both vices before Cook's arrival. They well knew how to prepare an intoxicating drink from the well-known pepper plant called *kava* ['awa], and they had used it to excess.[6] This drink has a most unpleasant and foul taste and could not be to everyone's liking. On the other hand, all the Sandwich Islanders are exceedingly fond of European liquors.

Golovnin

COMMENTARY

1. Under Kamehameha's influence: Campbell, 1816:131.

2. See Narratives 83 and 113; also Turnbull, 1805, 2:62–63.

3. Broughton, 1804:34; Freeman, 1927:79 (wild goats as a nuisance around Honolulu); Campbell, 1816:146–47, 185–86; and Alexander, 1899:156–57 (the rum trade).

4. *Makahiki*, actually lasting four months.

5. See Narratives 107, 113 and 114 on gambling and cards.

6. On *Piper methysticum* ('awa) as an ancient drink of the *ali'i*, farmers, and others, see Titcomb, 1948.

89. *Late October 1818*

For making their outrigger-canoes, they employ a quite hard wood, taken from a tree that grows on the Islands.[1] To make large craft or war-canoes, that same wood and certain others too were used. But these are no longer being made now, and the natives are building brigs, schooners, gunboats, and armed launches on the European model.[2] The war-canoes of the Sandwich Islands were generally about eight fathoms long, but Vancouver saw one sixty-one and one-half feet long .... The Islanders fashion their eating vessels from gourds, coconut shells, and a wood called *etoe*,[3] or sacred wood.

Golovnin

COMMENTARY

1. Presumably *koa*. The timber was already scarce.
2. The original "model" was the *Britannia*, built by Vancouver's carpenters for Kamehameha I in 1793.
3. Apparently a typographical error made in 1821. The wood in question seems to be *koa*, whose soft grain made it suitable for carving into wooden food bowls (*'umeke la'au*).

90. *Late October 1818*

Tameamea [Kamehameha I] values these garments [red feather cloaks] so highly because of the labour and the considerable time needed to produce them. For every such cloak, after all, one must first catch several hundred small birds,[1] perhaps more than a thousand of them, then pluck their tiny feathers, sew them together, and at the same time attach them to a stuff resembling loose-woven cloth.[2] The Sandwich Islanders catch these birds by means of long poles, the upper extremity of which is smeared with a sticky substance obtained from a tree. Alighting on the rod, the birds stick to it and, lacking the strength to free themselves, become the hunter's prey ....[3] Eliot told me that the king alone may sell these cloaks [Plate 17], and that Tameamea will not accept less than 800 *piastres* for one.[4]

Golovnin

COMMENTARY

1. *I'iwi* (*Vestiaria coccinea*), in the first instance.
2. Technique described by Buck, 1957:215–17.
3. On these professional birdcatchers, or *po'e hahai manu*, see Brigham, 1899:3–4.
4. See Narrative 47. For discussion of the feather cloaks held at MAE in Leningrad, see Likhtenberg, 1960:182, 198–99; and Kaeppler, 1978.

91. *Late October 1818*

The waters surrounding the Sandwich Islands are rich in fish, but most are not too tasty, though the natives in fact prefer them to the varieties that we find more agreeable. Shark or dogfish, for example, is a delicacy of the local chiefs.[1] And the same is true of bonito, dolphin, grampus, etc.; but they dislike mackerel, sea bass, and two or three kinds that we, in Europe, would consider choice .... Turtles are also caught in a number of places on various islands, and crayfish are very plentiful indeed.[2]

Golovnin

COMMENTARY

1. Five kinds of shark were traditionally eaten, including the hammerhead and the great white shark (see Beckley, 1883:10ff.). On Oahu, they were noosed from canoes or even taken by hand when stupified by 'awa (Buck, 1957:289).
2. Bonito fishing was the sport of kings in Hawaii, and religious rites and kapu related to its consumption. See Malo, 1903:71–73 for remarks on turtles and dolphins.

92. 23–29 March 1821

It is a rare hut that has window openings, but nearly every one has two doors, one in each of two facing walls. These doors are covered only by mats. The huts of the commoners measure about three or four fathoms square, but the royal huts and those belonging to the grandees are far more spacious, measuring up to twenty fathoms square. The interior of these huts, however, is unvaried. There are clean, patterned grass mats over the floor, and at one end there is an elevation, divided off from the rest of the interior by a curtain made of the same stuff. This raised area is the bedroom ....[1]

The settlement [of Honolulu] seems large, because even the poorest Sandwich Islander should have two huts: one for himself and his sons, another for his wives and daughters. The king himself and his grandees have a separate hut for each wife and daughter ... And during our time there, polygamy was almost general, especially amongst the nobles.[2] The king had seven wives, as did the Island Governor, a handsome man not older than twenty-five.[3] No matter how much the missionaries may have been up in arms against this particular custom, it has remained in full force, as of old, regardless of the missionaries' efforts to adduce themselves as exemplars of their own doctrine and to assure the Vagu [Oahu] natives that they live very contentedly—with but one wife.[4]

It is a peculiarity that, on these Islands, the nobles differ strikingly in external appearance from the common people. The latter are of medium height and are lean, whereas the grandees are almost all of gigantic size, and very corpulent.

Golovnin

COMMENTARY

1. There are a number of similar descriptions of the Hawaiian dwelling by contemporary Russians; see Lisianskii, 1812, 1:208–09; and Vasil'ev, 1821:23–24. Gillesem's evidence is interesting in that it plainly states that, at Honolulu in 1821,

door openings (*puka*) were not fitted with (sliding or hinged) boards of traditional type (see Buck, 1957:101–02; and Malo, 1903:160). Gillesem's estimation of the floor area of a commoner's dwelling closely echoes Cook's of 1779 (Cook, 1784, III:140). By the standards of houses of *ali'i* seen by Cook and other early explorers, however, grandees' houses "measuring up to twenty fathoms square" were enormous.

2. Soviet scholarship has paid much attention to such assertions as this: see Tumarkin, 1954:110–16; and 1964:28–30. See also Narrative 119.

3. Boki Kamauleule was born circa 1785, so cannot have been the chief in question: see Ii, 1963:53 (his ancestry). Gillesem most likely confused Boki with Kuakini (1792?–1844), Governor of Hawaii and, at this period, a notorious "stealer of wives:" see Joseph Feher's *Hawaii: A Pictorial History* (Honolulu, B.P. Bishop Museum. Special Publ. No. 58, 1969):185.

4. See Bradley, 1968:124–25, and 158–59 (missionary successes against polygamy after 1823, etc.)

93. *29 March 1821*

The *maro* [*malo*], a sort of narrow girdle, one end of which is passed through the legs then tied at the back, is the men's only clothing.[1] It is made of a material which the natives produce, a sort of papyrus. Having stripped bark from a tree, they soak it in lime-water for about two weeks. Then, pulling it out, they stretch it on boards and bring the edges together. As many pieces are used as may be needed to produce the required breadth of material. Next, the stuff is beaten with flat cylinders till it is paper-thin.[2] In this form it is dried in the sun and restretched by hand until it is soft. It is finally embellished with various vegetable colouring agents, of extremely bright tones ....[3]

Women sometimes ornament themselves for dancing by placing a second, multi-coloured *pau* [*pa'u*], replete with festoons, over their ordinary one.[4] On these occasions, they also put wreathes woven from black, red and yellow feathers round the head and neck,[5] and wear plaited banana leaves round the shoulders. Ivy is also twisted round the leg just above the foot and round the arm at the wrist.[6]

Gillesem

COMMENTARY

1. Patently untrue: Russians saw cloaks of several sorts in use on Oahu in 1820, as earlier.

2. There are a number of secondary beaters (*i'e kuku*) in Leningrad, on permanent display: see Likhtenberg, 1960:200–01. "Flat cylinder" is a wretched description of *I'e kuku*, however, so *hohoa* clubs are doubtless meant: Buck, 1957:170–71.

3. See also Narratives 51 and 82 (colouring and impermeability).

4. See Narrative 69.

5. Depicted in Plate 11. The Russian evidence, fully complemented by data in Lahilahi Webb's study of featherwork in traditional Hawaiian culture (see Webb, 1933), underlines the persistence of such *lei hulu* in terms of technique, colour,

and use. No Russian saw the light green feathers of the *'o'u* bird in use as ornamentation, nor had colour schemes altered since Cook's time.

6. An error: ivy was not indigenous to the Hawaiian Islands. Gillesem was no botanist and was probably seeing garlands of sweet-scented *Alyxia olivaeformis* (*maile*) leaves, often worn around the neck or limbs during *hula* performances. See lithograph by Lauvergne given in Feher, 1969:171; and Buck, 1957:533.

94. *23–24 March 1821*

We saw taro roots used as food in the following manner. Having first been soaked in water from the sea, each root is individually placed and wrapped in banana leaves and put in a pit in the ground. The pit has been lined with hot cobblestones, and other hot stones cover the wrapped-up taro. The pit is filled in with earth, and the roots are cooked within a few hours.[1] The skins are then cleaned off and they are ground in troughs and mixed with hot water till there appears a jelly or, rather, a paste looking rather like diluted starch ....[2] This root has a strange property. If it is boiled, not baked, it causes intolerable burning pain in the mouth and throat. To avoid this, the Hawaiians boil it three times, allowing it to cool down completely each time. Thus treated, and sliced and fried in oil, the root makes a very tasty and nutritious food. Yams do not have this property, but the natives are less fond of them; they cannot be reduced to a paste by pounding.[3] In addition to these vegetables, the natives cultivate sizeable areas of *kava* or *'awa* ... but this is already going out of general use, particularly among the commoners. Nowadays, only the nobility drink the beverage prepared from it.[4] Fruits now cultivated on Vagu [Oahu] include coconuts, bananas, pisang, breadfruit, oranges, lemons, and grapes.[5]

Gillesem

COMMENTARY

1. Producing *'aipa'a*. See also Narratives 74, 97, and 108.

2. *Poi*. Technique described in Buck, 1957:20–21.

3. Yams (*uhi*) were in any case less important to the Hawaiians' health and sustenance than they were to the Western Polynesians. Several Russian accounts of the early 1800s make mention of Hawaiian yams, even so; and *Dioscorea alata*, in one or more of its many cultivated varieties (see Handy, *The Hawaiian Planter*: B.P. Bishop Museum Bull. no. 161, 1949:168–69), were certainly stowed aboard Russian ships that had called at the Islands in 1804–35.

4. Kotzebue asserts the opposite (Narrative 83), but Golovnin and Lazarev (Narratives 88 and 127) support Gillesem's position. Choris painted high-born imbibers: Plate 10.

5. Introduced to Oahu by Marin, like rice and coffee: see Narratives 102 and 108; and Bradley, 1968:240–41.

95. *Early April 1821*

The language of the Sandwich Islands is soft, pleasant to the ear, and very easily mastered by the foreigner. There are many vowels in its words, but the letter "r" is scarcely heard. The one common language is in use on all the Hawaiian Islands, there being merely certain differences in pronunciation or certain letters missing locally ... On Ovagi [Hawaii] Island, for example, a priest is *kaguna* [*kahuna*], but on Vagu [Oahu] he is *tahuna*. And on Vagu, Queens Kagumanna [Kaahumanu] and Kaligamega [Kalihameha] were known as Taahumanu and Talihameha.[1]

                                                                    Gillesem

COMMENTARY

1. The Russians on Oahu in 1821 were particularly aware of sound differences between the language they heard there and what they had heard on Hawaii Island. Lieutenant Aleksei Petrovich Lazarev, of Gillesem's own ship, collaborated with Lieutenant Pavel Zelenoi of the *Otkrytie* to compile a Hawaiian wordlist (see Kuznetsova, 1968:245 and Tumarkin, 1982:54). Chamisso published an early Hawaiian grammar in 1837, and worked on a dictionary also: details in Schweizer, 1973:20–27, and 31–32. Even earlier, in 1804, Lisianskii had taken the trouble to compile a Hawaiian word-list on the basis of what he and others from the ship *Neva* had heard at Kealakekua-Kaawaloa on the Kona Coast. There are interesting variants between his renderings of certain words or phrases and the equivalents recorded by Cook and his people. The Russian (or Russo-German) contribution to Hawaiian language studies cannot, indeed, be compared with the British contribution of the late 18th century. The very use of Cyrillic characters to convey Hawaiian sounds (a matter in which Reverend Hiram Bingham took a keen interest, to his credit), presents difficulties to the modern linguist; and there are various frustrating inconsistencies between Lisianskii's Russian- and English-language word-lists of Hawaiian, i.e. between his Russian list and his own translation of it. Chamisso's Russian- and German-language treatments of Hawaiian offer comparable problems. Even so, the Russians' and particularly Chamisso's contributions to our knowledge of the historical development of spoken Hawaiian do merit more attention. In the West there have been no attempts to build upon the work of Samuel H. Elbert, whose important commentary on Chamisso's Hawaiian grammar appeared in 1969 (see Chamisso, 1969). In the USSR, the manuscript of A.P. Lazarev's Hawaiian word-list lay undisturbed, in TsGAVMF (*fond* 213, op. 1, *delo* 43), until the early 1980s. It is now being edited for publication, together with related papers by the same lieutenant which are held at the Saltykov-Shchedrin Public Library in Leningrad (e.g., his diary and notes from the *Blagonamerennyi*: *fond* 17, 106″; kollektsiia I.V. Pomialovskogo, no. 72, etc.)

96. *Early December 1826*

Our native guide offered us his own travelling rations consisting of taro dough,[1] one small fish, and three coconuts, but we were looking forward to refreshments at Gonorura [Honolulu] and, understanding what the provident

Sandwich Islander really wanted to do, we let our little army settle down around a huge calabash full of earlier-prepared taro.[2] They filled their cheeks with the stuff, very skilfully and deftly using a single finger. This exercise allowed us to see that each of our bodyguards had one front tooth missing. The reason was that, on the death of Tameamea [Kamehameha I]—or rather when the news of it reached the people—nearly all his male subjects had quite willingly knocked out a front tooth. They thus performed a mourning rite for which a mere change of clothing would have been inadequate.[3]

Wrangel

COMMENTARY

1. *Pa'i'ai*, the doughy mass which, when water is added, produces *poi* (Buck, 1957:21; and Malo, 1903:67). On Oahu, this "hard *poi*" was formed into small balls and wrapped in *ti* leaves; on Hawaii, it was rolled into long cylinders.
2. This was an *ipu nui*, a very large gourd: Buck, 1957:33–35. Chamisso had seen *poi* eaten in this fashion in 1816 (Narrative 72).
3. Russians also saw tattooing associated with mourning for Kamehameha I (see Buck, 1957:565–66), but no signs of scarring caused by skin laceration (shark's teeth incision at a king's death).

For another view of Hawaiian customs, see Aleksei Lazarev's account of a March–April 1821 visit, Chapter 11 (Narrative 127).

CHAPTER NINE

Honolulu Village

97. *January–March 1809*

King Tomio-omio [Kamehameha I] draws great advantages from trade. He himself owns the best of the islands' productions, and ships calling in can provision themselves with everything they need in a very short time. Thanks to this trade that he has personally been conducting with foreigners for many years now, the king has accumulated such quantities of European goods of various sorts that many such wares lie unused.[1] Nor has he need of anything more except objects needed for his fleet. Since his own products are necessary if not indispensable to his visitors, however, he values them highly and will certainly not sell them cheap. Often, he will part with swine only for Spanish *piastres*.

Still, it is possible to bring these Islanders broadcloths of lesser quality, also walrus tusks, from which they make an ornament like a hook, to be worn at the neck.[2] And from the Hawaiians, for use in America or Kamchatka, one can take good salt, dried taro, and new *ti* [*ki*] tree rum. This rum improves in quality during the voyage and on being left for awhile.[3] As for the Hawaiian bast cordage, it is perhaps not as good as hempen cord but it can certainly be put to use in case of need, when hempen rope is wanting.[4]

These Islanders will purchase broadcloth whether it be heavy or fine, just so long as it is dense and close-woven; nor do they prefer one shade to another. All shades are equally acceptable.[5] They do not cut the cloth, however, or make any clothing from it in our sense. The men wear it in their *maro* [*malo*] or girdles, but for that purpose they need no more than a quarter of an *arshin* of material in length. The women, on the other hand, wrap a piece of cloth round themselves and then fix it just below the breast, so giving themselves cover down to the knee. The cloth thus makes a variety of attractive skirt ....

The dried and ground taro is hardly inferior to flour in any way.[6] It is important, in itself, in the natives' diet. Diligent hands can produce sugar and rum from the local sugar-cane.

Gagemeister

COMMENTARY

1. See Narratives 27 and 105 on the value of royal trade. Like Archibald Campbell, Gagemeister saw Kamehameha I's storehouse at Honolulu and was struck by the quantity and scope of wares and supplies: see Campbell, 1816:212. He himself added a few Russian goods to the "large stock of European articles of every description," (*ibid.*), rightly supposing that the king must become wealthy. Kotzebue saw the later development of this: see Chamisso in Kotzebue, *Voyage*, III:240; also Roquefeuil, 1823, II:341. What neither Gagemeister nor Campbell realized, however, was that high chiefs had always stored supplies and offerings, e.g., *makahiki* taxes, in this semi-public way: see Ii, 1963:120–21.

2. *Lei pala'oa*: The *lei pala'oa* was traditionally made of a sperm-whale tooth, suspended by two coils of braided human hair. Walrus tusks had been used for that purpose only in very recent years. Their introduction to Hawaii is associated with the arrival there of New Englanders. Buck is wrong, however, (1957:535) to suppose that the American traders in question were whalemen, for, as Gagemeister implies, *haole* were importing walrus tusks at least a decade before Captain Joseph Allen and his fellows became an important regular presence in Honolulu. The likeliest New England suppliers of walrus tusks in 1800–10 were those who sailed along the coasts of Russian North America. The Russian-American Company itself was exporting Pacific walrus tusk by 1804 at the latest: see Khlebnikov, 1976:139. In 1812, perhaps in response to Gagemeister's specific reference to the trade potential in Hawaii (in reports of 1809–10), the catch within the territory of the Company's Kodiak Office suddenly leapt to eight and one-quarter *pood* (298 lbs. avoirdupois). The walrus catch fluctuated wildly in this period, because the overhunting had depleted supplies in the North; but tusks were collected annually at Sitka and Kodiak, for sale in distant parts (*ibid.*, 12, 141; Okun', 1951:56). *Pala'oa* appeared in Hawaiian dictionaries, e.g., Parker's edition of Andrew's 1865 *Dictionary of the Hawaiian Language*, as simply "walrus"—a creature unknown to Hawaiians except through the tusks brought by Americans or Russians.

3. Gagemeister himself baulked at the price being asked at Honolulu in 1809: three *piastres* per gallon. With future Russian-Hawaiian trade in mind, he refused to buy: see Shemelin, 1818, 1:154; also Narrative 66, n. 3.

4. See Narrative 66; also Stokes, 1906:105–06; and Buck, 1957:290.

5. In June 1804, Lisianskii had found that on the Kona Coast red material was preferred to other kinds. By 1821, the Russians at Honolulu would find that their cloth was hardly wanted at all, only *kolomianka*, a striped and rather rough homespun woollen: see Lazarev, 1950:264.

6. Gagemeister took some back to Kodiak, where it was approved for use in the *promyshlennik* diet. Tikhmenev, 1939, 1:204; and Campbell, 1819:90.

98. *27 November 1816*

I met Mr. Marini [Marin], that is, Don Francisco de Paula Marini, (known to the natives as Manini), on the very first day.[1] He was in no great hurry to meet me, but I found him always helpful when I needed him and he gave me instructions in a kindly spirit. I hoped to see the whole island and learn everything there was to know. At a very tender age, Mr. Marini had been sent off in a ship about to leave port with fruits and vegetables. I believe it was from San Francisco harbour, on the Spanish-American coast of California.[2] The boy had fallen asleep under the influence of alcohol, administered by sailors once they had him aboard .... When left behind at these Sandwich Islands, he had become a chief of high repute. An industrious farmer, he had created wealth by making good use of imported animals and plants.[3] He was also a shrewd merchant, supplying the many vessels that cast anchor with all their requirements. Marini had realized that if meat was to be preserved in such a hot climate, it had to be pickled; the Spaniards had declared this an impossibility in the New World. He seemed to be independent of the king and not enjoying his particular favour. He was, in fact, more interested in the world of commerce ....[4] At our first meeting, he talked about recent events and about Napoleon, who would, he said, have done well in our Spanish America.

Chamisso

COMMENTARY

1. See also Narratives 54, 58, 102, 108 and 121 on Marin.
2. Mathison, 1825:427 (his wealth and shrewdness).
3. Marin arrived at the Islands in 1791, aboard the *Princessa real*, the former *Princess Royal*, seized by the Spaniards at Nootka Sound in 1789: Howay, 1973:10.
4. See Khlebnikov, K.T. LOII:96; and Vasil'ev, 1821:43.

99. *30 November 1816*

I set off for Gana-Rura [Honolulu], where the inhabitants behaved with great modesty and were glad when, out of curiosity, I went into their houses. All those at home then gathered around me, brought me various appetizers, talked a great deal and played like children. There was no hut without a tobacco-pipe, and smoking appears to be one of the principal pleasures here.[1] The houses of Gana-Rura, which in some places stand one beside the other in long and straight rows, but in other places are scattered about, are very like those on Ovaigi [Hawaii] Island.[2] A few Europeans who have settled here have built themselves houses that, so to speak, stand midway between our structures and the Hawaiians'.[3] The Spaniard Marini [Marin], who has built himself a stone house here, is to be recommended to every visitor to Vagu [Oahu] Island. He has introduced many useful plants and concerns himself greatly with their success. So far, he alone has a sizeable herd of oxen, cows, and sheep.[4] In the interior of the island, there are many wild cattle, brought by Europeans long ago. They multiply here very rapidly, I was told, but they have become so wild that they are actually hunted in the mountains and shot with muskets. The Spaniard Marini's herd is driven home every day, toward evening, by a naked Sandwich Islander [Plate 13]. There are also horses in his herd, which he obtained from America.[5] There has also lived on this island for some thirty years already, an Englishman named Goms [Holmes].[6] Earlier, he held Kareimoku's [Kalanimoku] position and his honest principles have brought him universal respect. But all the Europeans settling here marry Sandwich Island women, and so it is likely that, in time, the stock of the natives will vanish completely.[7]

Kotzebue

COMMENTARY

1. Locally grown and of high quality, tobacco was about to become an export item: see Bennett, 1840, 1:255; and *Sandwich Island Gazette*, 22 October 1836.
2. See Narrative 110.
3. See Narrative 129 and Map B, showing the Marin house.
4. See Mathison, 1825:426–27; and Tumarkin, 1964:83.

5. See Cleveland, 1850:204–05, and 208–10 (horses imported from California since 1803); and Broughton, 1804:34; Turnbull, 1805, 2:87; and Korobitsyn, 1944:171–72 (the problem of large herds of wild cattle).
6. Oliver Holmes, arrived in Hawaii in 1793, was a Massachussetts native, highly influential on Oahu since Isaac Davis had died in 1810: see Cox, 1832:38–39.
7. See Bingham, 1847:105–06; and Maria S. Loomis MS, 21 June, 4–14 September, 14 December 1820 (Half-caste children in Honolulu by 1820, their primary schooling, etc.)

100. *8 December 1816*

Foreseeing no danger whatever ashore, I decided to undertake a little excursion on foot to the river called Pearl River by the English, lying half a day's journey to the west of Gana-Rura [Honolulu].[1] The collecting of pearls there is prohibited on pain of death, the king alone enjoying the profits from it. But Kareimoku [Kalanimoku] had made me gifts of a few beautiful pearls from this river.[2] I ordered that he be told of my desire and he willingly gave me permission to go, appointing two guides for my greater protection .... I set out, with Dr. Eschscholtz[3] and First Mate Khramchenko, who was to assist me in surveying the coast, at 9 a.m. on 8 December. We called at the house of Mr. Bekli [Beckley], the commandant of the fort,[4] who had resolved to accompany us, and found waiting there a couple of soldiers. They were solidly-built men. For greater convenience, they had taken off all their clothing, merely retaining silver-mounted dirks as signs of their calling. As soon as we left Gana-Rura, we were obliged to cross a river of the same name, which flows from the mountains and surrounds the western portion of the small settlement itself. At some points, its width is as much as fifteen fathoms, and it is quite deep enough to take the boats that go there to water ....

On our way, we met now sugar plantations, now taro fields, now scattered huts; and so, without noticing it, we covered the five miles to the large village of Mauna-Roa [Mauna Loa], situated in a delightful valley on a mountain slope. From here, there winds to the sea a fast-flowing river of the same name. It is visible at a great distance and wanders through the mountains and cliffs in the most picturesque fashion.[5] In front of the village, consisting of pretty little reed huts, one encounters two groves, one of coconut palms, the other of breadfruit. We passed through these little groves, to take a rest on the hill lying immediately behind. And here, a general view of Honolulu Harbour opened up to us.[6] Our compass was set up and I took a number of angles with my sextant; but this caused great alarm among the inhabitants who had run up onto the hill with us, for they were expecting, so Bekli assured us, some kind of sorcery. Islanders regarded us with the greatest curiosity. These good-natured people indeed focused their attention on us, scrutinizing all our movements and actions; and they kept singing and dancing, expressing their absolute delight with the trifling presents they received from us. But they immediately changed and became displeased, when after awhile we prepared to leave them.

Kotzebue

COMMENTARY

1. See Narrative 74.
2. See Turnbull, 1805, 2:79; Peron, 1824, 2:146; Meares, 1790, App. V; and Wilson, 1930:25 and 120.
3. Johann Friedrich Eschscholtz (1793–1831), naturalist in both of Kotzebue's Pacific expeditions (*Riurik*, 1815–18 and *Predpriiatie*, 1823–26): biography and bibliography in Kotzebue, 1981:317.
4. On George Beckley, see also Narratives 8 and 12.
5. The Russians looked north from the fish-ponds: see Map A.
6. Kotzebue's route is discussed in Chapter 3; see also Ii, 1963:95.

101. *8 December 1816*

Having walked some two hours, we entered a quite delightful valley and settled down in the shade of some breadfruit trees by a salt-lake. The shores of this lake were covered with the most excellent salt, which brought the lake's owner, a distinguished *geri* [*ieri*], a large income.[1] On the lake was a species of diver which, though it cannot fly, is nonetheless very hard to shoot as it plunges under the instant it sees the flash in the priming pan. Wanting a few of these birds for our collection of natural history, I sent one of my guides to get them; and he, shooting a brace of them, proved simultaneously that the Sandvichane [Sandwich Islanders] are very good marksmen. Mr. Bekli [Beckley] had talked to me about a species of wild duck, similar to our European ones, which fly here in January, rear their young, and fly off again in early spring. This information—which I could not doubt as Beckli so loved to hunt that he would sometimes spend entire *days* by this lake—gave me the idea that there must exist some undiscovered land at latitude 45° or thereabouts, whence come these birds of passage. For one can scarcely suppose that these birds had made the journey down from the Aleutian Islands or from North America, to have a second summer here.

When we had rested a little here, we again went over a mountain. Now, we found ourselves in a beautifully cultivated valley full of taro fields, sugar-cane plantations, and banana tree groves.[2] At such a distance from the main town, Gana-Rura [Honolulu], we were yet greater objects of curiosity to the local natives .... We walked through one avenue which, I thought, was of aloe trees. The trees were twice as high as a man, perhaps four and a half *arshin*, and they had round red fruits. My guide, noticing that I paid these particular attention, picked a few of them and invited me to try them—little thinking that I had failed to recognize them. I bit off a piece from one fruit and was punished for my sweet tooth; for though I found the taste quite good, my whole mouth was full of little thorns, which caused me pain till the next morning .... Dr. Eschscholtz, who had lagged behind us ..., informed me that the fruit was not aloe but cactus or Indian fig.[3]

We went past the properties of Iung [Young] and Goms [Holmes],[4] which the king had presented to them, and noticed how very spacious and excellently cultivated they were. Though the sun still stood high in the sky, the air was filled with a kind of bat.[5]

Kotzebue

COMMENTARY

1. In 1809, Gagemeister had taken salt from this lake to Petropavlovsk-in-Kamchatka: Campbell, 1816:117, and 124–25; Golder, 1930:40; and Bradley, 1968:48. In 1821, *Thaddeus* would carry more from it, to the same place: *MHSP*, 44:37. The lake was called Aliapaakai, on the northeast of Halawa.

2. This was the 1"Wauiau" Valley, the headwater of which the Russians had approached from the northeast: see Chapter 3. See Ii, 1963:95–96 on the ancient trail to Halawa and Aiea.

3. 310 cm. These were *Opuntia ficus-indica*.

4. See Narratives 99 and 127 on Oliver Holmes; Narratives 1, 4–8 etc. on John Young. These estates lay on what is now the perimeter of Honolulu International Airport.

5. This was the *'ope'apa'a*, an indigenous Hawaiian mammal, not used for food.

102. Early December 1816

There are no bridges over the streams and rivers by Hana-Rura [Honolulu]. The fresh water itself provides a bath which is no less valued by the people living by the ocean than we, who live inland, value the saltwater. One is reminded of the fresh water at every opportunity and asked, "Would you like to bathe?"

I had once undressed to cross the stream that flows into the harbour behind Hana-Rura.[1] The water was up to my knees. A light canoe came near and I heard loud laughter. It was a woman who was enjoying teasing me. I behaved like an innocent maid whom a boor had bothered whilst she took a bath!

In the course of another walk, a guide led me through a broad, quiet stream. He went into it before me and it did not reach up to his chest; but I, though I could not really swim, got the idea of attempting to swim across. I tried and— surprise! The water bore me. I was well pleased with myself and thought that, though I was perhaps not a master of the natives' art of swimming, I would show them that I was not entirely unacquainted with it. I was rudely awakened from this dream: when I looked round to see what was happening (there were shouts of laughter from the river-bank), I observed a crowd laughing at the odd *kanaka haole* who, instead of wading through the water like any sensible man, was going to such trouble to demonstrate his own incompetence. However, the laughter had nothing hostile in it. Men have the right to laugh ....

Hiking through the fertile valley immediately behind Hana-Rura, on another day, I found at the edge of a taro-irrigation channel, a beautiful grass which I had not seen before. I picked a few samples, but a native approached me angrily and I had difficulty in calming him down. I talked about this to Mr. Marini [Marin] afterwards, and showed him my grass. The man had been his tenant and the grass was rice which, finally and after many mistrials, he had managed to grow this year.[2] Many a botanist might have laughed at me, but would not have fared better. In a herbarium, I could not have recognized *Oryza sativa*.

                                                                    Chamisso

COMMENTARY

1. See Narrative 70.

2. Marin persevered, in the early 1820s, but rice did not become an important crop on Oahu: see *Sandwich Island Gazette*, 22 October 1836; and Simpson, 1847, 2:124–27; see also Narratives 98 and 108 on his horticulture.

103. *December 1816*

In the cemetery for Europeans near Honolulu,[1] the following simple inscription may be seen on the grave of Mr. Davis:

"The remains
of
Mr. Isaac Davis,
who died at this
Island, April 1810
aged 52 years."

When we last sailed from Honolulu, we left Mr. Jung [Young] in a very enfeebled state because of his age. Both these friends, whose names have long shone in the history of these islands, will repose together.[2] Although indeed Mr. Jung's children will receive his estate as their inheritance,[3] they will still lack the respect of the populace inasmuch as they were born of a woman not of noble antecedents.[4]

Chamisso

COMMENTARY

1. At the intersection of modern Pensacola and Piikoi, at the southeastern foot of the Punchbowl: see Map A. Like Cleveland in 1803, Chamisso saw the 1802 gravestone of Captain Derby: see Cleveland, 1843, 1:233; Restarick, 1923:58–59. Ii, 1963:83–84 describes the funeral procession for Davis and explains the burial site.

2. See Narrative 8; also Bishop, 1827:49; Shaler, 1808:162; Vancouver, 1798, 3:65–66; and Bell, 1929:76.

3. See Narrative 105; also Maria S. Loomis MS: June 1820, *passim*; and Bingham, 1847:105ff.

4. Chamisso was mistaken: unlike the *kulu* offspring of many *haoles* on Oahu (Malo, 1903:82), who were given deprecating or even insulting names, Young's three sons and three daughters enjoyed wealth and standing in the Islands. John Young Jr., (Keoni Ana), was minister of the interior of the Hawaiian Kingdom in the 1850s: see Carter, 1923:51–53. Isaac Davis's own son, George Hueu Davis, likewise had a native mother of good birth and so enjoyed status.

104. *11 October 1817*

When, on 11 October, I heard the sound of a dull drum, I was seized with the urge to go into the temple;[1] but, supposing that entry was forbidden, I stopped a little distance from it. I also supposed, since it was not a *tabu [kapu]* day, that the people in it must be priests. The attention with which I was looking at them was noticed from the temple, and soon two Sandwich Islanders came out to me with the salutation, *Aroga [Aloha] ieri nui* ("Greetings, great chief!"), and invited me to enter. I was greatly surprised that they gave me this permission and, I confess, was even apprehensive at first lest the priests take it into their heads to offer me to their gods ....

I found only an area about fifty fathoms square, fenced in with a bamboo palisade; in the middle of the little square, six small huts[2] stood one beside another in the form of a semicircle. Each of these chapels was surrounded by a low fence of plaited reeds, above which protruded, like sentinels, the colossal heads of their idols.[3] The necks supporting these dreadful heads were hung around with swine, and several still bore the bones of hogs that had rotted away .... Near one particular hut stood two complete statues, the male and female sex of which could be discerned, crude though the carving was. Between them a pole had been fixed in the ground, its tip hung about with bananas. The woman, who was facing the man, had grasped the fruit with her left hand while the man extended his right hands towards it. Any observer, seeing it, would have had to think of Adam and Eve, and I greatly regretted having nobody with me who, knowing the language, might have explained the allegory to me. The priests pointed out to me that the open mouths of both statues were full of human teeth. One of the small chapels[4] was covered around by mats, and the dull sound of a drum reverberated from it, often interrupted by a man's pitiful cry. All this together produced on me such an impression that I was extremely glad when I was able to leave the place.

Kotzebue

COMMENTARY

1. This was almost certainly the *heiau* built hastily in 1816 to replace one defiled by the incursion of Scheffer's men: see Narratives 68 and 72. The temple drum (*heiau pahu*) produced a "dull" tone because it was generously covered with shark-skin.
2. The usual number of temple houses was four: see Buck, 1957:520–21; and Malo, 1903:213–14.
3. Choris drew a number of temple images in 1816–17: see Choris, 1822: Plates V–VI and discussion on pp. 12–13.
4. The *hale pahu*. Kotzebue's whole description makes an interesting comparison with the Russian descriptions of Hikiau *heiau* at Kealakekua, Hawaii, as it was in June 1804. See Barratt, 1987: Pt. 3, 4. The insertion of human teeth, usual in feather images, is a most unusual one in wooden god figures.

105. *Late October 1818*

Another principle of Tameamea [Kamehameha I] ... is not to give any of the foreigners who come to his islands special privileges but rather to act in the same way with all, allowing everyone to trade freely and equally with his subjects but forbidding the Europeans to establish their own settlements.[1] With this in view, he grants control of land to Englishmen and Americans in his service only on the condition that the grants will remain theirs only so long as they reside on the Islands.[2] They may not, under any circumstances, transfer these lands to another person; and the estates revert to the king on their death or departure ....

Children born of mixed marriages between these European settlers and native women will be of particular assistance in the development of this nation. While acquiring certain knowledge from the father, they will at the same time be attached to the native land through the mother and her customs. I saw many such children; they were running around almost naked as do the rest of the natives, but they understand English and they also know certain trades ....[3]

The Sandwich Islanders have in fact become very skilful and shrewd in their trade, especially their ruler, Tameamea. Proof of this is the fact that he has with him several men, chiefs of lower rank, who know English and whose duty it is to visit foreign ships and discover from their crews what the cargo is and of what volume. It is also their duty to calculate the number of people in the vessel, so that Tameamea may charge for his goods and provisions accordingly. The principal ware is now sandalwood, which they divide up into three or four grades. They always show the lowest grade first, then, if that is not taken, wood of a slightly higher quality. Only when dealing with connoisseurs, and after many arguments, will they sell the very best wood .... Americans transport it to Canton and sell it to the Chinese who use it for various boxes, cases and the like, and especially to make coffins and a type of oil that is burned in temples.[4]

Golovnin

COMMENTARY

1. This confirms statements by Shaler, 1808:171–72; Campbell, 1816:122, 150, and 160; Cox, 1832:40; and Corney, 1896:36 and 47.
2. See Bradley, 1968: 35–36.
3. See Narratives 99 and 103; on the trades, see Campbell, 1816:166.
4. See Narratives 27 and 127; and Bradley, 1968:55–57 (state of the sandalwood trade in 1818). Gillesem saw the narrow planks of sandalwood (6 feet long and 3 inches thick or less) that were being sold by New Englanders in Canton: Gillesem, 1849:223–24.

106. *29 October 1818*

The Sandwich Islanders have also introduced a tax on the sale of foodstuffs to foreigners, especially hens, pigs, and goats. Tameamea [Kamehameha I] fixes the prices, and no native may charge less—though he may charge more.[1] In consequence, warships needing provisions but carrying no trade goods must give the Islanders very large sums of money for everything they buy.[2] Conversely, the Americans who are constantly in these waters bring with them vast quantities of European trifles of all sorts, generally doing their best to bring something the Hawaiians have not seen before; and they use these trifles as payment for everything they obtain, though often quoting prices in *piastres*. Often enough, they will give a Sandwich Islander a bauble costing fifty *kopeks* in exchange for a pig, but will quote it at seven or eight *piastres*. The native takes the bauble from the American, not knowing its value but merely liking it and considering it worth his pig .... Today, a warship in need of a large quantity of supplies would be making a great mistake in calling at these islands to reprovision. Two medium-sized hogs cost me fifteen *piastres*.

Justice demands that I should here mention a very fine deed performed by Mr. William [Heath] Devis [Davis], a citizen of the North American Republic and owner and master of several vessels trading in the Hawaiian area.[3] Learning from the Spaniard Manini [Marin] that I had commissioned him to purchase cabbage and other greenstuffs for my crew, and realizing that I should have to pay for them in *piastres*, he gave Manini a sufficient quantity of his own trade goods to cover my purchase and refused to take any money from me in return, saying that the goods had cost him little enough ....[4] I had no way of showing gratitude to that worthy gentleman except by presenting him with some rockets and fireworks, of which he had need and we had a superfluity.

Golovnin

COMMENTARY

1. See Narrative 105.
2. See Narratives 108 and 129.
3. Davis (Narratives 17, 18 and 85), was master only of the *Eagle* in 1818, but had an interest in other vessels: see Pierce, 1965:232; Khlebnikov, 1976:7, 58.
4. On Marin's increasing wealth and interest in augmenting it further, see Narrative 121; Mathison, 1825:427; and Paulding, 1831:227.

107. Late October 1818

They [the Hawaiians] have yet another vice, which is their very own: a passion for gambling, in which they frequently lose all their property.[1] And now our cards have been introduced among them and they themselves have invented a game using them. It is a guessing game.[2] As yet, they are not sophisticated enough for Boston. Intemperance gives rise to arguments and fights among the natives, from which in turn springs a desire for vengeance. To get revenge, they employ various devious means. Since now, under a sole and powerful ruler, they do not dare to settle their arguments with weapons as they formerly did, they have recourse to libel and slander, each man watching the other and using spies. Eliot[3] [Elliot] told me that the system of espionage has been developed to a state of perfection, and that one spy is appointed to each European, the spy reporting to the chiefs .... Another vice, introduced by the

Europeans, causes great harm to this good people by spreading that infectious disease that is so damaging to persons of low morals. Kuk [Cook] himself concedes that venereal disease was brought to these isles by his crew ....[4] The Europeans who are now coming and settling here are not only making no effort to stamp out or diminish that vice, but are actually spreading it themselves. Today, every newly-arrived ship is immediately surrounded by craft bringing out young women who, as the principal trade article, are offered to seamen by their own fathers and husbands for a certain sum of money.[5] It must be said, however, that only the commoners indulge in this appalling practice; the chiefs and people of rank will not trade their daughters or wives for any sum .... Europeans may refer to Island women cohabiting with them as their wives, and even take proper care of the children resulting from such liaisons; but no marriage ceremony is ever performed.

Among the Europeans who have settled here, of course, there are some people of honesty and of good morals; but the majority of them cannot boast of their high moral standard and are, in the main, uneducated and without knowledge. Such people can teach the Sandwich Islanders only what they know, and their knowledge consists of various trades, the handling of boats, and the use of firearms.[6]

Golovnin

COMMENTARY

1. See Narratives 88, 107, 113 and 114.
2. See Narrative 127; also Malo, 1903:287 (older guessing games).
3. See Narrative 46; also Malo, 1903:266 (maka'i or spies).
4. Cook, 1785, 2:543ff.
5. Vasil'ev, 1821:18–19; also Vancouver, 1798, 2:40; Broughton, 1804:32; Lisianskii, 1812, 1:169–70; and Korobitsyn, 1944:166 (true prostitution takes root). See also Narratives 118, 127, and 129.
6. Golovnin has deserters and runaway sailors in mind; see Turnbull, 1805, 2:21–22; Langsdorf, 1813, 1:187; Franchère, 1854:69; and Bradley, 1968:35.

108. *29 October 1818*

Taro, which is the staple food here for people of all conditions and often almost the only food of the commoners, does not grow in great abundance on Hawaii Island, because it is difficult to bring water there; this plant must be constantly submerged in water up to half its own height. Therefore, much taro is brought there from other islands and from Voagu [Oahu] especially ....

Near Gonolulu [Honolulu] harbour, between the mountains and the sea, there extends a broad, level plain with a barely perceptible slope away from the mountains. At its edge, by the harbour, stands the main settlement with its fort. There is room enough on this plain, in fact, for a sizeable town. A small but quite swift river empties into the harbour, the tributary streams of which flow from the mountains behind, serving to irrigate numerous taro plantations. Voagu now produces such a huge quantity of that most necessary plant, that great amounts are shipped out annually ....[1]

Besides the native plants—taro, breadfruit, bananas, sweet potatoes, sugarcane, coconuts, plantain, and gourds—Voagu now produces great quantities of melons and watermelons, as well as some lemons, oranges, pineapples, figs, and grapes. The grapevines were brought from California. They are large and tasty: the wine from them is very pleasant when young. Manini [Marin] regaled me with both the grapes and the wine. He had also grown tobacco at Gonolulu, the cigars being not inferior to those from Panama.[2] Any difference that does exist may derive from ignorance in the manufacturing. European kitchen vegetables, such as cabbage, cucumber, garlic and mustard, grow very well here. Other sorts are being introduced. It is not hard to stock up on vegetables here nowadays; I gave 2 *piastres* for fifty head of cabbage and a Spanish *real* or 65 *kopeks* each for eight watermelons. One must say that we were charged too much, even so.[3] Watermelons grow here in such abundance that pigs are often fed on them .... Manini and other Europeans engaged in horticulture and husbandry here assured me that tea and coffee could be grown very easily on the Sandwich Islands.[4]

Golovnin

COMMENTARY

1. See Narratives 74, 94, and 97, on taro production on Oahu. Like Kotzebue, Golovnin saw the *lo'i* or pond fields near Honolulu.

2. See Narrative 99, n. 1; also Jarves, 1843:118.

3. Compare prices mentioned in Narratives 106, 127, and 129.

4. Bradley, 1968:240, n. 114 (the earliest attempts to grow coffee in the Islands, 1817 on).

109. *Early April 1821*

Certain of the Americans, we were told, were inhuman enough to have sold these good Sandwich Islanders to the Kolosh [Tlingit] Indians as sacrificial victims, just for profit.[1] If this is the truth, then those Americans merit every possible kind of censure. Considering the dishonesty of their commercial dealings, alas, one can well believe that it is true.[2]

Vasil'ev

COMMENTARY

1. See Narratives 14 and 16; Vancouver, 1801, 5:134–35 (the ship *Nancy* proceeding from Niihau to the Coast with no trade goods); Bradley, 1968:20, n. 74; Turnbull, 1805, 2:71 (Hawaiian seamen, labourers on the Northwest Coast).

2. A view shared by Chamisso (in Kotzebue, 1821, 3:315) and Kotzebue, 1821, 2:70–71, and assessed in detail by Tumarkin, 1964:60–62.

110. *21 March 1821*

A valley, clad in eternal verdure, is fringed by the water's edge with a narrow sandy strip behind which, in a semicircle, stands Gana-Rura [Honolulu] village. The village consists of native huts and two houses built in the European manner.[1] One of them, standing immediately by the quayside, was built by some American merchants. It is of planks, two storeys high. It has been sold to the king, but he does not live in it and has presented it to his stepmother, Kagumanna [Kaahumanu], whose private rooms are upstairs while her court staff stays below.[2] The second house, which stands on the northeastern limit of the village, is of stone and surrounded by a six-foot-high stone wall.[3] It used to belong to Marini [Marin], a Spaniard settled here. The native houses or, rather, huts, are not arranged to any plan but are sometimes clustered together, at other times built singly. They are constructed of roofing poles placed directly on the earth and then covered over with long grass ....[4]

To the right of the village, perhaps three *versts* distant and at the foot of a hill, American missionaries, members of the Moravian Brethren sect, have built their own dwelling with the late king's permission. It consists of two small plank houses with outbuildings and a little hut for use as a church.[5] Immediately behind the village proper start the residents' plantations: they grow sugar-cane, sweet potatoes—which reach the size of a human head and have a sickly-sweet flavour—melons, watermelons, pineapples, and cucumbers, which the Europeans have introduced. But the main crop is taro. This root is like our own swede in size and look, with the difference that its outer skin is black.[6]

Gillesem

COMMENTARY

1. Marin's and the shipmasters': see Map B. See also Narratives 54 and 129, on the building of several other frame houses in 1821–24.
2. See Narratives 54, n. 1 and 49 (the interior of this house).
3. See Narratives 1, n. 4 and 99.
4. Gillesem himself provides more detail in Narrative 92.
5. Compare Narrative 127. The plank houses had succeeded the original reed-and-grass huts by November 1821, the "church hut" being dedicated on 15 September that year: Maria S. Loomis MS: 15 September 1821; *Missionary Herald*, 18 (September 1822):272–73; Mathison, 1825:378 and 432; Bingham, 1847:117, and 132–35 (earliest services at the mission, structural developments).
6. See Narratives 94, 97, and 108.

111. *14 December 1824*

Behind the harbour, securely protected against the ocean waves by coral reefs, the mariner sees the town of Ganaruro [Honolulu]: irregular rows of dwellings stretch across its plain. Here and there among the native huts of various forms, there arise stone houses built in the European manner. The huts hide modestly in the cool shade of palms, whereas the houses stand forth boldly under the sun's burning rays, their white stucco walls reflecting in a blinding way.[1]

Right by the shore a fortress rears its massive quadrangular walls with their numerous cannon [Plate 13]; and over this fort waves the multi-coloured flag of the Sandwich Islands, with its bright stripes.[2] Plantations of taro, sugar-cane, and bananas extend behind the town and up, like a wonderfully handsome amphitheatre. Still higher, and soaring into the clouds, there are steep wild hills, thickly covered with large trees ....

It is on Vakhu [Oahu], the most fertile island of the archipelago and, moreover, the only one with a quite safe harbour, that civilization has made the most progress. A number of American and English merchants have now settled in Gana-Rura, shops have opened to sell every possible kind of ware,[3] and many stone and wooden houses have been put up in the European style. Some of the wooden ones were brought over in pieces from America and put together here. Thanks to the efforts of Marini [Marin], European vegetables have spread on Vakhu, as well as the grape that thrives so well here, and many kinds of fruit. Marini has developed a herd of cattle, and goats, sheep, and European domestic poultry are now being raised everywhere.[4]

Kotzebue

COMMENTARY

1. See Narratives 1 and 62 (Kaahumanu's half-stone house, the brightness of white walls).
2. See Narratives 1, 12, 13, 18, and 26 (the fort); and 127 (the Hawaiian flag).
3. Paulding, 1831:232, John C. Jones in *MHSP*, 44:45, and Hunnewell, 1880:xi–xii, as well as Beechey, 1831, 2:96–98 and Stewart, 1828:154–55, confirm that many retail stores had opened between 1821 and 1825.
4. See Narratives 102, 108, and 121.

112. *15 December 1824*

Our conversation was interrupted by the sound of wheels and loud voices. I looked out of the window and saw a little carriage to which a number of strongly built youths had harnessed themselves. They were in fine spirits. I asked Marini [Marin] what this meant, and was given the answer that Queen Nomakhanna [Namahana] was going to church.[1] Just then, a servant entered and announced that the carriage was ready. Nomakhanna kindly invited me to travel with her. I gratefully accepted this offer, fearing that a refusal might offend her; but I foresaw how comical I would look in the equipage with her. Nomakhanna put on a white calico hat embellished with artificial Chinese flowers, took hold of a large Chinese fan, and pulled a pair of clumsy sailor's boots onto her feet.[2] We then went on our way ... though it was some time before we could settle into the carriage. The trouble was that *it* was too narrow, and my companion—too wide. I had to squeeze up onto the very edge of the seat. In such a position, I could very easily have lost my balance on the ride. To avert that misfortune, however, the queen grasped me firmly around with a powerful thick arm .... Having thus driven through the whole of Ganaruro [Honolulu], we arrived safely, a quarter of an hour later, at a church situated on a desolate plain.[3]

Kotzebue

COMMENTARY

1. See Narratives 123–124 on Namahana's religious zeal, and *Missionary Herald*, 21 (July 1825):210–11; and Levi Chamberlain MS:3–15 April 1824 (queens' growing support of the mission in 1824; also Levi Chamberlain MS:4 December 1825; Bingham, 1847:277; and *Missionary Herald*, 22 (October 1826):309 (Kaahumanu's and Kalanimoku's admission to communion, December 1825).
2. See Narratives 7, 50, and 87 (use of clothing, etc.).
3. See also Narratives 110 and 127. Several early artists drew the Mission House and the chapels built, one after another in the 1820s, on Honolulu's empty eastern plain. See for instance Feher, 1969:174 (the second chapel in 1822). On Lydia Namahana (Piia), see Ii, 1963:53, 141, and 145. She altered greatly, to judge by contemporaneous records, under Bingham's influence: see Tregaskis, 1973:289.

113. *15–18 December 1824*

Daily visits to Ganaruro [Honolulu] convinced me, I am afraid, that the Vakhu [Oahu] Islanders were by no means those good-natured and innocent creatures that we had earlier known. The dregs of various nations, who have settled among them, as well as the crude seaman element that visits Ganaruro, have in fact had a sorry influence on the Islanders' morals.[1] Incidents of deceit, theft, and nocturnal robbery of houses, unheard of crimes in the time of Tameamea [Kamehameha I], now occur fairly often.[2] The debauchers of these good Islanders have not yet managed to push them to the point of committing murders ....

In Ganaruro, I saw signs put out inviting passersby to drink in certain houses, and it struck me as unpleasant that civilization should have produced such local fruits.[3] The keepers of these taverns are runaway sailors. Naturally, in their pursuit of a living they scorn no methods whereby the people might be made to want wine. All these dives are usually overflowing with patrons.[4] In more luxurious drinking establishments, to which seamen and commoners are not admitted, *geri* [*ieri*] and sea captains foregather. Here they too drink; but there are also cards for whist, and billiards are played. Whist has now become the Vakhu Islanders' favourite game and it has reached perfection here. It is played everywhere, even on the bare ground in the streets; and there is always money or other stakes ....[5]

In the large market-square of the town, Islanders now compete in running races for days on end. There too, horse-races are organized, in the course of which the people win or lose large sums. The natives of Vakhu have just as great a passion for horse-racing as the Malays do for cock-fighting.[6] Without hesitating, a punter will sometimes risk his entire property—which might well consist of a single horse. As horse-breeding, properly speaking, is not under-

244 PART II, Chapter 9

taken here yet, horses are brought from California and sold for 200, 300, or even 500 *piastres* each. The Vakhu Islander may save up his money for years, in order to buy a horse and so hope to win a great sum in the races. However, he may well lose his all in the first run-off. Horsemen prance about quite naked and without a saddle, a piece of string sometimes serving for a bit.

Kotzebue

COMMENTARY

1. Paulding, 1831:225–26; Beechey, 1831, 2:117–118; Charlton, *Correspondance*:15; Duhaut-Cilly, 1835, 2:319.
2. Compare Narrative 83.
3. Beechey, 1831, 1:317 and 2:97.
4. Furey, 1934:68; *MHSP*, 44:43; and Bradley, 1968:83–84.
5. Compare Narrative 127.
6. Levi Chamberlain MS: 5 August 1823; Beechey, 1831, 2:68; also Narrative 129.

114. *Mid-December 1824*

In Ganaruro [Honolulu], one may often see a game called "little ships." In this game, during which large bets are laid,[1] the Islanders demonstrate their penchant for maritime skills. The usual participants are clever boatbuilders. According to the rules, they construct pretty little boats,[2] even giving the underwater part such a form as to ensure speed. These tiny craft are equipped with full rigging and sails, and are embellished with pennants and flags.[3] Their owners gather by the bank of a large pond and, in the presence of a large crowd, launch them across the water with sails spread and helm held fast. The little ship that is built the most skilfully and has the finest qualities will outdistance the rest and arrive first at the opposite bank.[4]

Kotzebue

COMMENTARY

1. On local gambling, see also Narratives 88, 107, 113, and 127.
2. Liholiho had given Lieutenant A.P. Lazarev one, of traditional Hawaiian form, as a gift in 1821: see Narrative 127; also Vancouver, 1798, 3:17–18, and 51–52 (Kamehameha I and the building of the *Britannia*, the first European-style boat from the Islands).
3. As Nathaniel Emerson observed in 1898, in connection with the traditional Hawaiian love of string figures, knot-slipping, cat's cradle and related games, "the Hawaiian was ... a born rigger:" Malo, 1903:306.
4. John Adams Kuakini, Namahana's brother, was a devotee of this pastime, as was the king: see Ii, 1963:29–30. The Russians saw "little ships" being played on a shore pond (*loko kuapa*) in Honolulu.

115. Late December 1824

A passion for foreign wares, especially articles of clothing and ornament, gives rise here to the majority of crimes.[1] Shopkeepers try in every way to make their wretched goods seem attractive. Sometimes they sell on credit, then charge twice as much—even though they make huge profits without that.[2] I myself saw young girls paying two Spanish dollars for a string of ordinary glass beads that would hardly go round the neck. On top of this, the tradesmen here allow themselves to cheat their customers in every way and often enough succeed,[3] for as yet there are no laws on the Sandwich Islands ....[4] The old domestic utensils have now gone completely out of use [Plate 6]. Even in the very poorest native's hut, Chinese porcelain plates have ousted coconut or gourd containers, from which nobody wishes to eat any longer.[5]

                                                                  Kotzebue

COMMENTARY

1. See Narratives 113 and 129; also Stewart, 1828:153–54; and MHSP, 44:47.
2. Paulding, 1831:232; and Beechey, 1831, 2:97 confirm that there was much money circulating in Honolulu by 1825–26; in 1821 its scarcity had boosted barter: Hunnewell, 1880:xiii; and Freycinet, 1839, 2, pt. 2:617.
3. Confirmed by John C. Jones, Thomas Brown, and other interested parties: Marshall MSS: Brown to Marshall & Wildes, Oahu, 6 July 1821, etc.; also MHSP, 44:34–38.
4. Untrue: Honolulu port regulations were promulgated on 2 June 1825 (text in Graham, 1826:159), and Liholiho's prohibition of desertion from visiting vessels was published on 8 March 1822 (text in Kuykendall & Gregory, 1928:128).
5. Perceptible by 1816, this development had accelerated at Honolulu since 1818: see Narrative 89.

116. Mid-September 1825

Not long before our sailing, an order was issued to the effect that country inhabitants with all their children aged eight or more should present themselves in Ganaruro [Honolulu] to learn reading and writing.[1] The poor farmers were very discontented but did not dare to disobey, so, submissively abandoning their fieldwork, they hastened to Ganaruro.[2] On the streets we saw whole families. With spelling-books in hand, they sat in little huts which had hastily been built of branches. Those who could read already were obliged to endlessly learn parts of the Bible by heart.

There are several school buildings on each and every street in Ganaruro now. They are long reed huts, quite devoid of any internal partitioning. In each one, a Sandwich Islander teaches about a hundred male and female students. Standing on a raised platform, he loudly pronounces every letter separately, and those gathered round him repeat that letter, yelling with all their might. The sound of human voices reverberating in such schools is audible at a quite considerable distance.[3] On other streets, by contrast, complete silence reigns, and people are scarcely to be seen unless it be a group of scholars going, with their teachers, to church. Gaiety of every kind is forbidden; any manifestation of joy in living is prosecuted .... Had Tameamea [Kamehameha] I lived twice as long as he did, and had Stiuart [Stewart] undertaken his work with that monarch's protection, the Sandwich Islanders might already have earned the just respect of other nations.[4] As it is, these natives are now regressing culturally and are forced into hypocrisy and bigotry.

Taking a walk once with an American trader settled here, I met a naked old man with a book in his hand. The book greatly surprised my companion, who knew the old man for a decided opponent of the new ways .... Having made sure that no one else could hear him, the man said with a roguish but bitter smile, "Don't think that I really want to learn to read. Just let Kagumanna [Kaahumanu] think that I'm following the example of the rest.[5] If I didn't do this, I would lose my access to the queen—and then it would go badly with me, a miserable old man. But why do we have nothing but this cursed 'b', 'a', 'b'? Will it make the yams or taro grow better? To the contrary, the field workers are being forced to leave the fields untended; they can barely work half their land. How will it end? If there is a famine, *palapala* will not feed us."[6]

Kotzebue

COMMENTARY

1. Emerson, 1928:48; *Missionary Herald*, 27 (April 1831):117; Levi Chamberlain MS: August 1825.

2. Beechey, 1831, 2:101–02; and Duhaut-Cilly, 1835, 2:283–84 (abandoned fields and irrigation canals, etc.).

3. See also Delano, 1846:23; and Bingham, 1847:257.

4. See Narrative 125 on Reverend Charles S. Stewart; also Bradley, 1968:138, and 175, n. 36 (Russian approval of Stewart).

5. See Westervelt, 1912:20; Bradley, 1968:135–36, and 146–49.

6. Such fears were not unfounded: see Bradley, 1968:150.

   For additional observations on Honolulu Village, see Chapter 11, Narratives 127–129 (the journals of Ferdinand Wrangel and Aleksei Lazarev).

CHAPTER TEN

The Missionary Impact

Broadly speaking, Russian visitors to Honolulu in the early 1820s much disliked the *practice* of conversion to the Christian faith—as this was understood by Bingham—while in principle approving of the missionary effort there. As honest men, Wrangel and Kotzebue did not hide their deep misgivings about Bingham's true objectives in the Islands. Both well recognized his liking for authority, and his ruthless willingness to use the native aristocracy as, in effect, an instrument for shattering traditional religious practices. Though Lutherans themselves, both looked askance at an extreme Protestant movement which, they saw, had little time for secular enjoyment of the Island world.

Golovnin preceded Bingham and his fellow missionaries by just two years and, in a prophetic vein, foretold the miseries that Kotzebue was to witness six years later (1824). It seemed improbable, wrote Golovnin (Narrative 119) that free persuasion would convert Hawaiians to an alien, *haole* faith. That being so, would missionaries use force which would imply "recourse to bloodshed, and ... lead not to enlightenment but to destruction?" Wrangel and his people were to witness the results of a deliberate destruction of a large part of the fabric of traditional religion on Oahu. As he drily observed: "They say ... there are generally few zealous Christians on Oahu" (Narrative 129).

Chamisso predictably took deep exception to the very possibility (as it remained in 1817) that Christian priests would undermine Hawaiian culture and religion. As an older, sicker man, he sadly recognized that all his fears had been realized by Bingham and his colleagues:

> Putting aside all other charges, the missionaries carried out their duties in Hawaii without spirituality, as is shown by all reports .... The quiet celebration of the sabbath and the enforced visit to church and school do not ensure Christianity .... (*Werke*, 1836, 1:350).

117. *Late November 1816*

Up to now, no missionaries have come to the Sandwich Islands, nor, indeed, can they anticipate great successes among this people given over to sensuality. The introduction of Christianity to the islands of Eastern Polynesia can only be based on the destruction of the entire order of things now existing there ....[1] Now, in fact, in the reign of the high-minded Kamehameha I, and with the help of Europeans settled in his kingdom whose knowledge and experience might serve as important aids to the scholar, now, I say, is the time to begin the undertaking of recording on paper all that the Hawaiians know about themselves ....[2]

As Kareimoku's [Kalanimoku's] guests, we were witnesses of the celebration of the *tabu-pori* [*kapu pule*], which lasted from sunset to sunrise on the third day.[3] It is known what sort of sanctity is imparted to the man participating in this communion with the gods, for as long as this *tabu* [*kapu*] lasts. Should he happen to touch a woman, even accidentally, she must at once be put to death. Should he enter the dwelling-place of women, it must immediately be consumed by flames.[4]

Chamisso

COMMENTARY

1. A prescient comment: see Narratives 125–126, and 129.
2. Mahr, 1932:13–14; and Chamisso, 1836, 1:227 (the naturalist's unsuccessful attempt to remain on Oahu after the *Riurik*'s departure for the Arctic, to be picked up later).
3. See Narratives 68, 72, and 104.
4. See Narrative 78; Korobitsyn, 1944:172; Ellis, 1826:394. The *kapu* about to begin was that of *Ku*, *kapu pori* or *pule* being, despite Chamisso's remark, a general term.

118. *27–28 November 1816*

I cannot pass in silence over the first thing that all foreigners encounter in these Islanders; the obtrusive and grasping manners of the fair sex that are general there and the offers openly made by married women.[1] Modesty, it seems, is inborn; but chastity is a virtue only according to our customs and in this respect the woman is bound by the will of the man, whose property she has become .... Chastity as a virtue was unknown to these people. We ourselves are guilty of having inspired them with greed and removed modesty. Only on the more northerly part of O-Wahu [Oahu] Island, which is separated by mountains from the sinful harbour town, did I find more patriarchal and unspoiled customs.[2]

Chamisso

COMMENTARY

1. Compare Narratives 107, 127, and 129 (development of true prostitution at Honolulu); also Tumarkin, 1964:76–78, for discussion based on primary sources.
2. Chamisso, 1836, 1:229 (his excursion of 8–9 December 1816). Also Chapter 3 above.

119. *Late October 1818*

It would be rash, however, to assert that all these natives are very honest; there are thieves among them too, and many of them at that, but at least, along with the other European arts, they have learned to steal as it is done among civilized nations. Nowadays, I mean, the Sandwich Islander will not steal a single object that he does not need, and if he does decide to pilfer sonething, he awaits his opportunity and does it in such a way as to leave no traces of his theft. Earlier, the Islanders would carry off whatever happened to come their way, and would do it right under the victims' eyes. At Voagu [Oahu] Island, the natives stole from me—right from their craft—a small but costly cellaret and a leather cover for a case; and they did it so skilfully that, even though we had sentries posted round the sloop expressly to keep an eye on the craft coming out to us, I did not notice the loss till the next day. It should be noted, though, that none of this applies to the chiefs, who would now regard such acts as shameful and dishonourable .... [1]

Various factors hinder the Sandwich Islanders from adopting a European code of civil laws ..., the greatest of all being the religion of these people, which openly prescribes for them actions completely contrary to our European customs and laws—such as human sacrifice to their deities, polygamy,[2] the exclusion of women from various privileges accorded to men, and so forth. But it is not easy to introduce a foreign religion to a free and strong people! One must employ persuasion on a free people; but would one soon succeed in that? Use of any force would imply a recourse to bloodshed, and that would lead not to enlightenment but to destruction.

Golovnin

COMMENTARY

1. Compare Narratives 76 and 113 (theft increasing in Honolulu).
2. See Narratives 78 (human sacrifice), and 92 (polygamy). Also on polygamy and the usual virtue of noblewomen, Lisianskii, 1812, 1:211; Ellis, 1828:444; Golovnin, 1822:300; Jarves, 1847:89–90; and Tumarkin, 1954:110–116.

120. Late October 1818

Vancouver tried to suggest the idea of accepting Christianity to Tameamea [Kamehameha I]. The latter ..., believing that Vancouver was exalting his own god but defaming the Sandwich Islanders', proposed that Vancouver go up onto a very high and rocky cliff situated near Karekekua [Kealakekua] Bay, whither he would also send one of his chief priests. They could both jump off together. The god of him who remained alive would be shown stronger and more just, and the king would recognize him as the true deity. This test did not appeal to Vancouver, who not only declined to take it but also omitted so much as to mention it in his *Voyage*. And so ended the discussion of religion. This story had been told to many American captains by Iung [Young],[1] the Englishman mentioned in numerous published voyages, and a man who lived more than twenty-five years on the Sandwich Islands. At the time, Iung had been acting as interpreter for Vancouver and the king. I heard it from Devis [Davis] ....[2]

With regard to the offering of human sacrifices, a gradual change has taken place. Today, according to Eliot [Elliot] and the captains of American vessels, only criminals who deserve death are killed in the temples, where they are left as sacrificial offerings as on a place of execution.[3]

Golovnin

COMMENTARY

1. In another version, recorded by Richard Cleveland in 1803 (Cleveland, 1850; and Taylor, 1925:134–35), the would-be proselytizer was not Vancouver, but (more plausibly) the Reverend John Howell (see Restarick, 1924:28–31; and Bradley, 1968:34, n. 129). Certainly, Vancouver himself makes no mention of any such incident in 1793.
2. William Heath Davis: see Narratives 85 and 106.
3. See Narratives 46 (John Elliot de Castro), 78 and 119 (human offerings, etc.). On these human offerings (*mohai*), see Buck, 1957:527; also Malo, 1903:223 and 242 (the controversy as to whether criminals were admissible victims, not being pure and blameless).

121. *March 1821*

Notwithstanding his enlightened attitude toward religion, the late King Tameamea [Kamehameha I] had not wanted to introduce the new faith into the islands that he had subdued; not, that was, in his lifetime. But on his death bed, he had charged his son and the effective ruler, Kagumanna [Kaahumanu], to attempt gradually to introduce it. And their first actions after his death had been to break *tabu* [*kapu*], burning idols and razing *morais*. So the natives found themselves with no religion at all; for, having abandoned the old one, they did not adopt the Christian faith—even though they had mentors already.

The missionaries ... were called Bin'iam [Bingham] and Ferster, the former being the senior man. They had with them a deacon called Lamis [Loomis] and a single gardener. Lamis had, in addition to his other duties, the management of a small printing-press, on which a short Catechism and a letter-book were printed in Latin characters. The missionaries themselves had just translated the Catechism into Hawaiian. When they arrived in the year 1818, the king had granted them lands and given them workers, allowing them to preach the Gospel and to baptize anyone willing to receive baptism. He himself had not accepted the new faith, however, perhaps from laziness. The missionaries then established a school, in which they have taught reading, writing, the basic elements of sacred history, and the Divine Laws to as many as thirty pupils. The adults and especially the grandees, though, following the example of their king, have kept away from the missionaries. They have, in fact, not only declined to accept Christianity, but also declined any instruction whatsoever concerning government, or husbandry, or grain growing; and this despite the fact that they have clearly seen with their own eyes that Europeans work the soil better than they! And yet a rich harvest could be expected from fields cleared and sown with wheat and maize, which, incidentally, was not to be found on these islands before the missionaries came.

The reasons for this indifference on the part of the natives to what was clearly better, were not to be found in mere idleness or adherence to the past, but rather in the teaching of Europeans living on the Islands. Among the latter, a particular case was a certain runaway French sailor named Rives. These Europeans found it convenient for themselves that the natives should remain in a state of ignorance, and feared lest the missionaries' teaching improve the morals of the native people, the women especially, who led a pretty debauched life. For in *that* eventuality, they would no longer be able to satisfy their passions: licentiousness and an avidity to enrich themselves, through deceit, with money obtained from Americans or other shipmasters calling at Ganaruro [Honolulu] Harbour. In this period, debauchery reigned unfettered on the Islands and particularly on Vagu [Oahu], so often visited by Europeans, and most of all by American whalers. Unmarried females knew no shame; married ones, for fear of being unmasked before their husbands, were more constrained—and had relations only with foreigners. Often enough, wives would be sold out of cupidity by their lords and masters.[1]

Gillesem

COMMENTARY

1. This passage well illustrates the strengths and weaknesses of Gillesem's entire memoir, as published in 1849 (details in Chapter 13, vi). Weaknesses predominate. It is readable, and covers plenty of ground, to be sure; but it is also flawed by factual errors, worsened by the author's complete ignorance of English. The names of Bingham and his associates are mangled, indeed, a missionary (Ferster) is invented; the time and circumstances of their arrival in Honolulu are misrepresented; even the chronology of events thereafter—the resistance of certain *ali'i* to the new teaching, Liholiho's actions in that connection, etc.—is out of focus. Gillesem so uses past tenses, in his text, as to cast doubt on the period he is describing. Clearly, he supposes that American whalers were in Oahu and spreading immorality some years before 1820; yet nothing is made plain. However, the passage is of value as a record of the version of recent history that Russian visitors were being told by their (mostly British or New England) informants. Gillesem is more reliable when he deals with agriculture or material culture on Oahu, i.e., objects and procedures that he saw with his own eyes. On Rives, see Narratives 49 and 50. On Loomis and his press, see Bradley, 1942:133–35.

122. *15 December 1824*

It is most surprising that a people who had so deeply revered their gods and priests, as I myself had earlier witnessed more than once, should so quickly have reconciled themselves to the destruction of their sanctuaries and the announcement that their faith was a delusion. Nor is it less remarkable that the populace should have lived quietly without any observances of religious rituals. Kareimaku [Kalanimoku] understood, however, that such a state of affairs could not long be preserved and that the people needed a new faith .... In this very year, 1819, the island of Vakhu [Oahu] was visited by Captain Freycinet, on his voyage round the world. There was aboard his ship a priest, who baptised Kareimaku and his brother Boki according to the Catholic rite

....[1] In April 1820 a ship with missionaries arrived at Vakhu. However, Liolio [Liholiho] learned of these foreigners' intention and, forbidding them to land, required that they leave. On this occasion, too, Kareimaku interceded.[2]

The newcomers directed their main efforts to the conversion of the king, his family, and the most noble *ieri* [*ali'i*] to Christianity. Once this had been accomplished in a short time, the missionaries felt solid ground under their feet and could proceed with greater confidence toward the fulfilment of their plans. Learning the local language quickly and thoroughly, they began to teach the Islanders to read and write; and the latter easily mastered this.[3] Even by 1822, a book was printed on the island of Vakhu in the language which it is now usual to call Hawaiian, after the name of the largest island. This book contains songs of a spiritual content.[4]

Kotzebue

COMMENTARY

1. Freycinet, 1839, 2:587ff. on Boki's subsequent support of French Catholic missionaries on Oahu, and its political meaning: Yzendoorn, 1927:20, 41; and Bradley, 1968:184–85, and 203–06.
2. Bingham, 1847:81–90; *Missionary Herald*, 17 (April 1821):114–20; and Christison, 1924:650–51.
3. Survey in Bradley, 1968:133–37.
4. Bingham, 1847:155–56; *Missionary Herald*, 19 (February 1823):42; and Spaulding, 1930:28–33. The book seen by Kotzebue was presumably Bingham's eight-page elementary reader: Dibble, 1909:416

123. *15 December 1824*

Queen Nomakhanna [Namahana] informed me, with evident self-satisfaction, that she had become a Christian and visited chapel several times a day. In order to ascertain the extent of her acquaintance with Christian teaching, I asked her, through Marini [Marin], why she preferred our religion to the previous one. Nomakhanna answered that the reason was not entirely clear, truth to tell, but that the missionary Bingkhem [Bingham], whose command of *palapala* (reading and writing) was marvelous, had assured her that the Christian religion was, in fact, the best.[1] Besides, the queen added, the Europeans and Americans who visited the Islands far excelled her countrymen in their knowledge; and since all these better educated people confessed Christianity, it could only be concluded that the faith was indeed the most reasonable one. "However," added Nomakhanna, "if we see that the faith in question does not suit our people, we shall exchange it for another."[2] From this, it is plain that the local missionaries have not succeeded in explaining properly to the Islanders the essence of Christianity. In conclusion, the queen triumphantly made mention of yet another superior side of the new faith: previously, women had been compelled to be satisfied with dog-meat, but now they could regale themselves on pork.[3]

Kotzebue

COMMENTARY

1. See also Narratives 54 and 112, n. 1 (Bingham's hold over the queen).
2. Many visitors heard such comments: Mathison, 1825:372, 422; Ellis, 1826:57; Montgomery, 1831, 1:404–05; *Missionary Herald*, 18 (June 1822):190 (Reverend Asa Thurston to Worcester).
3. See Narratives 78 and 84; and survey in Tumarkin, 1964:25.

124. 15 December 1824

In the church there had gathered a very small congregation. The representatives of the fair sex were Nomakhanna [Namahana] and one other old woman. Besides the women, Khinau [Kinau][1] and a few other men were present. Even those who had brought us there did not enter the church building: it was evident that the influence of the missionaries on Vagu [Oahu] was not yet as great as in Otaiti [Tahiti] and that the local people were not yet driven to prayer meetings with sticks.[2]

The missionaries, however, will hardly be able to work on the minds of these natives to the extent that they have managed it in Otaiti, where foreigners seldom go. For the presence of the latter is by no means conducive to the missionaries' activity. The Sandwich Islanders are in constant contact with foreigners coming either to replenish supplies or simply out of the passion for gain. When concluding their trade deals, these strangers habitually permit themselves every kind of trickery—and for that very reason are not at all interested in the propagation of Christian ideas among the natives ....
For runaway sailors, there is nothing sacred, for they have already broken the Lord's commandments, whatever may befall them.[3] Therefore, they allow themselves to mock the teachings of the missionaries who, for their part, compromise themselves by various ridiculous rules and prescriptions.

Mr. Bingkhem [Bingham] delivered a sermon in the Hawaiian language which possibly had very great distinction, but which was, essentially, delivered to empty benches.[4] The minds even of those few present in the church were obviously occupied with other things, and I myself understood nothing whatever.

Kotzebue

COMMENTARY

1. See Narratives 54 and 56, on Kamehameha I's son, Kahoanoku Kinau.
2. Naturally, Kotzebue compared Bingham's activities and influence with those of Reverend Henry Nott and his fellow-missionaries from the London Missionary Society, whom he had encountered at Matavai Bay, Tahiti, in early April 1824. Kotzebue had much disliked the ways in which religious pressure was applied on the Tahitians. His experience at Matavai Bay made him more sensitive to Bingham's own ambition for Hawaii: see Kotzebue, *New Voyage*, II: Chap. 5; and Tyerman & Bennett, 1832, II:216–17.

   Kotzebue's disapproval of Reverend Bingham's means, if not perhaps of *all* his ends, contrasted starkly with Vasil'ev's approval of three years earlier. One may wonder if Vasil'ev himself would have voiced enthusiasm for the missionaries' work at Honolulu, had he called again in 1825. The fact remains, however, that he had, by conscious choice, assisted Bingham in important ways in 1821, and that the *Predpriiatie* was visiting an altered town. Here is Bingham:

> Commodore Vascilieff, of the Russian Exploring Squadron, ... treated the missionaries very courteously, gained their high esteem, and aided their cause .... He assured the chiefs he should report to the Emperor Alexander the happy arrival and favourable reception of the mission established there, and the good system of instruction which the missionaries had commenced among the people .... (Bingham, 1847:150).

Vasil'ev was a Russian patriot and military conservative in a style quite unlike Otto von Kotzebue. Russian-speaking, Orthodox, and dour, he had not had wide experience of foreign navies or indeed made distant voyages in early life: Sevastopol' and Corfu were the farthest points he reached as a lieutenant: see Lazarev, 1950:27–28. He was not a brilliant sea-officer like M.P. Lazarev or Golovnin. He did his duty; and on reaching Honolulu he considered it a duty to be civil and polite to Reverend Bingham.

> The civility and kindness of the Commodore and his officers to the mission family, manifested in various ways, are well illustrated in the following note, in Russian and English:
> H. Imp. Maj. S. Otkritie, December 19th, O.S. 1821
> Dear Sir—I thank you from all my heart and soul for the opportunity given me and the officers under my command, to be sharers in promoting the business of this Christian mission. The collection of seven golden ducats and eighty-six Spanish dollars I take the pleasure of sending with this letter, of which you will make use as you think proper. Please to receive our most sincere wishes that your good intention and the glorious design in which you are engaged may be prospered and increased. Remaining, with my respects to you and your respectable society,
> > Your humble servant,
> > Michael Vascilieff.

3. See Narratives 107, 113–115; and Bradley, 1968:83 (deserters and their evil influence).
4. See Narratives 122 and 127 (Bingham learning Hawaiian, etc.). Levi Chamberlain (Journal MS 3 & 10 October 1824) confirms that the Honolulu congregation was small towards the close of 1824; but within a year, it had grown to 3,000 (*ibid.*, 20 November 1825).

125. *Mid-September 1825*

On his own initiative, Bingkhem [Bingham] has made himself tutor of the young king,[1] whom he keeps under strict observation. He interferes in all affairs of state, and from him come all new directives, which are made public by Kagumanna [Kaahumanu] or even, on occasion, by Kareimaku [Kalanimoku]. Bingkhem's particular attention is drawn to business matters, in which he has a great interest. This missionary, in fact, has quite forgotten his priestly calling and the object with which he arrived at this island. He finds it more to his liking to rule than to preach Christianity.[2] Even this might have been pardonable, if he had been possessed of the necessary qualities to instruct the people and render them happier; if he had but approached the unsophisticated Islanders like a skilful craftsman who, by polishing a diamond, enhances its value and gives it an external lustre. But, alas, nothing of the sort may be said of Bingkhem. He is unable to proceed as he ought and is, besides, pursuing secret objects which draw him further from the right path. One can only regret deeply that the physical and spiritual well-being of this good-natured people should now be in the hands of so untalented a madcap.

A second missionary, Stiuart [Stewart], who arrived here more recently than Bingkhem, is a very sensible and well informed man.[3] He might have done much of use for the Islanders, had his activities not been hampered by Bingkhem who, now ruling the roost in spiritual matters, can tolerate no independence. Despite all his zeal and intelligence, Stiuart can do nothing to enlighten the natives of Vakhu [Oahu] and therefore does not want to stay.[4]

Kotzebue

COMMENTARY

1. Kauikeaouli: see Narratives 62–63, and 129; Bingham, 1847:346–47, and 403ff.; *Missionary Herald*, 28 (February 1828):40–41; and Levi Chamberlain MS:26–27 December 1825.
2. A sentiment secretly shared by several fellow-missionaries: see Bishop, 1916:51; and Anderson, 1874:232–34. See Narrative 129 on Bingham's purchasing of clothing, etc. from visiting shipmasters; and Bradley, 1968:174–75 on local hostility towards Bingham by 1825.
3. Reverend Charles S. Stewart, missionary at Lahaina, Maui, since 1823: see Narrative 116.
4. In the event, Reverend Stewart did leave the Islands in 1825. His journal was published in London in 1828.

126. *14 September 1825*

In all the houses and huts of Ganaruro [Honolulu], people pray several times a day in accordance with the sovereign edict. Even the foreigners settled here are forced to submit to this order, so that, under the cover of piety, they may busy themselves unhindered with their affairs—which are often enough very dark. Streets formerly full of life are now deserted. All games, even the most innocent, are strictly forbidden. Singing is a punishable offence, and the person who dares to dance cannot expect tolerance on the part of his harsh judges.[1] On Sundays, fires may neither be lit nor even prepared. The entire day is spent in praying (with what piety can be imagined).[2] Kagumanna

[Kaahumanu], who is enchanted by her adviser, will hear no objections; and since it is in her power to put those who disobey her to death, everyone bows beneath the iron sceptre of that power-loving old woman ....[3]

Here is an example of the amazing severity with which Kagumanna is realizing her objects in the field of enlightenment. On one of her parcels of land, situated several hours journey from Ganaruro, a seventy-year-old man lived as a tenant. He had always paid his rent punctually, but in view of his advanced age and the considerable distance involved, he did not consider himself obliged to pay visits to school and church. On learning this, Kagumanna had driven him from his land. The hapless man appeared before the queen as suppliant ... but all his pleadings were vain.[4] Kagumanna yelled at him, with a malicious grimace, "If you don't want to learn to read, go and drown yourself."

Kotzebue

COMMENTARY

1. This disapproval of missionary policy is shared by Beechey, 1831, 2:101–03; Duhaut-Cilly, 1835, 2:290–91; and resident Honolulu merchants. See also Dibble, 1839:101–02 (ban on *hula*); Ellis, 1826:48–50; *Missionary Herald*, 25 (December 1829):372; Maria S. Loomis MS, 30 January 1821 (ban on ancient songs, etc).

2. Edict by Kaahumanu, from Lahaina, 8 June 1824: see Stewart, 1828:319; and *Misssionary Herald*, 22 (August 1826):240.

3. Levi Chamberlain MS, 20 November and 5 December 1825.

4. Supporting data in Bradley, 1968:146–50.

   Further on missionary activity in 1821, see the narrative of Aleksei Lazarev, Chapter 11, Narrative 127. On missionary activity in 1826, see the narrative of Ferdinand Wrangel, Chapter 11, Narrative 129.

CHAPTER ELEVEN

The Honolulu Narratives of Aleksei P. Lazarev (1821) and Ferdinand P. Wrangel (1826)

ALEKSEI PETROVICH LAZAREV

Aleksei Petrovich Lazarev (1791–1862), the youngest of the three Lazarev brothers in the Russian Navy, was appointed Second Lieutenant of the sloop *Blagonamerennyi* (1818) on the strength of his acquaintance with her new commander, Gleb S. Shishmarëv. Gingerly disengaging from St. Petersburg society, in which he had already made a place for himself, Lieutenant Lazarev thus joined the "Northern Division" of the Navy's two-pronged polar expedition that was shortly to begin. The commander of his division was Mikhail Nikolaevich Vasil'ev. Lazarev was a gifted writer and maintained a full and even lively diary, as well an an official service journal, from the first day of his voyage (3 July 1819) to the last (2 August 1822). Because the *Blagonamerennyi* and the *Otkrytie* twice called at Honolulu, in March–April and November–December 1821, that diary and journal both contain "Oahu passages." The following account, also in two parts to reflect the double visit, was written up by Lazarev on the basis of the earlier material in 1822 or shortly thereafter. It is entitled, *Zapiski o plavanii voennogo shliupa Blagonamerennogo v Beringov proliv i vokrug sveta dlia otkrytii, v 1819, 1820, 1821, i 1822 godakh* (*Notes on the Voyage of the Naval Sloop "Loyal" to Bering Strait, and Round the World on Discovery, in the Years 1819–1822*). The holograph, now held at TsGAVMF under reference: *fond* 1153, *delo* 1, is of 325 pages in fine copperplate. Having long remained in the Lazarev family, that holograph was missing more than thirty years before it surfaced in Smolensk Regional Archive (1948?). It was annotated and severely edited both by its finder, Tamara G. Timokhinaia, and by Professor A.I. Solov'ev, and was published in 1950. For further data, see next chapter ("Aleksei Petrovich Lazarev").

Unlike the *Riurik* before her and perhaps two dozen Russian vessels after her, the *Blagonamerennyi* did not arrive at Honolulu the worse for wear after a period in sub-Arctic and Arctic waters. More than most New Englanders who reached the Islands after passages around Cape Horn, most Russians needed rest, fresh fruit, and viands on Oahu. Their reactions to the free availability of these necessities were correspondingly positive. It is not often that a Russian memoir of Honolulu has a disapproving tone; Lazarev's is no exception, fully rested though he was after a California sojourn. More importantly, Lazarev was a perceptive visitor to Oceania and sought out opportunities to pick up natural historical and ethnographic data, on Oahu as in Arctic North America. His narrative thus complements Midshipman Gillesem's, and gains additional importance by the fact that the Vasil'ev accounts (see Part Three, Chapter 12) were never published by imperial authority.

For details of the *Blagonamerennyi*'s southward route from Unalaska— first to Novo-Arkhangel'sk and then to San Francisco (where she wintered very comfortably: 10 November 1820–10 February 1821)—the reader may consult Ivashintsev, 1980:51–52. Of the westward passage to Oahu from Upper California, suffice it to note it was delayed by futile searching for the (fictional) "Maria Laxara Islands" then shown on European charts.

127. Visit of March–April 1821

At 8 p.m., being twenty miles offshore, we spotted a fire and made straight for it. Moving nearer, we saw a rocket and surmised that it must be from the sloop *Otkrytie*, so we kept on our course, answering with a blue light. Two blue lights, set off one after the other, confirmed us in our supposition, for this was the signal for us to keep closer to the *Otkrytie*. We came upon her about twelve miles off the south cape[1] of Vagu [Oahu] Island and, taking off all canvas except topsails, lay southwest like her. Thus passing the whole night, at 5 a.m. both sloops headed for Vagu Island; but a calm soon fell. Taking our bearings during this time, we noted that Maratai [Molokai] Island had not been very accurately fixed by Vancouver[2] and should, in fact, be positioned on the chart a little to the northwest. By 9 a.m. a little breeze had sprung up from the north-northwest and, using it, we began to tack. Around noon, however, we were again becalmed.

Having lost twenty-four hours without any benefit, thanks to this unbroken calm, we managed only at 9 a.m. the following day, 20 March, (sic) to reach Ganaruru [Honolulu], taking advantage of a following wind. One had to suppose that the sloop *Otkrytie*, which was now far away from us, would not reach shore till evening and so must stand at anchor overnight; but we had already decided not to wait for her but, because we were being helped by a following wind, to go straight into harbour. For if we acted otherwise, and postponed this till the following morning, we might well need to be towed in; and for that it would be necessary to hire Sandvichevye [Sandwich Island] double canoes, paying up to forty *piastres* for each canoe.[3] For such was the weight of our sloop that her own rowing-boats would not be able to bring her in. Besides all this, we ourselves might be able to assist the *Otkrytie* with our boats, at the harbour entrance, and thereby again avoid unnecessary expense.

We had hardly rounded the southern cape of Vagu Island before two Englishmen, fulfilling the functions of pilot, came out to us. Having questioned us in the customary way as to what ship we were, whither bound, on what mission, etc., in order to inform the elders ashore, one of these Englishmen[4] remained with us while the other went off to the Island for permission for us to enter the harbour. And while we were actually moving in, there came out

to us one of the most important chiefs on this island, a friend of the king and
nephew of the senior chief of all these islands, Krai-Moku [Kalanimoku], who
had called himself Tamegamega [Kamehameha I] in honour of the late king
of that name. He came out accompanied by the Englishman Bikli [Beckley][5],
who introduced himself as one occupying the post of harbour-master at Ganaruru. At the time of the brig *Riurik*'s visit here, he had held the postion of
commandant of the fort, and so his name was already familiar to the captain
of our sloop.[6]

After the initial greetings on both sides, Bikli asked Shishmarev if we would
salute the fort. We answered that we could not do so in view of the *Otkrytie*
and, pointing out that sloop to him, explained that he must await a salute
from her. This was translated for the chief, who was still present and who
was apparently satisfied by it. Shortly afterwards, we were rejoined by the
pilot who had gone ashore for permission to bring us into harbour. We were
by now right by its entrance, where the least depth of water is at least three
sazhen [fathoms] at low-tide but where the bottom, coral-strewn, is perfectly
visible. At 11 a.m. we dropped anchor in five *sazhen*, soft bottom, right
opposite Kagumana [Kaahumanu] Fort.[7] In this place, vessels may stand on
a single anchor, for the wind blows from two directions only: from land and
from sea. The current is almost imperceptible and, in any case, the harbour
is such an enclosed one that neither a swell nor even the slightest rippling is
felt. Finally, because of the harbour's compactness, vessels stand so close to
each other that, lying on moorings, it is difficult for them to swing—so very
little cable is let out. The excellence of the bottom assists, in this respect.
In the channel, a kedge-anchor is used with the mooring-swivel. We ourselves
used one.

We had scarcely got into the harbour before we were surrounded by numerous elders[8] who had come out to us merely to say *Aroga!* [*Aloha*] and drink off
a glass of wine each, as they have been taught to do by the visiting Americans.
Even while we were still a couple of miles from Ganaruru Harbour, indeed,
we ourselves had been met by a large number of Islanders, some of whom
had come out in their craft, others swimming. These natives had escorted the
sloop, she being under very gentle way, right to her anchoring place. We next,
out of politeness, invited just a few chiefs to come on board. They came with
their wives and daughters and at once began to make us immoral propositions, which were decisively turned down. We were much amused by the fact
that the Sandvichane [Sandwich Islanders] unanimously mistook our priest,[9]
a seventy-year-old man in his long and capacious cassock and skullcap, for a
woman, and it was only with great difficulty that we managed to correct that
delusion.

In the harbour itself we found four American vessels, two of which had
come to trade with the Sandvichane and on the Northwest Coast of America,
while the other two were readying for a whale hunt off the shores of Japan
and the Kuril Islands.[10] The captains of some of these craft paid us a visit,
inviting us back.

The sea wind that allowed us to enter the harbour did not persist for long,
however, but veered round to northeast, so that only the next morning was the
Otkrytie able to anchor by its entrance. While waiting for her, we conducted

an examination of our rigging and found very slight damage. Everything else was in first-rate condition.

On the afternoon of 21 March, officers and other officials from our sloop went ashore to visit Chief Buke [Boki], then governing the Island in the king's absence.[11] We learned from him that His Sandwich Majesty had long since gone off to the island of Muve [Maui] but would very soon be returning thence with his whole fleet, consisting of eight or ten brigs and other sailing craft.

From the very first moment of our arrival in harbour, we were surrounded by a quantity of canoes and Islanders bringing out various trifles for sale and demanding *thalers* for them. And thus have Europeans taught them to act! When evening fell, trade of another sort manifested itself—a trade of which all voyagers in these parts have already written. This was a trade in beauties who, surrounding the sloop, awaited reiterated permission to come aboard. Not receiving the reply they sought, these females grew very angry and shouted, then sang songs and made various grimaces, but nothing helped and we gestured to them that they should go home. They submitted to this rejection with obvious regret and did go back to shore; but they appeared again the next evening and every evening for as long as we remained at Ganaruru, though always in vain.[12]

Meanwhile, the contrary wind continuing to prevent the *Otkrytie* from entering the harbour, there appeared, at about noon, the royal fleet of four brigs[13] and the same number of schooners. All flew a flag consisting of seven stripes, which represented the seven islands,[14] and, as the English had been the first Europeans with whom the Sandvichane had grown acquainted, the latter had the English Jack in one corner of their own flag, to commemorate that fact. On these craft, the king had brought whole families—4,500 persons in all—to settle on Vagu, the island he had chosen as his residence.[15] The choice of this island, rather than Ovagi [Hawaii], had great advantages for him; for not one of the Sandwich Islands has a better harbour than Ganaruru, which is suitable for the maintenance of his fleet and is defended by a fort mounting, in our time there, 49 cannon of three-pound to twelve-pound calibre.

Because of the contrary wind, the royal flotilla dropped anchor at midday. In the evening, though, taking full advantage of a slight breeze that had just sprung up from seaward, the craft all entered the harbour under tow. We were much entertained by this spectacle, in which we saw the efforts of a people still almost savage to attain or, rather, to emulate European culture. And one must certainly concede that the Sandvichane, who are indebted for all this to Tamegamega [Kamehameha I], are, in fact, advancing toward civilization by swift steps. Let us only recall in what state they were left by the immortal Kuk [Cook] who, on one of their islands, paid the greatest sacrifice a man can pay for the good of science and trade, and in what condition they are now less than fifty years after his death. Let us also recall what a sorry picture of barbarity and ignorance all other natives of the South Sea still present even now; and yet *then* the Sandvichane were on a level with them![16]

Ahead of the fleet entering the harbour went the yacht carrying the king. She fired a five-gun salute, to which the fort and the other craft all replied with the same number of shots. That night, a perfect calm descended. At 5 a.m., the *Otkrytie* called for our rowing-boats by a shot and, with their help, entered the harbour within two hours. There she dropped anchor beside our sloop. Even before the *Otkrytie*'s arrival however, the royal yacht having dropped anchor in the harbour, we had sought permission to present ourselves to the king; but the latter told us, through an official, that because of the untidiness and disorder on his yacht he would be unable to receive us that day. He postponed the audience till 10 a.m. next morning. When the appointed hour came round, the captains and other officers of both sloops, dressed in new uniforms and accompanied by Bikli, who had volunteered to serve as our interpreter, set off for the king's residence. He had already gone ashore.[17]

The king received us in a spacious hut, far larger than all the others surrounding it, the interior appointments of which, however, consisted merely of mats strewn on the floor [Plate 14]. As we told him our surnames, he took each of us by the hand and greeted us with the word *Aroga*. He wore coffee-coloured cloth breeches and a white flannel jersey. His hair was cut almost in the European way, and plaited behind. In his presence were three servants, two of whom were driving flies away with fans, (which cooled the hut somewhat), while the third carried behind his sovereign a bowl containing aromatic grasses.[18] The king spat or blew his nose into this almost incessantly. These attendants who, we afterwards learned, had been chosen from among the chiefs, must remain inseparably with the king and if he talks with anyone, no matter who it may be, they will stand beside His Majesty. Besides the king and these three servants, there stood in the hut only one chief and, amongst the men, the king's favourite queen.[19] The king's suite, as such, consisted of several men with straw helmets and muskets in their hands. Some of them were completely naked, others in shirts only, while others again wore only waistcoats or trousers; some wore nothing but shoes or boots. It was their duty to stand by the door but not enter the hut. Since they thus blocked the entrance to the royal chamber, it was only a small window in the wall[20] that spared us from remaining in total gloom. Once the initial greetings were over, the king invited us to look over his yacht and, taking some of his officials with him, went with us and them together in our launches.

On reaching the yacht, the king informed Captain Vasil'ev that we were to receive a five-gun salute. The leader of our expedition thereupon sent instructions that both our sloops should respond to the royal salute with an equal number of guns. Since the guns were not loaded aboard the *Blagonamerennyi*, however, she did not manage to reply to this royal salute at the same time as did the *Otkrytie*. She did so a little later—whereupon the yacht fired off another five rounds, in response. As well as by the yacht, guns were fired by the fort, the flotilla, and even, a few minutes later, on several American vessels.

The king invited us into his cabin, where we were asked to be seated round a large table covered with a cloth. He himself sat at the head, placing Captain Vasil'ev at his right hand and Captain Shishmarev at his left, while the rest of us sat beside them without any distinctions of rank. For the king's favourite wife, a chair was placed beside him; and behind them, on the floor, sat a fly chaser and a functionary with a spittoon. At this juncture, we observed a certain distinction between the appointed attendants of the king and queen. The former, as I have already said, was fanned by two common straw fans, the latter by one fan only; but it was a sultan and very beautifully and neatly made with red feathers.[21] She had no spittoon-bearer. Bikli, who remained present as interpreter, did not sit but remained standing by the king's left side, between him and Captain Shishmarev.

Several chiefs, probably of the highest nobility, likewise entered the cabin but had no place at the table. Conversation began with our praising the royal yacht, which was in fact justified, while an African Negro was bringing several tumblers, wine-glasses and, finally, four carafes full of liquid to our table. He had most likely got to the Sandvichevye Islands from some American ship or other, as was shown by his peculiar words and knowledge of English. He was dressed only in a white shirt. Saying, "Rum, brandy, gin, wine," he went off. The king then began to regale us, offering us our choice of drink and pouring a glass of wine for himself.[22] We followed his example and drank his health, which obviously pleased him for he thanked us with the word *Aroga*; and so ended all our Sandvichevye Island courtesies.

The queen, who afterwards died in London, was named Kamegamega [Kamehameha] and was a woman of unusual height and size.[23] Although a chair had been placed for her, she did not sit on it long. Instead, she constantly paced about the cabin and struck the seated chiefs with her heavy hand. Though indeed they winced in pain, the chiefs tried to give the impression of being well pleased with this sign of attention.

The leader of our expedition asked the king if, as we had called at Ganaruru only for fresh provisions and did not mean to stay long in harbour, he would meet our requirements more quickly by appointing a man to bring the supplies out to both our ships. In response to this, the king undertook to furnish us with swine himself, and entrusted the provision of greenstuffs to the Englishman Bikli. As a result of this order we wanted for nothing, every day receiving fresh meat from the king and sometimes, in small quantities, fish also. Except for the swine, for which the king charged us three *thalers* each, everything went out to us as a gift.

The yacht on which we found ourselves would have done honour to an owner other than a half-savage Islander. She had been built in America by a wealthy citizen and, on his death, had been sold to other Americans then trading with the Sandvichane. These new owners in turn sold her to the local king for 80,000 *piastres*, or 400,000 roubles. The sum was indeed an appalling one, but it must be noted that the Americans did not receive hard cash for the yacht, but rather sandalwood, one *picul* or 133 pounds in English measure being regarded as worth ten *piastres*. They intended to sell this wood in Canton for twelve or even fifteen *piastres* per *picul*. Such profits do not seem so huge when it is seen that the seller was obliged to wait several months for this timber, which was standing far from Ganaruru Harbour and in the north of the island, so that people were obliged to carry it a good distance on their backs and then load it up for transferal to the harbour. If one believes Captain Torner [Turner],[24] who was to obtain sandalwood in exchange for this yacht, he was forced to wait at Vagu at least one year. Naturally, this had caused him some considerable loss, but he did not leave the Sandvichevye Islands in the interim, fearing that, if he did, he would lose his payment altogether. With this in mind, it is not surprising that the Americans here sell their vessels for such high prices. The entire royal flotilla has been purchased from them even so, also in exchange for sandalwood and most likely plenty of it.

The yacht of which I speak was built of solid oak as a schooner and had all the qualities of a good sea-going vessel. She was armed simply and well, and beautifully fitted out on the exterior, with fine carving on bow and stern. She had fourteen gunports, only eight of her guns being loaded while we were there. We also much admired her internal arrangements. At her stern were a salon finished with pink and deep blue mountings and gilt, a bedroom, a buffet, and a stairway leading up to her deck. Midship was a captain's cabin and, forward, quarters for a crew, a storage area for tackle and so forth, a galley above and, finally, a spacious lounge containing tables of the finest workmanship, inlaid with palm and lacquered redwood. The walls of this lounge were embellished with a number of carved gilt designs, and the floor was spread with good English carpets. Seeing all this painstaking work and fitting, one could only regret that such a beautiful craft had fallen to the Sandvichane and not to devotees of order and cleanliness; for the interior of that yacht no doubt resembled a stable shortly after our departure.[25]

Taking our leave of the king, we next went ashore to look over the village, where we were met by Bingam [Bingham], a missionary who had come from the United States of America.[26] He invited us to his house, showed us his establishments and dwelling, and asked us to take tea with him on 25 March. Returning to the sloops, we let off ten rockets as the king had desired, then occupied ourselves with work started earlier.

On the 24th, the king visited both sloops at our invitation. He went first to the *Otkrytie* which, like our own vessel, saluted him from five guns. The royal yacht, the fort, and the entire Sandvichanskii [Sandwich Island] flotilla responded with an equal salute. The king wore a light blue cloth uniform covered with gold lace and with gold epaulettes, just like those worn by our rear-admirals but for the difference that our admirals do not have a black eagle but a golden one. These epaulettes had been presented to the king by our consul, Dobelli [Dobell], who had specially ordered them from St. Petersburg.[27] The king's hat, which was carried behind him by one of his attendants, was a tricorne with plain white feather plume, trimmed with gold braid. At first we supposed that the king's uniform was the one he had received as a gift from the King of England, but one of the functionaries in the royal suite informed us that it, together with the king's other apparel, had been sewn on Vagu Island, probably to an American design.

From the *Otkrytie*, the king came over to us on the *Blagonamerennyi*, and after him came two queens and a number of chiefs and servitors who, on entering the cabin, arranged themselves as they pleased. The king himself simply sat on a divan. Having allowed the monarch a little time to rest, we conducted him all over the ship, and every part and object was examined by him with great attention. His retinue, however, seemed to pay attention to nothing whatever. The ruler of the Sandvichane went into almost all the officers' quarters and tested the comfort of a bunk in his full-dress uniform, remained there a minute or so, stood up, shouted for his suite, and went off without saying a word to anyone. The other Islanders, following their king's example, had spread out anywhere and anyhow. One of them carelessly broke a thermometer. Though of small importance, the loss was the more unpleasant because it had been our last remaining thermometer; we had to bring out one of our barometers and suspend it in the air. That evening, following the orders of the leader of our expedition, we again let off ten rockets for the entertainment of the king, to whom Vasil'ev later gave more than half of our remaining supply of fireworks.

On 25 March, we accepted an invitaton from Bingam and set off to his house for tea at 4 p.m. This estimable priest, a Bostonian by birth, had not been sent by the government of the United States, as we had first believed, but by a Bostonian philanthropic society,and not directly to the Sanvichevye Islands either, but rather to the South Sea Islands in general. Thus, he had initially been in the Society Islands but, learning that English missionaries were there already, he had set off for Ovaga and had been kindly received by the king with whom he had come to Vagu.[28] Together with Bingam, there came to the Sandvichevye Islands another priest, Brooks by name, who was making ready to go to Otuvai [Kauai] even while we were present.[29] There were also a number of other clergymen, one of whom could print books (a particularly useful thing for the educated natives), and various tradesmen and farmers or gardeners. Most of these people were married, having settled amongst the Sanvichane [Sandwich Islanders] with their own families. While we were there, their number had reached thirty; they were not all living together but were scattered over the Islands. Bingam himself had with him only one assistant and a gardener with three children.

This missionary had arrived on Ovagi Island almost immediately after the death of Tamegamega[30] and, moving to Vagu, had received from the new king a parcel of land one *verst* from the settlement [of Honolulu]. According to the local custom, Bingam had then built three huts connected by a gallery. These were of sticks interwoven and covered with grass. There was a kitchen-garden by them, and Bingam had laid it out. Almost every sort of vegetable was growing in it, only not in such quantity that the good priest could share them with others.

Bingam had also brought with him a fully finished two-storey wooden house, six or eight *sazhen* long and about four *sazhen* wide, which had only to be put together. The estimable missionary was intending to establish in this building a church, a school, and a room in which to reside himself; but he had not been able to get the king's permission. The king, we were told, did not want to see structures other than the usual Sandvichevye sort. The true cause of the difficulty, however, would seem to be foreigners who, no doubt out of envy, are hindering the missionary's useful intentions here.

These foreigners have been here a long time, are close to the king, and know the Sandvichanskii language, so Bingam has been obliged to speak to the king through them. Still, we were sure that when Bingam, who had already made progress in learning that tongue, was able to talk to the king directly, the latter would permit him to build a house in the European manner. We were not mistaken in this.[31] Settling on Vagu Island, Bingam had immediately established at his home a little school, where he had taught not only almost all the children of both sexes born to Europeans of Sandvichanki [Sandwich Island women], but also the offspring of the Islanders themselves. Even the king had been starting to attend it, to learn English, but that had soon bored him and so he sent two men along in his stead. But these followed his example and, after a few days, ceased to attend the school altogether.[32]

When we visited Bingam, we found that he had readied the children for the occasion and was putting questions to them in our presence. We liked very much the politeness that he had instilled in these semi-savage children. When he summoned them into the hut where we were, they bowed to us civilly upon entering, one after another, and the girls even curtseyed in the European way. After this, they took their places on benches. Although poorly dressed, they were dressed tidily and entirely in the European fashion, a matter to which their instructor paid particular attention, purchasing for them—from ships visiting the Sanvichevye—dresses, kerchiefs, and materials for suits, etc. These things were given out as rewards to those of especial diligence. Mrs. Bingam, who seemed to be still a very young woman, was an energetic and zealous assistant for her husband. She questioned with particular gentleness those children, few in number, who were still learning the alphabet; and they, smiling, answered her without shyness. Afterwards, Bingam himself put questions to the remaining children in English, the subjects being the ten commandments and the basic tenets of the Christian catechism.[33] Pupils apparently answered very well, and in the Sandwich Island tongue, which especially caught our attention. We asked Bingham how, not knowing that language himself, he had managed to get his charges to express themselves in it where rules of Christian life were concerned. He drew our notice to two Sandvichane also present who, having lived in Boston for several years, had returned to their native country with him and settled down in the same house as him. Knowing English well, they had served him as extremely useful assistants. Bingam was hoping to convert them also to Christianity, without forcing them in the least, or even making his desire apparent, but merely waiting till they themselves, persuaded of the high truths of the Christian faith, should wish to accept it. He is studying the Sandwich Island language with their aid,[34] and, as the English tongue is not equal to the expression of certain words in that language, he is employing letters from other European languages too. In this connection, he even asked us about our Russian alphabet, learning the pronunciation of its letters and diphthongs. Bingam also requested our artist to prepare some elementary sketches for the children, which Karneev did extremely well,[35] with the permission of the leader of our expedition. We did not doubt that, with such principles, Bingam would succeed in attracting all the Sandwich Islanders to himself, thereby forcing the avaricious and immoral Europeans surrounding the king and using his trust only for their own advantage, to take themselves off. Certainly, the conduct and princples of this worthy missionary stood in striking contrast to those that we had observed among the Catholic priests of California. The latter had not given the least thought to inspiring the savages there with the principles of the Christian faith and, thinking only of the external rites of that religion, had demanded that an Indian kiss their sleeve on approaching, kneel down on hearing the sound of a church bell, and recite prayers while not even understanding them. All the efforts of those priests, indeed, are directed towards making the greatest possible number of conversions to Christianity, to which end they even use force.[36] Bingam, on the other hand, desires that those introduced by him to Christianity should be Christians in the full sense of the word. It is to that noble aim that he had dedicated his time on the Sandvichevye Islands and, perhaps, his whole life; for, as he said, it was up to the king if he was to stay forever in his domain.

The examination over, the children were told they could go and play. On receiving this permission, they all stood up in their places and left the room with the greatest order, taking their leave of us in the European way. What especially pleased us was that they did everything they were told quite willingly, with a smile and without the slightest embarrassment or stubbornness. Bingam told us that in all the time his school had existed, which was about a year, not one of his students had ever been subjected to a scolding, let alone any more serious punishment.[37] The behaviour of these children well shows the modesty and gentleness of nature of the Sandvichane, of which I shall speak below. Our pleasant talk with this respected missionary lasted till late evening, when we were finally forced to go home.

On the 26th the king, escorted by four queens and many officials, again went out to the *Otkrytie* to look at the fireworks put on for him by Vasil'ev. At first, they all paid great attention to this display, raising a shout with each new rocket; but they soon grew weary of it, some of them even lying down to sleep, and the king went off home very soon after the fireworks were over. On this same day, there arrived an American vessel which, because of a contrary wind, could only be brought into the harbour on the 27th. She was preparing for a voyage to the shores of Japan, there to hunt the whales from which whale-oil is obtained.[38]

After this, as we worked on the sloops, chiefs paid us very frequent visits, and once the king himself came, very simply, with his suite. The chiefs brought with them mats, spears, and other objects, for which they would accept almost nothing in return but *thalers*. Thus in savage nations does the love of money arise together with the first sprouts of enlightenment. The commoners also visited us in great numbers.

Bikli, whom the king had appointed to supply us with provisions, saw that he alone would not manage to purchase everything we needed, so he announced to the chiefs that they could all trade with us directly.[39] As a result, we were daily surrounded by craft carrying provisions, from morning till evening. We took on more here than anywhere else on our voyage. Among other goods, we obtained for our people nineteen swine, three goats, and a large amount of cabbage, onion, etc. This was in exchange for things we had brought as gifts, among which the Sandvichane mostly preferred striped woolen cloth and little adzes.[40] They would not even look at our other wares, which is proof that they are becoming more and more the shopkeeper with every passing day. We fermented and salted down three casks of cabbage from what we had acquired.

Our shipboard work would have been completed very quickly, had we not been forced to get water from a river flowing down from the mountains.[41] This river proved to be so shallow that, even at full tide, neither our launch nor even a little skiff could get down it laden. For this reason, our people were obliged to carry the water in small casks over a distance of almost one *verst* before they could get it to the launches at the quayside, where it was poured into casks. This was certainly rather exhausting labour, but thanks to good fresh food, a pleasant climate, and the fact that we had practically no other tasks to fulfil, we had not a single sick man during our stay in the Sandvichevye Islands.

Vasil'ev bought two kegs of rum for our sloop from one American vessel, at two and a half *piastres* a gallon or, by our measurement, thirty half-cups. Thus a barrel would have cost us thirty-two roubles. Each cask of resin cost fifteen *piastres*. While at Ganaruru we made the acquaintance of all the American skippers and visited their vessels, which were used in whaling. We were curious to learn the particulars of that industry, so we asked these skippers to tell us about it and obtained the following information from a Captain Allen, commanding the ship *Maro* (*Mariia*).[42]

Almost right up to the time of our arrival in the Sandvichevye Islands, the Americans had not engaged in whaling at all in the Pacific Ocean but had usually gone for whales along the coasts of Tierra del Fuego, or off Patagonia and Khili [Chile]. As the whales producing spermaceti had become very scarce in those parts, however, Captain Allen and his companions had decided to try their luck in the Pacific off the shores of Japan where, he had heard, such whales might be found in quantity. This had been in 1820. Allen's first attempt proved a success and he had grown quite wealthy. In the next year, 1821, nine vessels had set off there after his example and had hunted most successfully, especially Allen himself, who had taken as much as 200 tons of pure spermaceti in a total of seventeen months. The hunters take their catch off to Mexico where they get from seven to nine *piastres* a gallon for the oil; in the United States themselves, it sells for no more than one *piastre* a gallon. From the spermaceti the hunters themselves make candles, but these are not as good as factory-made ones and are sold for one *piastre* a foot. Captain Allen believed that his share of the cargo collected by him and his comrades in 1821 would be about 12,000 *piastres*. And besides this profit, the construction of ships and the upkeep of his people had cost him nothing. The hunt of which I here speak is conducted between 30° and 35°N and longitudes 160° and 170°W from Greenwich; and the whalers have selected the Sandvichevye Islands as their resting place.[43] The spermaceti thus obtained is poured into casks and so taken away for sale. The candles are made in the following fashion.

The whale-oil is poured into a vessel and left to stand several days, after which fat remains on the surface. This is skimmed off and burned in lamps, for which purpose it is highly suitable, giving a bright flame and producing neither soot nor an offensive smell. What remains in the vessel is heated again. When it cools down, it becomes as white as snow, all impurities having settled to the bottom. The upper layers of this fat are next carefully taken off, so that they do not mingle with these impurities, and again boiled two or three times. Every time, they are poured through a canvas bag; the remaining fat passes through this strainer. When there is no more liquid, the fat is heated one final time, mixed with potash, and poured into candle moulds. We ourselves saw candles thus made, and they were very clean and of good quality. In order to boil the blubber, brick stoves are placed between the mainmast and foremast of these American whalers' vessels. The stoves contain cemented boilers, into which the cut-up blubber is put. What remains after this heating process is used as fuel, instead of firewood, under those same cauldrons and even in the cook-house.

The construction of such a stove in the waist of a vessel does not allow a launch to be placed aboard her, so the whalers take four or five ships' boats along instead. These are suspended over the vessel's sides, perfectly ready to be launched for the actual hunt. Sometimes these gigs are lashed together at the sides, and so serve instead of a launch. If a large anchor is to be carried, a raft is made of the casks on board and that raft, with the anchor on it, can then be towed by the gigs to the required spot. It seems to me that it would be extremely advantageous to our American Company to conduct such a hunt. It would, after all, be far easier for that company, inasmuch as the hunt is conducted near its possessions; the whales themselves, if I am not mistaken, being found all over the Eastern [Pacific] Ocean and even occasionally being washed up, alive or dead, on Unalashka [Unalaska Island], where, however, the natives fear to hunt them from their *baidarki*.[44]

When returning from his first hunting voyage to the Sandvichevye Islands, Captain Allen discovered in latitude 19°17′N and longitude 165°33′E a low coral island and a coral reef. He assured us that he had fixed its position by careful observations, adding that there must surely be other islands in those parts. This he said on the basis of signs of nearby land, which he had often noted. Bikli, of whom I spoke earlier, also told us that one of the king's vessels had once been at sea and carried far to the north of the Sandvichevye Islands by a powerful southwest wind. There, during the night, breakers had been observed only a short distance off to windward. Turning on the other tack and passing that spot where the breakers had been sighted, the commander of the vessel was entirely satisfied that it existed and deduced that there must be, in the vicinity, some as yet unknown island or reef.[45] After this, he proceeded with a following wind to southward and, almost twenty-four hours later, reached the island of Muve [Maui]. In general terms, it can be said with some confidence that those parts of the Eastern [Pacific] Ocean will yet offer numerous discoveries, if not perhaps important ones.

I may boast of having been shown greater goodwill than our other officers by His Sandwich Majesty. The cause of this was the various gifts that he received from me, including new and beautifully sewn suspenders, a forage cap of ancient form made of red cloth, sewn with gold and embellished with a gold tassel, and other articles. When inviting some American shipmasters to dine with him simply once, the king invited me along too, in the queen's name; but he desired that it be done in secret, lest my comrades learn of it. The invitation gave me a good chance to see a Sandvichankii repast, and its preparation. Nine of us dined: the king, Queen Kamegamega [Kamehameha], three chiefs, John Mik [Meek], Thomas Mik [Meek], Deviz [Davis],[46] (all three captains of American vessels), and I. Such an honour did not come to the Americans *gratis*, however, for they were taxed—in wine and rum—for the meal. We ate on the ground but in the cleanest conditions, and our food was pork and dog meat, the preparation for which I had managed to observe before this dinner. It was carried out as follows. Plenty of firewood is placed and lit in a hole dug in the earth and neatly lined with stones. When the latter have been sufficiently heated through by this fire, the pit is cleaned out, clean leaves are placed in it, followed by a stifled animal, which has been carefully disemboweled and stuffed with other hot stones. A covering is then laid on top. The meat is thus cooked, being left for several hours in great heat and steam. The animal is removed, cleaned of the stones, placed whole on clean leaves, and so brought to the table or, rather, to the ground.

When we had been regaled, the queen, tearing off a piece of roast meat with her own hands, offered a piece first to me, then to the other guests. Instead of plates we used one clean leaf each; and we ate with our hands, with taro instead of bread. The Sandvichane prefer dog meat to pork. I deduced this from the fact that it was served to the queen alone, who gave very little indeed of it to the rest of us. I was in any case bound to decline any more, out of politeness. The meat was very pleasant, and tasty.[47] On leaving the hut, we found that the royal retainers had also dined, only instead of the rum and wine that we had all drunk from a single tumbler, they had a large plaited goblet full of *kava*. Out of curiosity I sampled that too, and found that it was like watery milk in flavour, only bitter and unpleasant, for which reason the Sandvichane themselves do not drink it much. According to the king (and I myself confirmed this at first-hand), the beverage is prepared in the following manner. *Kava* root is taken, chewed, and spit out together with saliva into a small bowl. Water is then added.[48]

Soon after this meal was over, the king said *Aroga* to us and proceeded to busy himself, together with one of his chiefs, with a game of cards. The Americans and I went off to take a wander through the village. On another occasion, when I dined with the king in the open air, together with our other officers, everything was arranged in the European manner; but all the tableware had been hired from the Americans and the king seemed to take great pride in the entertainment he was offering.

Rio-Rio [Liholiho] did not limit himself to mere external gestures of goodwill towards me: on the day of our sailing from Vagu, he presented me with a Hawaiian craft as a gift.[49] If the king tried to express his benevolence toward me, however, his subjects acted less civilly with me. One day before our departure from Ganaruru, they stole from me a beautiful Newfoundland dog, which my brother M.P. Lazarev had given to me, and two other dogs besides. All three, no doubt, were destined to be roasted.

While buying various livestock, poultry, etc. for the company of our sloop at Vagu, I paid the following price:

For a large hog	5 *piastres*
For a small hog	2 *piastres*
For a piglet	1 *piastre*
For a goat	1 1/2 *piastres*
For a kid	1 *piastre*
For 5 hens	1 *piastre*
For 25 eggs	1 *piastre*
For 12 melons, watermelons, or gourds	1 *piastre*

We were offered large quantities of sugar-cane at two *piastres* a cane. I did
my best to purchase sows in farrow and goats similarly placed, and these
did in fact give us piglets and kids on our voyage, so that we needed to buy
very little livestock after leaving the Sandvichevye Islands but could simply
use what we had bought at Ganaruru. Some of these animals remained even
when we reached Kronstadt and so we could offer them as gifts, for instance
to the frigate *Kreiser*, then about to leave on a distant voyage.[50]

In concluding this chapter, I will make some mention of the Sandvichevye
Islands themselves. Constantly visited by Europeans, they have been described by almost all the mariners who have sailed round the globe and are
so well known that to describe them here would be merely to repeat what
the public was told long before me. Since those Islanders' striving for civilization and the times themselves offer new material for statistics and history,
nevertheless, I too, in my turn, propose to make remarks. They may serve
to supplement what was written before my time about those islands insep-
arable from the sad fate of the celebrated Kuk. I will begin my account of
the Sandvichane with the entertainment with which they used to amuse their
king.

Every day throughout our entire stay, early in the morning at sunrise and
again at sunset in the evening, as many as 150 women would dance before
the king's residence; and they would sometimes be joined by 20 or 30 men,
presumably chiefs. The women were very likely their wives, daughters, or
female relations. This dance was described by Kuk and is very accurately
and well depicted in the atlas of his *Voyage*. But at other times of the day,
the natives—and the chiefs in particular—did nothing at all, unless, wearied
by their very idleness, they played games; rolling stones, casting bones, or
divining a stone under a cushion.[51] The Europeans have introduced the use
of playing-cards to the chiefs and they, male and female alike, now play with
them incessantly. Unfortunately, the natives' educated guests have introduced
their own vices together with civilization. Thus, quite apart from his incessant
card playing, no Sandvichanin having an opportunity to get hold of rum will
let it slip by. He will want to get drunk. The king himself, who has that
alcoholic drink in abundance and who is continually purchasing wines, so we
were told, is no exception in this regard but frequently drinks after dinner
until he completely loses his senses. Those who do not have any imported
rum drink the rum produced on the Islands, which is far worse and has a bad
smell.[52] The well-known *kava* drink is also much used by the Sandvichane;
one can tell a man who drinks it at a glance. The skin on his body is whitish,
rough, and covered with wrinkles and cracks. It is unpleasant to see even the
face of such a man. To the credit of the Islanders, however, one must say that
for all their passion for rum, they will never exchange a good article for it,
but only some trifle. Still, they certainly like to get rum as a gift. Besides
this, one must add that if we happened to meet a drunken Sandvichanin on
the street, it never once occurred that the drunk caused any of us the least
offense or insult.

One of these rum-lovers would often come to our tent while we were making
observations; but he never did anything bad, was always obedient, and would
move away quietly when we drove him off. In its way, this indicates the

quietness of these Islanders' temperament. And to this must be added the fact that, for twelve years before our own arrival among them, there had not been a murder nor even a large fight, though fights could well have been anticipated on Vagu Island because of the large number of Europeans resident there. We assuredly had considerable arguments with the Sandvichane who, during our observation periods, and while we checked the chronometers at Kagumanu Fort, would gather in crowds to watch our activities (which seemed like sorcery to them); for they would shake the instruments. But this in no way contradicts what I have just said about these people.

It is a regrettable fact that the avaricious custom of letting foreigners have one's daughters does still prevail at full strength among the Sandvichane. And Europeans, far from dissuading them from that shameful commerce, themselves support it.

Let us now move on to the famous Tamegamega, the transformer of the Sandvichane, who, born a savage in the full sense of that word, by the strength of his own genius perceived the benefits of enlightenment and shed its first rays upon his subjects. Tamegamega is the true name of that great son of the kingdom of the Sandwich Islands. In its pronunciation, however, the letter "g" is extremely soft, indeed almost imperceptible, so that all the mariners call him Tamagamea.[53] I make the following statements about him on the basis of the Islanders' own words. He was the first ruler of this people to begin to receive foreigners in a friendly way, the first to begin regular trade with them, and the man who united all the Sandvichevy Islands under one rule. The Europeans many times suggested to him that he abandon his idolatry for the Christian religion and receive missionaries, but Tamegamega always rejected those proposals and showed himself unwilling to accept another faith in any form, saying that his people were happy in the religion with which they had been born.

This worthy king died, to the general regret of his whole people and of the Europeans who had known him, in the year 1819. He was succeeded by his son Rio-Rio or Lio-Lio, whom he had named as his successor during his lifetime and whom I mentioned above. Since he was still very young, however, his father appointed as his governor or guardian one of his relatives who was also of the high nobility of the Island, Kraimoku, known in English as Mr. Pitt.

Rio-Rio or Lio-Lio, which in the Sandvichanskii tongue means dog or lion, is called Tamegamega II [Kamehameha] by the English and loves the Europeans even more than did his father. He strives to adopt from them everything that he thinks good. Immediately upon his succession as king, he wished to destroy idolatry. He signalized his succession to the royal title by a complete destruction of the risible custom known by that familiar word, tabu [kapu], which is found on all the South Sea Islands. Among the Sandvichane, the word is not so much as mentioned now. Previously, there were days on which it was tabu for the natives to go out to sea or even launch their craft. Numerous religious rites were similarly tabu and to break it was punishable by death. In earlier times, women could neither eat together with men, nor even enter a hut where men were eating. They were also prohibited from touching pork and had to nourish themselves on dog-meat, etc. All this has now been changed. Every man has complete liberty to live in the manner he chooses, and the women eat with the men as in Europe.

Immediately after his accession, the new king wished to destroy idolatry, saying: "How imprudent we are to worship a piece of wood that we ourselves have carved!" But his cousin, who was next in line to the throne, objected strongly to this intention, and he had all the priests on his side. Open warfare resulted from their frequent and violent arguments on that subject. The heir to the Sandvichanskii throne was supported not only by the priests but also by the greater part of the populace who, in their superstition and ignorance, dreaded even the thought of seeing their gods destroyed. As for the king, he had only a few adherents, but on the other hand numerous Europeans were on his side, and all his troops were armed with pistols and rifles, whereas his opponents either completely lacked, or at best were very poorly supplied with, such weaponry. The war that flared up in this way might have proved a very long and bloody one, had the king's cousin, the head of the resisting party, not lost his life in the first battle. This took place on the island of Vagu and was an extremely cruel one. Wounded in one hand, the heir proceeded to load his rifle with the other one, defending himself bravely against his attackers. He took another bullet in the leg but still fought on, until a third, striking him in the chest, felled him on the spot.[54] The Sandvichane whom he had led out thereupon surrendered unconditionally to the lawful king who, in the first moment after his victory, gave orders for the destruction of idols on all the islands then under his authority. This order was executed with such speed that on Vagu less than half an hour (sic) elapsed before all the idols on the island had been broken and committed to the flames. Thus did the decisive action of one individual overcome, in the very shortest time, the age-old monuments to the Islanders' ignorance—memorials hallowed by prejudice and by antiquity—and shed the rays of Christian faith in a place earlier shamed by pagan sacrifices. The chief who had killed the leader of the insurgent party was rewarded for the important service rendered, and occupies the first place under the royal protection. His name is Kege-Kukui [Kehekukui], and at the time of our visit he was considered the first warrior in the Sandvichanskaia army which Chief Adams[55] commanded on Vagu Island.

Having completely destroyed their idols and dismissed the word *tabu* the Sandvichane were, immediately after the event, without any religion whatsoever. But missionaries from the United States who had come to the Islands with the object of converting the king and his people to Christianity failed; for although Rio-Rio certainly wished to adopt it, he would be converted only by English priests. No matter how long the Americans explained the oneness of the faith offered by them, and that practised in England, nothing helped, and the king remained silent instead of giving an answer.

A number of Europeans who were in the Sandvichevye Islands when we were, including the Spaniard Marini [Marin],[56] who had served in the royal presence, assured us that the king, knowing the proximity to him of the Russian colonies, had very nearly had it in mind to get missionaries from Russia. For although the Spanish possessions in California were yet closer, he was *not* well disposed to the Spaniards. Not long before our arrival, he had received from the then Commandant of Kamchatka, Captain Rikord,[57] a letter in English with a Russian translation attached. He showed it to us, asking us to explain the contents, and doubtless wishing to collate it with the version offered to him by the English. In this letter, Rikord congratulated the king on his accession to the throne of the Sandvichevye Islands, assured him of our Sovereign's benevolence and protection, thanked him for his kind reception of Russian vessels and, in conclusion, proposed trade links in view of their proximity. Rikord requested the king to begin by sending to Kamchatka, that summer, a vessel laden with salt. The king was well pleased with this letter from Rikord and decided that he would indeed send the requested vessel to Kamchatka. He told us, in this connection, that he wanted war with nobody but desired to live at peace with all in the world, especially with the Russians who had always offered him signs of friendship. The actions of Dr. Sheferd [Scheffer] were certainly bound to give the king the idea that Russians meant to take possession of his islands. "However," said the king, "I have already written about those actions to your Emperor through Dobelli.[58] I asked for his protection and therefore I rely on his magnanimity, of which I have always heard a great deal." Turning to me, he then added: "I shall instruct my secretary to make a copy of this letter."[59]

The secretary in question, a Frenchman named Rives[60] who had fled from a French merchantman on which he had been serving as assistant mate, did in fact bring me the letter the following day. The king was wanting to write again to our Emperor but he did not tell us what about. Recognizing the might of Russia, he probably hoped to obtain her protection, which, as the following will show, he needed.

In 1820, when insurgents razed Monterey in New California from a squadron consisting of two frigates under the command of a Captain Buksard [Bouchard], that same Buksard came to the Sandvichevye Islands and caused their king much unpleasantness, even committing aggressions.[61] Among other things, he took away from him [the king] a brig purchased from the Americans, insisting that she belonged to him. It was of no interest to him, he said, how the brig had come to be in the royal fleet. And he added the threat that if the brig were not voluntarily ceded to him, he would take her by force. The king lacked resources to resist him and so was obliged to give the vessel up, losing his own purchase. On top of this, Buksard brought many natives out to his vessels by force and, in general, treated the Sandvichane Islanders as a conqueror might treat the conquered.[62] For collaboration in these shameful proceedings, he gave the Spaniard Marini the king's senior interpreter, a patent to officer's rank. In the year 1821 the royal fleet, then commanded by the runaway English seaman Adams, consisted of ten or twelve vessels and was constantly being enlarged by fresh purchases. Still, all these vessels were small; and though the fort boasted many guns, there was nobody to work them, which led the king himself to remark: "I see that my fleet and fort are not for Europeans." The protection of a great Power was necessary to him.

When the late Tamegamega had learned that the Americans who bought sandalwood from him sold it in Canton at a far higher price, he himself had resolved to send a ship similarly laden to that city, as from himself but in the name of the American Consul there.[63] The goods were sold and the vessel returned, actually after the death of Tamegamega. But then his heir learned that 500 *piastres* tax had been charged merely so that the vessel could stand in Canton harbour, and said to those around him: "Why should I not impose duties? The water by my islands is the same as at Canton." And from then on, it was established that foreign vessels stopping outside Ganaruru Harbour must pay forty *piastres*, while those inside must pay eighty. Warships were exempted from this duty.

All the time we remained at Ganaruru, the trade-wind blew day and night from the northeast, sometimes quite hard. In the mornings, though, it blew feebly or else there would be a complete calm in that quarter; vessels obliged to approach the harbour in a contrary wind would sometimes wait five or six days for such a calm, or for a helpful wind. The weather remained fine and it rained very little. Natives told us that in the winter months—December, January and February—they do have a northeast wind, which sometimes rises to a storm and is often accompanied by rain. The sea-wind takes hold in March and blows till December.

At length we were ready to depart and at 9 a.m. on 5 April, under a gentle north-northeast wind, we began to pull out of the harbour; there was too little room to put on canvas in it. Having left the harbour, we raised sail and set a course south-southwest. The *Otkrytie* was pulled out after us. We passed through a depth of four *sazhen*, with sand and coral bottom, moved around an underwater rock, and so went out to sea. There we lay to, waiting for the *Otkrytie* and hoisting up the rowing-boats that we had kept in readiness in case towing were needed. The good Sandvichane long stood on the shore, waving goodbye to us ...

TRANSLATOR'S REMARKS

Lazarev concludes his Chapter IX with brief remarks on the two sloops' position, on 6 April, according to Vancouver's chart, and on the course set for the North (details given in Ivashintsev, *Russian Round-the-World Voyages*:52–55). The heights of Kauai were in sight all day on 7 April. Sitka was reached on 11 May, and there a specially made boat and interpreters were taken aboard for the coming Arctic work. What Vasil'ev and Shishmarev hoped to do was an impossibility; but circumstantial factors made their Northern failures the more certain. Neither was of Kotzebue's calibre as a scientific officer, their vessels were less suited to high-Arctic survey work than the *Riurik* had been, and on coming to the North, where the *Otkrytie* was forced to tow.her slower-sailing boat, they quickly parted. Vasil'ev reached a point close to the modern settlement of Wainwright (by his far from certain reckoning, $70°41'$N by $161°27'$W), before turning back from what he viewed as pack-ice. On the Asian littoral, Shishmarev and Lazarev went only to Cape Serdtse Kamen' before meeting solid ice and turning back. The expedition had some small achievements. It discovered Nunivak, an island in the Bering Sea, and in the Ellices it sighted and surveyed a group of sixteen little islands—the "Blagonamerennyi cluster." In the main, however, it was certainly a disappointing venture. Leaving Petropavlovsk-in-Kamchatka in mid-October 1821, Vasil'ev intended to round Cape Horn as soon as feasible. But three days after their departure, the sloops were separated yet again, in heavy mist. Both proceeded to the designated rendezvous, Honolulu Harbour. The *Blagonamerennyi* arrived there on 24 November, three days before the *Otkrytie*. Lazarev takes up the narrative in Chapter XII of his manuscript.

COMMENTARY

1. Barber's Point.
2. Vancouver, 1798, II:201. The Russians had a copy of Vancouver's chart of the Sandwich Islands (*ibid.*, IV: no. 15), by Lieutenant Joseph Baker.
3. The Russians leave a good account of the development of port dues at Honolulu: see Narratives 4 and 10. The local canoes in question were *wa'a kaulua*.
4. One of these was John Harbottle: see Alexander, 1907:14 (Peter Corney's meeting with him in 1818, etc.); also Narrative 1. The other, judging by the contemporaneous evidence of Karl Gillesem (Gillesem, 1849:217), was William Warren (Russian: Uorn). Harbottle appears in various Russian texts as Gebottel, Garbottl', and even Botl'; but then his countrymen had him as Hairbottle.
5. George Beckley, pioneer settler on Oahu; commandant of Fort Kaahumanu since 1816.
6. The *Blagonamerennyi* carried a copy of Kotzebue's *Puteshestvie*, 1821. Beckley appears in Pt. I:65–66, in a favourable light.
7. See Map A. The *Blagonamerennyi* evidently stood where the *Riurik* had, in 1816–17, due west of the fort.
8. Russian: *mnozhestvom starshin*. Lazarev employs the term *starshina*, meaning "village elder".
9. Father Mikhail Ivanov.
10. Details in Judd, 1929; and Starbuck, 1876:232–35.
11. Liholiho had briefly returned to Lahaina, where he had paused two months earlier when returning from Kailua, Kona, to establish his seat at Honolulu: Kamakau, 1961:250; Hawaiian Mission Children's Society Library, Honolulu: Maria S. Loomis Journal, February–March 1821.
12. Compare Cook, 1784: II:543; Vancouver, 1798, II:40; and Kotzebue, *A Voyage*, I:327; also Narratives 4 n. 3 and 9 n. 3 on sexual abstinence.
13. The *Albatross*, *Columbia*, *Krymakoo* (ex-*Bordeaux Packet*), and *Cahoo-mah-noo* (ex-*Forester*). On the Hawaiian acquisition of the *Bordeaux Packet*, see *The Friend* (Honolulu, January 1867):6; and J. Hunnewell, ed., "A Voyage in the Brig *Bordeaux Packet* ... and a Residence in Honolulu, 1817–1818," *HHS Papers*, no. 8 (1895):8–17. On the French-built *Forester*, see Pierce, 1965:233–34. Sailing under British colours, she had visited Sitka and Kamchatka repeatedly in 1813–15: see Porter, 1931, II:640–41.
14. Lazarev stresses that the Hawaiian flag being flown by Liholiho's fleet did have the Union Jack in the upper quarter by the masthead. Certainly, the Union Jack *had* been retained: Choris had drawn it, together with the seven (?) stripes, in 1817 (Choris, 1822: "Port d'Hanarourou"). And it was still in evidence in the 1820s (see Mathison, 1825:464). For a different assessment, see Westervelt, 1922:36 and Corney, 1896:88.
15. Sinclair, 1976:31–32.
16. Further on this reverence for Cook among Russian naval officers see Armstrong, 1979; and Barratt, 1979c:1–3.
17. To pay a visit to Kaahumanu at her house where King and Punchbowl Streets later met. New houses were built for her, Liholiho himself, and Kalanimoku on that site, known as Halehanaimoa, in 1824; and there Kotzebue called on Namahana in December 1824: see Narrative 112. Beckley was acting as interpreter be-

cause Captain Shishmarev spoke neither Hawaiian nor English (see Mahr, 1932:13, for Chamisso's wry description of the former second-in-command of the *Riurik*). Lazarev himself, by contrast, was an amateur linguist and drew up a Hawaiian word-list in April 1821; details below, Bibliography: Soviet Archival Sources for the History of Honolulu, 1809–1826: TsGAVMF, *fond* 213.

18. The scrap bowl (*ipu 'aina*), into which Liholiho might place superfluous scraps of food, was carried by a courtier of high rank: see Malo, 1903:85; and Buck, 1957:53–54. In the Leningrad "pre-1828" Hawaiian collection at the N.N. Miklukho-Maklai Institute of Anthropology and Ethnography (Peter-the-Great Museum), there are no such bowls; but there are four *kahili*: Nos. 505–2, 3, 4, 736–207. See Likhtenberg, 1960:197–98 and Plate VII. "Unfortunately," as Miss Likhtenberg writes (p. 168–69) "it is impossible to determine precisely by which of the first Russian circumnavigators the items in Collection No. 736 were collected." On *kahili*, feathered staffs of state that also served as fly-whisks see Buck, 1957:578–80.

19. Kamamalu, who died in London on 8 July 1824.

20. An innovation, showing *haole* influence. There were of course Hawaiian houses without walls, in pre-contact times (Buck, 1957:78–79); but Lazarev speaks plainly of a window (*nebol'shogo okna.*) and five plaited coconut or pandanus leaf fans (*peahi*: Nos. 736–208, 209, 294a, 294b, 750–4).

21. The Russian, *sultan*, makes plain that Kamamalu's attendant bore a *kahili*, a fan of the sort drawn by Choris (Plate 2). See Buck, 1957:578–80 and Malo, 1903:107 on the *kahili* as "emblem and embellishment of royalty."

22. The Russians confirm that Liholiho was drinking heavily in March 1821. His intemperance worsened over the next three months: *MHSP*, LIV:35; Harvard University Library: Marshall MSS: Thos. Brown to Marshall, Oahu, 6 July 1821.

23. Lazarev confuses Kamehameha with Kamamalu, on whom see Sinclair, 1976:18–20, 72 (English impressions of the queen, etc.).

24. Captain John Suter, Bryant & Sturgis's ablest shipmaster since 1817, who had supervised the sale of *Cleopatra's Barge* to Liholiho (November 1820): see Bradley, 1942:61–62.

25. Lazarev had learned, it seems, of her wrecking on the coast of Kauai (1824): details in Alexander, 1906:29; and Bingham, 1847:218.

26. Hiram Bingham (1789–1869), *de facto* senior missionary at Honolulu, New England Calvinist, preacher, translator, educator. For a survey of Bingham's religious (and political) aims in the Islands, see Bradley, 1942:121–31.

27. Peter Dobell, an Irish-American who had taken Russian citizenship while in China and who, like Scheffer, had unsuccessfully urged the Russian government to seize a Hawaiian Island as a mid-Pacific base: see Golder, 1928:39–49; and Mehnert, 1939.

28. Incorrect: see Bradley, 1942:122–24.

29. Probably a reference to Amos S. Cooke, a teacher at Honolulu in 1821, who did indeed visit the missionary Samuel Whitney on Kauai, but did not remain there. The printer mentioned was Elisha Loomis: see Dibble, 1909:139–40.

30. Actually, on 30 March 1820, ten months after the king's death but only a few days after the Battle of Kua'mo'o near Kailua, where Liholiho's forces had destroyed the traditional faction led by Kekuaokalani.

31. The Russians were quite aware of John Young's lack of enthusiasm for American commercial and political influence in the mid-Pacific. Lazarev was more correct,

in this respect, than Stewart, *Private Journal of a Voyage* (1828):158; Sir George Simpson, 1847, II:156; or Henry Restarick, 1924:42–43, all of whom supposed Young to have assisted Bingham's cause in 1820. On the missionaries' lack of any European-style house until the time of the *Blagonamerennyi*'s visit to Honolulu, see *Missionary Herald*, XVII (April 1821):114–20; and Bingham, 1847:69ff.

32. Details in Bingham, 1847:103–07; and Diell, 1838:22–24.

33. Mrs. Bingham was effectively directing the school, using "Watt's Catechism" and "Webster's spelling-book": Maria S. Loomis Journal, 9 June 1821; Bingham, 1847:104; and Holman, 1931:29–30. On the quarterly public examinations at Oahu Charity School, see *Missionary Herald*, XIX (August 1823):272 and XX (October 1824):317; also Westerveld, 1912:19–20.

34. *Columbian Centinel*, 27 October 1819; Thurston, 1921:3–6; and Lyman, 1906:2–3 (on Hawaiian assistants from the mission school at Cornwall, Connecticut). Dibble names the three "assistants" met by the Russians as Opukakaia, Kanui Hopu, and Honori (Dibble, 1909:119).

35. Emel'ian E. Karneev, or Kornéev (1778–183?), artist in the *Otkrytie*, graduate and prizewinner of the St. Petersburg Academy of Arts. For surveys of his career, see N.N. Goncharova, "Vidopisets E. Korneev," *Iskusstvo*, 1972, no. 6:60–64; and, by the same writer, "Khudozhnik krugosvetnoi ekspeditsii 1819–1822 godov E. Korneev," *IVGO*, 105 (1973), no. 1:67–72.

   Korneev worked in pen and aquarelle while in the Hawaiian Islands in 1821. So much is clear from papers, formerly held by the Academy of Arts, which are now at TsGIAL (*fond* 789, op. 20, *dela* 7, 9, 17, 21, 28, 30, 36, 48 etc.). Microfilm copies of these papers are held at Elmer E. Rasmuson Library, University of Alaska at Fairbanks, Alaska (Shur Collection: reel 85). That same library also acquired, in 1983, complementary materials from TsGAVMF (e.g., *fond* 162, op. 1, *delo* 44: *fond* 205, op. 1, *delo* 644—reel 98), that bear directly upon Korneev's illustrative work while in the Pacific. TsGIAL papers include detailed lists of two portfolios, of 36 and 61 drawings respectively, that were submitted to the Admiralty Department of the Naval Ministry in 1822, as well as correspondence between the Academy's Director, Olenin, and the Navy Hydrographic Depot, regarding the publication of some of those drawings in works by Captain M.N. Vasil'ev, by Korneev himself, or even by Karl Gillesem, formerly midshipman on the *Blagonamerennyi* (but by 1830 a "retired major in Riga"). Korneev quixotically sought a Crown subsidy of 45,000 roubles to defray the costs of publishing his own well-illustrated, *Voyage*. He had to be satisfied with a pension of 720 roubles a year. His Hawaiian material was never published; most was lost in the appalling inundation of St. Petersburg of 7 November 1824 (TsGIAL, *fond* 789, op. 20, 1823, No. 30), which the poet Pushkin graphically describes in *The Bronze Horseman* (*Mednyi Vsadnik*).

36. Lazarev had visited Catholic missions in the San Francisco area in January 1821, following in Kotzebue's and Chamisso's footsteps of 3–4 October 1816 (see Kotzebue, *Voyage*, I:278–84). His negative impressions echoed those of Vasil'ev, whose unpublished "Notes on San Francisco and the Californian Missions," now at TsGAVMF (*fond* 213, *delo* 105 and 107), likewise contrast starkly with a generally favourable account of Bingham's contemporaneous proselytizing on Oahu ("Notes on the [Gavaiiskie] Hawaiian Islands," *fond* 213, *delo* 113).

37. See Bingham, 1847:105–07; and Diell, 1838:23.

38. See Judd, 1929.

39. The Russians well recognized that royal monopolies on trade articles had survived Kamehameha I: details in Roquefeuil, 1823, II:360; Franchère, 1854:60; and Kuykendall, 1938:88–90.

40. Russian: *kolomianku i shliakhty*. Russian texts rarely give such specific indications of trade goods brought by Russian vessels to Polynesia, (see Barratt, 1979c:102–03). *Kolomianka*, acceptable to the Hawaiians at Honolulu as late as 1821, was a striped homespun woollen cloth, of fairly coarse texture. *Shliakhty* were small adzes, the working part being attached transversally across the haft top, i.e., having the same general shape as the Hawaiians' traditional stone adzes, illustrated by Choris.

41. Nuuanu Stream.

42. Lazarev adds (*Mariia*), apparently supposing that the *Maro*, as he first and correctly names that celebrated Nantucket whaler of 315 tons, was a Hawaiian version of *Mariia* or *Mary*.

43. These data confirm and supplement those in Bingham, 1847:134; and Starbuck, 1876:95–98. Such Russian material may be collated with American, e.g., *Missionary Herald*, XVII (September 1821):280, in the tracking of Captain Joseph Allen's pioneering routes of 1820–21.

44. Aleut craft of skins stretched over a frame. See Khlebnikov, 1976:55, on products from beached whales at Unalaska.

45. This is a puzzling passage. The "low coral island" and reef that Allen said he had found in the given latitude and longitude would have been in the Loyalty Group or at the northern tip of New Caledonia. No such discovery was accredited to him in the last century, or is today. On the other hand, Allen did, on 2 June 1820 and in latitude 25°3′N, longitide 167°40′W, discover the barren, rocky outcrop that he named Gardner Island (see Sharp, 1960:196). And a day or two later, he apparently also discovered Maro Reef, in latitude 25°24′N, 170°20′W (details in *Directory of the North Pacific Ocean*, ed. Findlay, 3rd ed., 1886:1112; and R.G. Ward, ed., *American Activities in the Central Pacific, 1790–1870*, Ridgewood, N.J., Gregg Press, 1967, IV:193). It was doubtless this reef that was sighted and heard by the Hawaiian vessel mentioned by Beckley. Lazarev seems, absentmindedly, to have omitted a sentence connecting Captain Allen's claim and the reef in the northwest of the Hawaiian Chain. Allen certainly did announce the existence of Maro Reef, and the Russian naval ministry was aware of it; for the sloop *Moller* (Captain Mikhail N. Staniukovich) searched for it in February 1828, sighting it at a distance of six miles in 25°32′N, 185°15′E (see Ivashintsev, 1980:88–89). Partly because of the opinion of officers aboard the *Otkrytie* and the *Blagonamerennyi* that, as Lazarev put it, that part of the Pacific basin would yet "offer numerous discoveries," Staniukovich had orders to sweep along the entire known length of the Hawaiian chain, from southeast to northwest. In the process, he duly sighted Captain Allen's "Gardner Island" in latitude 25°03′N, longitude 191°58′E.

46. William Heath Davis, Sr., who in 1812 had briefly shared a monopoly of the Hawaiian sandalwood trade with the Winship brothers: see Bradley, 1942:29–30, and Pierce, 1965:232. As captain of the *Isabella*, Davis had made many Russian acquaintances; at Honolulu, he was at pains to be pleasant and useful to

Russian visitors (see Golovnin, 1949:374, etc.). So, too, was his father-in-law and fellow-settler there, Oliver Holmes: see Pierce, 1965:107 and 169. On Davis, see Narratives 17–18, and 85; on Thomas Meek, who was master of Davis's *Eagle* but now commanding the *Arab*, see Narratives 15, 17, and 129; and Howay, 1973:119–21, and 144–45.

47. A false deduction: Kamamalu was forbidden nothing and possibly preferred dog, but most Hawaiian women appear not to have shared that preference in the 1820s.

48. An excellent two-line summary of the traditional process: see Buck, 1957:66–67. The Russian visitors to Hawaii of 1804 had shown far more interest in the making of 'awa than did those of 1821.

49. Lazarev's choice of words here (*natsional 'niu svoiu lodku* makes plain that Liholiho gave him a model of a canoe with outrigger: see Lazarev, 1950:269. The gift was itself a reflection of a Hawaiian infatuation with model craft of all kinds, which reached a peak in the reign of Liholiho. John Papa Ii (1963:29–30) records that the king himself and several powerful chiefs encountered by the Russians and other Europeans were very fond of playing on an ocean pool with fine models of *haole* men-of-war, complete with tiny flags and cannon; and that John Adams Kuakini did so even in old age. Kotzebue saw model ships being used in this fashion in December 1824: see Narrative 114. Liholiho doubtless thought a model canoe more suiatable as a small gift for a Russian junior officer. MAE in Leningrad holds two such models (Likhtenberg, 1960:194 and Plate 2), both acquired after 1845.

50. To Sitka by way of Hobart Town in Van Diemen's Land and Matavai Bay, Tahiti: see Ivashintsev, 1980:70–71. The transfer of livestock occurred in Kronstadt roads between 3 and 16 August, 1822, sixteen months after these Honolulu purchases. Well might Kotzebue, who stowed his Hawaiian livestock on the 180-ton *Riurik*, a brig far smaller than the 130-foot long *Blagonamerennyi*, complain (*Voyage*, II:203) that it was like sailing in Noah's Ark.

51. The "cushion" was a bundle of *kapa*, the game being *no'a*, described in Malo, 1903:203, 295–96 and Ii, 1963:64. The rolling stones or disks were used in a variety of the ancient game of *ulumaika* (Ellis 1839:198). By "casting bones," Lazarev possibly means jack-stones.

52. Russian evidence here confirms the journal of Levi Chamberlain (Hawaiian Mission Children's Society Library: Chamberlain MS), April–July 1823 *passim*; and Stewart, *Private Journal* (1828):91, in suggesting that Liholiho was disposed to drunkenness.

53. In fact, Kamehameha was known less often as Kamehameha (or Tamehamea) than as Tameamea or Kameamea, in this period. Lazarev's own language, however, put him at a disadvantage, where such questions of received pronunciation were concerned. By "the letter g," he obviously meant aspirate "h".

54. The chief Kekuaokalani indeed perished, at Kua'mo'o near Kailua on the Kona Coast, as the Russians were told; but he was not "heir to the throne," despite being a son of Kamehameha's younger brother: discussions in Jarves, 1847:107–09; Dibble, 1909:130–35; and Alexander, 1917:37–45.

55. Kuakini, brother of Kaahumanu.

56. Francisco de Paula Marin.

57. Captain (later Admiral) Petr Ivanovich Rikord (1776–1855); rescued Golovnin from captivity on the Kuril Islands, 1813; commandant at Petropavlovsk-in-

Kamchatka, 1817–22. L.I. Rikord, *Admiral Petr Ivanovich Rikord: biograficheskii ocherk* (St. Petersburg, 1875), touches on the question of Pacific supply routes.

58. Peter Dobell, an Irish-American who had taken Russian citizenship while in China and who, like Scheffer, unsuccessfully urged the Russian government to seize a Hawaiian island as a Pacific base: see Golder, 1928:39–49.

59. It is reproduced as an appendix to Lazarev, 1950. The vessel in question was the *Thaddeus* (Captain William Sumner). She carried salt north, returning with cordage, canvas, ironware, and dried fish: *Missionary Herald*, XVIII (September 1822):273–74; and *MHSP*, LIV:44.

60. Jean Rives (Ioane), secretary and companion of Liholiho: see Ii, 1963:86–87, and 128; and Narratives 49 and 50.

61. Captain Hypolito Bouchard, of the Revolutionary Republic of La Plata,: see Corney, 1896:83–84, and 90–92; and Porter, 1931, II:1149–50.

62. *Columbian Centinel*, 2 April, 6 December 1817. The vessel in question was the *Santa Rosa*.

63. For literature on the 1817 Canton adventure of the *Kaahumanu*, see Bradley, 1942:57.

128. *Visit of November–December 1821*

On 12 November, we spotted flying-fish for the first time on this return passage, and on the morning of the 22nd, to the general delight, we caught sight of the northern point of Vagu [Oahu] Island away to the southeast. Passing through the narrow strait that separates that island from Maratai [Molokai],[1] we were caught by a violent squall that forced us to put two reefs in our topsails. However, it soon died away and we were able to tack round to Ganaruru [Honolulu] under topgallants, with a soft northwest wind. While still five or six miles from that harbour, we were met by the pilot, Varren [Warren], an American.[2] He had come out to escort the sloop. At 2 p.m. on the 24th, being one mile offshore, we dropped anchor with a chain in sixteen *sazhen* [fathoms]; the bottom—coral. As we soon began to drift here, we put down another anchor; but we saw that even this was not helping, so were obliged to raise sail again and make for the harbour.

It was at this juncture that Chief Kamegamega [Kamehameha I][3] the Governor of Vagu Island, came out to us. I have mentioned him before. Shishmarev asked him to send double-canoes out to tow us in next day and to furnish us with fresh provisions and greenstuffs until the arrival of the *Otkrytie*, whom we impatiently awaited. Kamegamega willingly undertook to fulfil our requests but informed us that he would be able to send only one boat, since there were no others in the harbour at that time. At 7 p.m. we again dropped anchor in a depth of fourteen *sazhen*, coral bottom, now being two-and-a-half miles southeast of the entrance into Ganaruru Harbour. That night the weather was clear and a calm descended. Seeing that the calm would continue, we fired a gun at 4 a.m. to request rowing-boats and a pilot. An hour later, we repeated the signal; and at 6 a.m., with the assistance of eleven rowing-boats and Sandvichanskie [Sandwich Island] double-canoes, we successfully entered the harbour. There we moored on a kedge anchor. There already stood there five North American merchantmen, lately trading on the Northwest Coast of America, one English vessel on her way to the coasts of Japan to hunt sperm-whales, and three brigs and three schooners of the Sandvichanskii fleet. This time we did not stand where we had earlier; that had been a very inconvenient spot, for the depth surrounding it would suddenly increase greatly, quite often causing the sloop to drift.

We were escorted into the harbour by Chief Kamegamega himself, once he had inquired whether or not our sloop would salute the fort. We explained to him that we really had no right to do so, but that the fort's salute would not go unanswered. Hardly had we dropped anchor before the fort duly fired seven shots, receiving an equal number from us.

Ganaruru now presented a very dull picture; the king had for some reason gone off to Ovagi [Hawaii] Island, all the chiefs were presently in the interior of Vagu to fell sandalwood, for which purpose a large number of natives had also been sent, and the fields around the harbour had emptied.[4] There were not even any dances, though these were the constant relaxation of the Sandvichan. The natives who had remained at home received permission to take foodstuffs out to us, but they charged pretty steeply for them; altogether in the European manner indeed, demanding several *thalers* for any trifle. All this was probably a result of the chiefs' desire to please the king, for he, when he returns to Vagu Island, sometimes taxes them one *thaler* each for the right to visit his residence.

The missionaries' house had already been built but it was not yet com-pletely finished inside. They and the craftsmen who had come with them had moved into it, however. The church and school were in special huts. Another two-storeyed house in the European style had been built by Broun [Brown], the skipper of an American vessel, probably with a view to selling it to the king in due time.[5] For the king had already purchased from him, while we were present, a fully-armed brig, paying in sandalwood to the value of 36,000 *piastres*. A *picul* was reckoned to be worth ten *piastres*.[6] On Vagu Island, we found Dzhons [Johns], who had been sent there as consul from the United States. He had been left in complete idleness, however, as the king did not know the significance of the word "consul," and traded only in the company of Broun.

We had called at Ganaruru with the intention of recaulking our entire sloop, inside and outside, for the high winds that had blown during our voyage from Kamchatka had opened her up. The firewood that we had taken aboard in Petropavlovsk port had given rise to dreadful dampness, rank air, and a smell of rottenness in the hold, so we found ourselves obliged to remove it and busy ourselves in drying the sloop out. Finally, we had to take on water, for which purpose we hired Sandvichan. We paid them in goods, but even so their services were not cheap. For the same goods, and at the same exorbitant rate, we acquired provisions: swine, goats, cabbage, sweet potatoes, and so forth. Occasionally the chiefs would send us fish of various sorts as a gift. We stowed away twenty-seven hogs and six goats and pickled down eight casks of cabbage.

It was while this bartering and work was proceeding, on the morning of 26 November, that our spirits were raised by the appearance of the sloop

Otkrytie. She approached the harbour but, in view of the calm, fired a shot to request a tow by rowing-boats which both we and some American vessels duly sent out to her. With their aid, she was pulled into harbour and there dropped anchor. The king arrived with one of his brigs on the morning of the 28th.

On 16 December, the king paid a visit to the sloops *Otkrytie* and *Blagonamerennyi*, which received him with all the honours due to his rank. He much admired our arms drill and, as a mark of his pleasure, he next day sent us ten hogs as a gift.

During this stay of ours in Ganaruru Harbour, the winds blew first from seaward, then later from the land; and perfect calms sometimes fell. In the first days of December, though, the winds began to blow steadily from the shore, and on the 10th a strong wind set in from the northeast which persisted until the day of our departure. The barometer rose from 29 inches, 9 lines to 30 inches, 2 lines, and the thermometer, from 72° to 81°.

By 18 December we were completely ready to make sail, but since the wind was blowing from east-northeast we could only leave the harbour. Our sloop touched on a shoal at the bow. She moved off it all right. Meanwhile the wind had shifted to the northeast, so we raised sail and went out of the harbour. Then, while waiting for the *Otkrytie*, we lay to and hoisted our boats. She too came out at 3 p.m. and, being ready for the voyage, indicated a south-southwest course to us. From the point where we left, we reckoned the place where we had lain at anchor in Ganaruru to lie in latitude 21°18′30″N, longitude 202°9′29″E ....

COMMENTARY

1. Kaiwi Channel.
2. William Warren, ex-seaman, early American settler on Oahu: see *Columbian Centinel*, 6 November 1816.
3. Kalanimoku.
4. On the hardships caused by this enforced cutting of sandalwood, see Bradley, 1942:70–71; and Narrative 27.
5. Thomas Brown, Honolulu agent for Marshall & Wildes and associate of John C. Jones. See Narrative 54 on imported frame houses.
6. Thus, sandalwood was being bought for $170 a ton.

FERDINAND PETROVICH WRANGEL (RUSSIAN: VRANGEL')

Baron Wrangel (1796–1870) was, like Ferdinand Petrovich Lütke (Russian: Litke), a particularly shrewd and able Baltic German officer in Russian service. Founding member of the Russian Geographical Society, surveyor, and admiral, he was in 1829–35 Governor of Russian North America. In that capacity, he fought a rearguard and generally successful action with Sir George Simpson and John H. Pelly of the Hudson's Bay Company. (In 1838, Sir George could describe him, exasperatedly, as "an extraordinary looking ferret-eyed, red whiskered and mustachioed little creature in full Regimentals ...": see Barratt, *Russian Shadows*:36.) But this was long after the Honolulu visit of the *Krotkii*, which a younger and more physical Captain-Lieutenant Wrangel deftly handled in the final weeks of 1826. Of Wrangel's earlier experience in Oceania, suffice it to note that he had sailed as midshipman aboard the *Kamchatka* (Captain V.M. Golovnin) in 1817–19, and had been commended to the Naval Ministry. Thus he had spent five busy days at Honolulu (26–30 October 1818) at the age of twenty-two. It was a visit that had left a deep impression.

The *Krotkii* carried a cargo of supplies and naval stores to Petropavlovsk-in-Kamchatka and to Sitka. She was a specially built transport, sailed well in heavy seas, and, when she called at Honolulu on her homeward passage, had a relatively modest crew of forty-nine including officers. Wrangel had spent a mere three weeks at Sitka (21 September–12 October 1826), before gladly moving south; he would have reached Oahu Island even earlier if he had not, like Gleb Shishmarev and other Russian captains, wasted time searching in vain for Maria Laxara Island, "given by Norie," Ivashintsev observes (*Russian Round-the-World Voyages*:85), "in latitude 27°6'N, longitude 139°20'E." In his subsequent account of this Hawaii visit, Wrangel claimed that his chronometers were much in need of checking and his stores of food depleted by the first week of November, so that duty made that visit unavoidable. No doubt his men did need fresh foodstuffs. It is also plain, however, that he relished the idea of returning to Oahu and, in fact, enjoyed himself at Honolulu. From there, he proceeded to Manila, dropping anchor on 13 January 1827.

Wrangel wrote easily and well. He was the author of large travel works and ethnographic-cum-statistical compendia, as well as numerous reports, papers, and essays on a range of naval, mercantile, and scientific topics. His account of the *Krotkii*'s Honolulu visit, here translated into English for the first time, was based on her log and his own official journal, and appeared in the periodical, *Severnyi arkhiv* (St. Petersburg, 1828), vol. 12:86–105.

129. Visit of November 1826

At 5.30 a.m. the southern tip[1] of Uagu [Oahu] emerged, northeast 41°, through the mist. We then laid to and tacked northwest, hoisting all possible canvas. It transpired at this point that during the night we had been carried along by the powerful current that flows here and that, in the night, we had not spotted the southeast cape[2] at all but the south cape. Thus we had so fallen below the wind that it was only by tacking that we could reach our anchorage, which was then seven miles north-northeast of us. It was cloudy, and a wind was blowing from the northeast with squalls, but often enough dying away completely, which made tacking very difficult. Despite all this however, at 4 p.m. we reached the roadstead in front of the entrance into Gonoruru [Honolulu] Harbour. The royal pilot, an Englishman by birth,[3] came out to us and brought us to anchor half a mile from the reef in twenty-five *sazhen* [fathoms] of water, so that the centre of the village was 5° northwest of us. The bottom was fine whitish sand with shell, and we let out sixty-eight *sazhen* of rope. We stood quietly in this spot even though, for the first two days, the wind was blowing with violent squalls.

In the *Voyages* of Captains V.M. Golovnin and Kotzebue,[4] one can find all the necessary instructions regarding the approach of ships to the roadstead and entry into Gonoruru Harbour itself, which lies two and a quarter miles west of Vaititi [Waikiki] settlement, three and a half miles northwest of the southern cape, and thirteen miles east of the southwest cape of Uagu Island. According to Vancouver's chart, this harbour lies in longitude 157°51'40"W from Grinvich [Greenwich]. According to our own reckonings, the latitude of the quay there is 21°18'23"N.[5]

One of the reasons that had led me to call at these islands had been a wish to check the movement of our chronometers, which had not been done since our departure from Kamchatka. Another and equally important necessity was that of obtaining fresh provisions for our crew; for our stores had so dwindled that saltmeat[6] and pease were being served now even at the officers' table.

For better communication with the shore, I had meant to move right into the harbour itself. However, this was possible only during a complete calm, such as usually occurs at dawn, and as there was no such calm for two consecutive mornings, I decided to answer our needs by standing in the roadstead and taking advantage of the obligingness of Captain Dzhones [Jones] of the United States of America.[7] Captain Dzhones, who had already been here a month and a half with his twenty-four-gun corvette, the *Pavlin* [*Peacock*],[8] and 180 men, gave orders for fresh water to be brought to us in his own boats. Our chronometers were taken ashore the next day and put in a trader's house, where Navigator Kozmin continued to make the observations necessary for their correction for as long as we remained.[9]

Early in the morning, the royal pilot brought us out a hog, some fruit and some vegetables, as a gift from the king.[10] I went ashore with some of my officers at 10 a.m. About twenty-five merchantmen were in the harbour, (one English whaler, all the rest flying the United States flag), besides the naval corvette, mounting twenty-four 32-pounders, also under the flag of the United States of America.[11]

In the village itself we were surprised by the quite considerable number of houses built in the European manner, with two storeys,[12] and by the neat appearance of the natives who crowded around us with particular pleasure on their faces. Some of them wore cloths but many were dressed in the European way. Neither now nor later did I see a single individual completely naked, or any of those comical states of semi-dress that had so often amused us during my previous stay here in 1818, with the *Kamchatka* [Plate 23].[13]

Accompanied by the pilot we made our way to the king, who resides a half *verst* from the quay. His house, as is the local custom, resembles a great barn.[14] A simple palisade encircles it. At the gate, I was met by the present Governor of Uagu, Buke [Boki] by name, who was dressed in a jacket in the European way.[15] Buke introduced me to King Tameamea [Kamehameha] III, a younger son of the famous Tameamea [Kamehameha] I, now a boy of perhaps twelve.[16] We walked between two rows of correctly dressed warriors, perhaps 150 of them, who formed a guard of honour in their own fashion.[17] We seated ourselves, in this barn, on chairs round a large table covered by a blue cloth. The king alone occupied its far end. He was dressed as an English midshipman, and throughout our audience he uttered not one word, the whole conversation being conducted by the aforementioned Buke, a brother of the celebrated Pitt [Kalanimoku]. He was managing affairs of state now because of Pitt's illness. We thanked him and the king for the gift sent out that same day and obtained the royal permission to supplement our supplies by making purchases from his subjects. We would then have taken our leave, but Buke ordered wine to be brought out in decanters and glasses,[18] proposing a toast to the health of King Tameameà III, which we drank with much pleasure.

Governor Buke then conducted us to his sick brother, who was living three houses away from the king. Mr. Pitt was seated on a sofa in his shirt, smoking a cigar. A decanter of Madeira wine stood on a little table in front of him. Two Sandvichane [Sandwich Islanders] were massaging his feet with their hands. For more than a year already, Pitt had been suffering from water on the knee, and the affliction had even altered his facial expression. I had difficulty in recognizing the old Pitt.[19] Our ship's surgeon, Dr. Kiber, went into details about the cruel ailment, at the sufferer's own request. I myself hastened to take my leave in order to meet Captain Dzhones of the United States corvette, *Pavlin*. USS *Pavlin* had already spent two years in these waters. Her mission was to protect the merchant shipping of the United States from pillage, which is by no means uncommon along the coasts of South America.[20] Having looked about the whole coast from Val'pareizo [Valparaiso] up to Acapulco, Captain Dzhones had made for Otaiti [Tahiti] by way of the Washington [Marquesas] Islands and the Nizmennyi [Low or Tuamotu] Archipelago, and so the Sandvichevy [Sandwich] Islands. It would seem to be his object to determine these islands' degree of independence from England and from the United States. Certainly, it is with that object in mind that an English Consul, Navy Captain Charlton [Mr. Charlton] is here.[21] He had also been in Otaiti.

I had the pleasure of meeting Mr. Charlton at Captain Dzhones' quarters. Gonorura Harbour has become such an important one for American trade now, that the United States government finds it necessary to protect its merchants there by guaranteeing access to the Sandvichevye Islands regardless of

England. Otaiti, Mr. Dzhones told me, was in a state of general rebellion; two parties, the king's and the queen's, were warring and the natives, taking full advantage of the disorders produced by this internecine dissension, had lately plundered an English whaler, without however killing one soul.[22] The teaching of the English missionaries has put down weak roots.

As is well known, missionaries from the United States of America have undertaken the task of saving souls on the Sandvichevye Islands. Looking at the matter one way, it is impossible to deny the beneficial effect that these pastors have had on the Islanders' morality. But, alas, that love of power which is innate in all men has deflected even these teachers of meekness from the true ends of their own teaching. Captain Dzhones, having now learned the large ambitious designs of these missionaries, thinks it necessary to send the head of the local mission off to America, and, in the name of his government, to limit its other members' field of activity.[23]

Only the lower class of women can be reproached here with licentiousness, for the missionaries have managed to instil in the females some idea of the merit of chastity. One old lady of very advanced years but very noble descent,[24] forgetful of the long ago times of her own sportive youth, now watches with a tireless vigilance over the virtue of the young women of the Island. This severe Vestal forbids the young to walk out on the streets and insists that, when at home, the women shall wear long shirts to cover up their neck and breasts or else wrap themselves in their cloths.[25] The nobility of her antecedents gives her full rights to lay down prohibitions of every kind.

We noticed no theft and heard from Europeans resident here that the Islanders have, in fact, almost abandoned that vice. The reason for this, however, is of course the natives' frequent contact with Europeans, rather than the missionaries' brief presence. I would even think that, in their observation of the rules of honesty, the Islanders excel the local merchants. There are no longer any idols in the *morais* [*heiau*, or temples]; churches and institutes are being erected instead. It is the utility of the latter, recognized by the king's counsellors, that has persuaded him to tolerate the former. They say, though, that there are generally few zealous Christians here. The native schools are attended quite assiduously, and in Gonoruru it has been decreed that entire families shall go to school in turn.[26] In these schools, young and old and men and women alike all study reading and writing under the instruction of teachers, of both sexes, whom the missionaries have well tested.[27] The king can write pretty well, read no worse, and even exercises himself by studying rudiments of arithmetic and English grammar. His orders are nowadays disseminated in written form on the State printing press.[28]

Having made mention of changes and novelties introduced by the missionaries, I will now mention a few other changes. It is no longer Ovaiga [Hawaii], but Uagu, that is considered the principal island of this group; and the port of Gonoruru which serves as the only haven for merchant shipping in the Islands, has now become the seat of the king and the focal point of his power. I was assured that the royal forces number 10,000 men on all the islands, 1,500 being on Uagu, in various villages and in batteries on elevations round the harbour and settlement of Gonorura itself. His Majesty's personal bodyguard, consisting of some 200 men, occupy positions round his residence and always carry loaded firearms by night. Tameamea III's household troops have a uniform of white cloth trousers, and white jacket with red collar and cuffs; black tie, with clean shirt visible behind; and round shako of stiff dark leather. The shako has a red top and a plume of straight white feathers. A bandolier is worn across the left shoulder, and the gun is held in the right hand. The soldiers are strong, well-built, and far more impressive looking than the Brazilian Regiments at Rio [de] Janeiro.[29] A soldier's pay consists of his food and clothing, that is, he receives no fixed wage; but he is exempted from all labour duty and is not even employed on public works unless these be immediately linked to the martial calling.[30]

As for the royal naval forces, they now consist of five brigs and ten sailing single-deckers.[31] The latter only voyage between the Islands, but the brigs go to California, Otaiti, and other places, to hunt the amphibious animals whose fat is so prized on the Canton mart.[32]

At about 2 p.m., a bell was struck and I learned on enquiry that it was thus that persons wishing to partake of a *table d'hôte* were summoned into an eating-house. Our own meal time had long since passed, so we hastened into the spacious eating-house in question and sat at a huge, neatly laid table. It offered the best dishes in Spanish style; the establishment was maintained by a son of the famous Manini [Marin]. One can take breakfast, lunch, or supper for one *piastre*.[33] I would advise a visitor to settle his account with the proprietor promptly and on a daily basis, for there is double-entry book-keeping there— in chalk. While at table, I got to know several merchant captains who had been at Okhotsk, Kamchatka, and Sitka,[34] and were presently engaged in the Canton trade, which brought them an annual profit of thirty-three percent overall.

After this meal, a certain Mr. Mik [Meek], captain of one of those United States merchantmen we had found at Sitka, invited me to his own house. Mr. Mik had first met us here while we were still tacking in the Gonorura roadstead, and he tried to be of use to us, as and where possible, right through our stay.[35] On our way to his house, we passed by a billiard-room, two drinking establishments, and a shop selling Chinese and European wares. I also learned that there is now a sugar refinery at Gonorura,[36] that excellent roads are being laid down to neighbouring villages, and that for a certain sum one can take a ride in a carriage or ride out on "trained horses"![37] All these amusements are essentially, of course, consequences of the active trade and enterprising spirit of the citizens of the United States of America.

The sudden descent of darkness detained us ashore; the coral reefs make it very risky to leave the harbour, at night especially, when the darkness prevents one from making out objects at a sufficient distance. We wanted to derive some benefit, at least, from this turn of events, so we decided to take a walk round the island next day, setting off at dawn. Having made the necessary arrangements, we abandoned ourselves to slumber on the cold mats spread out in the local manner on the floor of our friend Captain Mik's clean and attractive house. Mik himself moved to another building.[38]

The cock had hardly crowed before a drummer from Tameamea III's bodyguard was rapping his way along all the village streets. We immediately dressed and were told that, hearing of our intention, the Governor had ordered that a guard of honour and some good guides be allocated to us. This guard consisted of four handsome members of the queen's household troop in full military dress. They formed up in twos and our guide indicated that we should walk between them, so our ceremonial progress took on the appearance of a walk by arrested men under very close escort! The village natives, however, who ran out of their houses in droves, saw nothing so offensive in all this, but merely followed behind us in silence, the elders alone venturing to greet us with an *Arokho!* [*Aloha!*], that is, "Hello, friend!" [Plate 27].

We waded across the Gonorura stream, then made for the northeast, gaining height insensibly as we followed paths winding over man-made plantations of that useful plant, taro.[39] The valley here offered no pleasant views. At a distance, the bare tops of hills could be seen on either side; and as for the plain lying between them, it was covered by a faded yellow grass and devoid of that variegated and strongly contoured nature with which tropical lands are usually beautified. And added to this absence of natural beauties that we had expected to see was an extremely muddy road, areas of bog, and almost impassable thickets. This all combined to make our excursion a wearisome one for body and spirit alike. However, Surgeon Kiber[40] found objects in the plant kingdom even here that merited his attention, while I found some entertainment in the originality of the many natives, men and women, who came up to us with bundles of bananas, sugar-cane, hens, swine, and other supplies meant to be sold down in Gonorura.[41]

After two hours' walk, we spotted a little house in an open place. Entering it, we were refreshed with watermelons that the perspicacious mistress offered us. The interior of her house was, essentially, a spacious shed on the walls of which hung calabashes, bananas, and nuts on a string which served instead of candles.[42] A little way off grew taro, cabbage, watermelons, and melons. From here, after another hour and a half of really hard going on an extremely difficult track, we descended finally into a shady ravine. Here, our guide offered us his own provisions for the journey; taro dough, one fish, and three coconuts; but we were looking forward to delicacies brought from Gonorura and, recognizing the true wish of this provident Sandvichanina, permitted our entire little brigade to lie on the grass around a huge calabash full of taro dough.[43] Using a single finger, they very deftly and quickly stuffed their cheeks with this dough. This exercise by our bodyguard gave us opportunity to observe that each man was missing a front tooth, a result, as I afterwards learned, of the death of Tameamea I.[44] For as soon as it became common knowledge that the king had died, almost all his male subjects willingly knocked out one tooth, so following a mourning ritual for which a mere change of clothing is insufficient. We were not left as suffering witnesses to others' dinner, however; for three Sandvichanina ran up with wine, gin, a dish of tasty sauce made from chicken and duck, yams, potatoes, and cooked taro instead of bread. We turned nothing down, attempting to build up our strength so that we might continue our expedition without another stop.

At first we were obliged to force our way through thickly intertwined bush; but then we suddenly came out into an open place, whence it was necessary to go up a steep elevation. Our army halted, removed hats on command, and took hold of the guns with both hands; and our guide gave us a sign to remove our hats too, fasten up all buttons, and prepare to meet a great gust of wind. Only then did we ascend, and no sooner did we reach a summit than the eternally blowing trade-wind suddenly roared dreadfully. Up to now, the mountains had been protecting us from it. We were subjected to its full fury. Ahead, to the northeast, surged the ocean. Below our feet, back to the southwest, extended the whole valley that we had traversed, Gonorura Harbour with its ships looking like little boats, and the distant sea. To either side, we were surrounded by jagged and sharp-sided cliffs. As we turned to the right, the wind struck us in the back and, passing through little ravines, we attained an even greater height where we were obliged to hang onto a cliff lest the strength of that wind cast us down into the fathomless abyss that lay directly beneath us.[45] We could not even hear our own voices, such was the noise of ocean rollers smashing against the coral reefs that encircle the eastern shore of this island and the howling, whistling, and roaring of the winds as they struck the steep walls of these pyramidal cliffs. Certainly we had not noticed that behind us there had gathered many Islanders, no doubt going to the settlement on the east coast, below the mountain on which we now stood. We smiled involuntarily, seeing this crowd of men and women take on assorted caricature-like poses as they strove to defend themselves, and their burdens, against that savage wind. The men, being less concerned with the newly introduced notions of modesty here, and fearful of losing every ornament and covering that they might wear, simply stood there in all their nakedness, their long hair flying in the wind; they seemed like eternal dwellers of these wild rocks. The women, however, were more troubled by the observances of propriety. I gazed wonderingly as one young girl in a long shirt[46] struggled hard with the rude zephyrs as they insolently snatched at the edges of her simple clothing. She held it by hands and by standing on it, too; and, swollen like a sail, her shirt tried to lift the terrorstruck girl into the air!

The sun was already passing through the meridian, and we were still seven miles distant from Gonorura; and so, wasting no further time, we were obliged to leave these picturesque heights and descend into the muddy valley. On our way back we called in again at the little house where we had earlier rested and where there now awaited us a tasty dinner, brought out from Gonorura. We got home at 5 p.m., weary and filthy to the knees but nonetheless well pleased with our campaign and with the adventures of the day. On reaching the *Krotkii*, I found everything shipshape. The work had been completed successfully.

Next day, those officers who had hitherto remained aboard, Lavrov and Matiushkin,[47] went ashore. The former I commissioned to present certain articles to the king and Governor[48] as gifts in my name: a silver watch of English make, two cut-glass decanters complete with glasses, three Morocco hides of different hues, and a large looking-glass. To these articles were later added, at the Governor's request, a supported jib-boom and a royal-mast boom, which were rather expensive things in these parts. I mention these gifts to give a true idea of the high prices of foodstuffs; for in return, I received from the king and his Governor only five goats, a hog, forty hens, and a small quantity of greens.[49] It was explained to me that other animals destined for us had perished on the way to Gonorura from other villages.

All this day, and the next, I remained aboard the sloop, and we duly completed all necessary tasks, watering with Captain Dzhones' assistance, purchasing and bringing aboard livestock and greenstuffs. All we lacked was grass for our goats, which was to be cut on a hillside and could not be handed to us before the 19th. We used this unavoidable delay to give a dinner for our Gonorura acquaintances, Captain Dzhone, Consul Charlton, and the American Consul, Mr. Dzhons.[50] On leaving, Captain Dzhones invited me and all my officers to call on him next day aboard the *Pikok* [*Peacock*]. We could scarcely decline, and spent from 3 p.m. till a late hour on board her, passing the time quite pleasantly among educated people. We were glad of this chance to examine a United States Navy corvette, and we found everything in perfect order and well arranged in her. At last, they brought out the hay. There was no wind till 10 a.m., but then we weighed anchor and, with the gentle trade-wind that had blown up, moved out to sea, steering southwest.[51]

COMMENTARY

1. Modern Barber's Point.
2. Diamond Head is meant, not Koko Head.
3. Kotzebue's *Puteshestvie v Iuzhnyi okean* (St. Petersburg, 1821) and Golovnin's *Puteshestvie vokrug sveta ... na shliupe "Kamchatka"* (St. Petersburg, 1822) were among the *Voyages* carried aboard the *Krotkii* on her two Pacific expeditions (1825–27 commanded by Wrangel; 1828–30 commanded by Gagemeister).
4. Alexander Adams, who also commanded the royal brig, *Kaahumanu*: see Narrative 29.
5. The *Riurik* reckoned this anchorage to lie in latitude 21°17′57″N. According to the *Blagonamerennyi* it was latitude 21°18′30″N. The *Neva* and *Kamchatka* made reckonings within this range, so that disparities in latitudinal fixings for Honolulu Harbour were less than 1′. By contrast, the differences in longitudinal reckoning were as much as 40′ in this period. The *Riurik* read longitude 157°52′00″W, the *Blagonamerennyi*—157°90′71″W, for two points within 100 yards of each other. Longitudinal error margins were universally greater than latitudinal ones, however, even in the early 1800s when improved chronometers were used in conjunction with lunar observation to calculate longitude.
6. *Solonina*, saltmeat.
7. Captain Thomas ap Catesby Jones, USN (1790–1858).
8. USS *Peacock* had actually arrived at Honolulu on 10 October 1826; details in U.S. Dept. of the Navy, Naval Records and Library: Thos. C. Jones, "Report of the *Peacock*'s Cruise to the Sandwich, Society, and other Islands in the Pacific, performed in the Years 1826 and 1827 ...":17–19. On Captain Jones's mission and instructions to investigate American traders' "claims for property" on Oahu, etc., see *United States Congress, House Reports: XXVIII Congress*, 2nd Session, No. 92: 8ff.
9. Prokopii I. Kozmin, a veteran of the *Kamchatka*'s visit of 1818. The "trader's house" was probably John or Thomas Meek's; on their dealings with the Russians from 1816 on, see Narrative 17.

10. This was Kauikeaouli (Kamehameha III), Liholiho's younger brother: see Bingham, *Sandwich Islands*:203, on his accession in 1824. The young king was ruler in name only until the death of Kalanimoku, joint-regent with Kaahumanu, in 1827. See Bradley, 1942:143, n. 99.

11. For details of shipping, see Judd, 1929; and Starbuck, 1876; tart comments on the New England whaling fleet of 1822–26 in Bingham, 1847:134. Wrangel's figures corroborate Richard Charlton's data (*Correspondence relative to the Sandwich Islands*:11) regarding Honolulu's primacy as a Pacific port of call for whalers, and underline the relative unimportance of Lahaina on Maui in 1826–27.

12. These were frame houses of the type imported first by Marshall & Wildes and the American Board of Commissioners for Foreign Missions in 1821: Harvard University Library, Marshall MSS: Jones to Marshall & Wildes, Oahu, 5 October 1821.

13. Golovnin, 1822: Chap. XI.

14. Kauikeaouil's "great barn" (Russian: *ogromnyi sarai*) had been erected on the orders of Kalanimoku. He had received Lord Byron and the officers of HMS *Blonde* in it (May 1825): see Stewart, 1828:277ff; and Bingham, 1847:264–65. It stood in an enclosure known as Pohokaina, near the corner of King and Punchbowl Streets, and was therefore doubly pallisaded (see Ii, 1963:143 and 148).

15. Boki had escorted Liholiho and Queen Kamamalu to London in 1823–24 and so been exposed to heavy British influence: see Sinclair, 1976:52–54, and 69–75. He was guardian of the youthful king until, in 1829, he left the Islands forever (he is commonly supposed to have drowned in the Fiji Islands: Bradley, 1942:196). The Russian evidence confirms that Boki, the inveterate opponent of Kaahumanu, exerted a powerful influence on the court, perhaps aspiring to the regency himself in 1826–27. On Kaahumanu's and Bingham's opposition see Levi Chamberlain MS, 11–16 November 1826 and Beechy, 1831, 2:110.

16. The king had actually been born in 1814: see Kamakau, 1961:260; also Alexander, 1899:158.

17. These were known as the Okaka Guards (Ii, 1963:149) and had developed from the royal bodyguard established by Kamehameha I at Vancouver's suggestion (*ibid.*, 139).

18. Boki encouraged the king's heavy drinking and even owned saloons in Honolulu, according to Charlton: *Correspondence relative to the Sandwich Islands*:23.

19. Kalanimoku's edema worsened and he died, in Kona, in February 1827: Harvard University Library, Marshall MSS: Jones to Marshall, Oahu, 6 March 1827; see also Sinclair, 1976:88.

20. See n. 8.

21. For surveys of these matters, J.I. Brookes, *International Rivalry in the Pacific Islands, 1800–1875* (Berkeley, 1941):50–51; and Bradley, 1942:105–09. Wrangel was aware of Consul Charlton's anti-American animus.

22. Details in C.W. Newbury, ed. *History of the Tahitian Mission, 1799–1830, written by John Davies, missionary ...* (Cambridge, Hakluyt Society, 2nd series, No. CXVI, 1961):334ff and J.A. Moerenhout, *Voyages aux îles du Grand Océan* (Paris, 1942: 2nd ed.), 2:504–08.

Charlton and John C. Jones told Wrangel what they knew about the struggle that had developed between Pomare III's and Almata's parties on Tahiti. Political and religious tensions had increased greatly on Tahiti since the *Predpriiatie* had left

Matavai Bay, on 23 March 1824. Wrangel's full report to the Russian Admiralty came too late however (17 September 1827) to be useful to the captain of the sloop *Moller*, (Captain Mikhail N. Staniukovich). Unaware of the Tahitian crisis (which in any case was lessening by then), Staniukovich arrived at Matavai Bay on 29 April 1827. Having passed a pleasant fourteen days at anchor, he proceeded to Hawaii in his turn, but passed between Oahu and Kauai without making a call (13–14 June 1827). Visits to Oahu made it possible for Russian officers to keep abreast of the political and other action in Tahiti in 1821–28, just as calls at Matavai Bay produced Hawaiian news (e.g., for Bellingshausen in July 1820)

23. Charlton's hand is discernible here. Despite what Wrangel seems to have been told, Jones had nothing of the sort in mind and was, indeed, sympathetic toward Bingham: U.S. Dept. of the Navy, Naval Records and Library: Jones, "Report of the *Peacock's* Cruise," 14 May 1827.

24. Kaahumanu, the favourite wife of Kamehameha I.

25. This was in keeping with the American missionaries' edict or "Code of Laws" of August 1825. Kaahumanu was supporting Bingham in "a general prohibition of lewdness in the Sandwich Islands": cited by Bradley, 1942:174 (from Letters to the American Board, 31, No. 25). See also Dibble, 1909:101–02, on prohibitions of lewd behaviour; and Narratives 125–26 (Kotzebue's poor opinion of religious fervour at Honolulu two years before the arrival of the *Krotkii*; Kaahumanu's extremism in religious discipline).

26. See *Missionary Herald*, XXIV (April 1828):104. Such attendance by turns was necessary because of a shortage of textbooks: *ibid.*, XXV (February 1829):55; and Bingham, 1847:257. Wrangel is typically cautious in his criticism of enforced and almost universal attendance of schools, compared with other foreign visitors of the period, e.g., Beechey, 1831, II:101–02; and Duhaut-Cilly, 1835, II:283–84.

27. See Narratives 122 and 125–26, for Kotzebue's reactions to this.

28. This side of Kauikeaouli's character, and his friendliness towards the missionaries (see Journal of Levi Chamberlain, 26–27 December 1825, and *Missionary Herald*, XXVIII:41), are generally stressed less than his pleasure in billiards, horses, and rum. Wrangel objectively records the success of the missionaries in educating the young king (Bingham, 1847:346–47, and 430ff.), whose brother Liholiho had shown less patience with schooling (Mathison, 1825:428) and more indolence. More significant, however, is Wrangel's identification of the printing press by which the royal edicts were disseminated, in 1826, as *Gosudarstvennaia* (State). The press in question was that brought by the missionaries and first used to run off a Hawaiian speller on 7 January 1822 (see Bingham, 1847:156; and *Missionary Herald*, XIX:42). The Russian evidence thus supports the assertion of the missionary historian Sheldon Dibble that, by 1826, a union of church and state "did exist to a very considerable extent": Dibble, 1909:78), despite all Bingham's heated disclaimers. Other Russian narratives of the period show how the mission's monopoly of printing afforded it potent opportunities to mould the Hawaiians' lives.

29. Wrangel had called at Rio de Janeiro twice, in November 1817 with the *Kamchatka* and in November 1825 with the *Krotkii*. The Portuguese (Brazilian) troops made a poor impression on him and many other Russian visitors: see Shur, 1971:40 and 96 (1817 diaries of Fedor F. Matiushkin and Litke). In general, the Russian narratives of sojourns on Oahu in 1816–36 are rich in descriptions of military protocol and uniforms.

30. This was a major privilege, since Kaahumanu had habitually sent religious back-sliders and all social outcasts to work on roads upcountry; see Malo, 1903:87–88 (the hard lot of the Makaainana).

31. Further on the growth of the Hawaiian Navy, see Narratives 52 and 127; also W.D. Alexander, "Early Trading in Hawaii," *HHS Papers*, 11 (Honolulu, 1904):23; and Bradley, 1942:56 and 62.

32. Pinnipeds, the suborder of marine carnivores including seals (*phocidae*), elephant seals (*mirounga*), and Pacific walrus (*odobenidae*).

33. On the personal and business links between Don George, the son of Francisco de Paula Marin, or Marini, and the other main partner in this particular eating-house, Captain Thomas Meek, see Bradley, 1942:112, n. 326 (joint trading venture with Boki in 1828, etc.); also Narratives 15, 17, and 127. Beechey visited the same establishment a year after Wrangel (Beechey, 1831, II:97) and found that prices had fallen.

34. These included John Ebbets, now commanding J.J. Astor's new brig *Tamaahmaah* (Narrative 17; and Howay, 1973:165) and Captain Kelly of the brig *Owhyee*. (On Ebbets' many connections with the Russian Northwest Coast since 1802, see Pierce, 1965:232–33.) Such Nor'westers were far outnumbered, at the time of the *Krotkii*'s visit, by the 107 whalers at Honolulu that year, some of which Wrangel inspected: see Richards, 1834:358; and Wyllie, 1844:49; also Narrative 34.

35. See Appendix B on Meek's role in Oahu and Sitka trade in 1809–26.

36. Operated by an English settler, John Wilkinson, who had reached the Islands in 1825 with HMS *Blonde* at the invitation of Boki: see Paulding, 1831:220–22; Thrum, 1875:35; and Levi Chamberlain MS: 3, 10 August 1826 and 30 November 1826.

37. See Beechey, 1831, II:68. Details of the trade in Harvard University Library, Marshall MSS: Thompson to Marshall, Oahu, 19 November 1830.

38. On Meek, see Narratives 15 and 17; and *MHSP*, XL:44 (John C. Jones on the early Hawaiian ban on the construction of permanent houses by *haole*).

39. These were on either side of the Waolani Stream.

40. Dr. August Kiber, botanist and physician, surgeon aboard the armed transport *Krotkii*.

41. At inflated prices, by 1826: see Narratives 106 and 108.

42. *Kukui* nut candles, from the tree *Aleurites moluccana*. The nuts were lightly baked, the hard shells cracked, and the oily kernels threaded on lengths of stiff, dry, coconut leaf: see Ellis, 1839: 374. The Russian text (*na nitke nanizannye orekhi* ...) shows that these nuts were threaded on a string-like substance.

43. The "calabash" or gourd container (*'umeke pohue*) was full of *pa'i'ai*. Full details in Buck, 1957:20–21, and 33–35.

44. 8 May 1819. Survey of traditional grieving practice in Dibble, 1909:68–69.

45. Probably Puu Konahuanui (3,105 feet).

46. Russian: *rubakha*, a shirt or chemise.

47. Fedor Fedorovich Matiushkin (1799–1872), school friend of the poet A.S. Pushkin at Tsarskoe Selo *lycée*; sailed in the *Kamchatka* to Hawaii in 1818; Second Lieutenant of the *Krotkii*, 1825–27; saw action in Russo-Turkish War, 1828–30, with Admiral P.I. Rikord, the promoter of Hawaiian-Kamchatkan trade. Details in Shur, 1971:14–16.

48. Boki.

49. The previous year (1825), such prices had driven many whalers from Honolulu to Lahaina on Maui: *Correspondence*, 1843:10–11; Wyllie, 1844:49.

50. John C. Jones, Jr., agent of Marshall & Wildes since 1821, ally of Boki, critic of Reverend Hiram Bingham, and since 1823 the U.S. commercial agent at Honolulu. Though he so designated himself when signing official documents and meeting foreign officers like Wrangel, Jones was not in fact U.S. Consul: see Bradley.

51. The *Krotkii* then made for the Northern Mariana Islands and, passing between Sarigan and Anatahan on 28 December, entered the Philippine Sea. She returned to Kronstadt on 14 September 1827.

I.F. Kruzenshtern (1770-1846)

Iu.F. Lisianskii (1773-1837)

The Ship *Neva* in 1805: (Lisianskii)

L.A. Gagemeister (1780-1834)

V.M. Golovnin (1776-1831)

Armed Sloop of the *Kamchatka* class

Armed Transport of the *Blagonamerennyi* class

Otto Evstaf'evich von Kotzebue (1787-1846)

Adelbert von Chamisso (1781-1838)

Hawaiian dwelling and natives

Hawaiian natives wearing *kihei*, with animals (rough draft by Choris)

Preliminary sketch for portrait of Queen Kaahumanu, by Choris

Chief Kalanimoku in 1825, near his death (pencil study by Dampier)

John Young, Viceroy of Hawaii Island, adviser to Kamehameha I;

Mission House and Chapel

Gleb Semenovich Shishmarev

Ferdinand Petrovich Wrangel

Mikhail Nikolaevich Vasil'ev

Fedor Petrovich Lütke

The Brig *Riurik* at Tongareva, 1816

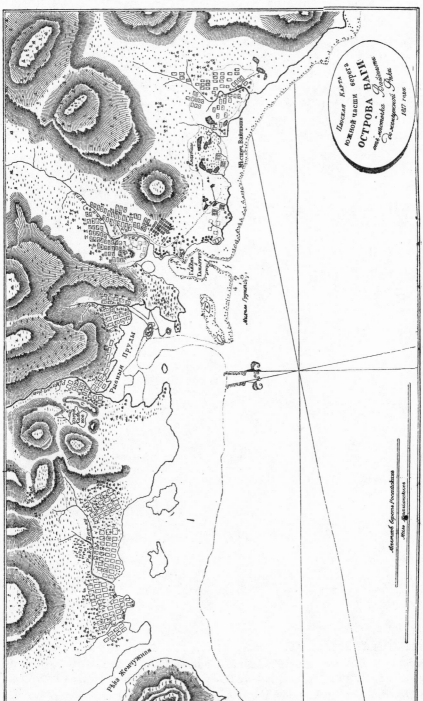

Пиоская Карта
южной части берега
ОСТРОВА ВАГИ
отъ мѣстечка Вайтити
до жемчужной Рѣки
1817 года

Рѣка Жемчужная

Рѣка Ваитити

Рыбныя Пруды

Масштабъ версть Россійскихъ

Мили Аглинскихъ

The South Part of the Coast of Oahu Island from Waikiki Hamlet to the Pearl River, 1817

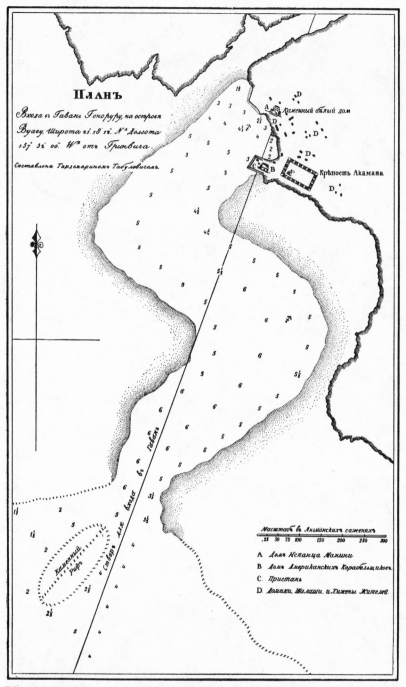

Plan of the Entrance into Honolulu Harbour, on Oahu Island,
in latitude 21°18′12″N, longitude 157°52′, 1818: (Midshipman Tabulevich)

A The house of the Spaniard Marini.   C The landing-place.
B The house of American shipmasters. D Houses and Huts of the natives.

Part Three

THE SOURCES

CHAPTER TWELVE

Notes On Narrators and Printed Texts Selected

LEONTII ADRIANOVICH GAGEMEISTER 1790–1833
(GERMAN: CARL AUGUST LUDWIG VON HAGEMEISTER)

Captain Gagemeister's earlier career and the circumstances that surrounded his Oahu visit have been summarized elsewhere in this book. Suffice it to add that his career flourished thanks to his proven competence at sea, as demonstrated on Pacific expeditions (with the *Neva*, 1807–09, the *Kutuzov*, 1816–19, and the *Krotkii*, 1828–30). He was the first of many Russian naval officers to serve as Governor of Russian North America (1818–20), and held the crosses of St. Anna and St. George in recognition of his service to the Crown, not just the Company, in the Pacific. As an officer, he was deliberate and thorough, avoiding unwanted risk. Despite his somewhat dashing mien [Plate 22] he was a cautious man, well able to survive the administrative squalls that struck the Company to which he was seconded for a decade.

Unlike most other officers who made their name in the Pacific while in Russian service, Gagemeister made no effort to instruct and entertain the reading public with a *Voyage*. His reports to the directors of the Russian-American Company describing his impressions of, and economic dealings on Oahu, were not meant for publication. They were accordingly placed in the Company's own files: one copy at Novo-Arkhangel'sk, and one at St. Petersburg. For this reason, it was servants of the Company, notably K.T. Khlebnikov and F.I. Shemelin, who transcribed and annotated them in 1810–17. The originals of several letters from Gagemeister to the Company directors (of 1807) remain to this day in the K.T. Khlebnikov Collection at the Perm' District State Archive, Perm', USSR (*fond* 445, op. 1, *delo* 58). Microfilm negatives may be consulted at the Elmer E. Rasmuson Research Library of the University of Alaska at Fairbanks.

Shemelin's own interest in Gagemeister's reports on Oahu was fired by a passing visit to the Hawaiian Islands in 1804. He was the Company *prikazchik* (clerk) aboard the *Nadezhda* (Captain I.F. Kruzenshtern). Because his loyalty was to the Company (represented on that ship by Nikolai Petrovich Rezanov) and by no means to the Navy (as embodied by the captain), Shemelin had an uncomfortable time on the voyage. His journal, which contains interesting entries on Hawaii Island and Hawaiian-*haole* relations, clearly reflects the tensions between Rezanov, Russian envoy designate to the Mikado, and the *Nadezhda*'s officers, which adversely affected its chances of publication at the end of the *Nadezhda*'s expedition (1806). (The original journal is preserved at the Saltykov-Shchedrin Public Library, Leningrad, Manuscript Department—Rukopisnyi otdel—reference: F.IV.59.) Shemelin eventually succeeded in publishing an account of his travels around the world: in 1816–18 there appeared, in two parts, his 1803–06 *Zhurnal pervogo puteshestviia Rossiian vokrug zemnago shara, sochinennyi ... Rossiisko-Amerikanskoi Kompanii glavnym kommissionerom, Moskovskim kuptsom Fedorom Shemelinym* (*A Journal of the First Voyage of Russians round the Globe, Composed ... by the Chief Factor of the Russian-American Company, the Moscow merchant Fedor Shemelin*: (St. Petersburg, Meditsinskaia tipografiia). Permission to print, however, had been granted only after his compliance with requests to omit or amend certain references to these tensions between Company and Navy representatives. It is significant that neither the Company itself nor the naval press saw fit to print it and that, being a Muscovite and an uninfluential stranger in St. Petersburg, Merchant Shemelin was obliged to make his terms, so to speak, with an independent press.

While composing a faircopy of his own Pacific journal (which, it seems, had been intended from the outset for the public eye), Shemelin made a copy for his own use of the Gagemeister-Company reports of 1809–10. He himself had not set foot on the Hawaiian Islands, to his obvious regret. For that reason, he was willing to make use of other, primary material to fill such gaps as would remain in his account. There were good reasons for including Captain Gagemeister's comments. In the first place, they were recent; in the second, they bore directly on the "productions," agricultural potential, trade and commerce of the Islands, Oahu in particular, which, at the time of writing, Russians had not subsequently visited; and in the third, they had been made at the suggestion of Chief Manager Baranov with a view to later use by servants of the Company. As chief factor of the Company, it was appropriate, in his opinion, that he transcribe and publish Gagemeister's "Honolulu Passages," at least in part.

Shemelin included Gagemeister's eye-witness account of the commercial situation and the native husbandry and agriculture on Oahu in that section of his *Zhurnal* headed, "O Razvode Skota i Ogorodnykh Ovoshchei na Ostrove Ovagii" ("On the Breeding of Cattle and Cultivation of Vegetables on Hawaii Island"). It covered pages 153–57 of Part I of the printed edition of 1818. The translations offered here are based on that text. Shemelin was scrupulous in his acknowledgement of Gagemeister's authorship; the section in question was provided with the following introduction:

> Fleet Lieutenant and *Chevalier* Gagenmeister (*sic*), who was formerly in the service of the Russian-American Company and who wintered in those Islands, writes the following, *inter alia*, about the Islanders' principal productions ... (p. 153, para. 2).

On his return to European Russia, Shemelin had made good use of data provided by the Hawaiian Kanekhoia, or Kanehoa (?), who had only lately reached the capital from Eastern Siberia. It is apparent from internal textual evidence, that the native, known in St. Petersburg as Vasilii Moller, was the major source of information for that section of the *Zhurnal* immediately preceding the section based on Gagemeister, i.e., "A Brief Description of the Inhabitants of Hawaii" (pp. 149–52). Equally apparent, however, is that data provided by Kanehoa and other sources played *no* part in Shemelin's adaptation of the Gagemeister text. The lines publicly attributed by Shemelin to Gagemeister are consistent in terms of style and thematic development, with Gagemeister's other known writings. The reader's attention is drawn to two letters by Gagemeister, dated 1 May and 20 June 1809, translated and published by Richard A. Pierce in his study, *Russia's Hawaiian Adventure, 1815–17* (Berkeley, 1965:37–40). In short, there are reasons to believe that Shemelin did not tamper with the Gagemeister narrative of 1809.

Shemelin's *Zhurnal* sold well, at a time when travel literature was exceedingly popular in Russia. Publication rights to it were acquired in 1821–22 by the owners of the periodical, *Russkii invalid* (*The Russian Veteran*), and Gagemeister's comments on Oahu and the Islands regularly re-appeared in a "literary supplement" to that periodical (*Literaturnye pribavleniia k Russkomu Invalidu*) in 1822. Gagemeister's observations on Oahu thus found an extensive readership, despite his reticence in playing the role of writer.

OTTO EVSTAF'EVICH KOTSEBU 1788–1846
(GERMAN: OTTO AUGUST VON KOTZEBUE)

Kotzebue was the first of many Russian naval officers who, in the early nineteenth century, reported accurately and at length on Honolulu to the Russian government. Like Kruzenshtern, his mentor in the service, Kotzebue was a Baltic German and Northern European cosmopolitan at ease in German, French, and Russian. From his father, the distinguished German advocate and dramatist August Friedrich von Kotzebue (1761–1819), he inherited not only deeply royalist political and social attitudes, but also a facility with words. It was a legacy that smoothed his path in later dealings with Hawaiian aristocracy and monarchy and, more importantly today, enabled him to leave a sober, balanced, yet above all highly readable account of what he saw at Honolulu. From the standpoints of ethnography and ethno-history especially, Lieutenant Kotzebue's naming to the *Riurik* was regarded as most fortunate.

Having lost his mother as an infant, and been periodically ignored by his intensely restless father[1] (whom a student shot to death for his ultramonarchism), Kotzebue was enrolled at the Imperial Cadet Corps in St. Petersburg aged only eight. He was intended to be a soldier. Fate, however, intervened in the unlikely person of his stepmother's favourite brother, I.F. Kruzenshtern. Early in 1803 both Otto and his brother Moritz were appointed as "volunteers" to the *Nadezhda*, then about to leave the Baltic for the far side of the world.[2] As a recent Soviet historian observes, "the first Russian expedition round the globe, commanded by Kruzenshtern, was for Kotzebue a variety of floating academy. Having no preparatory training whatever, he assimilated the science of naval service on the high seas, in practice; and acquaintance with the expeditionary naturalists awoke in him an interest in scientific research."[3] "I had occasion," recalled Kruzenshtern in 1818, "to note that Kotzebue applied himself with particular zeal to coastal surveys, astronomical observation, and the drafting of charts."[4] Kruzenshtern himself, by his example when the *Nadezhda* stood in Taio-hae Bay ("Anna-Maria"), Nukuhiva, in the Washington-Marquesas group (7–8 May 1804), had introduced the youthful Kotzebue to another branch of knowledge that attracted him—ethnography.

Kruzenshtern's "Marquesan Orders," read aloud as the *Nadezhda* was approaching Taio-hae Bay, where for the first time an entire Russian company was to have dealings with a South Pacific people,[5] rested solidly on Cook's similar orders of another generation. In turn, those orders were recalled by Kotzebue twelve years later, when commanding a Pacific expedition of his own.[6]

In every line of the "Marquesan Orders"—which were to shape Russian dealings with Pacific Islanders for years to come—Cook's influence is felt. It was also responsible, too, for the interest shown in native goods and artefacts by Kruzenshtern, Lisianskii, G.H. Langsdorf, W. Tilenius von Tilenau, and a number of lieutenants on the *Nadezhda* and the *Neva*.[7] Day after day, through peaceful barter, artefacts were gathered by the visitors, including Kotzebue and his brother, and were stowed aboard[8] in the presence of an expeditionary artist, Stepan Kurliandtsev. Day by day, Kurliandtsev—like another Parkinson—depicted artefacts and natives using them, while Kotzebue and his friends looked on.

A factor always present in Hawaii but conspicuously missing from the Taio-hae Bay the Russians visited—the voice of European residents—exerted a modest influence on Kotzebue's public dealings with Kamehameha and *ali'i* in Oahu (for example, predisposing him against some settlers), but led to no real divergence from the attitude of 1804. As he intended, Captain Kruzenshtern had set a standard of behaviour or, at least, had reinforced expectations concerning the behaviour of intelligent and erudite, as well as feeling, individuals.

On returning to the Baltic Sea in 1806, Kotzebue was appointed midshipman. In 1811 he became lieutenant, and commanded small vessels in the White Sea port of Arkhangel'sk. Appointment to the *Riurik* came when he was twenty-six, through his step-uncle's connection with Count Nikolai Petrovich Rumiantsev (1754–1826), Russian Chancellor since 1809, and wealthy patron of the coming expedition.

A man of sixty, who had served the State in very senior positions, Count Rumiantsev felt entitled to retire from the chancellorship in May 1814, and to devote his leisure to the execution of an exploration project, among other things. Napoleon had been dispatched to Elba. Europe was a peaceful continent. It seemed a propitious time for the launching of the little brig for which he had personally paid the builder, Erik Malm of Abo, more than 30,000 roubles. From the outset, it was understood that Rumiantsev, not the Naval Ministry, had overall control of her. A student of her 1816 San Francisco visit, A.C. Mahr, makes important observations in that connection:

> The *Riurik* carried his portrait bust .... The fact that [it] was carried on board reveals his personal vanity as a third motive for sending the *Riurik* on her way, the two others being, first, to impress the world with the prestige of the Imperial Russian Navy by dispatching the *Riurik* under the war flag and, ... second, to achieve the scientific purpose of new geographic discoveries.
>
> This last purpose appears to have been of the least importance since, according to Chamisso's statement, Kotzebue permitted a comparatively slight disturbance of his health to interfere with execution of the original plans for the investigation of a Northeast Passage.[10]

Whether or not the *Riurik*'s naturalist, Chamisso, was justified in such insinuations has been argued for a century. The evidence, however, is still weighted in Kotzebue's favour.[11] What is pertinent to the Hawaiian visits of the *Riurik*, and, more importantly, to the historic record of those visits, is the very fact—implicit in Professor Mahr's remarks— that there *was* tension between Chamisso and Kotzebue at the time. As will be seen, the lack of ease in their relations directly influenced the timing and form of Chamisso's later account of his experiences on Oahu.

Kotzebue, for his part, began to rearrange, edit, and polish his journal, with a view to publication, shortly after his return to Baltic duty on 30 August 1818. Although he was temporarily distracted from the project by his marriage in December to Amalia von Zweig of Reval, circumstances evolved which favoured its resumption. First, the court confirmed its interest in him: he was promoted in the service and rewarded with an audience. Second, a post was offered on the staff of Admiral A. Spiridov, commander of the naval base at Reval, that provided him with leisure to write.

Peculiarities inherent in his situation now grew more pronounced. Because the *Riurik* had not been governed by instructions from the Naval

Ministry, her scientists and crew owing allegiance to Rumiantsev, Kotzebue was denied the automatic right of access to earlier subordinates'
journals, logs, and notes guaranteed under normal Navy regulations,
even though the *Riurik* was sailing under the Russian Navy's flag by
imperial consent. As it was, both Chamisso and Choris had gone abroad
within six months of their return, Choris to Paris to pursue his studies
and to engage in radical discussions of the sort that Kotzebue loathed,
and Chamisso back to Berlin, to marry, to botanize, and to write his own
account of the voyage. Eschscholtz alone was close at hand.[12] As if to
underline the fact that Kotzebue's narrative, although "official," would
be written independently without the useful underpinning of associated
journals, I.Ia. Zakhar'in, one of his two former lieutenants (put ashore,
sick, in Kamchatka in July 1816, before Hawaii could be reached), remained unwell and out of touch in 1820.[13]

For political and private reasons, Kotzebue wished his *Voyage* to appear in German and in Russian simultaneously or, at least, within a
month. He planned accordingly, translating systematically, approaching
likely publishers. By 1820, he had come to terms with Nikolai Ivanovich
Grech, an old acquaintance, fellow Protestant, Germanophile, and since
1812 the editor of *Syn otechestva (Son the Fatherland)*, a leading periodical that gave much space to travel literature. Grech himself had written
about Germany, in 1806, and was the future author of three works of
travel.[14] As well, German publishers were approaching Kotzebue as the
son of August Friedrich Ferdinand who had been murdered so recently
and dramatically. He took private satisfaction in a contract signed with
Hoffmann brothers, publishers in Weimar, a town from which his father
had been virtually ousted by political and literary enemies.[15] Both Grech
and the *Gebruder* Hoffmann undertook to print two volumes straightaway, and a third, containing articles by Chamisso, Eschscholtz and
others, at a later date, since the necessary manuscripts had not arrived.
It was agreed that coloured plates, from drawings done by Louis Choris
during the *Riurik*'s Pacific enterprise, would be included.[16]

*Puteshestvie v Iuzhnyi okean i v Beringov proliv dlia otyskaniia Severo-
Vostochnago morskago prokhoda, predpriniatoe v 1815, 1816, 1817 i
1818 godakh ... na korable Riurike pod nachal'stvom Kotsebu* appeared,
in St. Petersburg, in 1821 (*A Voyage into the Southern Ocean and the
Bering Strait for the Discovery of a Northeastern Passage: Undertaken
in the Years 1815, 1816, 1817 and 1818 ... on the Riurik, Commanded by
Kotzebue*). It was bound in red morocco, with gold tooling by Zweidler,
and was aimed at an exclusive, wealthy market. The *Riurik*'s first visit
to Honolulu, of November–December 1816, was covered on pp. 42–72 of
Volume II, her second, of October 1817, on pp. 242–49 (Chapter 13) of
the same volume. Material was presented chronologically reflecting the
original sequence of the 1816 journal. The Weimar edition appeared—

with the title and chapter headings exactly translated into German—as *Entdeckungs-reise in die Süd-see und nach der Berings-strasse zur erforschung einer nordostlichen durchfahrt: unternommen in den Jahren 1815, 1816, 1817 und 1818* ....

The books were enthusiastically received. Within a month of publication by the *Gebruder* Hoffmann, they were in the hands of paraphrasts, translators, and adaptors. The first fruit of their hurried work was an edition *für die Jugend bearbeitet von C. Hildebrandt*, an abridged version of the Weimar text: what might frustrate or weary "youth" was simply excised. It sold briskly in Hanover, where it was printed, in a small two volume set, by Hahn Verlag.[17] Later in 1821, the complete English translation of the Russian text appeared: *A Voyage of Discovery in the South Sea, and to Behring's Straits, in search of a north-east passage* ... (London, R. Phillips). The two volumes were published in a single edition of 230 pages (23 cm.) by the radical and self-made bookseller, Sir Richard Phillips (1767–1840) who, being anxious to exploit a likely winner with the public, promoted it energetically.[18] To Sir Richard's disappointment, its sales were limited by the publication of a fine English translation of the recent German text by the philologist and diplomat, Hannibal Evans Lloyd (1771–1847).[19] Lloyd's version, *A Voyage of Discovery into the South Sea and Beering's Straits* (London, Longman, Hurst, Rees, Orme & Brown), became the standard English text. Thus Lloyd, who had lived in Hamburg for a twelve-year period, whose wife was German, and whose command of Russian was extremely good, brought Kotzebue's Honolulu to a large and continuing British readership.[20]

Chamisso, meanwhile, had dispatched his contribution for the third volume of the Kotzebue-Grech *Voyage* to Reval. It was edited in a way that angered him, and was published in 1823.[21] A Dutch translation of the 1821 text was already being sold in Amsterdam.[22]

Returning to Admiral Spiridov's staff in August 1826, at the conclusion of the voyage of the armed sloop *Predpriiatie*, Kotzebue slipped into a now-familiar routine. He was again promoted (Captain, 2nd rank), again made contact with the court and high society, and once more settled down to write a narrative; this time, however, to be published by the Naval Ministry at State expense. Kotzebue's official report on his second Pacific voyage appeared in St. Petersburg in 1828. *Puteshestvie vokrug sveta, sovershennoe ... na voennom shliupe "Predpriiatie" v 1823, 24, 25 i 26 godakh*, a work of a mere 200 pages, discharged its author's obligations to his government.[23] Professional successes at this juncture, almost burdened Kotzebue, who was anxious to start work on a more circumstantial, German-language work about his time on the *Predpriiatie*. He was to oversee construction of a powerful new frigate, to command a naval unit based at Kronstadt, to attend a hundred meetings.[24] Finally, uncertain health encouraged him to resume the quiet life in Reval. There, in 1829, he wrote and studied—while his lungs were giving out; coastal Estonia is cold and damp in winter. Kotzebue was again promoted and retired from the service on 12 February 1830. Three months later there appeared, in Weimar, *Neue Reise um die Welt* ... (W. Hoffmann).[25] It was his crowning work. His health remained uncertain so, unwillingly, he settled on his small estate near Reval. There, after a six-month illness, he died.[26]

The extracts from Kotzebue's writings offered here are taken from pp. 42–72 and 242–49 of Part II of the 1821 (St. Petersburg) text of *Puteshestvie v Iuzhnyi okean i v Beringov proliv,* ... and from pp. 242–94 (Ch. XIII) of Part II of the 1981 Soviet edition (D.D. Tumarkin and Ia.M. Svet) of the 1830 Weimar text. A new English translation is offered, on these bases, of the "Honolulu passages" on pp. 319–55 (Vol. I) and pp. 195–204 (Vol. II) of the Longman, Hurst, Rees edition of *A Voyage of Discovery into the South Sea* (London, 1821), and on pp. 156–248 and 251–65 of the Colburn and Bentley edition of *A New Voyage round the World* ... (London, 1830). It may be noted that D.D. Tumarkin's 1981 text, entitled *Novoe puteshestvie vokrug sveta v 1823–1826 godakh* (Moskva, Nauka), is provided with detailed commentaries (pp. 317ff.) replete with biographical data on members of the *Predpriiatie* expedition active at Honolulu in 1824–25: Heinrich Seewald, Johann Friedrich Eschscholtz, Wilhelm Preis, E.K. Lenz, and Ernst Hoffman.

LOUIS CHARLES (ADELBERT) VON CHAMISSO 1781–1838

The second major source on the *Riurik*'s stay at Honolulu, Louis Charles Adelaide de Chamisso (Adelbert was a German adaptation, chosen by himself), was born in Champagne of an ancient and noble French family. Stripped of their property and expelled from France in 1790—because of their extreme Royalist sympathies—his family wandered through Europe until finally, in 1796, they found a refuge in Berlin. Adelbert became a page to the Queen of Prussia and received a lieutenancy in the Prussian army (1801). Napoleon's elevation to First Consul precluded the possibility of a return to France, and so the boy remained in Germany. Disgusted by his ignorance, he started on a massive course of studies of his personal devising, at the age of twenty-one. He was already, as he recognized, a man without a country. When, in 1806, he wished to resign from the army, Prussia was beseiged by the First Consul. Chamisso was saved from the necessity of shooting at his own (ex-)countrymen by falling into French hands as a prisoner-of-war. He was permitted to return to Prussia nine months later.[27]

Chamisso had started writing poetry, in French and German, as an antidote to barracks life. In 1810, during another stay in Paris, he was introduced to Madame de Staël and her son, with whom he spent a vital year in Switzerland (1811–12). There, he seriously took up botany, which was in due course his profession, and studied English and other modern languages. He was the *Riurik*'s interpreter at Honolulu by necessity and by acclamation; but he undertook that task most willingly.

The year 1812, and a botanical excursion to the foothills of Mont Blanc, were ended violently by the Prussian National War of Liberation. Once again, Chamisso's awkward and ambiguous position grew apparent; while approving of the Prussian fight for liberty from French political and military oppression, he would not himself bear arms against his country. With events fast closing in on him, he fled Berlin and found a new refuge in the quiet provinces with friends. Involuntarily secluded, he studied botany and wrote fantasies. His high Romantic tale, *Peter Schlemiehl*, the story of a man searching for his shadow, was an internationally acclaimed success, securing Chamisso, the rootless cosmopolitan, a lasting place in German literature. To his contemporaries, it was obvious that Chamisso's own wretched situation, disconnected and unique, had been imposed—with some improvement—on his hero. Chamisso, like Peter, had no option but to move from place to place, now drawn by Paris, now by Prussia or some far remoter country.[28]

Tempted to remove himself from Europe even in 1812, he felt almost compelled to do so three years later, when Napoleon's escape from Elba once again stirred up the nationalistic cauldron in Berlin. The University, where he was studying zoology and medicine, philosophy, geology, and even magnetism ("I have no country but the Republic of Science and I can have none; so I dream of becoming naturalized and so perhaps enjoying a degree of liberty in peace")[29] suddenly seemed restricting. Chamisso discussed his problems with his friend, the advocate, *littérateur*, and publisher, Jules-Edouard Hitzig (1780–1849). Hitzig, a widely-travelled man, had lived in Warsaw, visited Russia, and remained in friendly contact with a good number of Russo-German literary figures. One of these was August Friedrich Ferdinand von Kotzebue, now (1815) the Russian Consul General in Königsberg (and an extremely well paid spy).[30]

It was at this juncture that Chamisso's political embarrassment was ended by the Duke of Wellington. With France brought low at Waterloo (18 June 1815), and with the German *Tugendbund* rejoicing, he at last seemed free, indeed, impelled to travel as the characters had travelled in his stories. At Hitzig's, one evening, he chanced to read in a gazette that Count Rumiantsev, Russia's chancellor, was sponsoring a voyage of discovery to the North Pole. "I would like to accompany those Russians," said Chamisso. "Are you serious?" asked Hitzig, who reports the scene. "Yes, I am." "Well, you must at once get hold of certificates to prove your capability, and we'll see what can be done."[31] Hitzig

contacted the Russian Consul, recommending Chamisso as a *savant*, linguist, and writer, but above all as a scientist of note. The Consul sent
the letter on, with an endorsement, to Rumiantsev's office. It was read
by Captain Kruzenshtern, the Consul's own brother-in-law.[32] By chance,
Charles-Frédéric de Ledebour of Greifswald, the botanist whom Count
Rumiantsev had proposed to send in the *Riurik*, had declined the invitation. The precocious young director of the Greifswald plant garden
was ill, but hoped for other opportunities to work with the Russians.[33]
Chamisso's appointment was confirmed by Kruzenshtern. The *Riurik*
was expected to arrive at Copenhagen on 5 August, and he was directed
to join her there. He did so, plunging suddenly into a small *wandernde
Welt*.[34] Here is his description of that wandering society:

> There were Captain Otto Avstavich ("son of Augustus") von Kotzebue;
> and First Lieutenant Gleb Simonovich Shishmarev, a friend of the cap
> tain and, as an officer, his senior. Shishmarev spoke only Russian; had
> a face serenely beaming, like the moon, pleasant to behold; of robust
> and healthy build—a man who has not forgotten how to laugh. Second
> Lieutenant Ivan Iakovlevich Zakharin, sickly, irritable, but warm-hearted,
> with a slight acquaintance with French and Italian. The Ship's Surgeon,
> a scientist and entomologist, Ivan Ivanovich Eschscholtz, a young doctor
> from Dorpat, rather private, but true and noble as gold .... The painter,
> Loggin ("Ludwig") Andreevich Choris, German by descent, who, even
> while still young, accompanied Marshal von Bieberstein on his expedition
> to the Caucasus, as draughtsman. There was also a volunteer naturalist,
> Martin Petrovich Wormskjold. Three assistant navigators: Khramchenko,
> very good- natured and an industrious lad; Petrov, a witty and laughing
> fellow; and Koniev, who allowed himself to be less familiar with us ....[35]

As seen, tension arose between Chamisso and Kotzebue as the voyage of the *Riurik* unfolded; and in Chamisso's treatment of his captain,
particularly in his private journal, there is not a little irony. Even while
the *Riurik* stood under Honolulu fortress, there were tense, unpleasant scenes between the two, whom temperamental differences separated
quite as much as political differences. Here, for instance, is an echo of
a tiny storm that broke on the *Riurik*'s quarterdeck on Wednesday, 7
October 1817:

> I spent most of my days on botanizing trips up in the hills, while Es
> chscholtz, at least during the first few days, was forced to remain on
> board by an injured foot. He was taking care of the preparation of the
> plants. To guard the plants, as they hung in the sun, was an unpleasant
> and time-consuming business, but was vital. Once Eschscholtz missed
> one of the packages that he had put on deck. He talked about the loss
> to me. The captain intervened, wanting to know what had occurred. I
> calmly explained the matter, not expecting the storm that all at once

broke round my head. Angrily, he pointed out to me that he had no desire to punish *his* sailors for *my* plants ....[36]

Much of the same tension emerges in a comment made by Chamisso during his first Hawaiian stay, to the effect that he could do more useful scientific work if he were left at Honolulu till the ship returned, in six or nine months' time. ("One is sent round the world just like a cannonball .... The captain said *he* would not hold me back; I should resign from the expedition whenever I felt like it."[37] Of course, he stayed with the *Riurik*, keeping a detailed journal in addition to his scientific notes.

Back in St. Petersburg, it quickly grew apparent that Rumiantsev did not wish to underwrite the publication costs of any *Voyage* by a (foreign) naturalist. Kotzebue, on the other hand, was willing that the scientific commentaries be incorporated in his own forthcoming book, as an appendix. Chamisso accordingly used his notes to draft the *Bemerkungen und Ansichten* which finally appeared, two years later, in the third part of the Weimar text, *Entdeckungs-reise*. He was angry when he read his work, in which ethnography loomed large, and found it riddled with typographic errors of the sort that basic editing should have removed:

> The sole recompense that I could really promise myself for all the efforts I had made during and after the voyage, as a naturalist and as a writer, had been to see these memoirs—which I had been asked for—appear in correct and proper form before the public for whom they were intended. The results did not answer my expectation. What I had written was, in many places, altered and made unintelligible by countless typographic errors which ruined the sense. I was, moreover, positively refused the chance to indicate these, in an errata list.[38]

Illogically perhaps, but understandably, it was while in a state of heated indignation with his Weimar publisher that Chamisso felt most uncharitable toward Kotzebue, who, he felt, wanted to garner all the glory of their voyage for himself, and was accordingly unprompt and unprofessional in correspondence bearing on their (strained) collaboration. Chamisso relished the biting criticism of his former captain who was accused, in the London *Quarterly Review* for January 1822, of too quickly abandoning his attempt to find a passage through the Arctic ice: "It would not be tolerated in England that the ill health of the commanding officer should be urged as a plea for giving up ...").[39] Chamisso's *Bemerkungen und Ansichten*, meanwhile, were being carefully translated into Russian. Paradoxically, they were rendered more accurately in Slavic than in German. Grech did nothing, by including them as volume III of *Puteshestvie v Iuzhnyi okean* .... (St. Petersburg, 1823), to diminish the academic value of the work as a whole. On the contrary, the naturalist's "comments" both enhanced and complemented Kotzebue's own account. *Entdeckungsreise in die Südsee* ... was reprinted, with minor alterations only, by the Viennese house, Kaulfuss and Krammer, in the spring of 1825. Chamisso's comments on Oahu found new readers, both in Austria itself and in the Hapsburg lands to east and south, as part of the Kaulfuss and Krammer series, *Museum der neuesten und interessantesten Reisebeschreibungen für gebildete leser.* Among the twenty plates included in it were several showing Honolulu scenes.[40]

The "Hawaiian section" of the St. Petersburg edition of Kotzebue's *Puteshestvie v Iuzhnyi okean* ..., written by Chamisso appeared on pp. 289–316 of Vol. III, under the chapter heading: *Sandvichevy Ostrova— Dzhonstonovy Ostrova.*

Chamisso was awarded an honorary doctorate on his return to Berlin, married, and gained financial security as the keeper of the Royal Botanical Gardens in Berlin. His links with Russia lapsed. Apart from one visit to Paris in 1825, indeed, he hardly left his peaceful Prussian home or his study. Thanks largely to his publication of the botanical finds of the *Riurik* expedition, he was ultimately nominated for membership in the Royal Prussian Academy of Sciences by Alexander von Humboldt. It seemed, by the late '20s, that his separate edition of *Bemerkungen und Ansichten* in 1827, had brought the record of his tense associations with the Russians to a close. In 1831, his health gave out.[41]

Ten years had passed since his annoyances and disappointments in connection with the Weimar and St. Petersburg editions of his own official comments when, aware that a measure of dissatisfaction lingered in his private attitude toward the public accounts of his experience with the *Riurik*, Professor Chamisso was asked by his Berlin publishers, Reimer and Hirzel, if he wished to amplify those accounts.[42] He hesitated, then, in mid-December 1834, took out his *Riurik* notes and diary.

Chamisso's *Tagebuch* of 1815–18 formed the basis of a work entitled *Reise um die Welt, mit der Romanzoffischen Entdeckungs-Expedition in den Jahren 1815–18, auf der Brigg Riurik: erster Theil.* It was published in Leipzig by Weidemannische Buchhandlung in 1836, as Vol. I of a four-volume collection of his works (*Werke*). Two sections dealt with Chamisso's 1816 and 1817 visits to Oahu. They were, respectively, "Von Californien nach den Sandwich-Inseln," pp. 201–32, and "Von Unalaska nach den Sandwich-Inseln," pp. 331–53. Chamisso's more official *Bemerkungen und Ansichten* formed Vol. II of the same edition, "Die Sandwich-Inseln" appearing on pp. 292–322.

Though published as a *Tagebuch*, Chamisso's more personal and frank account of his stays at Honolulu did not rest on a diary in the strict sense of the word. For he had chosen, in 1815, not to keep a daily record of events, but instead to write occasional prose sketches, incorporating recent facts and impressions, and to send descriptive letters to Eduard

Hitzig as often as was feasible. It was therefore on the basis of these pen-sketches and letters to Hitzig, and not on any chronological series of notes, that Chamisso composed his *Reise um die Welt*, in 1834–35.

Not only do his *Tagebuch* and *Bemerkungen und Ansichten* accounts of Honolulu complement each other in tone, content, and form; they also complement and lend greater perspective to the Kotzebue narrative. Taken together, Kotzebue's 1821 account, the Choris illustrative record, and the 1821–24 and 1834–36 "Hawaiian Passages" by Chamisso, comprise a valuable body of material for the historical and ethnographic study of Oahu at a turning-point in its development: the moment when the presence of the *haole* became politically, as well as economically, decisive for the infant Honolulu.

VASILII MIKHAILOVICH GOLOVNIN 1776–1831

Vasilii Mikhailovich Golovnin was born in 1776, in the Central Russian province of Riazan', and died in St. Petersburg in 1831, a victim of the great cholera epidemic. Navigator, adminstrator, writer, and vice-admiral, he pursued a brilliant career in a period of decline for the Russian Imperial Navy: as corresponding member of the Academy of Sciences (1818), Assistant Director of the Naval Cadet Corps at Kronstadt (1821), Quartermaster-General of the Russian Navy (1823). It was Golovnin's double achievement not only to draw practical lessons from his experiences as a volunteer with the British Fleet in wartime (1802–05), but also to appreciate the value—in a deeply conservative time and place—of technical innovation. Steamships came into use during his office as Quartermaster-General, and naval signaling devices were dramatically improved.

Orphaned to all intents and purposes, Golovnin spent his adolescence in the Naval Cadet Corps, where he studied constantly and widely and graduated with highest honours in 1792. The harshness of his childhood combined with the examples of demanding but humane sea-officers made him equally humane towards subordinates, whose loyalty he won by precept and retained by steady conduct. Baron F.P. Wrangel, formerly a midshipman in Golovnin's *Kamchatka* (1817–19), was one of many to extol him:

> Spiritedness in danger, decisiveness and swiftness in taking steps to reach a given end, indefatigability in work, constancy in friendship and unchanging gratitude to zealous colleagues and subordinates: such were the qualities that characterized him, as naval commander and as private citizen.[43]

On returning to Russia from service abroad, Lieutenant Golovnin compiled a new code of naval signals. Both his circumnavigations of the globe, in the sloop *Diana* (1807–09) and with the *Kamchatka*, were skilfully executed on the technical and professional levels. Misfortune struck him twice on the earlier venture: he was taken prisoner at Cape Town and held there for thirteen months in a time of Anglo-Russian tension (1808–09), then taken captive again by the Japanese while surveying one of the Kuril Islands, Kunashiri (1811–13).[44] He could not be held responsible for these events, however, and in fact turned them to genuine advantage by reporting, in a thorough, sober fashion, on the British base at Cape Town and (far more importantly) on his experiences with the Japanese. For sixty years, his observations on the state and people of Japan remained the soundest and most factual available in Russian.[45] Published in 1816 in English, *The Notes of Naval Captain Golovnin on His Adventures as a Prisoner of the Japanese in 1811, 1812, & 1813* ...[46] was the first of several successful travel books by Golovnin. It was followed by accounts of his two circumnavigations, published in 1819 and 1822, and complemented by a sharp analysis of Russia's naval decline, *On the State of the Russian Fleet in 1824*.[47] This last work he published under the *nom-de-plume*, Midshipman Morekhodov. *The Notes of Naval Captain Golovnin* of 1816 have significance in a Hawaiian context. They represented Golovnin's first attempt at extended prose based on a journal and, as such, marked the end of his literary apprenticeship. Writing skills thus honed were used again, in 1820–21, to relate the *Kamchatka*'s stay at Honolulu of October 1818.

Golovnin was a pragmatic patriot. Admiring Cook, Vancouver, and other pioneers as seamen, he was far more willing than Kruzenshtern or Kotzebue to condemn them on political or moral grounds.[48] In this respect, he stood with Kruzenshtern's own First Lieutenant on the *Nadezhda*, Makar' Ivanovich Ratmanov, and with Kotzebue's on the *Riurik*, Gleb S. Shishmarev, representing the Great Russian rather than the Baltic German attitude towards those heroes of Pacific exploration.[49] Cook's behaviour at Hawaii, in the view of Golovnin (as of Ratmanov), had been wretched. Cook's own men had brought venereal disease, while he himself had acted cruelly and rashly. It did not follow from this that Cook was not a master seaman and superb naval commander; but in Golovnin's opinion the realities should all be faced by Russians and others. And the Russians would, and should, behave quite differently with their Polynesian hosts.[50] It was because he was a pragmatist as well as a determined patriot, that Golovnin undertook training sessions on the *Kamchatka*, day by day; wanting perfection, he approached it realistically.

> The sloop's crew went through the necessary training sessions, and the organizing of shipboard duties was attended to. In the instructions composed by Golovnin, which still retain their interest even today, the obligations of every single crew member were precisely fixed. Golovnin demanded prompt and accurate execution of all orders from superiors, the subordination of all actions to the commander's will .... He gave encouragement to all who excelled, but also saw to it that his seamen and officers always had good nourishment, fruits and vegetables .... The result of this exhaustive preparation and competent leadership was the successful completion of a long and hard voyage.[51]

Anxious to emulate their captain, the *Kamchatka*'s junior officers took great pains over their journals, all of which, in consequence, contain much useful and reliable material relating to Oahu in the period of 26–30 October 1818. Especially interesting, and unknown in the West, are the "Oahu sections" of the journals of Midshipmen F.P. Wrangel and F.P. Litke (Lütke). All these journals, in accordance with instructions from the naval ministry, and with contemporary practice, were entrusted to the naval minister and made available to Golovnin at the conclusion of the *Kamchatka*'s voyage (September 1819).[52] Golovnin was thus in a position to compare his facts and figures with the data his subordinates provided. That he did, in fact, consult selective journals and related papers while composing and redrafting his account over the next twenty-one months, is indisputable. It seems however, that he did so with a facts-and-figures section of his future book in mind, not with the aim of introducing major changes to his narrative itself. Even the extant drafts from early 1820 show that Golovnin had decided to relate the *Kamchatka*'s story in a comprehensive, lively way, placing technical or specialized material (statistics, detailed surveys, notes on navigation, extracts from her logbook) in a separate section. In this way, he hoped to satisfy the curiosity and expectations of two kinds of future readers.[53]

Even after his appointment as Assistant Director of the Naval Cadet Corps, in 1821, Golovnin continued to rework and polish his account of the *Kamchatka*'s voyage. Professional success made other demands on his time; as corresponding member, he was now expected to contribute to the working of the (then as now prestigious) Academy of Sciences.[54] What would appear to be the final draft of Part I of Golovnin's *Voyage* is now held in the Central State Archive of the Navy of the USSR (TsGAVMF), in Leningrad, under reference: *fond* 7, op. I, *delo* 16.[55] The text was submitted to the Admiralty Department in August 1821, and was approved for publication at departmental expense within a month.[56] When finally printed in January 1823, but with the impress 1822, (delays were caused by the need to deal with A.N. Olenin, President of the Academy of Arts, to whom the *Kamchatka*'s artist Mikhail Tikhanov had given his Pacific portfolio,[57] and perhaps by internal intrigues and jealousy also),[58] Part I of the *Voyage* differed hardly at all from that draft. Chapters 10 and 11 of the work, entitled respectively, "Ot Novogo Albiona do Sandvichevykh Ostrovov" ("From New Albion to the Sandwich Islands") and "O Sandvichevykh Ostrovakh" ("About the Sandwich Islands"), form the basis of the present translations. The book itself, *Puteshestvie vokrug sveta na shliupe "Kamchatka" v 1817, 1818 i 1819 godakh flota kapitana Golovnina* (St. Petersburg, Morskaia Tipografiia, 1822), was well received in official circles despite the absence of Tikhanov's drawings; still, engravings of thirty pen sketches or aquarelles selected by Golovnin two years earlier had not been produced by the Academy of Arts.[59] (On this, see Appendix C.) The book was described as "useful for the fleet, containing much that is interesting and indeed worthy of note."[60] The public, too, responded favourably. Outside Russia, however, the book attracted far less interest than had the energetic Golovnin's account of his captivity by the Japanese, which had been available in English and French since 1818. It remained untranslated, *in toto*, for 150 years; nor were Golovnin's detailed comments on his meeting with Kamehameha I made accessible to English-language readers until 1894, when they appeared in a somewhat altered form, in the Hawaiian periodical, *The Friend*.[61]

Chapter 10 of *Puteshestvie vokrug sveta* is based, unmistakably, on Golovnin's own journal. Events are described in proper sequence, with convincing reference to times and dates. It is good to bear in mind that, had he wished to do so, Golovnin could have attempted both to "rearrange" events and, by omission, to alter the emphasis. There are good reasons for thinking that the changes he made to his 1818 text were fundamentally stylistic and that he adhered to the truth as he perceived it. He was punctilious by nature, and in any case could not have "rearranged" whole patterns with impunity in 1821–22, since there were witnesses to almost all the scenes that he described.[62]

Chapter 11 of the 1823 (1822) text and of the TsGAVMF faircopy, by contrast, is not chronologically but rather thematically arranged. The opening paragraph sets the tone, by dispassionately viewing the Hawaiians as "thousands of grown and even white-haired children, so to speak, who are just coming of age."[63] It is both pleasant and interesting, Golovnin suggests, to see the child coming of age. Freely ranging over many topics while continuing to focus on the Kona Coast and Honolulu he himself had seen and studied, Golovnin offers an independent, well-rounded and polished travel essay of some sixteen thousand words. Style, length, and content all suggest, as do Golovnin's instructions to the printer (in red ink) on the TsGAVMF draft, that he was thinking of submitting "About the Sandwich Islands" to a periodical. Golovnin had many literary contacts and was friendly with both Pavel Petrovich Svin'in (1788–1839), whose *Otechestvennye zapiski* (*Fatherland Notes*) had started in 1818, and with Nikolai Ivanovich Grech (1787–1867), whose *Syn otechestva* (*Son of the Fatherland*) accepted new travel pieces throughout the 1820s. Grech became Golovnin's biographer.[64] In any event, the essay stayed inside the book, providing readers with the fullest and most entertaining survey of Hawaiian history, resources, politics, and prospects to appear since the works of Langsdorf, Kruzenshtern, Lisianskii and Shemelin (1812–16), which was based on materials from 1804 (the visits of the *Nadezhda* and the *Neva*) and so were out of date.[65]

Puteshestvie vokrug sveta ... was reprinted, in slightly abridged form and minus Part II, in 1949. Also included in this Soviet edition (overseen and introduced by I.P. Magidovich) were abridged texts of the *Voyage* of the sloop *Diana*, of the 1816 account of Japanese captivity, and of Golovnin's 1822 survey of noteworthy shipwrecks.[66] A second Soviet edition, edited and introduced by an expert on Russian naval activity in the Pacific basin, V.A. Divin, with assistance from K.F. Fokeev and S.D. Osokin, appeared in 1965. It contains prints of Hawaiian drawings made by Tikhanov, archival material bearing on the *Kamchatka*'s voyage, and useful annotation. In the 1949 edition, the "Oahu Passages" appear on pp. 374–97; in the 1965 edition, Chapter 11 is contained in pp. 200–21 and is complemented by an appendix (pp. 328–31) containing Golovnin's account of the Hawaiian Islander Lauri's stay in Russia (1819–21).[67]

ALEKSEI PETROVICH LAZAREV 1791–1862

Aleksei Petrovich Lazarev, lieutenant in the naval transport *Blago-namerennyi* (*Loyal*: 1819–22), was the youngest of three brothers in the Navy, all of whom visited the mid-Pacific. The eldest brother, Andrei, went with the *Ladoga* in 1823.[68] Mikhail visited three times, with the *Mirnyi*, *Suvorov*, and *Kreiser* (1814, 1820, 1823–24). Aleksei, who was more the courtier, enjoyed a less brilliant career than his brothers.[69] Nevertheless, he remained on active service until 1828, when he saw action in the Dardanelles as Captain-Lieutenant and commander of his ship. Alone of the three brothers, he had opportunity to study the infant Honolulu and has left us with an eye-witness report.

From the outset, Aleksei's career had a courtly lustre: barely sixteen, he was already serving in the Adriatic Sea aboard the large frigate *Avtroil* (Admiral Seniavin's flagship, based at Corfu). By 1810 he had a pleasant posting at Trieste and Venice; two years later, he was taking Russian warships to the River Thames, by London.[70] Courteous and polished, the lieutenant was appointed to the imperial yachts *Tserera* and *Neva* (1816) and, for the next three years, was in contact with *le grand monde* of the capital. Unburdened by the strains of sea-duty, he had the time and inclination to pursue at least one heiress, Dunia Istomina, while watching out for favour and promotion.[71]

His brothers' example, however, weighed upon him. In particular, he envied their extended cruises around the globe. Finally, late in 1818, he sought appointment to one of the two sloops bound for Arctic work and a Pacific cruise: the *Blagonamerennyi*. Her newly-named commander, Gleb Shishmarev, was a friend of ten years' standing. Lazarev was promptly accepted, together with Shishmarev's own nephew, Nikolai Dmitrievich.[72] Gingerly disengaging from St. Petersburg society and naval circles, he reported to the officer commanding the division heading north, while Bellingshausen and his own brilliant brother, Mikhail, headed for the far south.[73] That officer, who was to leave his own account of Honolulu (see below), was Captain Mikhail Vasil'ev. The *Blagonamerennyi* left Kronstadt roads in company with the *Otkrytie* (*Discovery*) on 3 July 1819, proceeding to the South Pacific Ocean by way of Portsmouth, Rio de Janeiro, and Sydney, New South Wales.[74] Lieutenant Lazarev maintained a full and careful diary, as well as his official journal, from the first day of his voyage to the last. Its "Oahu Passages" are dated 20 March–7 April and 24 November–20 December 1821.

Returning to the Baltic Fleet in 1823, Lazarev sailed in frigates for awhile, then re-established contact with the Court as adjutant to the tsarevich. The latter's accession to the throne as Nicholas I (1825), however, signaled the end of Lazarev's rapid professional advancement. He was sent off to look at Caspian and Black Sea ports, then (1828) banished to Greece. Successful action against the Turks was rewarded with another, last promotion; and in 1830, he was asked to accompany a Swedish prince on an important Russian tour. Clouds hung over his career, even so, and for whatever small professional success he did enjoy during the '30s and the '40s, he depended largely the influence of his brother Mikhail Petrovich. Thus, he was able to serve (1848–51) under the aegis of the Black Sea Naval Staff, headed by his brother. Benevolent until 1825–26, the official attitude towards him abruptly changed for reasons which, though not entirely clear, plainly influenced the fate of Oahu narrative. The change in attitude was permanent. The former favourite of admirals and princes died, in absolute obscurity, on an estate far from the capital and the sea.[75]

The fate of A.P. Lazarev's account illustrates how, in a larger way, the fate of source materials relating to Oahu or Hawaii depended on the overall success of a whole venture (in the course of which a visit had occurred), as perceived by the imperial authorities. Various factors might produce a "failure" verdict on a naval enterprise, militating against publication of its records by the State. Captain Shishmarev's account was completely overshadowed, at a time (1822–25) when much material relating to Oahu might otherwise have appeared in print, by the immense success of Bellingshausen's venture on the fringes of Antarctica.[76] Again, at least three warships in the North Pacific Basin in that period, the *Vostok*, *Kreiser*, and *Apollon*, had in their crews incipient Decembrists, that is, men associated with the Guard-led revolution which began the reign of Nicholas I (14 December 1825).[77] The presence of such "scoundrels," in conjunction with the fact that other rebels and Decembrist sympathizers were associated with the Russian-American Company in its Pacific enterprise, did not dispose the tsar to view such officers as A.P. Lazarev or the Shishmarevs kindly.[78] Though not directly implicated in the ill-fated revolt, the cosmopolitan and widely- travelled Lazarev had friends who were notably officers of the Izmailovskii Lifeguards (spring and summer 1825).[79]

Lazarev wrote his account of the *Blagonamerennyi*'s venture, on the basis of his own journal and diary, in 1821–22 or shortly after. It was entitled *Zapiski o plavanii voennogo shliupa Blagonamerennogo v Beringov proliv i vokrug sveta dlia otkrytii, v 1819, 1820, 1821, i 1822 godakh* (*Notes on the Voyage of the Naval Sloop "Loyal" to Bering Strait and round the World on Discovery, in the Years 1819–1822*). The faircopy, of 325 pages, was written in fine copperplate and bound in leather, with the title impressed in gold on the spine. Lazarev's efforts to publish this work, the first of two proposed volumes, were vain and ceased in 1830. The bound faircopy stayed in the family until this century. It was found in the Smolensk Regional Archive by a local researcher, Miss T.G. Timokhinaia, in 1948(?) and forwarded to A.I. Solov'ev, professor of historical geography at Moscow State University. Solov'ev and Timokhinaia annotated and edited the find, which was published, under the guidance of A.A. Samarov, by the Central State Archive of the Navy of the USSR (TsGAVMF) in 1950. Samarov's own staff added relevant archival materials in appendices. The title of Lazarev's holograph was kept, but certain passages "not holding any interest were omitted and marked with dots."[80] The bound faircopy itself was sent to TsGAVMF, and stored under reference: *fond* 1153, *delo* 1. The original of Lazarev's shipboard journal (*putevoi zhurnal*), meanwhile, had been identified in the Manuscripts Department of the Saltykov-Shchedrin Public Library, in Leningrad, so that collation was possible.[81] The present translation of Lazarev's *Zapiski o plavanii* rests on the 1950 text, pp. 253–73 (Chapter IX).

KARL GILLESEM 179?–1853 (GERMAN: HULSEN)

Midshipman Karl Gillesem, of the *Blagonamerennyi*, left one of only two known eye-witness accounts of (parts of) that voyage to be published in the lifetime of the participants. Unlike Gleb Semenovich Shishmarev's 1852 essay on the Chukchi,[82] his account bore directly on Hawaii and Oahu Islands. "Puteshestvie na shliupe '*Blagonamerennyi*' dlia issledovaniia beregov Azii i Ameriki za Beringovym prolivom s 1819 po 1822 god" ("The Voyage of the Sloop 'Loyal' to Investigate the Shores of Asia and America beyond Bering Strait, from 1819 to 1822"), was published in the St. Petersburg journal *Otechestvennye zapiski* (*Fatherland Notes*), in three parts: vol. 55, no. 10; vol. 67, no. 11; and vol. 67, no. 12 in 1849. The third and final part, covering the expedition's movements from San Francisco to Oahu and the Northwest Coast (March–April 1821), appeared in the sub-section entitled "Smes" ("Miscellany"): no. 12, December 1849:215–28. The "Oahu Passage" was on pp. 217–25.

The inclusion of Gillesem's travel piece was a reflection of the changing tone of *Otechestvennye zapiski*, whose editor-proprietor, Andrei Kraevskii (1810–89), was at the time seeking a remedy to the defection of a group of ex-contributors and the formation of a major rival periodical in *Sovremennik*.[83] Responding to official nervousness and deepening reaction in the wake of 1848, a year of revolutionary upheavals in the West, he chose to publish solid, untendentious articles. Gillesem's was suitable in that regard and, as a bonus, was highly readable.

Gillesem's Honolulu memoir complements Lieutenant A.P. Lazarev's and Captain Mikhail Vasil'ev's contemporary pictures of the same places and individuals, producing sharply-focused images of 1821.

FERDINAND PETROVICH WRANGEL 1796–1870 (RUSSIAN: VRANGEL')

Born in December 1796, in Pskov, Admiral Wrangel died May 1870, in Tartu, Estonia. A distinguished Russian navigator, and senior member of the St. Petersburg Academy of Sciences, (1855), he was a founding member of the Russian Geographical Society.[84]

Wrangel graduated from the Naval Cadet Corps in 1815 and from 1817 to 1819 sailed with V.M. Golovnin in the sloop *Kamchatka*.[85] In 1820–24, he led an expedition in the Arctic, establishing that open sea lay to the north of Kolyma Peninsula in Eastern Siberia, and, from information acquired, determined the position of the large island now named after him. In 1825–27 he headed another round-the-world expedition, in the *Krotkii*. In 1829–35 he served as Governor of Russian North America. Maintaining an interest in the Russian-American Company, he joined its Board of Directors (1840–49). He was appointed naval minister in 1855, and held the post for three years. Shortly after his retirement, in 1864, he became involved in a campaign to oppose the sale of Russian North America (Alaska) to a foreign power.[86] Wrangel was the author of numerous articles, several books on the native peoples of Alaska, and *A Voyage Along the Northern Coasts of Siberia and in the Arctic Ocean* (1841).[87]

Wrangel's account of the *Krotkii*'s Honolulu visit of November–December 1826 appeared in the St. Petersburg journal, *Severnyi arkhiv* (*The Northern Archive*), vol. 12 (1828):86–105. It was entitled "Prebyvanie na Sandvichevykh Ostrovakh" ("A Sojourn on the Sandwich Islands"), and was essentially a transcript of Wrangel's log. F.V. Bulgarin and N.I. Grech, the editors of the journal, scarcely touched the text. Regrettably, dates are not indicated and are therefore doubtful, unless events are also recorded in local Hawaiian source materials. There are, however, letters addressed by Wrangel to F.P. Lütke and others, now held in Tartu, which help in establishing the dates of the *Krotkii*'s Honolulu visit. On 20 November 1826, for example, he wrote the following to Lütke:

> The young king Kamehameha III has his residence in Honolulu. The Governor of Oahu Island and the king's prime minister is called Mr. Pitt, but affairs are now managed by his brother because of his illness. I was received here with no little respect: several hundred grenadiers in full-dress coats (white uniform with red collar, low plumed shako) stood in ranks and, on the given command, performed some movement with their arms equivalent to presenting arms ...
>
> Missionaries from America are spoiling a good many things here; but trade has given this place a completely new look—there are roads, horses for riding, inns and drinking-taverns, stores, little shops, and a general marketplace for provisions...[88]

From Wrangel's own paper of 1828, it is clear that this reception by the youthful king and Boki took place the very day the *Krotkii* arrived at Honolulu.[89] This therefore was a day or two *before* the 20th. A few days in the town sufficed to convince Wrangel that Russian North America should be engaging in more regular and heavy trade with the Hawaiians. He made notes on the subject, on the spot:

> Trade with the Sandwich Islands: this has been tried by us only once, in case of need but quite advantageously. NB. I believe we should make more use of this branch of commerce. Furs are handled on the Sandwich Islands, at Honolulu to be precise, and it is always cheaper to buy from many than from one ....[90]

He was wrong in thinking the Russian-American Company had "only once" entered the market at Honolulu,[91] but correct in his approach. As seen (Chapter 3), his view did not result in an expansion of Hawaiian-Russian trade.

CHAPTER THIRTEEN

The Illustrative Records:

L. Choris and M. Tikhanov on Oahu, 1816–18

Russian narrative descriptions of Honolulu in its infancy are, like the large Hawaiian artefact collections now in Leningrad,[1] usefully complemented by the drawings made by artists aboard Russian ships. Two artists in particular, Ludovik or Choris (Khoris: 1795–1828) and Mikhail Tikhonovich Tikhanov (1789–1862), of Kotzebue's *Riurik* and Golovnin's *Kamchatka*, respectively, made important contributions to our knowledge of the growth of Honolulu. From Choris, we have twenty lithographs of Hawaiian scenes, from Tikhanov—four; both men, however, had assorted other Honolulu sketches and/or aquarelles in their portfolios, some of which have not appeared in print. Of the twenty illustrations by Choris published in 1822, eleven were of scenes, individuals, or objects drawn at Honolulu in 1816–17. Three others—of Kamehameha, Kaahumanu, and her brother "Teimotu"—were drawn on the Kona Coast on 24 November 1816 but have obvious relevance to Honolulu also. (For a cursory discussion of the Choris sketches now at the Academy of Arts in Honolulu, which were taken to Hawaii from Great Britain (1937) by Donald Angus, see Emory, 1946: 239–40.) All four of Tikhanov's drawings bear immediately on that infant town and its inhabitants. The work of other Russian artists remains unknown in the West to this day. It must be hoped that descriptions of the Honolulu drawings by Emel'ian Kornéev, artist in the *Otkrytie* (1821), which were apparently destroyed during the 1820s, will eventually be published by the Soviet authorities.[2] Other sketches remain, gathering dust, in files of the Central State Naval Archive of the USSR; it was not unusual for naval officers on round-the-world missions to be skilled draughtsmen and artists.[3] Observations follow here on Choris and Tikhanov, their careers, and their Honolulu legacies. Plates are then considered individually.

LOUIS CHORIS (LUDOVIK KHORIS) 1795–1828

Choris was of German descent but was raised and educated in Khar'-kov, in Southern Russia, where he was known as Loggin Andreevich Khoris and as a precociously brilliant artist. While still an adolescent, he made contact with another Russo-German in the area, Friedrich Marshal von Bieberstein (1768–1826). Bieberstein who, like Choris's own father, had entered Russian military service in the 1780s but maintained his German contacts, had in 1807 settled on his estate of Merefo, near Khar'kov, the better to work on his *magnum opus, Flora Taurico-Caucasica* (Khar'kov, 1808–18: 3 pts.). He invited the eighteen-year-old Choris to accompany him, as draughtsman, on a botanical trip to the Caucasus (1813). Thanks to Bieberstein, the young artist was in 1820 introduced to the great French naturalist, Baron Georges Cuvier (1769–1832); he and Bieberstein had studied together at Stuttgart in the pre-Napoleonic age.[4]

Choris's Caucasian portfolio of 1813 was admired by eminent Russian artists of the day, including A.N. Olenin, then President of the St. Petersburg Academy of Arts. When he applied to Count N.P. Rumiantsev in 1815 therefore, offering himself as painter to the expedition preparing to depart, he was promptly accepted.[5] In the course of the *Riurik*'s two visits to the Hawaiian Islands of 1816 and 1817, he produced a series of lifelike and unstylized sketches, some of great ethnographic value. These sketches remained in his possession on the *Riurik*'s return to St. Petersburg (1818), as he was not in naval service and his patron and employer, Count Rumiantsev, did not insist on his proprietorial rights. They went with Choris to Paris in the spring of 1819.

While in France, Choris re-established contact with Chamisso, who had also left Russia, and showed his *"Riurik* portfolio" to influential scholars, including Cuvier and Gall.[6] He corresponded with Kruzenshtern, Rumiantsev's unofficial maritime advisor and a highly influential naval bureaucrat at the time (1821), on the subject of publishing his sketches in the Kotzebue narrative or separately.[7] Finally, he opted for a separate account built around his drawings. Highly conscious of his limitations as an editor and author, especially in French, he turned to the publisher Firmin Didot for aid. M.J.B. Eyries edited the text that he, Georges Cuvier, and Dr. Gall presented in the early weeks of 1822. The "Honolulu section" was apparently his own.[8]

Voyage pittoresque autour du monde, avec des portraits de sauvages d'Amérique, d'Afrique, et des Isles du grand océan; des paysages, des vues maritimes, et plusieurs objets d'histoire naturelle ... appeared on 1 May 1822, with a (politic) introduction to Alexander I, tsar of Russia. "Never," wrote Choris in his introduction, had "so large a collection of portraits of different peoples" been seen. While on Oahu, as elsewhere, he had striven "to render faithfully the characteristic traits, the colour, in a word, the physiognomy, of the people" (p. iii). Hoping to increase their sales, Firmin Didot also issued the twenty-two sections that comprised the total work as booklets or *livraisons* (1821–23).[9] In its book form, however, *Voyage pittoresque* had seven parts, not twenty-two. Part II was entitled, "Les Iles Sandwich" and included the plates reproduced here. Firmin Didot put out a limited edition with coloured plates, and another, larger edition in black and white. Like the other six parts, "Les Iles Sandwich" was separately paginated. The "Hawaiian plates" followed an initial side-view of Hawaii and Oahu Islands from afar [Plate I], under the following titles:

II	Tammeamea, Roi des îles Sandwich
III	Reine Cahoumanou
IV	Taymotou, frère de la reine Cahoumanou
V	Temple du Roi dans la baie Tiritatea
VI	Idoles des îles Sandwich
VII	Idoles des îles Sandwich
VIII	Idoles des îles Sandwich
IX	Vue du port hanarourou
X	Habitants des îles Sandwich
XI	Armes et ustensils des îles Sandwich
XII	Danse des hommes dans les îles Sandwich
XIII	Bateaux des îles Sandwich
XIV	Bonnets et ustensiles des îles Sandwich
XV	Habitants des îles Sandwich (2)
XVI	Danse des femmes dans les îles Sandwich
XVII	Femme des îles Sandwich
XVIII	Port d'hanarourou
XIX	Intérieur d'une maison d'un chef dans les îles Sandwich

Several hands contributed to preparation of the sketches and lithographies of 1822. Choris himself lithographed several detailed drawings of Hawaiian artefacts, notably god-figures and canoes, and of single human figures (II, IV, VI–VIII, X, XI, XIII, XIV, XVII), for a total of ten. Nos. III, V, and XV were the work of the lithographer Norblin, and Nos. XII, XVI, and XIX, the work of Franquelin. Most distinguished of these French associates of Langlumé, however, was Jean-Victor Adam (1801–67). Later famous for his large-scale battle scenes, Adam was barely twenty-one when he was paid by Langlumé to work on Choris's two sweeping views of Honolulu settlement and harbour (Nos. IX and XVIII). To judge by attributions at the base of Plate XVIII ("Port d'hanarourou"), he actually reworked Choris's drawing, giving it greater contrast and tonality. As Jean-Baptiste Eyries (1787–1846) was the prism through which passed Choris's prose, so, in these instances, was Adam both the foreign intermediary and the true collaborator.

Choris made the sketches for Plates II–VIII inclusive while at Kailua, Hawaii, on 24–25 November 1816. Details of images may have been checked or improved during his second fleeting visit to the same bay on 28–29 October 1817. Plates VI, VIII, and IX cannot be connected exclusively with Honolulu, but circumstantial evidence suggests such a link. Plates IV, V, VII, X–XIV are unquestionably of Honolulu provenance.

Voyage pittoresque was well received in France, and Choris remained in Paris. There, in 1826, he produced his second illustrative work: *Vues et Paysages des régions equinoxiales, recueillis dans un voyage autour du monde ...* (Paul Renouard, 32pp., 24 coloured plates). As the title suggests, it had only incidental ethnographic interest.

Restless by temperament, Choris held strong republican views on first coming to France, at the age of twenty-four. He continued to shun political conservatives, to the displeasure of his erstwhile companions on the *Riurik*, and despite the dedication of his *Voyage pittoresque ...* to Tsar Alexander I. Early in 1828, he was inspired by reports of revolutionary events in South America to make another major journey. It resulted in his murder, at the hands of bandits, outside Vera Cruz in eastern Mexico. He left no children.

MIKHAIL TIKHONOVICH TIKHANOV 1789?–1862

The life and work of the *Kamchatka*'s artist have been studied at some length by L.A. Shur and R.A. Pierce, and more briefly by others.[10] To avoid repetition, only brief comments are offered here.

Tikhanov was born a serf about 1789. His talent was obvious and in 1806, aged seventeen, he was sent off by his master, Prince Golitsyn, to the St. Petersburg Academy of Arts. In 1815 he was granted his freedom and decided to remain at the Academy which was his haven in that city. In May 1817, the President of the Academy, A.N. Olenin, recommended Tikhanov to Captain V.M. Golovnin as a potential expeditionary artist. Tikhanov left in the *Kamchatka* that same August.[11]

During the voyage, Tikhanov painted at least forty-three pictures, including four of Hawaiian scenes. His most celebrated work is also the best-known portrait of A.A. Baranov, founding father and effectively the first Governor of Russian North America.[12] Specializing in human portraiture, Tikhanov took the opportunity to draw both chiefs and commoners while in Honolulu in October 1818.

Shortly after the *Kamchatka* left Manila in the Philippines, on her return voyage, Tikhanov fell seriously ill and showed the first signs of mental disturbance. These were serious by the time the *Kamchatka* reached Europe. There being no known cure, Tikhanov was placed in the hospital of the Academy of Arts. He improved in October 1819 and was released. In 1820, he was granted a disability pension of 600 roubles per annum; but within months he suffered a relapse and was placed in Obukhovskaia Hospital, diagnosed as deranged. He never recovered his sanity or worked again. From 1824 until his death in 1862, he was cared for by the widow of a former colleague at the Academy of Arts. His drawings were not published in his lifetime, even though, in 1821–22, Golovnin had corresponded energetically with the Academy itself and with the Admirality on that subject.[13]

Tikhanov painted Kamehameha I, in watercolours, at Kailua on the Kona Coast on 24 October 1818. The sitting was by "the royal palace," and the king wore European dress. Two days later, immediately on arrival at Honolulu, the *Kamchatka* was visited by various *haole* settlers and New England captains.[14] Tikhanov ignored them. On the 27th, he went ashore and met the chiefs Boki and Hekiri (Kahekili Keeaumoku). When the two chiefs paid a visit to the sloop, next day, he drew them carefully as they amused themselves with deck hoses and scrutinized the *Kamchatka*'s cannon. On the same brief visit to Honolulu, the artist also drew a local girl holding a little dog.

Golovnin had selected fifteen of the forty-three sketches and watercolours in Tikhanov's portfolio for engraving and inclusion in his forthcoming narrative, in May–June 1822. The visit of the Hawaiian chiefs to the *Kamchatka* had been included among them. Not until 1831, however, did the engraver A.G. Ukhtomskii prepare twenty-two plates; and not until 1841 were prints made from these, one set being sent to the Academy of Arts' directorate, a second to its "prints cabinet" (*kabinet estampov*).[15] Ukhtomskii returned Tikhanov's aquarelles to Olenin, the President of the Academy, in 1842; and on Olenin's death the following year, they were placed in the Academy's own library. There they remained for almost a century, until put in the Academy's museum (1941), where they may be examined today. The "Tikhanov album" (*Al'bom Tikhanova*) is in good condition, the soft pastels having faded but little. It is held in the department of drawing (*Otdel risunka, Muzei Akademii Khudozhestv SSSR*, Leningrad).[16]

Tikhanov's Hawaiian aquarelles first appeared in the 1949 edition of Golovnin's works (*Sochineniia*), much to the credit of its editor, the geographical historian I.P. Magidovich. They reappeared in the 1965 second edition of Golovnin's *Puteshestvie vokrug sveta ... v 1817, 1818, i 1819 godakh*, first published in St. Petersburg in 1822 (see Chapter 12). Kamehameha I, the chiefs' visit to the *Kamchatka*'s quarterdeck of 28 October 1818, and a full facial study of Boki in feather cloak and helmet, appear on pp. 371, 373, 375 of the Magidovich edition; the Hawaiian girl with a puppy follows on p. 386. Midshipman Tabulevich's chart of Honolulu Harbour, omitted in 1949, made its first appearance in print in 1965. The plates reproduced here are from the black-and-white versions in these Soviet editions.

OBSERVATIONS ON THE PLATES: L. CHORIS

1. *"Kamehameha, King of the Sandwich Islands"*

The brig *Riurik* entered Kailua (Kotzebue's "Tiatatua") Bay at dawn on 24 November 1816, to a very cool reception. Fearful of an extension of the Scheffer adventure at his own expense, Kamehameha had 400 warriors armed and ready in the area of Kamakahonu Cove. Once Kotzebue had explained his wholly peaceable intentions, he and his officers were given leave to pay a visit to the king ashore. Choris accompanied the party, which landed at approximately 10 a.m., and spent the next seven hours intermittently in the king's company.[17] In the course of an immense and lengthy meal, he made quick sketches of several of the *ali'i* present. Kotzebue notes that these were much admired and were first-rate likenesses. From these, in 1822, came Plate IV (certainly) and Plate X (probably). It was now that Kotzebue asked Kamehameha to pose:

> Even Kamehameha looked with surprise at Mr. Choris's work, but for some time he resisted my requests to allow himself, as they say, to be transferred to paper. Very likely he associated the art with some notion of magic. Not till I observed how happy our emperor would be to have Kamehameha's likeness did he consent to sit. To my considerably surprise, Mr. Choris succeeded in making an excellent likeness of the king even though, to discomfort the artist, he would not sit still for a minute and, despite my entreaties, pulled all kinds of faces. We took our leave of the king at 5 o'clock ....[18]

Kamehameha is shown against a stylized but plausible Hawaiian background. The *Riurik* appears, in the distance, over his left shoulder, hard against the *Brutus*, a New England merchantman that had preceded her into the bay from Keakakekua.[19] The king had worn pantaloons, shirt and waistcoat on the morning of Choris's visit, changing into Hawaiian attire for a visit to the Ahuena *heiau* (temple) and/or his sitting.

2. *"Queen Kaahumanu"*

Though also painted at Kamakahonu, Kailua, this portrait is included because of the Russians' frequent subsequent contact with this queen at Honolulu. Choris spent some time with Kaahumanu on 24 November 1816 and again on 28 September 1817. On both occasions, she was sitting on fine mats and eating watermelon. Choris may have drawn Kaahumanu (together with two other wives of Kamehameha) on his first visit, but the absence of pipe-heads and all smoking apparatus, the reference by Kotzebue to a *kanaka* "with a tuft of red feathers to drive away the flies" in 1817, and the fact that in 1817 Kaahumanu was "seated in the middle of a tent of white canvas",[20] clearly point to a reworking or development of the picture on the later date.

Kaahumanu is shown sitting on two or more layers of fine *makaloa* matting, with coloured geometrical motifs on the upper surfaces.[21] Her *kapa* garment shows five stamp designs, including large lozenges and zigzags.[22] The *kahili*, emblem of her rank, is some thirty inches long. Both the one in her left hand and that held by her *paa-kahili* have handles inlaid with turtleshell rings.[23] Turtleshell also figures prominently in her ornaments: a pair of bracelets of the *kupe'e 'ea* sort, an ivory bead necklace (also a sign of social standing and wealth), and a circular head ornament. Chamisso describes the bleaching of hair over the forehead with a mixture of *ti* root sap and *kukui* gum (Narrative 79). The tassels hanging from the royal tent are reminders of the costly Chinese silks and other wares imported into the Islands and much used by the Hawaiian nobility by 1816 (Narrative 7). Kaahumanu remained "stout," but had adopted European dress by 1824–25 (Narrative 62).

3. *"Teimotu, Brother of Kaahumanu"*

Kotzebue and his people met Teimotu several times in November 1816. On the 30th, he was aboard the *Riurik* in company with Kaahumanu and John Young (Narrative 71). Chamisso was of the opinion that Teimotu was planning to possess himself of Maui, on Kamehameha's death, and that he would do it with Kalanimoku's support (Narrative 40). The figure shows the usual traditional hairstyle: short at the front, long on the shoulders.[24] The earring is ivory. The structure by the shore (right background) is a *kanaka*'s house without walls, the commonest structure seen by the Russians at Honolulu (see Plates 4 and 13).[25]

4. *"A View of Honolulu Harbour"*

This broad view, taken from a point south of modern Kewalo Basin and southwest of Ala Moana Park, was at least begun on board the *Riurik* on the morning of 27 November 1816. It reflects the situation described by Kotzebue.[26] Fort Kaahumanu stands in the centre, beneath the striped Hawaiian Islands flag.[27] Behind it stretch dozens of native houses, most structures without walls, some, however, with curved rafters and ground pegs.[28] At least four buildings of the European type are visible, including the fort's blockhouse. Of six double canoes depicted, two are pulled up on the shore (beside an outrigger canoe), while four are in use afloat. Two appear to have ten paddlers each. Eight such *wa'a kaulua* towed the *Riurik* into the inner harbour on the following morning. The two small outriggers moving from the right and away from the shore, each with two persons, are not carrying the three-sided pandanus leaf sail as depicted by Cook's artist, John

Webber.[29] A long steering paddle may be seen behind the outrigger craft furthest to the right, five oval *hoe* blades and a curved cross-boom on the double canoe nearest the observer. Choris offers more details of these in Plate VIII. Some if not most of the paddlers have their hair tied up in a topknot.

The three vessels shown are the *Makanimoku* (ex-*Albatross*), the *Kaahumanu* (ex-*Forester*) to the left, and the *Traveller*, nearer the middle and pointing east (Narratives 1 and 3). The Hawaiian flag is visible at the stern of *Kaahumanu*; the departure of the *Traveller* has been delayed—she has no canvas spread—by Captain Wilcox's interview with Kotzebue and, perhaps, by the lack of a land breeze at so early an hour (6 a.m.).

5. *"Natives of the Sandwich Isles"*

> The king's favourites show their affection for him by expressing the desire to be sacrificed to the gods the instant he himself dies. We saw one of these men, destined to end his days at the moment when the king expired [Plate X, fig. 1]. The man seemed happy at the idea and proud of the honour of serving his king even after this terrestrial life. He loved his wife amazingly and did his utmost to be pleasant to her, choosing for her the most handsome foreigners who had happened to please her.

The man in question, on the right, wears his mantle in the same style as Kalanimoku, that described by Kotzebue as "Roman toga." The figure to the left wears a cool-weather *kihei* and what appears to be a dyed wig—a rarity. Under-the-chin beards and ivory earrings were still much in evidence at Honolulu in 1816–18.

6. *"Arms and Tools of the Islands"*

Choris himself annotated this plate (*Voyage*, "Iles Sandwich", p. 24), as follows:

Fig. 1	Vessel made from a gourd, in which *paya* is kept. A native dance is represented on the exterior.
Fig. 2	Vessel to hold water, also made from a gourd. Goats and guns visible on its outer wall.
Fig. 3	Spittoon decorated with human teeth. The king alone makes use of this article.
Fig. 4	Coconut shell covered with sharkskin, used as a small drum in dances.
Fig. 5	Stick to strike this drum.
Fig. 6	Stone adze; no longer in use.
Fig. 8	A tattooing instrument. One frequently dips it in water in which charcoal has been dissolved, then applies it to the body parts where figures are

to be made. The instrument is lightly struck, many times, with the implement shown as Fig. 7, till the epiderm is penetrated. These pierced areas swell up, but the swelling disappears in three or four days at most.

Fig. 9   Musical instrument. It consists of a piece of bamboo along which transversal cuts have been made, and along which one passes a little stick (Fig. 10), thus producing a noise like that of a child's hand rattle.

Figs. 11, 12   Assegais or javelins.

Fig. 13   Spear.

Brief observations may be made on the plate itself and on these accompanying comments, with a view to emphasizing their combined ethnographic value.

Fig. 1   By *paya*, Choris means *pa'i'ai*, the firm dough-like mass of pounded *poi* to which water is added when it is to be eaten. The gourd vessel itself is an ornamental *'umeke pohue*. A large bird is cut on the lid; three dancing figures, one with a long hula stick, on the lower part.

Fig. 2   *Huewai* with *pawehe* decoration associated principally, though not exclusively, with Niihau Island. Comparatively few and small geometrical motifs and extensive dyed background, in classical Hawaiian style.[30] The two long-barreled flintlocks are shown with bayonets. Goat designs like the pair visible on this gourd reappear on the upper right arm of the figure on the left of Plate 10 (XV by the 1822 schema). Suspensory loop, a simple cord tied in a knot around the neck, but no cord supports.

Fig. 3   *Ipu 'aina*. These were in fact used by high chiefs as well as kings, but if this one was for exclusively royal use, Choris may be presumed to have drawn it at Kailua. Eight molars are visible around the upper rim of this fluted scrap bowl, to give a probable total of 22–24. Highly polished with pumice and *kukui*-nut oil.

Fig. 4   *Puniu* or coconut knee drum lacking all signs of past or potential attachment to the knee, e.g., bottom cords. The Russians saw such little drums being played on the hard ground. Probably an unfinished article, since side cords are not attached, in the typical zigzagging manner, to the sharkskin overlap. There is, in fact, no cover fixation visible; and such drum membranes were not sewn.

Fig. 5   Wooden drumstick. Knee-drum beaters were usually(?) of thick coir fibre cords in pre- and immediate post-contact days.

Fig. 6   *Koi-pohaku*, the ancient stone adze. The upper, working part is generously lashed to the wooden haft in the traditional manner.[31]

Fig. 8   Also obsolescent by 1816, at least at Honolulu. Choris depicts tattooing on Plates 7, 10, 14, and Chamisso describes it (see Narrative 79).

Fig. 9   Neither a bamboo pipe, nor a bamboo rattle (*pu'ili*), but a Polynesian ancestor of the washboard popularized in the 1950s. Choris observes (*op. cit.*, p. 19) that it was played by women: "the women ... have pieces of reed with notches cut into them crosswise, along which, from one end to the other, they pull little pieces of wood. This produces a clattering noise like that of a child's rattle."

Figs. 11–13   Three varieties of short spear (ihe), two with barbs. Fig. 13 shows
three horizontal rows and a thicker shaft; the barbs appear to form
lanceolate points. Cook's people saw precisely such a hardwood spear in
1779.[32]

7.   "A Men's Dance in the Sandwich Isles"

The dance shown was arranged partly for the Russians' benefit, but
also as a normal aspect of the makahiki celebrations on Oahu, on 4
December 1816 (see Narrative 69). The three performers were professional dancers. They wore dog-tooth anklets, wider end uppermost,[33]
boar-tusk bracelets,[34] and festive outer wraps of kapa over the malo.

All three dancers hold gourd rattles. The dancer to the left carries an
early form of 'uli'uli mounted on a short stick. The seeds rattled. The
other two figures carry rattles with handsome kapa(?) ornamentation.[35]
Like the reclining chief of Plate 14, the one dancer who is tattooed has
patterning on one side of the torso only (left side for the dancer, right
side for the chief).[36] The Russians saw comparatively little tattooing
at Honolulu in 1816 and later years, and rightly recognized that the
practice was obsolescent.

Each of the four kneeling drummers has two instruments before him:
a composite ipu hula made of two gourds joined and gummed together,
the lower gourd being long and globular, and a knee drum or puniu. The
latter, however, are placed directly on the ground and are not attached to
the knee.[37] They are struck with sticks held always in the left hand, while
the right hand grips the cloth loop just below the junction of ipu hula's
lower and upper gourd. This is a classic study of traditional Hawaiian
musical practice, made the more valuable by Choris's own comments of
1822. Here is an extract from Voyage pittoresque ... ("Isles Sandwich,"
pp. 18–19):

> The dancing of these natives, the men especially, is extremely graceful. They do
> not move the feet a lot but merely make one step back, sideways, or forward; but
> the head, arms, and torso are constantly in motion which, far from being violent
> or excessive, produces always the most pleasant sense of harmony and infinite
> grace. The men do not normally dance together in groups larger than three,
> that is, before a circle of spectators; but the women often gather in numbers
> up to fifty to dance. It is an amusement for them. The men, on the contrary,
> are professional dancers and dance for payment. When they dance well, women
> throw whole pieces of material to them, as recompense. Like the women, the
> men have a special costume for the dance. They carry light shields, covered
> with the feathers of cocks and other birds, to the handle of which is attached
> a little calabash containing pebbles. When the shield is shaken, it makes a not
> unpleasant sound, especially when it is done in time with the dance air.
>   The musicians accompanying these dancers have, by their left hand, a large
> hollow calabash. They lift this gently into the air and let it fall to the earth. The

result is a hollow sound, not without some charm. With their right hand they strike a little drum made of coconut shell and covered with sharkskin. Apart from these instruments, the women also have pieces of stick which they strike one against another, in time .... The men wear on the forearm bone ornaments, and around the legs—several rows of teeth which, when they move, make a noise. All dances are accompanied by an air that is always the same ....

We often heard the people shouting to the dancers, when they had finished, to dance like the *kanaka haole*, i.e., foreigners. And the dancers would obey this command, making leaps and cabrioles and then waltzing, while the spectators exploded with laughter.

Choris does not depict the women's hula sticks (*ka la'au*) which he mentions, but does show women with *kahili* among the admiring audience, suggesting their high rank. Taken together, the use of *ka la'au*, gourd rattles with stones, composite *ipu hula*, coconut-shell drums, and rattles with frames (or "shields") decorated with cock feathers, all suggest continuity and conservatism in Hawaiian music. John Webber had drawn similar scenes, and heard very similar music, in 1779.[38] That fact, in turn, lends importance to the four-bar fragment of the air sung on 4 December 1816, recorded by Choris and printed in 1822 (p. 19) but omitted here.

8. *"Sandwich Islands Craft"*

"The canoes of these natives," observes Choris (*op. cit.*, p. 14), "are very long and either double or equipped with an outrigger on one side. They are normally paddled. It is only in very favourable winds that these Islanders put up sails."

Both the upper *wa'a kaulua* and the lower *wa'a kaukahi* are shown in use in Plate 4. The double canoe, used for towing large vessels into and out of Honolulu's inner harbour until they were replaced by bullocks in the 1830s,[39] has three heavy cross booms of the curved type used to raise the height of the central platform (*pola*), so keeping cargo dry. Such craft carried large quantities of taro from Honolulu to the Kona Coast and elsewhere. These booms rest on the gunwale strakes and project a few inches on the outboard sides of the hulls. Choris's outrigger canoe differs hardly at all from that drawn in 1804 by Lieutenant E.E. Levenshtern of the *Nadezhda*, then off the Kona Coast.[40] Median bow cover, thwarts, hull lashings, and *wiliwili* float with raised ends, are all strictly traditional in design and technique. The paddle shows a wide ovate blade with a pronounced shaft midrib.[41]

9. *"Helmets and Implements of the Sandwich Islands"*

Choris provides these terse notes to another of the plates that he himself lithographed (*op. cit.*, p. 24):

Figs. 1–2   Helmets made of *baquois* leaves.

Fig. 3   Pipe, used without a pipestem for smoking.

Figs. 4–5   Fish-hooks.

The material employed to make helmets was, in fact, the pliable aerial rootlet of *'ie'ie* (*Freycinetia arboras*). Choris's ignorance reflects the fact that the Russians saw no such helmets being made at Kailua or Honolulu in 1816–17. Fig. 2 represents a mushroom-ornamented helmet of the type also drawn by Arago, the artist with Freycinet (1817–20).[42] The technique is described by Peter Buck.[43] Fig. 4 represents a simple bone or whale-ivory hook, Fig. 5—a *makau mano*(?) for sharks. Fig. 6 appears to be the small chiefly fan (*peahi*) that Liholiho casually holds in Plate 14.

10. *"Natives of the Sandwich Islands"*

Three figures wear *kapa* pieces over the left shoulder or round both shoulders, the two top corners being tied with a reef knot. Choris saw *kapa* being made and left a description of the process:

> Much paper mulberry is cultivated on these islands. When the tree is three years old, it is felled right by the roots. The outer bark, which is thrown away as useless, is first carefully scraped; the underbark is then lifted off. It is allowed to soak some fifteen days in water, to soften, then kneaded into balls about the size of an average apple. These are laid on a clean plank and beaten with wooden mallets, so that the mass is flattened, spread out, and made thin. One of these balls can become a piece of stuff seven or eight feet long and equally wide. As the paste can dry out while being worked, it is frequently moistened—constantly during the night, since the preparation process can last ten to twelve days. The material obtained by this process is yellowish grey. It is later dyed with colours extracted from leaves and plant roots. All the patterns made are executed, with extreme care and patience, by women, who use a little split reed for the purpose. Undyed stuffs are easily washed. The others are rubbed with an aromatic oil obtained from the timber and roots of the sandalwood tree.

The expression of the central figure depicted is also elucidated by the artist himself:

> Many older chiefs drink *kava*, or *'awa*, for the pleasure of it. They grow lean, and their eyes turn red. The use of this beverage gives them the air of half-drunk men ... (p. 15)

The ample quantity of *kapa* worn, together with the facial expressions, suggest individuals of rank. Both exposed right arms are tattooed (two goats, a palm). The figure on the right has false hair, plaited and dyed a lighter shade, of the sort seen by King and Webber.[44]

11. *"Women's Dance in the Sandwich Isles"*

This is the pictorial accompaniment to the texts by Kotzebue and Chamisso (Narratives 69 and 73), describing the *hulahula* of 4 December 1816. There are five rows of girls, each of three dancers. All wear dyed festive *kapa* above the *pa'u*, much as do the men dancing in Plate 7. All wear additional *kapa* pieces around the shoulders, dog-tooth anklets, and head ornaments described by Kotzebue as "wreathes of flowers." They are certainly *lei*, but not necessarily of flowers only. Necklaces are apparently of shell, not beads. All the dancers follow the example of Queen Kaahumanu, dying the hair in a band above the forehead. Choris looked into this Hawaiian custom:

> The women love to ornament themselves. Cutting their hair very short, they lift up the hair at the front and coat it several times a day with lime. This makes the hair blond or even quite white. We often saw hair that had been dyed pink but could not discover how that hue was produced. Several Europeans supposed that this fashion had not existed before Europeans visited the islands; but this opinion is likely untrue, since the hair on the goddess Hareopapa [at the Ahuena *heiau* in Kailua] is dyed in the same manner and the timber of which that image is made was felled at least a century before .... (p. 14)

The dance was accompanied by at least three instruments: the composite gourd drum or *ipu hula*, the little *puniu*, and the notched bamboo stem with stick (standing figure in the audience). A woman of high rank has two *kahili*-bearers behind her. Though this *hulahula* was performed on the same spot as the professional male dancers' [Plate 7], it is painted from the landward side. The air to which these fifteen girls danced, records Choris, was "chanted in a stammering way" (*en bredouillant*). They, and the men too, would often dance seated on the ground. "They accompany themselves by singing, clapping their hands, and striking time on their own chests" (p. 19).

12. *"Sandwich Island Woman"*

Besides the "motley *kapa* material" (admired by Kotebue), the dyed fringe of hair, and the prominent earrings, the most striking feature of this woman's personal ornamentation is the *lei palaoa* around her neck. It is a handsome example of the Hawaiian hook-shaped ornament made from thick coils of human hair and a sperm-whale tooth or, in post-contact days, walrus tusk.[45] The Russians saw many such ornaments in use in 1816, which points to widespread acceptance of walrus ivory brought to the Islands from the North by *haole* traders. Choris makes a point of noting, however, that in 1816 New Englanders were still satisfying a local demand by selling the traditionally preferred sperm-whale teeth:

Women often wear coils of men's hair at their neck, to which they suspend, in front, a piece of bone carved into the form of a tongue. It is normally a cachalot tooth, which the Americans sell at a very high price to the Islanders.

The hair coils are suspended by short cords at the back of the wearer's neck, so that the carved tooth may hang freely and be seen to full advantage. The better to show her wealth and/or sense of fashion, this woman is also wearing an ivory bead necklace. Some of these beads are spindle-shaped, others round. The former are ivory, the latter are very probably red glass.[46]

Dark red glass beads (explains Choris, op. cit., p. 20), are the only ones sought after. Nothing is thought of beads of any other colour ....

Kaahumanu is depicted [Plate 2] wearing a composite bead and ivory necklace of the same sort; and, again, her influence must be suspected.

13. *"The Port of Honolulu"*

This little masterpiece is Jean-Victor Adam's main contribution to Hawaiian studies, albeit one that rests on Choris's own work. Unlike Plate 4, it represents the scene found by the Russians on their visit of October 1817. On the first of that month, records Kotzebue,

we found everything in motion in the harbour. Eight ships stood at anchor. Six of them flew the North American flag, one flew the flag of Kamehameha, and the eighth, belonging to the Russian-American Company, was sitting on a sandbank .... (Narrative 15)

Half-a-dozen canoes, containing from six to fourteen figures, ply between the anchored vessels and the shore. Other aspects of the composition similarly underline the element of reprovisioning. A native riding bareback with a string bridle, a sight seen again by Kotzebue in 1824 (Narrative 113), drives before him two cows. Cattle were becoming abundant by 1817, though Marin's remained the only large herd in the Honolulu area (Narrative 99). Pigs forage freely in the foreground. Two individuals carry a pair of gourd food containers each or, more probably, a pair of *huewai*. They are approaching Fort Kaahumanu from the north and hence from the Nuuanu Stream, and are using carrying poles (*'auamo*) of the type commonly used to convey sweet water. The gourds' necks are attached to either end of the poles by long suspensory loops.[47]

A lookout stands by the blockhouse of the fort, above which waves the Hawaiian flag, as described by A.P. Lazarev in 1821 (see Narrative 127). The seven stripes and indented Union Jack are clear. The sloping ends of the fort's coral-stone walls are emphasized, dramatically, by the sloping (and so harmonious) roofs of eight native structures clustered by the shore. Only the ninth and largest native structure, which the water-carriers approach, does not have a roof extending straight to the earth. That structure, moreover, has an alien, *haole* feature by the entrance: a rectangular awning.[48] While pointing up the independent existence of horserider and cattle, the two central figures peering out across the harbour to the ships reinforce the basic notion of the link between those vessels and the shore. The point is further strengthened by the crowd of natives standing by the strand. The waiting vessels need the shore and the natives, and cannot move off until their needs have, once again, been met.

14. *"Interior of a Chief's House in the Sandwich Isles"*

This scene is a mingling of Choris's memories of visits to at least two chiefly houses. One occurred at Kailua, Kona on 24 November 1816. Kotzebue records that the Russians entered a small, neat structure to find Liholiho, "a tall, corpulent, naked figure, stretched out on his stomach." The prince indolently raised his head to look at the intruders. "Near him sat several naked soldiers armed with muskets, guarding the monster; a handsome young native drove flies away from him with a bunch of red feathers."[49] The *peahi* (fan) of lozenge form, in the "prince's" right hand, reappears as Fig. 6 in Plate 9. Choris himself remembered the scene slightly differently:

Liholiho was sitting on the ground, on a beautiful mat, almost completely naked. He received us very coldly, uttered not a word, and had the air of paying us almost no attention. He was surrounded by several chiefs .... (*op. cit.*, p. 5)

The muskets leaning against the structure's interior, the "several chiefs," the "beautiful mat," and the prince's indolent and unwelcoming expression all link the drawing to that visit. At Honolulu, however, there were other chiefly houses and other visits. Choris took a look inside several and made comments on the subject in 1822:

The houses are spacious and clean, those of the women in particular. They are built of hurdles which are covered with earth and they have dry grasses on top and on the sides. A window serves to let in air rather than daylight. Doors are very low. These houses always face northeast-southwest (p. 20).

The central figure of the drawing, almost certainly to be identified with Liholiho, rests on fine *makaloa* mats and a plaited pandanus pillow (*uluna*).[50] Two *kahili*-bearers attest to his rank by their presence.

OBSERVATIONS ON THE PLATES: M. TIKHANOV

15. *"Girl from the Sandwich Islands"*

The original aquarelle of this plate is described by a recent Soviet émigré scholar as "wonderful in its range of colours."[51] The sheer skin area and bulk of *kapa* suggest that this was one of Tikhanov's main studies in colour composition in the Islands. The girl wears a bulky shell necklace and has the lime-dyed fringe of hair so common at the time.[52]

16. *"Kamehameha, King of the Sandwich Islanders"*

Tikhanov drew his protrait of the king at Kailua, Kona, on the morning of 24 October 1818. Golovnin has left details of the entire visit, beginning with the Russian longboat's landing, at 10 a.m., "on the sandy beach right next to the king's houses" at Kamakahonu.[53] The site where Kamehameha sat is now part of the Ahuena *heiau* reconstruction project, a complex of replica buildings completed in 1983 and standing behind the King Kamehameha Hotel at Kona.[54] The king, writes Golovnin,

> was dressed in European style but very simply: his dress consisted of pale green velvet trousers, a white shirt, a silk kerchief round his neck, a coffee-brown silk waistcoat, white stockings and shoes, and a soft round felt hat. He was holding in his hand a slender and very highly polished cane, the thinner extremity of which was split. Into this split had been inserted the leaf of some plant. I at first mistook this cane for some sign or emblem of authority, like our sceptre, but later gathered that it was actually for use in a local game ....

The silk kerchief, white shirt, and brown vest are shown in Tikhanov's aquarelle, now held in the museum of the Academy of Arts of the USSR (*Muzei Akademii Khudoshestv SSR*) and known by its original title, "Tameamea, korol' Sandvichan." The "Tikhanov album" (*al'bom Tikhanova*) is, like many items in the *Otdel risunka* of that museum, not on public display but may be examined, under surveillance, by visitors with proper scholarly and/or official identity papers. Golovnin approved of the portrait and included it in the seventeen earmarked for publication in his narrative of 1822–23: it was to have appeared as Plate XI. As noted in Chapter 12, Golovnin's *Voyage* appeared in 1823 without illustrations. Still, he fully expected that the Academy of Arts would shortly engrave the plates in question.[55] "Kamehameha, King of the Sandwich Islanders" was one of twenty-two plates finally engraved, in 1831, by the St. Petersburg craftsman A.G. Ukhtomskii.[56] It appeared in print 118 years later, and is here reproduced from p. 371 of that work: I.P. Magi-

dovich's 1949 edition of Golovnin's two *puteshestviia vokrug sveta* ...,
entitled *Sochineniia* (see Bibliography).

The portrait of the king has several points of interest in relation to
Golovnin's text, for the precise circumstances of the sitting are hinted
at.[57] In the royal "dining-room," for instance, stood a round table "covered with a blue cloth." Tikhanov paints it. On this table "stood a
quart of rum, a decanter half filled with red wine, a large glass of water, and three or four empty glasses." Tikhanov paints the decanter,
three-quarters empty now, because the Russians have drunk red wine.
The polished cane in Kamehameha's right hand was for use in the game
of *no'a*; having guessed beneath which of five *kapa* bundles a piece of
wood or stone was hidden, one flicked that bundle with the cane.[58] The
leaf drawn through a slit at the end of the king's rod was *ti* leaf, used
as an alternative to dogskin with a tuft of hair.[59] The game was still
very popular on the Kona Coast in the time of Reverend William Ellis
(1825).[60] Lastly, the king's haircut is noteworthy. The *Riurik*'s people
had found him with a full but very close-cut head of hair in 1817. Now,
he wore his hair in a fashion described by King in 1784: "they cut it
close on each side of the head, down to the ears, leaving a ridge of about
a small hand's breadth, running from the forehead to the neck; which,
when the hair is thick and curling, has the form of the crest of the ancient helmet."[61] The lack of stubble clearly indicates that Kamehameha
had had his hair cut very recently. Golovnin mentions, in passing, that
the king's sister had died the previous day, 23 October 1818, and that
signs and sounds of grief and mourning were obtrusive at Kailua.[62] It
was customary to cut the hair during mourning periods, to show respect
for the dead.[63]

17. *"Chiefs of Oahu Island Visiting the Sloop Kamchatka"*

This plate was to have appeared in Golovnin's own volume, of 1823,
as Plate XII: "Portrait of the Sandwich Island Chiefs Boki, Hekiri, and
Retinue."[64] Golovnin met both chiefs almost immediately upon his arrival at Honolulu, on 27 October 1818, the former as Governor of Oahu
to whom he himself owed some courtesy, the latter in his capacity as
commander of the royal naval forces.[65] Both spoke English and so did
not depend on Captain William Heath Davis, at whose house they and
Golovnin all dined that evening, as an interpreter. The Russian officers found them highly intelligent and civil. With Boki in particular
they had frequent contact, since it was he who arranged the provisionment of the *Kamchatka* with live hogs and newly picked vegetables, as
well as arranging entertainment for Golovnin with an evening *hulahula*
and, subsequently, a sham battle, a traditional boxing match, and even
a demonstration of pig-strangling and cooking. Boki and Hekiri (Ka-

Hekili Ke'eaumoku) paid their visit to the sloop on the afternoon of 28 October, remaining aboard several hours and dining with their hosts:

> Boki brought me a gift of ten hogs and I gave him a telescope in return. They wore their celebrated feather capes and each of the chiefs had with him a number of officials dressed in the same manner. They were very pleased to have our artist depict them on paper. Our guests stayed almost till evening. They were particularly struck by the working of our fire-hose, which the chiefs themselves directed into the native craft near the sloop ....[66]

In Tikhanov's painting, Boki stands to the right holding a bottle and glass. He wears a circular feather cloak with lozenge motif very similar to the Baranov cloak in Leningrad and the Kalanikauikalaneo cloak in the Bernice P. Bishop Museum, Honolulu.[67] However, it has a double lower (yellow) border. The crescent motif is not visible. Boki's cloak shows a considerable area of yellow 'o'o or, less probably, mamo feather work against the deep red background.[68] Together with its sheer length and volume, this fact emphasizes his rank and social prestige. Yellow is less in evidence on the cloak worn by Hekiri (with his back to the viewer). Boki's helmet is wide-crested and covered with the braid form of feather attachment.[69] His hair falls in ringlets on the shoulders.

Hekiri holds a hardwood thrusting spear (ihe) over his right shoulder. It is some six feet long, with three (?) rows of barbs, and highly polished.[70] Colour, function, and ownership all point to an object made of kauila wood. Golovnin's eye was caught, as King's had been forty years earlier, by this particular Hawaiian timber. To King, it had had "much the appearance of mahogany"; to Golovnin, it looked "as hard and black as ebony."[71] Hekiri also wears a wide-crested feather helmet and capacious cloak or cape.

Two females at the left, one sitting on a mortar, wear pa'u and, in one case, the lei niho palaoa (sperm-whale tooth pendant on human hair coils). The same woman also wears a feather lei on her head, so exploiting the sole exception to the classical Hawaiian restriction making ornamental use of feathers a male monopoly. A third attendant, at her right, holds a kahili inlaid with rings of turtleshell or human bone.

18.   "The Chief Boki"

A portrait serving, simultaneously, as a study in the Hawaiian feather helmet (mahiole). Chief Boki wears and stands behind wide-crested helmets, the insignia of high chiefs. Hekiri, whose height is obvious, wears a helmet with low median crest, the anterior concave curve defining a blunt point while the height of crest diminishes gradually towards the back. It resembles the so-called Kaumualii helmet, studied in detail by Peter Buck.[72] The helmet in the foreground is covered with the braid form of feather attachment, the sides being decorated both with an upper feathered braid running lengthwise and, unusually, with four spoke-like vertical or near-vertical braids. The sides of the crest itself are formed of yellow feathers.[73]

The *ihe* held by a pensive Hekiri appears to have no butt enlargement, as is usual in this short spear. Such a weapon was emblematic of Hekiri's military post and it was appropriate that he should be painted with it. As a "chief below the king," he and his staff were to be "constantly practised in the arts of war with the short spear, *ihe* ..." etc.[74]

19. *I.F. Kruzenshtern*

Captain I.F. Kruzenshtern (1770–1846), commander of the *Nadezhda* at Hawaii Island, May–June 1804.

He wears orders presented by the Emperor at the conclusion of that first round-the-world venture by the Russian Navy (1803–06). Accounts of the fleeting visit to Hawaii were left by several members of the *Nadezhda*'s company, including Lieutenants E. Levenshtern and M. Ratmanov, astronomer J.C. Horner, Russian-American Company Clerk F.I. Shemelin, Envoy Designate to Japan N.P. Rezanov, and the naturalists Tilenius von Tilenau and G.H. Langsdorf. The 1804 visit provided interest in the Hawaiian Islands at Petropavlovsk-in-*Kamchatka* and along the Russian Northwest Coast, where food was scarce.

20. *Iu.F. Lisianskii*

Captain Iu.F. Lisianskii (1773–1837), commander of the *Neva*, the first Russian ship to anchor and barter in the Islands (Kealakekua-Kaawaloa, 1804).

Lisianskii's own account of that visit and of the Hawaiian people, published in 1812 and translated into English by the author himself (1814), was complemented by the writings of Lieutenant V.N. Berkh, later historian of the Russian North Pacific venture, and Russian-American Company Clerk N.I. Korobitsyn, among others. Lisianskii's people collected many artefacts at Kealakekua, and some remain in Leningrad to this day.

21. *The Ship Neva in 1805*

The *Neva*, first Russian vessel at the Islands, was purchased in London (as the *Thames*) in 1802, and made two Pacific expeditions (1803–06, 1806–09) before being wrecked on a voyage from Okhotsk to Sitka (1813). This plate, based on a drawing done at Kodiak early in 1805 by Lisianskii, is taken from the 1814 (London) edition of this *Voyage Round the World*: 190.

22. *Left: Captain Leontii Adrianovich Gagemeister, circa 1818*
Right: Captain Vasilii Mikhailovich Golovnin, circa 1830

Captain Leontii Adrianovich Gagemeister (German: von Hagemeister), in full dress uniform of the Imperial Russian Navy, with Cross of St. Anna. This portrait, of circa 1820, hung in the Board Room of the Russian-American Company main office on Moika Quay in St. Petersburg.

Captain Vasilii Mikhailovich Golovnin, circa 1814. The hero of Japanese captivity (1811–13) was painted on his return to St. Petersburg, with orders but, at his request, in regular sea-duty uniform.

23. *Armed sloop of Kamchatka type, circa 1820*

Armed sloop of the *Kamchatka* class; from Lars Gronstrand, Gånga Tiders Skepp (Åbo, 1965).

24. *Armed Transport of the Blagonamerennyi class*

This sketch was made in the late 1940s by M. Semenov, a Soviet researcher, on the basis of archival materials that had been brought together in connection with the coming publication (1950) of Lieutenant A.P. Lazarev's account of the *Blagonamerennyi*'s round-the-world voyage of 1819–21 and with preparations for A.I. Andreev's (1949) edition of F.F. Bellingsgauzen's narrative of 1831 (*Dvukratnye izyskaniia v Iuzhnom ledovitom okeane ...*). It accurately shows an armed transport of the *Blagonamerennyi-Mirnyi* type, of 530 tons displacement. The *Blagonamerennyi* visited Honolulu twice in 1821, under the command of Captain G.S. Shishmarev. She was built outside St. Petersburg by the shipwright Kupreianov, and measured 36.5 metres in length. She flies the Russian Navy's blue-and-white cross of St. Andrew and is sloop-rigged.

25. *Otto Evstaf'evich von Kotzebue*

Otto Evstaf'evich Kotzebu, commonly known as Otto von Kotzebue, as a newly-posted Captain-Lieutenant of the Fleet. Kotzebue sat for the successful portraitist, Alexander Varnek (1728–1843), in St. Petersburg in 1819. Varnek's portrait was engraved, by Aleksei Ukhtomskii, for the frontispiece of Kotzebue's *Puteshestvie v Iuzhnyi okean ...* (St. Petersburg: Grech, 1821).

26. *Adelbert von Chamisso 1781–1838*

This portrait of the poet-scientist Adelbert von Chamisso was painted by Reinick in the 1830s, engraved by L. Heine and C. Barth, and used as the frontispiece to the first part of the 1836 Leipzig edition (Weidman-nische Buchhandlung) of Chamisso's *Werke*. It shows a man already ill, and conscious of the little time left for his numerous academic projects— including a grammar of the Hawaiian language, which was published in part in 1837.

27. Hawaiian Dwelling and Natives

A drawing of a chief's house by Choris, probably done on Oahu. This is one of several drawings taken to the Honolulu Academy of Arts in 1937 by Donald Angus, who had purchased them in England. In build and dimensions, this house is like that of Plate 14, but the larger-than-usual door opening (*puka*) with traditional wooden framing posts, here made below an oval air-vent of the variety described by the artist (Choris, 1822: 20), indicates another structure. The palisade or fence running in front of this building is associated with it. First published in Feher, 1969:68.

28. Hawaiian Natives Wearing Kihei, with Animals

Preliminary sketch by Choris done at Honolulu and illustrating the prevalence and ways of wearing rectangular *kapa kihei*, or cloak. The sketch was made in early winter. Several figures have the cloak tied over the right shoulder. Also shown are Hawaiian dogs (*'ilio*), a pig, and the outlines of three wall-less structures of the sort generally used by the common people (see Brigham, 1908: 88–89; and Ellis, 1827: 314).

29. Preliminary Sketch for Portraits of Queen Kaahumanu,. Chief Kalanimoku in 1825

At the left, a portrait of Kaahumanu by Choris. In 1816, the queen was about forty-eight years old and had another sixteen years to live. At the right, Kalanimoku (1768?–1827), a pencil study by Dampier made in 1825, at the time of HMS *Blonde*'s visit to Honolulu. The chief was then within two years of death and suffering from edema of the leg. "A God-fearing chief, he was the iron cable which held fast the nation; at his death that stay was broken." Published in Feher, 1969:183–84.

30. Mission House and Chapel, John Young

The second chapel hut on Honolulu's eastern plain, shown as it was when visited by Captain Mikhail N. Vasil'ev and the officers of the *Otkry-tie* in December 1821. The stone-built mission house, at left, was com-pleted in time for Kotzebue's visit of 1824, in the sloop *Predpriiatie*. Below is Pellion's portrait of John Young in old age.

31. *Left: Captain Gleb Semeonovich Shishmarev*
   Right: Captain Ferdinand Petrovich Wrange(l), or Vrangel'

Captain Gleb Semeonovich Shishmarev (1781–1835), a veteran of
Kotzebue's expedition in the *Riurik* (1815–18), later Rear-Admiral; commander of the armed transport *Blagonamerennyi* in 1819–22, in which
he visited Honolulu twice in 1821.

Captain Ferdinand Petrovich Wrangel(l), or Vrangel' (1796–1870),
midshipman on the *Kamchatka* (1817–19), commander of the sloop
Krotkii (1825–27), later Governor of Russian North America (1829–35).

32. *Left: Captain Mikhail Nikolaevich Vasil'ev*
   Right: Captain Ferdinand Petrovich Lütke (Litke)

Captain Mikhail Nikolaevich Vasil'ev (1770–1847), the commander of
the "Northern Division" of the 1819–21 double polar expedition. He visited Honollu twice in 1821, with the armed sloop *Otkrytie* (*Discovery*);
later Vice-Admiral and General Intendant of the Fleet.

Captain Ferdinand Petrovich Lütke (1797–1882), also a promising
midshipman aboard V.M. Golovnin's *Kamchatka*, in which he called
at Honolulu in 1818. Eminent hydrographer, founding member of the
Russian Geographical Society, and President of the Imperial Academy
of Sciences (1864–81).

33. *The Brig Riurik in 1816*

The brig *Riurik* off the coast of Tongareva, May 1816. This aquarelle
by Choris shows "a meeting with the inhabitants of the Penrhyn Islands": Eschscholtz and Chamisso are clearly portrayed by the *Riurik*'s
stern. Lithographed by de Bové and published in *Voyage pittoresque* ...
(Paris, 1822), this is the best surviving illustration of the little fir-built
brig as she was at the time of Kotzebue's first Pacific expedition.

MAPS

A. *Map of the South Part of the Coast of Oahu Island from
   Waikiki Hamlet to the Pearl River, 1817*

The mapping of Honolulu harbour was started by Vasilii Stepanovich
Khramchenko (1792–1849), mate of the brig *Riurik*, on the morning of
29 November 1816, and very nearly led to an armed clash. The sight of
survey poles with pennants attached reminded the natives vividly of recent attempts by the adventurer Georg Anton Scheffer to take possession
of at least part of Oahu.[75] The crisis is described by Chamisso (Narrative 5). Mistakenly supposing that the harbour had never been surveyed,
Kotzebue himself contributed sextant readings. By 8 December, indeed,

he had decided that Russians should produce the first accurate map of the surrounding area and was alarming other natives, west of Moanalua Stream, by setting up his compass and gazing incomprehensibly at the horizon. He was believed to be engaging in sorcery (Narrative 100). From his perch on this height just east of the Salt Lake, Kotzebue had a clear view southeast across the fish-ponds to the Kapalama Peninsula and, beyond it, Honolulu Harbour. To the west, his view was blocked; and the 1817 map offers greater detail and accuracy for the area east of Moanalua Stream than for the highlands west of it.

The map is, *sui generis*, a record of Kotzebue's own shore movements, showing the paths he took across the Kalihi Valley, the Moanalua Stream and north around the Salt Lake and, in the opposite direction, east to the settlement of Waikiki. Rectangular taro fields, many 160 feet long, are marked along the coast and in the valleys of the Moanalua, Kalihi, Nuuanu, and Manoa Streams. Again, Kotzebue gives a detailed description to accompany the map (Narrative 74). Numbers of native structures indicated by trapeziums amongst miniscule palms, make it possible to estimate the relative sizes of local settlements in 1816–17. Other features marked include Kaahumanu Fort on the east side of Honolulu Harbour, the Europeans' burial ground (now at the makai corner of King and Piikoi Streets), and the series of large ponds in swampy ground (west of the old Manoa streambed, later drained into the Ala Wai canal).

Comparison of the 1817 map with a recent map of the same area makes evident how much the shoreline has changed, thanks to persistent *haole* intervention. The low and dangerous sandbars and coral outcrops shown as "The Middle Ground" west of the harbour entrance, for example, have yet to rise and merge, forming the modern Sand (Anuenue) Island. With their protective wall of coral-stones, the old fish-ponds are obvious, at centre. Not until the early 1840s were plans devised to dam the Nuuanu Stream (the mud from which was silting up the bay), and then fill in the ponds.[76] As for the coastline west of Keehi Lagoon, where airport runways now receive *haole* visitors by the million, the changes caused by landfill and the bulldozer are obvious. The Wauiau Stream which once flowed west-southwest across the site of modern Hickam Air Force Base, no longer exists. Two drainage canals now run north–south between Ahua Point and Pearl Harbour Entrance.

The Kotzebue-Khramchenko map covers a two-and-a-half mile stretch of Oahu's south coast and country, up to one mile inland behind Diamond Head. It was one of twenty-one maps included in an atlas accompanying the three-volume original Russian-language edition of Kotzebue's *Puteshestvie v Iuzhnyi okean i v Beringov proliv ...* (St. Petersburg, N. Grech, 1821–23), but omitted from the same publisher's compact single-volume (23 cm.) edition, also of 1821–23.

B. *Plan of the Entrance into Honolulu Harbour, on Oahu Island, in Latitude 21°8'12" N and Longitude 157°52'00" from Greenwich*

The upper, northern half only is reproduced here, in order to magnify details of physical features on the eastern side of the inner harbour. The key, omitted here, reads as follows:

A The house of the Spaniard Marini.
B The house of American shipmasters.
C The landing-place.
D Houses and Huts of the natives.

This information is amplified on the plan proper. Beside the house of "Manini," that is, Francisco de Paula Marin (the three front upper windows and roof of which are discernible), is written "white stone house." Beside the large square structure east of B is written, "Fort Akamana," i.e., Fort Kaahumanu. The representation of the fort's embrasure layout is, like that of the "American shipmasters' house," stylized: twenty embrasures are indicated (five on the long facades, three on the short, and one at each corner), but in reality, as Choris shows us (see Plate 4), there were eleven on the south wall, none on the east. Even so, the plate and this map of 1818 combine to throw useful light on the development of Fort Kaahumanu—and on N.B. Emerson's 1900 study of it.[77]

Comparison of Maps A and B reveals interesting discrepancies, notably in the shape of the fort and the number of native huts by the shore north of it. One must conclude that the representation of the fort on the 1817 map is also a stylized one, and that the number of huts (suggested by three or four symbols in 1817, two dozen the next year), was rapidly increasing in this period. Thanks to Choris [Plate 13], we not only know what these structures looked like, but also understand why they were springing up north of the landing-place. For the Hawaiian populace, that stretch of waterfront was central in the business of provisionment and bartering. As is apparent from the Choris plate and from the anchorage selected for the *Kamchatka* (anchor sign, Map B), most ships stood at anchor facing it or, more precisely, with their stern holds facing it. Discrepancies, however, are outweighed by similarities between the maps; for instance, in the depths of water shown.

The map both illuminates and is illuminated by the literature on the infant Honolulu. Chamisso was one of many visitors struck by the blinding white reflection off Marin's house (Narrative 1): hence the description on the 1818 map. As for the ownership and provenance of the "American shipmasters' house" beside the quay, they have been touched on by at least three generations of historians.[78]

This elegant and simple "plan" was prepared on 27–30 October 1818 by Vikentii Tabulevich, one of four naval cadets aboard the *Kamchatka*, taken on at the conclusion of their courses at the Naval Cadet Corps in

Kronstadt (1817), because of their distinction.[79] It was Golovnin's policy to take larger than usual numbers of midshipmen and naval cadets on his Pacific expeditions and, as this plan illustrates, to let them continue their training in a practical and useful way.[80]

APPENDICES

APPENDIX A

Lauri, Second Hawaiian Visitor to Russia
to Return to Honolulu

Vasilii Mikhailovich Golovnin did much to bring the peoples of the Great South Sea, in particular Polynesia, to the notice of his countrymen. In 1808, while being forcibly detained with the sloop *Diana* at Cape Town, he became the first known Russian to encounter and describe a Maori.[1] His comments on Matara, son and heir of the chief Te Pahi of the Bay of Islands, ran to seven hundred words and formed a colourful excursus in his *Puteshestvie Rossiiskago Imperatorskago shliupa Diany (Voyage of the Russian Imperial Sloop "Diana" from Kronstadt to Kamchatka ... in the Years 1807, 1808 and 1809*: St. Petersburg, 1819).[2] By then, however, he was well known to the Russian reading public for descriptions of New Hebridean natives (Tana islanders, Vanuatu), the Ainu of the Japanese-exploited Kuril Islands, and the Tlingits of the Russian Northwest Coast.[3] The *Diana*'s four-day stay at Tana Island (1809) had been related in the journal *Syn otechestva (Son of the Fatherland*: 1816),[4] and been enthusiastically received. If he had not described Hawaiians, it was not for lack of personal experience with those seafaring natives; he had encountered them while at Novo-Arkhangel'sk with the *Kamchatka* in July 1818, if not in 1809–10 at the conclusion of his mission with the *Diana*.[5]

Golovnin could not have been surprised to see Hawaiian seamen on the Northwest Coast. He was acquainted with Vancouver's, Broughton's, Langsdorf's, and Lisianskii's narratives, in all of which such travel had been mentioned.[6] Both the *Nadezhda* and the *Neva*, he knew, had been approached in 1804 by would-be crew members and globe-trotters.[7] Even while Golovnin was looking over Novo-Arkhangel'sk (with an unfriendly eye) in May–June 1810,[8] New England vessels with Hawaiians in their crew were in the area.[9] Among such vessels there when he returned with the *Kamchatka* (28 July–19 August 1818) were the *Volunteer* (Captain James Bennett) and the *Brutus* (Captain David Nye).[10] Nye, who spent some time with Golovnin (whom he was unexpectedly to meet again at Honolulu two months afterward),[11] had left in late December 1817. Thus the Hawaiians in his crew had been at sea eight months or more, reaching the Russian Northwest Coast by way of Chile.[12] Golovnin was not, perhaps, a true *savant* in Chamisso's or even Bellingshausen's mould. He had a keen eye and encyclopaedic interest in the Pacific and its peoples even so, and was by temperament and training disposed towards ethnography. As a lieutenant on secondment to the British (1802–1805), he had visited Jamaica and (like Kruzenshtern before him) had studied a social and administrative system that revolved around the fact of Negro labour.[13] As a visitor to Tana (1809), he had deliberately followed Cook's and Forster's very steps along "Port Resolution's" shore,[14] like them describing native structures, dress and ornament, canoes, diet, and language.[15] His eloquent and comprehensive essay "On the Sandwich Islands," which comprised Chapter XI of his 1822 account of the *Kamchatka*'s voyage around the globe,[16] is flattered by comparison with any other survey of the subject then available to European readers.

The Hawaiian known to Russians as Terentii, but to his own people as Lauri, approached the *Kamchatka* on the evening of 29 October 1818 (see Narrative 19). The sloop was on the point of leaving Honolulu. The man asked Golovnin to take him on and let him work his passage to some other country.[17] Golovnin agreed to do so, thinking of his possible utility to the Russian-American Company at Novo-Arkhangel'sk (in its commercial dealings with the Islands), if he could master Russian.

Since arriving at Oahu three days previously, Golovnin had come to recognize how necessary it had become that Russian interests and Russia's reputation, be effectively defended in a virtually Anglophone-free port. New England traders might be anglophobes, as well as anglophone, but this did not prevent them from representing Russia's North Pacific settlements as all of Russia to some credulous Hawaiians, as well as suggesting that Russians were the hungriest, most beggarly of *haole*. (How could they not be starving, since they lived in endless winter?)[18] Shortly after his return to Kronstadt (5 September 1819), Golovnin discussed this problem in a wide-ranging report to Traversay, the naval minister.[19] The fact serves, in itself, to underline the strength of Golovnin's annoyance with American belittlers of Russia's true position in the world. He was, in general, unfriendly to New England merchant interests.[20]

There was a precedent for his acceptance of a young Hawaiian seaman, though perhaps he did not know it. Here is an extract from the 1818 printed text of a journal kept in 1804 by Fedor Ivanovich Shemelin, Company clerk aboard the *Nadezhda* and an able amateur ethnologist:

> These islanders make long voyages of their own free will, and the king not only does nothing to prevent it but does not even want to know about it .... Captain Wolf of Boston had as many as six Sandwich Islanders in his crew aboard *Iunona* when at the port of Novo-Arkhangel'sk on Baranov Island, which belongs to the Russian-American Company. Among the six was a youth of perhaps sixteen whose name was Kenokhoia Kanehoa(?), who, at the invitation of *Kammerherr* and Chevalier Rezanov who was on the island at the time, agreed to travel to Russia with him. The youth had already been in both Canton and Boston. He is at present (1810?) in St. Petersburg and in the care of the government, as desired by His Majesty the Emperor. He has accepted the Christian faith and is known, after his godfather, as Vasilii Fedorovich Moller. Moller has

been taught to read and write Russian and is now studying shipbuilding and other sciences, including grammar, law, sacred history, arithmetic, geography, history, English, marine draughtsmanship, civil architecture, and sketching ....[21]

Shemelin's "Wolf" was the Rhode Island merchant and ship-master John d'Wolf, whose 250-ton ship *Juno (Iunona)* was bought by Chief Manager Baranov, together with her cargo, in October 1805.[22] Rezanov was a courtier, grandee, and chief official of the Russian-American Company, who had arrived in the Pacific with the *Nadezhda*.[23] Kanehoa did not travel to St. Petersburg with him; Rezanov died at Krasnoiarsk, Eastern Siberia, in 1807.[24] For a short time, the Hawaiian's situation was accordingly precarious. But as Shemelin writes, he did—in due course—reach the capital and find another patron and protector. Moller was a high State dignitary, with an interest in naval matters. Kanehoa's baptism was followed by traditional Hawaiian name-exchange, and he subsequently answered to the name Vasilii Moller. He remained in European Russia for eight years, taking passage from St. Petersburg to Sitka in the Company vessel *Kutuzov* (Captain-Lieutenant Gagemeister) in September 1816. He reached the Russian Northwest Coast fourteen months later, and apparently went on to Honolulu by the Company transport *Otkrytie* (Sitka to California) and some other craft. At least, Gagemeister's orders to Lieutenant Ia.A. Podushkin to that effect, are extant. Of his subsequent fate in the Islands, nothing is known.

Lauri proved popular aboard the *Kamchatka* and became attached to members of her crew. He reached St. Petersburg, in his turn, in September 1819, having paused to see Guam, Manila, St. Helena, Fayal, and Portsmouth.[25] Golovnin takes up the tale, in a narrative composed, judging by textual and circumstantial evidence, before 1821:

The Sandwich Islander Lauri is about twenty-five years old, of good height, well-built and lively. He is quite good looking and his skin tone is dark chestnut, which is common to all Sandwich Islanders. He has a gay disposition, a kind heart, and he is very intelligent and adaptable by nature. While still on the sloop, and here in St. Petersburg, he liked to follow our customs and tried to please all his acquaintances; and for this, he was loved by all who knew him. On the sloop, he became especially fond of one of the non-commissioned artillery officers who, for that very reason, was assigned to take care of him upon our arrival in Russia and to show him everything of interest to him in the city. It should be added that this under-officer could converse with him better than all the rest of us.

Lauri lived near the Semenovskii Bridge in a house of the Russian-American Company, but he often came to see me. He was so intelligent that within a few days he had learned where the quarters of all his friends were, and was walking without an escort even to Galernaia Harbour. Once

he bought a hat in a shop on Sennaia Street and brought it to show me.
Seeing that he had been cheated, I sent a non-commissioned officer back
to the shop with him to get his money refunded. Lauri led him directly
to the place where he had purchased the hat.

Some of his actions would surprise me very much and leave me in a state
of puzzlement. In society, for example, he could not bring himself to sit
down if he saw even one man whom he regarded as important; and when
tea or anything else was being handed around, he would always attempt
to be served last of all. He would watch carefully to be sure that he did not
sit or stand with his back towards anyone. I knew that nobody had taught
him all this and that he could not possibly have picked it up in Russia
in so short a time. It seemed, therefore, that he must have acquired such
politeness among his own countrymen. When asked to sing or to dance
in his native way, he would do so straightaway without any excuses and
always, moreover, with an air of pleasure. Our soft and subdued music
was not at all to his liking, but drums and the sound of trumpets delighted
him. Once, a certain celebrated female singer performed in my own house.
We led Lauri to the fortepiano, to see what impression the music, from
which everyone else was in raptures, would make on him. Having listened
for a couple of minutes, he said, "Enough, no good," which was his usual
phrase when something displeased him.

He loved to be of service to others and was prepared to do anything to
please. Once in the Mariana Islands several Spanish officials came out to
our ship. Lauri noticed that they kept their hats on while addressing our
officers and, having never seen anyone aboard presume to do so previously,
immediately snatched the hats off their heads and handed them to them.
We laughed; but the Spaniards found little amusing about it, till it was
explained to them who had taken the action.

In St. Petersburg, Lauri saw so many things that surpassed his understanding that he did not know what to wonder at most: mountain-like
buildings, huge ships, the splendour of attire (especially in churches), carriages, all these enraptured him equally. But best of all he liked a cavalry
parade. When the infantry marched by he would watch in amazement
and silence; but when the cavalry started forward and trumpets sounded,
he was beside himself. He would put a hand to his mouth in imitation
of a trumpet, make the appropriate sounds, and prance about with his
neck bent down like a horse's. It is easy to understand that people watching him took him for a lunatic—for he was always well-dressed and his
appearance bore no resemblance to that of a savage.

Lauri did not like to be laughed at. When we had reached the temperate zone and, for the first time in his life he saw a hailstorm, he
hurled himself forward and started collecting hailstones, doubtless mis-
taking them for pebbles. At the same time he gave us to understand by
gestures that he would take them off to Oahu, the island where he had
been born. As soon as he noticed that these pebbles were turning into
water and vanishing, he was the first to laugh at his mistake; but when
our seamen collected hailstones and brought them over to him, he at once
grew angry at the joke and complained to me. I recall another occasion

when our ship's cook, who usually brought the seamen's soup for me to taste, was carrying it back to the galley and Lauri also wanted to sample it. The cook gave him the cup and Lauri, not knowing what it was, took a mouthful and scalded himself. First he cried out, then, noticing that the seamen were laughing at him, he began to weep and came to me with a complaint against the cook.

He did not like strong drinks and he detested drunken people, but of sweet things he was particularly fond. He had only one noticeable vice: miserliness. On the sloop, we had provided him with clothing, underwear, everything necessary. The officers were always giving him gifts, and he had many superfluous things, yet he was always picking up bits of rag, pieces of string, broken needles and other such trifles, hiding them away in his trunk. In St. Petersburg he loved to dress well when going out, but at home he would wear the most dilapidated clothing, which should have already been thrown away. For the winter, the Company supplied him with excellent winter clothes, which he liked very much—especially a wolfskin fur coat. But he took such good care of this that, when calling on me, he would carry it over his arm and only put it on as we were ascending the staircase. He would then put it away in a safe place. As a result, he frequently suffered from colds and coughs and we were compelled to tell him that these things were not his own property, but had only been loaned to him temporarily by the Company—and so would be taken back on his departure and replaced by other, new clothes. Only then did he stop saving them and start wearing them more freely. Once some ladies purposely lost a few roubles to him in a game of dominoes. He was delighted and very gladly took the money; but as soon as he himself began to lose, he refused to pay anyone, saying "Don't know how," pocketing the money, and leaving the game. "Don't know how" was his usual negative expression, meaning "not so," "that is untrue," "I don't want to," etc.

At first, Lauri liked Russia very much and did not even want to hear about his homeland; but later, when all the new objects had lost their novelty, and especially when winter had given all nature a more deathly aspect than he could possibly have imagined before, our Lauri began to recall Oahu and to complain about the local climate. In the end, he frankly said he wished to live here no longer and would die if he could not return home. He particularly disliked ice and snow, of which he was always complaining. He also had no liking for beards, grey beards particularly.

At the time of Lauri's departure from St. Petersburg, I was in Riazan'. He would often come to visit our officers and ask about my return. At first, he thought we would again sail in the same ship back to the Sandwich Islands, taking him along; and learning that he would have to sail in a different vessel, with people unknown to him, he became very upset, wept, and was even ready to stay in Russia forever. Fortunately for him, four of the seamen on tis new ship had served aboard the *Kamchatka* and were thus well known to him.

If Lauri has returned safely to his homeland, his trip will be a great boon to the Russian-American Company and to our navigators generally, who may call at the Sandwich Islands. For there is no doubt that his gratitude and devotion to Russians will create a friendly feeling towards us among his fellow-countrymen, while the impression of Russia's power, which he will impart to the chiefs, will make them entertain more respect for a nation of which they had previously gained a very unfavourable impression.[26]

To judge by Kotzebue's conversation with Queen Lydia Nomahana of 21(?) January 1825, Golovnin's hopes were at least partially realized. Upon returning to Oahu, Lauri had spoken in awed tones of the size of the Russian capital, the vastness of its houses, and the horrors of its winter. He had also, to Kotzebue's pleasure, so spoken of Tsar Alexander I as to arouse Nomahana's interest in the portrait of the sovereign that hung in the *Riurik*'s wardroom. Kotzebue added the following remarks to the description of his meeting with Nomahana (see Narrative 61):

Having praised us for the remarkable invention that permitted us to keep heat in a house with the aid of fire, the queen announced that, were she to find herself in St. Petersburg in the season of frosts, she would not go out onto the street at all but would drive about indoors. Nomahana then wished to know why there were cold and warm times of the year in Russia. I tried to explain the cause of this phenomenon in a way that she could understand, and in fact quite satisfied her. "Lauri was right," she remarked amicably. "In Russia, there are very clever people."[27]

APPENDIX B

A Note on Trade Between Oahu and
the Russian Northwest Coast (1806–1826)

The Sandwich Island group is a very welcoming one for all vessels calling in on their passage to the Northwest Coast of America, the Aleutians, or Kamchatka. It has very safe bays and offers an abundance of hogs, breadfruit, bananas, coconuts, taro, yams, sweet potato, salt ... and other things highly desirable as ships' supplies.

G.H. Langsdorf[1]

In the course of their visit to the Hawaiian Islands of June 1804, both officers and others aboard the ships *Nadezhda* (Captain I.F. Kruzenshtern) and *Neva* (Captain Iu.F. Lisianskii) noted the Islands' commercial possibilities. Men of the *Neva* especially, who spent six busy days (11–16 June) at Kealakekua-Kaawaloa on the Kona Coast of Hawaii, trading 90 pounds of iron for eleven hogs, axes for fruit, and clothes for yams,[2] had time to recognize the possible utility of the Hawaiian Islands as a mid-Pacific food source and/or depot for Kamchatka and the Russian Northwest Coast. The feeding of those farflung settlements, where even hard grain cereals refused to ripen, was a major, longterm problem for the Russians to which no complete solution would be found.[3] Lieutenant Vasilii Nikolaevich Berkh, of the *Neva*, was one of several officers to emphasize the value of the Islands to Chief Manager A.A. Baranov in the spring of 1805. "One Russian naval vessel," he urged, "should be sent down to those Islands every autumn from Kamchatka. That vessel should winter in the Islands, returning to the peninsula in May."[4] Nikolai Ivanovich Korobitsyn, clerk (*prikazchik*) of the Russian-American Company also sailing in the *Neva*, was more specific in regard to Hawaiian resources that could be exported to Kamchatka and the Russian Northwest Coast. Included in his list were breadfruit, coconuts, hogs, goats and chickens, sweet potatoes, sugar-cane, and even cabbages.[5]

While on the Kona Coast, Lisianskii met New England beachcombers who had made voyages to Sitka in American Nor'westers, and indeed were well acquainted with the Russians' problems there; with the warlike Tlingit Indians, shipbuilding, and provisionment.[6] New Englanders, he learned, had linked the Islands and the Russian Northwest Coast at least since 1792. The Bostonian Joseph O'Cain, mate of the merchant vessel *Phoenix* (Captain Moore), which had paused to trade in Nuchek Sound that summer, had become a trading partner and a good friend of

Chief Manager Baranov.[7] Other Boston shipmasters provided intermittent contact between Sitka and Oahu.[8]

Insofar as it is possible to trace the genesis of a direct trade between Sitka and Oahu, it would seem to have resulted from American, not Russian, propositions to Kamehameha, made in 1805–06. In 1806, in any case, a Russian-American Company servant, the *promyshlennik* Pavel Slobodchikov, came to Oahu in a lately-purchased sloop, was kindly treated by Kamehameha, purchased foodstuffs, and returned with handsome presents from the king for the Chief Manager.[9] The visit, which was the first of many by Company ships (see Table 1), was mutually useful and passed off very pleasantly.

Table 1
Russian-American Company Vessels at Oahu and their Captains
1807–25

1807	*Nikolai*	Slobodchikov
1809	*Neva*	Gagemeister
1815	*Bering*	Bennett
1815	*Isabella*	Tyler
1816	*Otkrytie*	Podushkin
1816	*Il'mena*	Wadsworth
1823	*Golovnin*	Etolin
1824	*Riurik*	Khromchenko
1825	*Okhotsk*	Ingestrom

Slobodchikov reached Lower California in June 1806, as a result of an arrangement reached by the Chief Manager and Captain Jonathon Winship of the ship *O'Cain*. Winship, who had reached the Russian settlements by way of Honolulu two months earlier, had agreed to take Aleut hunters to the fur-rich shores of Spanish California and later split the profits of the voyage. *O'Cain* sailed south with four cossacks, twelve women, and no less than a hundred Aleuts with fifty *baidarkas* crammed onto her deck. The motley company anchored just north of Trinidad Bay on 10 June 1806, and, sea-otter and fish both being very plentiful, remained there for twelve days. They then proceeded south, sighting the Farallones Islands—where the Russians were to place a hunting post in 1812—to Cedros Island in Sebastian Vizcaino Bay (115°10'W, 28°12'N). Here and at San Quinton, sea-otter hunting and illicit trade continued satisfactorily.

In July, however, Winship and Slobodchikov fell out, apparently over the question of authority over the crucial Aleut hunters; and Slobodchikov, in his vexation and anxiety to break all contact with the Winship brothers, bought a little Yankee schooner or sloop for the modest price of 150 otter skins. (When the *O'Cain* returned to Sitka in late August, she had aboard 5,000 skins worth $60,000.) This little vessel, renamed the *Nikolai* at Cedros Island, was almost certainly the former *Tamana*, obtained from Kamehameha in exchange for the *Lelia Byrd* in 1805. Named for Queen Kaahumanu, the *Tamana* had been sent to California, under Captain John T. Hudson, in order to sell off the remainder of the *Lelia Byrd*'s cargo. In short, she was well known to the Hawaiians—and associated with a hopeful enterprise and friendly dealings. Kamehameha received the cossack chief hunter, the two or three New England hired hands, and the Hawaiian crew of *Nikolai*, with generosity. One of these hired hands, or conceivably another American beachcomber-sailor on Oahu at the time, named George Clark, was entrusted by the king with a variety of diplomatic missions on the Russian Northwest Coast when, after pleasant days and nights, the schooner *Nikolai* sailed from the Islands. (Such, in early nineteenth-century Oahu, was the disadvantage—suffered by Slobodchikov and his associates—of not speaking some English.) When the Chief Manager had been presented with the royal gifts and greetings, Mr. Clark was to propose a treaty whereby taro, breadfruit, coconuts, livestock, and rope would be exchanged for Russian ironware, timber, and textiles. Clark duly reached Sitka, and Baranov formalized the goods exchange with pen and paper.

Russian and American primary sources disagree as to the time of the *Nikolai*'s return. Kiril T. Khlebnikov and the historian P.I. Tikhmenev baldly state that it was August 1807, implying that Slobodchikov remained a year in the Islands. There are reasons to treat Russian sources gingerly, however, where the whole *O'Cain*-and-*Nikolai* venture is concerned. They are silent on the matter of the argument, are vague about the *Nikolai*'s course, and even claim that Winship was forbidden by Baranov to hunt otter off the Californian coast without particular permission from the Spanish (i.e. regional) authorities to that effect. The New England sources, which appear more trustworthy, all offer 1806 as the year both of Clark's *and* of the *Nikolai*'s reception by Baranov.[10] But however that may be, it is quite clear that Baranov was as pleased with King Kamehameha's gifts and friendly offer, as with Winship's and the Aleuts' haul of peltry. Thanks to George Clark's and Slobodchikov's effective work as intermediaries, plans were made in 1806-07, to give substance to the prospect of Hawaiin-Russian trade. Early in 1809, Captain-Lieutenant Gagemeister took the *Neva* back to Oahu for that purpose.

Gagemeister was the first Russian to make a comprehensive study of the market and the economic promise of Oahu. By extension, he was also first to feel the broadly jealous and/or anti-Russian attitudes of certain British residents already settled on Oahu. John Ii, the Hawaiian courtier-historian, even implies that the arrival of the *Neva* at Honolulu played its part in the disagreement between Isaac Davis and the (far less Russophobic) king (Ii, *Fragments of Hawaiian History*, 1963:79).

The stay, of almost three months (12 January–April 1809), was long enough for a full and careful reconnaissance. Kamehameha willingly gave twenty-two tons of high-grade salt, a little sandalwood, some pearls, salted pork, and dried taro in exchange for 1,805 fur-seal pelts and a number of walrus tusks.[11] The ivory tusks were used in the Islands to make ornaments and implements alike. Gagemeister recognized the potential value of Oahu to the Russian settlements, observing that any one of the Hawaiian Islands could provide everything that Russian America needed, including sugar-cane, livestock, and wheat. Even so, he cautioned against expansion of trade with the Islands controlled by King Kamehameha, whose monopoly of most trade areas had led to inflated prices.[12] Baranov accepted the argument and looked to Upper California for foodstuffs; in 1811, Ivan Aleksandrovich Kuskóv was sent to reconnoitre there. Fort Ross(iia) was built (1812–13) just north of San Francisco Bay.[13] Late in 1814, King Kaumualii, ruler of Kauai and Niihau, wrote to Baranov offering to trade sandalwood, taro, "anything on the island that you may want," in exchange for articles with which to keep Kamehameha and his well-armed troops at bay: guns, ammunition, gunpowder, carpenter's tools, blacksmith's equipment, canvas, and a ship.[14] Baranov responded in 1815. The consequence was the ill-starred Scheffer affair. All trade and commerce between Russia's Northern outposts and Oahu ceased, at least as far as both the Company and King Kamehameha were concerned.

For five years thereafter (1817–21), direct Russo-Hawaiian trade was stymied by political and practical considerations. Chief among the former was Kamehameha's lingering distrust of Russia's longterm aims and policies in the mid-Pacific; chief among the latter were the relatively steep prices of foodstuffs and supplies at Honolulu, thanks in essence to the fast-growing demand of foreign ships,[15] and the necessity to pound and dry taro (for export flour) before loading could begin.[16]

Such contact as existed between Company officialdom at Sitka and Kamehameha, in the three-year period from 1817–1819, was maintained by the obliging agency of North American (New England) shipmasters with business in the Islands and along the Northwest Coast alike. Chief among these were Thomas Meek, Henry Gyzelaar, and David Nye, all three of whom sailed to Sitka (in the *Eagle*, *Clarion*, and *Brutus* respectively) in 1818–19, incidentally delivering messages and economic news from Honolulu. Meek and Nye had homes in Honolulu (October 1818); and nearby they stored the Chinese goods brought to the Islands from Canton, where they had profitably sold the fur-seal peltry lately picked up on the Russian Northwest Coast. For statistics, we consult reports by Kirill T. Khlebnikov (1776–1838), administrator and historian of the Russian-American Company (see Bibliography under Khlebnikov, K.T., and Gibson, J.R.)

The 190-ton brig *Brutus* and her captain, David Nye, had particularly frequent contacts with the Russians and Hawaiians in these economically intense post-Scheffer years. Finally, in the spring of 1819, the Company purchased the brig, complete with guns and cargo, for 5,000 fur-seal pelts. Shortly thereafter, she was sent to Honolulu and Waimea, Kauai with a supercargo, under Karl Johann Schmidt (Russian: Shmit), to buy provisions and, if opportunity arose, to lay the groundwork for resumption of Hawaiian-Russian trade. Schmidt had not been long in the Pacific but had made a good impression on the officialdom at Sitka. (He became Company Manager at Fort Ross in Upper California and much expanded agriculture there in 1821–24, so that that post was for awhile self-sufficient.) Khlebnikov (1976:65–66) takes up the story:

> Schmidt carried out the first part of his instructions; he reached the island ... and met King Kamehameha, [*sic*] who said among other things that although the items which the doctor [Scheffer] had given him were still intact, he was willing to pay for them. He said that he had eight bolts of frieze, four bolts of blue wool, 80 axes, 10 flagons of powder, a schooner with arms and sails, two cast iron cannon and two bronze cannon. The king agreed to pay 200 pikuls of the best sandalwood for these items, on condition that he be paid 15 barrels of English powder in exchange for the maintenance of Company personnel ....

Khlebnikov passes in silence over Schmidt's passage from Kauai to Oahu as, indeed, over the failure of the mission as a whole (which would appear to have dragged on many months). It is clear from a letter from the acting Company Chief Manager, S.I. Ianovskii, dated 20 April 1820, that in fact Schmidt had obtained no satisfaction from King Kaumualii, who perhaps would be more helpful "if a well-armed ship or two" went to Waimea. The materials appear, in English translation but in extract, in Pierce (1965:155–56). As for *Brutus*'s short visit to Oahu, it is totally ignored by Ianovskii and Khlebnikov, despite the fact that a New England pilot, Stevens, had been taken on at Honolulu Harbour. If the visit was of any use whatever in restoring trade relations between Sitka and Oahu, now controlled by Liholiho, then materials to prove the point are lost.

By 1820, most fresh provisions could be had cheaper from Boston or New York than from Oahu. Nonetheless, it was in 1821 that Captain Petr Ivanovich Rikord, Governor of Kamchatka (1817–22), wrote to Liholiho to propose that a direct trade be resumed between Kamchatka and/or Sitka and Oahu. Rikord, a former comrade of Golovnin and a man with much experience of British and New England enterprise

abroad, wrote to the youthful king in English. The letter was examined
by officers of the Russian sloop *Blagonamerennyi* at Honolulu in March
1821, (see Narrative 127). Rikord proposed a straight exchange of furs
for salt. The brig *Thaddeus* (Captain William Sumner) duly sailed from
Oahu for Kamchatka with a cargo of salt and other goods.[17] The salt,
obtained from the Aliapaakai lake, a little west of Honolulu, was approved by the Governor; but fresh foodstuffs were no less welcome in
Kamchatka. Since the fall of 1820, the authorities at Petropavlovsk and
at Novo-Arkhangel'sk had been obliged, despite their wishes, to enforce
an isolationist and even xenophobic policy whereby all foreign ships and
traders were excluded from the Company's own settlements and waters. Semi-isolation from the outside world, and periodic hunger in the
settlements became inevitable.[18] Then, in September 1821, came two
provocative imperial ukazes. By the first, Russia claimed sovereignty
over territory in America down to 51°N, extending to 115 miles offshore
on both the North American and Asian sides of the Pacific Ocean. By
the second, the Company was granted a monopoly of fur hunting, trading, and fishing, in those seas and on their islands for a further twenty
years. Foreign merchantmen were liable to seizure and their goods to
confiscation. In particular, New England shipmasters were warned not
to attempt to trade with Indians, for furs or other goods, on shores
in Russian jurisdiction. Russian warships would patrol the coasts in
question.[19]

In reality, American free traders at Kamchatka or at Sitka had, since
1817 or slightly earlier, been steadily diversifying their (already well assorted) trade goods. Even in the early 1800s, most Nor'westers carried
far more varied wares up to the Coast than had "King George's men,"
their rivals. Some New Englanders, notably Thomas Meek, Henry Gyzelaar, Andrew Blanchard, and David Nye, made a large part of *their*
profit in the Northwest Coast or "Sitka trade" of 1817-20, not from
furs but by supplying the beleaguered Russian settlements with food,
supplies, and stores from Honolulu.[20] Russian visitors of 1821 and later
years were hospitably received and given practical assistance on Oahu
by the Meeks, Blanchard, and Nye (see Narratives 132 and 134). In
an invaluable twelve-part survey of Russian America in 1833, published
in 1834, K.T. Khlebnikov gives details of this New England-managed
Honolulu-Russian Coastal trade.[21] According to Khlebnikov, twelve of
the eighteen foreign ships that called at Novo-Arkhangel'sk in 1818-23
inclusive, had the Islands as their final destination; and no less than
five had also *started* trading voyages at Honolulu (Table 2). The Russian ban on international trade of 1820, never recognized officially by
Congress or by Yankees in the North Pacific trade, was an annoyance
to the latter: in a single twelve-week cruise from Honolulu to the settlements and back, allowing sixty days at sea, a little brig like the *Clarion*

(Captain H. Gyzelaar) could make a sale worth 4,000 Spanish dollars (June 1819). To the Russians and their servants on the Coast, the ban gave substance to the prospect of starvation.[22]

Table 2
Foreign Shipping and Related Trade Values
at Novo-Arkhangel'sk
1818–26

Year	Ship	Captain	Origin	Destination	Purchase Value*
1818	Le Bordelais	De Roquefueil (Fr)	California	Canton	5,514
1818	Brutus	Nye	New England	New England	n/a
1818	Columbia	Robson (Brit)	England	California	n/a
1818	Mentor	Suter	New England	New England	n/a
1818	Volunteer	Bennett	New England	Canton	n/a
1818	Eagle	T. Meek	Hawaiian I.	Hawaiian I.	2,346
1819	Brutus	Nye	New England	Hawaiian I.	2,707
1819	Eagle	T. Meek	Hawaiian I.	Hawaiian I.	?
1819	Clarion	Gyzelaar	Hawaiian I.	Hawaiian I.	4,149
1819	Volunteer	Bennett	New England	Hawaiian I.	930
1820	Thaddeus	Blanchard	New England	Hawaiian I.	11,601
1820	Pedler	Pigot [Piggott]	Kamchatka	Hawaiian I.	4,135
1821	Arab	T. Meek	Boston	Hawaiian I.	12,939
1822	Sultan	Clark	New England	Hawaiian I.	893
1822	Pedler	J. Meek	Canton	Hawaiian I.	7,776
1822	Arab	T. Meek	Canton	Hawaiian I.	21,177
1823	Pearl	Stevens	Hawaiian I.	Hawaiian I.	680
1823	Arab	T. Meek	Hawaiian I.	Hawaiian I.	34,203
1824	Tamaahmaah	J. Meek	New England	California	n/a
1825	Lapwing	Blanchard	Boston	Hawaiian I.	42,655
1825	Parthenon	Valdes	Hawaiian I.	Hawaiian I.	1,212
1826	Sultan	Allen	Boston	Hawaiian I.	17,550
1826	Chinchilla	T. Meek	Boston	Canton	19,092
1826	Tally Ho	McNeill	New England	Hawaiian I.	2,873

*In Spanish piastres.
Sources: Khlebnikov, 1972:7–12; Ivashintsev, 1980:1.

By 1822, the colonies were in desperate straits.[23] Captain Matvei Ivanovich Murav'ev, the Governor of Russian North America, appealed urgently to the directors of the Company for foodstuffs. Since, however, their response could not be felt for twelve or even fifteen months (such

was the distance of the colonies from European Russia), he dispatched
Lieutenant Adol'f Kárlovich Etólin (or Etholen: 1790–1876) to Oahu for
a cargo of provisions. Ostensibly, Etolin was to concentrate on buying
salt at Honolulu, having first bartered a load of furs for grain in California. In reality, his orders were to get whatever foodstuffs were available
and not beyond his means at Honolulu. A veteran of the *Kamchatka*
expedition (1817–19), Etolin was a physically resilient and enterprising
officer. In 1821–22 he and Vasilii Stepanovich Khromchenko, who had
been Kotzebue's mate aboard the *Riurik*, had done distinguished survey work in Bristol Bay. By 1840, he would be the Governor of Russian
North America, a true "lord of the Indians" at Novo-Arkhangel'sk.[24]
Sailing by way of San Francisco, Etolin took the Company-owned brig
Golovnin (ex-*Brutus*) to Honolulu. An American-built merchantman,
she had been bought by Chief Manager Baranov (1818) only months
before his death.[25] The voyage was successful, incidentally returning
Thomas Meek to Honolulu. Here is Khlebnikov (1976:66):

> Etolin had bought the brig *Arab* from Meek, together with its cargo; he
> had come to Sitka with both ships. Meek and his crew had to be taken
> to the Islands, and so the *Riurik* was sent for that purpose. Meek agreed
> to load it with salt in the Sandwich Islands ... .

Like the *Brutus*, Meek's brig *Arab* served the Company far better
for the next several years than any vessel built at Sitka or Fort Ross
(see Gibson, 1976:39–40), connecting Honolulu with the Russian Northwest Coast and California. An oak-built ship of 230 tons unladen, she
was renamed *Baikal*. As for the *Riurik*, she was the heroine of Kotzebue's expedition (1815–18) and, like Adol'f K. Etolin, came from Finland
(Kotzebue, *Voyage*, I:15). Satisfied with the results of *Golovnin's* Hawaiian call, Governor Murav'ev repeated the experiment in 1824. This time,
Lieutenant Khromchenko was sent to Honolulu in the *Riurik*; for him
and for the brig, it was a happy return to scenes and friends of 1817.
It was perhaps true, as the Company Head Office claimed in 1822, that
"of the Island products, none are to be had for our possessions ... but
salt, which can be bought more cheaply, nearer base, and at the same
time as some grain, in California."[26] Even so, it seemed expedient to
Murav'ev to build goodwill, buy certain foodstuffs, and maintain the
Russian presence at Oahu. Like Etolin, Khromchenko was highly capable and destined to pursue a long career in the service of the Company
and Crown in the Pacific.[27] The *Riurik* was laden with a thousand quintals (rather more than fifty tons) of salt, as well as foodstuffs.[28] On her
return to Sitka, Khlebnikov's assistant listed those supplies and other
goods, as follows (Klebnikov, 1976:66):

217	gallons rum
133	gallons cognac
1,270	English lbs. of sea biscuits
500	English lbs. of sperm candles
18	barrels tar
39	barrels coconut oil

The price was 3,086 *piastres*, of which only 300 were immediately paid in cash, the rest being translated into 2,000 good fur-seal skins for sale in Canton. The spermaceti candles, tar, and cognac that were carried up to Sitka were, of course, not of Hawaiian manufacture; but the oil and the rum were very likely from Oahu, like the high-grade salt from the Aliapaakai Lake, of which the Russians had by now seen many shipments. Of the other likely exports from that island, Khlebnikov made special note of taro root and good jute cordage, meaning coir or *olona* twine such as New Englanders (and Captain Golovnin) had bought and praised. It was the taro that was needed on the coast, rather than rope; nor can the value to the Russians of continuing *entente* with men like Meek, Davis, and Nye be understood, unless one is aware of the wretched state in which the Company possessions found themselves as a result of the imperial ukazes banning international trade along the Russian Northwest Coast. Russo-Hawaiian trade was carried on, by the New Englanders and servants of the Company themselves, within the grim context of shortages and hunger in the North.[29] The point is eloquently made by naval visitors to Sitka in their private correspondence. Here, for instance, is an extract from a depressing note from Midshipman Pavel Nakhimov of the *Kreiser* (Captain Mikhail P. Lazarev) to his service friend, Lieutenant Mikhail F. Reineke:

> We finally reached Sitka on 23 September 1823. A sorry place it is, with a wretched climate—cruel winds and incessant rain. One can get practically nothing there, and even if there is something available, it's only for an exorbitant sum. No fresh food except fish, and precious little even of that in the winter months! But we had plenty of work, at least: an amazing number of rats had bred aboard, spoiling absolutely everything without discrimination. We had no choice but to unlade the whole frigate, fumigate her, then relade her. And *that* took up three weeks ....[30]

For the companies of the *Kreiser* and the *Ladoga*, the voyage out to Sitka had been hard. But in comparison with problems faced by Murav'ev in 1822–24, those of the seamen had been small. Murav'ev did not rebel against his orders, unavoidable though the resultant hardships were, and finally he was constrained by his own conscience to infringe upon them. By the time he had dispatched Lieutenant Khromchenko to

Honolulu in the *Riurik*, the failures of the new supplying policies and of
the trade bans had become too obvious to be ignored in St. Petersburg.
Too late, the Company Main Office sent permission for employees of the
Company to trade with North Americans and others, if such trade was
"necessary" and would not "result in loss."[31] Tired and disillusioned with
the Coast and his appointment, Murav'ev was looking forward to a swift
return to Europe. The decision to replace him had, in any case, been
taken in the capital.[32] Meanwhile, however, Company servants needed
food and so, in April 1825, he sent another brig to buy it in Oahu.

Once again, a Yankee merchantman fitted the bill; and once again,
the Company agreed to "rental with a view to purchase" terms, whereby
her master, Andrew Blanchard, would surrender his command but take
a share in whatever profits came. His brig, the *Lapwing*, was the size
and length of the *Riurik*, but had considerably greater cargo space. She
made the voyage to Oahu from the Coast, carrying fur-seal skins in bundles, with Andrei Ingestrom or Ingestrem commanding. On arrival, she
was known as the *Okhotsk*. Despite a crisis in Hawaiian State affairs,
(Captain Lord Byron had returned to Honolulu with the corpse of Liholiho and his queen in early June, and the Hawaiians' independence of
Great Britain was itself not very clear), Ingestrom found ways of doing
normal business. The *Okhotsk* (ex-*Lapwing*) was in due course laden,
in the words of Khlebnikov, with "1,160 *quintals* of local lake salt ... as
well as various other items of local production."[33]

Among the "other items," were locally-grown produce and a store of
sugar candy. The former was for use aboard the brig and for immediate consumption when she reached the colonies; the latter was for use
as a convenient and easily transported source of sugar, in the winter
months. More than a quarter century earlier, Lieutenant Peter Puget of
the *Chatham* had predicted that Hawaiian sugar-cane would soon "repay
in quantity" whatever "Labour was bestowed on it, in Sugar ...."[34] If the
candy that the *Okhotsk* carried to Sitka had itself not been produced
from the Oahu sugar crop, it was a sign of things to come. Within nine
months of her departure, an ambitious British settler named Wilkinson would have begun the enterprise in the Manoa Valley east of Honolulu that the officers of the *Krotkii* (Captain F.P. Wrangel) were to
see (Narrative 129). Controlled by Boki Kamauleule, after Wilkinson's
untimely death, that sugar mill increased production (1826–28); and as
before some sugar found its way to Oregon and to the Russian Northwest Coast.[35] As for the salt from the Aliapaakai and/or Aliamanu Lake
east of Halawa—also carried north by the Okhotsk in 1825—it was both
stored and used in Novo-Arkhangel'sk.[36]

Disrupted by the Russian trade bans and ukazes of 1820–21, New England seaborne commerce between Sitka, Petropavlovsk-in-Kamchatka,
and Oahu, gained another lease of life upon the conclusion of a Russo-

American convention (17 April 1824) that resolved the trade and sovereignty issues on the Northwest Coast.[37] Four of the five New England ships that called at Novo-Arkhangel'sk to trade in 1825–26 (see Table 2) had Honolulu as their home port and/or final destination. In conjunction with Oahu-Sitka trade in Russian bottoms (*Nikolai* and *Neva*), it was a commerce that not only reinforced the Russian factor in Pacific trade and commerce as a whole, but also kept Hawaiians' consciousness of Russia and her colonies alive. That consciousness could only shrink when, after 1826, the naval Governors of Russian North America looked to Old Oregon and Upper California, and not to Honolulu, for supplies. How little even Khlebnikov knew of the real economic and political position on Oahu by the early 1830s is apparent from the fact that he was ignorant of terms whereby the chiefs' sandalwood debts of long before had been resolved.[38] Only in 1845–54, as a result of the collapse of agriculture on the fertile West Coast of North America (during the California gold rush), did the Company resume its trade with Honolulu. Then, once more, salt and a range of local foodstuffs were exchanged for fish and timber from the Coast.[39]

APPENDIX C

The Honolulu Aquarelles of Emel'ian Kornéev

The Hawaiian aquarelles painted by Louis Choris of the *Riurik* in 1816–17, and first published in Paris in 1822 or 1826, have long been recognized as an important ethnographic legacy, discussed in print, and reproduced in popular and learned works alike.[1] The "Honolulu" drawings of *Kamchatka*'s serf-born artist, Mikhail Tikhanov, are perhaps not universally acclaimed like Choris's, but have attracted much attention nonetheless.[2] By contrast, Emel'ian Mikhailovich Kornéev, expeditionary artist in the sloop *Otkrytie* (Captain Mikhail N. Vasil'ev), who called at Honolulu twice in 1821 (25 March–7 April, 27 November–20 December), remains unknown to Western scholarship. That his Hawaiian work should be so unfamiliar is not surprising; most of it was lost during the flooding of St. Petersburg in November 1824, and what was saved was later lost, to all intents and purposes, in departmental chanceries and archives.[3] The destruction of that 1821 material was, to be sure, a loss for Polynesian studies. Thanks, however, to researches by Miss N.N. Goncharóva of the Soviet Academy of Arts (1969–73), it has for twelve years been possible to reconstruct the "Honolulu portion" of Korneev's lost portfolio.[4] This appendix merely reports the fact, adding some detail of long-lost watercolours on the basis of archival documents in TsGIAL and TsGAVINF, and an outline of Korneev's life and work.

Emel'ian Mikhailovich Korneev (1780–184?) was of merchant antecedents. His father had, however, been acknowledged *dvorianin*, or noble, from Poltava. Korneev had been enrolled at the St. Petersburg Academy of Arts in 1789 and remained there until 1800, under the guidance of the landscape painter Grigorii Ugriúmov, who also specialized in large-scale classical canvases. He was then appointed "pensioner" of the Academy, which gave him travel and financial privileges. In 1802–04, he served as artist in the Siberian expedition led by the Finnish-born General G.M. Sprengtporten (1741–1819). He acquitted himself well as a recorder of local scenes, costumes, materials, and individuals, and was rewarded by the Crown. Many of his Siberian pieces were published, handsomely engraved, in Karl Rechberg's edition of *Les Peuples de la Russie* (Paris, 1812–13). Korneev had been named an Academician in 1807, for a large painting on a mythological theme, now lost. Twelve years later, according to the President of the Academy of Arts, A.N. Olenin, a latent *Wanderlust* induced him to volunteer as one of the artists required on the two-pronged polar expedition that was then being prepared.[5]

Messrs Kornéev and Mikhailov, [wrote Olenin to the minister of education, Prince A.N. Golitsyn] both personally expressed a desire to take
part in this venture ... Mr. Kornéev, who is an Academician, some time
ago travelled for many years across Asia and Europe, and the fruits of his
work will be known to your committee through the descriptive volume of
costumes of peoples inhabiting Russia, published by Count Reichberg ....[6]

A middle-aged man of established reputation but in straitened circumstances, Korneev was not the likeliest of candidates for his position; but
his talents and Olenin's warm recommendation secured him a berth
aboard the *Otkrytie*. Olenin himself wrote "Instructions Regarding
Artistic Duties," article (i) of which began as follows:

> Your duty as artist on this expedition now setting out for a distant voyage
> is to draw everything that you may chance to meet during the voyage that
> is of interest, in whatever area it may be. Views of islands, shores, towns,
> settlements, structures of all kinds, representations of natives, their attire,
> ornament, domestic utensils, weaponry, sacred rites, solemn and other
> ceremonies, entertainments, gymnastic games, instruments and so forth,
> animals, birds, fish and insects, in sum, curious products of Nature of
> every variety should be the subjects of your labours.[7]

Like Pavel N. Mikhailov, who was appointed to the *Vostok* (Captain
Faddei F. Bellingshausen), bound for the farthest South,[8] Korneev was
enjoined by Olenin "under no circumstances ever to draw anything from
memory alone, when it is impossible to compare your sketch with the
original." Imaginative flights were to be halted at the outset; it was
scrupulous accuracy that was needed by the Navy.

Korneev returned to Kronstadt with his portfolio on 2 August 1822.
The portfolio was already in Captain Vasil'ev's keeping.[9] Vasil'ev forwarded it to the naval ministry which, shortly after, sent it back to
Korneev for reworking with a view to lithography. No little time and
energy was needed. Korneev had at least 300 sketches with which to
deal, and he was given just twelve months in which to do it. That
year elapsed on 5 March 1823. Korneev asked for more time, observing
that the ministry had been presented with sixty-five completed drawings at the time of his return from the Pacific, and had since then been
handed three dozen more, for a total of 101. The ministry expressed
some reservations, but was swayed by formal letters from Olenin and
Vasil'ev requesting that Korneev be allowed more time to "work up his
account," and have his expeditionary salary extended until the work
should be complete.[10]

No money was forthcoming, however, and by 1824 the harried artist
was in dire need. He sought a monetary pension like Tikhanov's: the
Kamchatka's artist, he observed, received 600 roubles annually, and had

earned that sum. Not until 1826 did the authorities award Korneev 720 roubles per annum.[11] By then his situation in St. Petersburg was desperate. His aquarelles and drawings from the *Otkrytie*, on which he had been staking his security, had mostly been destroyed in the appalling inundation of 7 November 1824. "During that flood, I lost my property and my wife's too."[12] It was a matter of considerable urgency, accordingly, that the 101 drawings in Crown possession be returned to him. He could then publish an assortment—a delayed Pacific echo of *Les Peuples de la Russie*—and so, with luck, recoup his fortunes and his health. But such a book would need support from the imperial authorities. Quixotically, Korneev estimated that he needed an advance of 45,000 roubles from the Crown to publish 300 copies of an Atlas containing 150 sheets. That sum was speedily denied him. He was left to struggle on, because (Prince A.N. Golitsyn learned from the naval minster, Admiral A.V. Moller), it was possible that an account of the *Otkrytie–Blagonamerennyi* Pacific venture by the leader, Captain Vasil'ev, might be approved and published; and in that event, Korneev's illustrations would be used.[13] Vasil'ev's narrative was, in fact, never published.

By this time, the "Korneev files" at the St. Petersburg Academy of Arts and the Naval Ministry were growing thick. They continued to expand for several years, while Korneev's health and prospects were declining. Relevant *fonds* from the Academy of Arts are held today at the Central State Historical Archive of the USSR (TsGIAL) in Leningrad. The principal *fond* is 789. Materials relating to the participation of Korneev, Pavel N. Mikhailov, and Mikhail T. Tikhanov in Pacific expeditions are to be found in: op. i, pt. 1, *dela* 1854, 1949, 1961, 2460, 2952; op. 1 pt. 2, *dela* 123, 207, 249, 262, 546, 595, 1660, 2557; op. 2, *delo* 28; op. 20, *dela* 7, 9, 17, 19, 28, 30, 36, 48 & 74. Complementary documents are held in TsGAVMF, *fond* 205, op. 1, *delo* 644 and *fond* 213, op. 1, *dela* 52, 101, 104. These materials were microfilmed by the Soviet authorities during the 1960s. Copies were acquired by the University of Alaska at Fairbanks in 1982, and are now held there in the Elmer E. Rasmusen Research Library, under reference: Shur Collection, reels 85, 98, 102, 105.

As observed, the naval ministry received sixty-five drawings from Korneev in August 1822, and another thirty-six within a year. Report 351 offers cursory descriptions of both collections. The first list, (of sixty-five drawings finished at sea), contains four Oahu items; the second, (of thirty-six drawings completed in St. Petersburg by 1823), contains another seven. A third list, which apparently does not overlap the earlier two, contains two more. We thus know of thirteen of the drawings begun by Korneev on Oahu in 1821. They are:

1.	List 1: 25	Sandwich Islanders Rolling Round Stones
2.	List 1: 32a	The Interior of a Sandwich Island House
3.	List 1: 32b	The King of the Sandwich Islands In a Boat
4.	List 1: 33	A Sandwich Island Dance on the Island of Vagu [Oahu]
5.	List 2: 19	A Sandwich Island Dance in the Fort on the Island of Vagu
6.	List 2: 20	Preparation for the Dance
7.	List 2: 21	A Sandwich Island Dance on the Island of Vagu
8.	List 2: 32	The Rich Attire of Well-born Sandwich Islanders
9.	List 2: 33	Kamegamega [Kamehameha], King of the Sandwich Islands, on a Visit to the Sloops
10.	List 2: 59a	Tropical Fish on the Sandwich Islands
11.	List 2: 59b	A Fire that Occurred on Vagu Island, 13 December 1821
12.	List 3: 16	A Sandwich Island Dance
13.	List 3: 17	Dinner of the Younger Queen of the Sandwich Islands On the Island of Vagu

No less than five of the thirteen drawings, one sees, are of Hawaiian dances in progress or in preparation. Another five would necessarily have shown Hawaiian dress. Thus, only Nos. 10 and 11 stand outside an essentially anthropocentric sub-collection. Korneev's emphasis reflects, and is complemented by, the same emphasis in his countrymen's narrative evidence of Honolulu. The Russian verb selected in No. 1 (*kataiushchie*) indicates that the game in question was *'ulumaika*: the discs were being bowled as far as possible across a prepared level area (Ellis, 1839:198). The Russians saw the game being played in Honolulu. The "younger queen" of Liholiho may be taken to mean Kamamalu. The king's own visit to "both sloops," accompanied by two wives and a large retinue (24 March 1821), is described by Lazarev, 1950:259–60 and Gillesem, 1849:222–23 in sufficient detail for very cautious reconstruction of Korneev's drawing No. 9 to be feasible. The dance of No. 5 took place inside Fort Kaahumanu because of Kalanimoku's dual role as commandant there and main intermediary between Shishmarev and the Hawaiian *ali'i*. Feather cloak is certainly subsumed by the Russian term, *odeianie*, describing Korneev's drawing No. 8. Tikhanov too, in October 1818, had succumbed to the urge to paint such a cloak, familiar though it was to Europeans (see Plate 17).

NOTES and BIBLIOGRAPHY

Abbreviations

AGO	Arkhiv Geograficheskogo Obshchestva (Leningrad)
AHR	American History Review (Washington, D.C.)
AVPR	Arkhiv Vneshnei Politiki Rossii (Moscow) Correspondence. Great Britain: Parliamentary Papers. Correspondence Relative to the Sandwich Islands (London, 1843)
BM	Bernice P. Bishop Museum (Honolulu)
CHQ	California Historical Quarterly (San Francisco)
DNB	Dictionary of National Biography (London, 1885–1912)
DLL	Deutsches Literatur-Lexicon, ed. B. Berger (Bern, 1968–84)
ES	Entsiklopedicheskii slovar' (St. Petersburg, F.A. Brokgauz and I.A. Efron, 1890–1907)
HAA	Hawaiian Almanac and Annual (Honolulu)
HHS	Hawaiian Historical Society (Honolulu)
IVGO	Izvestiia Vsesoiuznogo Geograficheskogo Obshchestva (Leningrad)
LOII	Leningradskoe Otdelenie Instituta Istorii Academii Nauk SSSR
MAE	Miklukho-Maklai Institute of Anthropology and Ethnography (Leningrad)
MHSP	Massachusetts Historical Society Proceedings (Boston)
NUC	National Union Catalog (pre-1956 imprints)
OMS	Obshchii morskoi spisok (St. Petersburg, 1885–1907)
PHR	Pacific Historical Review (Berkeley)
PNQ	Pacific Northwest Quarterly (Seattle)
PRO	Public Record Office (London)
PSZRI	Polnoe sobranie zakonov Rossiiskoi Imperii (St. Petersburg)
RAK	Rossiisko-Amerikanskaia Kompaniia
Razr.	Razriad (category)
SMAE	Sbornik Muzeia Antropologii i Etnografii (Leningrad)
TsGIAL	Central State Historical Archive (Leningrad)
TsGADA	Central State Archive of Ancient Acts (Moscow)
TsGIAE	Central State Historical Archive of the Estonian Republic (Tartu)
TsGAVMF	Central State Archive of the Navy of the USSR (Leningrad)
ZAD/ZADMM	Zapiski Admiralteiskago Departamenta Morskago Ministerstva (St. Petersburg)
ZGDMM	Zapiski Gidrograficheskago Departamenta Morskago Ministerstva (St. Petersburg)
ZUKMS	Zapiski Uchonogo Komiteta Morskago Shtaba (St. Petersburg)
USNA	United States National Archives (Washington, D.C.)

Notes to the Chapters

NOTES TO THE PREFACE

1. Barratt, 1984; Lisianskii, 1812, 1:164–216.
2. Gibson, 1976:209–10; Andreev, 1944:171.
3. Howay, 1973:27–57; Khlebnikov, 1973:8; Gibson, 1976:154–58; Morison, 1961:52–57.
4. Howay, 1930:11–21; Langsdorf, 1813–14, 1:187–88.
5. Rezanov, 1825; Tikhmenev, 1939:432.
6. Pierce, 1965:5–33.
7. Berkh, 1818:162; Sheffer Papers, Rossiisko-Amerikanskaia Kompaniia (translation by G. Lantzeff): Bancroft Library at University of California, Berkeley, MS P–N 4:11–12.
8. Tikhmenev, 1861, 1:166; Khlebnikov, 1835:161–62; Campbell, 1816:81; Barratt, 1981a:155–56.
9. On this, see Gibson, 1976:44–52.
10. I touch on this question in Barratt, 1981b:5–10.
11. Barratt, 1981a:140–41, 176–80.
12. See Bibliography on Hannibal Evans Lloyd's 1821 (London) version of Kotzebue's *Voyage* of that year, Victor S.K. Houston's 1939 rendering of parts of Chamisso's accounts of the Hawaiian Islands, and Ella Wiswell's recent and excellent translation of V.M. Golovnin's *Voyage* in the sloop *Kamchatka* (1818–21).

NOTES TO CHAPTER ONE

1. *PSZRI*, vol. 6, doc. 3682.
2. Lebedev, 1950:133–35.
3. Sokolov, 1848:175–83; *PSZRI*, vol. 22, doc. 16530.
4. Armstrong, 1979:1–15.
5. Sopikov, 1813: nos. 9206–08 for Russian translations of Cook; see also Hotimsky, 1971:3–12.
6. Anderson, 1956; Cross, 1980.
7. Beaglehole, 1967, pt. 1:447–58; pt. 2:1242, 1338–39.
8. Okun', 1951:10ff.; Barratt, 1981a:75–89.
9. TsGADA, *fond* Vorontsova, A.R., d. 367; Grenader, 1957:25–35; Penrose, 1959:88–96.
10. For entertaining commentary on this matter, see Nabokov, 1964, 2:162–64.
11. See Barratt, 1979a:2.
12. Okun', 1951:14; Barratt, 1979b:228.
13. Kotzebue, 1821, 1:6, 155.
14. Gennadi, 1876, 1:232.
15. Sopikov, 1813, no. 9206; Hotimsky, 1971:7.
16. Barratt, 1979b:228.
17. See n. 5.
18. Beaglehole, 1967, pt. 1:654, 714; pt. 2, appendix.

19. Ledyard, 1966: intro.; *Gentleman's Magazine*, 55 (1785), 2:570–71; Ts-GADA, *fond* Gosarkhiva, *razr.* 24, d. 61 (possible employment of Willem Bolts, et al).
20. TsGADA, *fond* Gosarkhiva, *razr.* 10, op. 3, d. 16 (orders for Mulovskii's people); TsGAVMF, *fond* 172, d. 376:261ff (Admiralty collation of recent British charts of the North Pacific Ocean, by V.P. Fozdezin).
21. Barratt, 1979b:218–19.
22. TsGAVMF, *fond* I.G. Chernysheva, d. 376:20–40 (P.P. Soimonov, "Notes on Trade and Hunting in the Eastern Ocean"); also 322–23 (orders of 22 Dec. 1786 regarding the Pacific routes and activities of "two vessels armed like those employed by Captain Cook").
23. Beaglehole, 1967, 1:700–01, 703.
24. Grenader, 1957:22–35 (Russian reactions to news of La Pérouse's movements).
25. See Barratt, 1979b:229.
26. Sopikov, 1813, no. 9218, with notes.
27. See Bibliography, under Vancouver.
28. Vancouver, 1798, 2:96.
29. On this, see *Gentleman's Magazine*, 62 (1792), 269–70.
30. Vancouver, 1798, 2:215.
31. *Ibid.*, 216.
32. Krusenstern, 1813, 1:xxv; Veselago, 1869:5ff.; Barratt, 1981a:108–12.
33. Nevskii, 1951:32–35; Lisianskii, 1814, chaps. I–VI.
34. Penrose, 1959:98–99; Barratt, 1981a:108.
35. See Beaglehole, 1955, 1:cclxxxiii, for his orders.
36. Rozina, 1966.
37. Barratt, 1981a:140–41.
38. Gibson, 1976:76; Lensen, 1959:142–55.
39. Krusenstern, 1813, 1:183; Lisianskii, 1814:67, 70–71.
40. Okun', 1936:181–86; Tumarkin, 1964:146–52; Mehnert, 1939:25ff.; Pierce, 1965:7–14.
41. Lisianskii, 1814:99–104; Korobitsyn, 1944:173–74.
42. Howay, 1973:13.
43. Severgin, 1804.
44. Lisianskii, 1812, pt. 1:216.
45. Andreev, 1952:165–66.
46. Berkh, 1818:159–60; RAK, Sheffer Papers, pp. 11–12.
47. Berkh, 1818:162; also Okun', 1951:153. For an English translation of Berkh's paper, Pierce, 1965:113–21.
48. Berkh, 1818:162.
49. See Bibliography, under Berkh, V.N.
50. Berkh, 1818:161, 164.
51. Tikhmenev, 1939, 1:176ff.; Davydov, 1810, 1:194–96; *Materialy*, 1861, pt. 3:136–37.
52. Langsdorf, 1813–14, 1:187.
53. Howay, 1973:55, 70.
54. Barratt, 1981a:125–26, 148; *Materialy*, 1861, 3:13; Gibson, 1976:157–58.

55. *Columbian Centinel* (Boston), 31 May and 21 June 1809, 18 June 1808; "Solid Men of Boston" MS:11–13, 25–26; Bradley, 1968:30; Pierce, 1965:245.
56. Golder, 1928:40; Bancroft, 1886:471.
57. Ivashintsev, 1980:13–14; Lenz, 1970:284–85; Barratt 1981a:154.
58. See Barratt, 1981a:107–09.
59. PRO Adm. 1 1927, cap. 9–10 (Capt. Hallowell from St. Thomas); Nicolas, 1844, 5:448–49 and 6:42–43.
60. Ivashintsev, 1980:13–14.Gagemeister's letters to Company Head Office of 1806–07 (originals in Perm District State Archive, Perm, *fond* 445 (Khlebnikova), op. 1, d. 58), are being edited by the present writer.
61. Tikhmenev, 1938:334–35; Barratt, 1981a:148–49.
62. See Barratt, 1981a:143–44.
63. Valaam Monastery, *Ocherk*, 1894:138–40; Langsdorf, 1813–14, 2:96–100.
64. Khlebnikov, 1973:32–33; Lisianskii, 1814:218; Andreev, 1952:176–78.
65. Tikhmenev, 1861, 1:146; Langsdorf, 1813–14, 2:89; Rezanov, 1926:4–6; also D'Wolf, 1861:38–41.
66. *Vneshniaia politika Rossii*, 6:279–80; U.S. Congress, *American State Papers*, 1858, 5:439; Gibson, 1976:158–60.
67. *Materialy*, 1861, 3:86, 93–94 (V.M. Golovnin's 1818 paper, "A Note on the Present Condition of the Russo-American Company").
68. Khlebnikov, 1973:74; Mehnert, 1939:19; Pierce, 1965:3; Bradley, 1968:48.
69. U.S. National Archives, Washington, D.C., "Records of the Russian-American Company," 1942: reel 1.
70. *Ibid.*, dated "*Neva*, at sea, 1 May 1809."
71. See Bradley, 1968:47–48; Pierce, 1965:3–4.
72. Mehnert, 1939:20; Golder, 1930:39–40.
73. Campbell, 1816:117, 124–25.
74. See Tumarkin, 1964:138, n. 119.
75. This is supported by the text of those orders printed in *K istorii*, 1957:160–66, in which there are no obvious references to colonizing.
76. Tikhmenev, 1861, 1:166; Pierce, 1965:4; Tumarkin, 1964:138.
77. Campbell, 1816:130; Gibson, 1976:142–43.
78. Khlebnikov, 1835:107–08; Tikhmenev, 1861, 2:280 (Rezanov on Kamehameha's inclination to go himself to Novo-Arkhangel'sk in 1807).
79. Barratt, 1981a:174–75, 185–89.
80. Bradley, 1968:48.
81. Cox, 1832:38; Taylor, 1925:197–200; Tumarkin, 1964:138.
82. See Pierce, 1965:4ff.; Khlebnikov, 1835:161–62; Kotzebue, 1821, 1:312–13; and Tarakanoff, 1953, on the king's increasing coolness towards Russians in 1810–16.
83. Pierce, 1965:155.
84. Howay, 1973:48, 55, 72.
85. Khlebnikov, 1973:86–87; Barratt, 1981a:174.
86. *Columbian Centinel*, 3 March 1802; Howay, 1973:43.
87. Howay, 1933:70–80.
88. Pierce, 1965:5.
89. Barratt, 1981a:175.

90. Ivashintsev, 1980:20–23; Gibson, 1976:143. On Scheffer, see Schaeffer, 1959 and Mazour, 1937.
91. Tikhmenev, 1938:309–16; Okun', 1951:100.
92. Pierce, 1965:5, 108.
93. *Ibid.*, 41–44.
94. Corney, 1896:46; also Snyder, 1937:366.
95. Pierce, 1965:8
96. Barnard, 1900:96; Gibson, 1976:144–45; AVPR, *fond* St. Petersburg Glavarkhiva, 1817–1819, d. 1:29 (Report from Company Head Office to Nesselrode, 19 January 1818).
97. Khlebnikov, "Zapiski o koloniiakh" MS:14–15; TsGIAL, *fond* 18, op. 5, d. 1239 ("Izvlechenie iz zhurnala ...");35–36.
98. Pierce, 1965:68.
99. TsGIAL, *fond* 18, op. 5, d. 1239:36; Golovnin, 1822, 1:327.
100. TsGIAL, *font* 18, op. 5, d. 1239:37.
101. Golovnin, 1822, 1:327; Tumarkin, 1964:147.
102. Corney, 1896:71–72; Pierce, 1965:14; Emerson, 1900:11–18.
103. TsGIAL, *fond* 18, op. 5, d. 1239:37; AVPR, *fond* St. Petersburg Glavarkhiva, 1–10, 1817–19, d. 1:32–37 ("conventions" made by Scheffer and Kaumualii in 1816); Pierce, 1965:15–16.
104. Kotzebue, 1821, 1:322.

NOTES TO CHAPTER TWO

1. Kotzebue, 1821, 1:12–16.
2. Dobrovol'skii, 1953:10–18; Veselago, 1939:290ff.
3. Ivanovskii, 1871:96–120; Tumarkin, 1981:5–6.
4. Kotzebue, 1821, 1:29–30.
5. Barratt, 1981a:176–77.
6. Kotzebue, 1821, 1:7, 10.
7. *Ibid.*, 1:16; Veselago, 1939:291.
8. Bibliographical data in Tumarkin, 1981:7, 317.
9. Kotzebue, 1821, 1:29–30.
10. *Ibid.*, 1:93; Ivashintsev, 1980:24.
11. Kotzebue, 1821, 1:271–74; Chamisso, 1856, 2:10–50.
12. Kotzebue, 1821, 1:272.
13. *Ibid.*, 1:297–99.
14. *Ibid.*, 1:319; Chamisso, 1836, 3:215.
15. Kotzebue, 1821, 1:324; Corney, 1896:46; Howay, 1973:107–08.
16. Kotzebue, 1821, 1:328.
17. *Ibid.*, 1:338–48; Chamisso, 1836, 3:230.
18. Tarakanoff, 1953:29–32; Gibson, 1976:146–48; Tumarkin, 1964:148–49; Kuykendall, 1938:87–88.
19. Nevskii, 1951:57–58.
20. Ivashintsev, 1980:25–26; Sharp, 1960.
21. Kotzebue, 1821, 1:355; Tumarkin, 1964:148–49.
22. TsGIAL, *fond* 18, op. 5, d. 1231 ("Mnenie Soveta RAK ot 26 mar. 1818"); Tikhmenev, 1861, 1:187–88.

23. TsGIAL, *fond* 18, op. 5, d. 1239 ("Izvlechenie iz zhurnala"):47.
24. Khlebnikov, "Zapiski o koloniiakh", 23–34; Golovnin, 1822, 1:313–14.
25. TsGIAL, *fond* 18, op. 5, d. 1231:44–45 ("Izvlechenie iz doneseniia ... ot 7 iulia 1817"); Tikhmenev, 1861, 1:190–91; Corney, 1896:89–90.
26. Ivashintsev, 1980:28; Svet, 1966:217–21.
27. Chamisso, 1836, 3:56 (with citation from the *Quarterly Review* for January 1822); but see Tumarkin, 1981:8, n. 12.
28. Kotzebue, 1821, 2:179.
29. *Ibid.*, 2:195; Chamisso, 1836, 3:340–341.
30. Arkhiv LOII, koll. 115, ed. kr. 447 (Khlebnikova, "Zapiski o koloniiakh v Amerike ..."):24–25; Kotzebue, 1821, 2:197–98.
31. Ivashintsev, 1980:31; Barratt, 1981a:184–85.
32. Barratt, 1981a:174–76.
33. Tikhmenev, 1939, 1:232–33; AVPR, *fond* St. Petersburg Glavarkhiva, 1–10 (1817–19), d. 1:29–33; Tumarkin, 1964:154–62.
34. *Materialy*, 1861, 3:2 (doc. 1510); Golovnin, 1822, 1:5ff.; Ivashintsev, 1980:36.
35. Barratt, 1981a:190–98.
36. *Materialy*, 1861, 1:70–77 (Golovnin's "Zapiska o nyneshnem sostoianii RAK"); Gibson, 1976:159–60.
37. TsGAVMF, *fond* 7, op. 1, d. 2 ("Zapisnaia knizhka"):240–54; Golovnin, 1961:iii–vi; Laird-Clowes, 1904, 4:395, 408–12.
38. TsGAVMF, *fond* 7, op. 1, d. 2:241–43.
39. Nevskii, 1951:33.
40. Langsdorf, 1813–14, 1:100–08; Lisianskii, 1814:88ff.; Andreev, 1952:213–16 (N.I. Korobitsyn's journal); Barratt, 1981a:119–21.
41. Golovnin, 1949:153ff.
42. The list first appeared in *Syn otechestva* (St. Petersburg, 1816), no. 33:20–21.
43. Bezobrazov, 1888, chap. 2; Lenz, 1970:478, 886; Ivashintsev, 1980:139.
44. Barratt, 1981a:198–99.
45. Golovnin, 1949:357ff.
46. *Ibid.*, 371–73.
47. See Ella Wiswell's recent translation, Golovnin, 1978.
48. Pierce, 1976:40–49.
49. Golovnin, 1965:328–31; Kotzebue, 1830, 2:239–40.
50. Gough, 1973:4.
51. Edinburgh, 1816.
52. Kotzebue, 1821, 1:325–26; Montgomery, 1831, 1:392, 435.
53. See *Historical Records of Australia: Series* 1, 7:474–76; 8:626; Bradley, 1968:51–52.
54. Bradley, 1968:96–97.
55. *Ibid.*, 51–53; Mathison, 1825:462–63; Montgomery, 1831, 1:471–72.
56. Cited in Kirwan, 1960:77.
57. Details in Bellinsgauzen, 1960:9–12.
58. See Barratt, 1981a:202–06; Christie, 1951:108–09; Sharp, 1960:198–99; Sementovskii, 1951.
59. Lazarev, 1950:5–7, 21–30; Gillesem, 1849, sect. 8; Ivashintsev, 1980:50–51; Kuznetsova, 1968:237–45.

60. Shur, 1974:167–68; Ivashintsev, 1980:140–41.
61. Kuznetsova, 1968:237.
62. *Ibid.*, 241.
63. *Materialy*, 1861, 2:98–99; AVPR, *fond* RAK, d. 284:22ff.; Choris, 1822:9; AGO, *razr.* 99, op. 1, d. 29 ("Kratkaia istoricheskaia Zapiska"):4–5.
64. Huculak, 1971:127–31 (texts); U.S. Congress, Senate, *Proceedings*, 1904, 2:25ff.; Barratt, 1983:5–18.
65. Gibson, 1976:182–89; AVPR, *fond* Kantseliarii Ministerstva Vneshnikh Del:1823, d. 8735:5–6; Barratt, 1981a:212–14.
66. Tumarkin, 1964:155–59; Kuznetsova, 1968:238, n. 8.
67. Gibson, 1976:181–82.
68. AVPR, *fond* Kantseliarii Ministerstva Vneshnikh Del:1823, d. 8735:5–6 (P.I. Poletika to Nesselrode); *ibid.*, d. 3646:22ff. (Russian "legal" purchase of Fort Ross from Chu-gu-an *et al.*, September 1817.)
69. *Vneshniaia politika Rossii*, 7:280; Gibson, 1976:113–16; Tikhmenev, 1939, 1:264–65; Okun', 1951:127–32.
70. Tikhmenev, 1861, 1:221–22; Barratt, 1981a:212–15.
71. Perkins, 1923:656–62.
72. Tikhmenev, 1861, 1:222.
73. TsGAVMF, *fond* 213, op. 1, d. 113 (M.N. Vasil'ev, "Zapiski o prebyvanii na Gavaiskikh Ostrovakh"):32ff.; TsGIAL, *fond* f18, op. 5, d. 1231 ("Mnenie Soveta RAK ot 26 mar. 1818"):17–19.
74. Gillesem, 1849:218.
75. *Ibid.*, 221; Marshall MSS, Harvard University Library, John C. Jones to Marshall & Wildes, Oahu, 5 Oct. 1821 (arrival of the frame houses seen by Russians).
76. Gillesem, 1849:217.
77. See Emerson, 1900:16ff.
78. Maria S. Loomis MS (typewritten copy of journal), Hawaiian Mission Children's Society Library, Honolulu: 9 February 1821; see also *Missionary Herald*, XVIII (July 1822):206.
79. Gillesem, 1849:222.
80. Bradley, 1968:63–66.
81. Montgomery, 1831, 1:415.
82. Bradley, 1968:62.
83. Gillesem, 1849:221; Alexander, 1907:29; Jarves, 1847:112–13.
84. Gillesem, 1849:223.
85. Marshall MSS, Harvard University Library, W. Cole to Marshall & Wildes, Kauai, 25 May 1821; John C. Jones to same, Oahu, 23 December 1821; Stewart, 1828:313; Porter, 1931, 2:657–58.
86. Porter, 1931, 2:641–46; Bancroft, 1886:537–39; *MHSP*, 44:40–42.
87. Gibson, 1976:77–85; Okun', 1951:67–68; Lazarev, 1950:233–34.
88. Bradley, 1968:54, 61–62.
89. *Missionary Herald*, 18 (September 1822):273–74; *Materialy*, 1861, 3:74; *Boston Commercial Gazette*, 25 March 1822.
90. Marshall MSS, Harvard University Library, Jones to Marshall & Wildes, Oahu, 20 November 1821; 10 August 1822; *The Friend* (Honolulu), January 1867:6.

91. Ivashintsev, 1980:55–56; Kuznetsova, 1968:243–45.
92. Tikhmenev, 1861, 1:335–48; Okun', 1951:68–69; Barratt, 1981a:211–12, 222–24.
93. Lazarev, 1950:41ff.; Ivashintsev, 1980:56.
94. AVPR, *fond* Kantseliarii Ministerstva Vneshnikh Del:1822, d. 3645:30–33 (Nesselrode to Gur'ev, 3 June 1822); Barratt, 1983:13–18.
95. Okun', 1951:224–26.
96. Shabel'skii, 1826, chap. 1; Khrushchev, 1826:201–04.
97. AVPR, *fond* Kant. Min. Vneshnikh Del:1822, d. 3645:32; Ivashintsev, 1980:65–66.
98. Lazarev, 1832:4–14; Samarov, 1952:2; Zavalishin, 1877, no. 5:54–67; Barratt, 1975:566–68.
99. Anon., "Kratkaia istoricheskaia zapiska":6–7v.
100. Khlebnikov, 1835:64; Gibson, 1976:163–65.
101. Barratt, 1983:18–33.
102. Tumarkin, 1981:9.
103. *Ibid.*, 317–18 (on Eschscholtz, Seewald and Lenz).
104. Kotzebue, 1821, 2:191–92; Kotzebue, 1830, 2:158.
105. Kotzebue, 1830, 2:227–30.
106. Gillesem, 1849:224–25.
107. Bradley, 1968:99.
108. Graham, 1826:103–61; Bloxam, 1925:23–49; *Correspondence relative to the Sandwich Islands*, 1843:13ff. (Byron to Croker, Oahu, 30 May 1825 etc.).
109. See Kotzebue, 1830, 2:255.
110. *Ibid.*, 258–59.
111. *Ibid.*, 263.
112. Until 1853 and the Crimean War, at least: see Gough, 1971, chap. 3.
113. Marshall MSS, Harvard University Library, Jones to Marshall, Oahu, 30 October 1827.
114. U.S. Congress, *Senate Documents: XXV Congress*, 3rd sess., no. 1:70.
115. Ivashintsev, 1980:84 (Logbook for 15 April 1826); *Severnyi arkhiv* (St. Petersburg, 1828), pt. 36, "Prebyvanie":59ff.
116. Wrangel, 1828:89–90.
117. Bradley, 1968:105–06, 109–14.
118. *House Reports: XXII Congress*, 2nd sess., no. 86:1–6 (Instructions regarding debt liquidation for Lieutenant J. Percival, USS *Dolphin*, 1825); Kuykendall, 1938:434–36; Bradley, 1968:109–116.
119. *House Reports: XXVIII Congress*, 2nd sess., no. 92: Commodore Isaac Hull, USN to Navy Secretary Southard, 25 May 1826.
120. Jarves, 1847:135–36, 167; Bradley, 1968:102–03.
121. Marshall MSS, Harvard University Library, John C. Jones to Wildes, Oahu, 30 September 1827.
122. Wrangel, 1828:93.
123. *Ibid.*, 98–99; Howay, 1973:165; Porter, 1931, 1:195ff.
124. Wrangel, 1828:91; Bingham, 1847:203–04; Bradley, 1968:142–43.
125. But see Bradley, 1968:182–84.
126. Wrangel, 1828:92.
127. Ivashintsev, 1980:115; Zavoiko, 1840, pt. 1 (Letter X):112–17.

128. Barratt, 1981a:209–19.
129. Barratt, 1983:48–52, 55–57.

NOTES TO CHAPTER THREE

1. Tikhmenev, 1939, 1:206; Khlebnikov, 1973:60–61; *Niles Weekly Register*, 1820, 18:418 (Winship-Slobodchikov venture in *O'Cain*, argument at Ceros Island, Lower California, Russian purchase of small vessel and departure for Hawaiian Islands, July 1807, etc.).
2. Malo, 1903:321; Jarvis, 1849:92–98.
3. Gibson, 1972:10–13.
4. Ivashintsev, 1980:115, 119.
5. Kotzebue, 1821, 1: "Prigotovleniia", 11 May 1815 (use of the imperial flag, ship's status).
6. Pierce, 1965:40.
7. Nevskii, 1951:54–55.
8. *Russkaia starina*, 1895, bk. 7:125–26; Kruzenshtern, 1809, pt. 1:3–4.
9. Ivashintsev, 1980:137.
10. Campbell, 1819:90; Tikhmenev, 1939, 1:204; Golder, 1930:40.
11. Kotzebue, 1821, 1:14ff.
12. Howay, 1973:97–111.
13. *Ibid.*, 115–16 and Pierce, 1965:23, 205–06.
14. Kotzebue, 1821, 1:9ff. (introduction by Kruzenshtern).
15. Ivashintsev, 1980:139–41; Golovnin, 1965:306–07 (*Kamchatka*'s company).
16. Bellinsgauzen, 1960:9–10; Lazarev, 1950:25–26.
17. Lazarev, 1950:25.
18. Kotzebue, 1981:9; Gibson, 1976:162–65.
19. Kotzebue, 1981:9, 24; Ivashintsev, 1980:74.
20. Details in Barratt, 1981a, chap. 9.
21. *Ibid.*, 221–24, 228–32.
22. Chamisso, 1836, 1:230.
23. Kruzenshtern, 1809, 1:18–19; Nevskii, 1951:56–60.
24. Korobitsyn, 1944:169–70; Nevskii, 1951:60, n. 1; Barratt, 1981a:115–16.
25. Kruzenshtern, 1809, 1:2.
26. Barratt, 1981a:115.
27. Admiralty College Order of 13 March 1819, cited in Lazarev, 1950:25.
28. See Lenz, 1970, for biographical data.
29. Barratt, 1981a:140–41; Kohl, 1843, 2:200–02; Lenz, 1970:40–41, 468.
30. Survey by D.D. Tumarkin in Kotzebue, 1981:317–18; see also Bibliography below.
31. Ivashintsev, 1980:61–65; *Severnyi arkhiv*, 1826, vol. 24. Klochkov's journal describing *Riurik*'s second Pacific voyage, of 1821–22, has yet to be published. It is held in the archive of the Russian Geographical Society (AGO), in Leningrad, under ref., *razriad* 99, *delo* 139.
32. Lazarev, 1950:29–30 and Kuznetsova, 1968:237–38 (on Shishmarev's career and reports); Khlebnikov, 1979:276 (survey of Khromchenko's maritime career).
33. Obshchii morskoi spisok, 14 v., St. Petersburg, 1885–1907.

34. See Barratt, 1981b:17.
35. Lisianskii, 1812, 2:172–77; Shemelin, 1818, 1:144–50.
36. Malo, 1903:56, 187.
37. New England sources concur: see Mathison, 1825:424 and *MHSP*, 44:33.
38. See Narrative 127, but also Golder, 1930:44ff.
39. Howay, 1973:91–110.
40. Survey in Bradley, 1968:80.
41. *Ibid.*, 106–09.
42. Golder, 1926:462–69; Bailey, 1934:39–49.
43. See Malo, 1903:56, 281 on the social and religious implications of this timing.
44. *Ibid.*, 186.
45. *Ibid.*, 54–57.
46. *Ibid.*, 187, 93, 281.
47. *Ibid.*, 88.
48. Wrangel, 1828:100–03.
49. Gillesem in 1821: Narrative 92.
50. Restarick, 1923:58–59; Cleveland, 1843, 1:233.
51. Chamisso, 1836, 1:219.
52. Howay, 1973:194, 201; Pierce, 1965:232–33; Bradley, 1968:112–13.
53. Chamisso, 1836, 1:219.
54. *Ibid.*, 1:222.
55. The ethnographic significance of these excursions is considered by Kelm, 1951.
56. Malo, 1903:39, 270–73.
57. Chamisso, 1836, 1:222.
58. Malo, 1903:56ff.
59. Thrum, 1917:47; Alexander, 1907:13; Westervelt, 1910:25–27; Pierce, 1965:17.
60. Chamisso, 1836, 1:222.
61. Malo, 1903:54, 281, and Narratives 42, 88, 96 here.
62. Wrangel, 1828:100–04.
63. *Ibid.*, 100. Wrangel's route can be retraced with the aid of the U.S. Department of the Interior Geological Survey map (N2115–W15754/7.5), Puuloa Quadrangle, and (N2115–W15746.5/75) Honolulu Quadrangle, of 1959. The 1:24,000 scale is adequate to the purpose.
64. Malo, 1903:53.
65. Wrangel, 1828:101.
66. These matters are discussed by Peter Buck in his incomparable study of the arts and crafts of early Hawaii. See Buck, 1957:21, 33–34.
67. Wrangel, 1828:103.
68. *Ibid.*, 104.
69. On Beckley, see Narratives 8, 12, 113.
70. Kotzebue, 1821, 2:60–61.
71. See Map A and discussion thereof in Chapter 13 above.
72. Chamisso, 1836, 1:344.
73. *Ibid.* The German text implies that a specific mountain was the objective of the expedition.
74. *Ibid.*, 1:345.

75. *Ibid.*, 1:346.
76. Chamisso, 1836, 1:346.
77. Gofman failed in a bid to climb Mauna-Loa. Fearful of its resident, quickly-angered spirits, his Hawaiian guides refused to climb higher than approximately 7000 feet. See Kotzebue, 1981:285.

NOTES TO CHAPTER FOUR

1. Kotzebue, 1821, 1:358.
2. Kruzenshtern, 1813, 1:192–98.
3. Wrangel, 1828:92ff.
4. E. Townsend, letter of 30 August 1798, in New Haven Colony Historical Society *Papers*, 4, (1888):74.
5. Kotzebue, 1830, 2:230.
6. Jarves, 1847:125.
7. Beaglehole, 1955:572.
8. Kotzebue, 1821, 1:302–03.
9. *Ibid.*, 1:344.
10. Houston, 1939:75.
11. Kotzebue, *op. cit.*, I:307.
12. Bradley, 1942:23.
13. Buck, 1957:535:38.
14. Lisianskii, 1814:99, 102, 115–16.
15. Kotzebue, 1821, 2:194.
16. Wrangel, 1828:105.
17. Bradley, 1942:23.
18. Pierce, 1965:39.
19. Kotzebue, 1821, 1:306.
20. Bennett, 1840, 1:255.
21. Hunnewell, 1880:xiii
22. Kotzebue, 1821, 1:302–03.
23. Golovnin, 1949:373.
24. Kotzebue, 1821, 2:203.
25. Lazarev, 1950:269.
26. Malo, 1903:85.
27. Pierce, 1965:37.
28. Langsdorf, 1813–14, 1:188–89; Lisianskii, 1814:128–29.
29. Pierce, 1965:37.
30. Bradley, 1942:24.
31. Khlebnikov, 1976:66.
32. Tikhmenev, 1939, 1:204.
33. Campbell, 1819:90.
34. Khlebnikov, 1976:66.
35. *Niles Weekly Register*, 27 August 1836, 50:440; *The Polynesian*, 12 September 1840.
36. Pierce, 1965:50.
37. *Ibid.*, 40.
38. *Ibid.*, 196.

39. Kotzebue, 1821, 2:199 and Hunnewell, 1895.
40. Beechey, 1831, 2:99.
41. Mathison, 1825:458.
42. Golovnin, 1949:384–85.
43. *Ibid.*, 380 n.
44. *Ibid.*, 376.
45. Pierce, 1965:43.
46. *Ibid.*, 49.
47. *Ibid.*, 196.
48. *Ibid.*, 155.
49. Bradley, 1942:29–31.
50. *Ibid.*, 56–65.
51. Kaeppler in Mitchell, 1979:168.
52. Braunholz, 1970:45.
53. Ryden, 1963:68.
54. Lysaght in Mitchell, 1979:9–80; Joppien, *ibid.*, 81–136.
55. Barratt, 1979c; 1981b.
56. *"Zhurnal prikazov ...,"* TsGIAL, *fond* M.M. Buldakova, *delo* 1, no. 74.
57. Barratt, 1988.
58. Kotzebue, 1821, 1:11.
59. Kabo and Bondarev, 1974.
60. Barratt, 1979c:18–22.
61. N.I. Vorob'ev, E.P. Busygin et al., "Etnograficheskie nabliudeniia I.M. Simonova na ostrovakh Tikhogo Okeana," *IVGO*, 1949, 5:497–504.
62. Bellinsgauzen, 1960:77.
63. *Ibid.*, 80.
64. Mitchell, 1979:167.
65. Likhtenburg, 1960:168–69.
66. Golder, 1930:40.
67. Langsdorf, 1813–14, 1:14–165.
68. Andreev, 1952:162.
69. Campbell, 1819:90; Tikhmenev, 1939, 1:204.
70. Khlebnikov, 1976:10.
71. *Ibid.*, 19.
72. Pierce, 1965:40–41.
73. *Ibid.*, 50.
74. *Ibid.*, 195.
75. *Massachusetts Historical Society Proceedings*, LIV:37.
76. *USNA*, "Russian-American Company," 3:83.
77. *Ibid.*, 31:304.
78. Khlebnikov, 1976:66.
79. Ellis, 1827:28.
80. Tumarkin, 1964:76–77.
81. *Ibid.*, 77.
82. TsGIAE, *fond* 1414, op. 3, *delo* 3:83, on typewritten copy held at Eesti NVS Riikliik Ajaloomuuseum in Tallin, *fond* 225, op. 1, *delo* 20.
83. *s druz' iami svoimi*: Kotzebue, 1821, 2:72.
84. Broughten, 1804:32.

85. Lisianskii, 1812, 1:169–70.
86. Houston, 1939:64.
87. Vasil'ev, 1821:18.
88. Kotzebue, 1830, 2:256–57.
89. Bradley, 1942:164–65.
90. *Ibid.*, 176–77.
91. Houston, 1939:66.
92. Lisianskii, 1814:128.
93. Bradley, 1942:33.
94. Langsdorf, 1813–14, 1:187.
95. Langsdorf, 1813–14, 2:221; Khlebnikov, 1976:6.
96. "Solid Men of Boston in the Northwest":13ff.
97. Turnbull, 1805, 2:71.
98. Choris, 1822:15.
99. Kotzebue, 1830, 2:240.
100. Judd, 1929:80.
101. Ellis, 1826:465 and Golovnin, 1822, 1:340.
102. Wilkes, 1845, 3:386.
103. Shaler, 1808:162.
104. Houston, 1939:66; Malo, 1903:271.
105. Cox, 1822:38–39.
106. Pierce, 1965:54, 59.
107. *Ibid.*, 107, 182.
108. Vancouver, 1798, 2:140.
109. Morison, 1921:171ff.; Pierce, 1965:43.
110. Vasil'ev, "Zapiski o prebyvanii na Gavaiskikh ostrovakh," TsGAVMF, *fond* 213, op. 1, *delo* 104:27.
111. Khlebnikov, 1835:114.
112. Khlebnikov, 1976:58.
113. *Ibid.*, 57–60.
114. Bradley, 1942:172, n. 19.

NOTES TO CHAPTER FIVE

1. Dobrovol'skii, 1953, followed the example of L.G. Berg, in Fersman, 1926, and other Soviet historians of navigation and discovery in the Pacific, by suggesting the contrary. D.D. Tumarkin (Kotzebue, 1981) offers a truer picture: see pp. 15–20.
2. Biographical data in Lukina, 1975; see also Lenz, 1970:199–200; Kotzebue, 1981:318; and Fersman, 1926:138.
3. H.R. Friis, 1967:192–93; *Bol. Sov. Entsiklopediia* (Moscow, 1970–78), 7:189.
4. Ivashintsev, 1980:138, 146, 101–03.
5. Kotzebue, 1821, 1:60–83.
6. Mahr, 1932:12–13; Chamisso, 1836, 1:342.
7. By engaging Georg von Reichenbach (1772–1826), an instrument maker in Munich, Kotzebue's superiors showed themselves aware of the most recent advances in combinations of the transit instrument and mural circle.

8. See Barratt, 1981a:140–41 on the Baltic German element in the "Russian" enterprise in Polynesia in the early 1800s. On Eschscholtz's work as Curator of the Zoological Museum at the University of Dorpat, see I. Heidemaa, "Zooloogiamuuseumi Fondidest," *TUAK*, 11 (1981):87ff., and "Zooloogia kateedri," *ibid.*, 2 (1975):164–66.

9. Kotzebue, 1821, 3:234. Lithophilous strands and smooth lava sheets on which the Russians collected botanical and geological specimens in 1817 and subsequently, (provenance and accession records at the Academy's geological museum are fairly good), see Vaughan MacCaughey, "The Strand Flora of the Hawaiian Archipelago: Ecological Relations," in *Bulletin of the Torrey Botanical Club*, 45 (Honolulu, 1918):493–96.

10. Kotzebue, 1821, 1:13; Houston, 1940:78–79.

11. Kotzebue, 1821, 3:357–70.

12. W.J. Holland, *The Butterfly Book* (New York, 1931):154.

13. E.C. Zimmerman, *Insects of Hawaii* (Honolulu, 1948), 1:65.

14. Specimens, presented to the Academy of Sciences by the Navy, remain in the ornithological cabinets of the Academy's Institue of Zoology.

15. For a survey of the development of the Academy's Zoological Museum, which attracts large crowds of visitors today, see D.V. Naumov, *Zoologicheskii muzei Akademii Nauk SSSR* (Leningrad, 1980). The Pacific Ocean had been represented (by a few stuffed birds and insects from the Dutch East Indies and Japan) in the collection formed by Peter the Great (*ibid.*, 6–7) and which, when gutted by a fire in 1747, had expanded to a thousand birds and five hundred species of fish (details in *Katalog Zoologicheskago Razdela Akademii Nauk ...*, St. Petersburg, 1742). But, of course, there had been no Hawaiian creatures in St. Petersburg. The first acquisitions by exchange or purchase are unknown, but it is known that early ones—though very likely not the first—were linked with Aleksandr F. Sevast'ianov (1771–1824), a zoologist with many friends abroad. Sevast'ianov published more than once on the zoological results of Baudin's expedition to Australia and Oceania ("Izvestie o nekotorykh ... zhivotnykh," *Tekhnologicheskii zhurnal*, II, 1805, 2:159–61) and realized the importance of the natural history collections from Hawaii made on Vancouver's expeditions and on Cook's third expedition. Other Russian scientists with active interests in Polynesian fauna during this period were Georg Heinrich Langsdorf, who had personally visited Hawaii in the *Nadezhda*, and the early taxidermist T. Bornovolókov, who was anxious to improve the preservation of exotic birds and insects (see "O sokhranenii ptichnykh chuchel' i nasekomykh," *ibid.*, VI, 1809, 2:96–110. To these, by 1817, we may add the name of Eduard Ivanovich Eikhval'd (1795–1876) who had studied zoology and medicine in Berlin, then moved to London. He later became first Professor of Zoology at Kazan' in 1823. Like Sevast'ianov, Eikhval'd was particularly interested in the fauna and flora of Oceania; it was he who, despite his youth, in 1822–24 examined and classified the Australian and Pacific plants brought to St. Petersburg aboard the *Vostok* (Captain Bellingshausen: see Bellingshausen, 1945, 2:348).

Zoological specimens brought to the Academy by the 1819–22 double polar expedition included Hawaiian ones. But the museum was already so

short of space that they "had to be put into boxes between display cabinets" (Naumov, 1980:13). The need for a new and larger building to house
the Academy's zoological collections was discussed at the Konferentsii of
1830 and 1831; and shortly afterwards, F.F. Brandt, a young professor at
the University of Berlin, was appointed director of the future museum on
the recommendation of the celebrated Humboldt. Three halls opened to
the Russian public, offering Hawaiian birds and fish *inter alia*, in 1833.
Brandt's museum was also a preparation laboratory. He and two assistants
worked in it, unaided and with very modest funding, until 1875.

16. Bellinsgauzen, 1960:77–80.
17. Kotzebue, 1821, 1:11–15, 22–23.
18. E.V. Barsov, "O znachenii grafa N.P. Rumiantseva v etnograficheskoi nauke,"
    in *Materialy dlia istorii Rumiantsevskogo Muzeia* (Moscow, 1882), bk. i:93–
    95; T.V. Staniukovich, *Etnograficheskaia nauka i muzei* (Leningrad, 1978):
    74–75.
19. Meeting with Tamara V. Staniukovich of 21 May 1985. On the ethno-
    graphical component of the collection that remained in St. Petersburg un-
    til its noble owner's death, see *Piatidesiatiletie Rumiantsevskago Muzeia v
    Moskve, 1862–1912: istoricheskii ocherk* (Moscow, 1912):163–66.
20. See I. Heidemaa, "Zooloogiamuuseumi Fondidest," *TUAK*, 11 (1981):87.
21. TsGAVMF, *fond* 215, op. 1, *delo* 1203.
22. Lazarev, 1950:154. See also, in connection with natural history material
    brought to Russia in 1822 from the Pacific, Kuznetsova, 1968:244–45.
23. TsGAVMF, *fond* 213, op. 1, *delo* 52 holds a list of naturalia and ethno-
    graphica from Polynesia and other distant parts that entered the Museum
    of the Admiralty Department in the early 1800s and were transferred to
    the Academy of Sciences in 1827–28.
24. See n. 16.
25. See Shemelin, 1818:153–55.
26. M.C. Neal, *In Gardens of Hawaii* (Honolulu, 1965):662.
27. Further on these matters, see Barratt, 1981a:115–17.
28. Cited in Nevskii, 1951:37.
29. Krusenstern, 1813, 1:5–6; Nevskii, 1951:57 and 270–71 (the Russian career
    and publications of Tilesius von Tilenau of Leipzig); Barratt, 1979c:19–20
    (Baron von Zach's Russian connections and geodesy); Shemelin, 1816, 1:5ff.
30. Barratt, 1981a:108–11 and notes.
31. PRO Adm. 1/498, cap. 370 (Murray to Stephen, 16 August 1794); J. Ralfe,
    Naval Biography (London, 1828), 3:212 and 4:98–99; the holograph of
    Lisianskii's private journal for the period 1793–1800 is held at the Cen-
    tral Naval Museum (TsVMM), Leningrad (ref., No. 9170–1938), together
    with *Neva's* ships's journal for 1803–06 (No. 9170–8). As was made clear by
    V.V. Pertsmakher in 1972 (see "Iu.F. Lisianskii v Indii, 1799," in *Strany
    i narody Vostoka*, ed. D. Olderogge, bk. 12, Moscow: 248–59), TsVMM
    has long held those original materials, so important for study of Lisian-
    skii's British contacts and early science, IRLI merely holding copies. Also
    at TsVMM (Ref.:41820/2) is the 180-page *vakhtennyi zhurnal* is kept by
    Lisianskii aboard HMS *Raisonnable* and *Sceptre* in 1797–99. For Kruzen-
    stern's scientific and professional activities of that same period, see "Putesh-

estvie ot Mysa Dobroi Nadezhdy k Madrasu," *ZAD*, III (St. Petersburg, 1815). Both he and Lisianskii came to regard the optical and scientific equipment used in British frigates as the standard equipment for the age.

32. Krusenstern, 1813, 1:7–9; *DNB*, 1:581–82, 97; 19:1186–87.
33. *DNB*, 1:97.
34. Krusenstern, *op. cit.*, 1:8.
35. Bolkhovitinov, 1966:114; Pertsmakher, 1972:252–53; TsGAVMF, *fond* 406, op. 7, *delo* 62:62–64 (Lisianskii's journal aboard the East Indiaman *Royalist*).
36. See V.A. Vorontsov-Vel'iaminov, *Ocherki istorii astronomii v Rossii* (Moscow, 1956), on Shubert's naval links.
37. Kotzebue, *Voyage*, 1:16; *DNB*, 19:1186–87.
38. Portfolio ref., R–29001–306. The aquarelle described below is No. 29272 (270 by Mikhailov's original schema). Other Hawaiian illustrations in the portfolio include No. 29288 (286), showing two native structures, one half open or wall-less, and many human figures; and Nos. 29188–29196 (186–194), a set of Hawaiian portraits, most from waist or neck up, unfinished. A few of these provide personal names, e.g., 29196 is "Hitati." These views and portraits, from Parts IV and VI of the 1819–22 portfolio, have been attached by the Museum authorities to stiff blue folio sheets of cardboard. Occasional drawings of Hawaiian fauna enliven the whole. No. 29248 (245), for example, shows a "Frigate-bird or sea-eagle from Lisianskii Island." It measures 27 cm by 37 cm. Lisianskii (or Lisiansky) was the Hawaiian outcrop on which the *Neva* had almost come to sudden grief on the night of 15/16 October 1805 (Lisianskii, 1814:251–57; Sharp, 1960:189). Its discovery began the period of Russian hydrography within the chain of the Hawaiian Archipelago that was honourably closed by the *Moller's* sweep of February 1828 (see Ivashintsev, 1980:89). Further on Mikhailov, see Barratt, 1981b:13–14, 76–77.
39. Krusenstern, 1813, 1:9; on the instrument-making of Nicolas-Theodore de Saussure (1767–1845) and Jean-André de Luc (1727–1817), see *Biographie Universelle* (Michaud), 25:400–01 and 38:77–79.
40. Discussion in D.F. Rudovits, "Pervoe russkoe krugosvetnoe plavanie 1803–1806 godov," *Trudy Gosudar. Okeanograficheskogo Instituta*, 27 (36), Leningrad, 1954:5–7.
41. Iu.M. Shokal'skii, *Okeanografiia* (Leningrad, 1959, 2nd ed.):33.
42. Kruzenstern, 1809–12, 3:333–41 (Hörner's paper, "Udel'naia tiazhest' morskoi vody").
43. Kotzebue, 1821, 1:69 and 3:318.
44. H.R. Friis, 1967:191.
45. Kotzebue, 1828:7. On Dollond's work, *DNB*, 5:1102–04. Also Nevskii, 1951:42 (barometer selection).
46. See Kotzebue, 1981, for introductory remarks by D.D. Tumarkin on the previous confusion of the 1828 *Puteshestvie* and the 1830 *Neue Reise*.
47. H.R. Friis, 1967:193.
48. Emil Lenz, 'Physikalische Beobachtungen, angestellt auf einer Reise um die Welt ... in den Jahren 1823–1826,' *Académie des Sciences de St-Pétersbourg: Mémoires*, 1 (St. Petersburg, 1831):221–244; see also J. Prestwich, "Tables

of Temperatures of the Sea at Various Depths ...," *Philosophical Transactions*, 165 (London, 1876):587–674.

49. V.M. Pasetskii, *Geograficheskie issledovaniia dekabristov* (Moscow, 1977):71–73, 176; Ivashintsev, 1980:67, 71–73.

50. For details of archival holdings and access, see P. Kennedy Grimsted, *Archives and Manuscript Repositories in the USSR: Leningrad and Moscow* (Princeton, 1972).

51. Bibliography by V. Akhmatov in Fersman, 1926:110–12.

52. Fersman, 1926:98.

NOTES TO CHAPTER TWELVE

1. Brun, 1896:141; Kotzebue, 1981:5; *ES*, 31:460–61.

2. Kruzenshtern, 1809, 1:10–11; Lenz, 1970:410; Barratt, 1981a:140.

3. D.D. Tumarkin, in Kotzebue, 1981:5.

4. Kotzebue, 1821, 1:xii.

5. Details in Langsdorf, 1813–14, 1:100ff.; Lisianskii, 1812, 1:103ff.; Shemelin, 1816, 1:120–23; Nevskii, 1951:113–44.

6. TsGIAL, *fond* 853 (Buldakova), *delo* 1, item 74 ("Zhurnal prikazov kapitana Kruzenshterna komande sudov Nadezhda i Neva"); on these orders, see Gvozdetskii, 1947:85–88. For an excerpt from the text, see Chapter 4.

7. Kruzenshtern, 1809, 1:178–202; Nevskii, 1951:123–24, 130–34.

8. Details in Rozina, 1963:110–19; illustrations in Lisianskii, *Sobrankie kart* (1812).

9. Barratt, 1981a:112–14, 176–80; Kotzebue, 1981:6.

10. Mahr, 1932:13.

11. Chamisso, 1836, 3:5–6, 179–80; Brun, 1896:212–25; Mahr, 1932:14.

12. Brun, 1896:145–47; Mahr, 1932:17–19; *ES*, 74:572 and 77:133; Kotzebue, 1981:317.

13. Kotzebue, 1821, 1, chap. 6 (15 July 1816); Barratt, 1979b:16–17, 22 (commanders' use of subordinates' journals, etc).

14. *ES*, 18:686–87; Polevoi, 1855:3ff.

15. Doring, 1830, chap. 6; Rabany, 1893.

16. See NUC, 304:542, on the Hoffmann edition.

17. Details in Bibliography.

18. *DNB*, 45:210. This volume was No. 6 in Phillips' *New Voyages and Travels* series.

19. *Gentleman's Magazine*, 1847, 2:324–26.

20. *DNB*, 33:421–22; NUC, 304:542.

21. Chamisso, 1899, 3:2; Brun, 1896:212–14.

22. *Ontdekkingsreis in de Zuid-zee en naar de Berings-Straat, in de jaren 1815, 1816, 1817 en 1818 ...* (Amsterdam, Johannes van der Hey, 1822, 3 vols.). Like the Longman, Hurst, Rees (London 1821) edition, this work, which brought Kotzebue's Honolulu before a sizeable Dutch readership, contained several plates engraved from Choris's 1816 drawings.

23. Kotzebue, 1981:3; Tumarkin, 1956.

24. *OMS*, 7:319–20.

25. Two volumes in one: maps; see Bibliography.

26. *OMS*, 7:321; Kotzebue, 1981:15.
27. Hitzig, 1842, Bd. 5; *ES*, 77:133–34; Brun, 1896, chaps. 1–2; Mahr, 1932:15–17.
28. Bois-Reymond, 1888:335–49; Feudel, 1971, chaps. 2–4.
29. Hitzig, 1842, Bd. 5:349; see also Brun, 1896:138–40.
30. Hitzig, 1842, Bd. 5:355–56; Brun, 1896:140–41; *ES*, 31:460–61; Doring, 1830:148ff.
31. Hitzig, *op. cit.*, 356.
32. Kruzenshtern, in his introduction to Kotzebue, 1821, 1:xx; Chamisso, 1899, 3:7–10; Brun, 1896:141.
33. Kotzebue, 1821, 1:xix–xx; Brun, 1896:141.
34. Chamisso, 1899, 3:18; Mahr, 1932:12.
35. Mahr, 1932:12. I modernize the transliteration of names.
36. Chamisso, 1836, 1:342.
37. *Ibid.*, 1:227.
38. Cited by Brun, 1896:211–12.
39. Chamisso, 1899, 3:179.
40. NUC, 304:542. *Bemerkungen und Ansichten* formed Book 3 of this as of the 1821 Hoffmann edition of the work.
41. See introductory essay by A. Bartels in Chamisso, 1899; *ES*, 77:133; Mahr, 1932:18.
42. Details in Menza, 1960:53 ("Niederschift des 'Tagebuchs'.") Bibliography for Chamisso in *DLI*, 2:566–70; and NUC, 103:29ff. Certain works by Chamisso that bear on Hawaiian studies, e.g., *Ueber die Hawaiische Sprache: Versuch einer Grammatik* (Berlin, 1837), are now bibliographical rarities and little known to North American ethnology.
43. TsGIAE, *fond* 2057, op. 1, *delo* 444.
44. TsGAVMF, *fond* 7, op. 1, *delo* 2:23.
45. Lensen, 1959:196–214, 248; Barratt, 1981a:160–69; Golovnin, 1851, 1:6–110.
46. See Bibliography (*Zapiski flota kapitana Golovnina o prikliucheniiakh ego v plenu ...*, 1816: two parts).
47. Discussion in Golovnin, 1965:7–8.
48. See Armstrong, 1979:4–5.
49. *Ibid.*, 3–4; Barratt, 1981a:119–21.
50. Golovnin, 1949:376–77; Tumarkin, 1964:76–78.
51. Golovnin, 1965:9–10 (Introductory essay by V.A. Divin).
52. Komissarov, 1964:414–18; Shur, 1970:205–06.
53. Golovnin, 1965:10–11.
54. *Ibid.*, 18–19.
55. Further on such archival materials bearing on Oahu, see Appendix C here.
56. TsGAVMF, *fond* 166, op. 1, *delo* 2680. See also Golovnin, 1965:21; and Shur, 1974:177–78.
57. TsGAVMF, *fond* 166, op. 1, *delo* 2680:7–14.
58. Shur, 1974:178–79.
59. Golovnin, 1965:21; Shur, 1974:178.
60. TsGAVMF, *fond*, op. 1, *delo* 16.
61. July 1894:52.

62. On these considerations, Barratt, 1979c:16–17.
63. Golovnin, 1949:376.
64. *ES*, 22:414–16; Grech, 1851.
65. Barratt, 1988: pt. 2.
66. *Opisanie dostoprimechatel'nykh korablekrushenii* ... (St. Petersburg, 1822).
67. See table in Chapter 3.
68. Barratt, 1975:566–69.
69. Lazarev, 1950:30–32.
70. Veselago, 1939:246–47; Barratt, 1981a:178.
71. Lazarev, 1950:32.
72. *Ibid.*, 29–30; Kuznetsova, 1968:237–38; Berkh, 1823, pt. 1; Ivashintsev, 1980:141.
73. Bellingsgauzen, 1831, pt. 1; Barratt, 1979c:13, 26–28; Hunter Christie, 1951:100–01.
74. Ivashintsev, 1980:50–52; Gillesem, 1849, no. 9; Lazarev, 1950: chaps. 1–2; Kuznetsova, 1968:239–40.
75. Lazarev, 1950:33–34.
76. Kuznetsova, 1968:237, 243–45; Barratt, 1981a:202–06; Debenham, 1959:45–49; Sementovskii, 1951, *passim*.
77. Barratt, 1981a:231–32.
78. Gibson, 1976:84.
79. Azadovskii, 1926, 1:242; Lazarev, 1950:33–34.
80. Lazarev, 1950:8.
81. I thank I.A. Grigor'eva for facilitating access to A.P. Lazarev's works held in that Department, under ref., *fond* 17, 106":1–3, and *kollektsiia I.V. Pomialovskogo*, No. 72.
82. "Svedeniia o chukchakh," *Zapiski Gidrograficheskago Departamenta*, vol. XI (St. Petersburg, 1852).
83. *ES*, 43:414–15.
84. Bibliographical essay in *Russkaia starina*, 5 (St. Petersburg, 1872).
85. MS materials relating to the voyage, and the Hawaiian Islands in particular, are now held in TsGIAE, Tartu. These materials are discussed in Andreev, 1943 and used, incidentally, in Davydov, 1956 and Pasetskii, 1965.
86. *ES*, 13:337–39.
87. See Lipshits, 1956:319ff.
88. TsGIAE, *fond* 2057, op. 1, *delo* 443:109/obverse.
89. Wrangel, 1828:91.
90. TsGIAE, *fond* 2057, op. 1, *delo* 352 (Krotkii notebook No. 3):10/obverse.
91. Details in Appendix B.

NOTES TO CHAPTER THIRTEEN

1. Details in Likhtenberg, 1960:168–205.
2. Goncharova, 1973; Lazarev, 1950:87; and Kuznetsova, 1968:244–45 (the artist's qualifications, the fate and whereabouts of his portfolio, etc).
3. Barratt, 1988: pt. 4, sections d–f (the Hawaiian sketches of Iu.F. Lisianskii, E.E. Levenshtern, 1804).
4. *ES*, 6:658; 74:572.

5. Kotzebue, 1821, 1:24; Chamisso, 1836, 3:18; Mahr, 1932:12–13.

6. Brun, 1896:145–57, 211–17; Menza, 1978:52ff.; NUC, 108:24.

7. Original letters in TsGIAE (Central State Historical Archive of the Estonian SSR), Tartu, under ref., *fond* 1414 (I.F. Kruzenshterna), op. 3, *delo* 42.

8. "Iles Sandwich" (24 pp.; pp. 6–20 on the Oahu visit).

9. NUC, 108:24; Mahr, 1932:18–19.

10. Shur, 1974; Pierce, 1976; Fedorov-Davydov, 1953:219–20, 323; Gutmanis, 1963.

11. Shur, 1974:164–65.

12. Pierce, 1976:40–41.

13. TsGIAL, *fond* 789, op. 19:52–68.

14. Shur, 1974:177–78.

15. Rovinskii, 1895:1068, 1078.

16. For conditions of access, write to Secretary, Main Administrative Office, Ulitsa Kropotkina 17, Moscow.

17. Kotzebue, 1821, pt. 1:24–38.

18. *Ibid.*, 37.

19. See Choris, 1822:5, on *Brutus*, "a large three-masted vessel of Boston."

20. Kotzebue, 1821, 2:239.

21. Buck, 1957:132–35; Brigham, 1906:76–78.

22. See Narratives 51 and 93 (Gillesem on *kapa* making); also Buck, 1957:191–200 (*'ohe kapala* stamps, etc.)

23. Buck, 1957:447.

24. Cook, 1784, 3:134.

25. Brigham, 1908:87–89; Ellis, 1827:314.

26. See Narratives 1–3.

27. See Narrative 127.

28. On this, see Buck, 1957:76–79, 102–06.

29. Cook, 1784; Hornell, 1936:18.

30. Buck, 1957:36, 59–60.

31. Details in Malo, 1903:77–78.

32. Cook, 1784, 3:151–52.

33. Cook, 1784, 3:27; Buck, 1957:553–57.

34. See Narrative 69.

35. Cook, 1784, 2:236; Roberts, 1926:22ff.; Buck, 1957:411–14.

36. The Russian evidence of tattooing is usefully seen in conjunction with Emory, 1946:235–70.

37. Ellis, 1839:100; Buck, 1957:401–05.

38. Roberts, 1926:*passim*.

39. Alexander, 1907:13–14.

40. See Barratt, 1988: plates U and V.

41. Discussion in Hornell, 1936:14ff.; and Buck, 1957:277–80.

42. Reproduced in Buck, 1957:245, 248.

43. *Ibid.*, 246–47.

44. Cook, 1784, 3:134; Buck, 1957:562–63.

45. Buck, 1957:535–38.

46. *Ibid.*, 546.

47. Details in Stokes, 1906:150–51.
48. Buck, 1957:100 (thatched *lanai*, etc).
49. Kotzebue, 1821, 1:32.
50. Details in Brigham, 1906:32–34.
51. Shur, 1974:175.
52. See Narrative 51.
53. Golovnin, 1949:371.
54. For details of the restoration project at Kamakahonu, I thank Moana Ching, Director of Guest Activities, King Kamehameha Hotel at Kona (75-5660 Palani Rd., Kailua-Kona, HI 96740). The hotel issued a lengthy press release on the project on 28 June 1976.
55. Shur, 1974:178; Gutmanis, 1963:29.
56. Rovinskii, 1895:1068.
57. Golovnin, 1949:372.
58. Malo, 1903:295–96; Buck, 1957:366–67.
59. Cook, 1784, 2:236.
60. Ellis, 1839:81.
61. Cook, 1784, 3:134.
62. Golovnin, 1949:371.
63. Ellis, 1839:175.
64. Gutmanis, 1963:29.
65. See Narratives 25, 66, 85, and 129 on Boki.
66. Golovnin, 1949:374.
67. Illustrated in Buck, 1957:228–29.
68. *Ibid.*, 217–18, 230–31.
69. *Ibid.*, 237.
70. Cook, 1784, 3:151–52.
71. *Ibid.*, and Golovnin, 1822, 2:66.
72. Buck, 1957:238–40.
73. *Ibid.*, 240–41.
74. Malo, 1903:257.
75. Survey in Pierce 1965:14–18.
76. Alexander 1907:14–15.
77. A paper written by Emerson in 1898.
78. Not until 1942, however, did Harold W. Bradley publish on the basis of the essential Marshall mss.; see Bradley 1968:60–61.
79. TsGAVMF, *fond* 7, op. 1, *delo* 16:22ff.
80. Ivashintsev 1980:139.

NOTES TO APPENDIX A

1. Golovnin, 1961:140–42; Barratt, 1981b:160–61.
2. McNab, 1908:298–99; Elder, 1932.
3. In Golovnin, 1816; see also Lensen, 1959:212–48.
4. St. Petersburg, 1816, no. 31:177–200; no. 32:217–33; no. 33:3–23.
5. *Materialy*, 1861, 1:71–77; 3:92–113; Barratt, 1981a:162–64, 195–98; Gibson, 1976:159–60; Ivashintsev, 1980:19, 38–40.

6. Lisianskii, 1814:128; Langsdorf, 1813–14, 1:187; Howay, 1930:11–21; Tumarkin, 1964:61–62, 70ff.
7. Lisianskii, 1814:128; Barratt, 1988: pt. 3, p. 4; Tumarkin, 1979:129–30; also Franchère, 1854:85.
8. Barratt, 1981a:162–64; *Materialy*, 1861, 1:76–77.
9. Gibson, 1976:159–60, 169; Howay, 1973:83–87.
10. Morison, 1921:179; Corney, 1896:73; Roquefeuil, 1823, 2:93–97; *Columbian Centinel*, 3 April 1819.
11. Narrative 18.
12. Corney, 1896:73; *Columbian Centinel*, 6 June 1818.
13. Barratt, 1981a:109, 159; Nevskii, 1951:25, 33.
14. Beaglehole, 1974:395–402.
15. Golovnin, 1819:146–208 (part 3).
16. Golovnin, 1822, 1 ("O Sandvichevykh Ostrovakh").
17. Narrative 19.
18. Golovnin, 1822, 1:342.
19. TsGAVMF, *fond* 166, op. 1, *delo* 2537a:145ff.
20. *Materialy*, 1861, 1:71–77; 3:92–113; Barratt, 1981a:194–98.
21. Shemelin, 1818, 1:158; Barratt, 1988: pt. 2 (text), pt. 5, sect. A (observations on MS, provenance, etc.).
22. Khlebnikov, 1973:45, 54; D'Wolf, 1861:39–40; Langsdorf, 1813–14, 2:89; Howay, 1973:64–65.
23. Rezanov, 1825; Barratt, 1981a:114, 121–122.
24. Tikhmenev, 1861, 1:162; Barratt, 1981a:151; Gibson, 1976:45, 178.
25. Ivashintsev, 1980:39–41.
26. Golovnin, 1965:328–31.
27. Kotzebue, 1981:282. The date of Lauri's return remains unclear. The Soviet historian Daniel D. Tumarkin claims (*ibid.*, 332, n. 15) that Lauri took passage in the Company vessel *Suvorov*, sailing from Kronstadt in 1820. If so, he would presumably have reached the Islands in 1821.

NOTES TO APPENDIX B

1. Langsdorf, 1813–14, 1, chap. 8.
2. Lisianskii, 1814:99–103.
3. See Gibson, 1976:212–17.
4. Berkh, 1818:162.
5. Andreev, 1948:96.
6. Lisianskii, 1814:100ff.
7. Barratt, 1981a:126, 148.
8. Howay, 1973:*passim*; Tumarkin, 1979:128.
9. Tikhmenev, 1939, 1:206; Langsdorf, 1813–14, 1:188.
10. Tikhmenev, 1939, 1:204; Campbell, 1819:90; *New England Palladium*, 8 October 1805; *Niles Weekly Register*, 1820, 18:418; Patterson, 1817:76; Howay, 1973:70; Bancroft, 1885, 2:23–24, 39–40.
11. Gibson, 1976:210; Pierce, 1965, documents 1–2.
12. Tikhmenev, 1939, 1:203.
13. Barratt, 1981a:152, 181; Gibson, 1976:11.

14. Pierce, 1965:40–41.
15. See Narratives 106, 108, and 129.
16. Gibson, 1976:210–11.
17. *MHSP*, 44:36–37; *Missionary Herald*, 18 (September 1822):273–74.
18. Barratt, 1981a:210–12.
19. *Ibid.*, 216–20.
20. Gibson, 1976:157–58, 161–62.
21. Introduced and translated by Gibson as "Russian America in 1833":Gibson, 1972:1–13.
22. Barratt, 1981a:223.
23. Khlebnikov, 1835:64.
24. Pierce, "Alaska's Russian Governors," *Alaska Journal*, 2 (1972):19–23.
25. Gibson, 1972:7.
26. USNA, 3:83.
27. Khlebnikov, 1979:276.
28. Gibson, 1972:7; USNA, 31:304.
29. See Barratt, 1981a:211–12, 216–24; Gibson, 1976, chaps. 3 and 6.
30. TsGAVMF, *fond* 1166, op. 1, *delo* 9:5.
31. USNA, 4:6.
32. Tikhmenev, 1861, 1:339–40; AGO, *razriad* 99, op. 1, *delo* 29 ("Kratkaia istoricheskaia zapiska o sostoianii RAK,"):10–11.
33. Gibson, 1972:8; Khlebnikov, 1976:66, 79 (cost and condition of the *Brutus*, *Arab*, and *Lapwing* when purchased by the Company, etc.); Hunnewell, 1895:4–9 (Blanchard and *Bordeaux Packet*); Stewart, 1839:274ff. and Robert Dampier, ed. P.K. Joerger, *To the Sandwich Islands on HMS Blonde* (Honolulu, 1971):34ff. (Byron's actions in Honolulu, June 1825).
34. PRO Adm. 1: "A Log of the Proceedings of His Majesty's Armed Tender *Chatham* ...," 28 February 1793. In June 1804, several Russians had similarly been struck by the potential of Hawaiian sugar-cane and its obvious utility in the Russian settlements of the Pacific rim: see Lisianskii, 1814:128–29; and Langsdorf, 1813–14, 1:188–89.
35. Hawaiian Mission Children's Society Library: "Journal of Levi Chamberlain," 24 February, 3 August, and 30 November 1826; Paulding, 1831:220–22; Franchère, 1854:70.
36. USNA, 31:304. Data on salt and other supplies taken to Sitka from Honolulu appear in numerous isues of the *Sandwich Islands Gazette*; see issues for 6 August 1836 and 13 May 1837, for the 1830s, U.S. Department of State: "Consular Letters," Honolulu, Series 1, for 1825–30.
37. Details in Barratt, 1983:10–18.
38. In 1826, Khlebnikov supposed that "Kari-maku" had "promised to liquidate" debts to American subjects, but had not delivered fully on that promise (Khlebnikov, 1976:67). Only Wrangel (1828:106) had been in contact with Kalanimoku, Captain Thomas ap Catesby Jones, USN, and Consul Richard Charlton that year, and so was apprised of the true position (as summarized in Bradley, 1942:106–09). The Company's trade interests at Honolulu did not, however, justify the appointment of any Russian consul or commercial agent; nor was that matter ever seriously considered until

1847: see USNA, 52:486v–99, on Governor Mikhail Tebenkov's proposals to expand Russo-Hawaiian trade and appoint a commercial agent at Honolulu.
39. Tikhmenev, 1939, 2:193; F.C. Cordes, "Letters of A. Rotchev, Last Commandant at Fort Ross," *California Historical Quarterly*, 38 (June 1960):111.

NOTES ON APPENDIX C

1. *ES*, 6:658; Charlot, 1958; Feher, 1969:*passim*; also Chapter 4 here.
2. Shur, 1974; Tumarkin, 1983; Pierce, 1976; Fedorov-Davydov, 1953:219–20, 323; Gutmanis, 1963.
3. N.N. Goncharova, "Khudozhnik krugosvetnoi ekspeditsii 1819–1822 godov E. Korneev," *IVGO*, 105 (1973), bk. 1:72.
4. *Ibid.*, 67–70 and, by the same author, "Vidopisets E. Kornéev," in *Iskusstvo*, 1972, 6:60–64.
5. TsGIAL, *fond* 789, op. 2 (1823), *delo* 30; Barratt, 1979c:6–8; Bellinsgauzen, 1960:8–11; Lazarev, 1950:23–27 (preparations).
6. TsGIAL, *fond* 789, op. 20 (1819), *delo* 28v.
7. *Ibid*; see also Bellinsgauzen, 1960:77–78 (artists' orders).
8. Portfolio now held at the Russian State Museum in Leningrad, (Drawings Division), under ref., R–29001–29308; on Mikhailov, see Barratt, 1981b: index (under Mikhailov, P.N.). The *Vostok* and the *Mirnyi* revictualed and rested at Matavai Bay, Tahiti, not at Honolulu, in the southern winter of 1820 (Ivashintsev, 1980:45); but even so, Mikhailov's portfolio at the Russian Museum contains Hawaiian pen sketches and aquarelles, because he returned to Polynesia in 1826–29 as artist in the sloop *Moller* (Captain-Lieutenant Mikhail N. Staniukovich). More specifically, it contains a set of two dozen aquarelles done on Oahu between 6 December 1827 and 9 February 1828. In connection with these paintings, note that Nos. 186 to 194 inclusive—by Mikhailov's original enumeration—that is, Nos. 29188 to 29196 by the present schema, are of Hawaiians. Some portraits are accompanied by proper names; for example, the male shown on No. 194 is "Hitati." The ethno-historical value of such paintings is self-evident. Also in the Mikhailov portfolio are several detailed Hawaiian landscapes, showing scenes in or near Honolulu. No. 270 (29272), for example, shows "A Waterfall on the Hanarura River on the Island of Oahu" ("Vodopad rechki Ganarury na Ostrove Avagu"). A note in the corner of the 21 cm by 35 cm sheet records that the scene was "drawn from nature on 8 February 1828," the day before the artist left Oahu forever. Some thirty human figures are shown, many swimming in the river or leaping into it. Tones (blue, dark blue, dark green) remain bright after 160 years.
9. TsGIAL, *fond* 789, op. 20 (1823), *delo* 30.
10. *Ibid.*, and TsGAVMF, *fond* 213, op. 1, *dela* 55 and 99.
11. Details in Goncharova, 1973:70–71.
12. TsGIAL, *fond* 789, op. 1, *delo* 546.
13. TsGAVMF, *fond* 166, register 202, *delo* 691.

Textual Sources Translated

1. Kotzebue, 1821, 2:42–43.
2. Chamisso, 1836:215–16.
3. Kotzebue, 1821, 2:45–56.
4. Kotzebue, 1821, 2:47–48.
5. Chamisso, 1836:222–23.
6. Kotzebue, 1821, 2:49.
7. Kotzebue, 1821, 2:49–51.
8. Kotzebue, 1821, 2:53–54.
9. Kotzebue, 1821, 2:57.
10. Chamisso, 1836:230–41.
11. Kotzebue, 1821, 2:70.
12. Kotzebue, 1821, 2:71–72.
13. Chamisso, 1836:305.
14. Chamisso, 1836:319–20.
15. Kotzebue, 1821, 2:242–43.
16. Kotzebue, 1821, 2:244.
17. Kotzebue, 1821, 2:248.
18. Golovnin, 1949:374.
19. Golovnin, 1949:375.
20. Golovnin, 1949:377.
21. Golovnin, 1949:379.
22. Golovnin, 1949:383.
23. Golovnin, 1949:396.
24. Lazarev, 1950:265–66.
25. Gillesem, 1849:217.
26. Gillesem, 1849:217–18.
27. Gillesem, 1849:223–24.
28. Gillesem, 1849:221.
29. Kotzebue, 1981:243–44.
30. Kotzebue, 1981:270–71.
31. Kotzebue, 1981:276.
32. Kotzebue, 1981:279.
33. Kotzebue, 1981:285.
34. Kotzebue, 1981:292–93.
35. Gagemeister, 1818:155–56.
36. Kotzebue, 1821, 2:43–45.
37. Kotzebue, 1821, 2:46–47.
38. Chamisso, 1836:224–25.
39. Kotzebue, 1821, 2:54.
40. Kotzebue, 1821, 2:66–67.
41. Chamisso, 1836:303–04.
42. Chamisso, 1836:308–10.
43. Kotzebue, 1821, 2:243.
44. Kotzebue, 1821, 2:249.
45. Golovnin, 1949:378, 382.
46. Golovnin, 1949:385.
47. Golovnin, 1949:396.
48. Vasil'ev, 1821:34–35, 43–44.
49. Gillesem, 1849:221–22.
50. Gillesem, 1849:222.
51. Gillesem, 1849:224.
52. Gillesem, 1849:223.
53. Gillesem, 1849:223.
54. Kotzebue, 1981:265.
55. Kotzebue, 1981:266.
56. Kotzebue, 1981:268.
57. Kotzebue, 1981:268.
58. Kotzebue, 1981:276–77.
59. Kotzebue, 1981:277–78.
60. Kotzebue, 1981:277.
61. Kotzebue, 1981:281–82.
62. Kotzebue, 1981:284.
63. Kotzebue, 1981:287.
64. Kotzebue, 1981:290–91.
65. Kotzebue, 1981:292.
66. Gagemeister, 1818:153–55.
67. Kotzebue, 1821, 2:51.
68. Kotzebue, 1821, 2:54–55.
69. Kotzebue, 1821, 2:55–56.
70. Chamisso, 1836:221–22.
71. Chamisso, 1836:223–34.
72. Chamisso, 1836:225–27.
73. Chamisso, 1836:228–29.
74. Kotzebue, 1821, 2:59–60.
75. Kotzebue, 1821, 2:61.
76. Kotzebue, 1821, 2:64–65.
77. Kotzebue, 1821, 2:67–68.
78. Chamisso, 1836:310–13.
79. Chamisso, 1836:314–15.
80. Chamisso, 1836:317–18.
81. Chamisso, 1836:344–45.
82. Chamisso, 1836:345.
83. Kotzebue, 1821, 2:245.
84. Kotzebue, 1821, 2:248.
85. Golovnin, 1949:374.
86. Golovnin, 1949:387.
87. Golovnin, 1949:388.
88. Golovnin, 1949:388–90.
89. Golovnin, 1949:396.
90. Golovnin, 1949:396.

91. Golovnin, 1949:397.
92. Gillesem, 1849:218.
93. Gillesem, 1849:222, 224.
94. Gillesem, 1849:219.
95. Gillesem, 1849:224.
96. Wrangel, 1828:101–02.
97. Gagemeister, 1818:157.
98. Chamisso, 1836:218–19.
99. Kotzebue, 1821, 2:52–53.
100. Kotzebue, 1821, 2:58, 60–1.
101. Kotzebue, 1821, 2:62–64.
102. Chamisso, 1836:220, 221.
103. Chamisso, 1836:321–22.
104. Kotzebue, 1821, 2:246–47.
105. Golovnin, 1949:380, 384.
106. Golovnin, 1949:385.
107. Golovnin, 1949:389.
108. Golovnin, 1949:390.
109. Vasil'ev, 1821:41.
110. Gillesem, 1849:218.
111. Kotzebue, 1981:242, 260.
112. Kotzebue, 1981:268–69.
113. Kotzebue, 1981:271–73.
114. Kotzebue, 1981:273.
115. Kotzebue, 1981:273–74.
116. Kotzebue, 1981:290–91.
117. Chamisso, 1836:306, 312.
118. Chamisso, 1836:216–17.
119. Golovnin, 1949:384.
120. Golovnin, 1949:387.
121. Gillesem, 1849:220–21.
122. Kotzebue, 1981:264–65.
123. Kotzebue, 1981:267–68.
124. Kotzebue, 1981:269–70.
125. Kotzebue, 1981:289.
126. Kotzebue, 1981:289–90.
127. Lazarev, 1950:264, 269.
128. Lazarev, 1950:260–61.
129. Wrangel, 1828:89ff.

Notes on Archival Sources

General Remarks

All officers and midshipmen in Russian naval vessels at Oahu by 1826, e.g., the *Kamchatka*, *Otkrytie*, *Blagonamerennyi* and *Predpriiatie*, were obliged to keep records and, at the end of a Pacific expedition, to surrender all their journals, logs, and notes to the Naval Minister as representative of the imperial authority. So too, with some exceptions and under rather complex terms, were naval officers in Company-owned vessels, i.e., officers seconded to the Russian-American Company and charged with the delivery of Company-owned goods to Petropavlovsk-in-Kamchatka and/or Sitka (Novo-Arkhangel'sk). Such naval officers were also in the infant Honolulu, (e.g., Lieutenants Gagemeister, Moritz Berkh, and Kozlianinov of the *Neva*), although it was not until the late 1830s that, aboard such Company-owned transports as the *Nikolai* and *Elena*, they would visit it in numbers.[1] The officers aboard the Russian ships in Honolulu Harbour between 1809 and 1826 (who numbered fifty) were of course not academics or *savants* in Captain Bellingshausen's mould; nor in some cases were they under orders to concern themselves particularly with the native peoples they encountered. It is a striking fact, however, that one half of all those ships called at Oahu in the course of strictly scientific voyages or ventures of discovery, and that the captains of two others, V.M. Golovnin of the *Kamchatka* and Wrangel of the *Krotkii*, won celebrity among their countrymen as officers of scientific bent. In short, a large majority of officers who visited and spent some time in Honolulu in the early nineteenth century were highly educated men, selected carefully for scientific work, and predisposed toward objective treatment of the novel scene. From the perspective of Hawaiian studies, this is fortunate. So, too, is the strikingly high incidence of subsequent political-professional success among those visitors to infant Honolulu. By attaining flag-rank and wielding influence within their service, Gleb Shishmarev of the *Blagonamerennyi*, Lütke and Wrangel of the *Kamchatka*, Vasil'ev of the *Otkrytie*, Kordiukov and Rimskii-Korsakov of the *Predpriiatie*,[2] to name but half-a-dozen admirals, ensured that their papers would survive intact in named and numbered *fonds* in central archives, to be disinterred by later generations with an interest in earlier post-contact Honolulu.

It is worth observing, in this context, the appreciable Baltic German element within the Russian naval-scientific presence at Oahu in the early nineteenth century. Otto von Kotzebue of the *Riurik*, Lütke and Wrangel of the *Kamchatka*, Karl Hulsen (Gillesem) of the *Blag-*

onamerennyi, Lieutenant Pfeifer of the *Predpriiatie*, and Midshipman Deibner of the *Krotkii* did not comprise as solid and formidable a German block as had subordinates whom I.F. (Adam J. von) Kruzenshtern had placed aboard the *Nadezhda* and the *Neva* in 1803 (Berg, Loewenstern, and Bellingshausen, Kotzebue et al).[3] Nevertheless, they were a presence and, together with the German-speaking naturalists, botanists, and surgeons also sailing with the Navy to Oahu (Chamisso and Eschscholtz in the *Riurik*, Eschscholtz, Seewald, Hoffmann, and Lenz in the *Predpriiatie*, and Kaiber in the *Krotkii*), a reminder of the power still exerted by the Baltic German *Herrenvolk* in Russia.[4] For their contemporaries, such names as Kotzebue, Chamisso, and Lütke carried sociopolitical, as well as academic weight, and lent the Russian Navy's North Pacific enterprise an unmistakably prestigious aura.[5] By extension, modern students of the infant Honolulu must perforce note that the bulk of I.F. Kruzenshtern's and F.P. Wrangel's papers are today held, not in Leningrad or Moscow, but in Tartu (the Estonian State Historical Archive: see below).

In summary, first-hand accounts of Honolulu were in fact submitted to the Russian Naval Ministry by many naval officers and others who, by stipulated terms of their secondment or appointment to specific vessels, e.g., draughtsmen sent by the Imperial Academy of Arts,[6] had fallen partially within the pale of naval discipline. Of these reports, most stayed in Navy keeping and are held today by the Central State Naval Archive of the USSR (*Tsentral'nyi Gosudarstvennyi Arkhiv Voenno-Morskogo Flota SSSR*, Leningrad). Related papers, private letters, and draft articles, by contrast, are now held in a range of central and provincial archives, listed below.

Formal submissions of reports by serving officers by no means guaranteed that they would ever see the light of day again. It was the overall success of any given expedition, as then assessed by the imperial authorities, that determined the fate of such reports—certain of which may now be viewed as source materials for Honolulu. Many factors could produce a "failure" verdict on a naval enterprise, removing any prospect of its records being published, at least at State expense, and in the short term. Vasil'ev's and Gleb Shishmarev's Arctic and Pacific expedition, for example, was completely overshadowed by the brilliant success of Bellingshausen, and was correctly seen as more or less a failure. Far from finding any navigable passage over Asia, it had met a wall of solid ice, turned back, and happened on an unimportant islet in the Bering Sea called Nunivak and sixteen even smaller coral islets in the Ellises.[7] As a result, the journals of participants were not printed at a time, from 1822 to 1825, when such material might otherwise have been published at Government expense. To the frustration of ethnographers from Sydney to Alaska, firsthand ethnographic data are gathering dust in naval archives to this day. What the *Otkrytie* failed to do was left largely for the *Blossom* (Captain F.W. Beechey) to achieve.[8] Even to glance at Gleb Shishmarev's little essay on the Coastal Chukchi, "Svedeniia i Chukchakh" (which appeared more than thirty years after his visit to Chukotka),[9] is to recognize the loss to Polynesian studies. Aleksei Petrovich Lazarev's attempts to leave at least some public record of the voyage of the sloop *Blagonamerennyi* ended in failure. In the view of A.I. Solov'ev, his Soviet biographer, that failure was an indirect result of the Decembrist insurrection and political machinations in St. Petersburg in 1826. "It is hard to suppose that Lazarev had any link with the Decembrists, but a fact remains a fact: the decline of his career did start at the outset of the year 1826."[10]

In short, numerous records of (in some cases quite long) stays at Oahu by intelligent, well-educated men were never published. Some of these records may be of interest to the student of Hawaii, who is indebted to such Soviet historians (Ostrovskii, Lipshits, Kuznetsova, Shur: see Bibliography) as has been insisted in published papers. What happened to the records? With exceptions, the faircopies were deposited in some section of the Central Naval Archive in St. Petersburg.

It would be wrong for the potential Western student of the Russian Navy's earlier activity in the Hawaiian Islands to suppose, however, that that Central Naval Archive is the only source of relevant original material. In reality, a wealth of such material, which falls essentially into three categories—articles, letters, and despatches or reports—may be examined in a number of the main Soviet archives and in certain libraries. The following remarks concern eight central or provincial institutions which today hold documents bearing directly on the Russian naval presence on Oahu in the period 1809 to 1826. Bibliographies are mentioned, and specific items bearing on Oahu are described in brief. All students contemplating working visits to the libraries or archives listed are advised to first acquaint themselves with P. Kennedy Grimsted's guide, *Archives and Manuscript Repositories in the USSR: Leningrad and Moscow* (Princeton, 1972).

Central State Archives, USSR

Tsentral'nyi Gosudarstvennyi Arkhiv Voenno-Morskogo Flota

Among the best-organized ministerial archives of the nineteenth century, and a direct descendant of the Admiralty College Archive formed in 1718, TsGAVMF remains officially closed to foreign scholars. Increasingly, however, the administration shows itself prepared, if foreign visitors have ample time and excellent credentials, to make documents from earlier historical collections (*fonds*) available to them in the main reading-room of the *Tsentral'nyi Gosudarstvennyi Istoricheskii Arkhiv*

SSSR, known as TsGIAL (see below). Armed with a reader's pass or ticket, the researcher has his own archival worker or *sotrudnik* help him place specific orders for materials. Of special value to the student of Hawaii are materials in *fonds* relating to distinguished officers who played a major role in the Pacific in the early nineteenth century: I.F. Kruzenshtern (14), V.M. Golovnin (166 and 7), F.P. Lütke (15). Assuming that no Soviet researcher is at work on them when the request is made, dozens of items bearing indirectly or directly on the Russian Navy's contacts with Hawaii or Oahu may be made available by approval to the foreigner at TsGIAL. Other *fonds* of relevance to Honolulu's history include: 203 (*Voennaia po flotu kantseliariia*); 432 (*Morskoi Kadetskii Korpus*); and 402 (M.N. Staniukovich papers, *inter alia*). While waiting for the delivery of materials, the visitor may avail himself of TsGAVMF's own library of 15,000 volumes.

Major inconveniences for the would-be user of documents held at TsGAVMF are the unavailability (to the user) of detailed *opisi* of various constituent collections, and the non-existence of a modern, comprehensive, published outline of the archive's massive holdings. The secrecy with which the *opisi* are still surrounded must be accepted with resignation; there is, however, something to be done to lessen the inconvenience of having no contemporary guide. One can consult beforehand the now widely available work, *Arkhivy SSSR: Leningradskoe otdelenie Tsentral'nogo Istoricheskogo Arkhiva: putevoditel' po fondam* (Leningrad: Lenoblizdat, 1933). Compiled by M. Akhun, V. Lukomskii and others, and edited by A.K. Drezen, the guide covered the archive in question as then constituted. A good sixth of its holdings were naval (described on pp. 197–248 of the guide). Although soon afterwards moved and administered as TsGAVMF, these naval holdings were nowhere else described; nor has any subsequent list appeared to make the 1933 guide obsolete for the purposes of naval research in a Pacific context. Two or three of the ten volumes of *Opisaniia del arkhiva Morskago Ministerstva za vremia s poloviny XVII do nachala XIX stoletiia (Descriptions of the Collections of the Archive of the Naval Ministry over the Period from the Mid-17th to the Beginning of the 19th Century*: St. Petersburg, 1877–1906), have similarly retained their usefulness. Axiomatically, the fact that the archive housing these materials has had several names over the years does not affect the value of these volumes, since the organization of naval *fonds* has been maintained over the generations to a noteworthy extent.

Observations follow on a dozen items or groups of items, held in TsGAVMF, which bear on Honolulu. It must be stressed that the items represent a mere fraction of the original material of this sort which is in TsGAVMF.

- *Fond* 5, op. 1, *delo* 95. The travel diary of Midshipman, later Admiral, Loggin Logginovich Geiden of the *Predpriiatie*, 1823–26: "Oahu Passages" dated 14 December 1824–31, January 1825, and 13–19 September 1825. An excellent example of the value, to the student of Hawaii, of subsequent professional success by an early visitor to Honolulu. Count Geiden, a hero of the battle of Navarino (1827), served on the Naval General Staff and the Scientific Committee thereof, and so sustained official awareness of the Pacific Basin in the 1850s.

- *Fond* 7, op. 1, *delo* 16. Faircopy (holograph) of Captain Vasilii Mikhailovich Golovnin's narrative account of his voyage in the *Kamchatka*, headed "Puteshestvie na voennom shliupe Kamchatka: chast' I". On the publication of this, in 1823, see Chapter 12 above. Occasional words and comments from the "Oahu Passage" (26–30 October 1818) are missing from the first edition. Associated materials in this same collection relate to Golovnin's success as a commander e.g., op. 1, *delo* 2:22–23 (testimony by F.P. Wrangel *et al*). The *Kamchatka*'s log (*morskoi zhurnal*) is filed under op. 1, *delo* 17, and contains data recorded in Honolulu Harbour on the aforementioned days.

- *Fond* 14, op. 1, *delo* 192. Otto von Kotzebue's official account of the *Predpriiatie*'s expedition, completed in 1828. The presence of this copy of I.F. Kruzenshtern's *fond* reflects the latter's importance as Kotzebue's main sponsor (and his fellow-countryman). See Tumarkin, 1981:3 and 14–15, on past confusion between the printed verions of this MS, "Puteshestvie vokrug sveta, sovershennoe ... v 1823, 24, 25 i 26 godakh ..." and *Neue Reise um die Welt ...*"(Weimar, Bd. 1–2, 1830).

- *Fond* 15, op. 1, *delo* 8. The travel diary of Midshipman, later Admiral, Fedor Petrovich Lütke (Litke), of the *Kamchatka*. "Oahu Passages," dated 26–30 October 1818. On this valuable diary and its ethnographic and general descriptive content, see B.M. Komissarov, 1964. The MS is entitled, "Dnevnik leitenanta F.P. Litke, vedennyi vo vremia krugosvetnogo plavaniia na shliupe 'Kamchatka' ": held under ref., *delo* 8, 234 pp.; *delo* 9, 156 pp. The Honolulu stay and the story of Georg Anton Scheffer's recent Hawaiian adventure are covered on pp. 145–61 and 161–86 of the MS in *delo* 8. Elsewhere in it, e.g., pp. 233–34, there are observations on relations between "Mr. Pitt" (Kalanimoku) and John Elliot de Castro. Lütke follows Golovnin in disapproving very strongly of Scheffer, some of whose papers both officers had read whilst at Honolulu, and quotes from letters of which the originals were lost in the last century. These letters bear on Scheffer's efforts to entrench himself and the Russian-American Company on Kauai and Oahu in 1816. For a survey, see Shur, 1970:205–06 and Komissarov, 1964:417–18. Also among the Oahu-related papers in *delo* 9 of this same collection, under ref., *delo* 9, p. 149/obv., are unusually frank comments by Lütke to the effect that M.N. Vasil'ev, commanding the *Otkrytie*, was a good man but not altogether suited to his post in 1819–21, "having never, or hardly ever, gone to sea."

- *Fond*, 25, op. 1, *delo* 114. Preparations for the double Pacific venture of 1819–21, alluding to the suitability of the Hawaiian Islands as a rendezvous and revictualling point for the Russians. Initial instructions by

Jean-François, marquis de Traversay, then naval minister: pp. 50–67; correspondence, Kruzenshtern-de Traversay, November 1818–March 1819, re commands, best routes to and from the Northwest Coast, the need to winter in mid-Pacific and survey there. On Kruzenshtern's own familiarity with the Hawaiian Islands, see Barratt, 1988: pt. 1, sect. b and c.

– *Fond* 162, op. 1, *delo* 44. Internal and interdepartmental correspondence re the possible publication of an as yet unwritten account of the voyage of the *Otkrytie* by Captain Mikhail Nikolaevich Vasil'ev; lack of major discoveries by him, slight interest of data on places often described, e.g., Hawaiian Islands and California. For complementary materials, see *fond* 205, op. 1, *delo* 644.

– *Fond* 166, op. 1, *delo* 2537. V.M. Golovnin's report to the Naval Minister, dated 13 September 1819, on the completed voyage of the sloop *Kamchatka* (pp. 85ff.), and other papers on her route; article "O prebyvanii Lauri v Rossii" ("On Lauri's Sojourn in Russia"), pp. 146–54; op. 1, *delo* 2680, pp. 1–3: the submission of V.M. Golovnin's account of his voyage, including descriptions of the history, and the political and economic situation in Hawaii, to the naval authorities, August 1821; op. 1, *delo* 2680, pp. 5/obv.–6, submission of Mikhail T. Tikhanov's drawings of Honolulu scenes *inter alia*, for engraving; the Academy of Arts' possession of the originals, etc. Further on the fate of these 1818 drawings by Tikhanov, see Chapter 13.

– *Fond*, 203, op. 1, *delo* 7306. The travel journal kept aboard the *Blagonamerennyi* (1819–1822) by Midshipman (later Captain 2nd rank) Nikolai Dmitrievich Shishmarev, the captain's nephew. This manuscript journal, 264 pages in length, was prepared for publication shortly after Shishmarev's death in 1844 (see Kuznetsova, 1968:239). However, the editor's efforts were in vain. The "Oahu Passage" is on pp. 105–09 (20 March–7 April 1821), and contains descriptions of John Harbottle's functions at Honolulu Harbour, American commercial activities at Honolulu, traditional Hawaiian skills, and encounters with Liholiho. Complements M.N. Vasil'ev's contemporaneous account (see below here, *fond* 213).

– *Fond* 213, op. 1, *delo* 104:16–70. "Sandvichevy Ostrova," also referred to as "Zapiski o prebyvanii na Gavaiskikh ostrovakh" ("Notes on a Stay in the Hawaiian Islands") by Mikhail Nikolaevich Vasil'ev, of the *Otkrytie*. It is an important 54-page essay, covering many aspects of the two 1821 visits to Honolulu; it also deals with native diet (pp. 31–32), New Englanders trading on the Northwest Coast from a Honolulu base (pp. 25–27), and *haole* ambitions and wealth (pp. 43–44). Further on this piece, see Tumarkin, 1983:48–55.

This essay is based on notes taken by Vasil'ev and others on or shortly after the arrival of his squadron at the Hawaiian Islands (1821) and at Rio de Janeiro (March 1822). What appears to be a paper based on the same data is filed in *delo* 113. The materials in the two *dela* overlap to a considerable degree, and are complemented by related Hawaiian material also in *delo* 113. Of particular interest are notes taken at Honolulu by the *Otkrytie*'s lieutenants, Aleksandr Avinov, Pavel Zelenoi, and Roman P. Boil' or

Boyle. Lieutenant Boyle composed a brief but sound paper entitled, "Zapiska o prirode, istorii, nravakh i obychaiakh zhitelei Sandvichevykh Ostrovov" ("A Note on the Nature, History, Mores and Customs of the Natives of the Sandwich Islands":2–16 of d. 113). Boyle had been instructed by Vasil'ev to collect information from Hawaiian chiefs and commoners on the basis of a prepared set of questions. He took his questionnaire to Captain George Beckley, who agreed to help him by interpreting both questions and answers. Boyle's paper was based on the results. He considered social structure, land ownership, and religious belief and practice, *inter alia*, noting that Cook was venerated as the god Lono; the more ardently because he had arrived during the *makahiki* season (pp. 9–10). Also in *fond* 213, *delo* 52, is a file of correspondence regarding the contents and proper use of diaries and travel notes kept, at Honolulu and elsewhere, by officers of the *Otkrytie* and the *Blagonamerennyi*. These materials had been made available to Vasil'ev in 1822–23, having been submitted in due form to the naval minister (August 1822), and might under more propitious circumstances have been used, as F. Bellingshausen's officers' notes were then being used (see Barratt, 1979c:16–18, 22), in the preparation of a monograph. Also in this *fond*, under ref., op. 1, *delo* 44:1–17 is a list of some 800 Hawaiian words and phrases compiled by A.P. Lazarev and P. Zelenoi, of the *Blagonamerennyi* and the *Otkrytie* respectively, in 1821. There are supplementary remarks on Hawaiian pronunciation and Island peculiarities therein. Finally, it also contains, under ref., op. 1, *delo* 352, excerpts from several journals kept by officers of those two ships. For those relevant to Hawaii (12 February–14 October 1821), see Lazarev, 1950:394–400 (App. XXVI).

– *Fond* 213, op. 1, *delo* 116:2–6. Holographs of two letters addressed to M.N. Vasil'ev (dated 15 April and 30 December 1821) by Reverend Hiram Bingham. The mission's appreciation of Russian support and financial aid, etc.

– *Fond* 215, op. 1, *delo* 1203. List of Hawaiian and other Pacific artefacts and "natural specimens" which went, in 1827–28, from the museum of the Admiralty Department into the museum of the Academy of Sciences, the *Kunstkammer*, from which developed the modern Peter-the-Great Museum of the N.N. Miklukko-Maklai Institute of Anthropology and Ethnography: see Likhtenberg, 1960:168ff.

– *Fond* 402, op. 1, *delo* 104. Report by Captain-Lieutenant M.N. Staniukovich, of the *Moller*, on the success of his voyage and (pp. 44–45) the friendly reception given him at Honolulu, where he passed nine weeks (6 December 1827–9 February 1828). It usefully complements Wrangel's account of an 1826 stay in the *Krotkii*, with similar emphasis on commerce and the true situation of King Kauikeaouli vis-à-vis resident traders and missionaries.

– *Fond* 1153, op. 1, *delo* 1. Bound faircopy of Aleksei Petrovich Lazarev's "Zapiski o plavanii voennogo shliupa *Blagonamerennogo* v Beringov proliv ... v 1819, 1820, 1821 i 1822 godakh," i.e., the account found in the Smolensk

State Regional Archive and edited by A.I. Solov'ev at TsGAVMF in 1949–50. Variants between its "Oahu Passage" and that printed (pp. 253–73) in Lazarev, 1959, reflect Soviet notions of what is "of interest."

Tsentral'nyi Gosudarstvennyi Istoricheskii Arkhiv, Leningrad

Here, as in TsGAVMF, one is hampered by an absence of recent comprehensive guides to holdings, and thoroughly dependent on the efforts of *sotrudniki* who do have access to such typed inventories as are at hand. One can, however, make good use of A.K. Drezen's 1933 guide to the archive, earlier discussed. Among records that illuminate the Russian Navy's venture in the North Pacific Ocean in the early nineteenth century (and incidentally touch on its dealings with the monarchy and merchants of Hawaii), are papers relating to the secondment of naval officers to the Russian-American Company. *Fond* 853, for example, is that of Mikhail Buldakov, long chairman of that Company's Board of Directors.[11] Its contents throw considerable light on the beginnings of the Kruzenshtern-Lisianskii expedition, in the course of which the *Nadezhda* and the *Neva* came to the Islands (1804). TsGIAL also holds the former archive of the Department of Manufacture and Domestic Commerce, under whose jurisdiction the Company Board was placed in 1811 and remained for many years (see Okun', 1951:97–98). It is thus in TsGIAL that one finds materials relating to the Company's and Navy's attitudes towards the international tensions caused by Scheffer's colourful adventures on Oahu and, particularly, at Kauai. *Fond* 18, op. 5 contains Company-Department correspondence for 1816–20, and *delo* 1239 offers a selection of Company attacks on the characters of New England shipmasters trading, by way of Honolulu, on the Northwest Coast of North America. "The merchants always select as skippers of the vessels they are sending out ... the most dishonest individuals; for they cannot hope for profit from honest ones. And these skippers choose themselves crews from among persons of the same sort as themselves" (d. 1239, p. 32). Letters from Scheffer to Alexander I (1817) and to Count Nesselrode, minister of foreign affairs, are in this same folder. Finally, the student of early Hawaii should be aware of *fond* 789, containing papers of the Imperial Academy of Arts. These throw light both on the terms of employment, as it were, of official artists on ships that called at Honolulu, and, more significantly, on the fates of portfolios containing drawings of Honolulu scenes.

– *Fond* 15, op. 1, *delo* 13. Diary of an unidentified individual, written en route from Sitka (Novo-Arkhangel'sk) to the Hawaiian Islands, 1820. Possibly on a Company vessel based in the North Pacific. The urgency of securing fresh provisions for the Company settlements on Northwest Coast, Hawaiian produce, etc.

- *Fond* 789, op. 1 (Pt. 1), *dela* 1854, 1949, 1961, 2460. The appointment of Mikhail Tikhanov to the *Kamchatka*, his qualifications and duties, op. 20, *dela* 17, 19, 21, 28, 30, 36, 48: Tikhanov's progress, drawing emphases, contacts with A.N. Olenin. These MSS are the basis of L.A. Shur's 1974 article on Tikhanov (see Bibliography). Op. 1 (pt. 2), *dela* 123, 207, 249, 262, 546, 1660, 1904: participation of Emelian Korneev, also a graduate of the Academy, in the voyage of the *Otkrytie* (1819–22), his Hawaiian and other drawings, their whereabouts in 1822–23.

- *Fond* 18, op. 5, *delo* 1239. Extracts from a letter to Tsar Alexander I from Dr. Scheffer regarding the occupation by Russians of the Sandwich Islands; with additional comments in strong opposition to his proposals: pp. 17–19. The need for Russia to undermine New England dominance in the Hawaiian trade, 1817. The added comments are by P. Ostrogorskii, an official at the Department of Manufacture. *Delo* 1231: Scheffer on the activity of Captain James Bennett and the 1815 wreck of the *Atahualpa* (see Pierce, 1965:230). *Delo* 1231, pp. 42–43: details of Kaumualii's alleged cession of sovereignty of Kauai to the Russian-American Company, 21 May 1816, and promise to grant half of Oahu to it in return for military aid against Kamehameha I (large warship, 500 men, etc.) This is entitled, "Izvlechenie iz doneseniia Glavnomu Kompanii Pravleniiu byvshikh na Sandvichevykh Ostrovakh ... eio sluzhitelei ot 7 chisla iulia 1817 gods." Insights into Scheffer's intentions for Oahu Island. See Tumarkin, 1964:145–46, where good use is made of these materials.

Other Major Archives in Leningrad

Arkhiv Vneshnei Politiki Rossii SSSR (AVPR)

Since Russia's navy, like all other major navies, has repeatedly had dealings with the representatives of foreign governments, and since its officers have often served as agents or apologists for Russia overseas, this archive—of Russian foreign policy—cannot be ignored by the historian of earlier post-contact Oahu. At such a place as Honolulu, Russian diplomatic, naval, and commercial interests were so interwoven, in the age of sail, as to be almost inextricable. AVPR contains the diplomatic record of the Russian Crown and Empire from the time of Peter the Great until 1917. Important sections for the student of Hawaiian history—in its Russian context—are the *Sankt-Petersburgskii Glavnyi Arkhiv or Glavarkhiv* (1–10, 1817–1819) and the chancery of the Ministry of Foreign Affairs which, until 1923, had been retained in the old archive of the ministry itself, in Petrograd. These chancery papers are now arranged by year, with subdivisions for outgoing and incoming correspondence, and for embassies and missions overseas. Under the years 1818–21, a wealth of information may be found on the Navy's (and Crown's) changing attitude towards a forward policy in the North Pacific Basin and, incidentally, towards involvement in the political life of Hawaii.

- *Fond* St. Petersburg Glavnogo Arkhiva, 1–10, 1817–1819, *delo* 1. "Is-toricheskoe, klimaticheskoe i statisticheskoe svedenie o Sandvichevykh os-trovakh" ("Historical, Climatic, and Statistical Information on the Sand-wich Islands"): pp. 38–42. Impressions of Kamehameha I's personal wealth by 1817, stone storehouse on Oahu full of European wares, weapons and ammunition. "Izvlechenie iz podannogo doktorom Shefferom zhurnala ..." ("Extract from a Journal Submitted by Dr. Scheffer ..."): pp. 29–30. Ex-tracts included in a Company Board report to K.V. Nesselrode, dated 19 January 1818 and taken from pp. 35–36 of Scheffer's January 1815–March 1818 journal, i.e., 3 January–May 1816. Scheffer receives land-grants on Oahu from King Kamehameha I and starts agricultural experiments on one lot. (See Pierce, 1965:8, for background.) Pp. 29–31 of this same *delo*, 1, also submitted to Nesselrode that day, describe the settlement for Oahu proposed by Kaumualii on 21 May 1816, i.e., under Russian suzerainty.

- *Fond* Kantseliarii Ministerstva Vneshnikh Del: 1821, *delo* 2804, pp. 108–10. "Vypiski iz dnevnika kapitana Benneta, komandira sudna Rossiisko-Amerikanskoi Kompanii *Beringa*" ("Extracts from the Diary of Captain Bennett, Commander of the Russian-American Company vessel *Bering*"). Scheffer, James Bennett, and plans to occupy several Hawaiian Islands or parts of islands, 1815.

Arkhiv Leningradskogo Otdeleniia Instituta Istorii Akademii Nauk SSSR (LOII)

Published works describing the holdings of this archive, of the Lenin-grad Division of the Academy of Sciences' Institute of History, are avail-able in the Institute's own library. Moreover, photocopying facilities are now available and there is close liaison between LOII and the archive and library of the Academy of Sciences (known as BAN), which are equally accustomed to receiving foreign visitors. A useful starting point is the annotated guide by I.V. Valkina and others, *Putevoditel' po arkhivu Leningradskogo otdeleniia Instituta Istorii*, ed. A.I. Andreev (Moscow-Leningrad, 1958: 603pp). LOII holds materials relating to the fortunes of the Russian-American Company in the Pacific Basin, and the papers of many prominent and noble Russian families that produced admirals with Pacific interests, e.g., the Menshikovs, Vorontsovs, and Golovnins.

- *Kollektsiia* 115, No. 447, pp. 1–98. Kiril Timofeevich Khlebnikov, "Za-piski o koloniiakh v Amerike Rossiisko-Amerikanskoi Kompanii" ("Notes on the Russian-American Company's Colonies in America"). Khlebnikov was Chief Manager and second-in-command at Sitka (1817–32), later Com-pany Director, and was intimately acquainted with the Company's affairs in the Pacific.[12] These "Notes" reflect a knowledge of those affairs unpar-alleled by any contemporary, and touch on Company dealings on Oahu from 1816 through 1826; they also reflect on the considerable wealth of Don Francisco de Paula Marin, his estates, herds, and flocks near Hon-olulu, and his readiness to provision Company vessels. Also dealt with briefly (pp. 13–14) is Chief Manager A.A. Baranov's instruction to Scheffer of 15 February 1816, to be delivered by Navy Lieutenant Ia.A. Podushkin (Pierce, 1965:53–54), to the effect that he should "establish a factory" on Oahu or some other place, if possible.[13]

Saltykov-Shchedrin Public Library: Rukopisnyi otdel (ORGPB)

- *Kollektsiia I.V. Pomialovskogo*, No. 72. The diary kept by Lieutenant Aleksei Petrovich Lazarev, of the *Blagonamerennyi*, with an "Oahu section" dated 20 March–7 April 1821.

- *Fond* 17, 106, pp. 1/obv.–3. Notes re A.P. Lazarev's attempts to publish his 1819–22 journal, and his recognition of failure in 1830.

- *Fond* 211, k. 3620, *delo* 14. Materials reflecting friendly relations between Captain V.M. Golovnin and A.N. Olenin, President of the Academy of Arts whose protégé, M. Tikhanov, sailed in the *Kamchatka* to Honolulu; Olenin recommends Tikhanov as a first-rate draughtsman, etc. k. 3626, *delo* 25/4, p. 1: Golovnin's decision to present certain "rarities" (ethnographica) collected in the Pacific, to the Academy. See Likhtenberg, 1960:168–69, on the problems of establishing the exact provenance of Hawaiian artefacts, now in Leningrad, which were in the Admiralty Department's museum by 1828.

Institut Russkoi Literatury Akademii Nauk (Pushkinskii Dom): Rukopisnyi Otdel

- *Fond* 93, op. 2, no. 161. Fedor Fedorovich Matiushkin, "Zhurnal krugosvetnogo plavaniia na shliupe *Kamchatka*, pod komandovaniem kapitana Golovnina" ("A Journal of a Voyage Round the World on the Sloop *Kamchatka*, under the Command of Captain Golovnin"). Matiushkin was a close friend of the poet Alexander Pushkin (see Gastfreind, 1913:20–21 and Davydov, 1956:58–65), and his journal is officially treated as having particular literary associations and interest. The "Honolulu Passage" of the MS (pp. 109–11) covers, in a stylistically overwrought manner, the Hawaiians' readiness to take passage to Europe, Lauri's acceptance onboard the *Kamchatka*, local shipping, and American commercial zeal. Complementary letters from Matiushkin to friends in St. Petersburg (1818–19), formerly in the collection of Prince Sergei Oldenburgskii, are now in the Saltykov-Shchedrin Public Library, *Rukopisnyi Otdel*: main card-catalog, under Matiushkin, F.F.

Other Archives

Tsentral'nyi Gosudarstvennyi Istoricheskii Arkhiv Estonskoi SSR, Tartu

This is the main historical archive of Estonia, and contains materials relating to all aspects of the link between Estonia (*Estliandiia*) and imperial Russia since the Russian conquest in 1711. It holds family papers (Kruzenshtern, Bellingshausen, Loewenstern, Berg) of direct relevance to naval studies and Pacific history. These papers reflect the professional successes of many naval officers of Baltic German origin, some of whom, e.g., Kruzenshtern, Kotzebue, and Wrangel, visited the Hawaiian Islands and left accounts of them. Materials in Tartu are often complemented by similar records at the Estonian State Museum of History (*Eesti NSV Riiklik Ajaloomuuseum*) and the adjacent library of the Academy of Sciences of the Estonian SSR (*Teaduste Akadeemia Teaduslik Raamatukogu*), both in Tallin. The I.F. Kruzenshtern (1414) and F.P. Wrangel (2057) *fonds*, both extremely large, are of greatest value to Hawaiian history and ethnography.

- *Fond* 1414, op. 3, *delo* 42. Letters to I.F. Kruzenshtern from the artist of the *Riurik*, Ludovik (Louis) Choris, dated 1821–22, re the publication of (Hawaiian and other) illustrative material in book form, in Paris. Preparations for *Voyage pittoresque autour du monde*, obligations to Count Nikolai Petrovich Rumiantsev and others.

- *Fond* 2057, op. 1, *dela* 310 and 312. Journal notes from the voyage of the *Krotkii* (1825–27) kept by Captain, later Admiral, Ferdinand Petrovich Wrangel or Vrangel' (1796–1870), prominent scholar and student of Russian America, founding father of the Russian Geographical Society. Op. 1, *delo* 352, pp. 10/obv.–11: Notebook for 1830, with analysis of the advantages for the Russian-American Company of buying supplies and selling furs at Honolulu. Op. 1, *delo* 443: Wrangel's letters to F.P. Lütke from Honolulu (pp. 109–10 offers a description of Honolulu's markets in November 1826, published by Shur in 1970:209). Other letters elaborate on the baneful effect of American missionary work, and the frenetic rate of commercial expansion at Honolulu.

Gosudarstvennaia Publichnaia Biblioteka imeni V.I. Lenina, Rukopisnyi otdel (Lenin Library, Moscow: Manuscripts Department)

This manuscript collection contains materials relating to the *Nadezhda*'s brief visit to the Hawaiian Islands of June 1804, to Russian-American Company plans for reprovisioning at the Islands (1814–15), and to the reality of trade between Russian North America and Honolulu, then and slightly later.

- *Fond* 178, M 10693a-b contains the sketching albums of Wilhelm-Gottlieb Tilesius von Tilenau (1769–1857), the Leipzig-educated naturalist who sailed with Kruzenshtern in 1803–06.[14] The albums complement the naturalist's Pacific diary, held at the Archive of the Academy of Sciences, Leningrad (*Razriad* IV, op. 1, No. 800). Both diary and albums, however, concentrate on the Marquesas rather than the Hawaiian Islands; the latter are touched upon briefly.

- *Fond* 255, *karton* 15, *delo* 35 offers a set of letters sent to Count N.P. Rumiantsev, as Chancellor of Russia and a former minister of finance, by the chairman of the Russian-American Company's Main Board, M.M. Buldakov. The letters, most of 1814, bear on questions of trade and its expansion in the Pacific. Of more signficance to Hawaiian studies in the frame of 1816–26 is *Fond* 204.

- *Fond* 204 (*Arkhiv I.A. Kuskova*), *karton* 32. This box contains letters by, biographical papers on, and official reports by and concerning Chief Manager A.A. Baranov's principal assistant in the Russian-American Company's Pacific colonies, Ivan Aleksandrovich Kuskov (1765–1823). Kuskov, founder of Fort Ross in Upper California (1812), remained there as manager until 1821. Various materials reflect his awareness of the need to keep the Hawaiian Islands in mind as a possible place of provisionment and market for certain kinds of peltry.

Other Soviet archives and libraries also have holdings that bear directly on the Honolulu seen by Russian visitors in the early nineteenth century. Four will be mentioned, and observations offered on the prospects of finding other primary materials in the USSR.

- A variant copy of K.T. Khlebnikov's essay, "Zapiski o koloniiakh ... v Amerike" (see LOII above), together with related papers, is held in the archive of the Geographical Society in Leningrad (*Arkhiv Geografscheskogo Obshchestva Akademii Nauk SSSR*, or AGO), under ref., *Razriad* 99, op. 1. The archive's holdings are briefly summarized in a comparatively recent guide, *Russkie geografy i puteshestvenniki: fondy arkhiva Geografcheskogo Obshchestva*, compiled by T.P. Matveeva *et al.* (Leningrad, 1971). Other essays by Khlebnikov with incidental reference to Company trade in Honolulu are listed in Gibson, 1976:242. Gibson also quotes from Company reports now held at the U.S. National Archives in Washington, D.C. ("Russian-American Company Journals of Correspondence"), to illustrate the Company Head Office's persistent hope of possessing itself of one or more Hawaiian Island: see pp. 148–49, nn. 25, 28. These reports and Khlebnikov's "Zapiski o koloniiakh ..." are complementary.

- Another collection of Khlebnikov papers, some bearing on Company activities in the mid-Pacific, is in the Perm District State Archive, Perm'. Mention may be made of items in *fond* 445, op. 1: *delo* 43 is a biography of Captain L.A. Gagemeister, the first Russian officer to pay a visit to Honolulu (1809); and *dela* 143 and 381 hold letters to Khlebnikov from A.A. Baranov and Karl Schmidt (Company manager at Fort Ross in Upper California from 1821 to 1824), which make references to Hawaiian supplies and Russian-Hawaiian dealings. A large part of this Perm' collection of Khlebnikov's writings was microfilmed in the early 1970s by L.A. Shur, and may now be consulted in the Elmer Rasmuson Research Library at the University of Alaska in Fairbanks. It is described in three papers, of 1953–57, by the Soviet historical geographer, B.N. Vishnevskii (see Shur,

1970:211, n. 22).

- A third institution with Hawaiian material is the Academy of Arts (*Akadem-iia Khudozhestv SSSR*), in whose museum (drawing division, *otdel risunka*) is kept not only Mikhail Tikhanov's original portfolio of 1819–22 with its four Hawaiian scenes, but also related written material. There is, for instance, a list of all Tikhanov's works from the Pacific with annotations by Golovnin, apparently from June 1822.

- Finally, *Tsentral'nyi Gosudarstvennyi Arkhiv Drevnikh Aktov* (TsGADA) contains certain Lütke papers of Hawaiian relevance. The then midshipman's 1818 diary is bound in *Razriad* (Section) XXX, *delo* 53 of the large subdivision known as Gosarkhiv, i.e., the old *Gosudarstvennyi Arkhiv Rossiiskoi Imperii*, established in 1834.

Discoveries of documents by officers and others who visited Oahu in the course of expeditions in the early nineteenth century, continue to be made. No less important, from the standpoint of Hawaiian studies, is the very fact that such historians as V.V. Kuznetsova searched in TsGAVMF (1967–68) for other papers by participants in the Vasil'ev-Shishmarev Arctic venture, that is, A.P. Lazarev's companions, and found Midshipman Nikolai Dmitrievich Shishmarev's journal (see here, under Ts-GAVMF, and Kuznetsova, 1968:237). Impressed by Kuznetsova's success, L.A. Shur also returned to TsGAVMF. The *fonds* principally used by her, 203 and 213, had earlier yielded unknown primary material to the leading Soviet historian of Hawaii, Daniel Davydovich Tumarkin, who had used them in his 1964 study, *Vtorzhenie kolonizatorov v "Krai vechnoi vesny"* (*The Intrusion of Colonizers into "the Land of Eternal Spring"*: Moscow, Nauka). More specifically, Tumarkin had searched *fond* 213 and found Lieutenant Roman Pavlovich Boil's (Boyle's) "Note on the Nature, History, Mores, and Customs of the Natives of the Sandwich Islands" (see above, under TsGAVMF). Boyle was Third Lieutenant of the *Otkrytie* in 1819–22 and so was visiting Honolulu simultaneously with Aleksei Petrovich Lazarev. Though his interests were mainly South American, Shur found and microfilmed material of relevance to Oahu in several *dela* in *fond* 213, e.g., 104 and 113 (Vasil'ev's observations on the Hawaiian Islands and their people, in draft and finished form), and 52 (correspondence regarding the content and possible uses of diaries and travel notes kept by others aboard the *Otkrytie* and the *Blagonamerennyi*). Shur also microfilmed the travel diary of Midshipman Count L.L. Geiden, of the *Predpriiatie* (1824–25: *fond* 5, op. 1, *delo* 95), of which Western scholars were entirely unaware, and the *Kamchatka* journal of Midshipman F.P. Lütke (1817–19). The Hawaiian section of Lütke's journal was omitted from Shur's study, *K beregam Novogo Sveta* (*To the Shores of the New World*, Moscow, 1971); nor was any use made, in print, of Geiden's manuscript. Material discovered and microfilmed by Shur, as was mentioned, was acquired in 1982 by the Elmer Rasmuson Research Libary at the University of Alaska, Fairbanks.

AMERICAN ARCHIVAL SOURCES

United States National Archives (Washington, D.C.)

- "Records of the Russian-American Company, 1802–1867: Correspondence of Governors General." File microcopies of Records in the National Archives: No. 11, 1942: reels 1–65 (Vols. 1–49). For a guide to the contents of despatches, see *Records of the Russian-American Company, 1802, 1817–1867*, (Washington, D.C., National Archives and Records Service: General Services Administration, 1971). This pamphlet, produced by Raymond H. Fisher, describes the holdings of M11, records group 261, by item, chronologically. *Inter alia*, see Nos. 196 (the discharging of Dr. Scheffer required, March 1817); 120, 1818 (Russian reaction to Wilson Price Hunt's successful trade at Oahu with the *Pedler*); 487, 1819 (imperial views on correct Russo-Hawaiian relations, Gagemeister's obligation to inform Kaumualii that Alexander I will not accept his fealty as of August 1819 but has gifts for him, hopes that the king may yet sell Kauai to the Company, etc.); 206, 1819 (on the importance of maintaining warm relations with Kaumualii); 177, 1821 (Karl Schmidt's mission to the Hawaiian Islands as supercargo on the ship *Brutus*, Liholiho's uncertain attitude toward Kaumualii, the Russian need to deal with increasing numbers of New Englanders, and transport costs); 257, 1821 (on goods delivered to the *Riurik* at Oahu by Messrs. John Ebbets and Thomas Meek, their unpaid bill for $230 dating from 1817).

Few of the numerous items of this *fond* that relate to the Hawaiian Islands have yet been edited and published in English. Those that have, e.g., No. 196, 1817; 451, 1817; 120, 1818; and 60, 1818 in Richard A. Pierce's *Russia's American Adventure, 1815–1817*:108–09, 124 and 153–54, suggest the importance of a study of these USNA materials, not merely as they relate to Scheffer's adventure in the Islands, but in a wider Hawaiian context.

Office of the Department of State

- "Consular Letters," Honolulu Files, 1. John C. Jones to Secretary of State Adams, 1821–23: (Mostly trade matters, but politics and even naval policy occasionally emerge, e.g., on 20 and 31 December 1822, regarding the Russian ban on foreign trade off the Russian Northwest Coast, Russian naval patrols there, and the need for an American warship to protect U.S.

commercial interests between Oahu and the North Pacific trading centres).
The latter also contain his despatch to Adams of 1 July 1827, on the "hundred lawless seamen of every nation" then to be seen in Honolulu, and the
need for greater international—and internal—order on Oahu.

Harvard University Library, Boston

- Horatio Appleton Lamb MSS: "Notes on Trade with the North West Coast,
  1790–1810." These contain plans of the Boston company of J. and T.H. Perkins to carry supplies to the Russians based at Sitka, 1808; J.J. Astor's
  recognition of the promise of Russo-American trade in the Pacific basin;
  and New England reactions to Russian expansion there and activities in
  Hawaii.
- James Hunnewell MSS: "Journal of James Hunnewell, 1817–19": (Voyage
  in the *Bordeaux Packet* and her sale to Kamehameha I for sandalwood;
  American dominance in this kind of barter, and the need to suppress all
  foreign competition through commercial growth; foreign interest in Honolulu.)

Harvard University School of Business, Baker Library, Boston

- Bryant and Sturgis Letterbooks, 1814–18: (Honolulu and the sandalwood
  trade; Captain John Suter on the Northwest Coast 1817; Bryant and Sturgis vessels vie with J.J. Astor's in bringing mixed cargoes from Honolulu
  to Sitka, 1816–22; an alarum, in orders to Daniel Cross and Wm. Bryant of
  18 October 1823, lest U.S. citizens lose all trade rights along the Northwest
  Coast from Vancouver Island up; Russo-American trade generally in the
  Pacific, and Russian dependence on outside foodstuffs, e.g., from Hawaii.)
- Marshall MSS: "Letterbooks and Related Papers of Messrs. Marshall and
  Wildes," 1821–27: (The arrival of two frame houses, later admired by
  the Russians, in Honoluu, 1822; the *Cleopatra's Barge*; provisions, manufactured goods, and Chinese produce sent from Honolulu to Sitka—John
  C. Jones, Jr. to Marshall and Wildes, 22 January 1822, Wildes to Marshall,
  18 July 1825, etc.; Hawaiian goods suitable for disposal at Sitka, in Jones
  to Marshall and Wildes, 8 February 1826; the voyage of the *Thaddeus* from
  Honolulu to Kamchatka, and her return to Oahu with Russian cordage,
  canvas, and Kamchatkan dried fish, in Jones to Marshall and Wildes, 5
  and 20 November 1821.)

University of California, Bancroft Library (Manuscripts Room), Berkeley

C–D 10 Capitan José Fernandez, "Cosas de California"

P–K 29 Anonymous MS: "Early Commerce in the North Pacific"

P–N 4 "Sheffer Papers," translated by George Lantzeff and S.G. Stewart in 1939, from copies of documents transcribed in Cyrillic by H.H. Bancroft's research assistant, Alphonse Pinart. Pinart, a French ethnologist, worked in St. Petersburg in 1874–75. Further details in Pierce, *op. cit.*, vi–viii, 220.

P–C 31 Phelps, William D. "Solid Men of Boston in the Northwest".

Massachusetts Historical Society Library

"Log of the Atahualpa, October 1813–March 1814": (The sale of this New England trading vessel to Chief Manager A.A. Baranov for the Russian-American Company, 1813; Russo-American *entente* in the Pacific during the War of 1812, and Russian connections with Hawaii through Bostonians.)

Hawaiian Mission Children's Society Library, Honolulu

- "Journal of Levi Chamberlain," MS: 1823–28: (The foreign community on Oahu, including several met by Russian officers; Bingham and such officers; contacts with Wrangel as secular agent of the American Board's mission at Honolulu.)
- "Journal of Maria S. Loomis," MS, 1820–22: (Hawaiian-*haole* relations and foreign influences on them; mission school; French and Russian naval visitors, etc.)

BIBLIOGRAPHY

Adams, Alexander, 1906. "Extracts from an Ancient Log: Selections from the Logbook of Captain Alexander Adams in Connection with the Early History of Hawaii. Occurrences on Board the Brig *Forester*, of London, from Conception Towards the Sandwich Islands," (Honolulu), *Hawaiian Almanac and Annual*, pp. 66–74.

Akimov, Andrei S., 1914. "Lisianskii, Iu.F.," in A.A. Polovtsov and B.L. Modzalevskii, eds., *Russkii biograficheskii slovar'*, (St. Petersburg), vol. 10.

Alexander, W.D., 1894. "The Proceedings of the Russians on Kauai in 1814–1819," HHS *Papers*, 6, 20pp.

——, 1899. *A Brief History of the Hawaiian People* (New York, 2nd ed.). 1st ed. 1841.

——, 1904. "Early Trading in Hawaii," HHS *Papers*, 11:22–24.

——, 1906. "The Story of the Cleopatra's Barge," HHS *Papers*, 13:28ff.

——, 1907. "Early Improvements in Honolulu Harbour," HHS *Fifteenth Annual Report*, pp. 13–28.

——, 1918. "The Overthrow of the Ancient Tabu System in the Hawaiian Islands," HHS *Twenty-Fifth Annual Report*, pp. 37–45.

Anderson, M.S., 1956. "Great Britain and the Growth of the Russian Navy in the Eighteenth Century," *Mariner's Mirror*, 42, 1:132–46.

Anderson, Rufus, 1874. *A History of the Mission to the Sandwich Islands* (Boston).

Andreev, A.I., 1944. *Russkie otkrytiia v Tikhom okeane i v Severnoi Amerike v XVIII–XIX vekakh: sbornik materialov.* Revised edition, 1948 (Moscow-Leningrad).

Anonymous, n.d. "Early Commerce in the North Pacific," Bancroft Library, University of California/Berkeley, MS PK–29.

Arago, J., 1822. *Promenade autour du monde, pendant les années 1817, 1818, 1819 et 1820* (Paris).

Armstrong, Terence, 1979. "Cook's Reputation in Russia," in R. Fisher and H. Johnston, eds. *Captain Cook and his Times* (Seattle), pp. 121–28.

Bailey, T.A., 1934. "Why the United States Purchased Alaska," PHR, 3:39–49.

Ballou, Howard M., 1905. "The Reversal of the Hawaiian Flag," HHS *Papers*, 12:5–11.

Bancroft, H.H., 1884. *History of the Northwest Coast* (San Francisco, 2 vols.).

——, 1885. *History of California* (San Francisco, 7 vols.).

——, 1886. *History of Alaska, From 1730 to 1885* (San Francisco).

Barratt, Glynn R., 1975. *The Rebel on the Bridge: A Life of the Decembrist Baron Andrey Rozen (1800–84)* (London).

——, 1979a. *The Russian Navy and Australia, to 1825: The Days before Suspicion* (Melbourne).

——, 1979b. "The Russian Navy and New Holland," *Journal of the Royal Australian Historical Society*, 64:217–34.

——, 1979c. *Bellingshausen: A Visit to New Zealand: 1820* (Palmerston North, New Zealand).

——, 1981a. *Russia in Pacific Waters, 1715–1825: A Survey of the Origins of Russia's Naval Presence in the North and South Pacific* (Vancouver and London).

——, 1981b. *The Russians at Port Jackson 1814–1822* (Canberra, Australian Institute of Aboriginal Studies).

——, 1983. *Russian Shadows on the British Northwest Coast of North America: A Study in Rejection of Defence Responsibilities* (Vancouver and London).

——, 1984. Russian Exploration in the Mariana Islands: 1817–1828. *Micronesian Archaeological Survey Report Number 17.* (Saipan, Micronesia). Translated and edited by Barratt.

——, 1988. *The Russian Discovery of Hawaii, 1804: The Ethnographic Record* (Honolulu).

Beaglehole, John C., 1955. *The Journals of Captain James Cook: The Voyage of the "Endeavour," 1768–71* (Cambridge, Hakluyt Society). Edited by Beaglehole.

——, 1967. *The Journals of Captain James Cook: The Voyage of "Resolution" and "Discovery," 1776–1780* (Cambridge, Hakluyt Society). Edited by Beaglehole.

——, 1974. *The Life of Captain James Cook* (Cambridge, Hakluyt Society). Edited by Beaglehole.

Beckley, Emma M., 1983 *Hawaiian Fisheries and Methods of Fishing* (Honolulu).

Beechey, Frederick, W., 1831. *Narrative of a Voyage to the Pacific and Beering's Strait ... in the Years 1825, 26, 27, 28* (London).

Bell, Edward J., 1929. "The Log of the *Chatham*," *Honolulu Mercury*, 1, No. 4 (September) and No. 6 (November).

Bellinsgauzen, Faddei F., 1831. *Dvukratnye izyskaniia v Iuzhnom ledovitom okeane i plavanie vokrug sveta, v prodolzhenie 1819, 1820 i 1821 godov, sovershennye na shliupakh "Vostok" i "Mirnyi"* (St. Petersburg). 2nd ed. 1949 (Moscow), edited by A.I. Andreev; 3rd ed. 1960 (Moscow), edited by E. Shvede.

Bennett, F.D., 1840. *A Whaling Voyage Round the Globe* (London, 2 vols.).

Berg, L.S., 1949. *Pervye russkie krugosvetnye moreplavateli I.F. Kruzenshtern i Iu.F. Lisianskii: ocherk po istorii russkikh geograficheskikh otkrytii* (Moscow).

Berkh, Vasilii N., 1818. "Nechto o Sandvichevykh ostrovakh," *Syn otechestva*, 7:158–65.

——, 1823a. "Izvestie o mekhovoi torgovle, proizvodimoi Rossiianami pri ostrovakh Kurilskikh, Aleutskikh, i severozapadnom beregu Ameriki," *Syn otechestva*, Part 88, pp. 243–64; Part 89, pp. 97–106.

——, 1823b. *Khronologicheskaia istoriia vsekh puteshestvii v severnye poliarnye strany* (St. Petersburg).

Bezobrazov, V., 1888. *Graf F.P. Litke* (St. Petersburg).

Bingham, Reverend Hiram, 1847. *A Residence of Twenty-One Years in the Sandwich Islands* (Hartford, Connecticut).

Bishop, Artemas, 1827. "Journal ...," in *Missionary Herald*, 23 (February), pp. 48–51.

Bishop, Sereno E., 1916. *Reminiscences of Old Hawaii* (Honolulu).

Bloxam, Andrew, 1825. "The Diary of Andrew Bloxam, Naturalist of 'Blonde' on her Trip from England to the Hawaiian Islands, 1824–25," *Bishop Museum Special Publication* 10.

Blue, George Verne, 1930. "The Policy of France toward the Hawaiian Islands from the Earliest Times to the Treaty of 1846," in A.P. Taylor and R.S. Kuykendall, eds., *Hawaii: Early Relations with England-Russia-France. Official Papers read during the Captain Cook Sesquicentennial Celebrations, Honolulu, August 17, 1928* (Honolulu), pp. 22–39.

Bois-Reymond, E. du, 1888. "Adelbert von Chamisso als Naturforscher: Rede zur Feier des Leibnitzischen Jahrestages in der Akademie der Wissenschaften zu Berlin, am 28 Juni 1888," *Deutsche Rundschau*, (Berlin) 56:329–49.

Bolkhovitinov, Nikolai, 1966. *Stanovlenie Russko-Amerikanskikh otnoshenii, 1775–1815* (Moscow).

Bradley, Harold W., 1934. "The Hawaiian Islands and the Pacific Fur Trade, 1785–1813," PNQ, 30:275–99.

——, 1942. *The American Frontier in Hawaii: The Pioneers, 1789–1843* (Stanford). 2nd ed. 1968.

Braunholtz, H.J., 1970. "Ethnography since Sloane," in *Sir Hans Sloane and Ethnography* (London).

Brigham, William T., 1899. "Hawaiian Feather Work," *Bishop Museum Memoir* 1, Part 1, pp. 1–81.

——, 1906. "Mat and Basket Weaving of the Ancient Hawaiians," *Bishop Museum Memoir* 2, Part 1, pp. 1–105.

——, 1910. "The Ancient Hawaiian Home," *Bishop Museum Memoir* 2, Part 3, pp. 185–378.

——, 1911. "Ka hana kapa—The Making of Bark-Cloth in Hawaii," *Bishop Museum Memoir* 3.

——, 1918. "Additional Notes on Hawaiian Feather Work," *Bishop Museum Memoir* 7, Part 1, pp. 1–64.

Broughton, William R., 1804. *A Voyage of Discovery to the North Pacific Ocean ... Performed in His Majesty's Sloop "Providence," and Her Tender, in the Years 1795, 1796, 1797, 1798* (London).

Brun, Xavier, 1896. *Adelbert de Chamisso de Boncourt* (Lyon).

Buck, Peter H. (Te Rangi Hiroa), 1957. "The Arts and Crafts of Hawaii," *Bishop Museum Special Publication* 45.

Campbell, Archibald, 1816. *A Voyage Round the World, from 1806 to 1812, in which Japan, Kamchatka, the Aleutian Islands, and the Sandwich Islands were Visited* (Edinburgh). 2nd ed. 1819.

Carter, G.R., 1923. "A New Document of John Young," HHS *Thirty-First Report*, pp. 51–53.

Cartwright, Bruce, 1922. "The First Discovery of Honolulu Harbour," HHS *Thirtieth Report*, pp. 11–28.

Chamisso, Adelbert von, 1818. "Brief von A. von Chamisso an E. Hitzig während der Weltreise ..., etc.' in *Literarisches Wochenblatt*, 1, Bd. 13:97–99.

——, 1836–42. *Reise um die Welt mit der Romanzoffischen Entdeckungsexpedition in den Jahren 1815–18, auf der Brigg Riurik ...,* in *Chamissos Werke*, (Leipzig, 6 vols.). Edited by J.E. Hitzig.

——, 1969. *Über die Hawaiische Sprache.* (Amsterdam, Halcyon Antiquariaat). Reprint of 1837 edition, edited by and with introduction by Samuel H. Elbert.

——, 1898–1900. *Samtliche Werke*, (Leipzig, 4 vols.). Edited by A. Bartels.

Charlot, Jean, 1958. *Choris and Kamehameha* (Honolulu, Bishop Museum).

Choris, Ludovik, 1822. *Voyage pittoresque autour du monde* (Paris).

——, 1826. *Vues et paysages des régions équinoxiales* (Paris).

Christie, E.W. Hunter, 1951. *The Antarctic Problem: An Historical and Political Study* (London).

Christison, L.L., 1924. "From a Missionary Journal; Samuel and Nancy Ruggles," *Atlantic Monthly*, 134 (November), pp. 650–55.

Cleveland, Richard J., 1850. *A Narrative of Voyages and Commercial Enterprises* (Boston, 5th ed.). 4th ed. 1843.

Coan, Mrs. Titus, n.d. *Life of Mrs. Sybil Moseley Bingham* (n.p.).

Colnett, James A., 1798. *A Voyage to the South Atlantic and Round Cape Horn into the Pacific Ocean, for the Purpose of Extending the Spermaceti Whale Fisheries ...* (London).

Cook, James, 1784. *A Voyage to the Pacific Ocean, ... for Making Discoveries in the Northern Hemisphere in ... the "Resolution" and "Discovery" ...* (London, 3 vols.). Volume 3 by James King. See also J.C. Beaglehole, above.

Corney, Peter, 1896. *Voyages in the North Pacific. The Narrative of Several Trading Voyages, from 1813 to 1818, between the Northwest Coast, the Hawaiian Islands, and China ...* (Honolulu).

Cox, Ross, 1832. *Adventures on the Columbia River* (New York).

Craig, R.D., 1978. "The 1780 Russian Inventory of Cook Artifacts," *Pacific Studies*, 2, 1:94–95.

Cross, Anthony G., 1980. *By the Banks of the Thames: Russians in Eighteenth-Century Britain* (Newtonville, Massachusetts).

Damon, Reverend S.C., 1925. "The First Mission Settlement on Kauai," *The Friend* (Honolulu), (September), pp. 207–14; (October), p. 225ff.

Davydov, G.I., 1810. *Dvukratnoe puteshestvie v Ameriku morskikh ofitserov Khvostova i Davydova* (St. Petersburg).

Davydov, Iurii, 1856. *V moriakh i stranstviakh* (Moscow).

Debenham, Frank, 1959. *Antarctica* (London).

Delano, Reuben, 1846. *The Wanderings and Adventures of Reuben Delano* (Worcester).

Dibble, Sheldon, 1838. *Ka Mooolelo Hawaii* (Maui, Lahainaluna School Press).

——, 1909. *History of the Sandwich Islands* (Honolulu).

Diell, John, 1838. "Oahu Charity School," *Hawaiian Spectator*, 1, 1 (January) pp. 23–24.

Dixon, George, 1798. *A Voyage Round the World, But More Particularly to the North West Coast of America, Performed in 1785–1788 in the "King George" and "Queen Charlotte"* (London).

Dobrovol'skii, A.D., 1953. *Otto fon Kotzebu: russkie moreplavateli* (Moscow).

Dodge, Ernest S., 1969. "The Cook Ethographical Collections," in R. Duff, ed., *No Sort of Iron: Culture of Cook's Polynesians* (Auckland).

Doring, Heinrich, 1830. *August von Kotzebues Leben* (Weimar).

Dufour, C.J., Essig, E.O., *et al*, 1933. "The Russians in California," *CHQ*, 12:210–16.

Duhaut-Cilly, A., 1834–35. *Voyage autour du monde* (Paris).

Dumitrashko, Nikolai V., 1947. "Iu.F. Lisianskii i russkie krugosvetnye plavaniia," in Iu. Lisianskii, *Puteshestvie vokrug sveta na korable "Neva" v 1803–1806 godakh* (Moscow).

D'Wolf, John, 1861. *A Voyage to the North Pacific and A Journey Through Siberia* (Cambridge, Massachusetts).

Elder, J., 1923. *The Letters and Journals of Samuel Marsden, 1765–1838* (Dunedin, New Zealand). Edited by Elder.

Ellis, Reverend William, 1826. *Narrative of a Tour through Hawaii* (London). 2nd ed. 1827.

——, 1839. *Polynesian Researches, During a Residency of Nearly Eight Years in the Society and Sandwich Islands* (London, 4 vols.), 3rd. ed.

Emerson, John S., 1928. "Journal," (May 1832) in Oliver P. Emerson, ed., *Pioneer Days in Hawaii* (Garden City, New York).

Emerson, N.B., 1900. "The Honolulu Fort," HHS *Eighth Annual Report*, pp. 11–25.

Emory, Kenneth P., 1946. "Hawaiian Tattooing," *Bishop Museum Occasional Papers*, 18, 17:235–70.

Fedorov-Davydov, A.A., 1953. *Russkii peizazh XVIII–nachala XIX vekov* (Moscow).

Feher, J., 1964. "Hawaii: A Pictorial History," *Bishop Museum Special Publication* 58.

Fersman, A., 1926. *The Pacific: Russian Scientific Investigations* (Leningrad). Edited by Fersman.

Feudel, Werner, 1971. *Adelbert von Chamisso. Leben und Werk* (Leipzig).

Fornander, A., 1916–20. "Hawaiian Antiquities and Folk-lore," *Bishop Museum Memoirs*, vols. 4–6.

Franchère, Gabriel, 1854. *Narrative of a Voyage to the Northwest Coast of America in the Years 1811, 1812, 1813 and 1814* (Redfield, New York.).

Freycinet, L.C.D. de, 1827–39. *Voyage autour du monde ... sur les corvettes ... "L'Uranie" et "La Physicienne"* ... (Paris, 2 vols.).

Friis, H.R., 1967. *The Pacific Basin: A History of its Geographical Exploration* (New York). Edited by Friis.

Furey, Francis, 1934. *Records of the American Catholic Historical Society*, 45:67–69. Edited by Furey.

Gastfreind, N.A., 1913. *Tovarishchi Pushkina po imperat. Tsarskosel'skomu Litseiu* (St. Petersburg).

Gennadi, G., 1876–80. *Slovar' russkikh pisatelei i uchennykh* (Berlin, 2 vols.).

Gessler, G., 1943. *Tropic Landfall: The Port of Honolulu* (Garden City, New York).

Gibson, James R., 1972. "Russian America in 1833: The Survey of Kirill Khlebnikov," PNQ, 63, 1:1–13.

———, 1976. *Imperial Russia in Frontier America: The Changing Geography of Supply of Russian America, 1784–1867* (New York).

Gillesem, (Hulsen) Karl, 1849. "Puteshestvie na shliupe Blagonamerennyi dlia issledovaniia beregov Azii i Ameriki za Beringovym prolivom, s 1819 po 1822 god," in *Otechestvennye zapiski*, 66, sect. 8.

Gofman (Hoffmann), Ernst K., 1829. *Geognostische Beobachtungen auf einer Reise um die Welt in den Jahren 1823–1826* (Berlin).

Golder, Frank A., 1917. *A Guide to Materials for American History in Russian Archives*, 1 (Washington, D.C.).

———, 1926. "Russian-American Relations during the Crimean War," AHR, 31:462–77.

———, 1930. "Proposals for Russian Occupation of the Hawaiian Islands," in A.P. Taylor and R.S. Kuykendall, eds., *Hawaii: Early Relations with England-Russia-France*, (Honolulu), pp. 39–50.

———, 1937. *A Guide to Materials for American History in Russian Archives*, 2 (Washington, D.C.).

Golovnin, Vasilii M., 1819. *Puteshestvie Rossiiskago Imperatorskago shliupa Diany, iz Kronshtadta v Kamchatku ... v 1807, 1808, i 1809 godakh* (St. Petersburg).

———, 1822. *Puteshestvie vokrug sveta ... sovershennoe na voennom shliupe "Kamchatka" v 1817–19 godakh flota kapitanom Golovninym* (St. Petersburg). Revised edition, 1965 by V.A. Divin (Moscow).

———, 1851. *Zapiski Vasiliia Mikhailovicha Golovninia v plenu u Iapontsev v 1811, 1812, i 1813 godakh ..., pod redaktsiei N.I. Grecha* (St. Petersburg).

———, 1949. *Sochineniia. Puteshestvie na shliupe "Diana" iz Kronshtadta v Kamchatku ... V plenu u vokrug sveta na shliupe "Kamchatka" v 1817, 1818 i 1819 godakh ... pod redaktsiei I.P. Magidovicha* (Moscow-Leningrad).

———, 1961. *Puteshestvie na shliupe "Diana" iz Kronshtadta v Kamchatku* (Moscow).

———, 1979. *Around the World on the "Kamchatka," 1817–1819* (Honolulu). Translated by Ella Wiswell.

Gough, Barry M., 1971. *The Royal Navy and the Northwest Coast of North America, 1810–1914: A Study of British Maritime Ascendancy* (Vancouver).

Graham, Maria, 1826. *Voyage of H.M.S. "Blonde" to the Sandwich Islands, in the Years, 1824–1825* (London).

Grech, Nikolai I., 1851. *Zhizneopisanie Vasiliia Mikhailovicha Golovnina* (St. Petersburg).

Gronskii, P.P., 1928. "Les Russes aux îles Hawaii au début du XIXe siècle," *Le Monde slave*, 4 (October), 10:21–39.

Gutmanis, Jane, 1963. "Tikhanov in Hawaii," *The Conch Shell, Bishop Museum News*, 1, 3:27–30.

Gvozdetskii, N.A., 1947. "Pervoe morskoe puteshestvie Rossiian vokrug sveta," *Priroda* (Moscow), 8, 1:85–88.

Haddon, A.C., and Hornell, James, 1936–38. Canoes of Oceania, *Bishop Museum Special Publications* 27–29 (3 vols.).

Hall, Edwin O., 1838. "The Condition of Common Schools at the Hawaiian Islands," *Hawaiian Spectator*, 1 (October), pp. 350–58.

Handy, E.S. Craighill, 1933. *Ancient Hawaiian Civilization* (Honolulu).

——, 1940. The Hawaiian Planter, vol. 1, *Bishop Museum Bulletin* 161.

Hitzig, Julius E., 1842. "Leben und Briefe von Adelbert von Chamisso," in *Chamissos Werke* (Leipzig) Bd. V/VI. Edited by Hitzig.

Holman, Lucia R., 1931. *The Journal of Lucia Ruggles Holman* (Honolulu).

Hotimsky, Constantin M., 1971. "A Bibliography of Captain James Cook in Russian—1772–1810," *Biblionews and Australian Notes and Queries*, 5, 2:3–12.

Houston, S.K., 1939. "Chamisso in Hawaii," HHS *Forty-Eighth Annual Report*, pp. 55–82.

Howay, Frederic W., 1924. "James Colnett and the *Princess Royal*," *Oregon Historical Quarterly*, 25:36–52.

——, 1930. "Early Relations between the Hawaiian Islands and the Northwest Coast," in A.P. Taylor and R.S. Kuykendall, eds., *Hawaii: Early Relations with England-Russia-France*, pp. 11–21.

v.
——, 1933. "The Last Days of the *Atahualpa*, alias *Behring*," HHS *Forty-First Annual Report*, pp. 70–80.

——, 1934. "The Ship *Eliza* at Hawaii in 1799," HHS *Forty-Second Annual Report*, pp. 103–13.

——, 1973. *A List of Trading Vessels in the Maritime Fur Trade, 1785–1825*, (Kingston, Ont., Limestone Press: Materials for the Study of Alaskan History, vol. 2). Edited by Richard A. Pierce.

Hunnewell, James, 1880. *Journal of the Voyage of the "Missionary Packet," Boston to Honolulu, 1826* (Charlestown).

——, 1885. "Honolulu in 1817 and 1818: A Voyage in the Brig *Bordeaux Packet*, Boston to Honolulu, 1817, and a Residence in Honolulu, 1817–18," HHS *Papers*, 8:3–19. Printed separately in 1909 (Honolulu), 23pp.

Ii, John P., 1963. *Fragments of Hawaiian History*, (Honolulu). Translated by M.K. Pukui, edited by Dorothy B. Barrère.

Ikonnikov, S., 1873. *Graf N.S. Mordvinov* (St. Petersburg).

Ivanovskii, A.D., 1871. *Gosudarstvennyi kantsler graf Nikolai Petrovich Rumiantsev: biograficheskii ocherk* (St. Petersburg).

Ivashintsev, Nikolai A., 1980. *Russian Round-the-World Voyages, 1803-1849* (Kingston, Ont., Limestone Press: Materials for the Study of Alaskan History, vol. 14). Translated by Glynn R. Barratt.

Jarves, James J., 1847. *History of the Hawaiian or Sandwich Islands* (Honolulu, 3rd ed.).

_____ , 1843. "The Sandwich Islands or Hawaiian Islands," *Merchants' Magazine*, 9 (August), pp. 113-20.

Jewitt, John R., 1815. *Narrative of the Adventures and the Sufferings of John R. Jewitt, only Survivor of the crew of the ship "Boston," during a Captivity of nearly Three Years ...* (Middletown, Connecticut). Reprinted 1967 (Fairfield, Washington).

Judd, Bernice, 1929. *Voyages to Hawaii before 1860 ...* (Honolulu).

Judd, Laura F., 1928. *Honolulu: Sketches of Life Social, Political, and Religious, in the Hawaiian Islands from 1828 to 1861* (Honolulu).

Kaeppler, Adrienne, 1978a. "'Artificial Curiosities': Being an Exposition of Native Manufactures Collected on the three Pacific Voyages of Captain James Cook, RN," *Bishop Museum Special Publication* 65.

_____ , 1978b. "Cook Voyage Artifacts in Leningrad, Berne, and Florence Museums," *Bishop Museum Special Publication* 66.

_____ , 1979. "Tracing the History of Hawaiian Cook Voyage Artefacts in the Museum of Mankind," in T.C. Mitchell, ed., *Captain Cook and the South Pacific* (London, British Museum Yearbook 3) pp. 167-97.

Kamakau, S.M., 1961. *Ruling Chiefs of Hawaii* (Honolulu).

_____ , 1964. "Ka Po'e Kahiko: The People of Old," *Bishop Museum Special Publication* 51. Translated by Mary K. Pukui, edited by Dorothy Barrère.

Kelm, H., 1951. "Adelbert von Chamisso als Ethnograph der Südsee," (dissertation, Universität Bonn).

Khlebnikov, Kiril T., 1829. "Zapiski o Kalifornii," *Syn otechestva i severnyi arkhiv*, 9:208-27, 276-88, 336-47, 400-10.

_____ , n.d. "Zapiski o koloniiakh v Amerike Rossiisko-Amerikanskoi Kompanii," AGO, *razr.* 99, op. 1, *delo* 111.

_____ , n.d. "Zapiski o Amerike ...," in *Materialy dlia istorii*, pt. 3:88ff.

_____ , 1979. *Russkaia Amerika v neopublikovannykh zapiskakh K.T. Klhebnikova* (Leningrad). Edited by R.G. Liapunova and S.G. Fedorova.

Khrushchev, Stepan P., 1826. "Plavanie shliupa Apollona v 1821-1824 godakh," ZADMM, 10:200-72.

Kirwan, L.P., 1960. *The White Road: A Survey of Polar Exploration* (London).

Klochkov, E.A., 1826. "Puteshestvie vokrug sveta v kolonii Rossiisko-Amerikanskoi Kompanii," *Severnyi arkhiv* (St. Petersburg), 24:202-19.

Kohl, Johann, G., 1843. *Russia and the Russians in 1842* (London).

Komissarov, Boris N., 1964. "Dnevnik puteshestviia F.P. Litke na shliupe 'Kamchatka' v 1817–1819 gg.," IVGO, 96, 5:414–19.

——, 1975. *Grigorii Ivanovich Langsdorf 1774–1852* (Leningrad).

Korobitsyn, Nikolai I., 1944. "Zapiski," *Russkie otkrytiia v Tikhom okeane i Severnoi Amerike v XVIII–XIX vekakh: sbornik materialov* (Moscow-Leningrad). Edited by A.I. Andreev. Translated by Carl Ginsburg, 1952, as *Russian Discoveries in the Pacific and in North America in the 18th and 19th Centuries* (Ann Arbor).

Kotzebue, Otto E. von, 1821. *Puteshestvie v Iuzhnyi Okean i v Beringov proliv v 1815–1818 godakh* (St. Petersburg). English translation by H.E. Lloyd, 1821, as *A Voyage of Discovery into the South Sea and Beering's Straits, for the Purpose of Exploring a North-East Passage ...* (London, 3 vols.). German translation (no author available), 1821, as *Entdeckungsreise in die Süd-See und nach der Berings-Strasse ... in der Jahren 1815, 1817, 1817 und 1818 ...* (Weimar).

——, 1828. *Puteshestvie vokrug sveta, sovershennoe na voennom shliupe Predpriiatie, v 1823, 24, 25, i 26 godakh ...* (St. Petersburg).

——, 1830. *Neue Reise um die Welt in den Jahren 1823, 24, 25, und 26 ...* (Weimar). Russian translation, with an introduction by Daniel D. Tumarkin, 1981, as *Novoe puteshestvie vokrug sveta v 1823–26 godakh* (Moscow).

Kruzenshtern, Ivan F., 1809–12. *Puteshestvie vokrug sveta v 1803, 4, 5 i 1806 godakh na korabliakh "Nadezhda" i "Neva"* (St. Petersburg, 3 vols.). English translation by R.B. Hoppner, 1813, as *A Voyage Round the World ... in the Years 1803, 4, 5 and 6* (London).

——, 1813. *Atlas k Puteshestviiu vokrug sveta* (St. Petersburg).

Kuykendall, Ralph S., 1938. *The Hawaiian Kingdom, 1778–1854: Foundation and Transformation* (Honolulu).

Kuykendall, Ralph S., and Gregory, Herbert E., 1928. *A History of Hawaii* (New York).

Kuznetsova, V.V., 1968. "Novye dokumenty o russkoi ekspeditsii k Severnomu poliusu," IVGO, 100, 3:237–45.

Laird-Clowes, William, 1899–1904. *A History of the Royal Navy* (London, 7 vols.).

Langsdorf(f), Georg H., 1812. *Bemerkungen auf einer Reise um die Welt in den Jahren 1803 bis 1807* (Frankfurt, 2 vols.). Translated (no author available), 1813–14, as *Voyages and Travels in Various Parts of the World ...* (London).

Lazarev, Aleksei P., 1950. *Zapiski o plavanii voennogo shliupa Blagonamerennogo v Beringov proliv i vokrug sveta dlia otkrytii v 1819, 1820, 1821 i 1822 godakh* (Moscow). Edited by A.I. Solov'ev.

Lazarev, Andrei P., 1832. *Plavanie vokrug sveta na "Ladoga" v 1822, 1823, i 1824 godakh* (St. Petersburg).

Lazarev, Mikhail P., 1815. "Izvlechenie iz zhurnala puteshestvuiushchogo krugom sveta rossiiskago leitenanta Lazareva," *Syn otechestva*, 26:255–58.

——, 1918. "Pis'mo A.A. Shestakovu," *Morskoi sbornik* 1:53–63.

Ledyard, John, 1966. *John Ledyard's Journey through Russia and Siberia, 1787–88* (Madison). Edited by Stephen D. Watrous.

Lensen, George A., 1959. *The Russian Push Toward Japan: Russo-Japanese Relations, 1697–1875* (Princeton).

Lenz, W., 1970. *Deutsch-Baltisches Biographisches Lexikon, 1710–1960* (Köln-Wien). Edited by Lenz.

Likhtenberg, Iuliia M., 1960. "Gavaiskie kollektsii v sobraniiakh Muzeia Antropologii i Etnografii," SMAE, 19:168–205.

Lipshits, B.A., 1956. "Etnograficheskie issledovaniia v russkikh krugosvetnykh ekspeditsiiakh pervoi poloviny XIX veka," *Ocherki po istorii russkoi etnografii, fol'kloristiki, i antropologii* (Moscow), Bd. 1:298–321.

Lisianskii, Iurii F., 1812a. *Puteshestvie vokrug sveta v 1803, 1804, 1805, i 1806 godakh, na korable "Neva" pod nachal'stvom Iuriia Lisianskago* (St. Petersburg). Translated by the author, 1814, as *A Voyage Round the World in the Years 1803, 4, 5 & 6, ... in the ship "Neva"* (London).

——, 1812b. *Sobranie kart i risunkov, prinadlezhashchikh k puteshestviiu Iuriia Lisianskago na korable "Neva"* (St. Petersburg).

London Missionary Society, ?1890. *Catalogue of the Missionary Museum* (London).

Loomie, Maria S., 1820. "Journal," typewritten copy in Hawaiian Mission Children's Society Library, (Honolulu).

Lukina, T.A., 1975. *Iogann Fridrikh Eshchol'ts* (Moscow).

Lydgate, John M., 1916. "Ka-umu-alii, the Last King of Kauai," HHS *Twenty-Fourth Annual Report*, pp. 21–36.

Lyman, Henry M., 1906. *Hawaiian Yesterdays* (Chicago).

Lysaght, A.M., 1979. "Banks's Artists and his 'Endeavour' Collections," in T.C. Mitchell, ed. *Captain Cook and the South Pacific* (London, British Museum Yearbook 3), pp. 9–80.

Mahr, August C., 1932. "The Visit of the 'Riurik' to San Francisco in 1816," *Stanford Publications in History, Economics, and Political Science*, 2:2.

Malo, David, 1839. "On the Decrease of Population on the Hawaiian Islands," *Hawaiian Spectator*, 2 (April), pp. 125–27. Translation by Lorrin Andrews.

——, 1903. Hawaiian Antiquities (Moolelo Hawaii) *Bishop Museum Special Publication* 2. Translation by Nathaniel B. Emerson (dated 1898). 2nd ed. 1951.

Materialy dlia istorii russkikh zaselenii po beregam Vostochnogo okeana, 1861 (no author given). Supplement to *Morskoi sbornik* 1861, no. 1 (St. Petersburg).

Mathison, Gilbert F., 1825. *Narrative of a Visit to Brazil, Chile, Peru, and the Sandwich Islands* (London).

Mazour, Anatole G., 1937. "Doctor Yegor Scheffer: Dreamer of a Russian Empire in the Pacific," PHR, 6:15–20.

——, 1944. "The Russian-American Company: Private or Government Enterprise?" PHR, 13:168–73.

McNab, Robert, 1908–14. *Historical Records of New Zealand* (Wellington, 2 vols.). Edited by McNab.

Meares, John, 1790. *Voyages Made in the Years 1788 and 1789 from China to the North West Coast of America* ... (London).

Mehnert, Klaus, 1939. "The Russians in Hawaii, 1804–1819," *University of Hawaii Occasional Papers* (Honolulu), 38.

Menza, Gisela, 1978. "Adelbert von Chamissos 'Reise um die Welt mit der Romanzoffischen Entdeckungs-Expedition in den Jahren 1815–1818': Versuch einer Bestimmung," *European University Papers, Series 1, German Language and Literature*, 251 (Frankfurt and Bern).

Mitchell, T.C., 1979. *Captain Cook and the South Pacific* (London, British Museum Yearbook 3). Edited by Mitchell.

M'Konochie, Alexander, 1816. *Considerations on the Propriety of Establishing a Colony on One of the Sandwich Islands* (Edinburgh).

Montgomery, James, 1831. *Journal of the Voyages and Travels by the Rev. Daniel Tyerman and George Bennet, Esq.* (London). Compiled by Montgomery.

Morison, Samuel Eliot, 1921a. "Boston Traders in the Hawaiian Islands, 1789–1823," *Washington Historical Quarterly*, 12:166–201.

——— , 1921b. *Maritime History of Massachusetts, 1783–1860* (Boston). Revised edition, 1961 (Cambridge, Mass.).

Neal, Marie C., 1948. "In Gardens of Hawaii," *Bishop Museum Special Publication* 40.

Nevskii, Vladimir V., 1951. *Pervoe puteshestvie Rossiian vokrug sveta* (Moscow).

Nicolas, N., 1844. *The Despatches and Letters of Vice-Admiral Lord Nelson* (London, 8 vols.). Edited by Nicolas.

Novikov, P.A., 1962. "Zoologicheskie issledovaniia Shamisso i Ia. Eshchol'tsa vo vremia krugosvetnoi ekspeditsii O.E. Kotsebu na "Riurike" (1815–1818)," *Trudy Instituta Istorii Estestvoznaniia* (Leningrad), 40:248–82.

Ogden, Adele, 1941. *The California Sea Otter Trade, 1784–1848* (Berkeley).

Okun', Semen B., 1936. "Tsarskaia Rossiia i Gavaiskie ostrova," *Krasnyi arkhiv* (Moscow), 5:161–86.

——— , 1939. *Rossiisko-Amerikanskaia kompaniia* (Moscow). Translation by C. Ginsburg, 1951, as *The Russian-American Company* (Cambridge, Mass.).

Ostrovskii, Boris G., 1949. "O pozabytykh istochnikakh i uchastnikakh antarkticheskoi ekspeditsii Bellingsgauzena-Lazareva," IVGO (Leningrad), 81.

Pasetskii, B.M., 1965. *O chom sheptalis' poliarnye maki* (Moscow).

Patterson, Samuel, 1817. *Narrative of the Adventures, Sufferings, and Privations of Samuel Patterson, a Native of Rhode-Island* ... (Palmer, Mass.). 2nd edition, enlarged, 1825 (Providence, Rhode Island).

Paulding, Hiram, 1831. *Journal of a Cruise of the United States Schooner "Dolphin" Among the Islands of the Pacific Ocean* (New York).

Penrose, Charles Vinicombe, 1959. "A Memoir of James Trevenen, 1760–1790," *Navy Records Society*, CL (London). Edited by C. Lloyd and R.C. Anderson.

Perkins, D., 1923. "Russia and the Spanish Colonies, 1817–1818," AHR, 28:656–73.

Perkins. R.C.L., 1913. *Introduction to Fauna Hawaiiensis*, (Cambridge), pp. xv–ccxxviii. Edited by D. Sharp.

Peron, J., 1824. *Mémoires du capitaine Peron, sur ses Voyages aux côtes d'Afrique ..., aux Isles Sandwich, à la Chine, etc. ...* (Paris, 2 vols.).

Pierce, Richard A., 1965. *Russia's Hawaiian Adventure, 1815–1817* (Berkeley). Reprinted, 1976 (Kingston, Ontario).

——, and Shur, Leonid A., 1976. "Artists in Russian America: Mikhail Tikhanov (1818)," *Alaska Journal*, 6, 1:40–49.

Porter, Kenneth W., 1929–30. "John Jacob Astor and the Sandalwood Trade of the Hawaiian Islands, 1816–1828," *Journal of Economic and Business History*, 2:495–519.

——, 1931. *John Jacob Astor, Business Man* (Cambridge, Mass., 2 vols.).

——, 1932. "The Cruise of the *Forester*: Some New Sidelights on the Astoria Enterprise," *Washington Historical Quarterly*, 23:261–85.

——, 1934. "Notes on Negroes in Early Hawaii," *Journal of Negro History*, 19:194–97.

Portlock, Nathaniel, 1789. *Voyages round the World; but more particularly to the North West Coast of America, performed in 1785, 1786, 1787 and 1788 in the "King George" and "Queen Charlotte" ...* (London).

Puget, Peter, 1929. "The Log of the *Chatham*," *Honolulu Mercury*, 1, 4:9ff. Edited by E. Bell.

Pukui, M.K., and Elbert, S.H., 1957. *Hawaiian-English Dictionary* (Honolulu).

Rabany, C.G., 1893. *Kotzebue, sa vie et son temps* (Paris).

Restarick, Henry B., 1923. "The First Clergyman Resident in Hawaii," HHS *Thirty-First Annual Report*, pp. 58–59.

——, 1924. *Hawaii, 1778–1920 from the Viewpoint of a Bishop* (Honolulu).

Rezanov, Nikolai P., 1825. "Pervoe puteshestvie Rossiian vokrug sveta, opisannoe N. Riazanovym, polnomochnym poslannikom ko dvoru Iaponskomu ...," *Otechestvennye zapiski*, (St. Petersburg) 24:246–53.

——, 1926. *The Rezanov Voyage to Nueva California in 1806* (San Francisco). Translation by Thomas C. Russell.

Richards, Rev. William, 1834. "A Letter to the Reverend Ephraim Spaulding ..., Lahaina, December 7, 1833," *Sailor's Magazine*, 6:358–59.

Riegel, René, 1834. *Adelbert de Chamisso: sa vie et son œuvre* (Paris, 2 vols.).

Roberts, Helen H., 1926. "Ancient Hawaiian Music," *Bishop Museum Bulletin* 29.

Roquefeuil, Camille de, 1823. *Journal d'un voyage autour du monde, pendant les années 1816–1819 ...* (Paris, 2 vols.).

Rovinskii, D.A., 1895. *Podrobnyi slovar' russkikh graverov XVI–XIX vekov* (St. Petersburg).

Rozina, L.G., 1963. "Kollektsiia Muzeia Antropologii i Etnografii po Markizskim ostrovam," SMAE, 21:110–19.

——, 1966. "Kollektsiia Dzhemsa Kuka v sobraniiakh Muzeia Antropologii i Etnografii," *SMAE*, 23:234–53.

Ryden, Stig, 1963. "The Banks Collection: An Episode in Eighteenth Century Anglo-Swedish Relations," *Ethnographic Museum of Sweden, Monograph Series* 8 (Stockholm).

Samarov, A.A., 1952. *Russkie flotovodtsy: M.P. Lazarev: Dokumenty* (Leningrad). Edited by Samarov.

Schweizer, Niklaus R., 1973. *A Poet among Explorers: Chamisso in the South Seas* (Bern).

Sementovskii, Vladimir N., 1951. *Russkie otkrytiia v Antarktike v 1819–1821 gg.* (Moscow). Edited by Sementovskii.

Severgin, N.V., 1804. "Instruktsii dlia puteshestviia okolo sveta po chasti mineralogii i v otnoshenii k teorii zemli," *Severnyi vestnik* (St. Petersburg), 2–3.

Shabel'skii, Akhilles P., 1826. *Voyage aux colonies russes de l'Amérique fait à bord du sloop de guerre l'"Apollon", pendant les années 1821, 1822 et 1823* (St. Petersburg).

Shafranovskaia, Tamara K. and Komissarov, Boris N., 1980. "Materialy po etnografii Polinezii v dnevnike E.E. Levenshterna," *Sovetskaia etnografiia* (Leningrad), 6.

Shaler, William, 1808. "Journal of a Voyage between China and the North-Western Coast of America, Made in 1804," *American Register*, 3:137–75.

Sharp, Andrew, 1960. *The Discovery of the Pacific Islands* (Oxford).

Shemelin, Fedor I., 1816–18. *Zhurnal pervogo puteshestviia Rossiian vokrug zemnago shara* (St. Petersburg, 2 vols.).

——, 1823. "Istoricheskoe izvestie o pervom puteshestvii Rossiian krugom sveta," *Russkii invalid* (St. Petersburg), 146, nos. 23–28, 31–36.

Shur, Leonid A., 1970. "Dnevniki i zapiski russkikh puteshestvennikov kak istochnik po istorii i etnografii stran Tikhogo okeana (pervaia polovina XIX veka)," *Avstraliia i Okeaniia* (Moscow), pp. 201–12. English variant in *Ibero-Amerikanisches Archiv* (Berlin), 1, 45:395–401.

——, 1971. *K beregam novogo sveta* (Moscow).

Simpson, George, 1847. *Narrative of a Journey round the World in the Years 1841 and 1842* (London, 2 vols.).

Sinclair, M., 1976. *Nahi 'ena'ena: Sacred daughter of Hawaii* (Honolulu).

Smith, Bernard, 1960. *European Vision and the South Pacific, 1768–1850* (Oxford).

Snow, Elliot, 1925. *The Sea, the Ship, and the Sailor: Tales of Adventure from Logbooks and Original Narratives ...* (Salem). Introduction by Snow.

Snyder, J.W., 1937. "Voyage of the *Ophelia*," *New England Quarterly*, 10:364ff.

Sopikov, Vladimir N., 1813. *Opyt Rossiiskoi Bibliografii* (St. Petersburg). Edited by V.S. Rogozhin. Reprinted 1962 (London, Holland House).

Spaulding, Thomas, 1930. "The Adoption of the Hawaiian Alphabet," *HHS Papers*, 17:28–33.

Starbuck, Alexander, 1876. *History of the American Whale Fishery from Its Earliest Inception to the Year 1876* (Waltham, Mass.).

Stewart, Rev. Chas. S., 1828a. *Journal of a Residence in the Sandwich Islands During the Years 1823, 1824, and 1825* (London).

——, 1828b. *Private Journal of a Voyage to the Pacific Ocean and Residence at the Sandwich Islands ...* (New York).

Stokes, John F., 1906. Hawaiian Nets and Netting, *Bishop Museum Memoir*, 2, 1:105–63.

Sullivan, Josephine, 1926. *History of C. Brewer and Company, Ltd.* (Boston).

Svet, Ia.M., 1971. *Tret'e plavanie kapitana Dzhemsa Kuka: plavanie v Tikhom okeane v 1776–1780 godakh* (Moscow). Translation of Cook, 1784, *A Voyage ...*, vol. 3.

Tarakanoff, V.P., 1953. *Statement of my Captivity among the Californians* (Los Angeles).

Taylor, Albert P., 1926. *Under Hawaiian Skies: Narrative of the Romance, Adventure, and History of the Hawaiian Islands* (Honolulu).

——, 1928. "Lihiliho: A Revised Estimate of his Character," HSS *Papers*, 15:21–39.

Thrum, Thomas G., 1875. "Notes on the Sugar Industry of the Hawaiian Islands," *Hawaiian Almanac and Annual* pp. 32–36.

——, 1917. "A Brief Sketch of the Life and Labors of S.M. Kamakau, Hawaiian Historian," HSS *Twenty-Fifth Annual Report*, pp. 45–54.

——, 1924. "Heiaus (Temples) of Hawaii Nei," HSS *Thirty-Second Annual Report*, pp. 14–36.

Thurston, Lucy G., 1921. *Life and Times of Mrs. Lucy G. Thurston* (Honolulu).

Tikhmenev, P.A., 1861–63. *Istoricheskoe obozrenie obrazovaniia Rossiisko-Amerikanskoi Kompanii i deistvii eio do nastoiashchego vremeni* (St. Petersburg, 2 vols.). English translation, D. Krenov, 1939, as *The Historical Review of the Formation of the Russian-American Company* (Seattle, 2 vols.).

Titcomb, Margaret, 1948. "Kava in Hawaii," *Journal of the Polynesian Society*, 57, 2:105–71.

Tregaskis, Richard W., 1973. *The Warrior King: Kamehameha the Great* (New York).

Tumarkin, Daniel D., 1954. "K voprosu o formakh sem'i u gavaitsev v kontse XVIII-nachale XIX veka," *Sovetskaia etnografiia* 4:110–16.

——, 1956. "Zabytyi istochnik: o knige O.E. Kotsebu *Neue Reise um die Welt*," *Sovetskaia etnografiia* vol. 2.

——, 1958. "Iz istorii gavaitsev v kontse XVIII-nachale XIX veka," *Sovetskaia etnografiia*, 6:38–53.

——, 1960. "Novye arkhivnye materialy o gavaitsakh," *Sovetskaia etnografiia* 2:158–60.

——, 1964. *Vtorzhenie kolonizatorov v "Krai vechnoi vesny": Gavaiskii narod v bor'be protiv chuzhezemnykh zakhvatchikov v kontse XVIII-nachale XIX veka* (Moscow).

———, 1979. "A Russian View of Hawaii in 1804," *Pacific Studies*, 2:109–31.

———, 1983. "Materialy ekspeditsii M.N. Vasil'eva-tsennyi istochnik po istorii i etnografii Gavaiskikh ostrovov," *Sovetskaia etnografiia*, 6:48–61.

Turnbull, John, 1805. *A Voyage round the World, in the Years 1800, 1801, 1802, 1803 and 1804* (London, 2 vols.).

United States, Congress, Senate, 1858. *American State Papers*, (Foreign Relations), vol. V.

———, 1833. *House Reports: XXII Congress*, 2nd Session.

———, 1845. *House Reports: XXVIII Congress*, 2nd Session.

———, 1839. *Senate Documents: XXV Congress*, 3rd Session.

Valaam Monastery, 1894. *Ocherk iz istorii Amerikanskoi pravoslavnoi dukhovnoi missii (Kadiakskoi missii 1794–1837 godov)* (St. Petersburg).

Vancouver, George, 1798. *A Voyage of Discovery to the North Pacific Ocean and Round the World ... in the Years 1790–1795* (London).

Veselago, F.F., 1869. *Admiral Ivan Fedorovich Kruzenshtern* (St. Petersburg).

———, 1939. *Kratkaia istoriia russkogo flota* (Leningrad).

Vishnevskii, B.N., 1957. *Puteshestvennik Kirill Khlebnikov* (Perm').

Vishniakov, Nikolai, 1905. "Rossiia, Kaliforniia i Sandvichevye Ostrova," *Russkaia starina* (St. Petersburg), 124:249–89.

Vneshniaia Politika Rossii XIX i nachala XX veka: dokumenty Rossiiskogo Ministerstva Inostronnykh Del: seriia I, 1801–1815 1961–75 (Moscow).

Webb, Elizabeth L., 1933. "Featherwork and Clothing," in E.S. Craighill Handy et al., *Ancient Hawaiian Civilization* (Honolulu).

Westervelt, W.D., 1910. "Legendary Places in Honolulu," HHS *Seventeenth Annual Report*.

———, 1912. "The First Twenty Years of Education in the Hawaiian Islands," HHS *Nineteenth Annual Report*, p. 16ff.

———, 1922. "Kamehameha's Method of Government," HHS *Thirtieth Annual Report*, pp. 30–42.

Wheeler, Mary E., 1971. "Empires in Conflict and Co-operation: The Bostonians and the Russian-American Company," PHR, 40:419–41.

Wilson, W.F., 1920. *Hawaii Nei 128 Years Ago, by Archibald Menzies* (Honolulu). Edited by Wilson.

Wrangel, Ferdinand P., 1828. "Otryvok iz rukopisi, pod zaglaviem: Dnevnye zapiski o plavanii voennogo transporta *Krotkago* v 1825, 1826 i 1827 godakh," *Severnyi arkhiv* (St. Petersburg), 36:49–106.

———, 1839. *Statistische und ethnographische Nachrichten über die russischen Besitzungen an der Nordwestküste von Amerika* (St. Petersburg).

Wyllie, Robert C., 1844. "Whaling ... Statistics, Compiled from Records kept by Stephen Reynolds ...," *The Friend*, VOL. 2, 1 May, pp. 49–50.

Yzendoorn, Fr. Reginald, 1927. *History of the Catholic Mission in the Hawaiian Islands* (Honolulu).

Zavalishin, Dmitrii, 1877. "Krugosvetnoe plavanie fregata "Kreiser" v 1822–
1825 godakh pod komandoiu Mikhaila Petrovicha Lazareva," *Drevniaia i
novaia Rossiia* (St. Petersburg), 5:54–67; 6:115–25; 7:199–214.

Zavoiko, Vladimir S., 1840. *Vpechatleniia moriaka vo vremia dvukh puteshestvii krukom sveta: sochinenie leitenanta V. Zavoiko*, 1: "Puteshestvie v
1834, 1835 i 1836 godakh" (St. Petersburg).

Zubov, Nikolai N., 1954. *Otechestvennye moreplavateli-issledovateli morei i
okeanov* (Moscow).